Composers on Record

An Index to Biographical Information
on 14,000 Composers
Whose Music Has Been Recorded

Compiled by
Frank Greene

The Scarecrow Press, Inc.
Metuchen, N.J., and London, 1985

Library of Congress Cataloging in Publication Data

Greene, Frank, 1946–
   Composers on record.

   1. Composers--Biography--Indexes. 2. Composers--
Discography--Indexes. I. Title.
ML105.G78 1985   016.78'092'2   85-8238
ISBN 0-8108-1816-7

To my parents, Marguerite and Thomas William Greene.

TABLE OF CONTENTS

PREFACE

This book contains the names of the 14,000 composers
that have appeared in the 66 discographies and record
catalogues indexed plus those composers found in the
record collection of the Music Library of the University of Toronto. The composers in this book are
mainly those who have composed "serious music".
Although several of the sources indexed contain some
composers whose work could not be thought of as being
in that category, they have been included for the sake
of completeness.

To my knowledge this is the first time that a list has
been compiled of composers whose work has appeared on
commercially available recordings. I also believe this
to be the largest list containing composers only, apart
from the multivolume dictionary catalogues of such
institutions as the New York Public Library (R.200)
and the British Library in London (R.88), and
catalogues of printed music such as Pazdirek (R.89).
The previous largest list of composers seems to have
been in Bull´s Index to Biographies of Contemporary
Composers (R.14) with 8,000 names. Aaron Cohen´s
International Encyclopedia of Women Composers (R.7)
lists some 5,000 female composers. Most other biographical dictionaries combine composers with artists,
musicologists etc., and do not indicate how many
entries they contain. By way of comparison I have
estimated the following totals:

        The New Grove (R.1)   26,000
        Frank, 14th ed. (R.3)   22,000
        Frank, 15th ed. (R.4)   17,000
        Baker, 6th ed. (R.6)   14,000

The composers on this list form a distinct group and
are not merely a sub-set of the composers who have

vii

appeared in the hundreds of biographical dictionaries
that have been published over the years. This stems
from the fact that most biographical dictionaries are
compiled by musicologists whereas decisions about
recordings are made by people who are more marketing
orientated. This dichotomy may be illustrated by
considering the composers with entries in the <u>New Grove</u>
(R.1). By my estimate this 20 volume reference work
contains around 16,000 composers, however, no more than
6,000 of the composers in the New Grove are to be found
on this list. This leads one to the conclusion that 60
percent of the composers that the editors of that
prestigious publication considered worthy of mention
are unrepresented on the recorded medium or have appeared only on recordings with a limited distribution.

The corollary of this is that there are many composers
whose works have been recorded but who are not to be
found in any reference work. This may illustrated by
considering the recordings made by Enrico Caruso. In
addition to the standard operatic repertoire Caruso
made recordings of popular songs of the day. There are
two discographies giving details of all his recording
sessions and everything he recorded is available today
and yet for several of these songs all we seem to know
about the composer is their surname. The identity of
composers such as "Varel", "Michelena", "Posadas",
"Pennino" and "Souci" remains a mystery (to me at
least) despite the fact that their music has been
recorded by one of the greatest singers.

There is also the case of Max Niederberger. Three
operettas by him were staged in Berlin, "Fräulein Frau"
(1922), "Das Phantom" (1924) and "Die blonde Sphinx"
(1925), yet no biographical information about the composer is readily available. He appears in Steiger's
<u>Opernlexikon</u> (R.93) with no dates and a quick check in
27 biographical dictionaries failed to reveal any
mention of the gentleman.

There are also numerous composers whose music can be
bought on records today but who do not seem to have
appeared in any biographical dictionary since the last
century. There is, for example, Charles Kinkel
(b.1832). The only biographical information I have
come across was published in 1886 (see R.53) which
tells use that he spent 20 years teaching in Shelby-
ville, Kentucky. What he did after 1868 is not recorded and yet musically it was the most productive

part of this life. In the Catalogue of Printed Music
in the British Library (R.88) his compositions cover
several pages and were published in New York, London,
and Paris, most of them after 1868.

One of my main objectives in preparing this list has
been to provide a focal point where information may be
recorded about such forgotten (and perhaps forgettable)
composers as the compilers of the standard biographical
dictionaries are unlikely to ever take an interest in
these minor figures.

While this book is the work of just one person, I
believe that the information it contains is, in many
instances, an improvement over that currently available. Having said that perhaps I may be allowed a few
comments on a reference work at the other end of the
lexicographical spectrum.

>   "Ever since the first edition of Grove´s was
>   finished in 1890 it has been the definitive
>   musical reference book in the English language".

Thus spoke a reviewer writing about the New Grove
Dictionary of Music and Musicians (R.1) and indeed it
was a reputation that I did not think to question when
I set about verifying the information I had taken from
record catalogues and discographies. In cases where a
composer´s dates given in the New Grove were at var-
iance with those in another reference source, I
accepted the dates in the New Grove. However a few
weeks before the publisher´s deadline I became sus-
picious and decided to make further investigations.
Of the six names that I checked - Marion Bauer, Cathy
Berberian, Augustin Lara, Harry Partch, Harvey
Sollberger and Efrem Zimbalist - it would appear that
in every case the information in the New Grove is
incorrect. In the case of Efrem Zimbalist the conse-
quences of the error in the New Grove can already be
seen: the editors of the Algemene Muziek Encyclopedie
(R.25) have evidently used the incorrect information
from the New Grove in their article on that composer.
Unfortunately it has not been possible to go back and
re-check all the dates taken from the New Grove.

"The New Grove has been set by computer and
that has permitted the inclusion of material
and information uncovered as late as the
first half of 1980".

The words of another reviewer. However this use of
modern technology did not prevent the editors of the
New Grove from omitting information that had been
around for years. Several composers listed in the New
Grove as still living had in fact died up to ten years
prior to publication. These include Marius-Francois
Gaillard (1900-1973), Friedrich Schroder (1910-1972),
Rick Besoyan (1924-1970), Frank Loesser (1910-1969) and
Ottmar Gerster (1897-1969).

Of course errors are almost inevitable in any publication of this nature and I would not wish users of
this volume to believe that I consider my efforts to be
the exception. I would be most interested in hearing
from anyone who notices errors in this list of composers or who can supply information that is missing
from this first edition.

I mention elsewhere that this book represents the work
of one person in one library, however this book would
not have been possible without the help of my faithful
assistant Grace Ho. Grace was resposible for all the
typing and the numerous revisions that had to be made.
My gratitude to her is immense. I would also like to
thank the staff of the Music Library of the University
of Toronto who were always generous with their help and
advice: James Creighton, John Fodi and Kathleen
McMorrow.

GUIDE TO USE

Users of this book should be aware that it has been
compiled by a non-musicologist. This should be borne
in mind when judging the validity of assumptions that
have been made regarding the identification of composers
from incomplete information and especially while reading
the notes at the back of the book. Also to be borne in
mind is the fact that this is the work of one person
working in one library.

The names of the composers on this list are spelt as
they appear in the reference quoted. Where this
differs from that used in the source indexed a cross-
reference has been made. Alternate versions of a
composer´s name are given in brackets.

I have tried to find a bibliographic reference with
biographical information for every name on this list,
however, time constraints and sheer practicality have
prevented me from checking every name in every available reference work. The most obvious references were
checked first and once a reference had been found the
name was, with certain exceptions, crossed off the
list. I have been able to tabulate the number of
references given from each reference source and thus
users will be able to gauge the extent to which each
has been used.

Where no biographical reference has been found and
where the composer´s full name is not known the title
of the music recorded has been given.

The dates quoted for each composer generally come from
the reference indicated. The dates given are generally
the year of birth and the year of death. However for
many of the earlier composers these two facts may not
be known and the reference may be giving the date of

baptism, date of signing of the composer's last will
and testament or the date of his or her burial. In
addition some of the information given on dates in such
reference sources as the New Grove (R.1) have had to be
abbreviated. Statements such as "possibly died before
1560, probably died before 1571 and more than likely
was dead by 1585" have been shortened to, say, "died
c1570". Readers are urged to use the reference quoted
for fuller information regarding the life span of these
early composers. Further information about dates has
been taken from the "Index to Music Necrology" that
appears in the June issue of Notes: The Quarterly
Journal of the Music Library Association.

R   The number following is the reference where
        biographical information may be found.

S   The numbers following indicate the discographies
        that contain recordings of the composer's work.

S.c   This indicates that the composer's name has
        appeared in one or more of the current record
        catalogues indexed.

S.e   This indicates that recordings of the composer's
        work appear in one or more of the discographies
        of early recordings indexed. Generally this has
        been indicated when it is the only place record-
        ings have been found.

Most of the sources indexed list composers in alphabet-
ical order, when this has not been the case the approp-
riate page number has been indicated in parentheses.
This has not been possible with catalogues of early
recordings due to the huge number of references that
this would have entailed.

Where no source is given then the only place recordings
have been found is in the record collection of the
Music Library of the University of Toronto.

A name preceded by "***" indicates that the name or the
name-date combination is believed to be that of a fic-
titious person. This has usually come about when the
names of two distinct composers have been combined or
when the name of composer A has been combined with the
dates of composer B.

```
LANG, P. F.      [S.13] = LANG, Philip Emil Joseph
LUTSTSY, L.      [S.18] = LUZZI, Luigi
ZHORA, Mikhail [S.18] = JORA, Mihail
```

Entries such as the above are used when the name
appearing in a discography has been found to be an
incorrect spelling, typographical error or an unusual
transliteration. Many examples of the latter appear in
John R. Bennett's Russian Discography (S.18). The
person who did the transliteration from the Cyrillic to
the Roman alphabet was unaware sometimes that the name
in question had already been transliterated from Roman
to Cyrillic producing, as in the third example above, a
"Russification" of a common Italian surname.

In a work of this size the amount of time that could be
spent on each composer has obviously been limited.
Assumptions have been made and some of them will inev-
itably turn out to be incorrect. A name followed by
"[?]" indicates that the identification is highly
speculative. The greatest number of assumptions have
been made with regard to names taken from S.1x, 5x and
S.e. These sources list surnames only and identification has been made generally through catalogues of
sheet music such as R.89-92 and 112. R.89, though a
mine of information on 19th Century music, contains
numerous misattributions and information taken from it
needs to be treated accordingly. Another source used
for identifying these surname-only composers was R.88.
One should entertain no doubts about its accuracy but,
alas, the volumes published had reached only the letter
"K" at the time of going to press. S.32 is a special
case as not only are Christian names missing but in
most instances no titles are given either. With many
names an intelligent guess was the best that I could do
in deciding which composer was meant by entries such as
"Smith". S.24a was still on a card-index file when I
used the information. This source was added only when
the name did not appear in S.24 or when it contained
information about that was not in S.24.

REFERENCES

R.1   Grove, G. The New Grove Dictionary of Music
        and Musicians. Ed. S. Sadie, London:
        Macmillan, 1980.   [5497]

R.1.1   Grove, G. Grove's Dictionary of Music and
        Musicians (A.D. 1450-1889) by Eminent Writers
        English and Foreign. London: Macmillan,
        1878-89. Revised and reprinted, 1900.   [1]

R.1.5   Grove, G. Grove's Dictionary of Music and
        Musicians. 5th ed., ed. E. Bloom
        London: Macmillan, 1954.   [12]

R.2   Riemann, H. Musik Lexikon. 12th ed.,
        ed. W. Gurlitt.
        Mainz: B. Schott's Sohne, 1959-67.   [70]

R.2a   -------. Supplement. [3]

R.3   Frank, P. Kurzgefasstes Tonkunstler-
        Lexikon. 14th ed., ed. W. Altmann.
        Regensburg: Gustave Bosse, 1936. [314]

R.4   Frank, P. Kurzgefasstes Tonkunstler-
        Lexikon. 15th ed, ed. B. Bulling.
        Wilhelmshaven: Heinrichshofen, 1974. [503]

R.5   Eitner, R. Biographisch-Biblio-
        graphisches Quellen-Lexikon der Musiker und
        Musikgelehrten Christlicher Zeitrechung
        bis mitte des neunzehten Jahrhunderts.
        2nd ed. Graz: Akademische Druck, 1959.   [182]

R.6   Baker, T. Baker's Biographical Dictionary of
        Musicians. 6th ed., ed. N. Slonimsky.
        New York: Schirmer Books, 1978.   [-]

R.7   Cohen, A. I. International Encyclopedia of
        Women Composers. New York: R. R. Bowker 1981.
        [307]

R.8   Gatti, G. M. La Musica: Parte seconda:
        Dizionario. Turin: Unione Tipografico-
        Editrice Torinese, 1968-71. [152]

R.9   Pena, J. Angles, H. Diccionario de la
        Música Labor.
        Barcelona: Editorial Labor, 1954. [51]

R.10   Schmidl, C. Dizionario Universale dei
        Musicisti. Milan: Sonzogno, 1937. [86]

R.10s   ------. Supplement. [25]

R.10sa ------. ------. Appendix. [1]

R.11   Michel, F. Encyclopedie de la Musique.
        Paris: Fasquelle, 1958. [10]

R.12   Blume, F. Die Musik in Geschichte
        und Gegenwart.
        Kassel: Bahrenreiter, 1949-1967. [1]

R.13   Bull, S. Index to Biographies of
        Contemporary Composers. Vol.1.
        New York: Scarecrow Press, 1964. [14]

R.14   Bull, S. Index to Biographies of
        Contemporary Composers. Vol.2.
        Metuchen, N.J.: Scarecrow Press, 1974. [705]

R.15   Szabolcsi, B.; Toth A. Zenei Lexikon.
        Budapest: Zenemukiado Vallalat, 1965. [19]

R.16   Honegger, M. Dictionnaire de la musique.
        Paris: Bordas, 1970. [9]

R.17   Organizacion de los Estados Americanos.
        Compositores de America. [1]
        Washington, 1954-1979.

R.18   Cernusak, G. Cesko Slovensky Hudebni Slovnik
        Osob a Instituci. Prague: Statni Hudebni
        Vydavatelstvi 1963-1965. [52]

R.19   Anderson, E. R.   Contemporary American
        Composers: A Biographical Dictionary.
        2nd ed.   Boston: G. K. Hall, 1982.   [858]

R.20   Heard, P. S.   American Music 1698-1800:
        An Annotated Bibliography.
        Waco, Texas: Baylor University Press,
        1975.   [2]

R.21   Muller, R.   Anthologie des Compositeurs de
        Musique d'Alsace.
        Strasbourg: Federation des Societes
        Catholiques de Chant et de Musique
        d'Alsace, 1970.   [3]

R.22   Moncada Garcia, F.   Pequenas Biografias de
        Grandes Musicos Mexicanos.
        Mexico, D.F.: Ediciones Framong, 1966.   [4]

R.23   American Society of Composers, Authors and
        Publishers.   ASCAP Biographical Dictionary
        of Composers, Authors and Publishers.
        4th ed by Jaques Cattell Press, New York:
        R. R. Bowker Company, 1980.   [305]

R.24   Zimmerman, F. B.   Henry Purcell 1659-1695:
        An Analytical Catalogue of his Music.
        London: Macmillan, 1963.   [-]

R.25   Robijns, J. Algemene Muziek Encyclopedie.
        Bussum: Unieboek, 1979.   [86]

R.26   Arizaga, R.   Enciclopedia de la Musica
        Argentina.
        Buenos Aires: Fondo Nacional de las Artes,
        1971.   [57]

R.27   Coral, J. A.   Compositores Mexicanos.
        Mexico, D. F.: Editores Asociados, 1971.   [1]

R.28   Vodarsky-Shiraeff, A.   Russian Composers and
        Musicians: A Biographical Dictionary.
        New York: H. W. Wilson, 1940.   Repr.
        New York: Da Capo Press, 1969.   [7]

R.29   Vasconcellos, J.   Os Musicos Portuguezes.
        Porto: Imprensa Portugueza, 1870.   [2]

R.30   Morin, C. Sohlman's Musiklexikon.
        2nd ed., ed. H. Astrand. Stockholm:
        Sohlman Forlag, 1975-1979. [130]

R.30a   Morin, C. Sohlman's Musiklexikon.
        Stockholm: Sohlman Forlag, 1948-52. [14]

R.31   Canadian Association of Music Libraries.
        Musicians on Canada: A Bio-bibliographical
        Finding List. Ottawa: Canadian
        Association of Music Libraries, 1981. [41]

R.32   Dennison, S. The Edwin Fleisher Collection
        of Orchestral Music in the Free Library of
        Philadelphia: A Cumulative Catalogue,
        1929-1977.   Boston: G. K. Hall, 1979. [-]

R.33   Cosma, V. Muzicieni Romani Lexicon.
        Bucharest: Editura Muzicala a Uniunii
        Compozitorilor, 1970. [12]

R.34   Vieira, E. Diccionario Biographico de
        Musicos Portuguezes: Historia e
        Bibliographia da Musica em Portugal.
        Lisbon: Moreira & Pinheiro, 1900-04. [2]

R.35   Murdoch, J. Australia's Contemporary
        Composers. Sydney: Macmillan, 1972. [3]

R.36   Japan UNESCO Ngo Council. Japanese
        Composers and their Works (since 1868)
        Tokyo, 1972. [22]

R.37   Ronald, L. Who's Who in Music. London:
        Shaw Publishing Co. Ltd., 1937. [25]

R.38   Kortsen, B. Contemporary Norwegian Music:
        A Bibliography and Discography.
        Bergen: Kortsen, B., 1980. [3]

R.39   Pratt, W. S. The New Encyclopedia of Music
        and Musicians. New York: Macmillan, 1924.
        [14]

R.40   Deale, E. M. A Catalogue of Contemporary
        Contemporary Irish Composers.   [5]
        Dublin: Music Association of Ireland, 1973.

R.41   Schuh, W.   Schweizer Musiker-Lexikon.
        Zurich: Atlantis Verlag, 1964.   [3]

R.42   Kovacevic, K.   Muzicka Enciklopedija.
        Zagreb, 1971.   [2]

R.43   Key, P.   Pierre Key´s Musical Who´s Who.
        New York: Pierre Key, 1931.   [9]

R.44   Brown, J. D. and Stratton, S. S.   British
        Musical Biography: A Dictionary of Musical
        Artists, Authors and Composers born in
        Britain and its Colonies.
        Birmingham: Stratton, 1897.   [35]

R.45   Abert, H. J.   Illustriertes Musik-Lexikon.
        Stuttgart: J. Engelhorns 1927.   [-]

R.46   Bernsdorf, E.   Neues Universal-Lexikon
        der Tonkunst.
        Dresden: Robert Schaefer, 1856-65.   [1]

R.47   Keldysh, Y. V.   Muzykalnaya Entsiklopedia.
        Moscow: Sovietski Kompozitor, 1973.   [103]

R.48   Londieux, J. M.   125 ans de Musique pour
        Saxophone. Paris: Leduc, 1971.   [6]

R.49   Berger, K.   Band Encyclopedia.
        Kent, Ohio: Band Associates, 1960.   [44]

R.50   Jablonski, E.   The Encyclopedia of American
        Music.   [38]

R.51   Eaglefield-Hull, A.   A Dictionary of Modern
        Music and Musicians.
        London: J. M. Dent, 1924.   [3]

R.52   De Angelis, A.   Dizionario dei Musicisti.
        Rome: Ansonia, 1922.   [12]

R.53   District of Columbia Historical Records
        Survey, Division of Community Service
        Programs Work Projects Administration.
        Bio-Bibliographical Index of Musicians in
        the United States of America from
        Colonial Times. Washington, D.C.:
        Music Division Pan American Union, 1941.   [59]

R.54   Pohlmann, E. Laute Theorbe Chitarrone.
        2nd ed. Bremen: Edition Eres, 1972. [2]

R.55   Mariz, V. Dicionario Bio-Bibliografico
        Musical. Rio de Janeiro: Livraria Kosmos
        1948. [3]

R.56   Mayer-Serra, O. Música y Músicos de Latino
        America. Mexico, D. F.: Atlante, 1947. [12]

R.57   Brown, J. D. Biographical Dictionary of
        Musicians with a Bibliography of English
        Writings on Music. London: Alexander
        Gardner, 1886.
        Repr. Hildesheim: Georg Olms, 1970. [15]

R.58   Olt, H. Estonian Music.
        Tallin: Perioodika, 1980. [16]

R.59   Ewen, D. Popular American Composers from
        Revolutionary Times to the Present.
        New York: H. W. Wilson, 1962. [4]

R.60   Claghorn, C. E. Biographical Dictionary of
        Jazz. Englewood Cliffs, N. J.:
        Prentice-Hall, 1982. [5]

R.61   Kinkle, R. D. The Complete Encyclopedia of
        Popular Music and Jazz 1900-1950.
        New Rochelle, N. Y.: Arlington House,
        1974. [7]

R.62   Comuzio, E. Film Music Lexicon.
        Amministrazione Provinciale di Pavia, 1980. [7]

R.63   Ravina, M.; Shlomo, S. Who is Who in Acum.
        Acum Ltd., Societe d'Auteurs, Compositeurs
        et Editeurs de Musique en Israel, 1965. [1]

R.64   Yates, J. V. Who's Who in Music and
        Musicians' International Directory 1972.
        6th ed. London: Burke's Peerage Ltd., 1972.
        [15]

R.65   Potterton, W. J. Who's Who in Music and
        Musicians' International Directory 1969.
        5th ed. Burke's Peerage, 1972. [-]

R.66   Townend, P.; Simmons, D. Who's Who in
        Music and Musicians' International
        Directory 1962.
        4th ed. Burke's Peerage, 1962. [1]

R.67   Cardoso, S. T. Dicionario Biografico de
        Musica Popular.
        Rio de Janeiro: S. T. Cardoso, 1965. [18]

R.68   Boltenstern, T. Musiklexikon: Svensk
        1900-talsmusik fan opera till pop.
        Stockholm: Bokforlaget, 1978. [6]

R.69   Goertz, H. Österreichische Komponisten der
        Gegenwart. Vienna: Doblinger, 1979. [2]

R.70   Mize, J. T. H. The International Who
        is Who in Music. 5th ed.
        Chicago: Who is Who in Music, 1951. [1]

R.71   Barone, J. Who is Who in Music: 1941 Edition.
        Chicago: Lee Stern Press, 1941. [1]

R.72   Spaeth, S. Who is Who in Music:
        1929 Edition. Chicago: Who is Who in
        Music, 1929. [-]

R.73   Vannes, R. Dictionnaire Universel des
        Luthiers. 3rd ed. Brussells:
        Les Amis de la Musique, 1972. [-]

R.74   Chominski, J. Slownik muzykow Polskich.
        Warsaw: Polskie Wydawnictwo Muzyczne, 1962. [1]

R.75   Bohlander, C.; Holler, K. H. Reclams
        Jazzfuhrer. Stuttgart: Philipp Reclam,
        1971. [1]

R.76   De Schrijver, K. Bibliografie der
        Belgische Toonkunstenaars sedert 1800.
        Leuven: Vlaamse Drukkerij, 1958. [2]

R.77   Pine, L. G. Who's Who in Music:
        First Post-War Edition (1949-50).
        London: Shaw Publishing, 1950. [13]

R.78   Kutsch, K. J.; Riemens, L. Unvergangliche
        Stimmen Sangerlexikon. 2nd ed.
        Bern: A Francke AG, 1982. [1]

R.79   Pierreuse, B. Flute Litterature.
        Paris: Editions Jobert, 1982. [1]

R.80   Gaster, A. International Who´s
        Who in Music and Musicians´ Directory.
        9th ed. Cambridge: International Who´s Who
        in Music, 1980. [97]

R.81   Winters, K. Poitvin, G. Encyclopedia of
        Music in Canada. Ed. H. Kallmann.
        Toronto: University of Toronto Press, 1981. [15]

R.82   Stern, S. Women Composers: A Handbook.
        Metuchen, N. J.: Scarecrow Press, 1978. [-]

R.83   Smith, R. Sixth Catalogue of Contemporary
        Welsh Music. The Guild for the Promotion
        of Welsh Music, 1975. [2]

R.84   Green, S. Encyclopaedia of the Musical
        Theatre. New York: Dodd Mead, 1976. [1]

R.85   Gammond, P.; Horricks, R. Music on
        Record 1: Brass Bands.
        Cambridge: Patrick Stephens, 1980. [41]

R.86   Hixon, D. L. Music in Early America:
        A Bibliography of Music in Evans.
        Metuchen, N. J.: Scarecrow Press, 1970. [1]

R.87   Sears, M. E. Song Index: An Index to more
        than 12,000 Songs in 177 Song Collections
        Comprising 262 Volumes and Supplement,
        1934. H. W. Wilson. Repr.
        The Shoe String Press, 1966. [-]

R.88   Baillie, L. The Catalogue of Printed
        Music in the British Library to 1980.
        London: K. G. Saur, 1981-. [-]

R.89   Pazdirek, F. Universal-Handbuch der Musik-
        literatur aller Zeiten und Volker.
        Vienna: Pazdirek, 1904-1910. Repr.
        Hilversum: Knuf, 1967. [-]

R.90   BBC Music Library. _Piano and Organ Catalogue._
        London: British Broadcasting Corporation, 1966.
        [-]

R.91   BBC Music Library. _Song Catalogue._ London:
        British Broadcasting Corporation, 1966. [-]

R.92   BBC Music Library. _Chamber Music Catalogue._
        London: British Broadcasting Corporation, 1966.
        [-]

R.93   Steiger, F. _Opernlexikon._
        Tutzing: Schneider, 1977. [-]

R.94   Shaw, M.; Coleman, H.; Cartledge, T. M.
        National Anthems of the World. 4th ed.
        Poole, Dorset: Blandford Press, 1975. [2]

R.95   Suppan, W. _Lexikon des Blasmusikwesens._
        2nd ed. Freiburg: Blasmusikverlag Fritz
        Schulz, 1976. [29]

R.96   Cook, K. _The Bandsman's Everything Within._
        London: Hinrichsen Edition, 1950. [9]

R.97   Pereira Salas, E. _Biobibliografia Musical_
        de Chile desde los Origenes a 1886.
        Santiago: Ediciones de la Universidad
        de Chile, 1978. [1]

R.98   Baker, T. _A Biographical Dictionary of_
        Musicians. New York: G. Schirmer, 1900. [9]

R.99   Baker, T. _Baker's Biographical Dictionary_
        of Musicians. 3rd ed., ed. A. Remy.
        New York: G. Schirmer, 1919. [1]

R.100   Baker, T. _Baker's Biographical Dictionary_
        of Musicians. 4th ed.
        New York: G. Schirmer, 1940. [-]

R.101   Baker, T. _Baker's Biographical Dictionary_
        of Musicians. 5th ed., ed. by N. Slonimsky.
        New York: G. Schirmer, 1958. [-]

R.102   Baker, T. _Baker's Biographical Dictionary_
        of Musicians. 1965 supplement by N. Slonimsky.
        New York: G. Schirmer, 1965. [-]

R.103   Baker, T.   Baker's Biographical Dictionary
         of Musicians.   1971 supplement by
         N. Slonimsky.   New York: G. Schirmer,
         1971.   [-]

R.104   Sagardia, A. S.   Musicos Vascos.
         San Sebastian: Editorial Aunamendi, 1972.   [10]

R.105   Weston, P.   More Clarinet Virtuosi of the
         Past.   London: Pamela Weston, 1977.   [4]

R.106   Bone, P. J.   The Guitar and Mandolin:
         Biographies of Celebrated Players and
         Composers.   2nd ed.   London: Schott, 1954,
         repr. 1972.   [7]

R.107   Love, J.   Scottish Church Music, its
         Composers and Sources.
         Edinburgh: William Blackwood, 1891.   [1]

R.108   Stewart-Green, M.   Women Composers:
         A Checklist of Works for the Solo Voice.
         Boston: G. K. Hall, 1980.   [-]

R.109   Baptie, D.   Musical Scotland Past and
         Present.   Paisley: J. & R. Parlane, 1894.
         Repr. Hildesheim: George Olms, 1972.   [3]

R.110   Subira, J.   Historia de la Musica Espanola
         e Hispano-americana.
         Barcelona: Salvat Editores, 1953. [1]

R.111   Norlind, T. Allmant Musiklexikon.
         Stockholm: Wahlstrom & Widstrand, 1927.   [10]

R.112   BBC Music Library.   Choral and Opera
         Catalogue.   London: British Broadcasting
         Corporation, 1967.   [-]

R.113   Hostos, A. de. Diccionario Historico Biblio-
         grafico Comentado de Puerto Rico.
         San Juan: La Academia Puertorriquena de la
         Historia, 1976.   [1]

R.200   New York Public Library Reference Department.
         Dictionary Catalogue of the Music Collection.
         Boston: G. K. Hall, 1964.   [72]

SOURCES

Discographies.

S.1   Gramophone Shop Inc. Encyclopedia of the
        World's Best Recorded Music. 2nd. ed.,
        ed. R. Gilbert.
        New York: Gramophone Shop, 1931.

S.1x   -------. Index

S.2   Gramophone Shop Inc. The Gramophone Shop
        Encyclopedia of Recorded Music.
        Ed. R. D. Darell. New York: Gramophone
        Shop, 1936.

S.3   Gramophone Shop Inc. The Gramophone Shop
        Encyclopedia of Recorded Music. 2nd ed.,
        ed. G. Leslie. New York: Gramophone
        Shop, 1942.

S.4   Gramophone Shop Inc. The Gramophone Shop
        Encyclopedia of Recorded Music. 3rd ed.,
        ed. R. H. Reid. New York: Gramophone
        Shop, 1948.

S.5   Clough, F. F. and Cummings, G. J.
        The World's Encyclopedia of Recorded Music.
        London: Sidgwick & Jackson, 1952.

S.5x   -------. Index

S.6   Clough, F. F. and Cummings, G. J..
        The World's Encyclopedia of Recorded Music.
        1st supplement. [Bound in with S.5].

S.7   Clough, F. F. and Cummings, G. J.
       The World's Encyclopedia of Recorded Music.
       2nd supplement. London: Sidgwick &
       Jackson, 1953.

S.8   Clough, F. F. and Cummings, G. J.
       The World's Encyclopedia of Recorded Music.
       3rd supplement. London: Sidgwick &
       Jackson, 1957.

S.9   Myers, K. Index to Record Reviews based on
       material origionally published in "Notes, the
       Quarterly Journal of the Music Library
       Association" between 1949 and 1977. Vols. 1-4.
       Boston: G. K. Hall, 1978.

S.10   -------. Vol. 5.

S.11   Hall, D. The Record Book. 5th printing.
       New York: Smith & Durrell, 1943.

S.12   Rowell, L. American Organ Music on Records.
       Braintree, Mass: The Organ Literature
       Foundation, 1976.

S.13   Oja, C. J. American Music Recordings:
       A Discography of 20th Century U.S.
       Composers. New York: Institute for
       Studies in American Music, Conservatory
       of Music Brooklyn College of the City
       University of New York, 1982.

S.14   Coover, J.; Colvig, R. Medieval and
       Renaissance Music on Long-Playing Records.
       Detroit Studies in Music Bibliography, No.6.
       Detroit: Information Service, 1964.

S.15   -------. First supplement (1960-1961).
       [Bound in with first edition].

S.16   -------. Renaissance Music on Long-Playing
       Records. Detroit Studies in Music Bibliography,
       No.26. Detroit: Information Coordinators, 1973.

S.17   Tinnell, R. D. An Annotated Discography
       of Music in Spain before 1650. Madison,
       Wisconsin: The Hispanic Seminary of Medieval
       Studies, 1980.

S.18 Bennett, J. R. Melodiya: A Soviet Russian
      L. P. Discography. Westport, Conn.:
      Greenwood Press, 1981.

S.19 Gilbert, R. The Clarinetists' Solo
      Repertoire: A Discography.
      New York: The Grenadilla Society, 1972.

S.20 Gilbert, R. The Clarinetists' Discography
      II. New York: The Grenadilla Society, 1975.

S.21 Walker, B. H. Recordings for the Clarinet
      and the Recording Artists.
      Augusta, Georgia: B. H. Walker, 1969.

S.22 Schleuter, S. L. Discography of Saxophone
      Music. Clear Lake, South Dakota: Meadowlark
      Publications, 1977.

S.23 Beaumont, F. Viola-Diskographie/
      Discographie sur l'Alto.
      Kassel: Bahrenreiter-Verlag, 1973.

S.24 Creighton, J. G. Discopaedia of the
      Violin (1889-1971). Toronto: University
      of Toronto Press, 1974.

S.24a -------. 2nd ed. (unpublished).

S.25 Stahl, D. A Selected Discography of Solo Song.
      Detroit Studies in Music Bibliography, No.13.
      Detroit: Information Coordinators, 1968.

S.26 -------. Supplement.
      Detroit: Information Coordinators, 1970.

S.27 -------. A Cumulation Through 1971.
      Detroit Studies in Music Bibliography, No.24.
      Detroit: Information Coordinators, 1972.

S.28 -------. Supplement 1971-1974
      Detroit Studies in Music Bibliography, No.34.
      Detroit: Information Coordinators, 1976.

S.29 Brumby, C. Discography of Australian Music.
      Australian Journal of Music Education, I.
      (Oct, 1967).

S.30   Frasier, J. Women Composers: A Discography.
        Detroit Studies in Music Bibliography, No.50.
        Detroit: Information Coordinators, 1983.

S.31   Gardavsky, C. Contemporary Czechoslovak
        Composers. Prague: Panton, 1965.

S.32   Purcell, R. C. Classic Guitar, Lute and
        Vihuela Discography. Melville, N.Y.:
        Belwin-Mills, 1976.

S.33   Rosenberg, H. Aksel Schiøtz: A Discography.
        Copenhagen,1966.

S.34   Mathews, E. G. Titto Ruffo - A Centenary
        Discography. Penybanc, Llandeilo, Dyfed:
        E. G. Mathews, 1977.

S.35   Kappel, V. Contemporary Danish Composers.
        2d ed. Copenhagen: Det Danske Selskab,
        1950.

S.36   Centre Belge de Documentation Musical.
        Music in Belgium - Contemporary Belgian
        Composers. Brussels: A. Manteau, 1964.

S.37   Callaway, F. and Tunley, D. Australian
        Composition in the Twentieth Century.
        Melbourne: Oxford University Press, 1978.

S.38   Bergendal, G. 33 Svenska Komponister.
        Falun: J. A. Lindblads, 1972.

S.39   Sublette, H. A Discography of Hispanic
        Music in the Fine Arts Library of the
        University of New Mexico. Albuquerque:
        University of New Mexico, 1973.

S.40   The Scandinavian Music Information Centres.
        Music from Scandinavia. Copenhagen: Nordic
        Council of Ministers, 1982.

S.41   Boren, C. van den. Geschiedenis van de
        Muziek in die Nederlanden. Amsterdam:
        Wereldbibliotheek, 1949.

S.42   Bontinck-Kuffel, I. Opern auf Schallplatten
        1900-1962. Vienna: Universal Edition, 1974.

S.43   Porter, J. W. and Henrysson, H. A Jussi
        Bjoerling Discography. Indianapolis, 1982

S.44   Bolig, J. R. The Recordings of Enrico Caruso.
        Dover, Delaware: 1973.

S.45   (Not used)

S.46   Arizaga, R. Enciclopedia de la Música
        Argentina. Buenos Aires: Fondo Nacional de
        las Artes, 1971. [R.26]

S.47   Wiley Hitchcock, H. American Music before 1865
        in Print and on Records: A Biblio-discography.
        Brooklyn: Institute for Studies in American
        Music, Department of Music, School of Performing
        Arts, Brooklyn College of the City University of
        New York, 1976.

S.48   Czigany, G. Contemporary Hungarian Composers.
        Budapest: Edito Musica, 1970.

S.49   Deale, E. M. A Catalogue of Contemporary
        Irish Composers. Dublin: Music Association of
        Ireland, 1973. [R.40]

S.50   Japan UNESCO Ngo Council. Japanese Composers and
        their Works (since 1868). Tokyo, 1972. [R.36]

S.51   Kortsen, B. Contemporary Norwegian Music:
        A Bibliography and Discography. Bergen:
        Kortsen, B., 1980. [R.38].

S.52   Cohen, A. I. International Discography of
        Women Composers. Westport, Conn.:
        Greenwood Press, 1984.

S.53   Kratzenstein, M. and Hamilton, J.
        Four Centuries of Organ Music:
        From the Robertsbridge Codex through the
        Baroque Era: An Annotated Discography
        Detroit: Information Coordinators, 1984.

S.54   Berger, K. Band Encyclopedia.
        Kent, Ohio: Band Associates, 1960. [R.49].

S.55   Gammond, P. and Horricks, R. Music on Record 1:
        Brass Bands. Cambridge: Patrick Stephens, 1980.
        [R.85]

S.56   Jacobsson, S. Musiken i Sverige
        Skivlyssnarens handbok i svensk musik
        fran aldsta tid till 1970-talet med utforlig
        skivforteckning. Vasteras: ICA-forlaget, 1975.

S.57   Jacobsen, E. and Kappel, V. Musikkens Mestre
        Danske Komponister. Copenhagen: Jul.
        Gjellerups Forlag, 1947.

Early Recordings.

        Voices of the Past, vol. 1. Ed. J. R. Bennet.
        Lingfield, Surrey: Oakwood Press, 1956.

        Moses, J. M. Collectors´ Guide to American
        Recordings 1898-1925. New York: American
        Record Collectors´ Exchange, 1949.

        Bauer, R. The New Catalogue of Historical
        Records 1898-1908/09. London: Sidgwick &
        Jackson, 1947.

Current Record Catalogues.

        Croucher, T. Early Music Discography. London:
        Music Library Association Publishing, 1981.

        Gramophone Classical Catalogue. London:
        General Gramophone Publications Ltd.
        Dec 76, Dec 78, Dec 83, Sept 84

        Diapason Catalogue General Classique. Paris:
        Dispason-Microsillon. 1982

        Bielefelder Katalog Klassik.
        Karlsruhe: G. Braun. Fruhjahr 1981.

ABBREVIATIONS

>	after	gui	guitar
<	before	hps	harpsichord
arr	arranged	orch	orchestra
b	born	org	organ
c	circa	p	piano
ce	cello	pseud	pseudonym
cl	clarinet	v	vocal
d	died	vi	violin
fl	flourished/flute	vla	viola

Arg	Argentina	Ire	Ireland
Arm	Armenia	Isr	Israel
Aus	Austria	It	Italy
Bel	Belgium	Lat	Latvia
Boh	Bohemia	Lith	Lithuania
Bul	Bulgaria	Mex	Mexico
Can	Canada	Neth	Netherlands
Cz	Czechoslovakia	Nor	Norway
Den	Denmark	Pol	Poland
Eng	England	Port	Portugal
Est	Estonia	Rum	Rumania
Fin	Finland	Scot	Scotland
Flem	Flemish	S. Neth	South Netherlands
Fr	France	Sp	Spain
Ger	Germany	Ven	Venezuela
Hun	Hungary	Yug	Yugoslavia

COMPOSERS ON RECORD

AACHEN, Hans von - pseud [see BEHR, Franż]
AAGAARD, Hans Thorvald (1877-1937), Den
   R.30   S.33,57
AAGESEN, Truid (fl 1593-1615), Den
   R.1   S.c
AARNE, Els - pseud [ie Elze Janova PAËMURRU]
   (1917-   ), USSR
   R.7   S.18,52
AARONSON, Irving (1895-1963), USA
   R.23   S.5,10
AAV, Evald (1900-1939), Est
   R.14   S.18
ABACO, Evaristo Felice dall´ [see DALL´ABACO, Evaristo]
ABACO, Giuseppe Clemente Ferdinando dall´
   [see DALL´ABACO, Giuseppe Clemente Ferdinando]
ABADES, J. Martinez
              S.e
ABAILARD, Peter [see ABELARD, Peter]
ABAZA, Arkadii Maximovich (1845 or 1848-1915), Russia
   R.47   S.18
ABAZA, Vladimir (1861-1918)
              S.5,18
ABBASOV, Ashraf Dzhelalogly (1920-   ), USSR
   R.14   S.18
ABBATINI, Antonio Maria (c1609-c1677), It
   R.1
ABBÉ, Joseph-Barnabe l´
   [see L´ABBÉ, le fils] (see note)
ABBIATI, Louis (1866-1933), Fr
   R.10   S.c
ABBOT, Lyman (1835-1922), USA
   R.53   S.24
ABBOTT - Just for today
              S.e
ABBOTT, Alan (1926-   ), Eng

ABDRAYEV, Mukash (1920-   ), USSR
   R.47   S.18

ABE, Komei (1911-   ), Japan
   R. 4   S. 50
ABEJO, Sister M. Rosalina (1922-   ), Philippines
   R. 7   S. 52
ABEL, Carl Friedrich (1723-1787), Ger
   R. 1   S. c,3,4,5,7,8,10,20,24
ABEL, Clamor Heinrich (1634-1696), Ger
   R. 1   S. c
ABEL, Otto (1905-   ), Ger
   R. 4   S. c
ABELARD [Abailard], Peter (1079-1142), Fr
   R. 1   S. c,5x
ABELE, Adolfs (1889-1967), Lat
   R. 30
ABELIOVICH, Lev Moiseyevich (1912-   ), USSR
   R. 47   S. 18,24a
ÅBERG, Jan Håkan (1916-   ), Sweden
   R. 30   S. c
ABLONIZ, Miguel (1917-   )
             S. c,10,32
ABRAHAM, Paul (1892-1960), Hun
   R. 1   S. c,9,10,24,43
ABRAHAMS, Maurice (1883-1931), USA
   R. 23   S. e
ABRAHAMSEN, Hans (1952-   ), Den
   R. 14   S. 40
ABRAMIAN, Eduard Aslanovich (1923-   ), Arm
             S. 24a
ABRAMSON, Robert M. (1928-   ), USA
   R. 19   S. 13
ABREU, Zeqhinha de - pseud
   [ie Jose Gomes de ABREU] (1880-1935), Brazil
   R. 67   S. 10
ABSIL, Jean (1893-1974), Bel
   R. 1   S. c,7,8,10,18,22,24,36
ABT, Franz Wilhelm (1819-1885), Ger
   R. 1   S. c,5x,10,24,28
ACCOLAY, Joan Batiste (1845-1905)
             S. 24a
ACCORDI, Pietro
             S. 24
ACCORETI - Die Verfuhrung (vi & p),
             S. 24
ACHLEITNER, Rudolf (1864-1909), Aus
   R. 95   S. 10
ACHRON, Joseph (1886-1943), USA
   R. 1   S. c,1x,4,5x,10,18,24
ACKERNLEY, Mabel
             S. 24,30

ACKLEY, Bentley Deforrest (1872-1958), USA
  R. 1   S. 10
ACOURT, Johannes [see HARCOURT, Johannes]
ACQUA, Eva dell [see DELL ACQUA, Eva]
ADACHI, Motohiko (1940-   ), Japan
  R. 4   S. 50
ADAM de ANTIQUIS VENETUS [see ANTIQUIS, Adam de]
ADAM de SAINT VICTOR (d. 1177 or 1192), Fr
  R. 1   S. c, 16
ADAM de la HALLE (c1245-c1306), Fr
  R. 1   S. c, 2-5, 7, 8, 10, 11, 14-16, 18
ADAM von FULDA (c1445-1505), Ger
  R. 1   S. c, 10, 16
ADAM, Adolphe (1803-1856), Fr
  R. 1   S. c, 2-11, 18, 24, 28, 43
ADAM, Carl Ferdinand (1806-1867), Ger
  R. 10   S. c
ADAM, Claus (1917-   ), USA
  R. 19   S. 10, 13
ADAM, Maitre (18th Cent) - Aussitot que la lumiere
  (Billant)   S. 5x
ADAMS, A. Emmet (?-1938)
            S. 24
ADAMS, A. Nelson
            S. 10
ADAMS, Alton A (1889-   ), USA
            S. 13
ADAMS, Stephen - pseud [ie Michael MAYBRICK]
  (1844-1913), Eng
  R. 44   S. c, 4, 5x, 10, 24, 28
ADAMS, Trayton
            S. 54(321, 34, 62)
ADAMYAN, G (1917-   )
            S. 18
ADASKIN, Murray (1906-   ), Can
  R. 1   S. 10, 24
ADDEY, Eileen L. L.
            S. e
ADDINSELL, Richard (1904-1977), Eng
  R. 1   S. c, 4, 10
ADDISON, John (1920-   ), Eng
  R. 1   S. c, 10
ADERHOLT, Sarah (1955-   )
            S. 30, 52
ADLER, Richard (1921-   ), USA
  R. 1   S. 9
ADLER, Samuel (1928-   ), USA
  R. 1   S. c, 10, 12, 13
ADLGASSER, Anton Cajetan (1729-1777), Ger
  R. 1

ADLINGTON - Au mois d'avril (vi & p)
        S. 24a
ADMONI, Iogann Grigorievich (1906-   )
    R. 14   S. 18
ADNEMAR (11th Cent) - Salve Regina, mater misericordiae
        S. c, 10
ADOLPHUS, Milton (1913-   ), USA
    R. 19   S. 10, 13, 20
ADORNO, Theodor Wiesengrund (1903-1969), Ger
    R. 1   S. c
ADRIAENSSEN, Emanuel (c1554-1604), S. Neth
    R. 1   S. c, 10
ADRIEN le ROY [see LE ROY, Adrien]
ADSON, John (d. 1640), Eng
    R. 1   S. c, 8, 10, 16
AERSCHOT, Oct. van - Moeder, ik je niet missen (vi & p)
        S. 24a
AFANASYEV, Leonid Viktorovich (1921-   ), Russia
    R. 14   S. 18
AFANASYEV, Nicolay Yakovlevich (1821-1898), Russia
    R. 1   S. 18, 24
AFFILARD, Michel l' [see L'AFFILARD, Michel]
AGA, Nazare
        S. 24a
AGABABOV, Sergei Artemievich (1926-1959)
    R. 14   S. 18
AGAPKIN, V. - Slav women's farewell
        S. 54(356)
AGAZZARI, Agostino (1578-1640), It
    R. 1   S. 7, 8, 10, 14, 16
AGER, Klaus (1946-   ), Aus
    R. 69   S. c
AGERBY, Aksel (1889-1942), Sweden
    R. 30   S. 4, 5x, 33, 35
AGINCOUR, François d' [see DAGINCOUR, François]
AGINCOURT, Perrin d' [see PERRIN d'AGINCOURT]
AGNEW, Roy (1893-1944), Australia
    R. 4   S. 5x, 29
AGOSTINI, Lucio (1913-   ), Can
    R. 31
AGOSTINO de CRUZ [see CRUZ, Agostino de]
AGOSTINO, Alfonso d' (1883-   )
        S. 24
AGRELL, Johan Joachim (1701-1765), Sweden
    R. 1   S. c, 10, 56
AGRÈVES, Ernest d' - pseud
    [see NIEUWENHOVE, Ernest Alfons van]
AGRICOLA, Alexander (?1446-1506), Neth
    R. 1   S. c, 15, 16

AGRICOLA, Martin (1486-1556), Ger
    R. 1   S. c, 10
AGUADOY y GARCIA, Dionysio (1784-1849), Sp
    R. 1   S. c, 3, 5x, 10, 32
AGUERAL - Plegaria a la Santisima Virgen
                  S. e
AGUILERA de HEREDIA, Sebastian (c1565-1627), Sp
    R. 1   S. c, 10, 16, 17, 39, 53
AGUIRRE, Julián (1868-1924), Arg
    R. 1   S. 5x, 7, 8, 10, 23, 24, 32, 46
AHLBERG, Gunnar (1886-1943) [pseud: Guy AMMANDT],
    Sweden   R. 30a   S. 43
AHLE, Johann Georg (1651-1706), Ger
    R. 1   S. 5x, 10
AHLE, Johann Rudolf (1625-1673), Ger

    R. 1   S. c
AHLERT, Fred E. (1892-1953), USA
    R. 23   S. 24a
AHLSTROM, David (1927-   ), USA
    R. 19   S. 10, 13
ÅHLSTRÖM, Olof (1756-1835), Sweden
    R. 1   S. c, 56
AHMED, Zakareia

AHO, Kalevi (1949-   ), Fin
    R. 1   S. 40
AHRENS, Joseph (Johannes Clemens) (1904-   ), Ger
    R. 1   S. c
AHROLD, Frank (1931-), USA
    R. 19   S. 13
AIBLINGER, Johann Kaspar (1779-1867), Ger
    R. 1   S. c, 2-4
AICH, Arnt von (d c1528-30), Ger [printer]
    R. 1   S. 9
AICHINGER, Gregor (1564-1628), Ger
    R. 1   S. c, 2-8, 10, 11, 14-16, 53
AIKIN, William Arthur (1857-1939), Eng
    R. 1. 5   S. e
AIM, Vojtěch Bořivoj (1886-1972), Cz
    R. 1   S. 31
AIN, Noa [formerly Susan AIN] (1924-   )
    R. 7   S. 10, 13, 30, 52
AITKEN, George (c1882-   ), Eng
    R. 3   S. e
AITKEN, Hugh (1924-   ), USA
    R. 19   S. 10, 13
AITKIN, Robert Morris (1939-   ), Can
    R. 1   S. 10
AIVAZYAN, Artemy Sergiviech (1902-   ), USSR
    R. 14   S. 18

AKBAROV, Ikram Ilkhamovich (1921-   ), USSR
    R. 14   S. 18,24
A KEMPIS, Nicolaus (c1600-1676), Flem
    R. 1   S. c
ÅKERLIND, Curt Ossian Nils (1912-   )
                 S. 24,24a
AKEROYDE, Samuel (fl. 1684-1706), Eng
    R. 1   S. 10
AKERS, Doris Mae (1922-   ), USA
    R. 23   S. 10,30
AKHINYAN, Grigor Mushegovich (1926-   )
                 S. 18,24a
AKHMETOV, Khusain Faizulovich (1913-   ), USSR
    R. 14   S. 18
AKHRON, Joseph [see ACHRON, Joseph]
AKHUNDOVA, Shafiga Gulam (1924-   ), USSR
    R. 7   S. 52
AKSES, Necil Kazim (1908-   ), Turkey
    R. 1   S. c
AKST, Harry (1894-1963), USA
    R. 23   S. 10
AKUTAGAWA, Yasushi (1925-   ), Japan

    R. 1   S. 10,18,50
ALA, Giovanni Battista (c1598-c1630), It
    R. 1   S. c
ALABIEV, Alexander [see ALYABYEV, Alexander]
ALADOV, Nikolai Ilyich (1890-1972), USSR
    R. 14   S. 18
ALAIN, Albert (1880-1971), Fr
    R. 16   S. c,4,5x
ALAIN, Jehan (1911-1940), Fr
    R. 1   S. c,5x,7-10
ALANUS, Johannes (d. 1373), Eng
    R. 1   S. c,14,16
ALARD, Jean-Delphin (1815-1888), Fr
    R. 16   S. c,10,24
ALARY, Giulio E. A. (1814-1891)
    R. 3   S. e
ALASSIO, Serafino
    R. 52   S. 24
ALBA, Alonso Perez de [Dalua] (d >1519), Sp
    R. 1   S. c
ALBANESE, Guido (1893-   ), It
    R. 8   S. 5x
ALBANO, Enrique (1910-   ), Arg
    R. 26   S. 8,46
ALBARTE - Pavan and galliard
                 S. 16
ALBELDA, Miguel (fl 1850), Sp
    R. 200   S. e[Albenda]

ALBÉNIZ, Isaac (1860-1909), Sp
R. 1   S. c,1-11,18,22,24,32,39,54(325)
ALBÉNIZ, Mateo Perez de (c1755-1831), Sp
R. 1   S. c,5x,8,10,32,39
ALBERCH VILA, Pere (1517-1582), Sp
R. 1   S. c,14,53
ALBERO, Sebastián (d. 1756), Sp
R. 8   S. 8,10
ALBERT - Tarantella de Blephegor
              S. 54(360)
ALBERT de RIPPE [see RIPA, Alberto da]
ALBERT, Charles Louis Napoléon d´ (1809-1886), Fr
R. 1   S. 10,47
ALBERT, Eugen d´ (1864-1932), Ger
R. 1   S. c,2-10,18,42
ALBERT, Heinrich (1870-1950)
R. 3   S. 18[Albert, G.]
ALBERT, Heinrich (1604-1651) Ger
R. 1   S. c,2-5,8,10,11,14,16
ALBERT, Henry - pseud [see POPP, Wilhelm]
ALBERT, Prince Consort (1819-1861), Ger
R. 1   S. c,9,10
ALBERT, Stephen (1941-   ), USA
R. 19   S. 13
ALBERTI, Domenico (c1710-1740), It
R. 1   S. c
ALBERTI, Giuseppe Matteo (1685-1751), It
R. 1   S. c,10
ALBERTIN, Alfons (18th Cent)

              S. c
ALBERTO, Luis (16th Cent), Sp
R. 9   S. c,10,16,39,53
ALBERTSEN, Per Hjort (1919-   ), Nor
R. 1
ALBERTUS PARISIENSIS, (12th Cent), Fr
R. 1   S. c,17
ALBICASTRO, Henricus (fl 1700-06), Swiss
R. 1   S. c,10,24
ALBINONI, Tomaso Giovanni (1671-1751), It
R. 1   S. c,5x,6-10,18,20,24,32
ALBRECHT, Alexander (1885-1958), Slovak
R. 1   S. 31
ALBRECHT, Christoph (1930-   ), Ger
R. 4   S. c
ALBRECHT, Georg von (1891-1976), Ger
R. 4
ALBRECHT, Kurt (1895-1971)
              S. c
ALBRECHTSBERGER, Johann Georg (1736-1809), Aus
R. 1   S. c,9,10

ALBRICI, Vincenzo (1631-1696), It
   R. 1   S. c,56
ALBRIGHT, William Hugh (1944-   ) USA
   R. 1   S. c,10,12,13
ALCALAY, Luna (1928-   ), Aus
   R. 7   S. 52
ALCOCK, John Sr. (1715-1806), Eng
   R. 1   S. c,10,53
ALCOCK, Walter Galpin (1861-1947), Eng
   R. 1   S. c,5x
ALDEMA, Gil (1928-   ), Isr
   R. 63   S. c
ALDER, Cosmas (c1497-1553), Swiss
   R. 1   S. c,10,16
ALDERIGHI, Dante (1898-1968), It
   R. 4
ALDOMAR, Pedro Juan (fl 1506), Sp
   R. 1   S. 10,16,17,39
ALDRICH, Henry (1648-1710), Eng
   R. 1   S. c
ALDROVANDINI, Giuseppe Antonio Vincenzo
   (c1672-1707), It
   R. 1   S. c,10,53
ALECIAN CARZOU, Eugenie (20th Cent)
            S. c
ALEJANDRO - Pavans vihuela, No. 2
            S. 39
ALEMANN, Eduardo
            S. 46
ALEMSHAH, Kourkene (1907-1947), Arm
   R. 4
ALESKEROV, Suleiman Eiub Ogli (1924-   ), USSR
   R. 14   S. 18
ALESSANDRO, Raffaele d´ (1911-1959), Swiss
   R. 1   S. c
ALETTER, Wilhelm (1867-1934)

            S. 5x,24
ALEWIJNSZ de VOIS, Pieter [see VOIS, Pieter Alewijnsz de]
ALEXANDER - The glory song
            S. e
ALEXANDER, Josef (1907-   ), USA
   R. 19   S. 10,13
ALEXANDER, Meister (fl 1250-1300), Ger
   R. 1   S. c,10,16
ALEXANDER, Russell USA
            S. 54(320)
ALEXANDRI - My thoughts (Trecui pe langa cruce)
            S. 24
ALEXANDROV - Mountains of the Caucasus
            S. 5x

ALEXANDROV, Alexander Vasilyevitch (1883-1946), USSR
    R. 1   S. 10,54(333,44)
ALEXANDROV, Anatoly Nikolayevich (1888-   ), Russia
    R. 1   S. 18
ALEXANDROV, Boris Alexandrovich (1905-   ), USSR
    R. 1   S. 10,18
ALEXANDROV, Yuri Mikhailovich (1914-   ), USSR
    R. 47   S. 18
ALEXANIAN, Diran (1881-1954), Arm
    R. 1   S. 10,18
ALEXIUS, Carl John (1928-   ), USA
    R. 19   S. c
ALFANO, Franco (1875-1954), It
    R. 1   S. 1-6,8,10
ALFONSO - Capricho en forma de bolero
              S. 5x
ALFONSO - Mis amores
              S. e
ALFONSO el SABIO (1221-1284), Sp
    R. 1   S. c,7-10,14,16,32,39
ALFONSO, Francisco (1908-   ), Sp
    R. 9   S. c
ALFONSO, Javier (1904-   ), Sp
    R. 1   S. 10
ALFONSO, Nicolas (1913-   )
              S. c
ALFORD, Harry L. (1880-1939), USA
    R. 49   S. 10,13[b. 1883],22
ALFORD, Kenneth J. - pseud [ie Frederick Joseph
    RICKETTS] (1881-1945), Eng
    R. 1   S. c,10,54
ALFVÉN, Hugo (1872-1960), Sweden
    R. 1   S. c,2-11,18,24,40,43,56
ALGAZI, Léon (1890-1971), Fr
    R. 14   S. c
ALI, Safar

ALI-ZADE, Akshin (1937-   )
              S. 18
ALIPRANDI, Bernardo (c1710-c1792), It (see note)
    R. 1   S. 24
ALIPRANDI, Paul (see note)
              S. 24a
ALISEDA, Jerónimo de (c1548-1591), Sp
    R. 1   S. c,17
ALISON, Richard (fl 1592-1606), Eng
    R. 1   S. c,5x,10,14-16,32
ALKAN, Charles-Henri-Valentin - pseud
    [ie C. H. V. MORHANGE] (1813-1888), Fr
    R. 1   S. c,9,10

AL-KHATIB, Abdur Rehman, Saudi Arabia

ALLAIN, Jean
    S. 24a
ALLAIRE, Ulderich S. (1901-1969), Can
 R. 31
ALLAN, Douglas R.
    S. 10, 13
ALLAN, Esther (1914-), USA
 R. 7   S. 52
ALLDAHL, Per-Gunnar (1943-), Sweden
 R. 30   S. 40, 56
ALLEGRI, Gregorio (1582-1652), It
 R. 1   S. c, 1x, 8, 10, 24
ALLEMAN, J. A.
    S. 10
ALLEN, Charles - pseud [see DE VITO, Albert Kenneth]
ALLEN, Gilbert (1918-), USA
 R. 14   S. 10
ALLEN, Georg Frederik Ferdinand (1856-1925)
    S. c
ALLEN, Henry Robinson (1809-1876), Ire
 R. 1   S. e
ALLEN, Judith Shatin [see SHATIN, Judith Allen]
ALLEN, R.
    S. 54(321, 34, 45)
ALLEN, T. Frank (fl c1884), USA
 R. 200   S. 10
ALLEN, Thomas S., USA
 R. 53   S. 13
ALLENDE, Pedro Humberto (1885-1959), Chile
 R. 1   S. 3, 4, 5x
ALLENDE-BLIN, Juan (1928-), Chile
 R. 1   S. 10
ALLEYN - If Mr. Cupid went on strike
    S. e
ALLIER, Gabrielle (fl 1918), Fr
    S. 54(337)
ALLING, John, USA
    S. 10, 13
ALLING, Vernon ?USA
    S. 10, 13
ALLITSEN [Bumpus], Mary Francis (1848-1912), Eng
 R. 1   S. 10 (see note)
ALMAND, Claude (1915-1957), USA
 R. 19   S. 10, 13
ALMANINANA - Flora
    S. e
ALMEIDA MOTT, Joan Pedro de
    S. 9

ALMEIDA, Carlos Vianna de
    S. 24a
ALMEIDA, Francisco António de (c1702-1755), Port
 R. 1
ALMEIDA, H. - Cuban dance
    S. 24
ALMEIDA, Juan (1927-)
    S. 18,24a
ALMEIDA, Laurindo (1917-), Brazil
 R. 80   S. 10,32,39
ALMOROX, Juan (fl. 1485-1504), Sp
 R. 1   S. c,17
ALMROTH, Knut O. W. [pseud: K.O.W.A]

ALMQVIST, Carl Jonas Love (1793-1866), Sweden
 R. 1   S. 10,56
ALNAES, Eyvind (1872-1932), Nor
 R. 1   S. c,4,5x,6-8,10,18
ALONSO - El dale dale
    S. e
ALONSO y ACEUEDO

ALONSO, (fl 1500), Sp
 R. 1   S. c,10,16,17,39
ALONSO, Francisco (1887-1948), Sp
 R. 9   S. c,8-10
ALPAERTS, Flor (1876-1954), Bel
 R. 1   S. c,7,8,10
ALPAERTS, Jef (1904-1973), Bel
 R. 1   S. 24,36
ALQUEN, Peter Cornelius Johann d´ (1795-1863), Ger
 R. 8   S. 5
ALSCHAUSKY, Francesco Serafino (1879-), Fr
 R. 10s   S. c[Josef Serafini]
ALSINA, Carlos Roqué (1941-), Arg
 R. 14   S. 10
ALT, Bernhard (1903-1945), Ger
 R. 4   S. c
ALTENBURG, Johann Ernst (1734-1801), Ger
 R. 1   S. c,10
ALTENBURG, Michael (1584-1640), Ger
 R. 1   S. c,2-4
ALTER, Louis (1902-1980), USA
 R. 23   S. 5x,10,11,13
ALTERMANN, E. - Petite annonce (vi & p)
    S. 24
ALTHEN, Ragnar (1883-1961), Sweden
 R. 30   S. 5x,10
ALTNIKOL, Johann Christoph (1720-1759), Ger
 R. 1   S. c

ALTSCHULER, Modest (1873-1963), USA
    R. 4   S. 1x
ALTUNYAN, Ruben (1939-   )
              S. 18,24
ALVA, Alonso de (d 1504)
    R. 1   S. c,10
ALVARADO, Diego de (c1570-1643), Basque
    R. 1   S. c,10,16,17,39,53
ALVAREZ, Fermin Maria (1833-1898), Sp
    R. 9   S. c,10,39
ALWOOD, Richard (16th Cent), Eng
    R. 1   S. c,53
ALWYN, William (1905-   ), Eng
    R. 1   S. c,4,5x,9,10,20,26,28,55
ALYABYEV, Alexander Alexandrovich (1787-1851), Rus
    R. 1   S. c,3-4,7,8,10,18,24
ALYN [S. 54 (323)] = ALWYN, William
AM, Magnar (1952-   ), Nor
    R. 38   S. 40,52
AMADEI, Albert (1851-1894), Hun
    R. 15   S. e
AMADEI, Filippo (fl 1690-1730), It
    R. 1   S. c,10 [PIPO, Filippo Amadei]
AMANI, Nikolai (1872-1904), Russia
    R. 47   S. 10,24
AMBROISE, Victor - pseud [see WRIGHT, Lawrence]
AMBROS, Vladimir (1890-1956), Cz
    R. 1   S. 31
AMBROSE, Robert Steel (1824-1908), Can
    R. 31   S. e
AMBROSE, Saint (c340-397)
    R. 1   S. c,2-4
AMBROSIO, Alfredo d´ [see D´AMBROSIO, Alfredo]
AMBROSIUS, Hermann (1897-   ), Ger
    R. 14   S. c,8,10,32
AMBRUIS, Honoré d´ [see DAMBRUIS, Honoré]
AMEMIYA, Yasukazu (1938-   ), Japan
    R. 23   S. c
AMERS, John Henry (?-1946), Eng
    R. 49   S. 54(365)
AMES, William T. (1901-   ), USA
    R. 19   S. 10,24
AMFITHEATROF, Daniele (1901-1983) It
    R. 1   S. 4
AMICUS - pseud [ie Peter Dodds McCORMICK] (1834-1916)
              S. 54(311)
AMIENS, Guillaume [see GUILLAUME d´AMIENS]
AMIRKHANIAN, Charles Benjamin (1945-   ), USA
    R. 19   S. 10,13

AMIROV, Fikret (1922-   ), USSR
   R. 1   S. 8,10,18,24a
AMMANDT, Guy - pseud [see AHLBERG, Gunnar]
AMMERBACH, Elias Nikolaus (c1530-1597), Ger
   R. 1   S. c,5x,10,11,16,53

AMNER, John (1579-1641), Eng
   R. 1   S. c,16,53
AMON, Johannes Andreas (1763-1825), Ger
   R. 1   S. c,10,24a
AMOR, Francisco
            S. 10
AMRAM, David (1930-   ), USA
   R. 1   S. 9,13,24
AMY, Gilbert (1936-   ), Fr
   R. 1   S. c,10,24
ANA, Francesco d´ [Varoter, Veneto] (c1460-c1502), It
   R. 1   S. c,10,14,16
ANCELIN, Pierre (1934-   ), Fr
   R. 14   S. c
ANCHIETA, Juan de (1462-1523), Sp
   R. 1   S. c,8,10,14,16,17
ANCLIFFE, Charles (1880-1952), Eng
   R. 1   S. 5x
ANDELIOFF - Het lied van den Smid
            S. e
ANDERSEN - God´s command
            S. 5x
ANDERSEN, Aksel (1912-1977), Den
   R. 30   S. 40
ANDERSEN, Ejvin (1914-1968), Den
   R. 30   S. 40
ANDERSEN, Karl August (1903-1970), Nor
   R. 14   S. 40,51
ANDERSEN, Karl Joachim (1847-1909), Den
   R. 1   S. c,10,11
ANDERSEN, Sophus (1859-1923), Den
   R. 3   S. 33,57
ANDERSON, B. - Ungdomsgladje
            S. 54(363)
ANDERSON, Beth (1950-   ), USA
   R. 19   S. 10,30,52
ANDERSON, C. A. - March of the Herald
            S. 54(341)
ANDERSON, C. S. - Kindergarten rhythms
            S. 54(336)
ANDERSON, Edmund (1912-   ), USA
   R. 23   S. 10
ANDERSON, G. (19th Cent) - The Battle of Waterloo

ANDERSON, Garland (1933-   ), USA
   R.19
ANDERSON, Laurie (1947-   ), USA
   R.19   S.13,30,52
ANDERSON, Lenough (20th Cent), USA
           S.c,12
ANDERSON, Leroy (1908-1975), USA
   R.1   S.c,9,10,24a,54(317,56)
ANDERSON, Muriel Bradford

ANDERSON, Robert (1934-   ), USA
   R.64   S.12,13
ANDERSON, Ruth (1928-   ), USA
   R.19   S.13,30,52
ANDERSON, Thomas Jefferson (´928-   ) USA
   R.1   S.10,13
ANDERSON, William Henry [pseud: Hugh GARLAND]
   (1882-1955), Eng
   R.4
ANDERSSON, (Ernst Christian) Richard (1851-1918),
   Sweden   R.1   S.c
ANDESPIN, Melchior d´ [see ARDESPIN, Melchior de]
ANDOLFI, Godfroy
           S.24
ANDORFF - Festival March
           S.5x
ANDRADE, Djalmi de [see SETE, Bola - pseud]
ANDRAS, Mihaly (1917-   )
           S.19
ANDRASOVAN, Tibor (1917-   ), Cz
           S.31
ANDRÉ, Emile
           S.e
ANDRE, Johann (1741-1799), Ger
   R.1   S.5x
ANDRE, José (1881-1944), Arg
   R.26   S.46
ANDRÉ, Ludwig (1858-1924), Ger
   R.3   S.24
ANDREA di GIOVANNI [see ADREAS de FLORENTIA]
ANDREAE, Volkmar (1879-1962), Swiss
   R.1   S.10
ANDREAS (16th Cent) - Jubilate Deo
           S.10,14
ANDREAS de FLORENTIA (d c1415), It (see note)
   R.1   S.c,10,16,53
ANDREAE, Padre Carolus (d.1627), Ger
   R.1   S.c,5x[Carolus],8,10
ANDRÉE, Elfrida (1841-1929), Sweden
   R.1   S.10,30,52

ANDREEV, Vasli [see ANDREYEV, Vasili Vasilyevich]
ANDREU, Francisco (17th Cent.), Sp
   R. 9   S. c
ANDREWS, Herbert Kennedy (1904-1965), Ire
   R. 1   S. c,8
ANDREYEV [Andreev], Vasili Vasilyevich (1861-1918),
   Russia   R. 1   S. 18
ANDRIASHVILI, Akaky (1904-   ), USSR
   R. 14   S. 18
ANDRIASYAN, R. - Etude (p)
            S. 18
ANDRICU, Mihail Gheorghe (1894-1974), Rum
   R. 1   S. 7,8,24a
ANDRIENSEN - Madonna ma pieta [S. 10]
   = ADRIAENSSEN, Emanuel
ANDRIESSEN, Hendrik (1892-1981), Neth
   R. 1   S. c,7,8,18,24
*** ANDRIESSEN, Hendrik (1913-) (see note)
ANDRIESSEN, Jurriaan (1925-   ), Neth
   R. 1   S. c,10
ANDRIESSEN, Louis (1939-   ), Neth
   R. 1   S. 10
ANDRIESSEN, Willem Christiaan Nicolaas (1887-1964),
   Neth   R. 14   S. c
ANDRIEU, F. (fl late 14th Cent.), Fr
   R. 1   S. c,10
ANDRIEU, Jean-François d´ [see DANDRIEU, Jean-François]
ANDRIX, George (1932-   ), USA
   R. 19   S. 13
ANDROZZO, Alma Bazel - pseud [see THOMPSON, Alma]
ANDRZEJOWSKI, Adam (1880-1920), Pol
   R. 1. 5   S. 18,24[Andzheyevsky]
ANEAU, Barthélemy (16th Cent), Fr
   R. 5   S. c
ANERIO, Felice (c1560-1614), It
   R. 1   S. c,2-4,5x,11,14,16,18
ANERIO, Giovanni Francesco (c1567-1630), It
   R. 1   S. c,9
ANET, Jean Jacques Baptiste (1676-1755), Fr
   R. 1   S. 5(379)
ANFOSSI, Pasquale (1727-1797), It (see note)
   R. 1   S. 5x
ANGEL PENA, d´ (1940-   )
            S. c
ANGELIS, Girolamo de (1858-1935), It
   R. 10,10s   S. 24
ANGELO, d´ - Sospiro (p)
            S.
ANGELOV, Vladimir
            S. 18

ANGERER, Paul (1927-   ), Aus
  R.1   S.c
ANGLADA - Polvillo de rape
           S.e
ANGLEBERT, Jean Henry d´ [see DANGLEBERT, Jean Henri]
ANGLÉS, Rafael (1730-1816), Sp
  R.1   S.c,5x,8,10,39
ANGULO - Cantos Yoruba de Cuba
           S.32
ANHALT, István (1919-   ), Can
  R.1   S.10,24
ANIDO, María Luisa (1909-   ), Arg
  R.26   S.18,32,46,52
ANIK, Harry

ANIMUCCIA, Giovanni (c1500-c1571), It
  R.1   S.c,15
ANISIMOV, Boris (1907-   )
           S.18
ANKERMAN, Khorkhe (1877-1941)
           S.18,24
ANNA AMALIA, Princess of Prussia (1723-1787)
  R.1   S.10,52
ANNA AMALIA, Duchess of Saxe-Weimar (1739-1807)
  R.1   S.10,28[Sachsen-Weimar],52
ANNIBALE PADOVANO [see PADOVANO, Annibale]

ANROOYI, Peter van (1879-1954), Neth
  R.25   S.8
ANSELMI - La villanella; L´infinito
           S.e
ANSERMET, Ernest (1883-1969), Swiss
  R.1   S.c
ANTEGNATI, Costanzo (1549-1624)
  R.1   S.c,10,16,53
ANTES, John (1740-1811), USA
  R.1   S.7-10,24,47
ANTHEAUME, l´Aîné (fl 1748-62), Fr - Regina Coeli [?]
  R.16   S.5x
ANTHEIL, George (1900-1959), USA
  R.1   S.c,2,3,5x,6-10,13,24
ANTHEUNIS, Gentiel Theodoor (1840-1907), Bel
  R.25   S.e
ANTHONELLO de CASERTA (fl 14-15th Cent), It
  R.1   S.c,5x[Marot de Caserta],10,16
ANTICO, Andrea (c1480->1539), It
  R.1   S.10
ANTIGA, Jean (1878-   )
           S.24
ANTILL, John Henry (1904-   ), Australia
  R.1   S.5x,6,10,29,37

ANTIQUIS, Adam de (fl early 16th Cent), It
R. 1   S. 16
ANTIQUIS, Giovanni Jacopo de (fl 1574-1606), It
R. 1   S. 14
ANTON, Ondrej, Boh
           S. c,10
ANTONELLI - O Salutaris
R. 1   S. 5x
ANTONET (15th Cent) - Anima Christi

ANTONI, Giovanni Battista degli
   [see DEGLI ANTONI, Giovanni Battista]
ANTONINI, Alfredo (1901-   ), USA
R. 19   S. 13
ANTONIO de SEBASTIAN, Padre J.
           S. c
ANTONIO, Fra
           S. 32
ANTONIOTTI, Giorgio (c1692-1776), Italy
R. 1   S. c
AORENA, Mme. - pseud
   [see LILIUOKALANI, Queen of Hawaii]
APERGHIS, Georges (1945-   ), Greece
R. 1   S. c
AP GLASLYN [see OWEN, John, called Ap Glaslyn]
           S. e
AP HUW, Robert (c1580-1665), Wales
R. 1   S. 10
APIARIUS, Mathias (c1500-1554), Ger
R. 1   S. 10,16
APKALNS, Longins (1923-   ), Lat
R. 30   S. c
APOLETON, Joan (1939-   )
           S. 24a
APOLLONI, Giuseppe (1822-1889), It
R. 10   S. e
APOSTEL, Hans Erich (1901-1972), Aus
R. 1
APOTHÉLOZ, Jean (1900-1965), Swiss
R. 14
APPEL - The young guard
           S. 54(367)
APPENZELLER, Benedictus (c1480->1558), ?Neth
R. 1   S. c,10,16
APPLEBAUM, Edward Everest (1937-   ), USA
R. 19   S. 9,10,13,19,20
APPLEBAUM, Louis (1918-   ), Can
R. 1   S. 10
APPLEBY, Thomas (fl c1535-63), Eng
R. 1   S. c

APPLETON, Jon Howard (1939-   ), USA
    R. 19   S. 9,13
AQUERRE, d´ - Maitena demande aux roses
                S. 24
AQUIN, Claude d´ [see DAQUIN, Claude]
AQUINO, Thomas de
                S. 10
ARAKISHVILI, Dmitri Ignatyevich (1873-1953), Georgia
    R. 1   S. 8,18
ARÁMBARRI, Jesús (1902-1960), Sp
    R. 1   S. 10
ARAMIS - Dernier voeu
                S. e
ARANDA, Luis de (b c1660), Sp
    R. 9   S. 17
ARANDIA NAVARRO, Jorge (1929-   ), Arg
    R. 26   S. 46
ARAÑÉS, Juan (d c1649), Sp
    R. 1   S. c,10,16
ARAPOV, Boris Alexandrovich (1905-   ), Rus
    R. 1   S. 18,24
ARAÚJO, Juan de (1646-1712), Sp
    R. 1   S. c,10
ARAUJO, Pedro (fl mid 17th Cent), Port
    R. 1   S. c
ARAUXO, Francisco Correa de
    [see CORREA de ARAUXO, Francisco]
ARBAN, Jean Baptiste (1825-1889), Fr
    R. 1   S. c,10   (see note under FROSINI)
ARBEAU, Thoinot pseud [Jehan TABOUROT] (1520-1595), Fr
    R. 1   S. c,2-4,5x,8,10,11,15,16,18,32
ARBÓS, Enrique Fernández (1863-1939), Sp
    R. 1   S. 1,4,7,10,11,24,39
ARBUCKLE, Dorothy M. (1910-   ), USA
    R. 7   S. 52
ARCADELT, Jacques (?1505-1568), ?Flem
    R. 1   S. c,1x,2-5,7,8,10,11,14-16,24
ARCADET - Chanson Lorraine
                S. e
ARCHANGELSKY, Alexander (1846-1924), Russia
    R. 8   S. c,2-4,5x,8-11
ARCHER, Harry (1888-1960), USA
    R. 61   S. 10
ARCHER, Violet Balestreri (1913-   ), Can
    R. 1   S. 24,30,52
ARCHILEI, Antonio (c1550-1612), It
    R. 1   S. c,16
ARCHILEI, Vittoria (née Concarini) [pseud: LA ROMANINA]
    (1550->1618), It   R. 7   S. 52

ARCHIMBAUD - March along mon ami
        S. e
ARDEN, Philip
        S. e
ARDESPIN, Melchior d´ (c1643-1717), Ger
  R. 1   S. c
ARDÉVOL, José (1911-   ), Cuba
  R. 1   S. 3,8
ARDITI, Luigi (1822-1903), It
  R. 1   S. c,2-4,5x,10,18,24
AREDES - Vienne clareando

AREFELDT, Sven (1908-1956), Sweden [?]
  R. 68   S. 5x
AREL, Bülent (1919-   ), Turkey
  R. 1   S. 10,24
ARENDS, Andrej Fedorovich (1855-1924), Russia
  R. 2s   S. c
ARENSKY, Anton Stepanovich (1861-1906), Russia
  R. 1   S. c,1-11,18,23,24
ARESTI, Floriano [see ARRESTI, Floriano]
ARESTI, G. E. (16th Cent) [?see ARRESTI, Giulio Cesare]
ARETINO, Paolo [Paul Antonio del BIVI] (1508-1584), It
  R. 1   S. 16 [Bivi]
ARETZ, Isabel (1909-   ), Arg
  R. 26   S. 46,52
AREZZO (i) [see Guido d´AREZZO]
AREZZO (ii) - Le plus joli reve (vi & p)
        S. 24a
ARGENTO, Dominick (1927-   ), USA
  R. 1   S. 9,10,13
ARIMINI, Vincent d´ [see VINCENZO da RIMINI]
ARIOSTI, Attillo (1666-?1729), It
  R. 1   S. c,2,3,5,8-11,24a
ARIZAGA, Rodolfo (1926-   ), Arg
  R. 26   S. 46
ARKAS, Nikolai (1852-1909)
  R. 47   S. 18
ARLBERG, George Efraim Fritz (1830-1896), Sweden
  R. 1.5   S. c
ARLEN, Harold (1905-   ), USA
  R. 1   S. 9,10,24a
ARMA, Paul (1905-   ), Fr
  R. 1   S. c,10,22
ARMAND, Jacques - pseud [see THIEL, Olof]
ARMANDOLA, José - pseud [see LAUTENSCHLÄGER, Willi]
ARMEGIANI - Dedans dehors (1976)

ARMENYAN, Gevork Artashesovich (1920-   )
        S. 18

ARMSDORFF, Andreas (1670-1699), Ger
   R. 1   S. c
ARMSTRONG, Harry (1879-1951), USA
   R. 23   S. 10
ARMSTRONG, Sir Thomas (Henry Wait) (1898-   ), Eng
   R. 1   S. c, 8
ARN, Tzvi (1927-)

ARNATT, Ronald (1930-), USA
   R. 19   S. 9, 12, 13
ARNAUD, Etienne Jean Guillaume (1807-1863), Fr
   R. 98   S. 5x
ARNAUD, Leon (1904-), Fr
           S. c, 10
ARNAUD, Pascal (18th Cent)
           S. c
ARNAUT de MAREUIL (fl 1170-1200), Fr
   R. 1   S. c
ARNAUT, Daniel (12th Cent)
   R. 11   S. c, 10, 14
ARNDT, Felix (1889-1918), USA
   R. 23   S. 10, 24
ARNE, Michael (c1740-1786), Eng
   R. 1   S. c, 2-5, 7, 8, 10
ARNE, Thomas Augustine (1710-1778), Eng
   R. 1   S. c, 2-11, 25-28, 42, 53
ARNELL, Richard (Anthony Sayer) (1917-), Eng
   R. 1   S. c, 5x, 6, 7, 10
ARNESTAD, Finn (1915-), Nor
   R. 1   S. c, 40, 24a, 51
ARNI, Thorsteinsson (1870-1962), Ice

ARNIM, Bettina von [see BRENTANO, Bettina]
ARNOLD von BRUCK [see BRUCK, Arnold von]
ARNOLD, Ernst (1892-), Aus
   R. 3   S. 10
ARNOLD, György (1781-1848), Hun
   R. 15   S. 24, 24a
ARNOLD, Hubert (1945-), USA
   R. 14   S. 22
ARNOLD, Malcolm (1921-), Eng
   R. 1   S. c, 8-10, 18-20, 32, 55, 24a
ARNOLD, Samuel (1740-1802), Eng
   R. 1   S. 10
ARONA, Colombino (1885-), It
   R. 10   S. 44
ARONOWICZ, Dan (1909-), Isr
   R. 14   S. 10
AROUTUNIAN, Alexander Grigori
   [see HARUTUNYAN, Alexander Grigori]

ARRAS, Moniot d´ [see MONIOT d´ARRAS]
ARRESTI, Floriano (c1660-1719), It
  R.1   S.c,53
ARRESTI, Giulio Cesare (1625-c1704), It
  R.1   S.c[Aresti, G. E.],53
ARRIAGA, Juan Crisóstomo (1806-1826), Sp
  R.1   S.c,1,5x,6-10,39
ARRIETE y CORERA, Pascual Juan Emilio (1823-1864), It
  R.8   S.c,1-3,8-10,39
ARRIEU, Claude - pseud [ie Louise Marie SIMON]
  (1903-   ), Fr   R.1   S.c,10,30
ARRIGO - Ave maria
          S.e
ARRIGO, Girolamo (1930-   ), It
  R.1
ARRO, Edgar Alexandrovich (1911-   ), Est
  R.4   S.18
ARSKY, Anatoli Mikhailovich (1912-   )
          S.18
ARTEMOVSKY [See GULAK-ARTEMOVSKY, Semyon]
ARTHUR, Gerald
          S.43
ARTHUYS, Philippe (1926-   ), Fr
  R.25   S.10
ARTSYBUSHEV, Nikolai Vasilevich (1858-1937), Russia
  R.1.5   S.18
ARUNDALE, Claude - pseud [ie Claude Arundale KELLY]
          S.13
ARUNTYUNYAN, Alexander Grigori
  [see HARUTUNYAN, Alexander Grigori]
ARUTYONYAN, Eric (1933-   )
          S.18,24
ASAFYEV, Boris Vladimirovich (1884-1949), USSR
  R.1   S.c,10,18,24a
ASCANIO, Josquin d´ [see JOSQUIN DESPREZ]
ASCHER - Birds of love
          S.54(316)
ASCHER, Joseph (1829-1869), Eng
  R.1.1   S.c,24
ASCHER, Leo (1880-1942), Aus
  R.25   S.10
ASCOLESE, Raffaele (1855-   ), It
  R.52   S.54(311)
ASENCIO, Vicente (1903-   ), Sp
  R.2s   S.c,10,32
ASENJO Y BARBIERI, Francisco
  [see BARBIERI, Francisco Asenjo]
ASEYEFF, E. - The Divine Liturgy of St. John Chrysostom
          S.10

ASHELM, Wilhelm Walter Conrad (1902-   )
    S. c
ASHFORTH, Alden (1933-   ), USA
  R. 19   S. 9,10,12,13,27
ASHLEIGH, Denis
    S. e
ASHLEY, Robert (1930-   ), USA
  R. 1   S. 10,13
ASHLYN, Quenton
    S. e
ASHRAFI, Mukhtar Ashrafovich (1912-   ), USSR
  R. 47   S. 18
ASHWELL, Thomas (c1478->1513), Eng
  R. 1   S. c
ASINS ARBO, Miguel (1916-   ), Sp
  R. 4   S. 39
ASIOLI, Bonifazio (1769-1832), It
  R. 1   S. 5x,9,10
ASKEW [Askue],   (fl c1595)
  R. 1   S. 10
ASLAMAZYAN, S. - Var on a theme from a caprice of
  Paganini (quartet)   S. 18
ASMA, Feike (1912-   ), Neth
  R. 25   S. c
ASOLA, Giammateo [Giovanni Matteo] (c1532-1609), It
  R. 1   S. c,7,8,10,14,16
ASPER, Frank Wilson (1892-1973), USA
  R. 19,71   S. 12,13
ASPLMAYR, Franz (1728-1786), Aus
  R. 1   S. 10
ASSAAIULO, Filippo [see AZZAIOLO, Filippo]
ASSALY, Edmund Phillip (1920-1983) Can
  R. 14   S. 24
ASSEMMACHES, Franz
    S. 24
ASSMAYER, Ignaz (1790-1862), Aus
  R. 1. 5   S. c
AST, Max - Es ist alles wie ein wunderbarer Garten
    S. 1x
ASTON, Hugh (c1485-?1558), Eng
  R. 1   S. c,10,15,16,53
ASTORGA, Emanuele d´ (1680-?1757), It
  R. 1   S. 5x
ASTROM, Axel (d 1940), Sweden
    S. 43
ASUAR PUIGGROS, Jose Vicente (1933-   ), Chile
  R. 30
ATKINS, Ivor Algernon (1869-1953), Eng
  R. 1   S. e

ATO EPISCOPUS TRECENSIS (12th Cent), Sp

ATRI, Raffaele d´ (1853-1924), It
  R. 10   S. e
ATTAIGNANT, Pierre (c1494-1551/2), Fr
  R. 1   S. c,7,8,10,14-16,24,32
ATTAWYL, Kamal, Egypt

ATTERBERG, Kurt (1887-1974), Sweden
  R. 1   S. c,1-7,23,24,40,43,56

ATTERBURY, Luffman (c1740-1796), Eng
  R. 1   S. 5x,7,10
ATTEY, John (fl 1622, d.1640), Eng
  R. 1   S. c,2-4,5x,8,10,14,16
ATTILA, Bozay [S.19] = BOZAY, Attila
ATTWOOD, Thomas (1765-1838), Eng
  R. 1   S. c,4,5x,10
AUBER, Daniel François Esprit (1782-1871), Fr
  R. 1   S. 1-11,18,24,42,54(327)
AUBERT, Jacques (1689-1753), Fr
  R. 1   S. c,9,10,19,21,24
AUBERT, Louis-François-Marie (1877-1968), Fr
  R. 4   S. c,2-5,7,8,10,24
AUBIN, Tony (1907-   ), Fr
  R. 1   S. c,20
AUDINOT, Nicolas Médard (1732-1801), Fr
  R. 1   S. 33
AUDOIRE, John Norman (1897-   ), Can
  R. 31   S. 54(343)
AUDRAN, Edmond (1840-1901), Fr
  R. 1   S. c,8,10,42
AUER, Leopold (1845-1930), Hun
  R. 1   S. 24
AUERNHAMMER, Josepha Barbara von (1758-1820), Aus
  R. 1   S. 30,52
AUFDERHEIDE, May (20th Cent), USA
               S. 30,52
AUFFMANN, Joseph Anton, (c1720->1773), Ger
  R. 1   S. c,10
AULETTA, Domenico (1723-1753), It
  R. 1   S. 8,10
AULETTA, Pietro (c1698-1771), It
  R. 1   S. 5x
AULIN, Tor (1866-1914), Sweden
  R. 1   S. c,4,5,18,24,56
AURIC, Georges (1899-1983), Fr
  R. 1   S. c,1-8,10,18,26,27
AUSTER, Lydia Martinova (1912-   ), Est
  R. 7   S. 18,24,30,52
AUSTIN, Egbert [see WILLIAMS, Bert]

AUSTIN, Frederic (1872-1952), Eng
   R. 1   S. 3
AUSTIN, Larry Don (1930-   ), USA
   R. 1   S. 10,13
AUSTIN, Ray (1915-   ), USA
   R. 23   S. 10
AUTENRIETH, Helma (1896-   ), Ger
   R. 7   S. c,52
AUVERGNE, Antoine d´ [see D´AUVERGNE, Antoine]
AVERY (?1470-?1543), Eng
   R. 1   S. c
AVIDOM, Menahem (1908-), Isr
   R. 1   S. 10,24a
AVILES, José
           S. 24
AVISON, Charles (1709-1770), Eng
   R. 1   S. c,5,9,10,24
AVKSENTYEV, Evgeny

AVNI, Tzvi (1927-   ), Isr
   R. 1   S. 10
AVOLO - Big guns
           S. 54(315)
AVON, Edmond
           S. 19,21
AVONDANO, Pedro Antonio (1714-1782), Port
   R. 1   S. 8,10
AVRAAMOV, Arseni Mikhailovich (1886-1944), USSR
   R. 47   S. 10
AVRIL, Edwin F - Arabic dance (accordion)

AVSHALOMOV, Aaron (1894-1965)
   R. 19   S. 10
AVSHALOMOV, Jacob (1919-   ), USA
   R. 1   S. 10,13
AXMAN, Emil (1887-1949), Cz
   R. 1   S. 5x,6,8
AXOLOTL - pseud [see MEISTER, Karl]
AYALA PEREZ, Daniel (1906-1975), Mex
   R. 1   S. c,10
AYALA, Hector (1914-   )
           S. c
AYER, Nathaniel Davis (1887-1952), USA
   R. 50   S. 10
AYLEWARD, Richard (1626-1669), Eng
   R. 1   S. c
AYLWARD, Florence (1862-   ), Eng
   R. 7   S. e
AYRTON - Allegamente (arr hps - H. Casadesus) (see note)
           S. 2,5x

AZALAIS de PORCAIRAGUES (12th Cent), Fr
   R. 7   S. c,30,52
AZARASHVILY, Vazha (1936-   )
           S. 18,24a
AZEEV, E. S. [see ASEYEFF, E.] [?]
AZIZ, El Shanan
           S. 10
AZZAIOLO, Filippo (fl. 1557-1569), It
   R. 1   S. c,2,3,10,11,14-16

BAAREN, Kees van (1906-1970), Neth
   R. 1   S. 10
BABADJANYAN, Arno Harutyuni (1921-   ), Arm
   R. 1   S. 7,8,10,18,24
BABAYEV, Andrei Avanesovic (1923-1964), USSR
   R. 14   S. 18
BABAYEV, Sabir (1920-   ), USSR
   R. 14   S. 18
BABBITT, Milton (1916-   ), USA
   R. 1   S. c,7,10,13,20,21,23,24a
BABCOCK, Edward Chester [pseud: James VAN HEUSEN]
   (1913-   ), USA
   R. 23   S. 22 [Van Heusen]
BABELL, William (c1690-1723), Eng
   R. 1   S. c,10
BABER, Joseph (1937-   ), USA
   R. 19   S. 10,13
BABIN, Victor (1908-1972), USA
   R. 1   S. 5x,10,13
BABITS, Linda (1940-   ), USA
   R. 7   S. 30
BABNIK, Johann (18th Cent)

BABNIK, Matya (19th Cent)
           S. 24a
BABOU, (fl 1710), S. Neth
   R. 25   S. c
BABOU, Thomas (1656-c1740), Fr
   R. 1   S. c,53
BABŮSEK, František (1905-1954), Cz
   R. 14   S. 5x,6,31
BACARISSE, Salvador (1898-1963), Sp
   R. 1   S. c,10,32
BACEWICZ, Grazyna (1909-1969), Pol
   R. 1   S. c,10,18 [Batsevich],24,52
BACH, Carl Philip Emanuel (1714-1788)
   R. 1   S. c,2,3,5-11,18-20,22-24,28,32
BACH, Erik (1946-   ), Den
   R. 95   S. 40

BACH, Georg Christoph (1642-1697)
R. 1   S. c, 10, 53
BACH, Heinrich (ii) (1615-1692)
R. 1   S. c, 10, 53
BACH, Johann (1604-1673)
R. 1   S. c, 10
BACH, Johann Bernhard (1676-1749)
R. 1   S. c, 10, 53
BACH, Johann Christian (1735-1782)
R. 1   S. c, 1, 2, 4-11, 18, 22-24, 53
BACH, Johann Christoph (1642-1703)
R. 1   S. c, 3, 6, 8, 10, 53
BACH, Johann Christoph Friedrich (1732-1795)
R. 1   S. c, 2, 4-11, 18, 23, 24, 53
BACH, Johann Ernst (1722-1777)
R. 1   S. c, 5, 10, 53
BACH, Johann Lorenz (1695-1733)
R. 1   S. c, 10, 53
BACH, Johann Ludwig (1677-1731)
R. 1   S. c, 10
BACH, Johann Michael (1648-1694)
R. 1   S. c, 2, 3, 5, 10, 11, 53
BACH, Johann Nicolaus (1669-1753)
R. 1   S. c, 10
BACH, Johann Sebastian (1685-1750)
R. 1   S. c, 1-11, 18, 21-28, 32, 33, 53, 54(335)
BACH, Johannes (see note)
              S. 10
BACH, Leonhard Emil (1849-1902), Ger
R. 3   S. c
BACH, Vincent (1890-1976), Hun (see note)
R. 1
BACH, Wilhelm Friedemann (1710-1784)
R. 1   S. c, 1, 3-11, 18, 20, 23, 24, 53
BACH, Wilhelm Friedrich Ernst (1759-1845)
R. 1   S. c, 10, 18
BACHELER, Daniel (?c1574->1610), Eng
R. 1   S. c, 10, 15, 16, 32
BACHELET, Alfred Georges (1864-1944), Fr
R. 11   S. c, 4, 5x, 10
BACHIXA, Francesco Xavier (d 1787), Port
R. 34   S. 8, 10
BACHMAN, Alberto Abraham (1875-1963), Swiss
R. 14   S. 24
BACHMANN, G. - pseud [see BEHR, Franz]
BACHMETEFF - Its my beard [see BAKHMETYEV, N. I.] [?]
BACHOFEN, Johann Caspar (1695-1755), Swiss (see note)
R. 1   S. c, 10
*** BACHOFEN, Johann Gottlieb Heinrich (1768-1839)
    (see note)

BACILLY, Bénigne de (c1625-1690), Fr
  R. 1   S. c,8
BÄCK, Sven-Erik (1919-), Sweden
  R. 1   S. c,5x,6,10,20,24,38,40,56
BACKER, David N. (1931-)

BACKER-GRØNDAHL, Agathe [see GRØNDAHL, Agathe]
BACKES, Lotte (1901-),Ger
  R. 7   S. c,24a,52
BACKOFEN, Johann Georg Heinrich (1768-1839), Ger
  R. 1   S. c,10,20,24a (see note)
*** BACKOFEN, Johann Gottlieb Heinrich (see note)
BACON, Ernst (1898-), USA
  R. 1   S. 8-11,13,25-27
BADAJÓZ el MÚSICO (fl.c1520), Sp
  R. 1   S. 10,16,17
BADARZEWSKA-BARANOWSKA, Tekla (1834-1861), Pol
  R. 1   S. 10,30,52
BADEN, Conrad (1908-), Nor
  R. 1   S. c,20,40,51
BADGER, Harold (1930-), Australia
  R. 14   S. 29
BADIJO - O tell again
          S. e
BADIN, Jacques (1916-)
          S. 24a
BADINGS, Henk (1907-), Neth
  R. 1   S. c,7,8,10,22,24
BADINSKI, Nikolai (1937-), Bul
  R. 1   S. c
BAENA, Lope de (fl c1475-c1508), Sp
  R. 1   S. 16,17
BAERMANN, Heinrich Joseph (1784-1847), Ger (see note)
  R. 1   S. c,19-21
BAERVOETS, Raymond (1930-), Bel
  R. 25   S. 24a
BAEYENS, August (1895-1966), Bel
  R. 1   S. 36
BAEZA, Garcia de (d 1560)
          S. 10,16
BAGDASARYAN, Eduard (1922-), USSR
  R. 14   S. 18,24a
BAGLEY, Edwin Eugene (1857-1922), USA
  R. 49   S. 10,54(344)
BAGLEY, Ezra Mahon (1853-1886), USA
  R. 49
BAGOT, Maurice (1896-), Fr
  R. 13   S. c
BAÏF, Jean-Antoine de (1532-1589), Fr
  R. 1   S. 18

BAILDON, Joseph (c1727-1774), Eng
   R.1   S.10
BAILEY, Derek (1932-   ), USA
   R.30   S.13
BAILEY, William Horace (1910-)
   R.200   S.3,5x
BAILLY, Henry de (d 1639), Fr
   R.5
BAIN, James Leith Macbeth
           S.5x
BAINBRIDGE, Simon (1952-   ), Eng
           S.c
BAINES, Francis Athelstan (1917-   ), Eng
   R.1
BAINES, William (1899-1922), Eng
   R.1   S.c,9
BAINTON, Edgar (1880-1956), Eng
   R.1   S.c,7,29
BAIRD, Tadeusz (1928-1981), Pol
   R.1   S.c,10,24
BAIRSTOW, Edward Cuthbert (1874-1946), Eng
   R.1   S.c,5x,7,8,10
BAJORAS, Felikas (1934-   )
           S.18,24
BAKALEINIKOFF, Vladimir Romanovich (1885-1953), USA
   R.19   S.5x,24[Balaleinikoff]
BAKALEINIKOV, Nikolai Romanovich (1881-1957), USSR
   R.47   S.24
BAKER, David Nathaniel (1931-   ), USA
   R.19   S.10,13
BAKER, Ernest John (1912-   ), Eng
   R.64   S.c
BAKER, George C. USA
           S.12,13
BAKER, John (19th Cent), USA - Coming home from the old
   campground (v)   S.10,47
BAKER, Larry (1948-   ), USA
   R.19   S.13
BAKER, Philip E. USA
           S.13
BAKER, Robert (1925-   ), USA
           S.10,13
BAKER, Thomas (1944-)

BAKFARK, Balint (1507-1576), Hun
   R.1   S.c,10,16,32,53
BAKHMETYEV, Nikolai Ivanovich (1807-1891), Russia
   R.28   S.e[Bachmeteff],4,11,18
BAKIKHANOV, Tofik (1930-   ), USSR
   R.47   S.18

BAKIROV, Enver (1920-   )
              S. 18
BAKRADZE, T. (1922-   )
              S. 18
BALABANOFF - In a garden
              S. e
BALADA, Leonardo (1933-   ), Sp
    R. 1   S. c,9,10,13,39,24a
BALADO, Juan (d. 1832)

BALAGUER - Sangre de reyes

BALAI, Leonid Petrovich [see BALAY, Leonid Petrovich]
BALAKAUSKAS, Osvaldas (1937-   )
              S. 24a
BALAKIREV, Mily Alexeyevich (1837-1910), Russia
    R. 1   S. c,1-11,18,24
BALALEINIKOFF, Vladimir [S. 24]
    = BAKALEINIKOFF, Vladimir
BALANCHIVADZE, Andrey (1906-   ), Georgia
    R. 1   S. c,10,18
BALANCHIVADZE, Meliton (1862-1937), Georgia
    R. 1   S. 18
BALASANIAN, Sergey Artemyevich (1902-   ), Russia
    R. 1   S. 18,24
BALASSA, Sándor (1935-   ), Hun
    R. 1   S. c,9,10,20
BALASSI, Bálint (1554-1594), Hun
    R. 15   S. c

BALAY, Guillaume (1871-1943), Fr
    R. 10   S. 10,21,18 [Balet],54
BALAY, Leonid Petrovich (1940-   )
              S. 10 [Balai],18,21
BALAZS, Frederic (920-   ), USA
    R. 19   S. 10,13
BALBASTRE, Claude Bénigne (1727-1799), Fr
    R. 1   S. c,4-10,18,53
BALDASSARE, Pietro (c1690->1768), It
    R. 1   S. c,10
BALDELLI, Antonio (1849-1922), It
    R. 4   S. e
BALDOMIR, José (1869-   ), Sp
    R. 9   S. e
BALDWIN, John (<1560-1615), Eng
    R. 1   S. c,5x,7,10
BALDWIN, John L. (1940-   ), USA
    R. 19   S. 10
BALES, Alfonso (d. 1635), Eng
    R. 5   S. c

BALES, Gerald Albert (1919-   ), Can
   R. 14
BALES, Richard (1915-   ), USA
   R. 19   S. 5x, 9
BALET, Guillaume [S. 18] = BALAY, Guillaume
BALFE, Michael William (1808-1870), Ire
   R. 1   S. c, 2-5, 7, 8, 10, 19, 24, 54(316)
BALISSAT, Jean (1936-   ), Swiss
   R. 4
BALL, Eric Walter John (1903-   ), Eng
   R. 14   S. c, 55, 54
BALL, Ernest   (1878-1927), USA
   R. 19   S. 10, 24, 43
BALL, Rae Eleanor
        S. 24, 30
BALLANTINE, Edward (1886-1971), USA
   R. 1   S. 9 12, 13
BALLANTYNE - Castles in the air (see note)
        S. e
BALLARD, Pierre (c1575-1639), Fr
   R. 1   S. c
BALLARD, Robert (ii) (c1575-c1650), Fr
   R. 1   S. c, 10, 16
BALLE - Christmas Bells
        S. 5x
BALLESTREM, Caspar (1934-   )
        S. c
BALLIF, Claude (1924-   ), Fr
   R. 1   S. c, 9, 20
BALLILA PRATELLA, Francesco
   [see PRATELLA, Francesco Ballila]
BALLON, Jean (1676-1739), Fr [dancer & choreographer]
   R. 11   S. c
BALLOU, Esther Williamson (1915-1973), USA
   R. 1   S. 10, 13, 30, 52
BALOGH, Erno (1897-   ), USA

   R. 19   S. 24
BALSYS, Eduardas (1919-   ), Lith
   R. 1   S. 18, 24
BALTAN, Kid ?USA
        S. 13
BALTIN, Alexander. (1931-   )
        S. 18, 24
BALTRUWEIT, Fritz
        S. c
BAMERT, Matthias (1942-   ), Swiss
   R. 19   S. 10, 13
BANAITIS, Kazimieras Viktoras (1896-1963), Lith
   R. 19   S. 18

BANCHIERI, Adriano (1568-1634), It
   R. 1   S. c,5x,7,8,10,14-16,53
BANCQUART, Alain (1934-   ), Fr
   R. 14   S. c
BANDO, Gyola (1903-   )
            S. 24,24a
BANFIELD, Raffaello de (1922-   ), Eng
   R. 14   S. 8-10
BANG, Mogens
            S. 33,57
BANISTER, John, Eng (see note)
   R. 1   S. c,5x,8
BANKS, Don (1923-1980), Australia
   R. 1   S. c,10,24,29,37
BANNER, Michael (1868-   )
            S. 24
BANNER, Philippo (c1700)
            S. c
BANSCHIKOV, Gennady (1943-   ), USSR
            S. 10,24a
BANTOCK, Granville (1868-1946), Eng
   R. 1   S. c,1-10,54(351),55
BAPTISTA, Gracia (17th Cent), It
            S. c,52
BAQUEIRO FÓSTER, Gerónimo (1898-1967), Mex
   R. 1   S. 39
BARA, George (1882-   )
            S. 18
BARAB, Seymour (1921-   ), USA
   R. 19   S. 8-10,13
BARABASHOV, V. (1901-   )
            S. 18
BARAHONA, Esquival [see ESQUIVAL BARAHONA]
BARANOVIĆ, Krešimir (1894-1975), Yug
   R. 1   S. 8,10
BARAT, Joseph Edouard (1882-   )
            S. 10
BARATI, George (1913-   ), USA
   R. 19   S. 8-10,13
BARAVALLE, Vittorio (1855-1942), It
   R. 10   S. 4[Barvalle]
BARAZZETTI, Luigi (1906-   )
            S. 23

BARBARINO LUPUS, Manfred (fl. 1557-61), Swiss
   R. 1
BARBAUD, Pierre (19??-   ), Fr (see note)
   R. 1
BARBE, Helmut (1927-   ), Ger
   R. 1   S. c

BARBELLA, Francesco (1692-1733), It
   R.8   S.c
BARBER, Samuel (1910-1981), USA
   R.1   S.c,3-13,18,24-28,42
BARBERIIS, Melchiore de (fl c1545-50), It
   R.1   S.c
BARBERIS, Mansi (1899-   ), Rum
   R.7   S.30,52
BARBETTA, Giulio Cesare (c1540->1603), It
   R.1   S.c,10,32
BARBIER, René (1890-   ), Bel
   R.1   S.c,20,36
BARBIERI, Francisco Asenjo (1823-1894), Sp
   R.1   S.c,8-10,39,42
BARBINGANT, (fl c1470)
   R.1   S.c
BARBION, Eustachius (d.1556), Neth
   R.1   S.c,10,16
BARBIREAU, Jacques (c1420-1491), Neth
   R.1   S.c,10,15,16
BARBIROLLI, Alfredo
           S.24a
BARBLAN, Otto (1860-1943), Swiss
   R.1   S.c
BARBOSA, Cacilda Campos Borges (1914-   ), Brazil
   R.7   S.52
BARBOSA, Luiz
           S.24
BARBOTEU, Georges-Yves (1924-   ), Fr
   R.80   S.10
BARBU, Filaret (1903-   ), Rum
   R.14
BARCHET, Siegfried (1918-   ), Ger
   R.15   S.c
BARCHUNOV, Pavel (1923-   )
           S.10
BARCLAY, Martin (see note)
           S.e
BARCLAY, Robert (1918-1980), USA
   R.19
BARCROFT, Thomas (16th Cent), Eng
   R.1.5   S.16
BARD, Leon - pseud [see LOMBARDO, Carlo]
BARDET, (15th Cent) - He, tres doux rossignol
           S.c
BARDI, Giovanni de (1534-1612), It
   R.1   S.c
BÁRDOS, Lajos (1899-   ), Hun
   R.1   S.c,5x,9,10

BAREN, Johann Chrysostomus (17th Cent)
      S. c
BARIE, Augustin (1883-1915), Fr
    R. 1. 5   S. c, 10
BARIERE, Etiennne-Bernard-Joseph
    [see BARRIERE, Etienne-Bernard-Joseph]
BARING GOULD, Sabine (1834-   ), Eng [?]
    R. 107   S. 54(325)
BARISONS, Peteris Martinovich (1904-1947), USSR
    R. 30   S. 18
BARK, Jan (1934-   ), Sweden
    R. 1   S. 38, 40, 56
BARKAUSKAS, Vytoutas (1931-   ), Lith
    R. 47   S. c, 18, 24
BARKER, George - Masonic march USA (see note)
        S. 10, 47
BARKER, George Arthur (1812-1876), Eng (see note)
    R. 44   S. 10, 47
BARKER, Paul (1956-   ), Eng
        S. c
BARKHOUDARIAN, Sergei Vasilievich (1887-   ), Arm
        S. 24a
BARKIN, Elaine (1932-   ), USA
    R. 19   S. 10, 13, 30, 52
BARLETTA, Alejandro (1925-   ), Arg
    R. 26   S. 24a, 46
BARLOW, Fred (1881-1951), Fr
    R. 1   S. 24
BARLOW, Samuel Latham Mitchell (1892-1982), USA
    R. 1   S. 10, 13
BARLOW, Wayne (1912-   ), USA
    R. 1   S. 3, 4, 8, 10-13, 19, 21, 23
BARNARD, Charlotte Allington (née Pye)
    [pseud: CLARIBEL] (1830-1869), Eng
    R. 1   S. 30
BARNARD, John (c1591-c1641), Eng
    R. 1. 5
BARNARD, d'Auvergne
        S. e
BARNBY, Sir Joseph (1838-1896), Eng
    R. 1   S. c, 10, 22, 24
BARNEKOW, Christian (1837-1913), Den
    R. 1   S. e
BARNES, Edward Shippen (1887-1958), USA
    R. 19   S. 12, 13
BARNES, Milton (1931-   ), Can
    R. 14   S. c
BARNES, Paul
        S. 54(329)

BARNHOUSE, Charles Lloyd Sr. (1865-1929), USA
   R.49   S.54(343)
BARNICOTT, Reginald S.
          S.e
BARNS - Lewis & Clarke
          S.54(337)
BARNS, Ethel (1880-1948), Eng
   R.7   S.24,30
BAROLSKY, Michael (1947-   ), USSR
   R.80   S.c
BARON, Ernst Gottlieb (1696-1760), Ger
   R.1   S.c,8,10,24,32
BARONVILLE (fl c1700) - Ordonnance des Dragons du Roy
          S.8
BAROZAI, Guy (Bernard de la Monnoye) (17th Cent)
          S.8
BARR, Albert Earl (1931-   ), USA
   R.23
BARRADAS, Carmen (1888/90-1963), Uruguay
   R.7   S.30,52
BARRAQUÉ, Jean (1928-1973), Fr
   R.1   S.c,9
BARRATT, William Augustus (c1874-   ), Eng
   R.109   S.5x,e
BARRAUD, Henry (1900-   ), Fr
   R.1   S.c,4-6,8,10,18,24
BARRE Joseph de la [see LA BARRE, Joseph de]
BARRE, Michel de la [see LA BARRE, Michel de]
BARRERA, Tomás (1870-1938), Sp
   R.9   S.10
BARRETT, John (c1674-1719), Eng
   R.1   S.c
BARRETT, Thomas Augustine (1866-1928), Eng
   [pseud: Leslie STUART, Lester THOMAS]
   R.3,4,8,25 S.e
BARRETT-LENNARD, Lady [see LENNARD, E. D., Lady]
BARRI, Odoardo - pseud [see SLATER, Edward]
BARRIÈRE, Etienne-Bernard-Joseph (1748-1816/18), Fr
   R.1   S.2,3,5x
BARRIÈRE, Françoise (1944-   ), Fr
   R.7   S.52
BARRIERE, Jean (c1705-1747), Fr
   R.1   S.c
BARRIGA - Hue a cancion Copihue Rojo
          S.e
BARRIOS - Fado das salas
          S.e
BARRIOS FERNANDEZ, Angel (1882-1964), Sp
   R.1   S.c,32

BARRIOS, Agustín Mangore (1885-1944), Paraguay
R. 1   S. c,10,39
BARRIOS, Jose
              S. 10
BARROLL - Laf-n-sax
              S. 22

BARRON, I. - Celaya
              S. 54(319)
BARRONET, Jean
              S. 10
BARROSO, Ary (1903-1964), Brazil
R. 55,67   S. 10,39
BARROSO, José (1901-   ), Mex
R. 25   S. 10
BARROSO, Paurillo Brazil
              S. 10,32,39
BARROW, Edgar L.

BARROWS, John Jr. (1913-1974), USA
R. 19   S. 13
BARRY - Lilies
              S. e
BARRY, John (1933-   ), Eng
R. 62
BARRY, Tom - Song of my heart

BARRYMORE, Lionel (1878-1954), USA
R. 19   S. 9,13
BARSANTI, Donato (1759-1823), It
R. 5   S. c
BARSANTI, Francesco (1690-1772), It
R. 1   S. c,8,10
BARSKOV, Oleg Vasilevich (1935-   )
              S. 18
BARSOTTI, Roger (1901-   ), Eng
R. 85   S. 55
BARSUKOV, Sergei Nikolayevich (1923-   ), USSR
R. 14   S. 9,18,24
BARTA - Rosa de Madrid

BÁRTA, Josef (c1746-1787), Cz
R. 1   S. c
BÁRTA, Lubor (1928-1972) Cz
R. 1   S. c,10,23,31,32,24a
BARTALI, Antonio [see BERTALI, Antonio]
BARTEVIAN, Ara (20th Cent)
              S. c
BARTH, Christian Frederik (1787-1861), Den
R. 1   S. c

BARTHE, Grat-Norbert (1828-1898), Fr
R. 39   S. 10,21
BARTHEL, Ursula (née Wegener) (1913-1977), Ger
R. 7   S. 52
BARTHELEMY, Richard (19-20th Cent)
             S. c
BARTHOLDY, Johann (1853-1904), Den
R. 3   S. 24
BARTHOLOMÉE, Pierre (1937-   ), Bel
R. 30   S c
BARTLES, Alfred H. (1930-   ), USA
R. 19   S. 10,13
BARTLET, John (fl 1606-10), Eng
R. 1   S. c,5,7,8,10,14,16,32
BARTLETT, Ethel Agnes (Mrs Rae Robertson)
(1900-   ), Eng
R. 37,15,43 S. 1x
BARTLETT, Harry (1922-   ), USA
             S. 10,13
BARTLETT, Homer Newton (1845-1920), USA
R. 3   S. 10
BARTLETT, James Carroll (1850-1929), USA
             S. 10,24,43
BARTÓK, Béla (1881-1945), Hun
R. 1   S. c,1-11,18-21,23,24,28,42
BARTOLINO da PADOVA (fl c1365-1405)
R. 1   S. c,10,16
BARTOLLI, Rene (1938-   )
             S. c,32
BARTOLOMEO de SELMA e SALAVERDE, Padre Francesco
(fl 1638), Sp
R. 5   S. c
BARTOLOTTI, Angelo Michele (17th Cent), It
R. 1   S. c
BARTOLOZZI, Bruno (1911-1980), It
R. 14   S. 10,24a
BARTOLUCCI, Domenico (1917-   ), It
R. 14   S. c,10
BARTON - Hawaii love song
             S. e
BARTON, Andrew - pseud (fl 1767), USA
R. 20
BARTON, George

BARTONCINI, Mario

BARTOŠ, František (1905-1973), Cz
R. 1   S. 5x,6,10
BARTOŠ, Jan Zdeněk (1908-   ), Cz
R. 14   S. 8,31,24a

BARTOW, Nevett (1934-1973), USA
  R. 23
BARTSCH, Charles (1907-   ), Bel
  R. 13
BARVALLE - Hymn degli Alpini Sciatori
          S. 54(333)
BARVALLE, Vittorio [S. 4] = BARAVALLE, Vittorio
BARVIK, Miroslav (1919-   ), Cz
  R. 18   S. 31
BASART, Robert (1926-   ), USA
  R. 19   S. 13
BASHINSKAS, Yustinas (1923-   )
          S. 18,24a
BASHMAKOV, Leonid (1927-   ), Fin
  R. 1   S. c,10,40
BASIRON, Philippe (15th Cent), Fr
  R. 1   S. 16
BASKETTE, Billy (1884-1949), USA
  R. 23   S. 10
BASMANS - Still night

          S. 5x
BASNER, Veniamin Efimovich (1925-   ), Russia
  R. 1   S. 18
BASS, George

          S. 24a
BASSA, Jose (1670-1730), Sp
          S. c,5x,10,39
BASSANI, Giovanni Battista (c1657-1716), It
  R. 1   S. c,5-8,10,27
BASSANO, Anthony (fl 1600-60)
          S. c,10,16
BASSANO, Giovanni (c1558-1617), It
  R. 1   S. c,8,14,53
BASSANO, Jerome (fl 1581-1631), It
  R. 1   S. c,10
BASSETT - Royal review
          S. 54(353)
BASSETT, Leslie Raymond (1923-   ), USA
  R. 1   S. 10,13,19,21,23,24a
BASSEVI, Giacobbe [see CERVETTO, Giacobbe]
BASSI, Luigi (1833-1871), It (see note)
  R. 10   S. c,19,21
BASSMAN, George (1914-   ), USA
  R. 23   S. 9
BASTIAANS, Johannes Gijsbertus (1812-1875), Neth
  R. 1   S. c
BASTON - Les yeux noirs
          S. e
BASTON, John (fl 1711-1733), Eng
  R. 1   S. c,10

BASTON, Josquin (fl 1542-63), Neth
   R. 1   S. c, 16
BATAILLE, Gabriel (c1575-1630), Fr
   R. 1   S. c, 5x, 8, 10, 14, 16
BATASHOV, K. (1938-   )
           S. 18
BATCHELAR, Daniel [see BACHELER, Daniel]
BATE, Jennifer Lucy (1944-   ), Eng
   R. 80   S. c, 52
BATE, Stanley (1913-1959), Eng
   R. 1   S. 4, 5
BATESON, Thomas (c1570-1630), Eng
   R. 1   S. c, 2, 3, 5, 7, 8, 10, 14, 16
BATH, Hubert Charles (1883-1945), Eng
   R. 1   S. c, 4, 5x, 10, 55
BATH, John Hubert - Cornish rhapsody [S. 10]
   = BATH, Hubert Charles
BATISTE - Andante in G
           S. 54 (313)
BATISTE, Antoine Edouard (18?0-1876), Fr
   R. 3
BATIZI, Andras (16th Cent)
           S. c
BATON, René [see RHENÉ-BATON - pseud]
BATSEVICH, Grazhina [S. 18] = BACEWICZ, Grazyna
BATSTONE, Philip Norman (1933-   ), USA
   R. 19   S. 10, 13, 27

BATSTSINY, Antonio [S. 18] = BAZZINI, Antonio
BATTEN, Adrian (1591-1637), Eng
   R. 1   S. c, 8, 10, 15, 16
BATTEN, Robert - pseud [see WILSON, Henry James Lane]
BATTISHILL, Jonathan (1738-1801), Eng
   R. 1   S. c, 5x, 7, 8, 10
BATUYEV, Zhigzhit (1915-   ), USSR
   R. 47   S. 18
BAUCHER, H. - Je t'aime; Reviens ma mie (vi & p)
           S. 24a
BAUD de la QUARRIÈRE (13th Cent)
   R. 5
BAUDACH, Ulrich (1921-   ), Ger
   R. 4   S. c
BAUDO, Serge (1927-   ), Fr
   R. 1   S. 10, 18 [Bodo]
BAUDREXEL, Philipp Jakob (1627-1691), Ger
   R. 1   S. c, 53
BAUER - Columella
           S. e
BAUER, Harold (1873-1951), USA
   R. 1   S. 13

BAUER, John (1947-   ), USA
          S. 13
BAUER, Marion (1887-1955), USA (see note)
     R. 1   S. 3,10,11,13,30,52
BAUER - Sokasodik (saxophone quartet)
          S. 22
BAUMANN, Erik Eugen (1889-1955), Sweden
     R. 30a   S. 43
BAUMANN - Kommt ihr Hirten; Quem pastores laudavere
          S. 10
BAUMANN, Herbert (1925-   ), Ger
     R. 80   S. c
BAUMANN, Max Georg (1917-   ), Ger
     R. 1   S. c
BAUMGÄRTNER (15th Cent), Ger
     R. 5   S. c [Boumgartner, Paumgartner],53
BAUMGARTNER, Wilhelm (1820-1867), Swiss
     R. 1   S. c
BAUMILAS, Vitolis (1928-   )
          S. 18
BAUR, Jean (1719->1773), Fr
     R. 1   S. c
BAUR, Jürg (1918-   ), Ger
     R. 1   S. c
BAUSTETTER, Johan Konrad (fl 1726-1752), Neth
     R. 5   S. 8
BAUSZNERN, Dietrich von (1928-   ), Ger
     R. 14   S. c
BAUTISTA, Julian (1901-1961), Arg
     R. 1   S. c,10,32
BAUTZ, G. - Chant de gaule; Chant de Pâques
          S. e
BAVICCHI, John (1922-   ), USA
     R. 19   S. 10,13,19,21,24a

BAVIKINE, Nikolai (18th Cent)
          S. c
BAX, Sir Arnold (1883-1953), Eng
     R. 1   S. c,1-11,18-20,23,24a
BAXTER, John (16th Cent)
          S. c,16
BAXTER, Leslie (1922-   ), USA
     R. 23   S. 9
BAY, Rudolph (1791-1856), Ger
     R. 3   S. 57
BAYCO, Frederic (1913-   ), Eng
     R. 66
BAYER, Joseph (1852-1913), Aus
     R. 1   S. c,5x,9,10
BAYES, Nora - pseud [see GOLDBERG, Doris]

BAYLE, François (1932-   ), Fr
   R. 1   S. c, 10
BAYLY, Thomas Haynes (1797-1839), Eng
   R. 44   S. 10, 24a
BAYNES, Sidney (1879-1938), Eng
   R. 1   S. 10
BAYNON, Arthur John (1889-   ), Eng
   R. 37   S. 5x
BAYNTON-POWER, Henry [see POWER, Henry Baynton]
BAZÁN, Oscar   Arg
   R. 26   S. 46
BAZANT, Jiri (1924-   ), Cz
   R. 18   S. 31
BAZEA, Juan
             S. 32
BAZELON, Irwin Allen (1922-   ), USA
   R. 19   S. 9, 10, 13
BAZIN, Francois (1816-1878), Fr
   R. 1   S. c, 5x
BÁZLIK, Miroslav (1931-   ), Slovak
   R. 1   S. 31
BAZZINI, Antonio (̄818-1897), It
   R. 1   S. c, 4, 5x, 10, 18 [Batstsiny], 24a
BEACH, Amy Marcy Cheney (1867-1944), USA
   R. 1   S. c, 4, 9-11, 13, 43, 52, 24a
BEACH, Bennie (1925-   ), USA
   R. 19   S. c, 13
BEACH, Perry (1917-   ), USA
   R. 19   S. 13
BEALE, David Brooks (1945-   ), USA
   R. 19   S. 13
BEALE, William (1784-1854), Eng
   R. 1   S. c, 2, 10
BEARCHELL, William   USA
             S. 54 (341)
BEAT, Janet Eveline (1937-   ), Eng
   R. 7   S. c
BEATRIZ de DIA (12th Cent), Fr
   R. 1   S. c, 10, 16, 52
BEAUHARNAIS, Hortense de [see HORTENSE de BEAUHARNAIS]
BEAULIEU, Eustorg de (c1495-1552), Fr
   R. 1   S. 10, 16
BEAULIEU, Girard de (see note)

BEAULIEU, Lambert de (fl c1576-90), Fr (see note)
   R. 1   S. 8
BEAUMONT - Caprice espagnol
             S. 54 (318)
BEAUMONT, Geoffrey (20th Cent), Eng
             S. 9

BEAUVARLET-CHARPENTIER, Jacques-Marie (1766-1834), Fr
    R. 1   S. c
BEAUVARLET-CHARPENTIER, Jean-Jaques (1734-1794), Fr
    R. 1   S. c
BEAVER, Jack (1900-1963), Eng
    R. 85   S. 55
BEAVER, Paul H. Jr. (1925-   ), USA
    R. 19
BEBEY, Francis (1929-   ), Cameroons
                S. c
BÉCAUD, Gilbert (1927-   ), Fr
    R. 1   S. c,9
BECCE, Giuseppe (1881-   ), It
    R. 3   S. 24
BECCHI, Antonio di (1522->1568), It
    R. 1   S. c
BECERRA SCHMIDT, Gustave (1925-   ), Chile
    R. 1   S. 10,39
BECHET, Sydney (1897-1959), USA
    R. 1   S. 9
BECHGAARD, Julius (1843-1917), Den
    R. 3   S. e,c
BECK, Christian Friedrich (18th Cent), Ger
    R. 5
BECK, Conrad Arthur (1901-   ), Swiss
    R. 1   S. c,5,7,10,20,22,23
BECK, Frederick W. (1928-   )

BECK, John Ness (1930-   ), USA
    R. 19   S. 13
BECK, Reinhold Immanuel (1881-1969), Ger
    R. 14
BECKER, Albert (1834-1899), Ger
    R. 3   S. c
BECKER, Charles (1944-   )
                S. c
BECKER, Dietrich (1623-1679), Ger
    R. 1   S. c
BECKER, Günther (1924-   ), Ger
    R. 1   S. c
BECKER, Jean (1833-1884), Ger
    R. 1   S. 24
BECKER, John Joseph (1886-1961), USA
    R. 1   S. 2,3,10,13,19,21
BECKER, Reinhold (1842-1924), Ger
    R. 3   S. e
BECKLER, Stanworth (1923-   ), USA
    R. 19   S. 13
BECKMAN, Bror (1866-1929), Sweden
    R. 4   S. 24a

BECKWITH, John (1927-   ), Can
  R.1   S.10
BECUCCI, Ernesto (1845-1905), It
  R.10   S.24
BEDELL, Robert Leech (1909-   ), USA
  R.19   S.12,13
BEDFORD, Brian
             S.10
BEDFORD, David (1937-   ), Eng
  R.1   S.c,10
BEDYNGHAM, Johannes (d.1459), Eng
  R.1   S.c
BEECKE, Ignaz von (1733-1803), Ger
  R.1
BEECROFT, Norma Marian (1934-   ), Can
  R.7   S.30,52
BEELBY, Malcolm (1907-   ), USA
  R.23   S.10
BEELER, Walter (1908-   ), USA
             S.10,13
BEELINI, J. - Katy, darling (fl 1854), USA
             S.10
BEER, Johann (1655-1700), Ger
  R.1
BEERHALTER, Aloys (1800-1852)
  R.46   S.c
BEERMAN, Burton (1943-   ), USA
  R.19   S.13
BEERS, Bob (1920-1972), USA
             S.13
BEESON, Elizabeth R.
             S.30
BEESON, Jack (1921-   ), USA
  R.1   S.9,10,13,27
BEETHOVEN, Ludwig van (1770-1827), Ger
  R.1   S.c,1-10,18-28,32,42,43,54(326,28)
BEGINIKER, Henricus (17th Cent)

BEGLARIAN, Grant (1927-   ), USA
  R.19   S.13
BEGUE, Nicolas-Antoine Le
  [see LEBEGUE, Nicolas-Antoine]
BEHR, Franz (1837-1898), Ger
  [pseud: Hans von AACHEN, G. BACHMANN
  W. COOPER, Charles GODARD, Charles MORLEY,
  Francesco d´ORSI, Edwin SMITH]
  R.3   S.1x
BEHREND, John Arthur Henry (1853-1935), Eng
             S.c

BEHREND, Siegfried (1933-   ), Ger
 R. 1   S. c,10,18,32
BEHRENS, Jack (1935-   ), USA
 R. 19   S. 13
BEHRMAN, David (1937-   ), USA
 R. 19   S. 10
BEIDERBECKE, Bix (1903-1931), USA
 R. 4
BEINES, Karl (1869-   ), Ger
 R. 3   S. c,e
BEKARYAN, T. - Sonata no. 2 (vi)
      S. 18
BEKKU, Sadao (1922-   ), Japan
 R. 1   S. 24a,50
BEKMAN-SHCHERBINA, Elena Alexandrovna (18??-1951), USSR
      S. 52
BELAUBRE, Louis Noel (1932-   ), Fr
 R. 14   S. c
BELCHER, Supply (1752-1836), USA
 R. 1   S. 10,47
BELKNAP, Daniel (late 18th Cent), USA
 R. 1   S. 10,47
BELL - Alert march
      S. 54(311)
BELL, Daniel (1928-   ), Sweden
 R. 30   S. 10,40,56
BELL, Firmin Le [see LEBEL, Firmin]
BELL, Leslie Richard (1906-   ), Can
 R. 14
BELLA, Jan Levoslav (1843-1936), Cz
 R. 18   S. 5x
BELLAK, James (19th Cent), USA
 R. 200   S. 10,47
BELLAVERE, Vincenzo (d 1587), It
 R. 1   S. c,16,53
BELLE, Jan (d <1552), Flem
 R. 1   S. c,8,10,14,16,41
BELLEVILLE, Jacques de (17th Cent)
 R. 1   S. 16
BELLINI, Vincenzo (1801-1835), It
 R. 1   S. c,1-11,18,20,24,28,34,42,
BELLINZANI, Paolo Benedetto (c1690-1757), It
 R. 1   S. c
BELLMAN - Drick or ditt glas
      S. e
BELLMAN, Carl Michael (1740-1795), Sweden
 R. 1   S. c,4,8,10,22,33,56
BELLOW, Alexander (1912-1976), USA
 R. 19   S. 10,13,32

BELLSTEDT, Herman (1858-1926), USA
   R. 49   S. 54(320,44)
BELMANS, Rafael - Legende

BELMONTE (15-16th Cent) - Pues mi dich non consiente
      S. 17
BELSAYAGA, Cristobal de
      S. 10
BELSTERLING, Charles
      S. 10,13
BELTON - Down the mall
      S. 54(324)
BELVILLE, Edward [see JAKOBOWSKY, Edward - pseud]
BEMBERG, Herman (1861-1931), Fr
   R. 11   S. 5x,10
BENARY, Barbara (1946-   ), USA
   R. 19   S. 13,30,52
BENARY, Peter (1931-   )
   R. 14   S. c,10 [Benary, Paul]
BENATZKY, Ralph (1884-1957), Aus/Ger
   R. 1   S. c,1x,5x,9 ⁻0,24
BENCINI, Giuseppe (fl 1723-27), It
   R. 1   S. 10,53
BENCRISCUTTO, Frank (1928-   ), USA
   R. 19   S. 10,13
BENDA, Franz [František] (1709-1786), Boh
   R. 1   S. c,2,3,5,9,10,18,24,32
BENDA, Friedrich (Wilhelm Heinrich) (1745-1814), Boh
   R. 1
BENDA, Friedrich Ludwig (1752-1792), Bohn
   R. 1   S. c
BENDA, George [Jiri] (1722-1795), Boh
   R. 1   S. c,4,5,8-10,24
BENDA, Johann (1713-1752), Boh
   R. 1   S. c,5,23
BENDER, Jan (1909-   ), USA
   R. 19   S. c,12,13
BENDINELLI, Cesare (d. 1617), It
   R. 1   S. c
BENDIX, Theodore (1863-1935), USA
   R. 53   S. 24a
BENDIX, Victor (1851-1926), Den
   R. 1   S. 33
BENDL, Karel (1838-1897), Cz
   R. 1   S. 1x
BENDUSI, Francesco (fl c1553), It
   R. 1   S. c,5x,10,11,16,53
BENEDETTI, Pietro (c1585-c1649), It
   R. 1   S. c,10

BENEDICENTI, Vera (Grottolo) (1913-   ), It
   R. 7   S. 52
BENEDICT, Sir Julius (1804-1885), Eng
   R. 1   S. c, 2-4, 5x, 7, 11, 18, 24
BENEDICTUS - Mijn liefkens bruin oghen
          S. c, 16
BENEKEN, Friedrich Burchard (1760-1818), Ger
   R. 1   S. 43
BENET, John (fl c1420-50), Eng
   R. 1   S. c, 2-4, 5x, 8, 10, 14
BENEVOLI, Orazio (1605-1672), It
   R. 1   S. c, 8, 9
BENGRAF, Joseph (1745/6-1791), Ger
   R. 1
BENGTSSON, Roland (1916-   ), Sweden
   R. 30
BENGUEREL, Xavier (1931-   ), Sp
   R. 1   S. c, 10
BENGZON - Viola
          S. e
BEN HAIM, Paul (1897-1984), Isr
   R. 1   S. c, 8, 10, 19, 21, 24
BENHAM, Earl
          S. e
BENIZZO, Franc. - pseud [see POENITZ Franz]
BENJAMIN, Arthur (1893-1960), Australia
   R. 1   S. c, 4-6, 8-11, 18, 19, 21, 23, 24, 54 (335)
BENJAMIN, Bennie (1907-   ), USA
   R. 23   S. 10
BENJAMIN, George (1960-   ), Eng
          S. c
BENNARD, George (1873-1958), USA
   R. 19   S. 10
BENNET, Charles William (1849-1926)

BENNET, John (fl 1599-1614), Eng
   R. 1   S. c, 5-8, 10, 14-16, 32
BENNETT, Arthur Christopher (1862-1925), Eng

BENNETT, David (1892-   ), USA
   R. 23
BENNETT, Frank, USA
          S. 10, 13, 20
BENNETT, Harold - pseud [see FILLMORE, Henry]
BENNETT, John (c1725-1784), Eng
   R. 1   S. c, 53
BENNETT, Richard Rodney (1936-   ), Eng
   R. 1   S. c, 9, 10, 21
BENNETT, Robert Russell (1894-1981), USA
   R. 1   S. c, 3, 4, 5x, 6, 9-13, 24

BENNETT, Thomas Case Sterndale
        S.c
BENNETT, William Sterndale (1816-1875), Eng
    R.1   S.c,10
BENO - Noel pour les gueux
        S.e
BENOIST, François (1794-1878), Fr
    R.1   S.10
BENOIT, Peter (1834-1901), Bel
    R.1   S.c,5x,7,36,41
BENSHOOF, Kenneth
        S.10
BENSON, Warren (1924-   ), USA
    R.1   S.9,10,13,19,21,22
BENT, R. - Swiss boy
        S.54(359)
BEN-TAYOUX, L. Frédéric (1840-   ), Fr
    R.57   S.10
BENTER, Charles (1887-1964), USA
    R.19   S.54(311,12)
BENTOIU, Pascal (1927-   ), Rum
    R.1   S.18,24
BENTSION, Eliezer (1920-   )
        S.24a
BENTZ - Berceuse (vi & ce)
        S.24a
BENTZON, Jørgen (1897-1951), Den
    R.1   S.4,5,10,22,35,40,57
BENTZON, Niels Viggo (1919-   ), Den
    R.1   S.c,4-9,20,24,35,40,57
BENTZON-GYLLICH, Oscar (1847-1899), Den
    R.111   S.e
BENVENUTI, Arrigo (1925-   ), It
    R.14   S.c
BEN YOHANAN, Asher (1929-   ), Isr
    R.14
BENZA, L. - Le passeur de la Moselle
        S.e
BEOBIDE, José (1884-1967), Sp [?]
    R.9   S.c
BÉRAT, Frédéric (1801-1855), Fr
    R.10   S.5x
BERBERIAN, Cathy (1925-1983), USA (see note)
    R.1   S.c,13,30,52
BERBERIAN, Hambardzum (1905-   ), Arm
    R.19
BERCHEM, Jacquet de (c1505-c1565), Flem
    R.1   S.c,1x,2-5,7,8,10,11,14-16,41
BERENGUIER de PALAZOL (12th Cent), Catalan
    R.1   S.c,10,16,17

BERESFORD - Margery Green
          S. e
BERETTA, Pietro (c1750)
  R. 5   S. c
BEREZOVSKY, Maxim Sozontovich (1745-1777), Russia
  R. 1   S. c,10
BEREZOWSKY, Nicolai (1900-1953), USA
  R. 1   S. 2,3,5,7,10,11,20
BERFF, Georg (17th Cent)
          S. c,53
BERG - Es steht ein Lind
          S. e
BERG, Alban (1885-1935), Aus
  R. 1   S. c,2,3-11,18-21,24,25,28,42
BERG, George (c1730-c1770), Eng
  R. 1   S. 10
BERG, Gottfrid (1889-1970), Sweden
  R. 14   S. 56
BERG, Gunnar (1909-   ), Den
  R. 1   S. c,20,40
BERG, Isak Albert (1803-1886), Sweden
  R. 1. 5   S. 10
BERG, J. A. - Herdegossen
          S. e
BERG, Jan van den (1929-   )
          S. c
BERG, Josef (1927-1971), Cz
  R. 1   S. 31
BERG, Natanael (1879-1957), Sweden
  R. 1   S. c,5x,6
BERG, Per (1897-1957), Sweden
  R. 30
BERG, Reinhard (1945-)

BERGAMIN, Luzi (1901-)

BERGAMO, Davide da [see DAVIDE, Felice Moretti]
BERGE, Sigurd (1929-), Nor
  R. 14   S. c,40,51
BERGEIM, Joseph USA
  R. 49   S. 54(319,44,56)
BERGEN, Eugene ?USA
          S. 13
BERGER - Amoureuse
          S. 54(313)
BERGER, Andreas (1584-1656), Ger
  R. 1   S. c
BERGER, Arthur Victor (1912-), USA
  R. 1   S. c,7,8,10,13,24

BERGER, Gunter (1929-   )
        S. c, 20
BERGER, Jean (1909-   ), USA
  R. 19   S. c, 8, 10, 13
BERGER, Ludwig (1777-1839), Ger
  R. 1   S. c, 10
BERGER, Rodolphe (1864-1916), Sp
  R. 3   S. e, 24a
BERGER, Theodor (1905-   ), Aus
  R. 1   S. c, 4, 5x, 9
BERGER, Wilhelm Georg (1929-   ), Rum
  R. 1   S. 24
BERGER, Wilhelm (1861-1911), Ger
  R. 8   S. c
BERGGREEN, Andreas Peter (801-1880), Den
  R. 1   S. c, 33
BERGH, Arthur (1882-1962), USA
  R. 14   S. 24
BERGH, Sverre (1915-1980), Nor
  R. 14   S. c, 40
BERGHMANS - La femme à barbe
        S. 10
BERGMAN, Erik Valdemar (1911-   ), Fin
  R. 1   S. c, 40
BERGMAN, Stefan (see note)
        S. 3, 5x
BERGSMA, William Laurence (1921-   ), USA
  R. 1   S. 7-10, 13, 24, 25, 27
BERGSON, Michal (1820-1898), Pol
  R. 1   S. 19, 21
BERGSTRÖM, Gurli Marie [see GULLMAR, Kai - pseud]
BERIO, Luciano (1925-   ), It
  R. 1   S. c, 9, 10, 20, 24
BÉRIOT, Charles Auguste de (1802-1870), Fr
  R. 1   S. c, 8, 24
BERKELEY, Lennox (1903-   ), Eng
  R. 1   S. c, 5, 8, 10, 20, 24, 32
BERKELEY, Michael (1948-   ), Eng
        S. c
BERKOWITZ, Sol (1922-   ), USA
  R. 19   S. 10, 13
BERLIJN, Anton (1817-1870), Neth
  R. 1
BERLIN, Irving (1888-   ), USA
  R. 1   S. c, 9-11, 24, 54(311)
BERLIN, Johan Daniel (1714-1787), Nor
  R. 1   S. c, 24a
BERLIN, Johan Henrik (1741-1807), Nor
  R. 1   S. c

BERLINSKI, Herman (1910-   ), USA
   R.19   S.9,10,12,13
BERLIOZ, Hector (1803-1869), Fr
   R.1   S.c,1-11,18,23-25,28,34,42,54(315,22)
BERMUDO, Juan (c1510-c1565), Sp
   R.1   S.c,10,15-17,32,39,53
BERNABE, (17th Cent), Sp
   R.9   S.c,10,53
BERNABEI, Giuseppe Antonio (?1649-1732), It
   R.1   S.c,4,5x
BERNAL JIMÉNEZ, Miguel (1910-1956), Mex
   R.1   S.c,8
BERNAL GONÇALEZ, ?José (16th Cent), Sp (see note)
   R.1   S.16
BERNAOLA, Carmelo (1929-   ), Sp
   R.1
BERNARD de CLUNY (14th Cent)
           S.c,10
BERNARD, Christoph [see BERNHARD, Christoph]
BERNARD, Felix (1897-1944), USA
   R.23   S.10
BERNARD, Jacques (20th Cent)
           S.c
BERNARD, Jean Emile-Auguste (1843-1902), Fr
   R.8   S.2,4
BERNARD, Matvey Ivanovich (1794-1871), Russia
   R.1   S.18
BERNARD, Paul (1827-1879), Fr
   R.3   S.26
BERNARDI, Steffano (c1585-1636), It
   R.1   S.c,2,5x,10,16
BERNARDINI, Marcello (c1740->1799), It
   R.1   S.c
BERNARDINI, Marcello (18th Cent)
   R.5
BERNART de VENTADORN (12th Cent), Fr
   R.1   S.c,2-4,5x,7,8,10,11,14-16
BERNAT, Robert (1931-   ), USA
   R.19   S.10

BERNER, Friedrich Wilhelm (1780-1827), Ger
   R.1   S.c
BERNERS, Gerald Hugh Tyrwhitt-Wilson (1883-1950), Eng
   R.1   S.c,1-5,7,8,10,11
BERNEVILLE, Gilebert de [see GILLEBERT de BERNEVILLE]
BERNGER von HORHEIM (fl 1180-90), Ger
   R.1   S.c
BERNHARD, Christoph (1628-1692), Ger
   R.1   S.c,5x,10,24
BERNIA, Vincenzo (16th Cent.), It
   R.10   S.c

BERNIAUX, Desire (1889-   )
           S.24,30
BERNICAT, Fermin (1841-1883), Fr
    R.98   S.e
BERNIER, Buddy (1910-   ), USA
    R.23   S.10
BERNIER, Nicolas (1665-1734), Fr
    R.1   S.c,4,5,8,10,24
BERNIER, René (1905-   ), Bel
    R.1   S.c,8,20,36
BERNOUX, Leon - pseud [see PERONNET, Amelie]
BERNSTEIN, Charles Harold (1917-   ), USA
           S.10,13,24a
BERNSTEIN, Leonard (1918-   ), USA
    R.1   S.c,4-10,13,19-21,24
BERRY, Wallace (1928-   ), USA
    R.1   S.9,13
BERSA, Blagoje (1873-1934), Croatia
    R.8   S.c,10
BERSOZZI, Alessandro [see BESSOZZI, Alessandro]
BERTALI [Bartali], Antonio (1605-1669), Aus
    R.1   S.c,10,24
BERTANI, Lelio (c1550-?1620), It
    R.1   S.7,10,14
BERTÉ, Heinrich (1857-1924), Aus
    R.1   S.c,2
BERTELSEN, Ankerstjerne
           S.33
BERTHEAUME, Isidore (c1752-1802), Fr
    R.1   S.24
BERTHELOT - L'amour de moy, Fr

BERTHIER, Jean-Jacques (1923-   ), Fr
           S.c
BERTHOLD, G. - pseud [see PEARSALL, Robert Lucas]
BERTHOMIEU, Marc (1906-   )
    R.14   S.c,5x,18
BERTI, Giovanni Pietro (d.1638), It
    R.1   S.10
BERTIN, Louise-Angélique (1805-1877), Fr
    R.1   S.10,30,52
BERTINI, Henri-Jérome (1798-1876), Fr
    R.1   S.c
BERTOLDO, Sperindo, (c1530-1570), It
    R.1   S.c,53
BERTOLI, Giovanni Antonio (fl c1639-45), It
    R.1   S.10
BERTON, Henri-Montan (1767-1844), Fr
    R.1   S.c,10

BERTON, Pierre Montan (1727-1780), Fr
   R. 1   S. c
BERTONCINI, Mario (1932-   ), It
   R. 30   S. 10
BERTONI, Ferdinando (1725-1813), It
   R. 1
BERTOUCH, Georg von (1668-1743), Nor
   R. 1   S. c
BERTOUILLE, Gérard (1898-   ), Bel
   R. 1   S. 36
BERTRAM, Hans George (1936-   ), Ger
   R. 80   S. c
BERTRAND, Antoine de (16th Cent), Fr
   R. 1   S. c,2,4,5x,8-10,14,16
BERTRAND, Henri-Joseph (b. 1768), Fr
   R. 5   S. c
BERVEILLER, Jean (20th Cent), Fr
          S. c,10
BERVILY - Isabella (vi & p)
          S. 24
BERWALD, Franz (1796-1868), Sweden
   R. 1   S. c,4,5,7,9,10,20,40,56
BERWALD, Johan Fredrik (1787-1861), Sweden
   R. 1   S. 24
BESARD, Jean Baptiste (c1567->1617), Fr
   R. 1   S. c,2,4,5x,7,8,10,11,14,16,32
BESOYAN, Rick (1924-1970), USA (see note)
   R. 1   S. 9
BESOZZI, Alessandro (1702-1793), It
   R. 1   S. c
BEST, William Thomas (1826-1897), Eng
   R. 3
BESTOR, Charles (1924-   ), USA
   R. 19   S. 13
BETHIER - Petite serenade (vi & p)
          S. 24
BETHUNE GREENE, Thomas (1849-1908), USA
   R. 1   S. 10
BETHUNE, Conon de [see CONON de BETHUNE]
BETTERTON, Ralph - pseud [see SANTLEY, Charles]
BETTINELLI, Angelo (1878-   ), It
   R. 3   S. e
BETTINELLI, Bruno (1913-   ), It
   R. 1   S. 8,10,24a
BETTS, Lorne M. (1918-   ), Can
   R. 4
BEUERLE, Herbert (1911-   ), Ger
   R. 4   S. c
BEUGNIOT, Jean-Pierre (1935-   )
          S. c

BEUTLER, Johann Georg Bernhard (1762-1814), Ger
R. 5   S. c
BEVAN, Frederick Charles (1856-1939), Eng
R. 39   S. e
BEVERIDGE, Thomas G. (1938-1981), USA
R. 19   S. 13
BEVERSDORF, Thomas (1924-   ), USA
R. 19   S. 10,13,24a
BEVIN, Elway (c1554-1638), Wales
R. 1   S. c,10,16
BEYDTS, Louis Antoine (1895-1953), Fr
R. 14   S. 4,5,8
BEYER, Frank Michael (1928-   ), Ger
R. 4
BEYER, Frederick H. (1926-   ), USA
R. 19   S. 13
BEYER, Johann Samuel (1669-1744), Ger
R. 1   S. 5
BEYER, Johanna Magdalena (1888-1944), USA
R. 7   S. 3,5x,13,20,30,52
BEZANÇON, Guy (1942-   )
              S. c
BEZANSON, Philip (1916-1975), USA
R. 19   S. 10,13
BIALAS, Günther (1907-   ), Ger
R. 1   S. c,10
BIALOSKY, Marshall H. (1923-   ), USA
R. 19   S. 10,13
BIALSKI, Joseph
              S. c
BIANCHI, Francesco (c1752-1810), It
R. 1   S. 8,18 (see note under ROSSI)
BIANCHINI, Domenico (c1510-c1576), It
R. 1   S. c
BIANCHINI, Francescho (fl 1547-8), It
R. 1   S. 16
BIANCHINI, Guido (1885-   ), It
R. 8   S. 10
BIANCIARDI, Francesco (c1571-1607), It
R. 1   S. 10
BIBALO, Antonio (1922-   ), Nor
R. 14   S. c,40,51
BIBER, Carl Heinrich von (1681-1749), Boh
R. 8   S. c,10
BIBER, Heinrich Ignaz Franz von (1644-1704), Boh
R. 1   S. c,3,4,5,8,9,18,24
BICALHO, (?Brazil) - Hino ao trabalhou
              S. 5x
BICK, Eva [pseud: BICKVOR] Sweden
              S. 43

BIDGOOD, Thomas
        S. 54(357,63,65)
BIEBL, Franz (1906-   )
  R. 14   S. c
BIECHTELER, Benediet (1689-1759), Ger
  R. 1   S. c
BIELAWA, Herbert (1930-   ), USA
  R. 19   S. 10,13
BIELING, Franz Ignaz (>1700-1757), Ger
  R. 1   S. c
BIENE, August van (1850-1913), Neth
  R. 10   S. 24
BIGAGLIA, Diogenio (c1676-c1745), It
  R. 1   S. c,10
BIGARD, Barney (1906-1980), USA
  R. 1
BIGELOW, Frederick USA
        S. 13,54(348)
BIGGS, Richard Keys (1886-1962), USA
  R. 23   S. 13
BIGNELL, Charles
        S. e
BIGOT, Eugène (1888-1965), Fr
  R. 1   S. 18
BILIK, Jerry H. (1933-   ), USA
  R. 19   S. 13
BILLAUT, L. - Tzarienne (vi & p)
        S. 24a
BILLI, Vincenzo (1869-1938), It
  R. 8   S. 1x,5x,10,24,34,44
BILLINGS, William (1746-1800), USA
  R. 1   S. 3,4,5x,6-11,47
BILLON - Sur tes levres
        S. 24a
BILSE, Benjamin (1816-1902), Ger
  R. 95   S. 54(343)
BILTON, J. Manuel (?-1935), Eng
  R. 49   S. 54(344)
BIMBONI, Alberto (1882-1960), It
  R. 4   S. e
BINCHOIS, Gilles de Bins dit (c1400-1460), Franco-Flem
  R. 1   S. c,2-4,5x,8,10,11,14-17,32,53,41
BINDER, Abraham Wolfe (1895-1966), USA
  R. 19   S. 10,13
BINDER, Carl (1816-1860), Aus (see note)
  R. 1
BINET, Jean (1893-1960), Swiss
  R. 1   S. c,4,7,10,19
BINGE, Ronald (1910-1979), Eng
  R. 1   S. c,54(321),55

BINGEN, von - O virga ac diadema
         S.14
BINGHAM - In your dear eyes
         S.e
BINGHAM, Seth (1882-1972), USA
   R.1   S.3,4,8,10-13,24a
BINKERD, Gordon Ware (1916-   ), USA
   R.1   S.8,10,13
BIONI, Antonio (1698->1739), It
   R.1   S.c
BIRCH - I Wondered...
         S.5x
BIRCH, Ernest
         S.e
BIRCHALL, Steven, USA
         S.10,13
BIRD, Arthur (1856-1923), USA
   R.1   S.10
BIRGISSON, Snorri Sigfos (1954-   ), Ice
         S.40
BIRKENSTOCK, Johann Adam (1687-1733), Ger
   R.1   S.24a
BIRTWISTLE, Harrison (1934-   ), Eng
   R.1   S.c,9,10,55
BISCARDI, Chester (1948-   ), USA
   R.19   S.13
BISCARDI, Luigi (d.1876), It
   R.10   S.10
BISCHOFF, John ?USA - Rendez-vous (released 1979)
         S.13
BISCHOFF, John W. (1850-1909), USA
   R.53   S.10,26
BISCHOFF, Kaspar Jakob (1823-1893), Ger
   R.3   S.e
BISCHOFF, Rainer (1947-   )
         S.c
BISCOGLI, Francesco (fl c1740), It
   R.1   S.10
BISH, Diane (20th Cent), USA
         S.52
BISHOP, Henry Rowley (1786-1855), Eng
   R.1   S.c,1x,2-8,10,11,18 24,28,47,54(332)
BISSELL, Keith Warren (1912-   ), Can
   R.14
BITCLIFF, Edwin
         S.10
BITGOOD, Roberta (1908-   ), USA
   R.19   S.12,13,52
BITSCH, Marcel (1921-   ), Fr
   R.14   S.10,22

BITTI, Martino (1655/6-1743),It
  R. 1   S. c,10
BITTNER, Jacques (fl 1683), Fr
  R. 5   S. c,8,10,32
BITTNER, Julius (1874-1939), Aus
  R. 1   S. c
BIUMI, Giacomo Filippo (c1580-1653), It
  R. 1   S. c,53
BIVI, Paolo Antonio del [see ARETINO, Paolo]
BIXIO, Cesare Andrea (1898-1978), It
  R. 62   S. 10
BIZET, Georges (1838-1875), Fr
  R. 1
  S. c,1-11,18,22,24,25,27,28,34,43,54(318,25,37)
BJERGBORG, Walther (1909-   ), Den
  R. 13   S. 33,57
BJERNO, Erling (1928-   ), Den
          S. 40
BJERRE, Jens (1903-   ), Den
  R. 1   S. 33,35,57
BJÖRKANDER, Nils (1893-1972), Sweden
          S. c,4,5,7,10,24,56
BLAAUW, Pierre
          S. 24
BLACHER, Boris (1903-1975), Ger
  R. 1   S. c,4,7,8-10,20,24a
BLACK, Frank J. (1896-1968), USA
  R. 19   S. 13
BLACK, John (fl 1546-87), Scot
  R. 1   S. c,10
BLACK, Johnny Stewart (1896-   )
          S. 10,24
BLACK, Stanley (1913-   ), Eng
  R. 4
BLACKBURN, Maurice (1914-   ), Can
  R. 14
BLACKFORD, Richard (1954-   ), Eng
          S. c
BLACKHALL, Andrew (1535/6-1609), Scot
  R. 1   S. c
BLACKMAN, Frederick J.
          S. e
BLACKWOOD, Easley (1933-   ), USA
  R. 1   S. 10,13,20,24
BLÁHA, Vaclav (1921-1959), Cz
  R. 18   S. 31
BLAHOSLAV, Jan (1523-1571), Cz
  R. 1   S. 5x
BLAINVILLE, Charles-Henri de (c1710-c1777), Fr
  R. 1   S. c

BLAKE, Charles Dupee (1847-   ), USA
   R. 53   S. 10,54(320)
BLAKE, David (1936-   ), Eng
   R. 1   S. 24a
BLAKE, Eubie (James Hubert) (1883-1983), USA
   R. 1   S. 10,24a
BLAKE, Howard (20th Cent)
           S. c
BLALOCK, R.
           S. 10
BLAMONT, François Collin de
   [see COLLIN de BLAMONT, François]
BLANC, Adolph (1828-1885), Fr
   R. 8   S. c,5x
BLANCAFORT, Manuel (1897-   ), Sp
   R. 1   S. 5x
BLANCHARD, Esprit Joseph Antoine (1696-1770), Fr
   R. 1   S. 5x,8-10
BLANCHE de CASTILLE (1188-1252), Fr
   R. 7   S. c,52
BLANCHET, Emile Robert (1877-1943), Swiss
   R. 4
BLANCHOT, Maurice (1934-   )
           S. c,10,24a
BLANCO, José (1750-1811), Sp
           S. c
BLAND, Dorothea/Dora [see JORDAN, Mrs. - pseud]
BLAND, James A. (1854-1911), USA
   R. 1   S. e,4,10,24
BLAND, William Keith (1947-   ), USA
   R. 19   S. 13
BLANE, Ralph [see HUNSECKER, Ralph Blane]
BLANGINI, Felice (1781-1841), Fr
   R. 1   S. c
BLANK, Allan (1925-   ), USA
   R. 19   S. 10,13,20,24a
BLANK, Gerhard
           S. c
BLANKE, H. B. - Marsovia waltzes
           S. 54(342)
BLANKENBURG, Hermann Ludwig (1876-1956), Ger
   R. 4,95(b. 1880) S. 54(311,25,28,29,47)
BLANKENBURG, Quirinus Gerbrandszoon van (1654-1739),
   Neth   R. 1   S. c
BLANTER, Matvey Isaakovich (1903-   ), Russia
   R. 1   S. 5x,10
BLARR, Oskar Gottlieb (1934-   )
           S. c
BLAS de CASTRO, Juan [see CASTRO, Juan Blas de]

BLASCO de NEBRA, Manuel (1750-1784), Sp
R. 1   S. 10,39
BLASCO, Manuel
              S. 10
BLASIUS, Mathieu-Frédéric (1758-1829), Fr
R. 1   S. 10
BLAT, Joseph
              S. 19
BLATNÝ, Pavel (1931-   ), Cz
R. 1   S. 31
BLAUFUSS, Walter (1883-1945), USA
R. 23   S. 24
BLAVET, Michel (1700-1768), Fr
R. 1   S. c,2-4,5x,6,8-11,22,42
BLAYE, (13th Cent.), Fr
              S. c
BLAŽEK, Zdeněk (1905-1974), Cz
R. 1   S. 5x,31
BLECH, Leo (1871-1958), Ger
R. 1   S. c,24
BLEEKMAN - At your feet; Song of Spring
              S. e
BLEICHMANN, Julius Ivanovich (1868-1909), Russia
R. 25   S. 18
BLEY, Carla (1938-   ), USA
R. 7   S. 52
BLEYLE, Karl (1880-1969), Ger
R. 14   S. 24
BLISS, Arthur (1891-1975), Eng
R. 1   S. c,2-11,18-20,23,24,55
BLISS, Philip Paul the Younger (1872-1933), USA
R. 19
BLISS, Philip Paul the Elder (1838-1876), USA
R. 1   S. 10
BLITHEMAN, John (c1525-1591), Eng
R. 1   S. c,8,10,14,16,18,53
BLITZSTEIN, Marc (1905-1964), USA
R. 1   S. 3-6,9,11,13
BLOCH, Andre (1873-1960), Fr
R. 8   S. 8,10
BLOCH, Augustyn (1929-   ), Pol
R. 1   S. c,24a
BLOCH, Ernest (1880-1959), Swiss
R. 1   S. c,1-11,13,18,23,24,32
BLOCKLEY, John (1800-1882), Eng
R. 44   S. 10
BLOCKX, Jan (1851-1912), Bel
R. 1   S. 36,41
BLODEK, Vilém (1834-1874), Cz
R. 1   S. 5x,6,8,10,42

BLOHM, Sven (1907-1956), Sweden
   R. 30   S. 5x
BLOM, Oscar (1877-1930), Sweden
   R. 30   S. 24
BLOMBERG, Erik (1922-   ), Sweden
   R. 14   S. 40
BLOMBERG, Gunnar (1906-   ), Sweden
   R. 30   S. 54(324,42)
BLOMDAHL, Karl-Birger (1916-1968), Sweden
   R. 1   S. c,5x,6,8-10,20,24,38,40,42,56
BLON, Franz (1861-1945), Ger
   R. 4,95   S. 24,54(363,65)
BLONDEAU, Pierre (16th Cent), Fr
   R. 1   S. 16
BLONDEL de NESLE (fl 1180-1200), Fr

   R. 1   S. c,2,3,5x,8,10,11,14
BLOOM, Marty
             S. 10
BLOOM, Rube (1902-1976), USA
   R. 23   S. 10
BLOW, John (1649-1708), Eng
   R. 1   S. c,5-10,42,53
BLUM, Robert (1900-   ), Swiss
   R. 30   S. 4
BLUME - Via riumphalis
             S. 54(363)
BLUME, Hermann (1891-1967), Ger
   R. 4   S. 24
BLUME, Karl (1883-1947), Ger
   R. 4
BLUMENFELD, Felix (1863-1931), Russia
   R. 1   S. c,10,18
BLUMENFELD, Harold (1923-   ), USA
   R. 19   S. 9,13
BLUMENTHAL, Jacob (1829-1908), Ger
   R. 3
BLUMER, Theodor (1882-1964), Ger
   R. 8   S. 4
BO, Victor de (1906-   ), Bel
   R. 25
BOATNER, Edward H. (1898-   ), USA
   R. 23   S. 4,10
BOATRITE, Howard (1923-   ), USA
   R. 19   S. 10[Boatrite, Harold]
BOCCALARI, E. - Patrol of the scouts; Dance of the
   serpents   S. 54(322,49)
BOCCHERINI, Luigi (1743-1805), It
   R. 1   S. c,1-11,18,21-24,32,54(343)
BOCCHINO, Alceu (1918-   ), Brazil
   R. 14   S. 24a

BOCHSA, Karl (d. 1821), Cz
   R. 10   S. c
BOCHSA, (Robert) Nicholas Charles (1789-1856), Fr
   R. 1   S. c, 10
BOCK, Jerry (1928-   ), USA
   R. 1   S. c, 9, 10
BOCKLET, Carl Maria von (1801-1881), Aus
   R. 15   S. c
BODA, John (1922-   ), USA
   R. 19   S. 10, 13, 21
BODART, Eugen (1905-   ), Ger
   R. 14   S. 4, 5x
BÖDDECKER, Philipp Friedrich (1607-1683), Ger
   R. 1   S. c, 4, 5, 10
BODE, Johnny (1912-   ), Sweden
           S. 43
BODEL, Jehan (c1165-1209/10), Fr
   R. 1   S. c
BODENHORN, Aaron (1898-   ), USA
           S. 13
BODENSCHATZ, Erhard (1576-1636), Ger
   R. 1   S. c, 2-4, 10, 15, 16, 18
BODGE, Peter
           S. 10
BODIN, Lars-Gunnar (1935-   ), Sweden
   R. 14   S. 40, 56
BODINUS, Sebastian (c1700-c1760), Ger
   R. 1   S. c, 10, 24a
BODKER, Walther
           S. 33
BODLEY, Seóirse (1933-   ), Ire
   R. 1   S. c, 10, 49
BODMAN, Christopher (1948-   ), Eng
           S. c, 24a
BODO, Serge [S. 18] = BAUDO, Serge
BODY, Jack (1944-   ), New Zealand

BOECK, Auguste de (1865-1937), Bel
   R. 1   S. c, 8, 24, 36, 41
BOECK, Ignaz von (1733-1804)
           S. c, 24
BOEDDECKER, Philip Friedrich
   [see BODDECKER, Philip Friedrich]
BOEHM, Karl [see BOHM, Karl]
BOEHM, Theobald (1794-1881), Ger
   R. 1   S. c, 10
BOEHM, Yohanan (1914-   ), Isr
   R. 14   S. c
BOEHME, John George
           S. 54(312)

BOEHME, Oskar Wihlelmovitch (1870-1938)
         S. c
BOEHMER, Konrad (1941-   ), Ger
  R. 4
BOELEE, Hans (1927-   )
         S. c
BOËLLMANN, Léon (1862-1897), Fr
  R. 1   S. c,1-5,7,8,10,18
BOËLY, Alexandre Pierre François (1785-1858), Fr
  R. 1   S. c,10
BOEN, Alex
         S. 19
BOERMAN, Jan (1923-   )

BOERO, Felipe (1884-1958), Arg
  R. 1   S. 2,3,5,8,46
BOESMANS, Philippe (1936-   ), Bel
  R. 1   S. c,24a
BOËSSET, Antoine (1586-1643), Fr
  R. 1   S. c,8,10,14,16
BOEX, Andrew J.
         S. 10
BOEZI, Ernesto (1856-1946), It
  R. 8   S. 1,2,4
BOGAR, Istvan (1937-   ), Hun
         S. c
BOGATIRYOV, Anatoly Vasilyevich (1913-   ), USSR
  R. 1   S. 18
BOGENHARDT, Helmut

         S. c
BOGOSLOVSKY, Nikita Vladimirovich (1913-   ), USSR
  R. 14   S. 18
BOGUSLAWSKI, Edward (1940-   ), Pol
  R. 1
BOHAČ, Josef (1929-   ), Cz
  R. 14   S. 10,31,24a
BOHDANOWICZ, Bazyli (1740-1817), Pol
  R. 1   S. c
BÖHM, Karl [pseud: Henry COOPER] (1844-1920), Ger
  R. 95   S. c,1x,4,5x,10,24
BÖHM, Georg (1661-1733), Ger
  R. 1   S. c,5-11,18,53
BÖHM, Karl (1894-   ), Aus
  R. 1   S. 28
BÖHM, Theobald [see BOEHM, Theobald]
BOHME, Franz Magnus (1827-1898), Ger
  R. 3   S. c
BOHME, J. A. - Eine schon Tageweis
         S. 5x

BÖHNER, Johann Ludwig (1787-1860), Ger
   R. 3   S. c
BOHRER, Anton (1783-1852), Ger
   R. 3   S. 24a
BOHRER, Max (1785-1867), Ger
   R. 3   S. 24a
BOIELDIEU, François-Adrien (1775-1834), Fr
   R. 1   S. c,2-5,7-11,42,54(318)
BOIKO, Rotislav Grigoryevich (1931-), USSR
   R. 14   S. 18
BOIS, Rob du (1934-), Neth
   R. 1   S. c
BOISDEFFRE, Charles-Henri René (1838-1906), Fr
   R. 8   S. 24
BOISMORTIER, Josef Bodin de (1689-1755), Fr
   R. 1   S. c,4-10,23,24,32
BOISSIÈRE, Frédéric

BOISVALLÉE, François de [DUCLOS, Pierre dit]
   (1929-1973) S. c
BOITO, Arrigo (1842-1918), It
   R. 1   S. c,1-11,18,42,54(342)
BOIX, Manuel Palau [see PALAU BOIX, Manuel]
BOLCOM, William (1938-), USA
   R. 1   S. c,9,10,12,13,24a
BOLDEMANN, Laci (1921-1969), Sweden
   R. 1   S. 38,40,56
BOLDI, Giuseppe - pseud [ie Jos. PREISSLER]
            S. 10
BOLDI, J. B. - Chanson bohemienne; Romance bohemiene
            S. 24
BOLDYREV, Igor Georgievich (1912-), USSR
   R. 14   S. 18
BOLEYN, Anne (c1507-1536), Eng
   R. 7   S. 10,52
BOLLE, James (1931-), USA
   R. 19   S. c,9,13
BOLLER, Carlo (1896-1952), Swiss
   R. 14
BOLLING, Claude (1930-), Fr
   R. 4   S. c,9,24a
BOLLING, Lennaus - The cannonade at Yorktown
            S. 10,47
BOLLIUS, Daniel (c1590-c1642), Ger
   R. 1   S. c
BOLOGNA, Jacopo da [see JACOPO da BOLOGNA]
BOLOGNA, Marco Antonio da
   [see CAVAZZONI, Marco Antonio]
BOLOGNINI, Ennio

BOLOTIN, Isidor Mikhailovich (1907-1961), USSR
  R. 47
BÖLSCHE, Jakob (d. 1684), Ger
  R. 5   S. c, 53
BOLTON, Edmund (16-17th Cent)
          S. 16
BOLTON, John - Canzon Pastoral
          S. c
BOLZONI, Giovanni (1841-1919), It
  R. 10   S. 4, 5x, 18, 24
BOMTEMPO, Joao Domingos (1775-1842), Port
  R. 1   S. 24a
BON, von - Heil Europa
          S. 54(331)
BON, Willem Frederick (1940-1983), Neth
  R. 4
BONAMICO, Pedro [see GUETFREUND, Peter]
BOND, Capel (1730-1790), Eng
  R. 1   S. c, 10
BOND, Carrie Jacobs (1862-1946), USA
  R. 7   S. 10, 24, 28, 30, 52
BOND, Victoria Ellen (1945-   ), USA
  R. 19   S. 10, 30, 52
BONDEMAN, Anders (1937-   ), Sweden
  R. 30   S. c
BONDEVILLE, Emmanuel (1898-   ), Fr
  R. 1   S. c, 8, 9
BONDON, Jacques (1927-   ), Fr
  R. 1   S. c, 10, 24a, 32
BONDS, Margaret (1913-1972), USA
  R. 19   S. 13, 30, 52
BONE, Gene, USA
  R. 23   S. 10
BONEFAAS, Jan (1926-   )
          S. c
BONELLI - Centenary
          S. 54(319)
BONELLI, Aurelio (1569-c1620), It
  R. 10   S. c, 8, 10, 16
BONET, Narcis (1933-   ), Sp
  R. 14   S. 24a
BONFA, Luiz Floriano (1922-   ), Brazil
  R. 23   S. 32, 39
BONI, Guillaume (c1545-1594), Fr
  R. 16   S. 8, 10, 14
BONI, Pietro Giuseppi Gaetano
  (fl 1st half of 18th Cent), It
  R. 1   S. 10, 22 [Boni, P.]
BONIME, Josef (1891-1959), USA
  R. 23   S. 10, 24

BONINCONTRO, Gabrielle (1878-   ), ?Fr
    R. 7   S. 24
BONNAL, Joseph Ermend (1880-1944), Fr
    R. 14   S. c, 4, 5, 10
BONNEAU, Paul (1918-   ), Fr
    R. 80   S. 5x, 6-8, 10, 22
BONNÉN, Helge (1896-1983), Den
    R. 30   S. c
BONNET, Joseph (1884-1944), Fr
    R. 14   S. c, 3, 4, 11
BONNET, Pierre (fl 1585-1600), Fr
    R. 1   S. c, 5x, 8, 10, 14-16
BONO, Pietro [see PIETROBONO]
BONONCINI, Antonio Maria (1677-1726), It
    R. 16   S. c, 5, 7, 10, 27
BONONCINI, Giovanni (1670-1747), It
    R. 1   S. c, 3-6, 8, 10, 24
BONONCINI, Giovanni Maria (1642-1678), It
    R. 1   S. c, 8, 10, 11
BONPORTI, Francesco Antonio (1672-1749), It
    R. 1   S. c, 4, 5x, 7-10, 18, 24
BONSET, Jacques (1880-1959), Neth
    R. 14   S. c
BONTA, Stephen
                  S. 10
BOONE, John William (Blind Boone)
                  S. 10
BOOTH, Margaret
                  S. 30
BOOY, Cor

BOPPE, Meister [see POPPE, Meister]
BOR, Modesta - Regreso al mar

BORCH, Gaston (1871-1926), Fr
    R. 4
BORCHGREVINCK, Melchior (?c1570-1632), Den
    R. 1   S. c
BORDEN, David (1938-   ), USA
    R. 19   S. 10, 13
BORDES, Charles (1863-1909), Fr
    R. 1   S. 1, 2
BORDESE, Luigi (1815-1886), It
    R. 3
BORDOGNI, Giulio Marco (1789-1856), It
    R. 1
BOREK, Krzysztof (d c1570), Pol
    R. 1   S. c
BOREL, Rene
                  S. 10, 22

BOREL-CLERC, Charles (1879-1959), Fr
   R. 4   S. 10
BORETZ, Benjamin (1934-   ), USA
   R. 1   S. 10,13
BORG, Kim (1919-   ), Fin
   R. 1   S. c
BORG, Thoralf
          S. 33
BORGANOFF, Igor - pseud [see NJURLING, Sten]
BORGES, Raul (1885-   ), Ven
          S. c,10,32
BORGHI, Giovanni Battista (1738-1796), It
   R. 1   S. c
BORGOVAN, Ion (1889-1970), Rum
   R. 33
BORGSTROM, Boris - Prelude (2 accordions)

BORIES - Consolation (vi & p)
          S. 24
BORISHANKY, Elliot (1930-   ), USA
   R. 19   S. 13
BORISOFF, Alexander (1902-   ), USA
   R. 23   S. 13
BORISOV, Lilcho (1925-   )
          S. 24a
BORISOV, Valentin Tikhonovich (1901-   ), USSR
   R. 14   S. 18
BOŘKOVEC, Pavel (1894-1972), Cz
   R. 1   S. 5,10,24,31
BORKOWSKI, Bohadan (1852-1901), Pol
   R. 1
BORKOWSKI, Marian (1934-   ), Pol
   R. 80   S. c
BORLET (14th Cent), Fr/Sp
   R. 1   S. c,8,10,14,16,32
BORMIOLI, Enrico
          S. 4
BORNE, Fernand le [see LE BORNE, Fernand]
BORNE, François (1840-1920)
          S. c
*** BORNE, François Ferdinand (1862-1929) (see note)
BORNEFELD, Helmut (1906-   ), Ger
   R. 1   S. c
BORNELH, Giraut de [see GIRAUT de BORNELH]
BORNEMISZA, Peter (16th Cent)
          S. c
BORNUM, Hans (1910-   ), Sweden [?]
   R. 68   S. 24
BORODIN, Alexander (1833-1887), Russia
   R. 1   S. c,1-11,18,22,24,28,42,43,54(351)

BOROES, Charles (1863-1909), Fr

BORONI, Alessandro
        S. 10
BOROS, David John (1944-1975), USA
    R. 19   S. 13
BOROVICKA, Antonin (1895-   ), Cz
    R. 18   S. 31
BOROWSKI, Felix (1872-1956), USA
    R. 1   S. 10,12,13,21,24
BØRRESEN, Hakon (1876-1954), Den
    R. 1   S. 4,5x,7,35,57
BORRIS, Siegfried (1906-   ), Ger
    R. 1
BORRONO, Pietro Paolo (fl 1531-49), It
    R. 1   S. c
BORSARI, Amédée Pierre (1905-   ), Fr
    R. 14
BORSHEL, Erich
        S. 24
BORTKIEWICH, Sergei Eduardovich (1877-1952), Russia
    R. 1   S. c,10,24
BORTNYANSKY, Dmitri Stepanovich (1751-1825), Russia
    R. 1   S. c,2-4,5x,8,10,11,18,24a
BORTOLAZZI, Bartolomeo (1773-   ), It
    R. 106   S. 32
BÖRTZ, Daniel (1943-   ), Sweden
    R. 14   S. c,40,24a,56
BORUP-JØRGENSEN, Axel (1924-   ), Den
    R. 1   S. 40
BOSC, Auguste (1868-1945)
        S. 10,24
BOSCO, Mwenda Jean (19-20th Cent), Congo
        S. c
BOSCÔLI, Ronaldo (1929-   ), Brazil (see note)
    R. 67   S. 39
BOSHKO, Natalie (1906-   )
        S. 24a
BOSKERCK - Semper paratus
        S. 54(355)
BOSKOVICH, Alexander Uriah (1907-1964), Isr
    R. 1   S. 8
BOSMANS, Henriette Hilda (1895-1952), Neth
    R. 7   S. 52
BOSSI - Dio siete buono

BOSSI, Marco Enrico (1861-1925), It
    R. 1   S. c,1-3,5x,10,11
BOSSINENSIS, Franciscus (fl. 1510), It
    R. 1   S. c,10,16,28

BOSSLER, Kurt (1911-1976), Ger
    R.14   S.c
BOSSU, Adam Le [see ADAM de La HALLE]
BOSWELL - Song

BOTREL, Theodore (1868-1925)
    R.3
BOTTACCHIARI, Ugo/Luigi (1879-   ), It (see note)
    R.10   S.4
BÖTTCHER - Hinunter
             S.e
BOTTEGARI, Cosimo (1554-1620), It
    R.1   S.c,10
BOTTESINI, Giovanni (1821-1889), It
    R.1   S.c,8-10,18,24
BOUCHARD, Victor (1926-   ), Can
    R.31
BOUCOURECHLIEV, Andre (1925-   ), Fr
    R.1   S.c,9
BOUGEOIS, Loys [see BOURGEOIS, Loys]
BOUGHITCH, L.- Scherzo (viola & p)
             S.23

BOUGHTON, Rutland (1878-1960), Eng
    R.1   S.c,2-5,10,28
BOUIN, Francois (17th Cent), Fr
    R.5   S.c,10
BOUININE [S.23] = BUNIN, Revol Samuilovich
BOULAHOV [S.23] = BULAKHOV, Pavel Petrovich
BOULANGER, Georges (1893-   ), Rum
    R.67   S.24[b.1892]
BOULANGER, Lili (1893-1918), Fr
    R.1   S.c,1,4,5x,7-10,24a,52
BOULANGER, Nadia (1887-1979), Fr
    R.1   S.18,52
BOULEZ, Pierre (1925-   ), Fr
    R.1   S.c,9,10,19,20,23,32
BOULOGNE, Joseph
    [see SAINT-GEORGES, Joseph Boulogne, Chevalier de]
BOULTON - All through the night

BOUMAN - Gy zoudt de liefste zyn

BOUMGARTNER (15th Cent) [see BAUMGARTNER]
BOURDEAU, E. - Premier solo (bassoon)
             S.10
BOURDIN, Roger (1923-1976)
             S.c,10,21
BOURGAULT-DUCOUDRAY, Louis (1840-1910), Fr
    R.1   S.c

BOURGEOIS, C. - Le coquet march
    S. 54(321)
BOURGEOIS, Derek (1941-   ), Eng
    R. 1   S. c, 55
BOURGEOIS, Emile (?-1922), Fr
    R. 3
BOURGEOIS, Loys (c1510-c1560), Fr
    R. 1   S. c, 10, 16
BOURGES, Clement de (16th Cent)
    R. 5   S. c, 53
BOURGET - Romance
            S. e
BOURGOGNE, Marie de (15th Cent), Fr
    R. 7   S. 32, 52
BOURGUIGNON, Francis de (1890-1961), Bel
    R. 1   S. c, 8, 24, 36
BOURNONVILLE, Armand (1900-   )
            S. 10
BOURREL, Yvon (1932-   )
            S. c, 24a
BOUSSET, Jean-Baptiste (1662-1725), Fr
    R. 1   S. c
BOUTMY, Guillaume (1723-1791), S. Neth.
    R. 1   S. c
BOUTMY, Jean Joseph (1725-1782), S. Neth.
    R. 1   S. c
BOUTMY, Josse (1697-1779), S. Neth.
    R. 1   S. c
BOUTMY, Laurent-François (1756-1838), S. Neth.
    R. 1   S. c, 24a
BOUTRY, Roger (1932-   ), Fr
    R. 1   S. c, 10, 18, 22, 24a
BOUVARD, François (c1683-1760), Fr
    R. 1   S. 5x, 6, 24
BOUVY, Johann
            S. 24
BOUZIGNAC, Guillaume (<1592->1641), Fr
    R. 1   S. c, 8, 10, 15
BOVET, Joseph Abbé (1879-1951), Swiss
    R. 4
BOVICELLI, Giovanni (fl 1592-4), It
    R. 1   S. c   [music theorist, author]
BOVY-LYSBERG, Charles Samuel (1821-1873), Swiss
    R. 1   S. 10
BOWEN, York (1884-1961), Eng
    R. 1   S. c, 20, 24
BOWERING, Klaus (1936-   )
            S. c
BOWERS, Frederick V. (1874-   ), USA
    R. 200

BOWERS, Robert Hood (1877-1941), USA
   R. 23   S. 54(343)
BOWLES, Paul Frederic (1910-   ), USA
   R. 14   S. 3-6,8,10,13,21,25,27
BOYCE, William (1711-1779), Eng
   R. 1   S. c,3-11,24,26-28,53
BOYD, Liona Maria (1950-   ), Can
   R. 81   S. 52
BOYD, Tod
            S. 24
BOYD, Wynn Leo (1902-   ), USA
   R. 19   S. 13
BOYDELL, Brian (1917-   ), Ire
   R. 1   S. 8,10,19,49
BOYER, Edmond
            S. 10
BOYER, Felix (1880-   ), Fr

BOYKAN, Martin (1931-   ), USA
   R. 19   S. 10,13
BOYKO, R. (1931-   )
            S. 24a
BOYLE, Malcom (1902-1976), Eng
            S. c
BOYLE, Rory David Alasdair (1951-   ), Scot
   R. 80   S. c
BOYVIN, Jacques (c1649-1706), Fr
   R. 1   S. c,10,53
BOZAY, Attila (1939-   ), Hun
   R. 1   S. c,10,18,19[ATTILA, Bozay],24a
BOŽIČ, Darijan (1933-   ), Yug
   R. 1   S. 10
BOZZA, Eugène (1905-   ), Fr
   R. 1   S. c,4-8,10,18-22,24
BOZZI, Marco Enrico [see BOSSI, Marc Enrico]
BRACCO, C. A. (fl. 1885-94), It - Serenata
   R. 106   S. 44
BRACHROGGE, Hans (d c1638), Den
   R. 1   S. c
BRACKETT - Saw we my savior, Shepherd show me

BRACONNIER, Jean [Lourdoys] (d. 1512), Fr
   R. 1   S. 15
BRADAPRANA, Pravrajika (1923-   ), USA
            S. 52
BRADBURY, William Batchelder (1816-1868), USA
   R. 50   S. 47
BRADE, William (1560-1630), Eng
   R. 1   S. c,10,14,16

BRADFORD, Alex E.
          S. 10
BRADFORD, John (1842-1897),Eng
  R. 3
BRADFORD-ANDERSON, Muriel
  [see ANDERSON, Muriel Bradford]
BRADSKY, Wenzel Theodor (1833-1881), Boh [?]
  R. 98
BRADWELL, Charles
          S. e
BRAEIN, Edvard Fliflet (1924-1976), Nor
  R. 1   S. 8,10,20,40,51
BRAGA, Ernani (1898-   ), Brazil
  R. 1. 5   S. 10,32,39
BRAGA, Francisco (1868-1945), Brazil
  R. 4   S. 24a
BRAGA, Gaetano (1829-1907), It
  R. 1   S. c,1x,4,5x,10,24
BRAGATO, Jose (1915-   )
          S. c
BRAGDON, Sarah Coleman

BRAGGINS - Alma mater

BRAHAM, John (1774-1856), Eng
  R. 1   S. c,5x,10

BRAHAM, Philip (1881-1934)
  R. 200   S. 10,24a
BRAHE, May - pseud [ie Mary Hannah MORGAN]
  (1885-1956), Eng
  R. 7   S. c,10,30,52
BRAHE, Per (1602-1680)

BRAHMS, Johannes (1833-1897), Ger
  R. 1   S. c,1-11,18-21,24-28,32,33,54(333)
BRĂILOIU, Constantin (1893-1958), Rum
  R. 4
BRAINE, Robert (1896-1940), USA
  R. 19   S. 11,13
BRAMIERI, Claudio (d. 1594)
  R. 5   S. c
BRAND, Geoffrey (1926-   ), Eng
  R. 85   S. 55
BRAND, Max (1896-   ), USA
  R. 19   S. 8,10,13
BRAND, Michael [see MOSONYI, Mihaly - pseud]
BRANDENSTEIN, Caroline [Charlotte] von (1754-1813), Ger
  R. 7   S. c,24a,52
BRANDL, Johann (1835-1913), Ger
  R. 8   S. 5x,10,24

BRANDMÜLLER, Theo (1948-   )
            S.c
BRANDT, Franz
            S.10
BRANDT, Hans Henrik (1944-   ), Den
    R.80   S.40
BRANDT, Jobst vom (1517-1570), Ger
    R.1   S.c,11,16
BRANDT, Vassily (1869-1923)
            S.c
BRANDTS-BUYS, Jan Willem Frans (1868-1939), Neth
    R.1
BRANDTS-BUYS, Ludwig Felix (1847-1917), Neth
    R.1   S.41
BRANDUSI, Francesco (16th Cent)
            S.c
BRANKA, Eugeniusz

BRANSON, Taylor (1880-   ), USA
    R.49   S.54(341)
BRANT, Henry Dreyfus (1913-   ), USA
    R.1   S.3,8-10,24
BRANT, Per (1714-1767), Sweden
    R.30   S.56
BRANT, von - Es steht ein Lind
            S.5x
BRANZI - La ma canzone

BRASSARD, François (1908-   ), Can
    R.4
BRASSART, Johannes (fl 1420-45), Neth
    R.1   S.c,2-4,5x,8,10,11,14,16,41
BRÄTEL, Ulrich (c1495-c1544), Ger
    R.1
BRATFISCH, Karl (1829-1901), Ger
    R.95   S.54(358)
BRATTON, John W. (1867-1947), USA
    R.23   S.54(360)
BRAUER, Ewald (1904-1961), Est
    R.58   S.18
BRAUN - Le coucou
            S.5x
BRAUN, Gunter (1928-   )
            S.c
BRAUN, Johann Georg Franz (c1630->1675), ?Boh
    R.1   S.c
BRAUN, Yeheztiel (1922-   ), Isr
    R.14   S.c
BRAUNFELS, Walter (1882-1954), Ger
    R.1   S.c

BRÄUTIGAM, Helmut (1914-1942), Ger
  R. 1   S. c
BRAVNICAR, Matija (1897-   ), Yug
  R. 14   S. 24a
BRAXTON, Anthony (1945-   ), USA
  R. 60   S. 10
BRAY, John (1782-1822)

BRAYSSING, Grégoire (fl. 1547-60), Ger
  R. 1   S. c
BRAZINSKAS, Algis (1937-   )
          S. 18,24
BREAU, Louis (1893-1928), USA
  R. 23   S. 24
BREDEMEYER, Reiner (1929-   ), Ger
  R. 1
BREE, Johannes Bernardus van (1801-1857), Neth
  R. 1   S. 10
BREEDLOVE, William P. (fl 1858), USA
          S. 47
BREGENT, Michel-Georges (1948-   ), Can
  R. 31
BREHM, Alvin (1925-   ), USA
  R. 19   S. 10
BREHM, Gunter - pseud [see LENGSFELDER, Hans]
BREHME, Hans (1904-1957), Ger
  R. 1   S. 18
BRÉHY, Hercule (1673-1737), S. Neth.
  R. 1   S. c
BREIL, Joseph Carl (1870-1926), USA
  R. 19   S. 13
BREILH, Fernande (20th Cent), Fr
  R. 7 (see note under DECRUCK)
BREMER, Marrie Petronella (1933-   ), Neth
          S. 30,52
BREMNER, James (d. 1780), Scot/USA
  R. 50   S. c,10,12,47
BREMNER, Robert (c1713-1789), Scot
  R. 1   S. c
BREMON RICAS NOVAS, Peire (13th Cent)
          S. c
BRENNENBERG, Reinmar von [see REINMAR von BRENNENBERG]
BRENTA, Gaston (1902-1969), Bel
  R. 1   S. 8,24,36
BRENTANO, Bettina (1785-1859), Ger
  R. 1   S. 10,24,30,52[Arnim]
BREPSANT, Engebert
          S. 54(315)
BRERO, Giulio Cesare (1908-1973), It
  R. 1   S. 10

BRESCIANELLO, Guiseppe Antonio (c1690-1758), It
   R. 1   S. 24
BRESGEN, Cesar (1913-   ), Aus
   R. 1   S. c
BRESNICK, Martin (1946-   ), USA
   R. 19   S. 13
BRESS - Le chant du forgeron
          S. e
BRESS, Hyman (1931-   ), Can
   R. 4   S. 10,13,24
BRETAN, Nicolae (1887-1968), Rum
   R. 33
BRETEUILL [see GOTTFRIED von BRETEUILL]
BRETON, Nicholaus (16th Cent)
          S. 16
BRETÓN, Tomás (1850-1923), Sp
   R. 1   S. c,1-4,5x,8-11,24,32,39,42
BREUER, Franz Josef (1914-   ), Ger
   R. 4   S. c
BREUNICH, Johann Michael (d >1756), Ger
   R. 1   S. c
BRÉVAL, Jean Baptiste Sébastien (1753-1823), Fr
   R. 1   S. 4,5,8,10,18,20,23
BREVI, Giovanni Battista (c1650->1725), It
   R. 1   S. c
BREVIK, Tor (1932-   ), Nor
   R. 4   S. 51
BRÉVILLE, Pierre de (1861-1949), Fr
   R. 1   S. 1-4
BREVILLE-SMITH, F. S. [see SMITH, F. S. B.]
BREWER, Herbert (1865-1928), Eng
   R. 1   S. c,1x
BREWER, Richard (1921-   ), USA
   R. 19
BRIAN, Havergal (1876-1972), Eng
   R. 1   S. c,9,24a
BRICCETTI, Thomas (1936-   ), USA
   R. 19   S. 10,13
BRICCIALDI, Guilio (1818-1881), It
   R. 1   S. c
BRICUSSE, Leslie (1931-   ), Eng
   R. 84   S. c
BRIDGE, Frank (1879-1941), Eng
   R. 1   S. c,1-6,8-10,24,28
BRIDGE, Frederick (1844-1924), Eng
   R. 1   S. c
BRIDGER - Shanghai sailor; Airborne division
          S. 54(311,55)
BRIDGEWATER, Ernest Leslie (1893-1975), Eng
   R. 14   S. 5,8,9

BRIEF, Todd (1953-   ), USA
   R. 19   S. 24a
BRIEGEL, Wolfgang Carl (1626-1712), Ger
   R. 1   S. c
BRIGGS, Ralph (1901-   ), USA
   R. 19
BRIGHT, Houston (1916-   ), USA
   R. 14   S. 10,13
BRIGNOLI, Giacomo (16th Cent)
   R. 10   S. 8,10,14
BRIHUEGA, Bernaldino (fl 1489), Sp
   R. 1   S. c,10,16,17,39
BRIK, Ester
            S. 10,30
BRINDLE, Reginald Smith [see SMITH BRINDLE, Reginald]
BRINGS, Allen (1934-   ), USA
   R. 19   S. 24a
BRIQUET, Marc (1896-1979)
            S. c
BRISTOW, George Frederick (1825-1898), USA
   R. 1   S. 7,9,10,12,47
BRITTEN, Benjamin (1913-1976), Eng
   R. 1   S. 3-10,18,23,24,26-28,32,42
BRITTENHAM, Robert USA
            S. 12,13
BRITTON, Dorothy Guyver (1922-   ), USA
   R. 7   S. 30
BRIVIO, Giuseppe Ferdinando (18th Cent), It
   R. 1   S. c
BRIXI, František Xaver (1732-1771), Cz
   R. 1   S. c,4,5,10
BRIXI, Simon (1693-1735), Cz
   R. 1   S. c,5
BRIXI, Vaclav Norbert (1738-1803), Cz
   R. 1   S. c
BROADVIEW, Lucy Ethelred (1858-1929), Scot
   R. 7   S. e
BROADY, Thomas E.
            S. 10
BROCARTE, Antonio de la Cruz (d >1716), Sp
   R. 1   S. 10,53
BROCCO, Giovanni (fl early 16th Cent), It
   R. 1   S. 16
BROCCO, Nicolo (fl early 16th Cent), It
   R. 1   S. c
BROCHE - Ma Patrie
            S. e
BROCKLESS, Brian (1926-   ), Eng
   R. 14

BROCKMAN, James (1886-1967), USA
R.23   S.24
BROCKMAN, Jane E. (1949-   ), USA
R.7   S.30,52
BROCKWAY, Howard (1870-1951), USA
R.1   S.10,13
BRODSZKY, Nicholas (1905-1958), USA
R.61,200   S.c,10
BROEK, Piet van den (1916-   ), Bel
R.25   S.c
BROEKHUISEN, Barend (17th Cent)
            S.c,53
BROERSE, Piet

BROGI, Renato (1873-1924), It
R.8   S.c,10,24,34
BROLLO, Bartolomeus (fl c1430-50), It
R.1   S.2-4,5x,11
BROMAN, Nathanael (1887-1966), Sweden
R.30   S.56
BROMAN, Sten (1902-   ), Sweden
R.1   S.5x,10,24,38,56
BRONS, Carel (1931-   ), Neth
R.1   S.10
BRONSART von SCHELLENDORF, Hans (1830-1913), Ger
R.1   S.c,10
BRONSART von SCHELLENDORF (née STARCK) Ingeborg von
(1840-1913), Ger   R.7   S.c,10,30,52
BROOKS, Richard James (1942-   ), USA
R.19   S.24a
BROOKS, Ruth
            S.24a
BROOKS, Sydney
            S.24
BROOKS, William (1943-   ), USA
R.19   S.c

BROQUA, Alfonso (1876-1946), Uruguay
R.1   S.c,10,11,32
BROQUET, Louis Chanoine (1888-1954), Swiss
R.14   S.c
BROSCHI, Carlo [pseud: FARINELLI] (1705-1782), It
R.1   S.c   [singer] (see note)
BROSCHI, Riccardo (c1698-1756), It
R.1   S.c
BROSSARD, Sébastien de (1655-1730), Fr
R.1   S.c,10
BROTT, Alexander (1915-   ), Can
R.1   S.24
BROUCK, Jacob de (fl 1568-83), Flem
R.1   S.c

BROUGHTON, W. - America
            S.54(312)
BROUSTET, Eduardo (1836-1901), Sp
    R.10   S.24
BROUWER, Leo (1939-   ), Cuba
    R.1   S.10,24,32
BROVSTIN, Boris Vasilyevich (1903-   )
            S.18
BROWN - Chin-chin
            S.54(319)
BROWN, Christopher Roland (1943-   ), Eng
    R.80   S.c
BROWN, Earle (1926-   ), USA
    R.1   S.c,9,10,13,24a
BROWN, Eddy (1895-1974), USA
    R.4   S.24
BROWN, Francis H. (?1818-1891), USA
    R.57,200
BROWN, Gladys Mungen (1926-   ), USA
            S.13,52
BROWN, J. Harold (1909-1981), USA
    R.19   S.13
BROWN, Marion (1935-   ), USA
    R.4   S.13
BROWN, Nacio Herb (1896-1964), USA
    R.1   S.10,24,54(323)
BROWN, Nettie Arthur
            S.10
BROWN, Newel Kay (1932-   ), USA
    R.19   S.10,13
BROWN, Obadiah Bruen (1829-   ), USA
    R.98   S.10
BROWN, Rayner (1912-   ), USA
    R.19   S.9 10,12,13
BROWN, Reginald Porter, USA
            S.10,13,19
BROWN, Rosemary (1917-   ), Eng
    R.1   S.c,9,52
BROWN, Thomas - Shepherd, thy demeanour vary

BROWN, William (fl 1782-87), USA
    R.20   S.10,47
BROWNE - That rag
            S.54(360)
BROWNE, Denis (1889-1915), Eng
            S.c
BROWNE, John (fl c1490), Eng
    R.1   S.c,10,16
BROWNE, Philip (1933-   ), USA
    R.19

BROWNE, Richard (c1630-1664), Eng
    R. 1   S. c
BROWNE, Philip (20th Cent), Eng
              S. 5x,19
BROWNELL, Leila M. (19th Cent), USA

BROWNSON, Oliver (18th Cent), USA
    R. 1   S. 10,47
BROZ, František (1896-1962), Cz
    R. 18   S. 23,31

BROZEN, Michael (1934-   ), USA
    R. 19   S. 10,13
BRUANT, Aristide ('851-1925), Fr
    R. 1   S. 10
BRUBECK, Dave (1920-   ), USA
    R. 1   S. c,9,13
BRUBECK, Howard (1916-   ), USA
    R. 19   S. 10
BRUBIER, Antoine [see BRUHIER, Antoine)
BRUCH, Max (1838-1920), Ger
    R. 1   S. 2-11,18-20,23,24,32
BRUČI, Rudolf (1917-   ), Yug
    R. 1   S. c
BRUCK, Arnold von (1500-1554), Neth
    R. 1   S. c,2-4,5x,10,11,14-16
BRUCKNER, Anton (1824-1896), Aus
    R. 1   S. c,1-11,18
BRUCKNER, Monika (1957-   ), Ger
              S. c,52
BRUDIEU, Joan (c1520-1591), Sp
    R. 1   S. 10,14-17
BRUGIER, Antoine [see BRUHIER, Antoine]
BRUGNEL, Ton (1934-   ), Neth

BRUGUIÈRE, Edouard (1793-1863), Fr
    R. 10   S. 10
BRUHIER, Antoine (fl early 16th Cent), Fr
    R. 1   S. c,10,15,16
BRUHNS, Nicolaus (1665-1697), Ger
    R. 1   S. c,2,6-10,53
BRUIN, B. (1912-1968)
              S. c
BRUINS, Theo (1929-   ), Neth
    R. 4
BRULÉ, Gace [see GACE BRULÉ]
BRÜLL, Ignaz (1846-1907), Aus
    R. 1   S. c,9,24a
BRUMBY, Colin (1933-   ), Australia
    R. 1   S. c,29,37

BRUMEL, Antoine (c1460-c1515), Fr
   R. 1   S. c,4,5x,7,8,10,14,16,41
BRUMEL, Jaches [see BRUNEL, Jacques]
BRUN - Je vous salue, Marie
           S. e
BRUN - Rhin et Danube
           S. 54(352)
BRUN, Bruno
           S. 20
BRÜN, Herbert (1918-   ), Ger/Isr
   R. 14   S. 10
BRUNA, Pablo (1611-1679), Sp
   R. 1   S. c,10,53
BRUNCKHORST, Arnold Matthias (1670-1725), Ger
   R. 1   S. c,9,10,53
BRUNDZAITE, Konstantsiya (1942-1971), USSR
           S. 18,52
BRUNEAU, Alfred (1857-1934), Fr
   R. 1   S. c,1x,2-4,8
BRUNEL [Brumel], Jacques (d. 1564), Fr
   R. 1   S. c,53
BRUNELL - Bonjour Marie
           S. e
BRUNELLI, Antonio (c1575-<1630), It
   R. 1   S. c
BRUNETTI, Gaetano (1744-1798), It
   R. 1   S. 8,10
BRUNNER, Adolf (1901-   ), Swiss
   R. 1   S. 7,10
BRUNOLD, Paul (1875-1948), Fr
   R. 4
BRUNSWICK, Mark (1902-1971), USA
   R. 1   S. 7,10,13
BRUSILOVSKY, Evgeny Grigoryevich (1905-   ), USSR
   R. 1   S. 18
BRUSLARD, Jacques (1618-1670), Fr
   R. 16   S. 8
BRUSSELMANS, Michel (1886-1960), Bel
   R. 1   S. 36
BRUSTAD, Bjarne (1895-1978), Nor
   R. 1   S. c,10,24,24a,51
BRUYNÈL, Ton (1934-   ), Neth
   R. 1   S. 10
BRUZDOWICZ, Joanna (1943-   ), Pol
   R. 7   S. c,52
BRYANT, Allan (1931-   ), USA
   R. 19   S. 13
BRYCE - Song

BRYER, Arthur
              S. 10
BRZEZINSKI, Franciszek (1867-1944), Pol
    R. 1. 5   S. 7,10
BUBALO, Rudolph (1927-   ), USA
    R. 19   S. 10,13
BUCALOSSI, Ernst (? -1933)
    R. 3   S. 54(330)
BUCALOSSI, Procida (?1859-   )
              S. 54(333)
BUCCHI, Valentino (1916-1976), It
    R. 1   S. 10,24
BUCCI, Mark (1924-   ), USA
    R. 14   S. 10,13
BUCHANAN - Little mother
              S. e
BUCHARDO, Carlos Lopez [see LOPEZ BUCHARDO, Carlos]
BUCHBINDER, Gunnar (1927-   )
              S. 24a
BUCHBINDER, Hazel Felman
              S. 10,24,30
BUCHER, Emanuel (1896-   )
    R. 200
BUCHNER, Hans [Johannes] (1483-1538), Ger
    R. 1   S. c,8,10,14-16,53
BUCHNER, Philipp Friedrich (1614-1669), Ger
    R. 1   S. c
BUCHT, Gunnar (1927-   ), Sweden
    R. 1   S. c,9,38,40,56
BUCHTEL, Forrest L. (1899-   ), USA
    R. 19   S. 13,21,54(361)
BÜCHTGER, Fritz (1903-1978), Ger
    R. 14   S. c,24a
BUCHWIESER, Balthasar (1765-   ), Ger
    R. 5   S. c
BUCIA, Nicolas
              S. 24
BUCK, Dudley (1839-1909), USA
    R. 1   S. c,4,10,12
BUCK, Ole (1945-   ), Den
    R. 1   S. 40
BUCK, Vera (fl 1935), Eng
              S. 5x
BUCK, Zechariah (1798-1879), Eng
    R. 1   S. c
BUCKLEY, Frederick (1833-1864), Eng
    R. 53   S. 10,47
BUCKLEY,   Bishop (1826-1867)
    R. 200

BUCKY, Frida Sarsen (1883/84-1974), USA   (see note)
          S.5x,13,30[Sarsen-Bucky]
BUCZYNSKI, Walter (1933-   ), Can
   R.4
BUDASHKIN, Nikolai Pavlovich (1910-   ), Russia
   R.14   S.5x,10,18
BUDD, Harold (1936-   ), USA
   R.19   S.10,13
BUDRYAVICHYUS, Viktoras (1934-   )
          S.18
BUDRYUNAS, Antanas (1902-1966), USSR
   R.14   S.18
BUEREN, R. F. G. van

BUFFARDIN, Pierre-Gabriel (c1690-1768), Fr
   R.1   S.c
BUGGERT, Robert W. (1918-   ), USA
   R.19   S.10,13
BÜHLER, Franz (1760-1824), Ger
   R.5   S.c,10,20,24a
BUICLIU, Nicolae (1906-   ), Rum
   R.14   S.24a
BUISSON, du [see DU BUISSON]
BUJARSKI, Zbigniew (1933-   ), Pol
   R.14   S.24a
BUKINIK, Mikhail Yevseyevich (1872-1947), USSR
   R.47   S.18
BULAKHOV, Pavel Petrovich (1824-1875), Russia
   R.47   S.5x,10,18,23[Boulchov]
BULL, Amos (c1741-1825), USA
   R.53
BULL, Edvard Hagerup [see HAGERUP BULL, Edvard]
BULL, John (c1562-1628), Eng
   R.1   S.c,2-4,6-11,14-16,18,53
BULL, Ole Bornemann (1810-1880), Nor
   R.1   S.c,2-4,5x,8,10,22,24
BULLARD, Frederic Field (1864-1901), USA
   R.10s
BULLER, John (1927-   ), Eng
   R.1   S.c
BULLOCK, Ernest (1890-1979), Eng
   R.4   S.c,8,10
BULMAN, Barick (fl c1600)
   R.1   S.c,10,15,32
BULOW, Hans von (1830-1894), Ger
   R.1   S.c,10
BULTERIJS, Nina (1929-   ), Bel
   R.7   S.30,24a,52
BUMPUS, Mary Francis
   [see ALLITSEN, Mary Francis - pseud]

BUNGERT, August (1845/6-1915), Ger
    R. 1   S. c, 5x
BUNIN, Revol Samuilovich (1924-   ), USSR
    R. 1   S. 18,23 [Bounine]
BUNIN, Vladimir Vasilievich (1908-1970)
    R. 14   S. 18,24a
BUNJES, Paul (1914-   )

BUONAMENTE, Giovanni Battista (d. 1642), It
    R. 1   S. c, 8, 10
BUONONCINI, Giovanni [see BONONCINI, Giovanni]
BURCH, Robert (1929-   )

BURCK, Joachim à (c1541-1610), Ger
    R. 5   S. c, 10, 16
BURCKHARD, Ursula
             S. 19
BURCKHARDI, J. (18th Cent)
    R. 5   S. c
BURG, Willem (Wim) ter (1914-   ), Neth
    R. 25   S. c
BURGE, David (1930-   ), USA
    R. 1   S. 10, 13, 20
BURGER, Siegfreid (1925-   )
             S. c
BURGESS - Love's descent
             S. 54(339)
BURGHARDT - Scherzando (recorder & hps)
             S. 6
BURGHAUSER, Jarmil (1921-   ), Cz
    R. 1   S. 10, 31, 32
BURGK, Joachim [see BURCK, Joachim a]
BURGKSTEINER, Joseph (18th Cent)

BURGMULLER, Friedrich (1807-1874), Ger
    R. 3   S. c, 9
BURGMULLER, Norbert (1810-1836), Ger
    R. 1   S. c, 10

BURGON, Geoffrey (1941-   ), Eng
    R. 14   S. c
BURGOS y JIMENEZ, J. de [see GIMENEZ, Jeronimo]
BURIAN, Emil Frantisek (1904-1959), Cz
    R. 1   S. 4, 5, 10, 24, 31
BURIAN, Karel (1870-1924), Cz [singer] (see note)
    R. 1   S. c
BURINSKAS, V. - Scherzino (vi)
             S. 18, 24
BURKE, James Francis (1923-   ), USA
    R. 70

BURKE, Joseph A. (1884-1950), USA
   R. 23   S. 10
BURKHARD, Paul (1911-1977), Swiss
   R. 1   S. c
BURKHARD, Willy (1900-1955), Swiss
   R. 1   S. c,4,5,7,10,23,24
BURKHARDT, Martin - Ihr Armen, hort es

BURKHART, Franz (1902-1978), Aus
   R. 14   S. c,10
BURLAS, Ladislav (1927-   ), Cz
   R. 14   S. 24a
BURLEIGH, Cecil (1885-1980), USA
   R. 19   S. 5x,10,13,24
BURLEIGH, Henry Thacker (1866-1849), USA
   R. 1   S. 4,10
BURMESTER, Willy (1869-1933), Ger
   R. 8   S. 24
BURNAND, Arthur Bransby (1859-1907), Eng
   [pseud: Anton STRELETZKI, Stepan ESIPOFF]
   R. 3   S. e
BURNARD, David Alexander (1900-1971), Australia
   R. 14   S. 29
BURNETT, Duncan (fl c1615-52), Scot
   R. 1   S. 16
BURNEY, Charles (1726-1814), Eng
   R. 1   S. c
BURNS, Robert (1759-1796), Scot
   R. 1
BURREL - Bay state commandery
            S. 54(315)
BURROWES, John Freckleton (1787-1852), Eng
   R. 1
BURT - Song of the Army Engineer; The Infantry
            S. 54(334,57)
BURTON, Charles P.
            S. 54(320)
BURTON, Eldin (1913-   ), USA
   R. 19   S. 7,9 ˙0,13,24
BURTON, John (1730-1782), Eng
   R. 1   S. c
BURTON, Stephen Douglas (1943-   ), USA
   R. 19   S. 13
BUS, Gervais du (fl 1310-14), Swiss
   R. 1   S. 3,4
BUSATTI, Cherubino (d. 1644), It
   R. 1   S. c
BUSCA, Lodovico (fl 1670-80), It
   R. 1   S. 3,4,5x,8

BUSCH, Adolf Georg Wilhelm (1891-1952), Swiss
R. 14   S. 24a
BUSCH, Carl (1862-1943), Den/USA
R. 30   S. 2,5x,11
BUSCH, Richard
               S. 20
BUSCH, William (1901-1945), Eng
R. 1   S. c,10,26,27
BUSCHMANN, Eberhard (1931-   )
               S. c
BUSH, Alan Dudley (1900-   ), Eng
R. 1   S. c,5,10,18,27
BUSH, Geoffrey (1920-   ), Eng
R. 1   S. c,7,10,18,24a
BUSH, Irving (1930-   ), USA
R. 19   S. 10,13
BUSNOIS, Antoine (c1430-1492), Fr
R. 1   S. c,9,10,14-16
BUSONI, Ferruccio (1866-1924), It
R. 1   S. c,1-5,7-11,18-20,24,42
BUSSANE, Anthony (16-17th Cent), It
               S. 10,16
BÜSSER, Paul Henri (1872-1973), Fr
R. 1   S. c,1-5,7,8,10,19
BUSSOTTI, Sylvano (1931-   ), It
R. 1   S. c,10,32
BUSTINI, Alessandro (1876-1970), It [?]
R. 8   S. 5x
BUSTON, Jean
               S. 32
BUTE, Cornelis Johan (1889-   ), Neth
R. 3   S. c
BUTERNE, Jean-Baptiste (c1650-1727), Fr
R. 1   S. c
BUTLER - Where go the boats
               S. e
BUTTERFIELD, James Austin (1837-1891), USA
R. 50   S. 10,24
BUTTERLEY, Nigel (1935-   ), Australia
R. 1   S. c,10,29,37
BUTTERWORTH, Arthur (1923-   ), Eng
R. 1   S. c,55
BUTTERWORTH, George Sainton Kaye (1885-1916), Eng
R. 1   S. c,4,5,7,8,10
BUTTING, Max (1888-1976), Ger
R. 1   S. 8,24
BUTTSCHARDT, Carl
               S. 24
BUTTSTETT, Johann Heinrich (1666-1727), Ger
R. 1   S. c,10,53

BUUCK, Paul (1911-   ), USA
          S. 13
BUXTEHUDE, Dietrich (c1637-1707)
   R. 1   S. c,1-5,7-11,18,23,24,32,33,35,53,57
BUYANOVSKY, Vitali Mikhailovich (1928-   )
          S. 18
BUZZI-PECCIA, Arturo (1854-1943), USA
   R. 8   S. 5x,10,18,34,44
BYERLY, William
          S. 10
BYRD, Charles (1925-   ), USA
   R. 4   S. 32
BYRD, J. - Conquest of the American wilderness
          S. 10
BYRD, William (1543-1623), Eng
   R. 1   S. 1-11,14-16,18,24a,32,53
BYREC, Louis

BYRT, John
          S. 10
BYSTROM, Thomas (1772-1839), Fin
   R. 30   S. 24a
BYTTERING (fl 1410), Eng
   R. 1   S. 8,10,14,16
CAAMAÑO, Roberto (1923-   ), Arg
   R. 1   S. 10,46
CABALLERO, Manuel Fernández
   [see FERNANDEZ CABALLERO, Manuel]
CABALLONE, Gaspare [see GABELLONE, Gaspare]
CABANILLES, Juan Bautista Jose (1644-1712), Sp
   R. 1   S. c,3,4,5x,8-10,39,53
CABESTAN, Guillaume de
          S. c
CABEZÓN, Antonio de (1510-1566),Sp
   R. 1   S. c,3-11,14-16,32,39,53
CABEZÓN, Hernando de (1541-1602), Sp
   R. 1   S. c,53
CABLE, Howard Reid (1920-   ), Can
   R. 14
CABRERA, José
          S. 24
CABUS, Peter (1923-   ), Bel
   R. 14   S. c
CACAVAS, John (1930-   ), USA
   R. 19   S. 13,21
CACCINI, Francesca (1587-1640), It
   R. 1   S. c,3,4,5x,10,52
CACCINI, Giulio (c1545-1618), It
   R. 1   S. c,1x,2-8,10,18,28

CACIOPPO, George (1926-   ), USA
  R. 19   S. 10,13
CADDIGAN, Jack (1879-1952), USA
  R. 23   S. 24
CADÉAC, Pierre (fl 1538-56), Fr
  R. 1   S. c,10,16
CADENAL, Peire [see PEIRE CARDENAL]
CADENAS, José Juan (1872-   ), Sp
  R. 200   S. e
CADENAT (1200-1230)
           S. c
CADMAN, Charles Wakefield [pseud: Charles C. WAKEFIELD]
  (1881-1946), USA
  R. 1   S. 2-4,5x,10,11,13,24,28
CAESAR - Waiting for your return
           S. e
CAGE, John (1912-   ), USA
  R. 1   S. c,4,5x,7,9,10,12,13,19,24a
CAGNARD, Gilles (20th Cent)
           S. c
CAGNONI, Antonio (1828-1896), It
  R. 1   S. e
CAHUZAC, Louis (1880-1960), Fr
  R. 1   S. 10,19,20
CĂIANU, Ioan (1627-1698), Transylvania
  R. 1   S. c
CAIAULY, W. - Csardas; Magudler (vi & p)
           S. 24a
CAILLET, Lucien (1891-   ), Fr
  R. 19   S. 4,10,11,13,21,22
CAIMO, Gioseppe (c1545-1584), It
  R. 1   S. c,10,14,15
CAIX d'HERVELOIS, Louis de (c1670-c1760), Fr
  R. 1   S. c,2-5,8,10,23
CALABRO, Louis (1926-   ), USA
  R. 19   S. 10,13,19
CALACE, Raffaele (1863-1934), It
  R. 8   S. c,10
CALCAGNO, Elsa (1910-   ), Arg
  R. 26   S. 46
CALCAÑO, José Antonio (1900-   ), Ven
  R. 4
CALDARA, Antonio (c1670-1736), It
  R. 1   S. c,1x,2-10,18,24,25,27,28,53
CALDUI - serenade a Lisette (vi & p)
           S. 24a
CALESTANI, Vincenzo (1589-c1617), It
  R. 1   S. c,8,10,28
CALIFANO, Arcangelo (fl 1733), It
  R. 5   S. 10

CALINE, Pierre (1900-   )

CALL, Leonhard von (1767-1815), Aus
R.1   S.10
CALLAERTS, Joseph (1838-1901), Bel
R.11   S.c
CALLAWAY, Ann (1949-   ), USA
R.14   S.30,52
CALLCOTT, John George (1821-1895), Eng
R.44
CALLCOTT, John Wall (1766-1821), Eng
R.1   S.c,10
CALLEJA y LLEÓ - Seguidillas
        S.e
CALLEJA, Francisco
        S.10
CALLEJA, Gomez Rafael [see GOMEZ CALLEJA, Rafael]
CALLEJA, Julian - Adios Granada

CALLHOFF, Herbert (1933-   ), Ger
R.4   S.c
CALMEL, Roger (1921-   ), Fr
R.14   S.c,24a
CALSTON, Nicholas (c 1550)
        S.c
CALVERT, Morley (1928-   ), Can
R.14   S.c
CALVI, Carlo (fl 1646), It
R.1   S.c
CALVIÈRE, Guillaume Antoine (c1700-1755), Fr
R.8   S.c
CALVISIUS, Sethus (1556-1615), Ger
R.1   S.2,3,8,11,15
CALZANERA, E. - Oremus Pro Pontefice
        S.e
CAMARA - Aires criollas
        S.e
CAMARATA, Salvador (1913-   ), USA
R.23
CAMARY, M. Brazil - Eu vou m'embora
        S.10
CAMBELL, S. Brunson
        S.10
CAMBINI, Giuseppe Maria (1746-1825), It (see note)
R.1   S.c,3-5,8-10,18,24
CAMBRAI, (13th Cent), Fr
        S.c
CAMERLOHER, Placidus Cajetan von (1718-1782), Ger
R.1   S.c,20

CAMERON, John

CAMEU, Helza (Helza Cameu de Cordoville)
    (1903-   ), Brazil   R.7   S.52
CAMIDGE, Matthew (1764-1844), Eng
    R.1   S.c,10,32
CAMIDGE, Michael C.
              S.10
CAMILLERI, Charles (1931-   ), Malta
    R.1   S.c
CAMINHA, Alda (20th Cent), Brazil
    R.7   S.10,52,24a
CAMONIN, Pierre (19th Cent)
              S.c
CAMOT - Le carillon magique (orch)
              S.24
CAMPAGNOLI, Bartolomeo (1751-1827), It
    R.1   S.c,10
CAMPANA, Fabio (1819-1882), It
    R.3
CAMPANUS, Jan (1572-1622), Cz
              S.c,5x,16
CAMPBELL, Kenneth (1922-   ), Can
    R.81
CAMPBELL, Mary Maxwell (1812-1886), Scot
    R.7   S.e
CAMPBELL, Sidney Scholfield (1909-1974), Eng
    R.64   S.c,10
CAMPBELL-TIPTON, Louis (1877-1921), USA
    R.19   S.5x,13,43
CAMPBELL-WATSON, Frank (1898-   ), USA
    R.19   S.10,12,13
CAMPENHOUT, François van (1799-1848), Bel
    R.1   S.54(317)
CAMPION, François (c1686-1748), Fr
    R.1   S.c,8,10
CAMPION, Thomas (1567-1620), Eng
    R.1   S.5x,7,8,10,14-16,26-28,32
CAMPO, Conrado del (1878-1953), Sp
    R.1   S.1x
CAMPO, Frank Philip (1927-   ), USA
    R.19   S.10,13,19,24a
CAMPOS, Juan Morel [see MOREL CAMPOS, Juan]
CAMPOS-PARSI, Héctor (1922-   ), Puerto Rico
    R.1   S.9,10
CAMPRA, André (1660-1744), Fr
    R.1   S.c,2-10,53
CAMPRODÓN y SAFONT, Francisco (1816-1870), Sp
    R.9

CAMPS, Pompeyo (1924-   ), Arg
   R. 26   S. 46
CAMUS, Sebastien le [see LE CAMUS, Sebastien]
CANALE, Floriano (fl 1579-1603), It
   R. 1   S. c,10,53
CANBY, Edward Tatnall (1912-   ), USA
   R. 19   S. 10,13
CANDAEL, Karel (1883-1948), Bel
   R. 1   S. 41
CANEVER, Ernest O.
           S. 54(326)
CANFIELD, David DeBoor (1950-   ), ?USA
           S. 13,24a
CANN, Richard, USA
           S. 10,13
CANNABICH, Christian (1731-1798), Ger
   R. 1   S. c,2-4,7,10,24a
CANNING, Thomas (1911-   ), USA
   R. 19   S. c,7,10,13
CANNIO, Enrico It
   R. 52   S. e
CANNON, Hughie - Bill Bailey, won't you come home
           S. 10
CANO, Antonio (1811-1897), Sp
   R. 10   S. c
CANO, Manuel Diaz
           S. 32
CANON de BETHUNE [see CONON de BETHUNE]
CANOVAS, Narciso
           S. 17
CANTALLOS (c1760-   ), Sp
           S. 5x,8,10,39
CANTELOUBE, Joseph (1879-1957), Fr
   R. 1   S. 2,3,8,10,27,28
CANTON, Edgardo Arg
           S. 46
CANTONI, Fortunato (1887-   ), It
   R. 10   S. e
CANTOR - O fair, O sweet and holy
           S. 24a
CAPEL, John Mais (1862-   ), Can
   R. 31   S. 10,28
CAPELLETTI, Daniel (1958-   )
           S. c
CAPELLI, Giovanni Maria (1648-1726), It
   R. 1   S. 5x
*** CAPIROLA, Giovanni Paolo (1474-1547) (see note)
CAPIROLA, Vincenzo (1474->1548), It
   R. 1   S. c,10,16,32

CAPLET, André (1878-1925), Fr
    R. 1   S. c,1-8,10,18
CAPOCCI, Gaetano (1811-1898), It
    R. 1   S. e
CAPOIANU, Dumitru (1929-   ), Rum
    R. 1   S. 24
CAPOLONGO, G.
    R. 52   S. 34
CAPON - Ad te levavi
           S. 16
CAPORALE, Andrea (fl mid 18th Cent), It
    R. 1   S. 18
CAPRI, Antonio (1901-   ), It
    R. 8   S. 24
CAPRICORNUS, Samuel Friedrich (1628-1665), Ger
    R. 1   S. c
CAPRON, Henri (fl 1785-95), USA
    R. 1   S. 10,47
CAPUA, Edoardo di (1864-1917), It
    R. 10   S. c,10,18,24,34,43,54(341,46)
CAPUA, Ernesto di
           S. c
CAPUA, Marcello da [see BERNARDINI, Marcello]
CAPUIS, Matilde (1912-   ), It
    R. 7   S. c,52
CAPUZZI, Giuseppe Antonio (1755-1818), It
    R. 1   S. c,10
CARA, Marchetto (c1470-?1525), It
    R. 1   S. c,6,8,10,14-16
CARACCIOLO, Luigi (1847-1887), It
    R. 10   S. e
CARCASIO, Giuseppe (18th Cent)
           S. c
CARCASSI, Matteo (1792-1853), It
    R. 10   S. c,10,32
CÁRCERES (16th Cent), Sp
    R. 9   S. c,16,17
CARDENAL, Peire [see PEIRE CARDENAL]
CARDEW, Cornelius (1936-1981), Eng
    R. 1   S. c
CARDILLO, Salvatore
           S. c,5x,10,18
CARDON, Jean-Baptiste (1760-1803), Fr
    R. 1   S. c
CARDON, Louis (1747-1805), Fr
    R. 9   S. c
CARDOSO, George (1949-   )
           S. c
CARDOSO, Lindembergue (1939-   ), Brazil
    R. 1   S. c

CARDOSO, Manuel (1566-1650), Port
   R.1   S.c,10,16
CARDUCCI - Ave Maria
          S.5x
CARELLI, Benjamino (1833-1921), It
   R.3   S.e
CARETTO - Pater Noster
          S.5x
CAREY, Elena (1939-   ), USA
          S.13,30,52
CAREY, Henry (c1689-1743), Eng
   R.1   S.5x,6,10,54(312,29)
CAREY, Lewis - pseud [see CONETTA, Lewis D.]
CARILLO - Sonata in e (vi & p)
          S.24a
CARISSIMI, Giacomo (1605-1674), It
   R.1   S.c,1-11,18,24-28
CARL, C. - Mussinan march
          S.54(344)
CARLES, Marc (1933-   )
          S.c
CARLETON - Song of Australia
          S.54(357)
CARLETON, Nicholas (c1570-1630), Eng
   R.1   S.c,16,53
CARLEVARO, Abel (1918-   ), Uruguay
   R.4   S.c
CARLID, Göte (1920-1953), Sweden
   R.1   S.10,40,56
CARLOS, Walter (1939-   ), USA
   R.19   S.c,9,10,13
CARLOSI - Hymn nacional portuguez
          S.e
CARLSON, Bengt Ivar (1890-1953), Fin
   R.14   S.10
CARLSON, Mark (1952-   )
          S.13
CARLSTEDT, Jan (1926-   ), Sweden
   R.1   S.c,10,24,38,40,56
CARLTON, Richard (c1558-?1638), Eng
   R.1   S.c,7,8,10,14
CARMEN, Johannes (fl 1400-20), Fr
   R.1   S.8,10,14,16
CARMER - Heat of Battle
          S.5x
CARMICHAEL, Hoagy (1899-1981), USA
   R.1   S.4,5x,10
CARMICHAEL, John ?USA
          S.13

CARMINES, Alvin A. (1938-   ), USA
  R. 19   S. 9 13
CARNE, Gerald [see KAHN, Gerald]
CARNEVALI, Vito (1888-   ), It
  R. 14   S. 10
CARNICER, Ramon (1789-1855), Sp
  R. 9   S. e
CAROL, Henri (1910-   )
         S. c
CAROLAN, Turlough (1670-1738), Ire
  R. 1   S. c
CAROLL - Rip van Winkle
         S. e
CAROLUS, Andreas [see ANDREAS, Carolus]
CARON, Philippe (fl 2nd half 15th Cent), Fr
  R. 1   S. c,14,16
CAROSI - Fontanella (p)

CAROSIO - Lauro soave (balletto)
         S. 5x
CAROSIO, Ermenegildo (1866-1928), It
  R. 10   S. 24a
CAROSO, Fabritio (c1527/35->1605), It
  R. 1   S. c,8,10,14-16,32
CAROUBEL, Pierre Francisque (d. 1611), Fr
  R. 1   S. c,8,10,14,16
CARPENTER, John Alden (1876-1951), USA
  R. 1   S. c,1-8,10,11,13,24a,25,27
CARPENTRAS [Elzear GENET] (c1470-1548), Fr
  R. 1   S. c
CARR, Benjamin (1768-1831), USA
  R. 1   S. 7,10,47
CARR, Edwin (1926-   ), New Zealand
  R. 1
CARR, Gordon (1943-   ), Eng
         S. c
CARR, Michael (i)
         S. 47
CARR, Michael (ii) - pseud [see COHEN, Maurice]
CARR, Richard (fl 1684-7), Eng
  R. 1   S. c
CARR, Robert (fl 1663-94), Eng
  R. 5   S. c,10

CARREIRA, António (c1525-c1589), Port
  R. 1   S. c,10,15,53
CARREÑO, Inocente (1919-   ), Ven
  R. 1
CARREÑO, Teresa (1853-1917), Ven
  R. 1   S. c,5x,30,52

CARRI, Ferdinand (1856-1927), USA
R. 3   S. 24
CARRIER - Mois de Marie
           S. e
CARRILLO, Julián (1875-1965), Mex
R. 1   S. 1-4,8-11,24,39
CARRION, Miguel Ramos (1845-1915), Sp (see note)
R. 200   S. 39
CARRIQUE, Ana (1886-   ), Arg
R. 26   S. 46
CARRODUS, Bernard Molique (1867-1936)
              S. 24
CARSE, Adam (1878-1958), Eng
R. 85   S. 55
CARSON, Philippe (1936-   ), Fr
R. 14
CARSTEN, Bert - pseud [see NOORDLANDER, Bert Carsten]
CARTAN, Jean (1906-1932), Fr
R. 1   S. 21
CARTER, Andrew (20th Cent), Eng
              S. c
CARTER, Elliott Cook (1908-   ), USA
R. 1   S. c,7-10,13,24a
CARTER, Stanley - pseud [ie Frederick J. REDCLIFFE]
              S. e
CARTER, Thomas M. (1841-1934), USA
R. 49   S. 10,54(317)
CARTIER, Antoine (fl 1552-88), Fr
R. 1   S. 5x
CARTUCCI, Pietro [S. 8] = CASTRUCCI, Pietro
CARULLI, Ferdinando (1770-1841), It
R. 1   S. c,10,18,23,24a,32
CARUSO, Enrico (1873-1921), It
R. 1   S. 43,44
CARVALHO, Dinorá de (1905-   ), Brazil
R. 4   S. 52
CARVALHO, Eleazar de (1915-   ), Brazil
R. 4
CARVALHO, João de Sousa (1745-1798), Port
R. 1   S. c,8-10,32,53
CARVER, B. - Devil m´cares
              S. 54(323)
CARYLL, Ivan - pseud [ie Felix TILKINS]
    (1861-1921), Eng/USA
R. 1   S. 54(324)
CASADESUS, Francis (1870-1954), Fr
R. 1   S. 4
CASADESUS, Henri (1879-1947), Fr (see note under
    AYRTON)   R. 1   S. c,3-5,10

CASADESUS, Marius Robert Max (1892-   ), Fr
    R. 1   S. c
CASADESUS, Robert Marcel (1899-1972), Fr
    R. 1   S. 4,5x,6,8-10,24
CASALI, Giovanni Battista (c1715-1792), It
    R. 1   S. 6
CASALS, Enrique (1892-   ), Sp
    R. 9   S. 10
CASALS, Pablo (1876-1973), Sp
    R. 1   S. c,5x,9,10,39
CASANOVA, André (1919-   ), Fr
    R. 1   S. 19
CASANOVAS, F. - La gata i el belitre
   = CASANOVAS, Fray Narciso
CASANOVAS, José (1924-   ), Sp
    R. 1   S. 10
CASANOVS, Narciso (1747-1799), Sp
    R. 1   S. c,5x,8-10,32,39
CASANTA, Joseph (fl 1919-42), USA
    R. 49   S. 54(332)
CASCARINO, Romeo (1922-   ), USA
    R. 19   S. 10,13
CASCIA, Giovanni da [see GIOVANNI da GASCIA]
CASCIOLINI, Claudio (1697-1760), It
    R. 1   S. c,5x,8,10
CASELLA, Alfredo (883-1947), It
    R. 1   S. c,1-11,18,24
CASENTINI, Marsilio (1576-1651), It
    R. 1   S. 10
CASERTA, Antonellus de [see ANTHONELLO de CASERTA]
CASES, Guillermo (1899-   )
              S. 5,8
CASIELLO - Estasi Estiva (p)

CASINI, Giovanni Maria (1652-1719), It
    R. 1   S. 10,53
CASLER - Honey bunch
              S. 54(332)
CASSADÓ, Gaspar (1897-1966), Sp
    R. 1   S. 4,5x,10,18,24,32,39
CASSADÓ, Joaquín (1867-1926), Sp
    R. 1   S. 8,10,39
CASSANOVAS - Sonata in F
              S. c
CASSINI, Leonard
              S. 5x
CASTALDI, Bellerofonte (1580-1649), It
    R. 1   S. c
CASTALDO, Joseph (1927-   ), USA
    R. 19   S. 13

CASTEGNARO, Lola (1905-   ), Costa Rica
    R. 7   S. 52
CASTELLANOS, C. - La morena de mi copla (orch)

CASTELLANOS-YUMAR, Gonzalo (1926-   ), Ven
    R. 1   S. c
CASTELLO, Dario (fl early 17th Cent), It (see note)
    R. 1   S. c,10,24
CASTELLON, Augustin [see SABICIAS - pseud]
CASTELNUOVO-TEDESCO, Mario (1895-1968), It
    R. 1   S. c,2-8,10,11,13,18,20,24,32
CASTÉRÈDE, Jacques (1926-   ), Fr
    R. 1   S. c,10
CASTIGLIONI, Niccolò (1932-   ), It
    R. 1   S. c,10
CASTILLEJA (16th Cent) - Cucu
                S. c
CASTILLEJO, Cristobal de
                S. 10,32
*** CASTILLO, Dario (mid 16th Cent) (see note)
CASTILLO, Diego del (16th Cent), Sp
    R. 8   S. 5x,16
CASTRO, Jean de (c1540-c1600), S. Neth
    R. 1   S. c,8,14,16,17
CASTRO, José María (1892-1964), Arg
    R. 1   S. c,8,46
CASTRO, Juan Blas de (c1560-1631), Sp (see note)
    R. 1
*** CASTRO, Juan de (1540?-c1600) (see note)
CASTRO, Juan José (1895-1968), Arg
    R. 1   S. 5x,10,46
CASTRO, Washington (1909-   ), Arg
    R. 1   S. 46
CASTRUCCI, Pietro (1679-1752), It
    R. 1   S. 5x
CASULANA, Maddalena (fl 1566-83), It
    R. 1   S. c
CATALANI, Alfredo (1854-1893), It
    R. 1   S. c,1-11,18
CATEL, Charles-Simon (1773-1830), Fr
    R. 1   S. 10
CATELINET, Philip Bramwell (1910-   ), Fr
    R. 14   S. 54(331,59)
CATHERINE, Alphonse (1868-1927), Fr [?]
                S. 24
CATHIE, Philip (1874-   ), Eng
    R. 51   S. 24
CATHY, Jules (1908-   )
                S. c

CATLIN, Edward N. (fl c1870-79)
R. 53   S. 10,47
CATO, Diomedes (<1570->1670), It
R. 1   S. c,7,8,10,14,16,18,53
CATOIRE, Georges Lvovich (1861-1926), Russia
R. 1   S. 18,24
CATURLA, Alejandro Garcia (1906-1940), Cuba
R. 1   S. 8,10,39
CAUDIOSO, Domenico (18th Cent)
        S. c
CAULERY, Jean (fl mid 16th Cent), Fr
R. 1   S. c,16
CAURROY, Eustache du [see DU CAURROY, Eustace]
CAUSTUN, Thomas (c1520-1569), Eng
R. 1   S. c,10
CAVACCIO, Giovanni (c1556-1626), It
R. 1   S. c,53
CAVALIERI, Emilio de (c1550-1602), It
R. 1   S. c,5,8-10,18
CAVALINI, Ernesto (1807-1874), It
R. 8   S. c,20,21
CAVALLI, Nicolo (18th Cent), It
R. 5   S. 7
CAVALLI, Pietro Francesco (1602-1676), It
R. 1   S. c,2-5,7-10,18,24,26,27
ÇAVALLOS, Rodrigo de [see CEBALLOS, Rodrigo de]
CAVANAGH, Kathleen - pseud [see WRIGHT, Lawrence]
CAVAZZONI, Girolamo (c1525->1577), It
R. 1   S. c,5x,8,10,14-16,53
CAVAZZONI, Marco Antonio (c1490-c1560), It
R. 1   S. c,15,18,53
CAVENDISH, Michael (c1565-1628), Eng
R. 1   S. c,5x,7,8,10,14,16
CAYMMI, Dorival (1914-   ), Brazil
R. 67   S. 39
CAZDEN, Norman (1914-1980), USA
R. 1   S. 10,13,24a
CAZZATI, Maurizio (c1620-1677), It
R. 1   S. c,10,24
CEBALLOS, Rodrigo de (c1530-1591), Sp (see note)
R. 1   S. c,10,16,17
CEBALLOS, Francisco de (fl 1554-71), Sp (see note)
R. 1   S. 16
CEBRIÁN, Antonio (16th Cent), Sp
R. 9   S. 10,16,17
CECCAROSSI, Domenico (1910-   ), It
R. 8   S. 10
CECCHINO, Tomaso (c1580-1644), It
R. 1   S. c

CECCONI-BOTELLA, Monic (1936-   ), Fr
  R. 7   S. c,10,52
CECERE, Carlo (1706-1761), It
  R. 1   S. c
CEELY, Robert Paige (1930-   ), USA
  R. 19   S. 10,13
CEJKA, J. V. - Divertimento in A maj: Adagio & minuet
              S. 5x
CELIBIDACHE, Sergiu (1912-   ), Rum
  R. 1   S. c
CELLA, Theodore (1897-1960), USA
  R. 14   S. 13
CELLES, Maurice Duclos de (1905-   ), Can
  R. 31
CELLIER, Alexandre (1883-1968), Fr
  R. 1   S. c
CELLIER, Alfred (1844-1891), Eng
  R. 1   S. 9
CELONIATI, Ignazio (<1740-1784), It
  R. 1
CENNICK, John (1718-1755), America
  R. 200   S. 10
CEREROLS, Joan (1618-1676), Sp
  R. 1   S. c,10
CERHA, Friedrich (1926-   ), Aus
  R. 1   S. c,24
CERNÉ, Charles
              S. 24
ČERNOHORSKÝ, Bohuslav Matej (1684-1742), Boh
  R. 1   S. c,7,8,53
CERRI, Luigi (1860-1930), It
  R. 10,10s   S. 5x,54(335)
CERTANI, Antonio (1879-   ), It
  R. 10s   S. 2-4,5x,11
CERTON, Pierre (d. 1572), Fr
  R. 1   S. c,5x,7-10,14-16
CERVANTES, Ignacio (1847-1905), Cuba
  R. 1   S. c,8,10,32
CERVEAU, Pierre (fl 1573-1604), Fr
  R. 1   S. 16
CERVELLINI, Giovanni (c1735-c1801), It
  R. 5   S. c
CERVETTI, Sergio (1941-   ), Uruguay
  R. 1   S. 13
CERVETTO, Giacobbe Basevi (c1682-1783), It
  R. 1   S. 7,10
CESANA, Otto (1899-1980), USA
  R. 19   S. 3,11,13
CESARE, Giovanni Martino (c1590-1667), It
  R. 1   S. c

CESARINI, Carlo Francesco (c1664-c1730), It
   R.1
CESARIS, Johannes (fl c1385-c1420), Fr
   R.1   S.c,16
CESEK, Hans (1868-   ), Moravia
   R.3   S.e
CESNOKOV, Pavel Grigoryevich
   [see CHESNOKOV, Pavel Grigoryevich]
CESTI, Antonio (1623-1669), It
   R.1   S.c,2-8,10,18,24,25,27,28
CEVALLOS, Rodrigo de [see CEBALLOS, Rodrigo de]
CHABANCEAU de la BARRE, Joseph
   [see LA BARRE, Joseph de]
CHABRAN, Carlo Francesco
   [see CHIABRANO, Carlo Francesco]
CHABRIER, Emmanuel (1841-1894), Fr
   R.1   S.c,1-11,18,24a,25-27,42,54(325)
CHADABE, Joel (1938-   ), USA
   R.19   S.10,13,24a
CHADWICK, George Whitefield (1854-1931), USA

   R.1   S.c,3,5,8-13,25
CHAGRIN, Francis (1905-1972), Eng
   R.1   S.c
CHAIKIN, Nikolai Yakovlevich (1915-   ), USSR
   R.47   S.10,18
CHAILLEY, Jacques (1910-   ), Fr
   R.1   S.c,5,8,10,23
CHAILLY, Luciano (1920-   ), It
   R.1   S.c
CHAITKIN, David (1938-   ), USA
   R.19   S.10,13
CHAIX, Charles (1885-1973), Fr
   R.14   S.c
CHAJES, Julius (1910-   ), Pol
   R.19   S.10,13,24
CHALAYEV, Shirvani (1936-   ), USSR
   R.1   S.18
CHALCOTT, John Wall [see CALLCOTT, John Wall]
CHALLAN, Annie
               S.30,52
CHALLAN, René (1910-1978), Fr
   R.14   S.c,8
CHALLONER, Robert (19th Cent), USA
               S.9
CHAMBERS, Joseph C. (1910-   ), USA
               S.5x,10,13
CHAMBERS, Stephen A. [see HAKIM, Talib Rasul]
CHAMBERS, William Paris (1854-1913), USA
   R.49   S.10,54(341)

CHAMBON - La Lyonnaise
        S. e
CHAMBONNIÈRES, Jacques Champion (1602-1672), Fr
   R. 1   S. c,2-5,7,8,10,11,53
CHAMINADE, Cécile (1857-1944), Fr
   R. 1   S. c,1-4,5x,8,10,18,24,52
CHAMPAGNE, Claude (1891-1965), Can
   R. 1   S. 24,32
CHAMPION, Thomas (d. 1580), Fr
   R. 1   S. c,16
CHAMPOREL - Berceuse (vi & p)
        S. 24
CHANCE, John Barnes (1932-1972), USA
   R. 19   S. 13
CHANCE, Nancy Laird (1931-   ), USA
   R. 7   S. 30,24a,52
CHANDLER, Thomas S. (1888-   ), Eng
   R. 49   S. 54(317,36)
CHANDOSCHKIN, Ivan Jestavievic (1747-1804), Russia
   R. 8   S. c
CHANÉ - Un adios a Mariquina
        S. e
CHANLER, Theodore Ward (1902-1961), USA
   R. 1   S. 8,10,13,25,27
CHANTAVOINE, H. - L'enfant dormira bientot

CHAPÍ y LORENTE, Ruparto (1851-1909), Sp
   R. 1   S. c,8-10,32,39,42,44
CHAPIN, Lucius (1760-1842), USA
   R. 50   S. 10,47
CHAPLIN, Charlie (1899-1977)
        S. 9 10
CHAPLIN, Saul [formerly Sol KAPLAN] (1912-   ), USA
   R. 23,50   S. 11,12[Kaplan]
CHAPPEL - The day
        S. e
CHAPPELL, Herbert (1934-   ),Eng
   R. 80   S. c,10
CHAPPLE, Brian (1945-   ), Eng
        S. c
CHAPUT, Roger (1909-   )
        S. c
CHARDAVOINE, Jehan (1538-c1580), Fr
   R. 1   S. c,10,14
CHARDON de REIMS (13th Cent), Fr
        S. 8,10,14
CHARITE (fl 1420-25), Fr
   R. 1   S. 16
CHARLAP, Morris Isaac (1928-   ), USA
   R. 23   S. 9

CHARLES d'ORLEANS
      S. 14
CHARLES, Ernest (1895-   ), USA
    R. 19   S. 3,4,5x,10,24
CHARLIER, Theo (1868-1944), Bel
    R. 25   S. 10
CHARLTON, Andrew (1928-   )

CHARPENTIER, Gabriel (1925-   ), Can
    R. 14
CHARPENTIER, Gustave (1860-1956), Fr
    R. 1   S. c,1-11,18,23,42
CHARPENTIER, Jacques (1933-   ), Fr
    R. 1   S. c,22
CHARPENTIER, Jacques Marie
  [see BEAUVARLET-CHARPENTIER, Jacques Marie]
CHARPENTIER, Jean Jacques
  [see BEAUVARLET-CHARPENTIER, Jean Jacques]
CHARPENTIER, Louise

CHARPENTIER, Marc-Antoine (1645/50-1704), Fr
    R. 1   S. c,2,3,6,8-10,24,53
CHARRIERE, Isabelle Agenta Elisabeth de (1740-1805)
    Swiss   R. 7   S. 52
CHARTES - Alleluia: Angelus Domini
        S. 5x
CHARTIER
        S. 32
CHASINS, Abram (1903-   ), USA
    R. 1   S. 1-3,5,6,10,11,13
CHASSAIGNES, Francis (c1850-   )
    R. 200   S. e
CHASTELAIN de COUCI (c1165-1203), Fr
    R. 1   S. c,2,3,5x,10

CHASTELLAIN, Charles (c1490-1578)
    R. 5   S. c,10,14
CHATAU, Henri
        S. e,24
CHATEAU-THIERRY, H. [S. 24] = CHATAU, Henri
CHATEAUMINOIS - Sonate pour 2 flutes et tambourins
        S. c
CHATILLON, Walter von [see WALTER von CHATILLON]
CHATMAN, Stephen (1950-   ), USA
    R. 19   S. 13,24a
CHAUCER, Geoffrey (c1434-1400), Eng
    R. 1   S. c
CHAUDOIR - La dame de pique
        S. e
CHAUMONT, Lambert (c1630-1712), S. Neth
    R. 1   S. c,9,53

CHAUN, Frantisek (1921-   ), Cz
    R.1   S.c,24a
CHAUSSON, Ernest (1855-1899), Fr
    R.1   S.c,2-11,18,24,26-28
CHAUVET, Charles-Alexis (1837-1871), Fr
    R.3   S.10
CHAVARRI, Eduardo [see ECHEVARRIA, Eduardo]
CHAVCHAVADZE, Georges (20th Cent)
                 S.8,10
CHAVERO, Mario [see YUPANQUI, Atahualpa - pseud]
CHÁVEZ, Carlos (1899-1978), Mex
    R.1   S.c,2-11,24,32,39
CHAYKOVSKY, Boris Alexandrovich (1925-   ), USSR
    R.1   S.10,18 24
CHAYNES, Charles (1925-   ), Fr
    R.14   S.c,9,10,24a
CHAZANOV - Farewell song
                 S.5x
CHÉDEVILLE, Esprit Philippe (1696-1762), Fr
    R.1   S.c,10
CHÉDEVILLE, Nicolas (1705-1782), Fr
    R.1   S.c,7,8,10
CHEDRINE, Rodion [see SHCHEDRIN, Rodion]
CHEETHAM, John (1939-   ), USA
    R.19   S.c,10,13
CHELLERI, Fortunato (c1690-1757), It
    R.1   S.c
CHELU, L. - Le drapeau tricolor
                 S.e
CHEMIN-PETIT, Hans (1902-1981), Ger
    R.1   S.c
CHEMIRANI, Djamchid
                 S.c
CHEN, Chien-Hwa
                 S.c,24a
CHEN, P'Ei-Hsun
                 S.c
CHENEY, Timothy (1913-   ), USA
    R.13   S.10,13,24
CHENG MAO YUN (fl 1928), China
                 S.54(319)
CHERKASSKY, Shura (1911-   ), USSR
    R.30   S.1x
CHERNETSKY, L. - Vengerka (Hungarian dance)
                 S.54(350,63)
CHERNIAVSKY, Leo (1890-   ), Russia
    R.4   S.24
CHERNOV, Alexander Abramovich (1917-1971), USSR
    R.47   S.18

CHERNY, Brian (1942-   ), Can
R. 31
CHERRY, Don (1936-   ), USA
R. 1   S. c
CHERRY, John William (1824-1889), Eng
R. 57   S. e
CHERTOK, Pearl (1918-   ), USA
R. 19   S. 10,30,52
CHERUBINI, Luigi (1760-1842), It
R. 1   S. c,1-11,18,24,25,27,42
CHESHAM, Edward Mills
              S. e
CHESLOCK, Louis (1899-   ), USA
R. 1   S. 19
CHESNOKOV, Pavel Grigoryevich (1877-1944), Russia
R. 1   S. c,6,8,10,11,18
CHESNUKOV, Konstantin Georgiyevich (1923-   )
              S. 18
CHETHAM, John (<1700-1746), Eng
R. 1
CHEVALIER de SAINT-GEORGES
   [see SAINT-GEORGES, Joseph Boulogne, Chevalier de]
CHEVALIER, Albert Onésime Britannicus Gwathveoyd Louis
   (1862-1923), Eng   R. 44   S. e
CHEVALIER, Auguste [see INGLE, Charles - pseud]
CHEVREUILLE, Raymond (1901-1976), Bel
R. 1   S. c,20,36
CHIABRANO, Carlo Francesco (b. 1723), It
R. 1   S. c,24
CHIAFFARELLI, Alberte (1884-1945)
R. 50   S. e
CHIARA di LUCCA
              S. c
CHIARA, Vincenzo di [see DI CHIARA, Vincenzo]
CHIARAMELLO, Giancarlo (1939-   ), It
R. 8   S. c
CHIARINI, Pietro (18th Cent), It
R. 1   S. 5x,8
CHIESA, C. - Pastorale for organ
              S. c
CHIESA, Melchiorre (fl 1758-99), It
R. 1   S. c
CHIHARA, Paul Seiko (1938-   ), USA
R. 1   S. c,9,10,13
CHILCOT, Thomas (c1700-1766), Eng
R. 1   S. c,9
CHILD, Ebenezer USA
              S. 47
CHILD, William (1606/7-1697), Eng
R. 1   S. 2,3,5x,8,16

CHILDS, Barney (1926-   ), USA
    R. 1   S. 9,13,20
CHILESE, Bastian (fl 1608), It
    R. 1   S. c,10
CHIMAKADZE, Archil Ivanovich (1919-   ), USSR
    R. 47   S. 18
CHIN Yen-Ping
              S. c
CHIN Yung-Ch'Eng
              S. c
CHION, Michel (1947-   )
              S. c
CHIRBURY, R. (fl c1400), Eng
    R. 1   S. c
CHIRESCU, Ioan Dumitru (1889-   ), Rum
    R. 1   S. c
CHISHKO, Oles Semyonovich (1895-   ), USSR
    R. 1   S. c,18,10[Tchishko]
CHISTYAKOV, Vladlen Pavlovich (1929-   ), USSR
    R. 47   S. 18
CHIZAT, Emile Abel (1855-   ), Fr
    R. 200   S. e
CHLUBNA, Osvald (1893-1971), Cz
    R. 1   S. 31
CHOPIN, Fryderyk Frantcizek (1810-1849), Pol
    R. 1   S. c,1-11,18,19,22-24,28,32,54(328)
CHORBAJIAN, John, (1936-   ), USA
    R. 19   S. c,10,13
CHOSTAKOVITCH, Dimitry [see SHOSTAKOVICH, Dimitry]
CHOTEM, Neil (1921-   ), Can
    R. 31
CHOU, Wei

CHOU, Wen-Chung (1923-   ), USA
    R. 1   S. c,9,10,13
CHOUDENS, Anthony (1849-1902), Fr
    R. 25   S. e
CHRENNIKOW, Tichon [see KHRENNIKOV, Tikhon]
CHRÉTIEN de TROYES (fl c1160-90), Fr
    R. 1   S. c
CHRÉTIEN-GENARO, Hedwige (1859-1944), Fr
    R. 7   S. e
CHRISTENSEN, Bernhard (1906-   ), Den
    R. 14   S. 4,5x,33,57
CHRISTGAU, Michael, Den
              S. 43
CHRISTIANSEN, Frederick Melius (1871-1955), USA
    R. 19   S. 13
CHRISTIANSEN, Henning (1932-   ), Den
    R. 1   S. 40,24a

CHRISTIANSEN, Paul (1914-   ), USA
R. 19   S. 10
CHRISTINE, Henri (1867-1941), Fr
R. 11   S. c,9,10,42
CHRISTMANN, Johann Friedrich (1752-1817), Ger
R. 1   S. c
CHRISTO, Pedro de (fl 1571-1618), Port
R. 9
CHRISTOV, Dobri (1875-1941), Rum
R. 3   S. c,18
CHRISTY - Where are you tonight?
              S. e
CHRZANOWA, Mikolaj z [see MIKOLAJ z CHRZANOWA]
CHU Chien-Erh
              S. c
CHUECA, Federico (1846-1908), Sp
R. 1   S. c,8-10,39,42
CHUKHADJIAN, Tigran (1837-1898), Arm
R. 1   S. 18
CHULAKI, Mikhail Ivanovich (1908-   ), USSR
R. 1   S. 18,24
CHUMLEIGH - Beloved at your feet
              S. e
CHURCH, John (1675-1741), Eng
R. 1   S. 10
CHURCHILL, Frank E. (1901-1942), USA
R. 23   S. 10
CHURKIN, Nikolai Nikolaiyevich (1869-1964), Russia
R. 47   S. 18
CHURLYONIS, Mikaloyus Konstantinas (1875-1911), Russia
R. 47   S. 18
CHVALY - Bohemian song
              S. e
CIABRANO, Carlo [see CHIABRANO, Carlo Francesco]
CIAJA, Azzolino Bernardino della
   [see DELLA CIAIA, Azzolino Bernardino]
CIAMAGA, Gustave (1930-   ), Can
R. 4
*** CIAMPI, Nina (see note)
CIAMPI, Vincenzo (?1719-1762), It (see note)
R. 1   S. c,2-5,10
CIBBINI, Katherina (nee Kozeluh) (1790-1858), Aus
R. 7   S. c,30,52
CICOGNINI, Alessandro (1906-   ), It
R. 14   S. 9
CICONIA, Johannes (c1335-1411), Neth
R. 1   S. c,4,5,7,8,10,14,16,41
CIFRA, Antonio (1584-1629), It
R. 1   S. c,10,28

CIKKER, Jan (1911-   ), Cz
    R. 1   S. c,5x,6,8,31
CILEA, Francesco (1866-1950), It
    R. 1   S. c,2-10,18,22,24,42-44
CILENŠEK, Johann (1913-   ), Ger
    R. 1   S. 24a
CIMA - Sonata for 3 flutes
                  S. c
CIMA, Andrea (fl 1606-27), It
    R. 1   S. c,53
CIMA, Giovanni Paolo (c1570, fl until 1622), It
    R. 1   S. c,10,16,24,53
CIMAGLIA-ESPINOSA, Lia (1906-   ), Arg
    R. 26   S. 46
CIMARA, Pietro (1887-1967), It
    R. 14   S. 1x,5x,10,24
CIMAROSA, Domenico (1749-1801), It
    R. 1   S. c,1-11,18,42
CIMELLO, Tomaso (c1500->1579),It
    R. 1   S. 10,14,16,32,53
CIMINELLI, Serafino de Aquilano (16th Cent), It
                  S. c[Dallaquila]
CIMMINO, Francesco (1864-   ), It
    R. 200   S. e
CINNA, Oscar de la
                  S. e
CINQUE, Vincenzo (1905-   ), It
    R. 8   S. 10
CIOCIANO - Cielo Turchino
                  S. 44
CIOCIANO, C. A.
                  S. 24
CIOFFI, Giuseppe
                  S. 10
CIORTEA, Tudor (1903-   ), Rum
    R. 4
CIRENEI, Fortunato (1868-   ), It [?]
    R. 10   S. 5x
CIRENEI, M. Luigi It
                  S. 5x,54(318)
CIRONE, Anthony (1941-   ), USA
    R. 19   S. 13
CIRRI, Giovanni Battista (1724-1808), It
    R. 1   S. c,7,8,10
CITKOWITZ, Israel (1909-1974), USA
    R. 1   S. 8,10,13
CIURLIONIS, Mikolajus Konstantinas (1875-1911), Lith
    R. 1   S. c
CIVIL, Alan (1929-   ), Eng
    R. 1

CLAFLIN, Avery (1898-1979), USA
   R. 19   S. 9,10,13
CLAIRLIE, Arnold - pseud [see SCHUTT, Eduard]
CLAPISSON, Louis (1808-1866), Fr
   R. 1   S. e
CLARE - L'anyerament: Romanza
           S. e
CLARIBEL - pseud [see BARNARD, Charlotte Arlington]
CLARK, Caroline (fl 1824)
           S. 30
CLARK, Frederick Scotson (1840-1883), Eng
   R. 1   S. 24
CLARK, Robert Keyes (1925-   ), USA
   R. 19   S. 10,13,20
CLARK, Thomas (1775-1859), Eng
   R. 5   S. c
CLARKE, Emily (1927-   ), ?Eng
   R. 7   S. 24,30
CLARKE, Henry Leland (1907-   ), USA
   R. 1   S. 13
CLARKE, Herbert Lincoln (1867-1945), USA
   R. 1   S. 10
CLARKE, Jeremiah (c1674-1707), Eng
   R. 1   S. c,5,7,8,10,53
CLARKE, Laurence Gordon (1923-   ), USA
   R. 19   S. 10,13
CLARKE, Rebecca [pseud: Anthony TRENT] (1886-1979), USA
   R. 7   S. c,11,13,30,52
CLARKE, Robert Coningsby (1879-1934), Eng
   R. 51   S. 4,5x,10,18
CLAUDE PETIT JEAN [see PETIT JEHAN, Claude]
CLAUDE le JEUNE [see LE JEUNE, Claude]
CLAUSEN - When a days work is over
           S. 5x
CLAUSSEN, Wilhelm (1843-1869), Ger
   R. 98   S. c
CLAUSSING, Franz

CLAVÉ, José Anselmo (1824-1874), Sp
   R. 1   S. 1
CLAVIJO del CASTILLO, Bernardo (c1549-c1626), Sp
   R. 1   S. 10,17,39
CLAY, Frederic (1838-1889), Eng
   R. 1   S. 9,10,24,28
CLAYPOOLE, Edward B. (1883-1952), USA
   R. 23   S. 10,54(312,51)
CLAYTON, William
           S. 10
CLEMENS NON PAPA (c1510-c1556), Franco-Flem
   R. 1   S. c,3,4,6,8,10,11,14-16,41,53

CLÉMENT, Charles-François (c1720->1782) Fr
  R. 1   S. c
*** CLÉMENT, Charles François (1780-1842) (see note)
CLEMENT, Fred W. - Song of the soldiers
            S. 54(357)
CLEMENT, Johan Georg (c1710-1794), Ger
  R. 1
CLEMENTI, Aldo (1925-   ), It
  R. 1   S. c, 10
CLEMENTI, Muzio (1752-1832), It
  R. 1   S. c, 1-5, 7-11, 18
CLEMMENSEN, Niels (1900-1950), Den
  R. 30   S. 33
CLÉRAMBAULT, Louis-Nicolas (1676-1749), Fr
  R. 1   S. c, 1-10, 18, 24, 53
CLERC - Nuit tragique
            S. e
CLERC, Borel
            S. 54(342
CLERGUE, Jean (1896-   ), Fr
  R. 11   S. 10
CLÉRICE, Justin (1863-1908), Arg
  R. 3   S. e
CLERISSE, Robert (1899-1973) Fr
  R. 48, 49, 95 S. c, 10, 22
CLESI, N. J.
            S. 24
CLEVE, Halfdan (1879-1951), Nor
  R. 1   S. c
CLEWING, Carl (1884-1954), Ger
  R. 8   S. c
CLIFFORD - Knights of Columbus
            S. 54(336)
CLIFTON, Arthur - pseud [see CORRI, Philip Anthony]
CLIFTON, John Charles (1781-1841), Eng
  R. 8   S. 5x, 7, 11
CLINTON, Larry (1909-   ), USA
  R. 23   S. 10
CLOSTRE, Adrienne (1921-   ), Fr
  R. 7   S. c
CLOTHIER, Michael (20th Cent)
            S. c
CLOUGH-LEITER, Henry (1874-1956), USA
  R. 1   S. 13
CLOWEZ - French march music
            S. 10, 54(324)
CLUTSAM, George H. (1866-1951), Australia
  R. 4   S. c, 10, 24
CLUZEAU-MORTET, Luis (1889-1957), Uruguay
  R. 1

COAN, Simeon
          S. 10,47
COATES, Eric (1886-1957), Eng
  R. 1   S. c,1x,2-4,5x,9-11,24,54(321,24,34)
COBB, George L. (1886-1942), USA
  R. 23   S. 10
COBB, Gerard Francis (1838-1904), Eng
  R. 39   S. e

COBB, James (d. 1697), Eng
  R. 1
COBB, John (fl 1630-60), Eng
  R. 1   S. 10
COBBOLD, William (1560-1639), Eng
  R. 1   S. c,7,8,10,14
COBERT, Robert (1924-   ), USA
          S. 13
COCAGNAC, A. M.
          S. c
COCCHI, Gioacchino (c1720->1788), It
  R. 1   S. 10
COCCHI, Goffredo (1871-1908), It
  R. 10
COCCIOLA, Giovanni Battista (fl 1610-20), It
  R. 1   S. c
COCHEREAU, Pierre Charles (1924-   ), Fr
  R. 1   S. c,10
COCKER, Norman (1880-1953), Eng
          S. c
COCLICO, Andrianus Petit (c1499->1562), Flem
  R. 1
COCO, Julian B.
          S. c
CODA, Charles (1874-1924)
          S. 24
CODAX, Martin (fl c1230), Galician
  R. 1   S. c,10,16,17,39
CODINA, Genaro (1852-1901), Mex
  R. 22   S. 10,39,54(367)
COE, Anthony (1934-   ), Eng
  R. 60   S. c
COELHO, Manuel [see RODRIGUES COELHO, Manuel]
COENEN, Willem (1837-1918), Neth
  R. 1   S. e
COERNE, Louis Adolphe (1870-1922), USA
  R. 1   S. 10
COERNER - Exaltation
          S. 54(325)
COGAN, Robert David (1930-   ), USA
  R. 19   S. 13

COGSWELL, Hamlin Elisha (1878-   ), USA
   R. 53   S. 54(357)
COHAN, George Michael (1878-1942), USA
   R. 1   S. 10,44,54(348,67)
COHAN, Gunter [see KOKHAN, Gunther]
COHEN, Linda
           S. 30
COHEN, Maurice [pseud: Michael CARR] (1905-   ), USA
           S. 10,13
COHENSOLAL, Robert (1943-   ). Fr
   R. 4
COHN, Arthur (1910-   ), USA
   R. 1   S. 10,13
COINCY [see GAUTIER de COINCY]
COKE-JEPHCOTT, Norman (1893-1962), Eng
   R. 19   S. c,10,12,13
COLACO, Alexander Rey (1854-   ), Port
   R. 3   S. 24
COLASSE, Pascal (1649-1709), Fr
   R. 5   S. 10
COLCORD - Stein song
           S. 54(358)
COLDING-JØRGENSEN, Henrik (1944-   ), Den
   R. 1   S. c,40
COLE, Hugo (1917-   ), Eng
   R. 1   S. 10
COLE, John (1774-1855), USA
   R. 200   S. 47
COLE, Robert A. (1863-1911), USA
   R. 50   S. 10
COLEMAN, Charles (c1605-<1664), Eng
   R. 1   S. c,10
COLEMAN, Cy (1929-   ), USA
   R. 4
COLEMAN, Edward (d. 1669), Eng
   R. 1   S. c
COLEMAN, Ellen (?1893-1973), Eng
   R. 7   S. 3,4,8,30
COLEMAN, Richard Henry Pinwill (1888-   ), Eng
   R. 3   S. 24
COLEMAN, James
           S. e
COLEMANN, Ornette (1930-   ), USA
   R. 1   S. 10,13
COLERIDGE-TAYLOR, Samuel (1875-1912), Eng
   R. 1   S. c,1-6,9,10,20,24,28
COLERUS-GELDERN, Olaf
           S. c
COLES, Bramwell
           S. 54

COLFS, Jan Josef (1708-1771)
        S. c
COLGRASS, Michael (1932-   ), USA
   R. 1   S. 10,13,24a
COLICO, Robert Petit [S. 10] = ? COCLICO
COLIN, Muset [see MUSET, Colin]
COLISTA, Lelio (1629-1680), It
   R. 1   S. c
COLLAN, Karl (1828-1871), Fin [?]
   R. 1   S. 5x
COLLIER, Ronald (1930-   ), Can
   R. 4
COLLIGNON - La barque volee
        S. e
COLLIN de BLAMONT, François (1690-1760), Fr
   R. 1   S. 3,4,5x
COLLIN, André (1898-   ), Bel
   R. 14
COLLINA, Francesco Saverio (1854-   ), It
   R. 10   S. e
COLLINS, Anthony (1893-1963), Eng
   R. 1   S. 4,5x,22

COLLINS, Walter R.
        S. 24
COLLISSON, William Alexander Houston (1865-1920), Ire
   R. 3   S. 5x
COLMAN, Gordon [see LANGFORD, Gordon]
COLOMB, André
        S. e
COLOMBIER, Michel

COLONNA, Giovanni Paolo (1637-1695), It
   R. 1   S. c,3,5x,9-11,53
COLOUTIER, Michel

COLTRANE, Alice (20th Cent), USA
        S. 52
COMBELLE, Alix (1912-   ), Fr
   R. 75   S. 10
COMES, Juan Bautista (1582-1643), Sp
   R. 1   S. 16,39
COMISEL, Florin (1922-   ), Rum
   R. 14
COMPANINO - Notte d'o corre
        S. 10
COMPÈRE, Loyset (c1455-1518), Fr
   R. 1   S. c,4,5x,8,10,14-16,41
COMPTESSA de DIA [see BEATRIZ de DIA]
CONCEIÇÃO, Coque da
        S. 32

CONCEIÇÃO, Diego da (fl 1695), Port
  R. 1   S. c,53
CONETTA, Lewis D. [pseud: Lew CAREY] (1927-   ), USA
  R. 23   S. c
CONFARLONIERI, Giulio (1896-1972), It
  R. 1   S. 10
CONFREY, Edward Elezear (1895-1971), USA
  R. 19   S. 9,10,24
CONGE, Michel (1912-   ), Sp
         S. c
CONINCK, Servaas de [see KONINK, Servaas de]
CONLEY, Eugene (1908-1981), USA
  R. 78   S. 10
CONNER, A. J. R. (fl 1844-60), USA
  R. 50   S. 10,47
CONNER, Thomas (1904-   ), Eng
  R. 37   S. 24
CONETTA, Lewis D. [pseud: Lew CAREY] (1927-   ), USA
  R. 23   S. c
CONNOLLY, Justin Riveagh (1933-   ), Eng
  R. 1
CONNOR, T. W.
         S. e
CONON de BÉTHUNE (c1160-1219), Fr
  R. 1   S. c,10,15
CONRAD, Con - pseud [ie Conrad K. DOBER] (1891-1938),
  USA R. 23   S. 10,24
CONRADI - Hymno national argentio
         S. e
CONRADI, Johann Georg (d. 1699), Ger (see note)
  R. 1
CONRADI, Johann Gottfried (1820-1896), Nor
  R. 1
CONRADI, Johann Gottfried (fl c1724), Ger
  R. 5   S. c,14
*** CONRADI, Johann Gottfried (?-1700?) (see note)
CONRADI, Johann Melchior (1675-1756), Ger
  R. 1
CONSEIL, Jean (1498-1535), Fr
  R. 1   S. 5x,10,14-16
CONSIGLIO - Hymn of Torino football club
         S. 54(333)
CONSILIUM, Johannes [see CONSEIL, Jean]
CONSOLI, Marc-Antonio (1941-   ), USA
  R. 19   S. 13
CONSTANT, Franz (1910-)

CONSTANT, Marius (1925-   ), Fr
  R. 1   S. c,9 10,20

CONSTANTEN, Thomas Charles (1944-   ), USA
  R. 23
CONSTANTINE - Songs of the village women
              S. 54(357)
CONSTANTINESCU, Dan (1931-   ), Hun
  R. 4
CONSTANTINESCU, Paul (1909-1963), Rum
  R. 1   S. c,18,24
CONSTANZI, (18th Cent) [Croucher]
  = COSTANZI, Giovanni Battista (1704-1778)
CONTANT, Alexis (1858-1918), Can
  R. 1
CONTI, Angelo (b c1603), It
  R. 5   S. c
CONUS, Julius Eduardovich
  [see KONYUS, Julius Eduardovich]
CONVERSE, Frederick Shepherd (1871-1940), Fr
  R. 1   S. 8,10,13
CONVERSI, Girolamo (fl 1571-5), It
  R. 1   S. 8,10,16
CONWAY, Marmaduke Percy (1885-   ), Eng
  R. 77
CONYNGHAM, Barry (1944-   ), Australia
  R. 1   S. 29,37
COOK, Eric Sydney - Bolivar
              S. 18
COOK, John (1918-   ), Eng
  R. 14   S. c,10,13
COOK, Will Marion (1869-1944), USA
  R. 1   S. 13
COOKE, Arnold (1906-   ), Eng
  R. 1   S. c,10,20,24a
COOKE, Benjamin (1734-1793), Eng
  R. 1   S. c
COOKE, J. [Old Hall Ms], (d ?1419), Eng
  R. 1
COOKE, James Francis (1875-1960), USA
  R. 19   S. 13
COOKE, Thomas Simpson (1782-1848), Ire
  R. 1   S. 5x,11
COOLEY, Carlton (1898-   ), USA
  R. 19   S. 10,13,23
COOLIDGE, Clark (1939-   )
              S. 10
COOLIDGE, Elizabeth Sprague (1864-1953), USA
  R. 1   S. 3,5,11,13,30
COOLIDGE, Peggy Stuart (1913-1981), USA
  R. 19   S. 9,13,30,52
COOLS, Eugène (1877-1936), Fr
  R. 8   S. 24

COOME, Eric

COOPER - Sweet Genevieve
          S. e
COOPER, Henry - pseud [see BOHM, Karl]
COOPER, John
          S. 10
COOPER, John Craig (1925-   ), USA
     R. 14   S. 13
COOPER, Kent (1880-1965), USA
     R. 23   S. 13
COOPER, Paul (1926-   ), USA
     R. 1   S. 10,13
COOPER, Robert [see COWPER, Robert]
COOPER, Rose Marie (1937-   ), USA
     R. 7   S. 30
COOPER, W. - pseud [see BEHR, Franz]
COOPER, Walter Gaze Thomas (1895-   ), Eng
     R. 14   S. 8
COOTE, Charles (the younger)
          S. 10
COOTS, John Frederick (1897-   ), USA
     R. 23   S. 10
COPE, David (1941-   ), USA
     R. 19   S. 10,13
COPE, Samuel (1856-1947), Eng [?]
     R. 85   S. 54(320,54)
COPLAND, Aaron (1900-   ), USA
     R. 1   S. c,2-13,18-21,24,25-27,54(348)
COPPINI, Alessandro (c1465-1527), It
     R. 1   S. 14
COPPOLA, Piero (1888-1971), It
     R. 1   S. 1,2,24
COPRARIO, John (c1575-c1626), Eng
     R. 1   S. c,8,10,14-16
CORBEIL, Pierre de [see PIERRE de CORBIE]
CORBETT, Felix (1861-   ), Eng
     R. 37   S. e
CORBETTA, Egidio

CORBETTA, Francesco (c1615-1681), It
     R. 1   S. c,3,4,8
CORDEIRO da SILVA, João (d c1790), Port
     R. 34
CORDEL, Andrew E. ?USA
          S. 13
CORDELL, Frank (20th Cent), Eng
          S. 10
CORDERO, Roque (1917-   ), Panama
     R. 1   S. 9,20,24a

CORDIER, Baude (fl early 15th Cent), Fr
   R. 1   S. c, 10, 16
CORDLE, Andrew E. ?USA
            S. 13
CORELLI, Arcangelo (1653-1713), It
   R. 1   S. c, 1-11, 18, 19, 21-24, 32
CORFE, Joseph (1741-1820), Eng
   R. 1   S. c
CORIGLIANO, John (1938-   ), USA
   R. 19   S. 10, 13, 24
CORKINE, William (fl 1610-12), Eng
   R. 1   S. c, 2, 3, 5x, 10, 14, 16, 32
CORNAGO, Johannes (fl c1455-85), Sp
   R. 1   S. c, 10, 14, 16, 17, 39
CORNAZANO, Antonio (c1430-1484), It [dancing master]
   R. 1   S. c
CORNELIUS, Peter (1824-1874), Ger
   R. 1   S. c, 1-10, 24, 25, 27, 28, 42
CORNELL, Klaus (1932-   ), Swiss
   R. 14
CORNER, David Gregor (1585-1648), Silesia
   R. 1   S. 5x, 8
CORNER, Philip (1933-   ), USA
   R. 14   S. 13
CORNET, Peeter (c1570-1633), Flem
   R. 1   S. c, 7, 8, 10, 14, 16, 53
CORNYSH, Robert (1465-1523)
            S. c, 10, 15, 16
CORNYSHE, William (d. 1523), Eng
   R. 1   S. c, 10, 16
CORRADINI, Nicolò (d. 1646), It
   R. 1   S. 53
CORREA BRAGA, Antonio (17th Cent)
            S. c
CORREA de ARAUXO, Francisco (c1576-1654), Sp
   R. 1   S. c, 9, 10, 15-17, 39, 53
CORREA, Padre Manuel (d. 1653), Port
   R. 1   S. 10, 39
CORREGGIO, Claudio da [see MERULO, Claudio]
CORRETTE, Gaspard (d <1733), Fr
   R. 1   S. c, 9, 10, 53
CORRETTE, Michel (1709-1795), Fr
   R. 1   S. c, 8-10, 24, 53
CORRI - Baby's sweetheart
            S. 54(314)
CORRI, Philip Anthony [pseud: Arthur CLIFTON]
   (1784-1832) R. 5   S. 10
CORSI, Giuseppe (d >1690), It
   R. 1   S. 2, 5x, 7

CORSIN (fl 1795-1800), Fr
   R. 5   S. c
CORTECCIA, Francesco (1502-1571), It
   R. 1   S. c,10,14,16
CORTÉS, Ramiro (1933-   ), USA
   R. 1   S. 10,13,24a,39
CORTI, Mario (1882-1957), It
   R. 14   S. 24
CORTOPASSI, Domenico (1877-1962), It
   R. 14   S. 5x,24,54(353)
CORY, Eleanor (1943-   ), USA
   R. 7   S. 52
CORY, George (1920-   ), USA
   R. 19   S. 10,13,25,27
COSACCHI, Stephan (1903-   )
   R. 14   S. c
COSLOW, Sam (1902-1982), USA
   R. 23   S. 10,24
COSSET, François (c1610->1664), Fr
   R. 1
COSSETTO, Emil (1912-   ), Yug
   R. 1   S. c
COSSMANN, Bernhard (1822-1910), Ger
   R. 1   S. c
COSTA (16-17th Cent) - Ricercare XXIV (Music de Joye)
           S. c
COSTA, Maria Helena da (20th Cent), Brazil
           S. 52
COSTA, Pasquale Mario (1858-1933), It
   R. 8   S. 24,34,44,54(311)
COSTA, Sir Michael (1808-1884), Eng
   R. 1   S. 10
COSTANTINI, Alessandro (1581-1657), It
   R. 1   S. c,10,16
COSTANTINI, Alessandro (1709?-1795) (see note)

COSTANZI, Giovanni Battista (1704-1778), It
   R. 8   S. c
COSTE, Gaspard (fl 1530-43), Fr
   R. 5   S. 16,32
COSTE, Napoléon (1806-1883), Fr
   R. 1   S. c,10
COSTELY, Guillaume (c1530-1606), Fr
   R. 1   S. c,2-8,10,11,14-16,53
COSYN, Benjamin (c1570->1652), Eng
   R. 1   S. c,5x,10
COTEL, Morish Moshe (1943-   ), USA
   R. 23   S. 13
COTTE, Rolland (1951-   )

COTTENET, Richard
   S. 24
COTTON, Frederick
   S. e
COTTONE - Cradle song
   S. 5x
COTTONI, Charles

COTTRAU, Teodoro (1827-1879), It
 R. 1   S. c,4,5x,10,34,44
COUCY, Chatelain de [see CHASTELAIN de COUCY]
COUILLART (fl 1534) - Viri Galilaei
 R. 5   S. 3-5
COULOMB-ST. MARCOUX, Micheline (1938-), Can
 R. 7   S. 30,52
COULTHARD, Jean (1908-), Can
 R. 1   S. 10,30,52
COUPELLE, Piereken de la [see PIEREKEN de la COUPELLE]
COUPERIN, Armand-Louis (1727-1789), Fr
 R. 1   S. c,24
COUPERIN, François (c1631-1708/12), Fr
 R. 1   S. 8
COUPERIN, François (1668-1733), Fr
 R. 1   S. c,2-8,10,11,18,23,24,32,53
COUPERIN, Gervais-François (1759-1826), Fr
 R. 1   S. c
COUPERIN, Louis (c1626-1661), Fr
 R. 1   S. c,3-8,10,11,32,53
COUPERIN, Pierre Louis (1755-1789), Fr
 R. 1   S. 2-5
COURBOIS, Philippe (fl 1705-30), Fr
 R. 1   S. 10
COURS, Niels La (1944-), Den
   S. 40
COURTOIS, Jean (fl 1530-45), ?Franco-Flem
 R. 1   S. c,10,16
COURVILLE, Joachim Thibault de (d.1581), Fr
 R. 1   S. c,5x
COUSINEAU, Jacques Georges (1760-1824), Fr
 R. 8   S. c
COUSINS, John (1943-), New Zealand

COUSINS, Major Thomas (1914-1972), USA
 R. 19   S. 10,13
COUTURE, Guillaume (1851-1915), Can
 R. 1
COVERLY, Robert (1864-1944), Port
 R. 4   S. e

COWAN, Marie - Waltzing Matilda
             S. 5x,10,54(364)
COWARD, James M. (1824-1880), Eng
   R. 3   S. 24
COWARD, Noël (1899-1973), Eng
   R. 1   S. 3,4,9-11,24
COWELL, Henry Dixon (1897-1965), USA
   R. 1   S. c,2-13,22,24,27
COWELS, Eugene (1860-1948), USA
   R. 53   S. 10,13,24a
COWEN, Frederic Hymen (1852-1935), Eng
   R. 1   S. c
COWIE, Edward (1943-   ), Eng
   R. 1   S. c
COWLES, Darleen L. (1942-   ), USA
   R. 19   S. 52
COWPER [Cooper], Robert (c1474-c1535), Eng
   R. 1   S. 10,15,16
COWPER, John [see COPRARIO, John]
CRACOVIENSIS, Nicolaus [see MIKOLAJ z KRAKOWA]
CRACOVIENSIS, N. Z. [see N. Z. CRACOVIENSIS]
CRADDY, Peter [see HAYSOM, Peter - pseud]
CRAGUN - Chicago, we´re true to you
             S. 54(319)
CRAMER - Waltz
             S. 5x
CRAMER, Georges (1909-   )
             S. c
CRAMER, Johann Baptiste (1771-1858), Ger
   R. 1   S. c,7,8,10,24
CRAMPTON, Ernest
             S. e
CRANDELL, Robert Eugene (1910-   ), USA
   R. 19   S. 8,10,12,13
CRANFORD, William (16th Cent), Eng
   R. 1   S. 5x,7,10
CRAPPIUS, Andreas (c1542-1623), Ger
   R. 1   S. 16
CRASSOT, Richard (b c1530), Fr
   R. 1   S. 14,16
CRAUS, Stephan (15th Cent)
             S. c,10,16,32
CRAWFORD (SEEGER), Ruth (1901-1953), USA
   R. 1   S. c,2,10,13,52
CRAWFORD, Robert McArthur (1899-1961), USA
   R. 19   S. 10,54(313,63)
CRAXTON, Harold (1885-1971), Eng
   R. 1   S. e
CRECQUILLON, Thomas (d. 1557), Franco-Flem
   R. 1   S. 7,8,10,14-16,53

CREMA, Giovanni Maria de [see GIOVANNI MARIA de CREMA]
CRÉMIEUX, Oktav (1872-   )
        S.18,24a
CRESCENZO, Costantino de (1847-1911), It (see note)
    R.10   S.10,44
CRESCENZO, Vincent de (1875-   ), It (see note)
    R.52   S.10
CRESHEVSKY, Noah (1945-   ), USA
    R.19   S.13
CRESPO, Enrique (1941-   )
        S.c
CRESPO, Jorge Gomes [see GOMES CRESPO, Jorge]
CRESTON, Paul (1906-   ), USA
    R.1   S.c,3-5,7-13,18,20,22
CRICHTON, Donald
        S.e
CRIMP, Herbert Edward (1870-   ), Eng
    R.37   S.e
CRIST, Bainbridge (1883-1969), USA
    R.1   S.4,5x,10,13
CRISTOFARO, A. de - Chiarastella; Vola, vola
        S.e
CRISTOFARO, Ferdinando de (fl 1890)
    R.10   S.24
CROCE, Giovanni (c1557-1609), It
    R.1   S.c,2-5,7,8,10,14-16
CROCHET, Evelyne
        S.10
CROES, Henri-Jacques de (1705-1786), S. Neth
    R.1   S.c,9,10,24
CROFT, William (1678-1727), Eng
    R.1   S.c,1x,5x,8-10,24,53
CROIX, de la [see PETRUS de CRUCE]
CROLEY, Randell (1946-   ), USA
    R.14   S.22
CRONER, Daniel (1656-1740), Transylvania
    R.1   S.c
CROOK, John (?-1922), Eng
    R.44   S.4
CROSLEY, Larry (Lawrence Eugene) (1932-   ), Can
    R.81
CROSS, Lowell (1938-   ), USA
    R.19   S.10,13
CROSSE, Gordon (1937-   ), Eng
    R.1   S.c,9,10,24
CROSSMAN, G. - Dancing down
        S.54(322)
CROTCH, William (1775-1847), Eng
    R.1   S.c,5x,10

CROUCH, Frederick Nicholls (1808-1896), Eng
   R.1   S.4
CROWTHER, John (1895-   )
              S.10,24[Crother]
CRUCE, Petrus de [see PETRUS de CRUCE]
CRUFT, Adrian (1921-   ), Eng
   R.1   S.c
CRÜGER, Johannes (1598-1662), Ger
   R.1   S.c,2,3,8,10,11
CRUMB, George (1929-   ), USA
   R.1   S.c,9,10,13,24
CRUSELL, Bernard Henrik (1775-1838), Fin
   R.1   S.c,10,20,40,56
CRUZ, Agostinho da (c1590-c1632), Port
   R.1   S.c,10,53
CSÁSZÁR, György (1813-1850), Hun
   R.15   S.24
CSERMÁK, Antal György (c1774-1822), Hun.
   R.1   S.24
CSEZMICEI, Janos

              S.10
CSUKEI, Istvan (16th Cent)
              S.c
CUCKSON, Robert (1942-   ), Australia
              S.29
CUESTA, Francisco (1889-1921)
              S.8,10
CUGLEY, Ian (1945-   ), Australia
   R.1   S.29 37
CUI, César (1835-1918), Russia
   R.1   S.c,1-8,10,11,18 23,24
CUMBERWORTH, Starling A. (1915-   ), USA
   R.19   S.24a
CUMMING, Richard (1928-   ), USA
   R.23   S.8-10,13,28
CUNDELL, Edric (1893-1961), Eng
   R.1   S.2,55
CUNDICK, Robert Milton (1926-   ), USA
   R.23   S.c,10,12,13
CUNNINGHAM, Arthur (1928-   ), USA
   R.1   S.10,13
CUPIS de CAMARGO, François (1719-1764), Fr
   R.5   S.5x
CURCI, Alberto (1886-1973), It
   R.14   S.9,24
CURILLIER [S.24] = CUVILLIER, Charles
CURRAN, Alvin (1938-   ), USA
   R.14   S.13
CURRAN, Pearl Gildersleeve (1875-1941), USA
   R.7   S.10,13,52

CURSCHMANN, Karl Friedrich (1805-1841), Ger
   R. 1   S. c
CURTI, Carlos
           S. e
CURTIS, Ernesto de (1875-1937), It
   R. 3   S. c, 5x, 10, 18 34, 43, 44
CURTIS, G. Battista de (1860-1926), It
   R. 10   S. c, 24
CURTIS-SMITH, Curtis (1941-   ), USA
   R. 19   S. 10, 13, 24a
CURWEN - Border ballad
           S. e
CURZIO, Elaine
           S. 30
CURZON, Frederic (1899-1973), Eng
   R. 1   S. c, 5x, 54(311, 17, 56)
CUSHING, Charles (1905-   ), USA
   R. 1   S. 8, 10, 13, 19, 21
CUSTER, Arthur (1923-   ), USA
   R. 19   S. c, 9, 10, 13, 20, 24a
CUTTING, Francis (fl 1608-13), Eng
   R. 1   S. c, 5x, 8, 10, 14-16, 32
CUVILLIER, Charles (1877-1955), Fr
   R. 1   S. e, 5x, 10, 24 [Curillier]
CUZENS - Two lawyers when a knotty cause were o'er
           S. 10
CYEAT, Renward (1545-1614)

           S. 16
CYR, Gordon Conrad (1925-   ), USA
   R. 19   S. 10, 13
CZAJKOWSKI, Michael (1939-   ), USA
   R. 19   S. 9
CZAPEK, Leopold Eustache (1840-   ), Pol
   R. 74   S. c
CZERNIK, Willy (1901-   ), Ger
   R. 4   S. 5x, 10
CZERNOHORSKY, Bohuslav Matej
   [see CERNOHORSKY, Bohuslav Matej]
CZERNY, Carl (1791-1857), Aus
   R. 1   S. c, 2-10
CZERNY, Frantisek

CZERNY, Joseph (1785-1842) [publisher] (see note)
           S. c
CZERWONKY, Richard Rudolph (1886-1949) , USA
   R. 19   S. 24
CZIBULKA, Alphons (1842-1894), Hun
   R. 1   S. c, 10, 24, 54(345, 66)
CZIFFRA, György (1921-   ), Fr
   R. 1   S. c, 10

DABROWSKI, Florian (1913-   ), Pol
  R.14   S.24a
DAÇA, Esteban [see DAZA, Esteban]
DACH, Simon (1605-1659), Ger
  R.1
DA COSTA, Noel George (1930-   ), USA
  R.19   S.10,13
D´ACOURT [see HAUCOURT, Johannes]
DACRE, Harry - pseud [ie Frank DEAN]
          S.10,54(335)
DADASHYEV - Scherzino
          S.24a
DADMUN, John William (1819-1890), USA
  R.53
DAETWYLER, Jean (1907-   ), Swiss
  R.41   S.c,24a
DAGGERE, William (15-16th Cent), Eng
  R.5   S.c,10,16
DAGINCOUR, François (1684-1758), Fr
  R.1   S.c,10,53
DAHL, Adrian (1864-1935), Sweden
  R.30   S.43
DAHL, Ingolf (1912-1970), USA
  R.1   S.7-10,13,20,22,24
DAHLGREN, Fredrik August (1816-1895), Sweden
  R.30   S.e
DAIGNEAULT, Robert (1940-   )

DAKIN, Charles (1930-   ), Eng
  R.4   S.22
DALAMONT, Gordon [S.10,22] = DELAMONT, Gordon
DALAYRAC, Nicolas-Marie (1753-1809), Fr
  R.1   S.c,2-5,10,18
DALBERG, Johann Friedrich Hugo (1760-1812), Ger
  R.1   S.c,24
D´ALBERT, Charles Louis Napoleon
  [see ALBERT, Charles Louis Napoleon]
DALBY, C. W. USA
          S.54(346)
DALBY, Martin (1942-   ), Scot
  R.1   S.c
DALCROZZE - Danse frivole (vi & p)
          S.24a
DALE, Benjamin (1885-1943), Eng
  R.1   S.c,5x,24
DALL ABACO, Evaristo Felice (1675-1742), It
  R.1   S.c,3-5,8,10,11,18,24
DALL ABACO, Giuseppe Clement Ferdinando (1709-1805), It
  R.8   S.8,10

DALLA CASA, Girolamo (d.1601), It
   R.1   S.c
DALLAPICCOLA, Luigi (1904-1975), It
   R.1   S.c,8-10,20,24
DALLAQUILA [see CIMINELLI, Serafino de Aquilano]
DALMANIS, Indulis (1922-   )
             S.18
DAL POZZO, Vincenzo (fl 1585-1612), It
   R.1
DALUA [see ALBA, Alonso de]
DALVIMARE, Martin-Pierre (1772-1839), Fr
   R.1   S.c
DALY, M. E. - pseud [see HAYMAN, Richard]
*** DALZA, Esteban (16th Cent) (see note)
DALZA, Joan Ambrosio (fl 1508), It
   R.5   S.c,5x,8,10,14,16,32
DAMARE, Eugene (1840-1919)

DAMAS, Tomás (fl 1860), Sp
   R.9   S.5x[Damas: Cantos]
DAMASE, Jean-Michel (1928-   ), Fr
   R.1   S.c,7,8,10,18
DAMBIS, Pauls (1936-   ), Lat
   R.1   S.c,18
DAMBOIS, Maurice (1889-1969), Bel
   R.25   S.24a
D´AMBROSIO, Alfredo (1871-1914), It
   R.8   S.5x,10,22,24
D´AMBRUYS, Honoré (17th Cent), Fr
   R.1   S.c
DAMETT, ?Thomas (?1389/90-1436/7), Eng
   R.1   S.c,2,3,5x,10,14,16
DAMIAN, Father (d.1729)

DAMJAKOB, Paul (1939-   )
             S.c
DAMMONIS, Innocentius (15-16th Cent)
             S.c
DAMPIERRE, Marc Antoine (1676-1756), Fr
   R.1   S.c,10
DAMROSCH, Walter Johannes (1862-1950), Ger
   R.1   S.2-4,10,13
DAN, Ikuma (1924-   ), Japan
             S.50
DANA, Mary Stanly Bunce (fl 1857), USA
             S.e
DANBÉ, Jules (1840-1905), Fr
   R.8   S.24
DANBY, John (c1757-1798), Eng
   R.1   S.c

DANCLA, (Jean-Baptiste) Charles (1817-1907), Fr
   R.1   S.10,24
DANDARA, Liviu (1933-   ), Rum
   R.33   S.24a
DANDELOT, Georges (1895-1965), Fr
   R.14   S.3,4
DANDRIEU, Jean-François (c1682-1738), Fr
   R.1   S.c,2-10,18,24,53
DANDRIEU, Pierre (d.1733), Fr
   R.1   S.10,53
DANGEL, Arthur (1931-   )
             S.c
DANGLEBERT, Jean-Henri (1635-1691), Fr
   R.1   S.c,7,8,10,53
DANICAN-PHILIDOR, Andre [see PHILIDOR, Andre]
DANIDERFF, Leo
             S.24
DANIEL, Arnaut (12th Cent), Fr
   R.1   S.c
DANIEL, John [see DANYEL, John]
DANIEL-LESUR, Jean Yves (1908-   ), Fr
   R.1   S.c,7-10,18,32
DANIELS, Charles [see MORET, Niel - pseud]
DANIELS, Mabel Wheeler (1878-1971), USA
   R.1   S.10,13,30,52
DANIELSSON, Christer (1942-   ), Sweden
             S.c,40
DANILOV, Viktor Petrovich (1932-   )
             S.18
DANKEVITCH, Konstantin Fiodorovich (1905-   ), USSR
   R.14   S.8,9,18,42
DANKOWSKI, Adalbert (Wojciech) (c1760->1800), Pol
   R.1   S.8
DANKS, Hart Pease (1834-1903), USA
   R.53   S.10,24,54(356)
DANNENBERG, Fr. - pseud [see KARK, Frederik]
DANNIBALE, Vincenzo
             S.10
DANNSTRÖM, (Johann) Isodor (1812-1897), Sweden
   R.1
DA NOLA, Giovanni Domenico del Giovane
   [see NOLA, Giovanni Domenico del Giovane da]
DANTY, Leopold
             S.e
DANYEL, John (c1564-c1626), Eng
   R.1   S.8,10,14,16
DANZI - Mattinata fiorentia; O mia bella madonna
             S.10[D´Arizi]
DANZI, Franz (1763-1826), Ger
   R.1   S.c,7-10,19,20,24a

DANZI, Margarethe (1768-1800), Ger
    R.1   S.c,30,52,24a
DAO, Nguyen-Thien (1940-   ), Vietnam
             S.c
DA-OZ, Ram (1929-   ), Isr
    R.1
DAQUIN, Louis-Claude (1694-1772), Fr
    R.1   S.c,1-11,18,24,53
DARASSE, Xavier (1934-   ), Fr
    R.1
DARCIER, J. - Versez-moi du vin bleu
             S.e
DARCY, Claude
             S.24
DARCY, Thomas Francis Jr. (1895-1968), USA
    R.23   S.54(341,45,63)
DARE, Elkanah Kelsey (1782-1826), USA
             S.10,47
DARE, Margaret Marie (1902-1976), Scot
    R.7   S.8
DAREWSKI, Herman (1883-1947), Eng
    R.1   S.24
DAREWSKI, Max (1894-1929)
             S.24
D´AREZZO, Guido [see GUIDO d´AREZZO]
DARGOMÏZHSKY, Alexander Sergeyevich (1813-1869), Russia
    R.1   S.c,1x,2-11,18,24,42
DARIEN - Ninon, voici des roses
             S.e
D´ARIZI [S.10] = ?D´ANZI

DARKE, Harold (1888-1976), Eng
    R.1   S.c,10
DARNLEY, Herbert
             S.e
DAROLZI BARDOS, Tamas

DARTER, Thomas Eugene Jr. (1949-   ), USA
    R.80   S.13
DARZINŠ, Emil (1875-1910), Lat
    R.1   S.18
DASCANIO, Josquin [see JOSQUIN DESPREZ]
DASER, Ludwig (c1525-1589), Ger
    R.1   S.c,10,16
DASHOW, James (1944-   ), USA
    R.19
DAUPRAT, Louis Francois (1781-1868), Fr
    R.1
DAUROV, A. (1940-   )
             S.18

DAUS, Avraham (1902-1974), Isr
   R.1   S.10
DAUVERGNE, Antoine (1713-1797), Fr
   R.1   S.c,9,10,24a
DAUVERGNE, Francois Georges Auguste (1800-1874), Fr
   R.57   S.c
DAVELUY, Raymond (1926-   ), Can
   R.14
DAVICO, Vincenzo (1889-1969), It
   R.1   S.c,5x,10
DAVID, Félicien César (1810-1876), Fr
   R.1   S.c,2-4,5x,10
DAVID, Ferdinand (1810-1873), Ger
   R.1   S.c,10
DÁVID, Gyula (1913-1977), Hun
   R.1   S.c,8-10,23,24a
DAVID, Johann Nepomuk (1895-1977), Aus
   R.1   S.c,10,18,24
DAVID, L. - Tents of arabs
              S.54(360)
DAVID, Lee (1891-1978), USA
   R.23   S.24
DAVID, N. - Benediction des abeilles
              S.5x
DAVID, Thomas Christian (1925-   ), Aus
   R.14   S.24a
DAVIDE da BERGAMO, (Padre) Felice Moretti (1791-1842),
   It (see note)   R.10   S.c
DAVIDENKO, Alexander Alexandrovich (1899-1934), Russia
   R.1   S.5x,18
DAVIDOFF - Trifle not with love; Night love and moon
              S.e
DAVÏDOV, Karl Yulievich (1838-1889), Russia
   R.1   S.c,3,4,10
DAVIDOV, Shalva (1934-   )
              S.18
DAVIDOVSKY, Mario (1934-   ), Arg
   R.1   S.10,13,21
DAVIDSON, Charles Stuart (1929-   ), USA
   R.23   S.13
DAVIDSON, Malcolm Gordon (1891-   ), Eng
   R.77   S.10
DAVIES, Dotie [see TEMPLE, Hope - pseud]
DAVIES, Evan Thomas (1879-   ), Wales
   R.51   S.5x
DAVIES, Henry Walford (1869-1941), Eng
   R.1   S.c,2-6,8,10,24,54(353)
DAVIES, Hubert (1893-1965), Wales
   R.83   S.5x

DAVIES, Peter Maxwell (1934-   ), Eng
   R.1   S.c,9,20,28
DAVIES, William (1859-1907), Wales
           S.5x,7
DA VIOLA, Paulinho
           S.c
DAVIS - A nation again
           S.e
DAVIS, Benny (1895-   ), USA
   R.23   S.24
DAVIS, Carl (1936-   ), USA
           S.c
DAVIS, Katherine K. (1892-1980), USA
   R.19   S.10,13,30,52
DAVIS, Roland
           S.54(335)
DAVIS, Sharon (1937-   ), USA
   R.19   S.13,30,52
DAVIS, Gussie L. (1863-1899), USA
   R.50   S.10
DAVISON, John H. (1930-   ), USA
   R.19   S.10,13
DAVISSON, Ananias (fl 1825), USA
   R.53   S.47
DAVITASHVILY, Meri (1924-   ), USSR
   R.47   S.18
DAVY, John (1763-1824), Eng
   R.1   S.e
DAVY, Richard (c1465-c1507), Eng
   R.1   S.c,8,9,14,16
DAVYDOV, Charles (1838-1889)
   R.10   S.18
DAWES, Charles Gates (1865-1951), USA
   R.53   S.1x,13,24
DAWSON, William Levi (1899-   ), USA
   R.1   S.9,10,13
DAY, J. M. USA
           S.47
DAY, Maude Craske (1876-   ), Eng
   R.37   S.e
DAZA, Esteban (fl 1575), Sp
   R.1   S.10,16,17,32,39
DEACON - Two eyes of grey
           S.e
DEAK, Csaba (1932-   ), Sweden
   R.14   S.20,40
DEAK-BARDOS, Gyorgy

DEAL, Edgar M. (1902-   ), Ire
   R.40   S.49

DEAN, USA - Consolation
          S.10,47
DEAN, Frank [see DACRE, Harry - pseud]
DE ANGELES - Se potessi
          S.e
DEARNLEY, Christopher (1930-   ), Eng
     R.1   S.c
DEBASQUE - Japanese Carnival
          S.54(335)
DE BELLIS, Giovanni Battista (c1585-c1623), It
     R.1
DE BOECK, August [see BOECK, August de]
DEBRAS, Louis (1938-   ) Bel
     R.25
DEBUSSY, Claude (1862-1918), Fr
     R.1   S.c,1-11,18-28,42,32,54(329)
DECHTJAREV, Stepan (1766-1813)
     R.47   S.c
DECIUS, Nikolaus (c1485->1546), Ger
     R.1   S.c
DECKER, Joachim (c1575-1611), Ger
     R.1
DECKER, Johann (1598-1668), Ger
     R.5   S.10,53
DECOURCELLE, Paul [pseud: Heinrich TELLAM] (1854-   ),
     Fr   R.3   S.24
DE CRESCENZO [see CRESCENZO]
DE CROES [see CROES, Henri Jacques de]
DECRUCK, Maurice (1896-1954), USA (see note)
     R.48   S.c,5x,10
DECSENYI [Descenyi], Janos (1927-   ), Hun
     R.1   S.c
DE CURTIS, Ernesto [see CURTIS, Ernesto de]
DEDEKAM, Sophie (1820-1894), Den
     R.7   S.e
DEDEKIND, Constantin Christian (1628-1715), Ger
     R.1   S.c
DEDLER, Rocus (1779-1822), Ger
     R.8   S.c
DEDRICK, Christopher (1947-   ), USA
     R.19   S.10,13,22
DEDRICK, Lyle Rusty (1918-   ), USA
     R.19   S.10,13,22
DEFAIX - Les Allobroges
          S.54(312)
DEFAY, Jean-Michel (1932-   ), Fr
     R.14   S.c,10,18
DE FESCH, Willem (1687-?1757), Neth
     R.1   S.c,5x,8,10,24,41

DEFFÈS, Louis Pierre (1819-1900), Fr
   R.3   S.e
DEFOSSEZ, René (1905-   ), Bel
   R.1   S.7,8,20,24,36
DEFRONCIACO (14th Cent), Fr
   R.1   S.c,16,32
DE FUENTAS, Eduardo Sanchez
   [see SANCHEZ de FUENTES, Eduardo]
DEGEMBLOUX, Johannes Franchois
   [see FRANCHOIS, Johannes]
DEGEN, Helmut (1911-   ), Ger
   R.1   S.c
DEGEN, Johann (c1585-1637), Ger
   R.1   S.c
DEGEYTER, Pierre (1849-1932), Fr
   R.4   S.c
DEGLI ANTONI, Giovanni Battista (1660->1696), It
   R.1   S.c,10
DE GREEF, Arthur (1862-1940), Bel
   R.1   S.c,8
DE GROOT, David (1881-1933)
           S.24a
DE HARTMANN, Thomas
           S.10
DEHLAVI, Hossein
           S.c
DEISS, Lucien (1921-   ), Fr
   R.21
DEJONCKER, Théodore (1894-1952), Bel
   R.4
DE KOVEN, Reginald (1859-1920), USA
   R.1   S.2-4,5x,10,13,24
DELA, Maurice (1919-1978), Can
   R.14   S.10
DELACHER, Hermann (1918-   ), Aus
   R.4   S.c
DELACROIX - Fantasia for cl & orch
           S.19
DELAGE, Maurice (1879-1961), Fr
   R.1   S.c,7,10,27
DELAHAYE (17th Cent)
           S.14
DELAHAYE, Jean (15th Cent), Fr
   R.11   S.10,14,16
DELALANDE, Michel Richard
   [see LALANDE, Michel Richard de]
DELAMONT, Gordon (1918-1981), Can
   R.81   S.10,22[Dalamont]
DELANGE, Edgar (1904-1949), USA
   R.23   S.10

DELANGE, Herman-Francois (1715-1781), S. Neth
    R.1   S.24a
DELANNOY, Marcel (1898-1962), Fr
    R.1   S.2,4,5,8,18,24
DE LA PUENTE - El Guitarrico (zarzuela)
                S.39
DE LARA, Isidore (1858-1935), Eng
    R.10   S.e
DELARUE, Gervais (1751-1833), Fr
    R.11   S.24
DE LA RUE, Pierre [see LA RUE, Pierre de]
DE LATRE, Petit Jean (c1510-1569), Neth
    R.1   S.7,8,10,14,16
DELAVIGNE, Philibert [see LAVIGNE, Philibert de]
DEL BORGO, Elliot Anthony (1938-   ), USA
    R.19   S.10,13,22
DELDEN, Lex van (1919-   ), Neth
    R.1   S.7,10,22
DE LEEUW, Ton [see LEEUW, Ton de]
DELEPLANGUE (1746-1801) [see DELLEPLANQUE]
DELERUE, Georges (1925-   ), Fr
    R.1   S.c
DELFIN - La Guinda
                S.e
DELFINO - Milonguita
                S.e
D'ELIA, Antonio (1897-1958), It
    R.8   S.54(312,25-28,34)
D'ELIA, N. N. - Hymn del Fianziere
                S.54(333)
DELIBES, Léo (1836-1891), Fr
    R.1   S.c,1-11,18,24,28,34,42,54(344)
DELISLE, Rouget [see ROUGET de LISLE, Claude-Joseph]
DELIUS, Frederick (1862-1934), Eng
    R.1   S.c,1-11,18,23-25,27
DELLA CIAIA, Azzolino Bernardino (1671-1755), It
    R.1   S.c,5x,8,10
DELL ACQUA, Eva (1860-1930), It/Bel
    R.7   S.4,5x,10,18,52
DELLA GOSTENA, Giovanni Battista (c1540-1598), It
    R.1   S.c
DELLA PORTA, Francesco (c1600-1666), It
    R.1   S.c
DELLA VALLE, Pietro (1586-1652), It
    R.1   S.c
DELLE CESE - Inglesina
                S.54(334)
DELLEPLANQUE (c1746-c1801), Fr
    R.5

DELLER, Florian Johann (1729-1773), Aus
    R.1
DELLINGER, Rudolf (1857-1910), Ger
    R.1   S.c,5x
DELLO JOIO, Justin (1954-   ), USA
                S.13
DELLO JOIO, Norman (1913-   ), USA
    R.1   S.4-7,9,10,13,18,20,24,25,27
DELL ORO
                S.e
DELMAR, Deszo (1891-   ), Hun
    R.19   S.7,10,13,24
DELMAS, Marc (1885-1931), Fr
    R.1   S.4
DELMET, Paul (1862-1904), Fr
    R.16   S.24
DEL MONACO, Alfredo (1938-   ), USA
    R.17   S.10,13
DELONEY, Thomas (16-17th Cent)
                S.c
DEL RIEGO, Teresa (Mrs. Leadbetter) (1876-1968), Eng
    R.7   S.10,24,28,39
DEL STAIGERS [see STAIGERS, Charles Delaware]
DEL TREDICI, David (1937-   ), USA
    R.1   S.c,10,13,24
DEL TURCO, Giovanni (1577-1647), It
    R.1   S.c,10]
DELUCA, Joseph Orlando (1890-1935)

DE LUCA, Severo [see LUCA, Severo di]
DEL VADO, Juan [see VADO, Juan del]
DELVAUX, Albert (1913-   ), Bel
    R.14   S.36,24a
DELVINCOURT, Claude (1888-1954), Fr
    R.14   S.c,5-8,10,22,24
DELYSSE, Jean - pseud
    [see ROESGEN-CHAMPION, Marguerite Sara]
DEMACHI, Giuseppe (1732->1791), It
    R.1
DEMACHY, Monsieur [see MACHY, Sieur de]
DEMANTIUS, Christoph (1567-1643), Ger
    R.1   S.c,5x,8-10,14,16
DEMAR, Johann-Sebastian (1763-c1832), Ger
    R.8   S.c,10
DEMAR, Therese (1801-   ), Fr
    R.7   S.52
DE MARINIS, Paul Michael (1948-   ), USA
    R.19   S.13
DEMARQUEZ, Suzanne (1899-1965), Fr
    R.7   S.30

DEMENA - Tres caprichios para vihuelas
      S.1x
DEMÉNYI, Dezsö (1871-1937), Hun
    R.15   S.2-4
DEMERSSEMAN, Jules August (1833-1866), Fr
    R.10   S.c,10
DEMESSIEUX, Jeanne (1921-1968), Fr
    R.1   S.c,9,30,52
DEMIDOV, Grigori Alexandrovich (1838-1871)
      S.18
DEMOIVRE, Daniel (c1710)
    R.5   S.c
DE MOL, Willem (1846-1874), Bel
    R.8   S.c,41
DEMON, J. Sp - Golondrina
      S.10
DEMOPHON, Alexander (fl 1507), It
    R.5   S.8,10,14,15
DEMPSTER, Stuart S. (1936-), USA
    R.19   S.13
DEMPSTER, W. R. USA
      S.47
DEMUS, Jörg (1928-), Aus
    R.1   S.10
DENCKE, Jeremiah (1725-1798), Moravia/America
    R.1   S.10,47
DENDRINO, Gherase (1901-1973), Rum
    R.4
DENIJN, Adolf (1824-1894), Bel
    R.25   S.c
DENIJN, Jef (1862-1941), Bel
    R.25   S.c
DENIS, Didier D. (1947-), Fr
    R.4
DENISOV, Edison (1929-), USSR
    R.1   S.c,10,24a
DENNI, Lucien (1886-1947), USA
    R.23   S.13,54(345)
DENNIS, P. - Joys of Sport
      S.54(335)
DENNIS, Robert (1933-), USA
    R.19   S.10,13
DENNY, William D. (1910-1980), USA
    R.19   S.10,12,13
DENSMORE, John Hopkins (1880-1943), USA
    R.19   S.1x
DENSS, Adrian (fl late 16th Cent), Neth
    R.1   S.c
DENZA, Luigi (1846-1922), It
    R.1   S.5x,10,18,24,43,44

DEPANSIS (14th Cent), Fr
R.1   S.c
DE PAUL, Gene (1919-   ), USA
R.23   S.9
DE PEDRO, Roque (1935-   ), Arg
R.26   S.46
DEQUIN, Leon
             S.24
DÉRÉ, Jean (1886-1970), Fr
R.14   S.19,21
DERENSART, Ed
             S.10
DERING, Richard (c1580-1630), Eng
R.1   S.c,1-3,5x,8,10,14,16
DE ROGATIS, Pascual (1880-   ), Arg
R.26   S.46
DEROO, Maurits Alfons (1903-   ), Bel
R.14   S.24a
DE ROSE, Peter (1900-1953), USA
R.23   S.10,24
DeRUBERTIS, Nicholas D. (1884-1957), USA
R.49   S.54(341,45)
DERVIZ, Nikolai Grigoryevich (1837-1880)
             S.18
DE SABATA, Victor (1892-1967), It
R.1   S.2,4,10
DESAIX - French march music
             S.10
DESCENYI, Janos [see DECSENYI, Janos]
DESCH, Rudolf (1911-   )
             S.c
DESDERI, Ettore (1892-1974), It
R.14   S.c
DESENCLOS, Alfred (1912-1971), Fr
R.14   S.c,5,10,22
DESFORGES, Pierre Louis Hus
   [see HUS-DESFORGES, Pierre-Louis]
DE SILVA, Andreas (b c1475-80), Sp
R.1   S.c
DESLANDRES, Adolph Eduard Marie (1840-1911), Fr
R.10   S.8
DESMARETS, Henry (1661-1741), Fr
R.1   S.c,2,5x,10
DESPARD, Marcel (1912-   )
             S.8
DESPAS - Poemes chinois notre bateau glisse
             S.1x
DESPLANES, Jean-Antoine [see PIANI, Giovani Antonio]
DESPONSATIONE, Justinus à
   [see JUSTINUS à DESPONSATIONE]

DESPORTES, Emile (1909-   ), Fr
        S.c,10,21,32
D'ESPÓSITO, Arnaldo (1907-1945), Arg
    R.26   S.46
DESPRET/DESPRES - Sourire d'avril
            S.e,24
DESPREZ, Josquin [see JOSQUIN DESPREZ]
DESSAU, Bernhard (1861-1923), Ger
    R.8   S.24
DESSAU, Paul (1894-1979), Ger
    R.1   S.c,9,10
DESSAUER, Joseph (1798-1876), Boh
    R.3

DESTINN - Poslendi Slzy (last tears)
            S.e
DESTOUCHES, André Cardinal (1672-1749), Fr
    R.1   S.c,1x,2-4,5x,10,24
DESVIGNES, Pierre
            S.10
DETEL, Adolf (1903-   )
            S.c
DETREE, Roberto
            S.c
DE TREJADA - Perjura
            S.34
DETT, Robert Nathaniel (1882-1943), USA
    R.1   S.1,3,4,5x,8,10,11,13
DEUTSCH - Poet's vision
            S.54(350)
DEUTSCH, Emery (1907-   ), USA
    R.23   S.24
DEVAUX - Le baiser de Mignon, Souvenir de venise
            S.e
DEVIENNE, Francois (1759-1803), Fr
    R.1   S.c,5x,9,10,19,24
DE VITO, Albert Kenneth (1919-   ), USA
    [pseud: Kenneth ROGERS, Kenneth LISBON,
    Charles ALLEN]   R.23
DE VOIS, Pieter [see VOIS, Pieter]
DEVREESE, Frederic (1929-   ), Bel
    R.1
DEVREESE, Godfried (1893-1972), Bel
    R.25   S.24a
DEVRIES, Herman (1858-1949), USA
    R.4   S.e
DEWANGER, Anton
            S.4
DEZÈDE, Nicolas (c1740-1792), Fr
    R.1   S.5x
D'HARDELOT, Guy [see HARDELOT, Guy d']

DIA, Comtesse de [see BEATRIZ de DIA]
DIABELLI, Anton (1781-1858), Aus
  R.1   S.c,8-10,18,19,21,23,32
DIACONESCU, Mircea (1929-   )
           S.c
DIACONUS, Paul (c770)
           S.2,3
DIAMOND, Arline (1928-   ), USA
  R.19   S.10,13,19,30,52
DIAMOND, David Leo (1915-   ), USA
  R.1   S.3,6-8,10,13,25,24a,27
DIAMOND, Stuart Samuel (1950-   ), USA
  R.19   S.13
DIANDA, Hilda (1917-   ), Arg
  R.26   S.46,52
DIAZ de la PEÑA, Eugeno (1837-1901), Fr
  R.9   S.2-4,8
DIAZ, Alirio (1923-   ), Ven
  R.1   S.39
DIAZ, Celso
           S.24
DIAZ GILES, Fernando (1887-1960)

DIBDIN, Charles (1745-1814), Eng
  R.1   S.5,8,10
DI CAPUA, Ernesto [see CAPUA, Ernesto di]
DI CAPUA, Rinaldo [see RINALDO di CAPUA]
DI CHIARA, Vincenzo (1860-1937), It
  R.10s
DICHLER, Josef (1912-   ), Aus
  R.14   S.5x
DICHMOUNT, William (1882-1943), Can
  R.31   S.e
DICK, Charles George Cotsford (1846-   ), Eng
           S.e
DICK, Hermann (1914-   )
           S.c
DICK, Marcel (1898-   ), USA
  R.19   S.10,13
DICK, Robert (1950-   ), USA
           S.13
DICK-STON - Désire; Recuerdos (Argentine tango)
           S.24
DICKINSON - Berceuse; Memories (vi & p)
           S.24
DICKINSON, Clarence (1873-1969), USA
  R.1   S.12,13
DICKINSON, Peter (1934-   ), Eng
  R.1   S.c

DICKS, Ernest Alfred (1865-   ), Eng
    R.37   S.e
DICKSON, Ellen [pseud: DOLORES] (1819-1878), Eng
    (see note) R.7   S.e
DICKSON, Stanley
                S.10
DI DOMENICA, Robert (1927-   ), USA
    R.19   S.13,24a
DIE, Beatrice [see BEATRIZ de DIA]
DIECK - Philadelphia all the time
                S.54(349
DIEGO da CONCEIÇÃO, Francisco (17th Cent)
                S.c,10
DIEKAMP, Heinz (1921-   )

DIEMENTE, Edward (1923-   ), USA
    R.19   S.10,13,22
DIEMER, Emma Lou (1927-   ), USA
    R.19   S.13,30,52
DIÉMER, Louis (1843-1919), Fr
    R.1   S.24
DIENEL, Otto (1839-1905), Ger
    R.3   S.c
DIENER, Theodor (1908-   ), Swiss
    R.14
DIENZL, Oskar (1877-1925)
                S.24

DIEPENBROCK, Alphons (1862-1921), Neth
    R.1   S.5x,8,10,41
DIEREN, Bernard van (1887-1936), Eng
    R.1   S.c,10,27
DIESEL, Paula
                S.30
DIESENROTH, Friedrich (19th Cent)

DIETER, Christian Ludwig (1757-1822), Ger
    R.1   S.c,10
DIETHELM, Caspar (1926-   ), Swiss
    R.14   S.c,24
DIETRICH, Albert Hermann (1829-1908), Ger
    R.1   S.5x,6,8,10,24
DIETRICH, P. - Abenlied (vi & p)
                S.24
DIETRICH, Sixt (c1493-1548), Ger
    R.1   S.c
DIETRICHSTEIN, Graf Moritz von (1775-1864), Ger
    R.5   S.c
DIETSCH, Louis (1808-1865), Fr
    R.1   S.8(6),24(845)

DIEUPART, Charles (>1667-c1740), Fr
R.1   S.c,10
DIJON, Guiot de [see GUIOT de DIJON]
DIKCHYUS, P. (1933-   )
             S.18,24a
DILETSKY, Nicolay (c1630-c1680), Ukraine
R.1   S.c
DILLEY - Hail Pennsylvania
             S.54(330)
DILLON, Fannie Charles (1881-1947), USA
R.19   S.10,12,13,52
DILLON, Henri (1912-1954), Fr
R.14   S.8
DILLON, Robert (1922-   ), USA
R.19   S.13
DIMA, Gheorghe (1847-1925), Rum
R.1   S.c
DIMITRESCU, Constantin (1847-1928), Rum
R.1   S.c,18,24
DIMITRESCU, Ion [S.7] = DUMITRESCU, Ion
DIMITRIYEV, Nikolai Dmitriyevich (1829-1893)
             S.18
DINEV, Petr Konstantinov (1889-   ), Bul
R.14   S.c
DINGEMANN, Gustav (1915-   )
             S.c
DINICU, Grigoras (1889-1949), Rum
R.8   S.c,3,4,5x,10,18,24
DINTRICH, Michel (20th Cent)
             S.c
DIOMEDES, Cato [see CATO DIOMEDES]
DIONISI, Renato (1910-   ), It
R.14   S.c
DI PASQUALE, James (1941-   ), USA
R.19   S.10,13,22
DIRKSON, Richard Wayne (1921-   ), USA
R.19   S.13
DIRUTA, Girolamo (c1554->1610), It
R.1   S.c,53
DIRVENSKAITE - Capriccio (vi & p)
             S.24a
DISSELHOFF, August
             S.10
DISSEVELT, Tom (20th Cent), Neth
             S.9,13
DISTLER, Hugo (1908-1942), Ger
R.1   S.c,8-10
DITTERSDORF, Carl Ditters von (1739-1799), Ger
R.1   S.c,1-5,7-11,18,23,24

DI VEROLI, Donato (1921-1943), It
   R.8   S.10
DIX, J. Airlie
             S.10
DIZI, François Joseph (1780-c1840), S. Neth
   R.1   S.10
DJABADANY - Rhapsodie Gregorienne (p & orch)
             S.4
DJABADARY, Heraclius (1891-1937)
             S.c
DJEMIL, Enyss (1917-   ), Fr
   R.1   S.c
DLUGORAJ, Wojciech (1557/8->1619), Pol
   R.1   S.c,4,10,16,32,53
DLUGOSZEWSKI, Lucia (1931-   ), USA
   R.1   S.10,13,30,52
DLUSKI, Erazm (1857-1923), Pol
   R.1   S.c,e
DOBER, Conrad K. [see CONRAD, Con - pseud]
DOBIAS, Václav (1909-1978), Cz
   R.1   S.5x,7,8,31
DOBIE, Janet (1936-   ), Australia
   R.7   S.29,52
DOBRODINSKY, Bedrich (1896-   ), Cz
   R.18   S.31
DOBROVEN, Issay Alexandrov (1894-1953), Russia
   R.1   S.c,24
DOBROWOLSKI, Andrej (1921-   ), Pol
   R.1   S.c
DOCHE, Joseph Denis (1766-1825), Fr
   R.1   S.c
DOCKER, Robert (20th Cent), Eng
             S.c,10
DOCKSTADER, Tod (1932-   ), USA
   R.19   S.9,13
DODGE, Charles (1945-   ), USA
   R.1   S.9,10,13
DODGE, Ossian E. USA
             S.47
DODGSON, Stephen (1924-   ), Eng
   R.1   S.c,10,32

DODWORTH, Allen (fl 1836-60), USA
   R.49   S.10,47
DOELLE, Franz (1883-1965), Ger
   R.1   S.33
DOERING, Georg (19th Cent)
             S.c
DOERR, Ludwig (1925-   ), Ger
   R.1   S.c

DOGA, Yevgeni Dmitriyevich (1937-   )
            S.18
DÖHL, Friedhelm (1936-   ), Ger
    R.1
DOHNÁNYI, Ernő (1877-1960), Hun
    R.1   S.c,1-11,18,20,24
DOIN, Gaston (1879-   )
            S.7
DOLAN, Robert Emmett (1906-1972), USA
    R.23   S.5x,9,13
DOLBY, Charlotte Helen
    [see SAINTON-DOLBY, Charlotte Helen]
DOLIN, Samuel (1917-   ), Can
    R.4   S.24a
DOLLÉ, Charles (fl 1735-55), Fr
    R.1   S.c
DOLORES - pseud [see DICKSON, Ellen]
DOLUHANIAN, Alexander Pavlovich (1910-1968), USSR
    R.14
DOMBROWSKI, Hans Maria (1897-1977), Ger
    R.14   S.c
DOMENICO del GIOVANE, Giovane da Nola
    [see NOLA, Giovanni Domenico del Giovane da]
DOMETIAN, Vlahul (16th Cent)

DOMINCHEN, Klementi Yakovlevich (1907-   ), USSR
    R.14   S.18
DOMINGUEZ, Alberto
            S.10
DONAGIO - Come sinfonia
            S.10
DONALDSON, Walter (1893-1947), USA
    R.1   S.10,24
DONALDSON, Will (1891-1954), USA
    R.23   S.10
DONATI - Primavera (p)

DONATI, Ignazio (c1575-1638), It
    R.1   S.c
DONATI, Pino (1907-1975), It
    R.4
DONATO da CASCIA (fl 2nd half of 14th Cent), It
    R.1   S.c,10,16
DONATO da FIRENZA [see DONATO da CASCIA}
DONATO, Baldassare (c1530-1603), It
    R.1   S.c,2-7,10,14-15,18
DONATONI, Franco (1927-   ), It
    R.1   S.c,8
DONAUDY, Stefano (1879-1925), It
    R.8   S.4,5x,10,18,25,44

DONAUROV, Sergei Ivanovich (1838-1897), Russia
   R.47   S.18
DONCEANU, Felicia (1931-   ), Rum
   R.7   S.52
DONDEYNE, Desire (1921-   ), Fr
   R.49   S.10
DONG, He (1948-   )
            S.24a
DONIZETTI, Gaetano (1797-1848), It
   R.1
   S.c,1-11,18,20,22,24,28,34,42,43,54(322,26)
DONIZETTI, Giuseppi (c1793-1856), It
   R.10   S.c
DONJON, Johannes (1839-1912)
            S.c,10
DONOSTIA, José Antonio de (1886-1956), Sp
   R.1   S.10,32,39
DONOVAN, Richard Frank (1891-1970), USA
   R.1   S.2,3,8,10,12,13
DONT, Jakob (1815-1888), Aus
   R.8   S.c,10,24
DOOLITTLE, Eliakim (1772-1850), USA
   R.50   S.47
DOPPELBAUER, Josef Friedrich (1918-   ), Aus
   R.14   S.c
DOPPER, Cornelis (1870-1939), Neth
   R.1   S.4,10,41
DOPPLER, Albert Franz (1821-1883), Pol
   R.1   S.c,10,18,24a
DOPPLER, Karl (1825-1900), Pol
   R.1
DORAN, Matt (1921-   ), USA
   R.19   S.10,13,19,20
DORATI, Antal (1906-   ), USA
   R.1   S.9,13
DOREL, Francis
            S.e
DORET, Gustave (1866-1943), Swiss
   R.1   S.5x
DORIA, F. - Chanson des peupliers
            S.e
DORING, A. (fl 1873-98) - Distant greeting
            S.54(323)
DORN, Sepp

DORNEL, Louis-Antoine (c1680->1756), Fr
   R.1   S.c,2-4,5x,8,10,11,24a,53
DOROUGH, Robert (1923-   ), USA
   R.60

DOROW, Dorothy (1930-   ), Eng
   R.7   S.c,10,30,40,52
DORSEY, Thomas (1905-1956), USA
   R.23   S.10
DORSON, Charles (1882-   )
            S.24
DORUMSGAARD, Arne (1921-   ), Nor
   R.1   S.8,9
DOS REIS, Gaspar [see GASPAR dos REIS]
DOSS, Adolf von (1823-1886), Ger
   R.1
DOSTAL, Hermann (1874-1930), Aus
   R.95   S.54(327)
DOSTAL, Nico (1895-   ), Aus
   R.1   S.c,9,10,18
DOTZAUER, Friedrich (1783-1860), Ger
   R.1
DOUBRAVA, Jaroslav (1909-1960), Cz
   R.1   S.5,24,31
DOUGHERTY, Celius (1902-   ), USA
   R.14   S.10,13,25,26
DOUGLAS, Clive Martin (1903-1977), Australia
   R.1   S.29,37
DOUGLAS, James (1932-   ), Scot
   R.80   S.c
DOUGLAS, Roy (1907-   ), Eng
   R.1   S.18
DOUGLAS, Shipley
            S.54(360)
DOUGLAS, William (1944-   ), USA
   R.19   S.10,13,20,24a
DOURIAN, Ohan (1922-   ), Isr
   R.13
DOURLEN, Victor Charles Paul (1780-1864), Fr
   R.1   S.4,5x
DOVZHENKO, Valerian Danilovich (1905-   ), USSR
   R.47
DOW, Daniel (1732-1783), Scot
   R.1   S.10,47
DOWLAND, John (1563-1626), Eng
   R.1   S.c,2-11,14-16,27-28,32,33,53
DOWLAND, Robert (c1591-1641), Eng
   R.1   S.c,5x,10,14
DOWLING, Eddie (1895-   ), USA
   R.61   S.24[b.1891]
DOWNEY, John (1927-   ), USA
   R.19   S.c,10,13
DOWNING, David L. (fl 1870-72), USA
   R.49   S.10

DOWNS, Hugh   USA
            S.13
DOYEN, Henry
            S.c
DRAESEKE, Felix August Bernhard (1835-1913), Ger
    R.1   S.c,8
DRAGHI, Giovanni Battista (c1640-1708), It
    R.1   S.c,10
DRAGOI, Sabin (1894-1968), Rum
    R.1   S.24a
DRAGONETTI, Domenico (1763-1846), It
    R.1   S.c,8-10
DRAGONI, Giovanni Andrea (c1540-1598), It
    R.1   S.c,16
DRANGOSCH, Ernesto (1882-1925), Arg
    R.26   S.46
DRAYTON, Paul (1944-   ), Eng
            S.c
DRDLA, Frantisek Alois (1869-1944), Cz
    R.1   S.1x,5x,10,18,22,24,54(355)
DRECHSEL, Bosse
            S.24,33
DRECHSLER, Joseph (1782-1852), Boh
    R.1   S.c,10
DREJSL, Radim (1923-1953), Cz
    R.18   S.31
DREMLIUGA, Nikolai Vasilievich (1917-   ), USSR
    R.14   S.18
DRESCHER - Ritirata Italiana
            S.54(353)
DRESDEN, Sem (1881-1957), Neth
    R.1   S.7,8,10,20,24
DRESE, Adam (c1620-1701), Ger
    R.1   S.8,10
DRESSER, Paul (1857-1906), USA
    R.1   S.10,43
DRESSLER, Gallus (1533-1580/9), Ger
    R.1   S.c,2
DRETZEL, Valentin (1578-1658), Ger
    R.1   S.c
DREWS, Steve (1945-   ), USA
    R.19   S.10,13
DREYFUS, George (1928-   ), Australia
    R.1   S.29,37
DREYSCHOCK, Alexander (1818-1869), Boh
    R.1   S.10
DRIESEN, Rene (1920-   )
            S.24a
DRIEST, Jan v.d.
            S.c

DRIFFILL, W. Ralph (fl 1892-1917)
           S.c[Ralph],7
DRIGO, Riccardo (1846-1930), It
  R.1   S.c,5x,10,18,24
DRING, Madeleine (1923-1977), Eng
  R.7   S.c,5x,30,52
DRISCHNER, Max (1891-1971), Ger
  R.1   S.c
DROGOZ, Philippe (20th Cent)
           S.c
DROSSIN, Julius (1918-   ), USA
  R.80   S.13
DROSTE-HÜLSHOFF, Annette von (1797-1848), Ger
  R.1   S.c,30,52
DROUET, Louis (1792-1873), Fr
  R.1   S.c,e
DRUCKMAN, Jacob (1928-   ), USA
  R.1   S.c,9,10,13,20,24a
DRUICK, Don (1945-   ), Can
  R.81
DRUMHELLER, C. - Banjo twang
           S.10
DRUMMOND, Frederick (19th-20th Cent), Eng
           S.c
DRUMWRIGHT, George USA
           S.13
DRUSCHETZKY, Georg (1745-1819), Boh
  R.1   S.c,10
DRUSCHININ, Fjodor (1932-   )
           S.c
DRUZECKY, Jiri [see DRUSCHETZKY, Georg]
DSERSCHINSKY, Ivan [see DZERZHINSKY, Ivan]
DUARTE, John William (1919-   ),Eng
  R.80   S.c,10
DÜBEN, Anders von (1673-1738), Sweden
  R.30   S.56
DÜBEN, Andreas (1558-1625), Ger
  R.30   S.c
DÜBEN, Andreas (c1597-1662), Sweden
  R.1   S.c,10,53,56
DÜBEN, Gustaf (c1628-1690), Sweden
  R.1   S.c,10,56
DUBENSKY, Arcady (1890-1966) USA
  R.19   S.c,1x,2-5,8,11,13,18
DUBLANC, Emilio (1911-   ), Arg
  R.26   S.46
DUBLE, Charles Edward (1884-1960), USA
  R.49   S.13,54(346)
DUBOIS, (François Clement) Theodore (1837-1924), Fr
  R.1   S.c,8-10

DUBOIS, Pierre Max (1930-   ), Fr
   R.1   S.c,10,20,22
DUBOYS, Jan (Jehan du Bois) (fl 1539), Fr
   R.5   S.c,10
DUBROVAY, Laszlo (1943-   ), Hun
              S.c,10
DU BUISSON (17th Cent) - Plaint sur la mort de Mr.
   Lambert   R.16   S.c
DUBUQUE, Alexander Ivanovich (1812-1898), Russia
   R.1   S.18
DUC de BOURGOGNE
              S.14
DUCASSE, Roger Jean [see ROGER-DUCASSE, Jean]
DU CAURROY, Eustache (1549-1609), Fr
   R.1   S.c,4,5,10,11,14,16,53
DUCH, O. Russia - Novgorod (v)

DUCHAMP, Marcel (1887-1968)

DUCHOW, Marvin (1914-   ), Can
   R.14
DUCKWORTH, F. - Rimington
              S.54(352)
DUCKWORTH, William E. (1943-   ), USA
   R.19   S.10,13,22
DUCOMMUN, Samuel (1914-   ), Swiss
   R.25
DUDNIK, Alexander Vasilyevich (1942-   )
              S.18
DUEBEN, Gustav [see DÜBEN, Gustave]
DUFAUT, Francois (d <1682/6), Fr
   R.1   S.c,10
DUFAY, Guillaume (c1400-1474), Fr
   R.1   S.1x,2-11,14-16,18,32,41
DUFF, Arthur (1899-   ), Ire
   R.49   S.10
DUFFAU, P. - Maggio valzer
              S.e
DUFFE, Helmut (1948-   )
              S.c
DUFFERIN, Helen Selina (Countess of Gifford)
   (née Sheridan) (1807-1867), Ire
   R.7   S.10,30
DUFORT, Charles - pseud [see KARK, Frederik]
DUFRENE, Francois (1930-   ), Fr
   R.25   S.10
DUGGER, Edwin (1940-   ), USA
   R.19   S.10,13
DUGORAJ, Wojziech [see DLUGORAJ, Wojziech]

DUIJCK, Guy (1927-   ), Bel
    R.25   S.22
DUISBERG, Robert Adamy (1953-   )

DUKAS, Paul (1865-1935), Fr
    R.1   S.c,1-11,18
DUKAY, Barnabas (1950-   )
                S.c
DUKE, John Woods (1899-   ), USA
    R.1   S.10,25,27,28
DUKE, Lewis Byron (1924-   ), USA
                S.13,24
DUKE, Vernon (1903-1969), USA
    R.1   S.9,13,24
DUKYEVICH, Georgi Nikolayevich (1887-   )
                S.18
DULICHIUS, Philipp (1562-1631), Ger
    R.1   S.c,10,16
DULOT, François (fl 1st half of 16th Cent), Fr
    R.1   S.14,15
DUMAGE, Pierre (1674-1751), Fr
    R.1   S.c,4,10,53
DUMANOIR, Guillaume (1615-1697), Fr
    R.1   S.8
DUMITRESCU, Gheorghe (1914-   ), Rum
    R.1
DUMITRESCU, Ion (1913-   ), Rum
    R.1   S.6[Dimitrescu]
DU MONT, Henry (1610-1684), Fr
    R.1   S.c,5,8-10,41,53
DUNAYEVSKY, Isaac Iosifovich (1900-1955), Russia
    R.1   S.c,18,24a
DUNCAN, John (1913-   ), USA
    R.19   S.10,13
DUNCAN, Ronald (1916-   ), Scot

DUNCAN, Trevor - pseud [ie Leonard TREBILCO]
    (1924-   ), Eng   R.64   S.c
DUNHILL, Thomas (1877-1946), Eng
    R.1   S.c,5x,18,24,25,27
DUNKELS, Ernest

DUNKLER, Eduard
                S.e
DUNKLEY, E. Charlwood
                S.e
DUNLAP, William Paul (1919-   ), USA
    R.23   S.5x,10,13
DUNN, James Philip (1884-1936), USA
    R.23   S.c,10,13

DUNN, John (1866-1940), Eng
   R.10s   S.24
DÜNSCHEDE, Hans (1907-   ), Ger
   R.13   S.24
DUNSTABLE, John (c1390-1453), Eng
   R.1   S.c,2-4,5x,8-11,14-16,53
DUO-VITAL, Arturo
         S.10
DU PAGE, Florence Elizabeth (1910-   ), USA
   R.23   S.30
DUPARC, Henri (1848-1933), Fr
   R.1   S.c,1-11,18,25-27
DUPHLY, Jacques (1715-1789), Fr
   R.1   S.c,4,5,9,10,24a
DUPLE - Hymn en l'honneur de general
         S.54(333)
DUPLESSIS [l'aîné] (fl 1704-48), Fr
   R.1
DUPONT - La Sidi Brahin
         S.54(356)
DUPONT, Auguste (1827-1890), Bel
   R.3   S.18
DUPONT, Gabriel Edouard Xavier (1878-1914), Fr
   R.3   S.2-4,5x,10,11
DUPONT, P. - Les boefs; Les sapins;
   Promenade du paysan   S.e
DUPORT, Jean-Louis (1749-1819), Fr
   R.1   S.c,10
DUPORT, Jean-Pierre (1741-1818), Fr
   R.1   S.c
DUPORT, Pierre Landrin
         S.10,47
DUPRÉ, Marcel (1886-1971), Fr
   R.1   S.c,3,4,5x,7-10,18
DUPUIS, Albert (1877-1967), Bel
   R.1   S.36
DUPUY, Jean Baptiste Edouard (c1770-1822), Swiss
   R.1   S.c,4,5,35,56,57
DURAND, Marie-Auguste (1830-1909), Fr
   R.1   S.8,10,18,24
DURAND, Paul (20th Cent), Fr
         S.8,10
DURANTE, Francisco (1684-1755), It
   R.1   S.c,2-5,7-11,18,24-28
DURANTE, Ottavio (fl 1608), It
   R.1   S.c
DUREY, Louis (1888-1979), Fr
   R.1   S.c,8,10,18
D'URFEY, Thomas (c1653-1723), Eng
   R.1   S.c

DURKÓ, Zsolt (1934-   ), Hun
   R.1   S.c,9,10,24
DURME, Jef van (1907-1965), Bel
   R.1
DURÓN, Diego (c1658-1731), Sp
   R.1   S.c,10
DURÓN, Sebastián (1660-1716), Sp
   R.1   S.c,10,53
DUROSOIR, Lucienn
            S.24,24a
DURUFLÉ, Marie-Madeleine
            S.10
DURUFLÉ, Maurice (1902-   ), Fr
   R.1   S.c,9,10
DUSEK, František Xaver (1731-1799), Cz
   R.1   S.c,5x,6,10
DUSIK, Gejza (1907-   ), Cz
   R.18   S.31
DUSSEK, Jan Ladislav (1760-1812), Boh
   R.1   S.c,4,5,7-10,24
DUSYSINX, F. - Exegi momentum

DU TERTRE, Estienne (fl mid 16th Cent), Fr
   R.1   S.c,8,10,14,16,32
DUTILLET, Jacques (1946-   )
            S.c
DUTILLEUX, Henri (1916-   ), Fr
   R.1   S.c,6,8,10,18
DUTKIEWICZ, Andrzej (1942-   )

DÜTSCH, Otto Johann Anton (c1823-1863), Den
   R.1   S.18
DUTSIS, Benedictus (c1480-1544)
            S.18
DUTTON, Frederic M. (1928-   ), USA
   R.19   S.10,13
DUVAL, Aimé
            S.c
DUVAL, François (1672-1728), Fr
   R.1   S.c
DUVERNOY, Charles (1776-1845), Fr
   R.8   S.c,10
DUVERNOY, Frédéric Nicholas (1765-1838), Fr
   R.1   S.24a
DUVERNOY, Henri-Louis-Charles (1820-1906), Fr
   R.8
DUVERNOY, Victor Alphonse (1842-1907), Fr
   R.1   S.c,10
DUYSSENS, Joseph (1845-   ), Bel
   R.76   S.e

DVARIONAS, Balys (1904-1972), Lith
R.1   S.7,18,24
DVARIONAS, Jurgis
           S.24a
DVOŘÁČEK, Jiří (1928-   ), Cz
R.1   S.31
DVORAK, Antonin (1841-1904), Cz
R.1   S.c,1-11,18,21-24,26-28,42,54(332)
DVORKIN, Judith (1930-   ), USA
R.7   S.10,13,30,52
DYER, Susan (1880-1922), USA
R.7   S.10,13,24,30,52
DYFF, Jean
           S.24
DYKES, John Bacchus (1823-1876), Eng
R.1   S.10
DYSON, George (1883-1964), Eng
R.1   S.c,5x,8
DYUTSH, Otto [see DÜTSCH, Otto]
DZERZHINSKY, Ivan Ivanovich (1909-1978), Russia
R.1   S.c,10,11,18
DZHABADARY, Erekle
           S.18
DZHANYBEKOV, A. (1934-   )
           S.18
DZHERBASHYAN, Stepan (1917-   )
           S.18
DZHUMAKHMATOV, A
           S.18
DZUTOYEV, Julian
           S.24
EAGLES, Moneta M. (1924-   ), Australia
R.7   S.29
EAKIN, Charles (1927-   ), USA
R.19   S.13
EARL, Mary - pseud [see KING, Robert A.]
EARLS, Paul (1934-   ), USA
R.19   S.10,13,28
EASDALE, Brian (1909-   ), Eng
R.1   S.5x,6,7,10
EAST, Michael (c1580-1648), Eng
R.1   S.c,2,3,5x,6-8,10,14,16
EAST, Thomas (c1540-1608), Eng [publisher]
           S.14
EASTHAM, Clark USA
           S.13
EASTWOOD, Thomas Hugh (1922-   ), Eng
R.14   S.c,32
EATON, E. K. (fl 1845-55), USA
R.57   S.10,47

EATON, John Charles (1935-   ), USA
   R.1   S.9,10,13,20
EBEL, Arnold (1883-1963), Ger
   R.4
EBELING, Johann Georg (1637-1676), Ger
   R.1   S.c,8
EBEN, Petr (1929-   ), Cz
   R.1   S.c,9,18[Ebyen],31
EBENHÖH, Horst (1930-   ), Aus
   R.4
EBERHARD von CERSNE (14th Cent)
          S.c
EBERHARDT, Johann Jakob (1852-1926) Ger
   R.25   S.24
EBERL, Anton (1765-1807), Aus
   R.1   S.24
EBERLE, Friedrich (1853-1930), Ger
          S.3
EBERLIN, Johann Ernst (1702-1762), Ger
   R.1   S.c,1x,2-4,6,10,53
EBHARDT, Gotthilf Friedrich (1771-1855), Ger
   R.5   S.c
EBNER, Wolfgang (1612-1665), Ger
   R.1   S.c,53
EBREO da PESARO, Guglielmo
   [see GUGLIELMO, Ebreo da Pesaro]
EBYEN, Petr [S.18] = EBEN, Petr
ECCARD, Johannes (1553-1611), Eng
   R.1   S.c,2,5x,6-8,10,14-16,32
ECCLES, Henry (?1675/85-?1735/45), Eng
   R.1   S.c,2,3,5,7,8,10,18,22-24
ECCLES, John (c1668-1735), Eng
   R.1   S.c,5,8,10
ECHARTE, Pedro Arg
          S.46
ECHEVERRIA, Eduardo (1871-1970), Sp

ECHEVERRIA, Ignacio de (d.1792), Basque

ECKERBERG, Axel Sixten (1909-   ), Sweden
   R.14   S.c,40
ECKERT, Carl Anton Florian (1820-1879), Ger
   R.3
ECKHARDT-GRAMATTÉ, Sophie-Carmen (1899-1974), Can
   R.1   S.24,30,52   (see note)
EDBAR - March Tartare
          S.54(341)
EDELMANN, Jean Frederich (1749-1794), Ger
   R.25   S.c,24

EDEN, Conrad William (1905-   ), Eng
    R.77   S.c
EDEN, Robert - Whats in the air today?

EDER, Helmut (1916-   ), Aus
    R.1   S.c
EDGAR - Mandy Lee
                S.e

EDLICHKO - Es wehen die Winde, Stormy breezes
                S.e
EDLUND, Lars (1922-   ), Sweden
    R.1   S.c,40,56
EDMONDS, Shepard N. (1876-1957), USA
    R.23   S.10
EDMUNDS, Christopher (1899-   ), Eng
    R.14   S.10,19,21
EDMUNDS, John (1913-   ), USA
    R.1   S.10,13,27
EDMUNDSON, Garth (1895-   ), USA (see note)
    R.19   S.c,7,8,10,12,13
EDSON, Lewis Sr (1748-1820), USA (see note)
    R.50   S.47
EDSON, Lewis Jr (1771-1845), USA
    R.50   S.10,50
EDWARDS, Clara (1887-1974), USA
    R.19   S.10,13,30,52
EDWARDS, George (1943-   ), USA
    R.19   S.10
EDWARDS, Gus (1879-1945), USA
    R.23   S.10
EDWARDS, Julian (1853-1909), Eng/USA
    R.1   S.e
EDWARDS, Richard (1524-1566), Eng
    R.1   S.c,2,3,5x,10,14,16
EDWARDS, Ross (1943-   ), Australia
    R.1   S.29
EDWARDS, Sherman (1919-1981), USA
    R.23
EEDEN, Jan van den (1842-1917), Bel
    R.1   S.41
EFFINGER, Cecil (1914-   ), USA
    R.1   S.9,10,13
EGENOLFF, Christian (1502-1555), Ger [printer]
    R.1
EGGE, Klaus (1906-1979), Nor
    R.1   S.c,7-10,24,40,51
EGGEN, Arne (1881-1955), Nor
    R.1   S.c,8,10
EGGLESTON, Anne (1934-   ), Can
    R.7   S.52

EGIAZARIAN, Grigory Egiazarovich (1908-   ), USSR
    R.14   S.24a
EGIDIUS de PUISEUS (fl c1344-48)
    R.1
EGIDIUS von THENIS (15th Cent)
        S.c
EGK, Werner (1901-1983), Ger
    R.1   S.c,4-7,9,10,24a
EGLI, Johann Heinrich (1742-1810), Swiss
    R.1   S.c
EGLIN, Arthur (1932-   )

EGNER, Philip (1870-1956), USA
    R.23   S.10
EGOROV, Alexander Alexandrovich (1887-1959), USSR
    R.14
EGUIGUREN, Ferdinando (b.1743), Basque
    R.104   S.c
EHMANN, Heinrich (1904-   ), Ger
        S.c,10
EHRET, Ernst (1911-   )

EHRHARDT, C. Michael (1914-   ), USA
        S.5x,6,8,10,13
EHRICH, J. - Liebesfrühling - Ländler, Op.32
        S.24
EHRICH, M. L. - pseud [see ELLMENREICH, Albert]
EHRLICH, Abel (1915-   ), Isr
    R.1   S.24a
EHRLICH, Jesse (1920-   ), USA
    R.14   S.10,13
EHRLICH, Karl Heinrich Alfred (1822-1899), Aus
    R.1   S.c
EICHENWALD, Philipp (1915-   ), Swiss
    R.4
EICHHEIM, Henry (1870-1942), USA
    R.1   S.1-3,11,13
EICHNER, Ernst (1740-1777), Ger
    R.1   S.c,10,18,23,24
EILENBERG, Richard (1848-1925), Ger
    R.2   S.24,54(315,39-41,43,53)
EIMERT, Herbert (1897-1972), Ger
    R.1   S.c,10
EINEM, Gottfried von (1918-   ), Aus
    R.1   S.c,5,7,8,10
EINFELDT, Dieter (1935-   ), Ger
    R.4
EISENHUT, Thomas (1644-1702), Ger
    R.1   S.c

EISENMANN, Will (1906-   ), Ger
   R.14   S.c
EISENSTEIN, Alfred (1899-   ), USA
   R.19   S.24
EISENSTEIN, Judith Kaplan (20th Cent), USA
   R.7   S.30
EISLER, Hanns (1898-1962), Ger
   R.1   S.2,3,8-10,20,24a
EISMA, Will (1929-   ), Neth
   R.4
EK, Gunnar (1900-   ), Sweden
   R.1   S.5x,6,20
EKIER, Jan (1913-   ), Pol
   R.14   S.c
EKLÖF, Joel Eznar (1886-1954), Sweden
   R.2   S.5x,43
EKLUND, Hans (1927-   ), Sweden
   R.1   S.c,10,38,40,56
ELBEL, Louis - The Victors
              S.54(363)
EL-DABH, Halim (1921-   ), Egypt
   R.1   S.10,13

ELDER - Echoes; Pearson's Song
              S.e
ELGAR, Edward (1857-1934), Eng
   R.1   S.c,1-11,18,24,43,55,54(336,37)
ELIAS, Jose (fl 1715-51), Sp
   R.9   S.c,10,39,53
ELIAS, Manuel de Santo (18th Cent), Sp
   R.5   S.c
ELIASSON, Anders (1947-   ), Sweden
   R.30   S.c,40,56
ELIES, Josep (17th Cent), Sp

ELIOD - pseud [see ODDONE SULLI-RAO, Elisabetta]
ELISCU, Robert
              S.c
ELIZALDE, Fred (1907-1979), Sp
   R.1   S.8,9,24
ELKIND, Rachel (1937-   ), USA
              S.52
ELKUS, Jonathan (1931-   ), USA
   R.19   S.10,13
ELLER, Heino (1887-1970), Est
   R.1   S.18,24
ELLERTON, Gustav
              S.24
ELLESKUDT - Drikkesangen
              S.e

ELLING, Catharinus (1858-1942), Nor
    R.1   S.24
ELLINGTON - Rockin´ in rhythm
             S.54(353)
ELLINGTON, Edward K. Duke (1899-1974), USA
    R.1   S.c,10,11
ELLINGTON, Mercer Kennedy (1919-   ), USA
    R.4
ELLIOT, Alonzo (1891-1964), USA
    R.19   S.24
ELLIOT, James William (1833-   ) Eng
    R.44   S.c,5x
ELLIOTT, Percy (1870-   )
    R.200   S.e
ELLIS, John Tilstone (1929-   ), Eng
    R.64   S.c
ELLIS, Merrill (1916-1981), USA
    R.19   S.10,13
ELLIS, Osian (1928-   ), Eng
    R.30
ELLIS, William (1620-1674), Eng
    R.5   S.8
ELLMENREICH, Albert [pseud: M. L. EHRICH] (1816-1905),
    Ger R.3   S.24a
ELLSASSER, Richard (1926-1972), USA
    R.19   S.8,10,12,13
ELLSTEIN, Abraham (1907-1963), USA
    R.19   S.c,13
ELMA - Auld Fisher
             S.e
ELMAN, Mischa (1891-1967), Russia
    R.1   S.c,1x,10,13,24
ELMORE, Cenieth Catherine (1930-   )
    R.7   S.30
ELMORE, Robert Hall (1913-   ), USA
    R.19   S.5x,8,10,12,13
ELOY, Jean-Claude (1938-   ), Fr
    R.1   S.c,10
ELSNER, Josef Antoni Franciszek (1769-1854), Pol
    R.1   S.c
ELSTON, Arnold (1907-1971), USA
    R.1   S.10,13
ELVEY, George (1816-1893), Eng
    R.1   S.c
ELWELL, Herbert (1898-1974), USA
    R.1   S.8-10,13,24,28
ELWYN-EDWARDS, Dilys (20th Cent), Wales (see note)
    R.7,83   S.c,52
EMER - Presque rien
             S.24a

EMERSON - Guarde republicaine marche
        S.54(328)
EMERSON, Luther Orlando (1820-1915), USA
    R.4
EMIDIO TAVORA, Florizinha (20th Cent), Brazil
        S.52
EMIL, Thoroddsen (1898-1944), Ice

EMMANUEL, Maurice (1862-1938), Fr
    R.1   S.c,8,10
EMMERSON, Simon (1950-   ), Eng
    R.4   S.c
EMMETT, Daniel Decatur (1815-1904), USA
    R.1   S.10,24,47,54(323)
ENCILLA - Tavira o la Romeria
        S.e
ENCINA, Juan del (1468-1529), Sp
    R.1   S.5x,8,10,14-17,32,39
ENDERS, Georg (1898-1954), Sweden
    R.30   S.43
ENDLER, Johann Samuel (1694-1762), Ger
    R.1
ENDSLEY, Gerald
        S.10
ENESCU, Georges (1881-1955), Rum
    R.1   S.c,2-11,18,23,24
ENEVOLD, P
        S.40
ENGEL, Carl (1883-1944), USA
    R.1   S.3,4,10,11,13,24
ENGEL, Joel (1868-1927), Russia
    R.1   S.c,10,24
ENGEL, K. - Allen voran
        S.54(312)
ENGELMAN, James
        S.10,13
ENGELMANN, Georg Sr. (c1575-1632), Ger
    R.1
ENGELMANN, Georg Jr. (c1601-1663), Ger
    R.1
ENGELMANN, Hans (1872-1914), USA
        S.54(334)
ENGELMANN, Hans Ulrich (1921-   ), Ger
    R.1   S.c
ENGELS, Adriaan (1906-   ), Neth
    R.14   S.c
ENGLAENDER, Ludwig (1859-1914), Aus
    R.53,59   S.e
ENGLERT, Giuseppe Giorgio (1927-   ), It
    R.14   S.10

ENGLISH - My Lagen Love
          S.e
ENGLISH, George Selwyn (1912-   ), Australia
     R.14   S.29
ENGLUND, Einer (1916-   ), Fin
     R.1   S.c,40
ENNA, August (1859-1939), Den
     R.1   S.4,57
ENRIQUE (15th Cent), Sp
     R.1   S.10,16,17,32,39
ENRIQUEZ de VALDERRABANO
     [see VALDERRABANO, Enriquez de]
ENRIQUEZ, Manuel (1926-   ), Mex
     R.1   S.24a
EPHRAM SYRUS (c306-373), Syria
     R.1   S.c
EPHROS, Gershon (1890-1978), USA
     R.14   S.9,13
EPIN de GROOT, Else-Antonia van [pseud: Derek LAREN]
     (1919-   ), Neth   R.7   S.52
EPISCOPIUS, Ludovicus (c1520-1595), S. Neth
     R.1   S.c,16
EPPELL, John Valentine
                 S.10
EPSTEIN, Alvin (1926-   ), USA
     R.19   S.10,13
EPSTEIN, David (1930-   ), USA
     R.19   S.9,13,20
ERB, Donald (1927-   ), USA
     R.1   S.c,9,13,24a
ERBACH, Christian (1568/73-1635), Ger
     R.1   S.c,2-4,5x,8,10,16,53
ERCHAN, P. - Prayer to the Holy Trinity
                 S.10
ERCOLANO, T. - Quell´augellin Canzone
                 S.c
ERDLEN, Hermann (1893-1972), Ger
     R.14   S.c
ERDMAN, Ernie (1879-1946), USA
     R.23   S.10
ERDMANN, Dietrich (1917-   ), Ger
     R.80   S.c,1x,24a
ERDMANN, Eduard Paul Ernst (1896-1958), Ger
     R.14   S.1
ERHARDT, Siegfried
                 S.24
ERICH, Daniel (c1660-c1730), Ger
     R.1   S.c,10,53
ERICKSON, Frank (1923-   ), USA
     R.19   S.10,13

ERICKSON, Robert (1917-   ), USA
    R.1   S.10,13
ERIKSSON, Josef (1872-1957), Sweden
    R.2   S.24,56
ERIKSSON, Nils Frederick (1902-1978), Sweden
    R.14   S.24,40
ERKEL, Ferenc (1810-1893), Hun
    R.1   S.c,2-5,7-10,24,42
ERKIN, Ulvi Cemal (1906-1972), Turkey
    R.1   S.c,18,24
ERLANGER, Baron Frédéric d´ (1868-1943), Eng
    R.1   S.3,4,24
ERLANGER, Camille (1863-1919), Fr
    R.8   S.24
ERLEBACH, Philipp Heinrich (1657-1714), Ger
    R.1   S.c,2-5,8,10,24a
ERMATOV, Tashtan (1928-   )
                S.18
ERNESAKS, Gustav (1908-   ), Est
    R.1   S.18
ERNST LUDWIG, Landgrave of Hessen-Damstadt (1667-1739),
    Ger R.1
ERNST, David (1945-   ), USA
    R.19   S.10,13
ERNST, Heinrich Wilhelm (1814-1865), Moravia
    R.1   S.10,18,24
ERÖD, Ivan (1936-   )
    R.14   S.24a
ERTL, Dominik (1857-1911), Aus
    R.3   S.10
ERWIN, Lee Orville (1908-   ), USA
    R.23
ERWIN, Ralph - pseud [ie Erwin VOGL)
                S.24
ESBERGER, W. - American spirit
                S.54(312)
ESCHER, Rudolf (1912-1980), Neth
    R.1   S.10
ESCOBAR, Andrés de (16th Cent), Sp
    R.9   S.8
ESCOBAR, Maria Luisa (nee Gonzalez-Gragirena)
    (1903 or 1908-   ), Ven
    R.7   S.52
ESCOBAR, Pedro (c1465->1535), Port
    R.1   S.c,8,10,14-17,39
ESCOBEDO, A. - Alfonso Gaona
                S.54(311)
ESCOT, Pozzi (1933-   ), USA
    R.7   S.30,52

ESCUDERO, Francisco (1913-   ), Sp
    R.1   S.c
ESCURIEL, Jehan de l´ [see JEHANNOT de l´ESCUREL]
ESHANOV, Godel Simkhovich
    [see YESHANOV, Godel Simkhovich]
ESHAVY, Rene
                S.1x
ESHPAY, Andrey Yakovlevich (1925-   ), USSR
    R.1   S.18,24
ESIPOFF, Stepan - pseud [see BURNAND, Arthur Bransby]
ESLAVA, Miguel Hilarión (1807-1878), Sp
    R.1   S.1,2
ESPEJO, Cesar (1892-   )
                S.10,18,24
ESPERANÇA, Pedro da (c1598-1660), Port
    R.1   S.c,10
ESPERÓN, Ignacio Fernandez
    [see FERNANDEZ ESPERON, Ignacio]
ESPINOSA de los MONTEROS, Gaspar
                S.54(340)
ESPLA, Oscar (1886-1976), Sp
    R.1   S.c,2,8,10,32,39
ESPOSITO, Arnoldo d´ (1907-1945), Arg
    R.26   S.5x[Esposito, E. d´]
ESPOSITO, Michele (1855-1929), It
    R.1   S.10,24
ESQUIVEL BARAHONA, Juan (c1563->1613), Sp
    R.1   S.c,16,17
ESTE, Michael [see EAST, Michael]
ESTEBAN de VALERA, María
                S.10,32
ESTELLET-BRUN, Michel (1943-   ), Eng
                S.c
ESTENDORF, Anton (1670-1711)
                S.c,53
ESTERHÁZY, Pál (1635-1713), Hun
    R.1   S.c,9
ESTEVE y GRIMAU, Pablo (d.1794), Sp
    R.1   S.c,5x,8,10
ESTEVEZ, Antonio (1916-   ), Ven
    R.4
ESTRÉE, Jean d´ (d.1576), Fr
    R.1
ESTRELLA, Blanca (1915-   ), Ven
    R.4   S.30
ESTVAD, Leo
                S.33
ESTVILLA, Manuel - pseud [see PLESSOW, Erich]
ETERARDI (18th Cent), It - Concerto mandolin,
    2 vi & continuo in D

ETIENNE de MEAUX (13th Cent)
        S.c,10
ETLER, Alvin (1913-1973), USA
   R.1   S.10,13,19,20
ETOVOS, Peter (1944-   ), Hun

ETT, Kaspar (1788-1847), Ger
   R.2   S.c,2
ETTEN, van - Go U Northwestern
        S.54(329)
EUGENIE, Charlotte Augusta Amalia Albertina,
   Princess of Sweden (1830-1889)
   R.7   S.52
EULENBERG, Philipp (1847-1921), Ger
   R.10   S.c,4
EUROPE, James Reese (1881-1919), USA
   R.1   S.10
EUSLER, Edmund (1874-1949), Aus

EUSTATIE de la PUTNA, Protopsalt (c1460-?1546)
   R.33
EVANGELISTI, Franco (1926-1980), It
   R.1   S.10
EVANS, David (1874-1948), Wales
   R.3   S.c
EVANS, David Pughe [see PUGHE-EVANS, David]
EVANS, George - In the good old Summertime
        S.54(334)
EVANS, Gil (1912-   ), Can
   R.1   S.10
EVANS, H. - Det Karaste Namnet
        S.54(323)
EVANS, Lindley (1895-1982), Australia
   R.14   S.8
EVANS, Meredydd (1919-   ), Wales
        S.5x
EVANS, Merle (1892-   ), USA
   R.49   S.10,13[b.1893]
EVETT, Robert (1922-1975), USA
   R.19   S.c,10,13
EVILLE, Vernon McAll (1878-1932)
   R.200   S.e
EVLAKHOV, Orest (1912-   ), USSR
   R.14   S.24a
EWALD, Victor Vladimirovich (1860-1935), Russia
   R.28   S.c,10
EWALDT [see HINTZ, Ewaldt]
EWING, Alexander (1830-1895), Scot
   R.1   S.c

EWING, Montague
         S.54(350)
EXAUDET, André-Josef (c1710-c1762), Fr
  R.1   S.c,1x,10,24a
EXCETRE, J. (fl c1410), Eng
  R.1   S.16

EXTON, John (1933-   ), Eng
         S.29,37
EYBLER, Joseph Leopold (1765-1846), Aus
  R.1   S.c,2,10
EYCHENNE, Marc (1933-   ), Fr
         S.22
EYCK, Jacob van (1589/90-1657), Neth
  R.1   S.c,5x,6,9,10,32
EYKEN, Ernest van der (1913-   ), Bel
  R.25
EYKEN, Johan Albert van (1823-1868), Neth
  R.25   S.c
EYSER, Eberhard Friedrich (1932-   ), Ger
  R.25   S.c,9,40
EYSLER, Edmund (1874-1949), Aus
  R.1   S.c,10
FABER, Johann Christoph (fl 1730), Ger
  R.1   S.c
FABINI, Eduardo (1882-1950), Uruguay
  R.1   S.1-3,11,18
FABRI, Stefano (c1606-1658), It
  R.1   S.c
FABRICIUS, Petrus (1587-1651), Ger
  R.1   S.c,10,16,32
FABRICUS, Werner (1633-1679), Ger
  R.1   S.c
FABRIS, Ausonio de Lorenzi
  [see LORENZI, Fabris Ausonio de]
FABRO, Louis - pseud [see SCHMIDSEDER, Ludwig]
FACOLI, Marco (fl late 16th Cent), It
  R.1   S.c,10,16,53
FAGAN, Gideon (1904-1980), South Africa
  R.1
FAGEL, Adrien Henri
         S.e
FAHNESTOCK, Karol

FAHRBACH, Philipp Sr. (1815-1885), Aus [?]
  R.1   S.54(358)
FAHRBACH, Philipp Jr. (1843-1894), Aus
  R.1   S.c
FAIDIT, Gaucelm (c1150-c1220), Fr
  R.1   S.c,8,14-16

FAIGNIENT, Noë (fl c1560-1600), Flem
  R.1   S.c,16
FAIN [Feinberg], Sammy (1902-   ), USA
  R.1   S.1,9,10,18,24
FAINI - Amore e Maggio
           S.e
FAIRCHILD, Blair (1877-1933), USA
  R.1   S.2,3,13,24
FAISST, Immanuel Gottlob Friedrich (1823-1894), Ger
  R.1   S.c
FAIT, Renato (1914-   )
           S.c
FAIXÁ, Manuel M. (1892-   ), Sp
  R.9   S.e
FAIZI, Dzhaudat Khraisovich (1910-   ), USSR
  R.14   S.18
FALB, Remigius (fl 1755), Ger
  R.5   S.c
FALCINELLI, Rolande (1920-   ), Fr
  R.7   S.52
FALCKENHAGEN, Adam (1697-1761), Ger
  R.1   S.c
FALCONIERI, Andrea (1585/86-1656), It
  R.1   S.c,2-5,7,8,10,11,18
FALIK, Yury Alexandrovich (1936-   ), USSR
  R.1   S.18,24a
FALK, Georg Paul (d.1778)
           S.8
FALL, Leo (1873-1925), Aus
  R.1   S.c,2,3,5x,9,10
FALLA, Manuel de (1876-1946), Sp
  R.1   S.c,1-11,18,24,28,32,39,42
FALLAMERO, Gabriele (fl 1584), It
  R.1   S.c,16
FALLAS, Diana
           S.30
FALVO, Rodolfo (1874-1936), It
  R.52   S.10,18
FAMPAS, Dimitri (1922-   )
           S.c
FANELLO, Giovanni Bernardino (16th Cent)
  R.5   S.14
FANSHAWE, David Arthur (1942-   ), Eng
  R.80   S.9
FANTINI, Girolamo (b c1600), It
  R.1   S.c,10,16,53
FARA, Giulio (1880-1949), It [editor]
  R.4   S.1x
FARADAY, Philip Michael (1875-   )
  R.200   S.e

FARBERMAN, Harold (1929-   ), USA
    R.1   S.c,8-10,13
FARHAS - Six short pieces
                 S.32
FARINA, Carlo (c1600-c1640), It
    R.1   S.c,10,24
FARINA, Guido (1903-   ), It
    R.4
FARIÑAS, Carlos (1934-   ), Cuba
    R.1   S.24a,32
FARINELLI - pseud [see BROSCHI, Carlo]
FARIS, Alexander (1921-   ), Eng
    R.64

FARJEON, Harry (1878-1948), Eng
    R.25   S.5x
FARKAS, Andras (16th Cent), Hun
    R.15   S.c
FARKAS, Ferenc (1905-   ), Hun
    R.1   S.c,8-10,18,24
FARKAS, Ödön (1851-1912), Hun
    R.1
FARLEY, Roland (1892-1932), USA
    R.19   S.10,13
FARMER, Henry (1819-1891), Eng (see note)
    R.99   S.10
FARMER, John (1836-1901), Eng
    R.3   S.e
FARMER, John (fl 1591-1601), Eng
    R.1   S.c,2-8,10,11,14-16
FARNABY, Giles (c1563-1640), Eng
    R.1   S.c,1x,2-11,14-16,18,53
FARNABY, Richard (b c1594), Eng
    R.1   S.c,8,10,14,16
FARNAM, Walter Lynnwood (1885-1930), Can
    R.1   S.8,10,12,13
FARNON, Robert Joseph (1917-   ), Eng
    R.14   S.c,10,24,55
FARQUHAR, David (1928-   ), New Zealand
    R.1   S.c,24a
FARR, Ian (1941-   ), Australia
    R.35   S.29
FARRAND, Noel (1928-   ), USA
    R.19   S.6,13
FARRANDINI (see note)
                 S.5x
FARRANT, Daniel (fl c1607-40), Eng
    R.1
FARRANT, Richard (c1530-1580), Eng
    R.1   S.c,7,8,10,14,16

FARRAR, Ernest Bristow (1885-1918), Eng
   R.1   S.c
FARRAR, O. R. (fl 1895), USA
   R.53   S.10,13
FARRELL, Dennis

FARRENC, Louise (1804-1875), Fr
   R.1   S.10,30,52
FARRINGTON, Adele
            S.e
FARTHING, Thomas (d.1520), Eng
   R.1   S.c
FARWELL, Arthur (1877-1952), USA
   R.1   S.3,10,11,13
FASANG, Arpad (1912-   ), Hun
   R.15
FASCH, Carl Friedrich Christian (1736-1800), Ger
   R.1   S.c,5
FASCH, Johann Friedrich (1688-1758), Ger
   R.1   S.c,10,24
FASOLO, Giovanni Battista (c1600->1659), It
   R.1   S.c,5x,6,8,10,27
FASSETT - G.A.R. Patrol
            S.54(328)
FASSLER, Guido (1913-   )

FATTORINI - Si vous m'aimez encore
            S.e
FATTORINI, Gabriele (fl 1598-1609), It
   R.1   S.c,53
FATUO, G., It
   R.52,200   S.e
FAUCHEY, Paul (1858-1936), Fr
   R.4   S.e
FAUGUES, Guillaume (fl c1460), Fr
   R.1   S.16
FAULT, François du [see DUFAULT, François]
FAURÉ, Gabriel (1845-1924), Fr
   R.1   S.c,1x,2-11,18,24-28,32
FAURE, Jean-Baptiste (1830-1914), Fr
   R.1   S.c,1-4,5x,10,18,44
FAUTH, Ulrich St. (1940-   )
            S.c
FAVART - La dame à la licorne
            S.c
FAVART-EXAUDET - Menuet
            S.e
FAWICK, Thomas L.
            S.13,24

FAWKYNER (fl late 15th Cent), Eng
R.1   S.c,10,16
FAX, Mark (1911-1974), USA
R.19   S.13
FAXON, Nancy Plummer (1914-   ), USA
             S.10,12,13,52
FAYDIT, Gaucelm [see FAIDIT, Gaucelm]
FAYE, P. de - Tell her I love her
             S.e
FAYRFAX, Robert (1464-1521), Eng
R.1   S.c,5,8,10,14,16
FEARIS, John Sylvester (1867-1932), USA
R.43   S.13
FEAUTRIER, Edouard
             S.e
FEBRIER
             S.e
FECKHLER, Joseph Paris (1666-1735)
R.5
FEDELI, Carlo (c1622-1685), It
R.1
FEDOR, Tsar (1661-1682)
             S.c
FEDRI - Ninna, nanna
             S.10
FEFERMAN, Boris Veniaminovich (1920-   )
             S.18
FEGUEUX, François le [see LEFEGEUEX, François]
FEHRES, Wilhelm (1901-   ), Ger
R.4   S.c
FEINBERG, Samuel [see FAIN, Sammy]
FEININGER, Leonore Helene (1901-   ), Ger
R.7   S.52
FEKETE, Zoltan (1909-   ), Hun
R.14   S.7,8,10
FELBER - Danza Slovacca Noil (vi & p)
             S.24a
FELCIANO, Richard (1930-   ), USA
R.19   S.c,9,10,12,13
FELD, Jindrich (1925-   ), Cz
R.1   S.c,10,24,31
FELDBUSCH, Eric (1922-   ), Bel
R.1   S.24a
FELDER, Hans - pseud [see LENGSFELDER, Hans]
FELDERHOF, Jan (1907-   ), Neth
R.1   S.10
FELDMAN, Ludovic (1893-   ), Rum
R.33   S.24a
FELDMAN, Morton (1926), USA
R.1   S.9,10,12,13,24

FELDMAYER, Johann Georg (b 1757), Ger
R.5   S.c
FELDSTEIN, Saul (1940-   ), USA
R.19   S.13
FELIS, Stefano (c1550->1603), It
R.1   S.14
FELIX, Hugo (1866-1934), Aus
R.25   S.24
FELIX, Václav (1928-   ), Cz
R.1   S.18,19,24a,31
FELLEGARA, Vittorio (1927-   ), It
R.1   S.10
FELSTED, Samuel (18th Cent), Eng
R.5
FELSZTYNA, Sebastian z [see SEBASTIAN z FELSZTYNA]
FELTAMAN, Oscar (1921-   )
           S.24a
FELTON, William (1715-1769), Eng
R.1   S.3-5,10,11
FELTZMAN, Oscar Borisovich (1921-   ), USSR
R.14   S.18,24
FENAROLI, Fedele (1730-1818), It
R.1
FENNELLY, Brian (1937-   ), USA
R.1   S.10,13
FENNIMORE, Joseph (1940-   ), USA
R.80   S.13
FEO, Francesco (1691-1761), It
R.1
FEONA, Alexei Alexeyevich (1919-1977), USSR
R.47   S.18
FERAGUT, Beltrame (c1385-c1450), It
R.1   S.c,10,16
FERANDIERE, Fernando (fl 1771-?1816), Sp
R.1   S.10,18,32
FERDINAND III, Emperor of Austria (1608-1657)
R.1   S.10
FERE, Vladimir Georgievich (1902-   ), Russia
R.14   S.18
FEREMANS, Jan-Jozef Francisca Gaston (1907-1964), Bel
R.14
FERENCZY, Oto (1921-   ), Slovak
R.1   S.c,24,31
FERGUSON, Howard (1908-   ), Ulster
R.1   S.c,4,5,8,10,20,24
FERGUSON, W. Harold (1874-1950), Eng
           S.c
FERLAND, Armand (1926-   ), Can
R.31

FERNÁNDES, Gaspar (c1570-<1629), Mex
R.1   S.10
FERNÁNDEZ ARBÓS, Enrique [see ARBÓS, Enrique]
FERNÁNDEZ CABALLERO, Manuel (1835-1906), Sp
R.9   S.c,1,8-10,39,42
FERNÁNDEZ ESPERÓN, Ignacio [pseud: Tata NACHO]
(1894-1968), Mex
R.27   S.24,S.54(346)
FERNÁNDEZ HIDALGO, Gutierre (1553->1620), Peru
R.1   S.10
FERNÁNDEZ de HUETE, Diego (fl 1699-1704), Sp
R.1   S.c,10,17
FERNÁNDEZ de MADRID, Juan (fl 1479)
           S.17
FERNÁNDEZ PALERO, Francisco (d 1597), Sp
R.1   S.c,7,10,16,17,32,53
FERNÁNDEZ, Diego (15-16th Cent), Sp
R.1   S.c
FERNÁNDEZ, Jesus

FERNÁNDEZ, Oscar Lorenzo [see LORENZO FERNÁNDEZ, Oscar]
FERNÁNDEZ, Padre Hipolito (c1762), Sp
           S.8,10,39
FERNANDIERE, Fernando [see FERANDIERE, Fernando]
FERNEYHOUGH, Brian (1943-   ), Eng
R.1   S.c
FERNSTRÖM, John Axel (1897-1961), Sweden
R.1   S.c,8,10,18,20,40,56
FERRABOSCO, Alfonso I (1543-1688), It
R.1   S.c,10
FERRABOSCO, Alfonso II (<1575-1628), It
R.1   S.c,2,3,5,8,10,14-16,24
FERRABOSCO, Domenico Maria (1513-1574), It
R.3
FERRABOSCO, Matthia (1550-1616), It
R.1   S.c
FERRANDIERRE, Ferdinand [see FERANDIERE, Fernando]
FERRANDINI, Giovanni Battista (c1710-1791), It
R.1   S.5x
FERRANDINI, Mario (1863-1907), It
R.10,52   S.34
FERRANTE, Arthur (1921-   ), USA
R.23
FERRARA, Franco (1911-   ), It
R.14   S.10,24
FERRARI - Strambetto
           S.5x
FERRARI, Benedetto (1603/04-1681), It
R.1   S.c

FERRARI, Giacomo Gotifredo (1763-1842), It
   R.1   S.10,24
FERRARI, Giorgio (1925-   ), It
   R.14   S.c
FERRARI, Luc (1929-   ), Fr
   R.1   S.c,9,10
FERRARI, Mario (1884-   ), It
   R.10   S.24
FERRARI, Serafino Amedeo de (1824-1885), It
   R.10   S.e
FERRARI-TRECATE, Luigi (1884-1964), It
   R.1   S.24
FERRER, Anselmo (1882-   ), Sp
   R.1
FERRER, Guillermo (fl c1790), Sp
   R.1   S.8
FERRER, Mateo (1788-1864), Sp
   R.1   S.10
FERREYRA, Beatriz (1937-   ), Arg
   R.7   S.52
FERRI, Nicola (1831-1886), It
   R.3   S.e
FERRITTO, John (1937-   ), USA
   R.19   S.10,13,20
FERRONI, Vincenzo (1858-1934), It
   R.10   S.24
FERROUD, Pierre Octave (1900-1936), Fr
   R.1   S.1-5,11
FESCA, Alexander (1820-1849), Ger
   R.1   S.c,10
FESCH, Willem de [see DE FESCH, Willem]
FESTA, Costanzo (c1490-1545), It
   R.1   S.c,2,3,5x,7,10,14-16
FESTA, Sebastiano (c1495-1524), It
   R.1   S.c
FESTING, Michael Christian (d.1752), Eng
   R.1   S.c,2,3,5x,7,10,14-16
FÉTIS, François-Joseph (1784-1871), Bel
   R.1   S.9
FETLER, Paul (1920-   ), USA
   R.19   S.10,13
FETRÁS, Oscar - pseud [ie Oscar FASTER] (1854-1931)
   Ger R.1,95   S.c,10
FEUCHTMAYR, Franz Seraph (1750-1798)
              S.c
FEUVRE, Guy le [see LEFEUVRE, Guy]
FÉVIN, Antoine de (c1470-1511/12), Flem
   R.1   S.c,2,3,5x,6,8,10,14-16,41
FEVRIER, Henry (1875-1957), Fr
   R.1   S.1-4,24

FIALA, George (1922-   ), Can
  R.4
FIALA, Jaromir (1892-1967), Cz
  R.1   S.24,31
FIALA, Joseph (1748-1816), Cz
  R.1   S.5x,10
FIALA, Petr (1943-   ), Cz
  R.14   S.c
FIBICH, Zdenek (1850-1900), Cz
  R.1   S.c,1x,2-10,18,24,42
FICARELLI, Mario (1937-   ), Brazil
  R.80   S.c
FICHER, Jacobo (1896-1978), Arg
  R.1   S.c,10,11,46
FICHTENHOLZ, Mikhail Israilevich (1920-   )
       S.18,24
FICKENSCHER, Arthur (1871-1954), USA
  R.19   S.7,10,13
FIEBIG, Kurt (1908-   ), Ger
  R.14
FIELD - North star (vi & p)
       S.24
FIELD, John (1782-1837), Ire
  R.1   S.c,2-5,8-11,24
FIELDING - A hunting we will go
       S.e
FIETZ, Siegfried
       S.c
FIGUEIREDO, Manuel Pinto de
       S.24
FIGUEREDO, Pedro (1819-1870), Cuba
  R.56,94   S.54(321,32)
FIGUIERA, Ghilhelm (13th Cent)
       S.c
FILIAMO, Girolamo (1473-1548)

FILIASI, Lorenzo (1878-   ), It
  R.3   S.e
FILIBERTO de LAURENTIIS [see LAURENZI, Filiberto]
FILIPPENKO, Arkady Dmitrievich (1912-   ), USSR
  R.14   S.c,18,24a
FILIPPI, Filippo (1830-1887), It
  R.10
FILIPPINI - Kleine Poppenice; Komm zu mir heut Nacht
       S.24a
FILLI RICCI [see RICCI, Frederico and Luigi]
FILLMORE, Augustus Dameron (1823-1870), USA
  R.57

FILLMORE, Henry (1881-1956), USA [pseud: Harold BENNETT
    Ray HALL, Harry HARTLEY, Al HAYES, Will HUFF]
    R.4,19,49   S.10,13,54(313,32,65)
FILLMORE, T. K. - Slim trombone; Lasses

FILOTEI (1368-1418) - Pripeala

FILTZ, Anton (1733-1760), Ger
    R.1   S.c,4,5,10
FINAROVSKY, Grigori Abramovich (1906-   ), USSR
    R.14   S.24a
FINCK, Heinrich (1444/45-1527), Ger
    R.1   S.c,2-4,5x,8-11,14-16,18,32,53
FINCK, Herman (1872-   ), Eng
    R.3   S.54(338,46)
FINCK, Hermann (1527-1558), Ger
    R.2   S.c
FINDEISEN, Theodore Albin (1881-1936), Ger
    R.3   S.c
FINE, Irving (1914-1962) USA
    R.1   S.c,7-10,13,25,27
FINE, Vivian (1913-   ), USA
    R.19   S.10,13,30,52
FINETTI, Giacomo (fl 1605-31), It
    R.1   S.c
FINGER, Gottfried (c1660-1730), Moravia
    R.1   S.c,10
FINK, Christian (1831-1911), Ger
    R.3   S.c
FINK, Heinrich [see FINCK, Heinrich]
FINK, Siegfried (1928-   ), Ger
    R.4   S.c,10
FINKBEINER, Reinhold (1929-   ), Ger
    R.14
FINKE, Fidelio Fritz (1891-1968), Ger
    R.4
FINKO, D. (1936-   )
                    S.24a
FINLAYSON, Walter Allan (1919-   ), USA
    R.23   S.13,54(359)
FINNEY, Charles H. USA
                    S.10,12
FINNEY, Ross Lee (1906-   ), USA
    R.1   S.10,12,13,25,27
FINZI, Gerald (1901-1956), Eng
    R.1   S.c,5,8-10,19-21,24a,25,27
FINZI, Graciane (1945-   ), Fr
    R.7   S.c,52
FIOCCO, Joseph-Hector (1703-1741), S. Neth
    R.1   S.c,2-5,8-10,18,22-24,41,53

FIORAVANTI, Valentino (1764-1837), It
R.1   S.c,7,9,42
FIORENTINO, Perino [see Perino FIORENTINO]
FIORENZA, Nicola (d.1764), It
R.1   S.c,10,30
FIORILLO, Dante (1905-   ), USA
R.4   S.13
FIORILLO, Federigo (1755->1823), It
R.1   S.c,2,3,10,24
FIORINO, Gasparo (fl 1571-4), It
R.1   S.c
FIORITO, Ted (1900-   ), USA
R.23   S.24
FIORONI, Giovanni Andrea (?1704-1778), It
R.1   S.4,5
FIRENZE, (12th Cent?), It - Aposte messe
             S.c
FIRENZE, P. de [see PAOLO de FIRENZE]
FIRESTONE, Idabelle (Mrs. Harvey S. Firestone)
(1874-1954), USA
R.23   S.13,43,52
FIRMIN le BEL [see LEBEL, Firmin]
FIRTH, Vic (Everett Joseph) (1930-   ), USA
R.23
FISCHBERG, Jascha
             S.24
FISCHER, Adolphe (1847-1891), Bel
R.3   S.13
FISCHER, Carl Theodore (1912-   ), USA
R.23   S.9,13
FISCHER, Ernst (1900-1975), Ger
R.14   S.c
FISCHER, Gotthelf (1928-   )

FISCHER, Irwin (1903-   ), USA
R.1   S.10,13
FISCHER, Jan Frank (1921-   ), Cz
R.1   S.c,31
FISCHER, Johann (1646-1716/17), Ger
R.1   S.c
FISCHER, Johann Caspar Ferdinand (c1670-1746), Ger
R.1   S.c,4,5,7-11,18,53
FISCHER, Johann Christian (1733-1800), Ger
R.1   S.c,8,10
FISCHER, Karl Ludwig (1816-1877), Ger
R.3   S.e
FISCHER, Matthäus Karl Konrad (1763-1840), Ger
R.25   S.5x
FISCHER, Michael Gottard (1773-1829), Ger
R.1   S.c,20

FISCHER, William Samuel (1935-   ), USA
    R.23   S.10,13
FISCHER, William Gustavus (1835-1912), USA
    R.1   S.10
FISCHOF, Robert (1856-1918), Aus
    R.3   S.e
FIŠER, Luboš (1935-   ), Cz
    R.1   S.c,10,24a,31
FISHBURN, Christopher (fl 1678-98), Eng (see note)
    R.1   S.5x
FISHER, Fred (1875-1942), USA
    R.23   S.24
FISHER, Gladys W.(1900-   ), USA
    R.7   S.30
FISHER, W. Howard
                S.24
FISHER, John Abraham (1744-1806), Eng
    R.1   S.5x,10

FISHER, Katherine Danforth (1913-   ), USA
    R.7   S.52
FISHER, Truman (1927-   ), USA
    R.14   S.13
FISHER, William Arms (1861-1948), USA
    R.23   S.2(141)
FISSINGER, Alfred (1925-   ), USA
                S.10,13
FITTIPALDI, Vincento
                S.24a
FITZENHAGEN, Wilhelm (1848-1890), Ger
    R.1   S.5x,10
FJODOR, Zar [see FEDOR, Tsar]
FLACKTON, William (1709-1798), Eng
    R.1   S.10,23
FLAGELLO, Nicolas (1928-   ), USA
    R.1   S.c,9,10,13,25,27,32
FLAGG, Josiah (1737-c1795), USA
    R.1   S.10,47
FLAMENT, Edouard (1880-1958), Fr
    R.14   S.2-4,24
FLANAGAN, William (1923-1969), USA
    R.1   S.7-10,13,23-27
FLECHA, Mateo el Viejo (1481-1553), Sp
    R.1   S.c,15,16
FLECHA, Mateo el Joven (c1530-1604), Sp
    R.1   S.10,17,39
FLÉGIER, Ange (1846-1927), Fr
    R.10   S.1x,5x,10,18,24
FLEGL, Josef (1881-1962), Cz
    R.18   S.31

FLEISCHER, Friedrich Gottlob (1722-1806), Ger
  R.1
FLEISCHMANN, Aloys (1910-   ), Ire
  R.1   S.49
FLEISCHMANN, Otto (1867-1924), Ger
  R.3   S.5x
FLEMING, Hans Friedrich von
             S.10
FLEMING, Robert (1921-1976), Can
  R.1   S.10
FLETCHER - Gridiron King
             S.54(330)
FLETCHER, Andrew (20th Cent), Eng
             S.c
FLETCHER, Grant (1913-   ), USA
  R.19
FLETCHER, John (fl 1884)
  R.200   S.e
FLETCHER, Percy (1879-1932), Eng
  R.1   S.c,5x,54(330,63),55
FLEURIE (14th Cent), Fr
  R.1   S.10
FLEURY, André (1903-   ), Fr
  R.1   S.c,10
FLICK-FLOOD, Dora (1885-   ), USA

  R.19   S.13,30,52
FLIES, Bernard (1770-   ), Ger
  R.5   S.c,5x,10,24
FLOQUET, Etienne Joseph (1748-1785), Fr
  R.1
FLOR, Christian (1626-1697), Ger
  R.1   S.c
FLORENCE, Paul (1864-1949)
             S.24a
FLORES, José Asunción (1904-   ), Paraguay
  R.4   S.18
FLORI, Jacob (fl 1571-99), Neth
  R.25   S.c
FLORI, Francesco (d.1588), Neth
  R.1
FLORIDIA, Pietro (1860-1932), It
  R.10   S.e
FLORONI, Giovani (1704-1778), It

FLOSMAN, Oldřich (1925-   ), Cz
  R.1   S.c,10,24a,31
FLOTHUIS, Marius (1914-   ), Neth
  R.1   S.c,10
FLOTOW, Friedrich (1812-1883), Ger
  R.1   S.c,1-11,18,34,42-44,54(342)

FLOYD, Carlisle (1926-   ), USA
R.1   S.10,13,26,27
FLOYD, Mont Keene (1941-   ), USA - Blues, horn & p

FLURY, Richard (1896-1967), Swiss
R.4   S.24a
FLYARKOVSKY, Alexander Georgievich (1931-   ), USSR
R.14   S.18
FLYNN, George (1937-   ), USA
R.19   S.10,13
FLYNN, John H.
             S.10
FLYNN, Norah
             S.e
FO, Jacopo [see FOGLIANO, Giacomo]
FOB, Harry

FOCK, Alfred
             S.e
FOERSTER, Adolph Martin (1854-1927), USA
R.4   S.13
FOERSTER, Josef Bohuslav (1859-1951), Cz
R.1   S.4-10,18,23,24
FOGGIA, Francesco (1604-1688), It
R.1   S.c
FOGLIANI, Lodovico (d c1539),It
R.1   S.16
FOGLIANO [da MODENA], Giacomo (1468-1548), It
R.1   S.c,5,10,16,17,53
FOLEY, David Francis (1945-   ), USA
R.19   S.10,13
FOLPRECHT, Zdenek (1900-1961), Cz

R.14   S.31
FOLQUET de MARSEILLE (1150/60-1231), Fr
R.1   S.c,16
FOLTIN, Gunter (1926-   )
             S.c
FOLZ, Hans (c1440-1513), Ger
R.1   S.10,14
FOMENKO, Mykola (1894-1961), USA
R.13   S.24[b.1895]
FOMIN, Evstigney Ipatovich (1761-1800), Russia
R.1   S.c,18
FONGAARD, Björn (1919-   ), Nor
R.14   S.c,10,40,51
FONTAINE, Pierre (?1390/95-c1450), Fr
R.1   S.c,10,16
FONTANA, Giovanni Battista (d c1630), It
R.1   S.c,10,24

FONTANA, Vincenzo (fl 1540-50), It
   R.1   S.c
FONTEI, Nicolò (d.1647), It
   R.1   S.c
FONTENLA, Jorge (1927-   ), Arg
   R.26   S.46
FONTENAILLES, H. de, Fr
             S.4,5x,10
FONTENAILLES, Nicolas de

FONTYN, Jacqueline (1930-   ), Bel
   R.7   S.30,24a,52
FONZO, Pasquale Ernesto (1860-1935), It
   R.10,10s,52 S.e
FOORT, Reginald (1893-   ), Eng
   R.1   S.10
FOOTE, Arthur (1853-1937), USA
   R.1   S.c,3-5,7,8,10-13,24a
FORBES, John (d.1675), Scot [publisher]
   R.1   S.c
FORBES, Sebastian (1941-   ), Eng
   R.1   S.c,10
FORD, Charles Edgar (1881-1961), Australia
   R.25   S.29
FORD, Eric

FORD, Thomas (d.1648), Eng
   R.1   S.c,2-6,10,14-16,27,28,32
FOREST, Jean Kurt (1909-1975), Ger
   R.1
FOREST, [?John] d.1446, Eng
   R.1   S.c,16
FORMAN, Joanne (1934-   ), USA
   R.19   S.13,30,52
FORMICHI, Pietro (1829-1913), It
   R.10   S.54(340)
FORNELLS - Mi jota
             S.e
FORNEROD, Aloÿs Henri-Gérard (1890-1965), Swiss

   R.1   S.2-4,8,24
FORNS y CUADRAS, José (1898-1952), Sp
   R.1
FORNSETE, John [see JOHN of FORNSETE]
FORQUERAY, Antoine (1671-1745), Fr
   R.1   S.c,9,10,24a
FORSBERG, Roland (1939-   ), Sweden
   R.80   S.40,56
FORSLAND, Rolf Bruce ?USA
             S.13

FORSMAN, John Väinö (1924-   ), Den
    R.14   S.24
FORST, Rudolf (1900-1973), USA
    R.19   S.13
FORSTER - On the field path
                S.1x
FÖRSTER, Christoph (1693-1745), Ger
    R.1   S.c,10
FORSTER, Dorothy (1884-1950), Eng
    R.7   S.24
FÖRSTER, Emanuel Aloys (1748-1823), Ger
    R.1   S.c
FORSTER, Georg - Son Ob & bc in c = FORSTER, Christoph
FORSTER, [?Georg] - I say adieu
                S.16
FORSTER, Glad USA
                S.13
FORSTER, John (17-18th Cent) - March & gigue
                S.c
FORSYTH, Malcolm Denis (1936-   ), Can
    R.31
FORSYTHE, Reginald (1907-   ), Eng
    R.30a   S.11
FORTEA, Daniel (1882-1953), Sp
    R.9   S.8
FORTNER, Wolfgang (1907-   ), Ger
    R.1   S.c,5x,7,8,10
FORTSCH, Wolfgang (1675-1743), Ger
    R.5   S.c
FOSCARINI, Giovanni Paulo (17th Cent), It
    R.1   S.c
FOSS, Harry
                S.c
FOSS, Lukas (1922-   ), USA
    R.1   S.4-6,8-10,13,18,24a
FOSSA, Johannes de (c1540-1603), Ger
    R.1   S.10
FOSTER, Dudley (1935-   ), USA
                S.12,13
FOSTER, Fay (1886-1960), USA
    R.7   S.13
FOSTER, Stephen Collins (1826-1864), USA
    R.1   S.1x,2-4,5x,9-11,18,19,24,28,47,54(346)
FOSTER, William USA
                S.10,47
FOTHERGILL, Frank - pseud [see TATE, Arthur Frank]
FOULDS, John (1880-1939), Eng
    R.1   S.c,5x
FOULKES, S. - Sérénade d'amour (vi & p)
                S.24

FOURDRAIN, Felix (1880-1923), Fr
  R.10   S.10
FOWLER, Jennifer Joan (1939-   ), Australia
  R.7   S.29,52
FOX, Aynsly
             S.e
FOX, George (?1854-1902), Eng
  R.44
FOX, James (1953-   ), USA
  R.19   S.13 [b.1913]
FRABIZIO, William (1929-   ), USA
  R.19   S.10,13
FRANCHISENA, César Mario (1923-   ), Arg
  R.26   S.46
FRACKENPOHL, Arthur (1924-   ), USA
  R.19   S.10,13
FRADKIN, Frederick (1892-1963), USA
  R.4   S.24
FRAGNA - Notte a S. Lucia
            S.5x
FRAJT, Ludmila (1919-   ), Yug
  R.7   S.52
FRANÇAIX, Jean (1912-   ), Fr
  R.1   S.c,3-11,18,19,22,24,42
FRANCE, William Edward (1912-   ), Can
  R.14
FRANCES - Saltiro de la cardina

FRANCESCATTI, Zino (1902-   ), Fr
  R.1   S.8,10,24a
FRANCESCHINI, Gaetano (18th Cent), USA
            S.7,10,47
FRANCESCHINI, Petronio (c1650-c1680), Fr
  R.1   S.c,10,24
FRANCESCO CANOVA da MILANO (1497-1543), It
  R.1   S.c,5x,8,10,14,15,17,18
FRANCESCO Veneto [see ANA, Francesco d']
FRANCHETTI, Alberto (1860-1942), It
  R.1   S.c,2-4,9,10,34
FRANCHETTI, Arnold (1906-   ), USA
  R.19   S.10,13,24
FRANCHOIS, Johannes (fl 1378-1415), Franco-Flem
  R.1   S.c
FRANCHOMME, August (1808-1884), Fr
  R.1   S.c
FRANCI, Rinaldo (1854-1907), It
  R.10   S.24
FRANCISCUS Raynaldus (14th Cent)
            S.16

FRANCISCUS, Magister (fl 1370-80), Fr
    R.1   S.4,5x
FRANCISQUE, Anthoine (c1575-1605), Fr
    R.1   S.c,5x,8,10,14,16,18,32,53
FRANCK, César (1822-1890), Fr
    R.1   S.c,2-11,18,21,24,27,36,41
FRANCK, Johann Wolfgang (1644-?c1710), Ger
    R.1   S.2-5,7,8,10,32
FRANCK, Johann Zacharias (1686-1756)
                 S.c
FRANCK, Melchior (c1579-1639), Ger
    R.1   S.c,2-5,8-11,14-16
FRANCO of COLOGNE (13th Cent), Ger
    R.1   S.2-4,10
FRANCO, Hernando (1532-1585), Sp
    R.1   S.10
FRANCO, Johan (1908-   ), USA
    R.1   S.10,13
FRANCO, José María (1894-   ), Sp
    R.9
FRANCO (attrib) - Ave, gloriosa mater salvatoris
                 S.5x
FRANCO-REBOLLO, Eustaquio (16-17th Cent)
                 S.c
FRANCOEUR, François (1698-1787), Fr
    R.1   S.c,2-5,8-10,18,19,21,24
FRANÇOIS, Samson [see SAMSON-FRANÇOIS]
FRANCUS de INSULA (fl 1420-25), Flem
    R.1   S.c,10,16
FRANK (15th Cent), Eng - Quene note
    R.1
FRANK, Alan (1910-   ), Eng
    R.1   S.3,4,5x,20
FRANK, Andrew (1946-   ), USA
    R.19   S.10,13
FRANKEL, Benjamin (1906-1973), Eng
    R.1   S.c,4,20,24
FRANKEL, Machelle (1936-   )

FRANKEN, Wim (1922-   ), Neth
    R.80   S.10
FRANKENSTEIN, Lutz - pseud [see HUSADEL, Hans Felix]
FRANKL, Ben (1912-   )

FRANKLIN, Benjamin (1706-1790), USA
    R.1   S.10,47
FRANKLIN-PIKE, Eleanor Baxter
    [see PIKE, Eleanor Baxter Franklin]
FRANKO, Sam (1857-1937), USA
    R.10,200   S.24

FRANKOWSKI, Hans (1888-   ), Aus
  R.3   S.10
FRANKSHTEIN, B. (1949-   )
          S.24a
FRANZ, A. - Der alte Dessauer
          S.54(312)
FRANZ, Robert (1815-1892), Ger
  R.1   S.c,1x,2-11,24,26-28
FRANZE, Juan Pedro (1922-   ), Arg
  R.26   S.46
FRANZEN, Olov Alfred (1946-   ), Sweden
  R.80   S.40
FRANZL, Ferdinand (1767-1833), Ger
  R.1   S.c
FRÄNZL, Ignaz (1736-1811), Ger
  R.1   S.c
FRASER, Jean (1920-   ), Can
  R.31   S.24
FRASER, Norman George (1904-   ), Eng
  R.14   S.10,24
FRASER-SIMSON, Harold (1872-1944), Eng
  R.1   S.c,2-4,24a
FRATELLI RICCI [see RICCI, Frederico and Luigi]
FRATER PETRUS [see PETRUS, Frater]
FRAUENHOLZ, Roman (1948-   )
          S.c
FRAUENLOB [Heinrich von Meissen] (c1250-1318), Ger
  R.1   S.c,8,14-16
FRAZEUR, Theodore (1929-   ), USA
  R.19   S.13,24a
FREDERICK II, King of Prussia (1712-1786), Ger
  R.1   S.c,2-10
FREDRICKSON, Thomas (1928-   ), USA
  R.19   S.13
FREED, Arnold (1926-   ), USA
  R.14   S.13
FREED, Dorothy Whitson (née Doorly) (1919-   )
  New Zealand R.7   S.52
FREED, Isadore (1900-1960), USA
  R.1   S.3,5x,11,13
FREEDMAN, Harry (1922-   ), Can
  R.1   S.10,24
FREEDMAN, Robert Morris (1934-   ), USA
  R.23   S.13
FREEMAN, John (1928-   ), USA
  R.19   S.13
FREESE - 'mong the green Irish hills
          S.e
FREIBERG, Gottfried (1908-1962), Aus
  R.4

FREIBERT, Joseph (1723-1799)

FREID, G. [S.23] = FRID, Grigori Samuilovich
FREILLON PONCEIN, Jean-Pierre (18th Cent)
      S.c,10
FREINSBERG, Jean Adam Guillaume [see GUILAIN]
FREIRE, Osman Perez (1878-1930), Chile
      S.c,5x,10,24,39,43
FREISSLICH, Johann Balthasar Christian (1687-1764), Ger
  R.1   S.c
FREITAS, Frederico de (1902-1980), Por
  R.1   S.18,24a
FREITHOFF, Johan Henrik (1713-1767), Nor
  R.1   S.c,24a
FREIXANET (18th Cent), Sp
      S.5x,8,10,39
FRENCH, Jacob (1754-1817), USA
  R.50   S.10,47
FRENCH, William Percy
      S.54(344)
FRENKEL, Benjamin Henrik (1713-1773)
      S.24a
FRESCOBALDI, Girolamo (1583-1643), It
  R.1   S.c,2-11,18,22,24,53
FRESNEAU, Henry (fl 1538-54), Fr
  R.1   S.16
FREŠO, Tibor (1918-　　), Slovak
  R.1   S.5x,6,24
FREUNDT, Cornelius (c1535-1591), Ger
  R.1   S.c,16
FREY, Hugo (1873-1952), USA
  R.23   S.54(345)
FREY, Jorg (1953-　　)
      S.c
FREYER, August (1803-1883), Pol
  R.1
FREYLINGHAUSEN, Johann Anastasius (1670-1739), Ger
  R.1   S.8
FREYNE, Rollo de
      S.24
FREYSTÄDTLER, Franz Jakob (1768-1841), Aus
  R.8   S.c
FRICKER, Herbert Austin (1868-1943), Eng
  R.4
FRICKER, Peter Racine (1920-　　), Eng
  R.1   S.c,8-10,24,32
FRID, Géza (1904-　　), Neth
  R.1   S.10
FRID, Grigori Samuilovich (1915-　　), USSR
  R.14   S.18,23[Freid, G.]

FRIDERICI, Daniel (1584-1638), Ger
R.1   S.c,8,14,16
FRIDL - Rosl waltz
             S.5x
FRIEBERG, Frans Alfred (1812-1913), Sweden
R.111   S.e
FRIEBERGER, Rupert Gottfried (1951-   )
             S.c
FRIEBERT, Joseph (1724-1799), Aus
R.1   S.c
FRIED, Alexej (1922-   ), Cz
R.14   S.c,31
FRIEDBERG, Carl (1872-1955), Ger
R.8   S.10,24
FRIEDELL, Harold William (1905-1958), USA
R.23   S.7,10,13
FRIEDEMANN, Carl Berthold Ulrich (1862-1952), Ger
R.95   S.54(356)
FRIEDHOFER, Hugo (1902-1981), USA
R.1   S.9,10
FRIEDMAN, Ignacy (1882-1948), Pol
R.1   S.c,24
FRIEDMAN, Leo (1869-1927), USA
R.23   S.10
FRIEDMAN, Stanleigh P. (1884-1960), USA
R.23   S.13
FRIEDMAN, Theodore Leopold [pseud: Ted LEWIS]
   (1892-1971), USA   R.23   S.10
FRIEDRICH, C. H.

FRIEDRICH, G. W. E. USA - The Lilly Bell Quickstep
             S.10
FRIEDRICH von HUSEN (c1150-1196), Ger
R.1   S.c,16,2-4,5x,11
FRIESE, Alfred USA
             S.13
FRIJS - Til min Gyldenlak
             S.e
FRIKLOFF, Harold (1882-1919)
             S.18
FRIML, Rudolf (1879-1972), USA
R.1   S.1x,2-4,5x,9-11,24,43,54(335)
FRITSCH, Johannes (1941-   ), Ger
R.1   S.c
FRITSCHELL, James (1929-   ), USA
R.19   S.10,13
FRITZ, Gaspard (1716-1783), Swiss
R.1   S.c,4,5,24
FROBERGER, Johann Jacob (1616-1667), Ger
R.1   S.c,4,5,7-11,18,32,53

FRODING, Ferdinand (1826-1881)
      S.c
FROES - Mimosa (v, Beniamino Gigli)

FRÖHLICH, Franz Joseph (1780-1862), Ger
   R.8
FRÖHLICH, Friedrich Theodor (1803-1836), Swiss
   R.1   S.c,10
FROHNE, Vincent (1936-   ), USA
   R.19   S.13
FROIDEBISE, Pierre (1914-1962), Bel
   R.1   S.c,36
FROISSART, Jehan (c1337-c1404)
              S.8,14
FROLOV, Markian (1892-1944), USSR
   R.4   S.18
FROMM, Herbert (1905-   ), Ger
   R.4   S.8,9,12,13,24a
FRONCIACO [see DEFRONCIACO]
FRONMULLER, Frieda (1901-   ), Ger
   R.7   S.c,52
FROSINI (see note)
              S.10
FRUCTUS del CASTILLO
              S.10
FRÜH, Huldreich Georg (1903-1945), Swiss
   R.1
FRUMERIE, Gunnar (1908-   ), Sweden
   R.1   S.c,4-6,24,38,40,56
FRY, William Henry (1813-1864), USA
   R.1   S.8,10,47
FRYBA, Hans

FRYE, Walter (fl c1450-75), Eng
   R.1   S.c,10,16
FRYKLÖF, Harald (1882-1919), Sweden
   R.1   S.c,24a,40,56
FRYXELL [Fryzell], Regina Holmen (1899-   ), USA
   R.19   S.10,13,30,52
FUCHS, K. E. - Ungarisches Märchen
              S.5x
FUCHS, Lillian (1903-   ), USA
   R.1   S.10,24,30,52
FUCHS, Robert (1847-1927), Aus
   R.1   S.c,24
FUČIK, Julius (1872-1916), Cz
   R.1   S.c,5x,10,54(319,25,27,52)
FUCITO, Salvatore (?1875-1929)
              S.44

FUENLLANA, Miguel de (16th Cent), Sp
   R.1   S.c,2-4,5x,8,10,11,14,16,18,32,39
FUENTES, Eduardo Sanchez de
   [see SANCHEZ de FUENTES, Eduardo]
FUERSTNER, Carl (1912-   ), USA
   R.4   S.13
FUGA, Sandro (1906-   ), It
   R.1   S.5x,24
FUHRMANN, Georg Leopold (fl 1606-15), Ger [publisher]
   R.1   S.c
FUKAI, Shiro (1907-1959) Japan
   R.4
FUKUSHIMA, Kazuo (1930-   ), Japan
   R.1   S.c,10,50
FUKUSHIMA, Yujiro (1932-   ), Japan
         S.50
FULEIHAN, Anis (1901-1970), USA
   R.1   S.10,13
FULKERSON, James (1945-   ), USA
   R.19   S.10,13
FULLER, Gilbert
         S.9
FULTON, James M. (1873-1940), USA
   R.49   S.54(315)
FULTON, Norman (1909-1980), Eng
   R.1   S.c
FUMET, Dynam-Victor (1867-1949), Fr
   R.1   S.c
FUMET, Raphael (1898-1979)
         S.c
FUNCK, David (c1630->1690), Ger
   R.1   S.c,4,5,24
FURBE, Johannes (fl 1760)
         S.c
FURGEOT, J. Fr - Marche de la Garde Consulaire à
   Marengo   S.54(340)
FURMANIK, Josef (1867-1953), Pol

FURRER, Franz (1943-   )

FÜRST, Fritz
         S.e
FÜRST, Georg (1870-1936), Ger
   R.95   S.54(314)
FÜRST, Paul Walter (1926-   ), Aus
   R.1   S.c,5x
FÜRSTENAU, Anton Bernhard (1792-1852), Ger
   R.1   S.c,10
FÜRSTENAU, Caspar (1772-1819), Ger
   R.1   S.c,8

FURTWÄNGLER, Wilhelm (1886-1954), Ger
  R.1   S.c,3,4,7-10,24a
FUSCO, Giovanni (1906-1968), It
  R.8   S.5x
FUSS, János [see FUSZ, Johann Evangelist]
FUSSAN, Werner (1912-   ), Ger
  R.1   S.c
FUSSELL, Charles (1938-   ), USA
  R.19   S.10,13
FUSTE - Háblame de amores
               S.5x,10
FUSTER VIRTO, Francisco (1887-   ), Sp
  R.13   S.e
FUSZ, Johann Evangelista [Fuss, Janos] (1777-1819), Hun
  R.1   S.10,24a
FUX, Johann Joseph (1660-1741), Aus
  R.1   S.c,7-10,24a,53
GABARAYEV, Ilya (1926-   )
               S.18
GABAYE, Pierre (1903-   ), Fr
  R.14   S.10
GABELLONE, Gaspare (1727-1796), It
  R.1   S.c
GABER, Harley (1943-   ), USA
  R.19   S.10,13,24a
GABETTI, Giuseppe (1796-1862), It
  R.3   S.54(353)
GABICHVADZE, Revaz Kondratyevich (1913-   ), Georgia
  R.1   S.18
GABRIEL, Charles Hutchison (1856-1932), USA
  R.1
GABRIEL, Mena [see MENA, Gabriel]
GABRIEL-MARIE - pseud [see MARIE, Gabriel]
GABRIELI, Andrea (c1510-1586), It
  R.1   S.c,2-6,8-11,14-16,18,32,53
GABRIELI, Giovanni (c1553-1612), It
  R.1   S.c,2-6,8-11,14,15,23,53
GABRIELLI, Domenico (1651-1690), It
  R.1   S.c,5x,6,8,10
GABRIELSKI, Johann Wilhelm (1791-1846), Ger
  R.2   S.8,10
GABRILOVICH, Ossip (1878-1936), USA
  R.1   S.13
GABRINSKY - Petite polonaise (vi & p)
               S.24
GABURO, Kenneth (1926-   ), USA
  R.1   S.9,10,13
GABUSSIO, Giulio Cesare (1555-1611), It
  R.1   S.c[Gabuzio],53

GACE BRULÉ (c1160->1213), Fr
   R.1   S.c,8,10,14,16
GADE, Jacob (1879-1963), Den
   R.14   S.c,4,5x,10,24,33
GADE, Niels (1817-1890), Den
   R.1   S.c,2-10,20,24,33,35,40,57
GADZHIBEKOV, Sultan [see HAJIBEYOV, Sultan]
GADZHIBEKOV, Uzeir [see HAJIBEYOV, Uzeir]
GADZHIBEKOV, Zulfugar Abdul Hussein (1884-1950), USSR
   R.14   S.18
GADZHIYEV, D. [see HAJIYEV, Akhmet]
GADZHIYEV, Rauf Soltanogly (1922-   ), USSR
   R.14   S.18,24[Gajiev]
GAETA, Giovanni [see MARIO, E. A. - pseud]
GAFFURIUS, Franchinus (1451-1522), It
   R.1   S.c,10,14-16
GAGLIANO, Marco da (1582-1643), It
   R.1   S.c,5x,6,8-10,14,16
GAGNEBIN, Henri (1886-1977), Swiss
   R.1   S.c,8,10,24

GAGNIER, Josephat Jean (1885-1949), Can
   R.49
GAGNON, Alain (1938-   ), Can
   R.4
GAGNON, Roland
             S.10
GAIGEROVA, Varvara Andrianovna (1903-1944), USSR
   R.7   S.18,52
GAILLARD, Marius-François (1900-1973), Fr   (see note)
   R.1   S.8,24
GAINSBORG, Lolita Cabrera (1895-1981), USA
   R.43   S.30,52
GAITO, Constantino (1878-1945), Arg
   R.1   S.8,46
GAIZHAUSKAS, Yurgis (1922-   )
             S.18,24a
GAJIEV, Rauf [see GADZHIYEV, Rauf]
GAL, Hans (1890-   ), Aus
   R.1   S.c,10
GALILEI, Michel Angelo (fl 1620), It
   R.5   S.c,10,15,16
GALILEI, Vicenzo (c1520-1591), It
   R.1   S.c,2-5,8,10,14-16,18,32
GALINDO, Aurello
             S.54(363)
GALINDO, Dimas Blas (1910-   ), Mex
   R.1   S.c,8,10,24a,39
GALINEN, Herman [see GALYNIN, Herman]

GALIOT, Johannes (fl 1380-95), Fr
R.1   S.c
GALKA, Jedrzej (fl 1450)
           S.c,16
GALKIN, Nikolai Vladomirovich (1850-1906), Russia
R.3   S.10
GALL, Jan Karol (1856-1912), Pol
R.1

GALLA, V. [see HALLA, V.]
GALLAGHER, Edward A. (1928-   ), USA
R.23   S.10
GALLATLY, James
           S.24
GALLAY, Jacques François (1795-1864), Fr
R.1   S.10
GALLES, Padre José (1761-1836), Sp
R.25   S.c,5x,8,10,32,39
GALLI, Mario
           S.24
GALLIARD, John Ernest (c1687-1749), Ger
R.1   S.c,5x,6-8,10,22
GALLICULUS, Johannes (16th Cent), Ger
R.1
GALLINI, Giovanni Andrea (1728-1805), It
R.5   S.c
GALLINI, Louis
           S.10
GALLO di INSULIS (Francus de Insulis) [see GALLO, R.]
GALLO, R. (fl 1420-30)
R.1   S.c,16,10
GALLOIS - Chanson de Barberine
           S.e
GALLOIS, Mme Philippe (19th Cent), Fr
R.7   S.24 [Gallos]
GALLOIS-MONTBRUN, Raymond (1918-   ), Fr
R.1   S.c,19,22,24
GALLON, Noël (1891-1966), Fr
R.1   S.4,7,8,10
GALLOT, Jacques le Vieux (d.c1690), Fr
R.1   S.c,2-4,5x,8
GALLOWAY, Tod B. (1863-1935), USA
R.23   S.10
GALLUPPI-CRAXTON [S.19]
   = GALUPPI, Baldassare, arr Craxton
GALLUS, Jacobus [see HANDL, Jacob]
GALUPPI, Baldassare (1706-1785),It
R.1   S.c,2-11,18,19,24,28,42,53
GALVES - Variantes de petenera y vives
           S.5x

GALYNIN, Herman Germanovich (1922-1966), USSR
   R.14   S.c,10,18
GAMARRA, Manuel de (fl 1753-72), Sp
   R.104   S.c
GAMBAU, Vincent (1914-   ), Fr
   R.11   S.c
GAMBINI, Carlo Andrea (1819-1865)
   R.8   S.5,8
GAMILLA, Alice Doria (1931-   ), Philippines
   R.7   S.52
GAMLEY, Douglas (1924-   ), Australia
   R.64
GANASSI dal FONTEGO, Silvestro (b.1492), It
   R.8   S.c,10,14,16
GANDINI, Gerardo (1936-   ), Arg
   R.1   S.10,39,46
GANDINO, Adolfo (1878-1940), It
   R.4
GANG, Chen (1935-   )
               S.24a
GANGI, Mario - Ut fabulae ferunt
               S.c
GANNE, Louis (1862-1923), Fr
   R.1   S.c,8-10,24,42,54(321,22,26)
GANSBACHER, Johann Baptiste (1778-1844), Aus
   R.1   S.c
GANZ, Rudolph (1877-1972), USA
   R.14   S.13
GANZ, Wilhelm (1833-1914), Ger
   R.1   S.c,24
GARAGULY, Carl von (1900-   ), Hun
   R.4   S.24
GARANT, Serge (1929-   ), Can
   R.1
GARAT, Pierre (1762-1823), Fr
   R.1   S.18
GARBIZU SALAVERRIA, Tomás (1910-   ), Sp
   R.104
GARCÍA - El roble y el ombu
               S.e
GARCÍA ESTRADA, Juan Augustin (1895-   ), Arg
   R.9   S.5,8
GARCÍA LORCA, Federico (1898-1936), Sp
   R.1   S.c,9
GARCÍA MORILLO, Roberto (1911-   ), Arg
   R.14   S.5x,10,46
GARCÍA MUÑOZ (16th Cent) [see MUÑOZ, García]
GARCÍA MUÑOZ, Carmen (1929-   ), Arg
   R.7   S.10,52

GARCÍA ROMAN, José (1945-   )
          S.c
GARCÍA, Eva
          S.24
GARCÍA, José Mauricio Nuñes (1767-1830), Brazil
    R.1   S.10[Nuñez García]
GARCÍA, Russell (1916-   ), USA
    R.23   S.10,13
GARDANE, Antonio (Antoine) (1509-1569), Fr
    R.1   S.c,8,10,14
GARDINER, Henry Balfour (1877-1950), Eng
    R.1   S.c,2,4,8,10
GARDNER, Johann von (1898-   ), Ger
    R.1   S.c
GARDNER, John (1917-   ), Eng
    R.1   S.c,18
GARDNER, Kay (1941-   ), USA
    R.19   S.30
GARDNER, Samuel (1891-   ), USA
    R.1   S.1x,4,5x,10,13,24
GÁRDONYI, Zoltán (1906-   ), Hun
    R.1   S.c

GARLAND, Hugh - pseud [see ANDERSON, William Henry]
GARLAND, Peter (1953-   ), USA
    R.19   S.10,13
GARNET, Horatio (fl 1789), USA
    R.53   S.47
GARNIER (fl 1538-42), Fr
    R.1   S.2-4,5x,8,11,14
GARNIER - Ça ne dure qu'un temps
          S.e
GARÔTO - pseud [ie Anibal Augusto SARDINHA],
    (1915-1955), Brazil R.67   S.c,10
GAROVI, Josef (1908-   ), Swiss
    R.95   S.c
GARREN - Just a girl that men like to forget (vi & p)
          S.24
GARRET, George (1834-1897), Eng
    R.1   S.c
GARRETA, Julio (1875-1925), Sp
    R.1   S.10
GARRIDO, Pablo (1905-   ), Chile
    R.1   S.10,24
GARROTIN, (19-20th Cent.), Sp

GARSHNEK, Anatoli Ivanovich (1918-   ), USSR
    R.14   S.18
GARSI da PARMA, Santino (1542-1604), It
    R.1   S.c,8,10,14,16

GARSTIN, Harold
          S.e
GART, John [John MARION] (1905-   ), USA
   R.23
GARTH, John (c1722-c1810), Eng
   R.1
GARTNER, Clarence G. - Love is mine
          S.44
GARTNER, Edward (1862-1918), Aus
          S.5x,10,24
GARUTA, Lucia Yanovna (1902-   ), Lat
   R.4   S.18,52
GARWIN, Joe - pseud [see SATTLER, Hermann]
GARZO (13th Cent), It - Altissima luce
          S.8,14
GASANOV, Gotfrid Alievich (1900-1965), USSR
   R.14   S.18
GASCOGNE, Mathieu (16th Cent), Fr
   R.1   S.c,5x,10,16
GASCON, Rafael
          S.54(320)
GASHIMOV - Prelude sher
          S.24a
GASPAR dos REIS (fl 1630), Port
   R.29   S.c,10,53
GASPARINI, Francesco (1668-1727), It
   R.1   S.c,8,10,24
GASPARINI, Quirino (1721-1778), It
   R.1   S.c,3,4,5x

GASS, Felix (18th Cent), Ger
   R.5   S.c
GASSMANN, Florian Leopold (1729-1774), Boh
   R.1   S.c,10
GASSMANN, Remi (1908-   ), USA
          S.13,24
GASTALDON, Stanislao (1861-1939), It
   R.8   S.c,10,18,24,44
GASTELDO - Fasciti Hymn
          S.e
GASTOLDI, Giovanni Giacomo (d.1622), It
   R.1   S.c,5x,7-10,14-16,24,53
GASTRITZ, Mathias (d.1596), Ger
   R.1   S.c
GATES, B. Cecil (1877-1941), USA
   R.23   S.10
GATES, Crawford (1921-   ), USA
   R.19   S.10,13
GATES, Everett (1914-   ), USA
   R.19   S.10,22

GATTY, Nicholas Comyn (1874-1946), Eng
  R.39   S.24
GAUBERT, Philippe (1879-1941), Fr
  R.8   S.c,1-3,5,7,10,19,21,24a
GAUCELEM FAIDIT [see FAIDIT, Gaucelm]
GAUDIBERT, Eric (1936-   ), Swiss
  R.4   S.24a
GAUDIOSI, Mario (1899-   )
  R.10sa   S.3-5
GAUJAC, Edmond-Germain (1895-   )
          S.c
GAUL, Alfred Robert (1837-1913), Eng
  R.3
GAULDIN, Robert (1931-   ), USA
  R.19   S.10,13
GAULTIER, Denis (1603-1672), Fr
  R.5,54   S.c,5x,8,10,16,18,32
GAULTIER, Ennemond (1575-1651), Fr
  R.1   S.c
GAUNTLETT, Henry John (1805-1876), Eng
  R.1   S.c
GAUTERIUS de CASTELLO RAINARDI (12th Cent)
  R.1
GAUTERIUS PREFATUS (12th Cent)

GAUTIER, Jacques (17th Cent), Fr
  R.1   S.8
GAUTIER, Leonard
          S.54(355)
GAUTIER d´ESPINAL (<1220-<1272), Fr
  R.1   S.c,10,14
GAUTIER de COINCY (c1177-1236), Fr
  R.1   S.c,5x,8,10,14,16
GAUTIER de MARSEILLE, Pierre (c1643-1697), Fr
  R.5   S.c,10
GAUTIER von CHATILLON [see WALTER von CHATILLON]
GAUTIER, Pierre (?1642-1696), Fr
  R.1   S.10
GAVARA, Valentin (16th Cent), It
  R.5   S.c
GAVEAUX, G. l´aîné (see note)

GAVEAUX, Pierre (1760-1825), Fr
  R.1   S.10
GAVEAUX, Simon (b.1759), Fr
  R.1   S.c
GAVINIÈS, Pierre (1728-1800), Fr
  R.1   S.c,10,24
GAVRILIN, Valeri Alexandrovich (1939-   ), USSR
  R.14   S.18

GAWARA-GUTEK, Walentyn [see GAVARA, Valentin]
GAY, Harry Wilbur , USA
             S.12,13
GAY, John (1685-1732), Eng
  R.1   S.c
GAY, Paul E. (1936-   ), USA
  R.19
GAYFER, James M. (1916-   ), Can
  R.4
GAYSON, Richard (1941-   ), USA
          S.13
GAZTAMBIDE, Joaquín (1822-1870), Sp
  R.1   S.c
GCKI-ALBI, G. N. - L´ours, valse (orch)
          S.24
GEARHART, Livingston (1916-   ), USA
  R.19   S.10
GEBAUER, François René (1773-1845), Fr
  R.1   S.c,10
GEBAUER, Johan Christian (1808-1884), Den
  R.1   S.33
GEBAUER, Michel-Joseph (1763-1812), Fr
  R.1   S.10
GEBHARD, Ludwig (1907-   ), Ger
  R.14   S.c
GEBHARD, Martin Anton (b c1770), Ger
  R.5   S.c
GEBHARD, Max (1896-   ), Ger
  R.14   S.c
GEBHARDI, Ludwig Ernst (1787-1862), Ger
  R.3   S.c
GEBHARDT, Hans (1897-   ), Ger
  R.14
GEDIKE, Alexander Fyodorovich (1877-1957), Russia
  R.1   S.10,18
GEEHL, Henry Ernest (1881-1961), Eng
  R.1   S.10,24,43,44,54(316,47),55
GEHLEN, Hermann (1937-   ), Ger
  R.4   S.c
GEHOT, Joseph (1756-c1820), Bel
  R.8   S.7,8,10,47
GEHRICKE, F. L. - Im Wald und auf der Heide
          S.10
GEIBEL, Adam (1855-1933), USA
  R.23   S.10
GEIERHAAS, Gustav (1888-1976), Ger
  R.14   S.c
GEIGER, O. - Une nuit (vi & p)
          S.24a

GEIJER, Erik Gustaf (1783-1847), Sweden
   R.1   S.c,10,56
GEISER, Walther (1897-   ), Swiss
   R.1   S.c,5,8,10
GEISSER, Kasimir (1899-1942)

GEISSLER, Frederick Dietzmann (1946-   ), USA
   R.19   S.10,13
GEISSLER, Fritz (1921-   ), Ger
   R.1
GEIST, Christian (c1640-1711), Ger
   R.1   S.c,10,56
GEIST, Konstantin Romanovich (1906-   )
           S.18
GELBRUN, Arthur (1913-   ), Isr
   R.1   S.9,10
GELD, Gary (1935-   ), USA
   R.23
GELD, Tom von der
           S.c
GELINEAU, Pater Joseph (1920-   ), Fr
   R.4   S.c
GELINEK, Josef (1758-1825), Cz
   R.1   S.c,5x
GELINEK, Johann (d.1780)
   R.2   S.c
GELLER, Mikhail Lazaryevich (1937-   )
           S.18,24a
GELLI, Ettore
           S.e
GELLMAN, Steven (1947-   ), Can
   R.31
GEMBLACO [Gembloux], Johannes Franchois
   [see FRANCHOIS, Johannes]
GEMINIANI, Francesco (1687-1762), It
   R.1   S.c,1x,2,3,5-11,18,24
GENA, Peter (1947-   ), USA
   R.19
GENÉE, Richard (1823-1895), Ger
   R.1   S.5x
GENERALI, Pietro (1773-1832), It
   R.1   S.c
GENET, Elzear [see CARPENTRAS]
GENTZ, Karl Emil Moritz (1852-1930), Fin
   R.2   S.5x,18
GENIN, Paul Agricola (1829-1904)
           S.c,8,10
GENSMER, Harold [see GENZMER, Harold]
GENTIAN (fl 1538-59), Fr
   R.1   S.c,2-4,5x,8,10,11,14,16

GENTILI, Giorgio (?1669->1731), It (see note)
R.1
GENTILUCCI, Armando (1939-   ), It
R.1   S.c
GENZMER, Harald (1909-   ), Ger
R.1   S.c,10,20
GEOFFRAY, César (1901-1972), Fr
R.4
GEOFFROY, Jean-Nicolas (d.1694), Fr
R.1   S.c,2-4,5x,11,53
GEORGE, Earl (1924-   ), USA
R.14   S.10,13
GEORGE, Graham (1912-   ), Can
R.14   S.10
GEORGES, Alexandre (1850-1938), Fr
R.8   S.2,3,5x
GERARD, Philippe (1924-   ),
            S.c
GERARD, d'Anella P.
            S.21
GERARDE, Derick (fl 1540-80), Flem
R.1   S.c
GERBER, Heinrich Nikolaus (1702-1775), Ger
R.1   S.c
GERBER, René (1908-   ), Swiss
R.1   S.c
GERENCSER, Ferenc
            S.10
GERGELY, Ferenc (1914-   ), Hun
R.15   S.c
GERHARD, Fritz Christian (1911-   ), Ger
R.14   S.c,22
GERHARD, Roberto (1896-1970), Sp
R.1   S.c,9,10,24a,39
GERHARDT, Paul (1607-1676), Ger [poet]
R.1   S.c
GERL, Franz Xaver (1764-1827), Aus
R.1   S.5x
GERLE, Hans (c1500-1570), Ger,
R.1   S.10,14
GERMAN, Edward (1862-1936), Eng
R.1   S.c,1-6,8-10,24,42,54(321,38,43)
GERMANI, Fabio - Cantata for Venice
            S.c
GERMETEN Jr, Gunnar (1947-   ), Nor
R.80   S.40
GERNSHEIM, Friedrich (1839-1916), Ger
R.1   S.10
GEROK, Karl (1906-1975)
            S.c

GEROV, Naiden Evlogiev (1916-   ), Bul
    R.14   S.24a
GERRARDE, Gervais (17th Cent)
              S.c
GERSCHEFSKI, Edwin (1909-   ), USA
    R.1   S.3,9,10,13
GERSHWIN, George (1898-1937), USA
    R.1   S.c,1-11,13,18,22,24,32,42
GERSTER, Ottmar (1897-1969), Ger (see note)
    R.1   S.8,18
GERSTER, Robert (1945-   ), USA
    R.19   S.10,13
GERTER, Franz (1793-1878)
              S.18
GERVAIS, Charles Hubert (1671-1744), Fr
    R.1   S.8,10
GERVAISE, Claude (fl 1540-60), Fr
    R.1   S.c,2-5,7,8,10,11,14-16,32,53
GERVASIO, Giovanni Battista (fl 1768-77), It
    R.5   S.c
GESENSWAY, Louis (1906-1976), USA
    R.19   S.10,13
GESIUS, Bartholomäus (c1560-1613), Ger
    R.1   S.c,10,15,16,32
GESUALDO, Carlo (c1561-1613), It
    R.1   S.c,2-11,14-16,18,53
GESZLER, György (1912-   ), Hun
    R.15   S.5x,24
GEVAERT, François-Auguste (1828-1908), Bel
    R.1   S.5x,41
GEVIKSMAN, Vitali Artemevich (1924-   ), USSR
    R.14   S.18
GEYER, Johann Egidus (1760-1808)

GHECIU, Diamandi (1892-   ), Hun
    R.4
GHEDINI, Giorgio Federico (1892-1965), It
    R.1   S.8-10
GHENT, Emmanuel (1925-   ), USA
    R.1   S.10,13
GHEORGHIU, Valentin (1928-   ), Rum
    R.1   S.8,24
GHERARDELLO da FIRENZE (14th Cent), It
    R.1   S.c,3,4,5x,8,10,11,14,16
GHERARDESCHI, Giuseppe (1759-1815), It
    R.3   S.c
GHEYN, Matthias van den [see VAN den GHEYN, Matthias]
GHEZZO, Dinu (1941-   ), USA
    R.19   S.9,13

GHIRARDO, Megan Roberts (1952-   ), USA
  R.19   S.13[Megan],30[Roberts],52
GHISELIN, Johannes (fl early 16th Cent), Flem
  R.1   S.c,10,14,16
GHIZEGHEM, Hayne van [see HAYNE van GHIZEGHEM]

GHRDN - Mashiroki fujino ne (vi & p)
          S.24
GHYOROS, Julien (1922-   ), Bel
  R.80   S.c
GHYS, Henri (1839-?1910)
  R.200
GIACOBBI, Girolamo (1567->1629), It
  R.1   S.c,16
GIAMBERTI, Giuseppe (c1600-c1662), It
  R.1   S.c
GIAMPIERI, Alamiro, (1893-1963), It
  R.14   S.c
GIAN DOMENICO, Il Giovane de Nola
  [see NOLA, Giovanni del Giovane da]
GIANELLA, Louis (?1778-1817), It
  R.1   S.10
GIANELLI - Olga: E lo sapevi
          S.e
GIANNEO, Luis (1897-1968), Arg
  R.1   S.c,8,10,24a,39,46
GIANNINI, Vittorio (1903-1966), USA
  R.1   S.9,10,13
GIANNINI, Walter (1917-   ), USA
  R.19   S.13
GIANONCELLI, Bernardo (fl 1650), It
  R.5   S.c,2,5x,8,10
GIARDINI, Felice (1716-1796), It
  R.1   S.c,4,5,7,10
GIAZOTTO, Remo (1910-   ), It
  R.1   S.c
GIBBONS, Christopher (1615-1676), Eng
  R.1   S.c
GIBBONS, Edward (1568-c1650), Eng
  R.1   S.c
GIBBONS, Ellis (1573-1603), Eng
  R.1   S.c,7,8,10,14
GIBBONS, Orlando (1583-1625), Eng
  R.1   S.c,1-11,14-16,18,22,53
GIBBS, Cecil Armstrong (1889-1960), Eng
  R.1   S.c,2-4,5x,10,18,25,27
GIBBS, Joseph (1699-1788), Eng
  R.1   S.c,24a
GIBBS, Michael (1937-   ), USA
  R.60

GIBBS, Thomas (17th Cent)
        S.c
GIBILARIO, Alfonso (1888-   ), It
   R.4   S.10
GIBSON, Archer (1875-1952), USA
   R.19   S.10,12,13
GIBSON, Henry (1882-   ), Eng [?]
        S.10
GIBSON, Jon (1940-   ), USA
   R.19   S.13
GIDASH, Fredesh (1928-   )
        S.18
GIDEON, Miriam (1906-   ), USA
   R.1   S.5x,10,13,30,52
GIELNIOVA, Ladyslaw [see LADYSLAW z GIELNIOWA]
GIENKO, Boris Fedorovich
   [see GIYENKO, Boris Fedorovich]
GIESEN, Willy (1911-   )
        S.c
GIESSEL, Alexander (1694-1766)
   R.5   S.c
GIFFORD, Helen Margaret (1935-   ), Australia
   R.7   S.52
GIGAULT, Nicolas (c1627-1707), Fr
   R.1   S.c,5x,10,18,53
*** GIGOUT, Eugène (1797-1828) (see note)
GIGOUT, Eugène (1844-1925), Fr
   R.1   S.c,1x,4,5x,8,10,18
GILABERT - La adoracion
        S.e
GILARDI, Gilardo (1889-1963), Arg
   R.1   S.8,24,46
GILBERT - All of the girlies
        S.54(312)
GILBERT - Marionettes
        S.24
GILBERT, David (1936-   ), USA
   R.19   S.13
GILBERT, Henry Franklin Belknap (1868-1928), USA
   R.1   S.4,5,10,13
GILBERT, James L. (fl 1866-92), USA
        S.e
GILBERT, Jean [pseud: Max WINTERFIELD] (1879-1942),
   Ger   R.1   S.c,10
GILBERT, John USA
        S.13
GILBERT, L. Wolfe (1886-1970), USA [author and
   publisher]   R.23   S.10
GILBERT, Pia (1921-   ), USA
   R.7   S.30,52

GILBERT, Robert (see note)
        S.10
GILBOA, Jacob (1920-   ), Isr
  R.1
GILES, Nathaniel (c1558-1634), Eng
  R.1   S.c,10
GILES, Thomas
        S.c
GILFERT, Charles H. (1787-1829), USA
  R.1
GILL, Harry (1897-   ), Eng
        S.c
GILLEBERT de BERNEVILLE (fl c1250-80), Fr
  R.1   S.c,10
GILLES de PUISEX, Henri
        S.c,10
GILLES, Henri (14th Cent)
        S.c
GILLES, Jean (1668-1705), Fr
  R.1   S.c,9
GILLESPIE, Haven (1888-1975), USA
  R.23   S.24
GILLET, Ernest (1856-1940), Fr
  R.4   S.5x,10,18,24
GILLIS, Don (1912-1978), USA
  R.1   S.5x,9,10,13
GILLMAN, Kurt (1889-   ), Ger
  R.4   S.18
GILMORE, Patrick Sarsfield [pseud: Louis LAMBERT]
  (1829-1892), USA   R.1   S.10,47
GILMOUR - Slumber song
        S.e
GILSON, Paul (1865-1942), Bel
  R.1   S.c,7,10,36,41
GILTAY, Berend (1910-1975), Neth
  R.1   S.24
GIMÉNEZ [Jiménez], Jerónimo (1854-1923), Sp
  R.1   S.c,1,8-10,28,39
GINASTERA, Alberto (1916-1983), Arg
  R.1   S.c,5x,7-10,18,24a,28,39,46
GINDRON, François (c1491->1560), Swiss
  R.1
GINTZLER, Simon (c1500->1547), Ger
  R.1   S.c,10,16,32
GIOE, Joseph Guiseppe (1890-1957), USA
  R.23   S.44
GIORDANI, Giuseppe (>1753-1798), It
  R.1   S.c,1-4,5x,6,8,10,11,25-27
GIORDANI, Tommaso (c1733-1806), It
  R.1   S.c,5,7,10,18,24

GIORDANO, Umberto (1867-1948), It
R.1   S.c,1-11,18,34,42,43,54(326)
GIORNI, Aurelio (1895-1938), USA
R.19   S.3,5,11,13
GIORNO, John (1936-   )

GIORNOVICHI, Giovanni Mane [Ivan Jarnovic]
(1735/45-1804), It R.1   S.24a
GIOVANNELLI, Ruggiero (c1560-1625), It
R.1   S.c,10,16
GIOVANNI MARIA da CREMA (fl 1540-50), It
R.1   S.c,14,16
GIOVANNI da CASCIA (da FIRENZE) (fl 1340-50), It
R.1   S.c,2-4,5x,8,10,11,14,16
GIOVANNI di CICONIA
              S.10
GIOVANNINI, Caesar (1925-   ), USA
R.23   S.13
GIRAUT RIQUIER [see RIQUIER, Giraut]
GIRAUT de BORNELH (c1140-c1200)
R.1   S.c,5x,8,10,14,16,39
GIROD-PARROT, Marie Louise (1915-   ), Fr
R.7   S.52
GIROUD, Jean (1910-   )
              S.c
GIROUST, François (1737-1799), Fr
R.1   S.c,9
GISTOU, Nicolo (d.1609), Den
R.1   S.c
GIUFFRE, James (1921-   ), USA
R.1   S.9,10
GIULIANI, Giovanni Francesco (c1760->1818), It
R.1   S.c,10,24,32
GIULIANI, Mauro (1781-1829), It
R.1   S.c,4,7,8,10,24,32
GIULIANI, V. - Divertimento for 6 instruments
              S.24a
GIULIANO, Giuseppe (18th Cent)
              S.c
GIULINI, Giorgio (1717-1780)
R.5   S.c
GIULIO da MODENA [see SEGNI, Julio]
GIUSSANI, Severo (18th Cent)
              S.c,10
GIUSTINI, Lodovico (1685-1743), It
R.1   S.c
GIYENKO, Boris Feodorovich (1917-   )
              S.18
GJERSTRM, Gunnar (1891-1951), Nor
R.14   S.7,24

GLAESER, Franz (Joseph) [see GLÄSER, Franz Joseph]
GLANVILLE-HICKS, Peggy (1912-   ), Australia
   R.1   S.4,8-10,13,23,29,30,52
GLAREAN, Heinrich (1488-1563), Swiss
   R.1   S.16
GLARUM, L. Stanley (1919-1976), USA
   R.23
GLÄSER, Franz (Joseph) (1798-1861), Boh
   R.1   S.e
GLASER, Werner Wolf (1910-   ), Sweden
   R.1   S.10,22,24a,40
GLASOW, Glen (1924-   ), USA
             S.10,13,24a
GLASS, Paul Eugène (1934-   ), USA
   R.4
GLASS, Philip (1937-   ), USA
   R.1   S.c,9,10,13,24a
GLAZUNOV, Alexander (1865-1936), Russia
   R.1   S.c,1-11,18,22,24
GLEBOV, Yevgeni Alexandrovich (1929-   ), USSR
   R.14   S.18
GLEESON, Horace (fl 1904-14)
             S.5x
GLEISSNER, Franz (1759-1818), Ger
   R.1   S.c
GLEN, Irma (1902-   ), USA
   R.7   S.52
GLICK, Srul Irving (1934-   ), Can
   R.14   S.22
GLIER, Reyngold Moritesevich (1875-1956), USSR
   R.1   S.c,2-11,18,20,21,23,24
GLINDEMANN, Ib (1934-   ), Den
   R.30   S.40

GLINKA, Mikhail Ivanovich (1804-1857), Russia
   R.1   S.c,1-11,18-21,23,24,28,42
GLITZ, W. - Larghetto (vi & p)
             S.24
GLOBOKAR, Vinko (1934-   ), Yug
   R.1   S.c,10,24a
GLODEANU, Liviu (1938-1978), Rum
   R.33   S.24a
GLOGAU, Jack (1886-1953), USA
   R.23   S.24
GLONTI, F.

GLORIEUX, François (1932-   ), Bel
   R.1   S.c
GLOVER, Charles William (1806-1863), Eng
   R.3   S.10,24,43

GLOVER, Stephen (1812-1870), Eng
   R.44   S.47
GLOVIRITZ - Polka brillante (vi & p)
           S.24
GLUCK, Christoph Willibald (1714-1787), Ger
   R.1   S.c,1-11,18,22-25,27,28,32,42
GLUCK, Herkulan (1776-1860)
           S.c
GLUSHANOK, Peter USA
           S.13
GNATALLI, Radamés (1906-   ), Brazil
   R.1   S.9,10,24a,32
GNAZZO, Anthony (1936-   ), USA
   R.14   S.10,13
GNECCHI, Vittorio (1876-1954), It
   R.1   S.e
GNECCO, Francesco (c1769-1810/11), It
   R.1   S.c
GNEIST, Werner (1898-   ), Ger
   R.4   S.c
GNESSIN, Michael Fabinovich (1883-1957), USSR
   R.14   S.24a
GOBBAERTS, Jean Louis (1835-1886), Bel
   [pseud: Maurice LECOCQ, G. LUDOVIC, STREABBOG]
   R.3
GODARD, Benjamin (1849-1895), Fr
   R.1   S.c,2-8,10,18,21,23,24,43
GODARD, Charles - pseud [see BEHR, Franz]
GODARD, Robert (fl 1536-60), Fr
   R.1   S.16
GODEFROID, Felix (1818-1897), Bel
   R.1   S.c,5x,10
GODFREY, Charles Sr. (1790-1863), Eng
   R.1
GODFREY, Charles Jr. (1839-1919), Eng
   R.49   S.54(327,35,56)
GODFREY, Daniel (1949-   ), USA
   R.19   S.13
GODOWSKY, Leopold (1870-1938), Pol
   R.1   S.c,2,4,5,7-10,13,18,24

GODOWSKY, Louis
           S.24a
GODRIC, Saint (c1069-1170), Eng
   R.1   S.10,14,16
GODRON, Hugo (1900-   ), Neth
   R.4
GODWIN, Joscelyn Roland (1945-   ), Eng
   R.80   S.10,13
GOEB, Roger (1914-   ), USA
   R.1   S.7,8,10,13

GOEBEL, Georg
        S.c
GOEDICKE, Alexander Fyodorovich
  [see GEDIKE, Alexander Fyodorovich]
GOEHR, Alexander (1932-   ), Eng
  R.1   S.c,9,10,26,24a,27
GOEHR, Walter (1903-1960), Ger
  R.1   S.4
GOENS, Daniel van (1904-   ), Fr
  R.3   S.5x,10,24
GOES, Damião de [see GOIS, Damião de]
GOETHALS, Lucien (1931-   ), Bel
  R.1
GOETZ, Alma
        S.e
GOETZ, Hermann (1840-1876), Ger
  R.1   S.c,4,7-10,24a,42
GOETZE, Walter Wilhelm (1883-1961), Ger
  R.4   S.c
GOEURY, Carlo (18th Cent)
        S.c
GOEYENS, Fernando (1892-   ), Bel
  R.14   S.24
GOEYVAERTS, Karel (1923-   ), Bel
  R.1
GOFFIN, Henry Charles (1883-1973), New Zealand
  R.85   S.54(345,54),55
GOFFIN, John Dean (1909-   ), New Zealand
  R.85   S.54(313,21,29),55
GOGEL, Georg Anton (1743-1802)

GOGOTZKY, Nicolai
        S.10
GOICOECHEA ERRASTI, Vicente (1854-1916), Sp
  R.1
GOIS, Damião de (1502-1574), Port
  R.1
GOLABEK, Jakub (1739-1789), Pol
  R.1   S.c,9
GOLD, Ernest (1921-   ), USA
  R.19   S.10,13,26
GOLD, Joe (1894-   ), USA
  R.23   S.10
GOLDBERG, Doris [pseud Nora BAYES] (1880-1928), USA
  R.23   S.10
GOLDBERG, Johann Gottlieb (1727-1756), Ger
  R.1   S.c,9,10,24
GOLDBERG, Leon
        S.24

GOLDENWEISER, Alexander Borisovich (1875-1961), Russia
R.1   S.c,18,24
GOLDFADEN, Abraham (1840-1908), USA
R.25,200   S.10,24
GOLDMAN, Edwin Franko (1878-1956), USA
R.1   S.c,13,54(319,21,29,31,35,47)
GOLDMAN, Richard Franko (1910-1980), USA
R.19   S.10,13,24a
GOLDMANN, Marcel (1936-   )
           S.c
GOLDMARK, Karl (1830-1915), Hun
R.1   S.c,1-12,21,24
GOLDSCHMIDT, Berthold (1903-   ), Eng
R.1   S.20
GOLDSCHMIDT, Otto (1829-1907), Ger
R.3
GOLDSMITH, Arthur Robert (1875-1948), Eng
R.96   S.54(355)
GOLDSTEIN, Edmund (1927-   )
           S.18
GOLDSTEIN, Malcolm (1936-   ), USA
R.19   S.24a
GOLDSTEIN, Mikhail [see note under
  OVSIANIKO-KULIKOVSKY, Nikolai Dmitrievich]
GOLEMINOV, Marin (1908-   ), Bul
R.30   S.18,24a
GOLESTAN, Stan (1876-1956), Rum
R.14   S.1-6,10,19,23,24
GOLITSÏN, Lev (1804-1871), Russia
           S.18
GOLITSÏN, Yury Nikolayevich (1823-1872), Russia
R.1   S.18
GOLLAND, John (1942-   ), Eng
R.85   S.55
GOLLER, Vinzenz (1873-1953), Aus
R.14   S.c
GOLOVANOV, Nikolay Semyonovich (1891-1958), Russia
R.1   S.18
GOLTERMANN, Georg (1824-1898), Ger
R.1   S.c,5x,10,24
GOLTZ, Boris Grigorievich (1913-1942), USSR
R.14   S.5x,18
GOLUBEV, Evgeny Kirillovich (1910-   ), USSR
R.14   S.18
GOMBAU GUERRA, Gerardo (1906-1971), Sp
R.14   S.c,10
GOMBERT, Nicolas (c1495-c1560), Flem
R.1   S.c,2-5,7,8,10,11,14-16,53
GOMES, Carlos (1836-1896), Brazil
R.1   S.c,1-8,10,18,39,44,54(330)

GÓMEZ CALLEJA, Rafael (1874-1938), Sp
  R.4   S.10,39
GÓMEZ CARRILLO, Manuel (1883-1968), Arg
  R.1   S.8
GÓMEZ CRESPO, Jorge (1900-1972), Arg
           S.c,7,8,10,32,39
GÓMEZ GARCÍA, Domingo Julio (1886-1973), Sp
  R.1   S.5,8,10
GÓMEZ - Alma andaluza
           S.54(312)
GÓMEZ, Alfredo
           S.54(322)
GÓMEZ, Jose Soler (1875-   )
           S.24
GÓMEZ, Vincente (1911-   ), USA
  R.30   S.5x,9,13
GOMOLYAKA, Vadim Borisovich (1914-   ), USSR
  R.14   S.8,18
GOMÓLKA, Mikolaj (c1539-1609), Pol
  R.1   S.c,2,4,5x,8-11,14
GONZAGA, Chiquinha (1847-1935), Brazil
  R.7   S.52
GOODALE, Ezekial (1780-1828), USA

GOODE, Daniel (1936-   ), USA
  R.80   S.13
GOODENOUGH, Forrest (1918-   ), USA
  R.19   S.10,13
GOODEVE, Mrs. Arthur [also Mrs. William] (19th Cent),
  Eng R.7   S.24
GOODMAN, Joseph (1918-   ), USA
  R.19   S.10,13
GOODMAN, Lillian Rosedale (1887-   ), USA
  R.23   S.24,30
GOODRICH, Lorraine
           S.10,30
GOODWIN, George H.
           S.10
GOODWIN, Ron (1925-   ), Eng
  R.62   S.c
GOODWIN, [? Starling] (fl 1790), Eng
  R.5   S.e
GOODWIN, Walter (1889-   ), USA
  R.23   S.24
GOODWIN, William (18th Cent)
           S.53
GOOSSEN, Frederic (1927-   ), USA
  R.19   S.13
GOOSSENS, Eugene (1893-1962), Eng
  R.1   S.c,1-3,5,8,10,21,24

GÖPFERT, Carl Andreas (1768-1818), Ger
    R.3   S.c,32
GORBULSKIS, Beniaminas (1925-   ), USSR
    R.14   S.18
GORCZYCKI, Grzegorz Gerwazy (c1667-1734), Pol
    R.1   S.c,1x,2,9
GORDELI, Otar Mihailovich (1928-   ), USSR
    R.14   S.10,18
GORDIGIANI, Luigi (1806-1860), It
    R.8   S.1x,10
GORDON, Gavin Muspratt (1901-1970), Scot
    R.14   S.c,4,10
GORDON, Philip (1894-   ), USA
    R.19   S.13
GORDON, Ramsey
             S.24a
GORDON, Westell
    R.43   S.24
GORECKI, Henryk (1933-   ), Pol
    R.1   S.c
GORLIER, Simon (fl 1550-84), Fr
    R.1   S.c
GÖRNER, Hans-Georg (1908-   ), Ger
    R.1
GÖRNER, Johann Gottlieb (1697-1778), Ger
    R.1   S.c
GÖRNER, Johann Valentin (1702-1762), Ger
    R.1   S.c
GORODOVSKAYA, Vera
             S.10,30
GORTER, Klaus (1901-   )

GORZANIS, Giacomo (1520-c1575), It
    R.1   S.c,8,10,14,16,32
GOSLEE, George ?USA
             S.13
GOSS, Sir John (1800-1880), Eng
    R.1   S.c,5x,8,10,54(350)
GOSSEC, Francois-Joseph (1734-1829), S. Neth
    R.1   S.c,2-8,10,18,21,22,24,41,32
GOSSWIN, Antonius (c1546-1598/99), Ger
    R.1   S.c,10
GOSTENA, Giovanni Battista della
    [see DELLA GOSTENA, Giovanni]
GOSTUSKI, Dragutin (1923-   ), Yug
    R.14   S.24a
GOT, Georgi Vasilevich (1861-1917)
             S.18
GOTKOVSKY, Ida-Rose Esther (1933-   ), Fr
    R.7   S.22,30,52

GOTOVAC, Jakov (1895-1982), Yug
R.1   S.c,10,42
GOTTFRIED von BRETEUILL (13th Cent)
          S.c
GOTTLIEB, Adolf Davidovich (1910-   )
          S.18
GOTTLIEB, Ernest (1903-1961), USA
R.4   S.24a
GOTTSCHALK, Arthur (1951-   ), USA
R.19   S.10,13

GOTTSCHALK, Louis Moreau (1829-1869), USA
R.1   S.c,4,7-10,47,54(324,37)
GOTTSCHE, Heinz Markus
          S.c
GOTTSCHICK, Friedemann (1928-   ), Ger
R.4   S.c
GOTTSCHOVIUS, Nikolaus (c1575->1624), Ger
R.1   S.c
GÖTZ, Johann (15th Cent)
R.5   S.c,10,16
GÖTZE, Carl (1836-1887), Ger
R.39   S.e
GÖTZE, Walter Wilhelm [see GOETZE, Walter Wilhelm]
GOUBIEL - Patrouille indiscrète (vi & ce)
          S.24a
GOUBLIER, Gustave
          S.4,34
GOUBLIER, Henri (1888-   ), Fr
R.13   S.24
GOUDIMEL, Claude (c1514-1572), Fr
R.1   S.c,2-5,7,8,10,11,14,16
GOUINGUENE, Christian (1941-   )
          S.c
GOULD, Glenn (1932-1982), Can
R.1   S.c,9,24
GOULD, John Edgar (1820-1875), USA
- Sans day carol [?]
R.53   S.c
GOULD, Morton (1913-   ), USA
R.1   S.c,3,4,5x,9-11,13,19-21,54(317)
GOULD, William Monk
          S.e
GOUNOD, Charles (1818-1893), Fr
R.1   S.c,1-11,18,23-28,33,34,42,54(326,28)
GOUPIL, Auguste USA
          S.13
GOURDIN - Acteon
          S.54(311)
GOUVY, Louis Théodore (1819-1898), Fr
R.1   S.c

GOWER, Albert E. Jr (1935-   ), USA
   R.23   S.13
GOWERS, Patrick (1936-   )
             S.c,32
GRAAF, Christian Ernst [see GRAF, Christian Ernst]
GRAAF, Tonnie de (1926-   ), Neth
   R.4   S.c
GRABERT, Martin (1868-1951), Ger
   R.14   S.c
GRABNER, Hermann (1886-1969), Ger
   R.1   S.c,10
GRABOVSKY, Leonid (1935-   ), USSR
   R.1   S.18
GRACE, Harvey (1874-1944), Eng
   R.1   S.c
GRACHEV, Mikhail Oskarovich (1911-   ), USSR
   R.47
GRAD, Toni (1903-   ), Ger [?]
   R.95   S.c
GRADWOHL, Pierre (1905-   )
            S.7,8,10
GRAENER, Paul (1872-1944), Ger
   R.1   S.c,2-5
GRAETTINGER, Robert (1923-1957), USA
   R.4   S.9
GRAF, Christian Ernst (1723-1804), Ger
   R.1
GRAF, Friedrich Hartmann (1727-1795), Ger
   R.1   S.10,24a
GRAFE, Friedebald
            S.c
GRAFFEO, Carlo (1851-1917), It
   R.10   S.e
GRAFULLA, Claudio S. (1810-1880), USA
   R.50   S.47,54(364)
GRAGNANI, Filippo (1767-1812), It
   R.10   S.c,10,18[Graiani],24
GRAHAM, Robert (1912-   ), USA
   R.23   S.9,13
GRAHN, Ulf (1942-   ), Sweden
   R.80   S.40
GRAIANI, Felipe [S.18] = GRAGNANI, Filippo]
GRAIN, Richard Corney (1844-1895), Eng
   R.44   S.e
GRAINGER, Percy (1882-1961), Australia
   R.1   S.c,1-11,13,22,23,24a,27,29,37
GRAM, Hans (1754-1804), USA
   R.1   S.8,10,47
GRAM, Peder (1881-1956), Den
   R.1   S.4,7,8,24,35,57

GRAMATGES, Harold (1918-   ), Cuba
  R.14   S.32
GRAMATTÉ, Sophie Carmen
  [see ECKHARDT-GRAMATTÉ, Sophie Carmen]
GRAMM, Arthur
            S.24
GRANADA, Louis Sanchez
            S.32
GRANADOS, Enrique (1867-1916), Sp
  R.1   S.c,1-11,18,22,24,25,27,28,32
GRANATA, Giovanni Battista (17th Cent), It
  R.1   S.c
GRANCINI, Michel Angelo (1605-1669), It
  R.1   S.c
GRANDERT, Jonny (1939-   ), Sweden
  R.14   S.40
GRANDI, Alessandro (c1577-1630), It
  R.1   S.9,10,16,24
GRANDJANY, Marcel (1891-1975), Fr
  R.1   S.c,4,10,13,18
GRANDRUE, Eustache (17th Cent)
  R.5   S.c
GRÄNER, Georg (1876-1945), Ger
  R.4   S.c

GRANIANI, Filippo [see GRAGNANI, Filippo]
GRANICHSTAEDTEN, Bruno (1879-1944), Aus
  R.2   S.c,1x
GRANIER, Jules - Hosanna
            S.44
GRANT, William Parks (1910-   ), USA
  R.19   S.5x,9,10,12,13
GRANTHAM, Donald (1947-   ), USA
  R.19   S.13,24a
GRAPPELLI, Stephane (1908-   ), Fr
  R.1   S.10,24a
GRASSE, Edwin (1884-1954), USA
  R.19   S.10,13,24
GRASSI, Antonio de (1880-   ), It
  R.53   S.24
GRASSI, Ciro (1868-   ), It
  R.10   S.10
GRASSO, G. - Polka militar
            S.54(350)
GRASZINSKY - An deinem Herzen
            S.e
GRATIANI, Bonifazio [see GRAZIANI, Bonifazio]
GRATTON, J. J. Hector (1900-   ), Can
  R.14   S.24
GRAU y HUGUET, Agustin (1893-   ), Sp
  R.43   S.c,10,32

GRAU, Alberto, Ven

GRAU, Eduardo (1919-   ), Sp
    R.26   S.10,46
GRAUBINS, Jekabs (1886-1961), Lat
    R.1   S.18
GRAUCINO - Mysterium ecclesiae
                S.c
GRAUER, Victor (1937-   ), USA
    R.19   S.10,13
GRAUMANN - Das erste Lied
                S.e
GRAUN, Carl Heinrich (1703/04-1759), Ger
    R.1   S.c,10
GRAUN, Johann Gottlieb (1702/03-1771), Ger
    R.1   S.10,24
GRAUNKE, Kurt (1915-   ), Ger
    R.4   S.c,24
GRAUPNER, Johann Christoph (1683-1760), Ger
    R.1   S.c,10
GRAVES, Milford (1941-   ), USA
    R.1   S.10
GRAVITIS, Olgerts (1926-   ), Lat
    R.1   S.18
GRAY, Alan (1855-1935), Eng
    R.1   S.c,5x,10
GRAY, George Charles (1897-   ), Eng
    R.64   S.c
GRAY, Hamilton
                S.e
GRAYSON, Richard (1941-   ), USA

    R.19   S.9,13
GRAZIANI [Gratiano], Bonifazio (1604/05-1664), It
    R.1   S.c,9
GRAZIANI, Carlo (d.1787), It
    R.1
GRAZIOLI, Giovanni Battista (1746-c1820), It
    R.1   S.4-7
GREAVES, Thomas (fl 1604), Eng
    R.1   S.c,7,8,10,14,16
GREBAN, Arnoul (c1420-c1471), Fr
    R.1   S.4
GRECHANINOV, Alexander (1864-1956), Russia
    R.1   S.c,1-8,10,11,18,20,22
GRECO, Gaetano (c1657-c1728),It
    R.1   S.8,10
GRECO, Jose (1919-   ), Sp
    R.30   S.39
GREEB, Benedict [see GREP, Benedict]
GREEF, Arthur de [see DE GREEF, Arthur]

GREEL - Laurbaer & Roser
           S.24
GREEN - Ellan Vannin
           S.5x
GREEN - The good fairy
           S.54(329)
GREEN, Bernard (1908-1975), USA
  R.19   S.13
GREEN, George (1930-   ), USA
  R.19   S.10,13
GREEN, H. R. - Hail to the orange
           S.54(330)
GREEN, Philip (1911-   )
           S.9,24
GREEN, Ray (1908-   ), USA
  R.19   S.2,3,5x,8,10,13
GREENE, Edwin
           S.10,24
GREENE, Maurice (1696-1755), Eng
  R.1   S.c,1,4,5,8,10,53
GREENHILL, James (19th Cent)
           S.5x,11
GREENWALD, Jan Carol (1952-   ), USA
  R.7   S.30,52
GREENWOOD, John A. (<1895-?), Eng (see note)
  R.85,96   S.54(335)
GREETING, Thomas (d.1682), Eng

  R.1   S.c
GREFFLINGER, Georg (17th Cent)
           S.c
GREFINGER, Wolfgang (c1470->1515), Ger
  R.1   S.c,10,16
GREGH, Louis (1843-1915), Fr
  R.39   S.e
GRÉGOIRE, Richard (1944-   ), Can
  R.81
GREGOR, Čestmír (1926-   ), Cz
  R.1   S.24a,31
GREGSON, Edward (1945-   ), Eng
  R.85   S.c,55
GREITER, Matthias (c1495-1550), Ger
  R.1   S.c,5x,10,14,16
GRELL, August Eduard (1800-1886), Ger
  R.1   S.c,55
GRELL, G. - Larghetto (Arizona Cello Society Orch)
           S.13
GRENON, Nicholas (c1380-1456), Fr
  R.1   S.c,4,5x,10,16,41
GREP, Benedict (d.1619)
  R.5   S.10

GRESHAM, Ann   USA
   R.7   S.22
GRESNICK, Antoine Frederic (1755-1799), S. Neth
   R.1   S.c
GRESSEL, Joel (1943-   ), USA
   R.19   S.10,13
GRETCHANINOV, Alexander [see GRECHANINOV, Alexander]
GRÉTRY, André-Ernest-Modeste (1741-1813), Fr
   R.1   S.c,2-11,24,36,41
GRETSCHER, Philipp (1859-1937), Ger
   R.4   S.e
GREVER, Maria (1885-1951), Mex
   R.7   S.10,24a,30,52
GREY - The Empire is marching
           S.54(324)
GREY, Frank Herbert (1883-1951), USA
   R.23   S.e
GREY, Geoffrey David (1934-   ), Eng
   R.14
GRIBOYEDOV, Alexander Sergeyevich (1795-1829), Russia
   R.47   S.18,23
GRIEG, Edvard (1843-1907), Nor
   R.1   S.c,1-11,18,22-25,27,28,33
GRIENINGER, August (1638-1692)
   R.5   S.c
GRIFFES, Charles Tomlinson (1884-1920), USA
   R.1   S.c,1-11,13,25-28
GRIFFIN, Frederick (20th Cent), Eng
           S.c
GRIFFIN, George (19th Cent), Eng - Surely the Lord is
   in this place   S.c
GRIFFIS, Eliot (1893-1967), USA
   R.1   S.13,24
GRIFFITH, Peter (1943-   ), USA
   R.19   S.10,13
GRIFFITH, Robert B. (1914-   ), USA
   R.19   S.10,13
GRIFSTRÖM - Pierette Dances
           S.5x
GRIGNY, Nicolas de (1672-1703), Fr
   R.1   S.c,4,5x,7-10,53
GRIGORIU, Theodor (1926-   ), Rum
   R.4
GRIGORYAN, Grant Aramovich (1919-1962), USSR
   R.14   S.18,24
GRILLER, Arnold (1937-   ), USA
           S.13
GRILLO, Giovanni Battista (d.1622), It
   R.1   S.c,10,16

GRIMACE (fl 1350-75), Fr
  R.1   S.c,10,16
GRIMANI, Marie Margherta (18th Cent), It
  R.7   S.30,52
GRIMES, David (1948-   )

GRIMM, Jim (1928-   )
            S.c
GRIMSHAW, Arthur Edward (1864-   ), Eng
  R.44   S.e
GRINGUIS, G. (1939-1970)
            S.c
GRINUPS, Arturs (1931-   ), USSR
  R.30   S.18
GRIPPE, Ragnar (1951-   ), Sweden
  R.68
GRISAR, Albert (1808-1869), Bel
  R.1   S.e
GRISELLE, Thomas (1891-1955), USA
  R.19   S.2,3,10,13
GRISEY, Gérard (1946-   ), Ger
  R.4   S.c
GRISON, Jules (19th Cent.), Fr
            S.c,7
GROBE, Charles (1817-1880), USA
  R.1   S.10
*** GROBE, Charles (1839-   ) (see note)
GROBET, Louis
            S.24
GROBOCZ, Miklos (1927-   ), Hun

GRODZKI, Boleslavs (1865-   ), Russia
  R.28   S.1x
GROENEWOLD, M. (1941-   )
            S.c
GROFÉ, Ferdinand (1892-1972), USA
  R.19   S.c,2-11,13,24
GROLL, Otto (1935-   )
            S.c
GRONAU, Daniel Magnus (c1700-1747), Ger
  R.1   S.c
GRØNDAHL, Agathe (1847-1907), Nor
  R.1   S.c,3-8,10,24,52[Backer-Grøndahl]
GRONEMANN, Albertus (1710/12-1778), Neth
  R.1   S.24
GROOME, Reginald
            S.e
GROOT, Cor de (1914-   ), Neth
  R.4

GROSS, Eric (1926-   ), Australia
   R.35   S.29
GROSS, Robert (1914-   ), USA
   R.1   S.10,13,24a
GROSS, Walter (1909-1967), USA
   R.23   S.24
GROSSE - Unter den Linden
             S.54(363)
GROSSE-SCHWARE, Herman (1931-   ), Ger
   R.4   S.c
GROSSI, Andrea (fl late 17th Cent), It
   R.1   S.10
GROSSI, Carlo (c1634-1688), It
   R.1   S.c,10
GROSSIN, Estienne (fl c1420), Fr
   R.1   S.4,5x,8,10,11,16
GROSSMAN - Zwei dunkeln Augen
             S.10
GROSSMAN, Ludwik (1835-1915), Pol
   R.1
GROSSMAN, Sasa [Sasha] (1907-   ), Cz
   R.14   S.4,7,31
GROSVENOR, Ralph L. (1893-   ), USA
   R.19   S.e
GROSZ, Wilhelm (1894-1939), Ger
   R.1   S.c
GROTH, Einar (1903-   )
             S.24
GROTHE, Franz (1908-1982), Ger
   R.1   S.5x,10,24
GROTTE, Nicolas de la [see LA GROTTE, NICOLAS de]
GROTTHUSS, Dietrich Ewald von
             S.10
GROUDIS, Josas [see GRUODIS, Juozas]
GROUYA, Theodore (1910-   ), USA
   R.23   S.10
GROVEN, Eivind (1901-1977), Nor
   R.1   S.c,8,10,51
GROVLEZ, Gabriel (1879-1944), Fr
   R.1   S.19,21,24
GRUA, Carlo Luigi Pietro (d c1665), It
   R.1   S.c
GRUBER - Caissons go rolling
             S.54(318)
GRUBER, Benno (1759-1796), Ger
   R.5   S.c
GRUBER, Franz Xaver (1787-1863), Aus
   R.1   S.c,4,5x,10,24,33,43
GRUBER, Ludwig (1874-1964), Aus
   R.14   S.24

GRUEN, John (1927-   ), USA
          S.8-10,13,25,27
GRUEN, Rudolph (1900-   ), USA
    R.43   S.lx
GRUENBERG, Louis (1884-1964), USA
    R.1   S.2-5,8,10,11,13,24
GRÜNBERGER, Theodor (1756-1820), Ger
    R.5   S.c,10
GRUNBLATT, Romuald (1930-   )
          S.18
GRUNDMAN, Clare Ewing (1913-   ), USA
    R.19   S.22,52,54(312,38,41,62,64)
GRUNENWALD, Jean-Jacques (1911-1982), Fr
    R.1   S.c,10
GRÜNER-HEGGE, Odd (1899-   ), Nor
    R.14   S.8,10,24a
GRÜNEWALD, Gottfried (1675-1739), Ger
    R.1   S.c
GRUNFELD, Alfred (1852-1924), Aus
    R.3   S.10
GRUODIS, Juozas (1884-1948)
    R.3   S.24a
GRÜTZMACHER, Friedrich Wilhelm Ludwig (1832-1903), Ger
    R.1
GRUYTTERS, J. de (fl 1772), S. Neth
    R.5   S.c
GUAMI, Gioseffo (c1540-1611), It
    R.1   S.c,8,10,14,16,53
GUARINO - Prince of Piedmont
          S.54(351)
GUARNIERI, Antonio (1880-1952), It
    R.1   S.8,10
GUARNIERI, Camargo Mozart (1907-   ), Brazil
    R.1   S.c,4,6,7,9,10,20,24,32,39
GUASTAVINO, Carlos (1914-   ), Arg
    R.14   S.c,8,10,18,24a,46
GUBARENKO, Vitali Sergeyevich (1934-   ), USSR
    R.47   S.18,24a
GUBAYDULINA, Sofiya Asgatovna (1931-   ), Russia
    R.1   S.18,52
GUDIASHVILY, Nikolai (1913-   ), USSR
    R.14   S.18
GUDMUNDSEN-HOLMGREEN, Pelle (1932-   ), Den
    R.1   S.40
GUÉDON de PRESLES, Honoré-Claude (d c1730), Fr
    R.1
GUÉDRON, Pierre (?1570/75-c1619), Fr
    R.1   S.c,5x,8,10,16
GUELL, Emilio
          S.24a

GUÉNIN, Marie-Alexandre (1744-1835), Fr
   R.1   S.c,8
GUERAU, Francisco (17-18th Cent), Sp
   R.1   S.c,10,39,32
GUERINI, Francesco (fl 1740-70), It
   R.1   S.2,3,5x
GUERRA PEIXE, César (1914-   ), Brazil
   R.1   S.18[Peishe, Guerra],24a

GUERRA, Gerardo Gombau [see GOMBAU GUERRA, Gerardo]
GUERRA, Nicola (1865-   )
            S.24
GUERRAU, Francisco [see GUERAU, Francisco]
GUERRERO y TORRES, Jacinto (1895-1951), Sp
   R.1   S.c,8-10,39,42
GUERRERO, Francisco (1528-1599), Sp
   R.1   S.c,5x,7,8,10,14-16,17
GUERRERO, Pedro (b c1520), Sp
   R.1   S.c,16
GUEST, Douglas (1916-   ), Eng
   R.1   S.c
GUETARY, Garme
            S.e
GUETFREUND, Peter (c1570-1625), Ger
   R.1   S.2,5x[Bonamico],16
GUETTLER, Knut Arne (1943-   ), Nor
   R.80   S.c
GUEVARA, Pedro de Loyola (fl.1575-82), Sp
   R.1   S.10
GUÉZEC, Jean Pierre (1934-1971), Fr
   R.1   S.10
GUGEL, Georg Anton (1743-1802)
            S.24
GUGLIELMI, Pietro Carlo (c1763-1817), It
   R.1   S.c
GUGLIELMO Ebreo da Pesaro (c1425->1480), It
   R.1   S.c,10,16
GUGO-NORIS, J. - Valse d´or (vi & p)
            S.24
GUI II, Chastelain de Courci [see CHASTELAIN de COURCI]
GUIDE, Richard de (1909-1962), Bel
   R.1   S.36
GUIDO (fl 1372-4), Fr
            S.c
GUIDO d´ARREZZO (c992->1033)
   R.1   S.c
GUIFFRE, Jimmy (1921-   )

GUIGNON, Jean-Pierre (1702-1774), It
   R.1   S.c

GUILAN [?Freinsberg, Jean Adam Guillaume] (fl 1702-39),
   Fr R.1   S.c,10,18,53
GUILD - Illinois loyalty
          S.54(333)
GUILHAUD, Georges
          S.20,21
GUILHEM de CABESTANH (12th Cent)

GUILLAUME d´AMIENS Paignour (13th Cent), Fr
   R.1   S.c,8,10,14,15
GUILLAUME de MACHAUT [see MACHAUT, Guillaume de]
GUILLAUME le HEURTEUR [see LE HEURTEUR, Guillaume]
GUILLAUME li VINIER (c1190-1245), Fr
   R.1   S.c,14,16
GUILLEBERT de BERNEVILLE [see GILLEBERT de BERNEVILLE]

GUILLELMUS MONACHUS (fl late 15th Cent), It
   R.1   S.c,10,16
GUILLEMAIN, Louis-Gabriel (1705-1770), Fr
   R.1   S.c,9
GUILLEMETTE - Volte (lute)
          S.16
GUILLERMIT - La Marseillaise brettone
          S.e
GUILLET, Charles (d.1654), S. Neth
   R.1   S.c,10,53
GUILLOU, Jean (1930-   ), Fr
   R.1   S.c
GUILMANT, Félix Alexander (1837-1911), Fr
   R.1   S.c,1,7,8,10
GUIMARAES, Joao
          S.10
GUINALDO, Norberto (1937-   ), USA
   R.19   S.12,13
GUINJOAN, Juan (1931-   ), Sp
          S.c
GUINOT, Georges (1922-   )
          S.c
GUION, David Wendell (1892-1981), USA
   R.19   S.2-5,8,10,11,13,26
GUIOT de DIJON (fl 1215-25), Fr
   R.1   S.c,8,10,14,15
GUIRAUD, Ernest (1837-1892), Fr
   R.1   S.10,24
GUIRAUT Riquier [see RIQUIER, Guiraut]
GUIRAUT d´ESPANHA de Toloza (fl 1240-70)
   R.1   S.c,15,17
GUIRAUT de BORNELH [see GIRAUT de BORNELH]
GULAK-ARTEMOVSKY, Semyon Stepanovich (1813-1873), Rus
   R.1   S.5x[Artemovsky-Yorish]

GULDA, Friedrich (1930-   ), Aus
   R.1   S.c
GULLBERG, Olof (1931-   ), Sweden
         S.40
GULLIDGE, A. W. - Divine Communion; Southern Australia
         S.54(323,57)
GULLIELMUS, Monachus (15th Cent)
   R.1   S.c,10
GULLMAR, Kai pseud [ie Gurli Maria BERGSTRÖM]
   (1905-   ), Sweden R.30   S.24
GULYÁS, László (1928-   ), Hun
   R.4
GUMBERT, Ferdinand (1818-1896), Ger
   R.2   S.5x
GUMBLE - Welcome Honey, to the old plantation
         S.e
GUMPELZHAIMER, Adam (1559-1625), Ger
   R.1   S.c,5x,8,16,32
GUNGL, Joseph (1810-1889), Hun
   R.1   S.c,5x,8-10,24
GUNSENHEIMER, Gustav (1934-   )
         S.c
GUREWICH, Jascha (1896-1938), USA
   R.48   S.22
GURIDI, Jésus (1886-1961), Sp
   R.1   S.c,5x,6-8,10,25,27,39,42
GURILYOV, Alexander Lvovich (1803-1858), Russia
   R.1   S.10,18
GURLITT, Cornelius (1820-1901), Ger
   R.30   S.10
GURNEY, Ivor (1890-1937), Eng
   R.1   S.c,5,10,24-27
GUSSAGO, Cesario (fl 1599-1612), It
   R.1   S.c,10,16,53
GUSTAF, Prince of Sweden & Norway (1827-1852)
   R.1   S.5x,43,56
GUTCHE, Gene (1907-   ), USA
   R.19   S.10,13
GUTIERREZ HERAS, Joaquin (1927-   ), Mex
   R.4
GUTIERREZ, Pedro Elias
         S.e
GUTTMAN, Newman
         S.10
GUTZEIT, Erich [pseud: James HONKY] (1898-1973), Ger
   R.95   S.54(366)
GUY de COUCY (d.1203)
         S.c,16,32

GUY, Harry
               S.10
GUY, Nicholas (d <1629), Eng
   R.1   S.c,10,16
GUYARD, (15th Cent)
               S.c,10,16
GUYMONT - Kyrie (Apt Ms.)
               S.16
GUYONNET, Jacques (1933-   ), Swiss
   R.1
GUY-ROPARTZ, Joseph [see ROPARTZ, Joseph Guy]
GWILT, David William (1932-   ), Scot
   R.14   S.c,24a
GYLDMARK, Hugo (1899-1971), Den
   R.30   S.43
GYRING, Elizabeth (1886-1970), USA
   R.19   S.10,13,30,52
GYROWETZ [Jirovec], Adalbert (1763-1850), Boh
   R.1   S.c,5,10
GYSELINCK, Franklyn (1950-   )
               S.24a
GYSIN, Brion (1916-   ), USA
               S.10
HA, Jae Eun (1937-   ), USA
   R.80   S.13
HAAG, Hanno (1939-   ), Ger
   R.4   S.c,24a
HAALAND, Ingebret (1878-1934), Nor
   R.30   S.24
HAAN, Stefan de (1921-   ),Eng
               S.c
HAARKLOU, Johannes (1847-1925), Nor [?]
               S.5x
HAAS, Joseph (1879-1960), Ger
   R.1   S.c,24a
HÁBA, Alois (1893-1973), Cz
   R.1   S.c,3-5,8-10,20,24,31
HÁBA, Karel (1898-1972), Cz
   R.1   S.5,31
HABER, Louis (1915-   ), USA
   R.19   S.10,13
HABERMANN, Frantisek Vaclav (1706-1783), Boh
   R.3
HABERT, Johannes Evangelista (1833-1896), Aus
   R.1   S.c
HACHIMURA, Yoshio (1938-   ), Japan
   R.4   S.50
HACK, Alfred d´ (1828-1892), Fr
   R.10s   S.e

HACKBARTH, Glenn (1949-   ), USA
            S.13
HACQUART, Carolus (c1640-?1701), Neth
    R.1   S.c,10,24
HACZEWSKI, Antoni (18th Cent)
            S.c
HADDAD, Donald (1935-   ), USA
    R.19   S.10,13
HADDOCK, George Percy (1860-   ), Eng
    R.39   S.e
HADER, Widmar (1941-   ), Ger
    R.4   S.c
HADJIDAKIS, Manos (1925-   ), Greece
    R.1   S.10
HADJIEV, Parashkev (1912-   ), Bul
    R.1   S.8,24
HADJU, Mihaly = HAJDU, Mihaly
HADLEY, Henry Kimball (1871-1937), USA
    R.1   S.3,5,8-11,13
HADLEY, Patrick (1899-1973), Eng
    R.1   S.c
HADULLA, Pius (1933-   )
            S.c
HADZHIBEKOV, Uzeir [see HAJIBEYOV, Uzeir]
HAEFFNER, Johann Christian Friedrich (1759-1833),
    Sweden   R.30   S.56
HAEMMERLEIN, Joseph Anton (c1721-1787)
            S.c
HAERTLING, Carlos (1875-1919), Honduras
    R.56,94   S.54(332)
HAESER, Georg (1865-1945), Ger
    R.41   S.5x
HAGEMAN, Richard (1882-1966), USA
    R.1   S.3,4,5x,10,13,24,25,27,28
HAGEN, Earl H. USA
            S.13
HAGEN, Francis Florentine (1815-1907), USA
    R.1   S.10,47
HAGEN, Joachim Bernhard (fl 1766), Ger
    R.5   S.c
HAGEN, Peter Albrecht von (c1779-1837), USA
    R.1   S.10[Van Hagen],47
HAGER, Frederick W. USA
            S.13,54(317,37,64,65)
HAGER, Ring
            S.10,22[Ring-Hager]
HAGER-ZIMMERMAN, Hilde (1907-   ), Aus
    R.7   S.52
HAGERUP BULL, Edvard (1922-   ), Nor
    R.14   S.c,51

HÄGG, Gustaf Wilhelm (1867-1925), Sweden
   R.30   S.c,10,56
HÄGG, Jacob Adolf (1850-1928), Sweden
   R.1   S.40,56
HAGIUS, Konrad (1550-1615), Ger
   R.1   S.16
HAGOBIAN, Edvard (1920-   ), Arm

HAGUE, Albert (1920-   ), USA
   R.23   S.9
HAHN, Bernard (1780-1852), Ger
   R.3
HAHN, Gunnar (1908-   ), Sweden
   R.14   S.c,40
HAHN, Hans Helmut (1913-   )
            S.c
HAHN, Reynaldo (1875-1947), Ven
   R.1   S.c,1x,2-11,18,20,24-28
HAIBEL, Jakob, (1762-1826), Aus
   R.1   S.c
HAIDEN, Hans Christoph (1572-1617), Ger
   R.1   S.c
HAIEFF, Alexei (1914-   ), USA
   R.1   S.7-10,13
HAIK VANTOURA, Suzanne [see VANTOURA, Suzanne Haik]
HAILSTORK, Adolphus (1941-   ), USA
   R.23   S.13
HAINDL, Franz Sebastian (1727-1812), Ger
   R.1   S.8
HAINES, Edmund (1914-1974), USA
   R.19   S.8,12,13
HAINES, Herbert E. (1880-1923)
            S.10
HAINLEIN, Paul (1626-1686), Ger
   R.1   S.c
HAIRSTON, Jester Joseph (1901-   ), USA
   R.23   S.10
HAISANIDE, Alexander [see HRISANIDE, Alexandru]
HAIT, Yulii Abramovich (1897-1966), USSR [?]
   R.47   S.5x
HAJDU, Mihály (1909-   ), Hun
   R.1   S.20[Hadju],24
HAJIBEYOV, Sultan (1919-1974), USSR
   R.1   S.18,24a[Gadzhibekov]
HAJIBEYOV, Uzeir (1885-1948), USSR
   R.1   S.18[Gadzhibekov]
HAJIYEV, Akhmet (1917-   ), USSR
   R.1   S.18[Gadzhiyev, D]
HAJKU, Michal (16-17th Cent)
            S.c

HÅKANSON, Knut (1887-1929), Sweden
   R.1   S.40,56
HAKIM, Talib Rasul [formerly Stephen A. CHAMBERS]
   (1940-   ), USA R.19   S.10,13
HALACZINSKY, Rudolf (1920-   ), Ger
   R.1   S.c,24
HALES, Robert (d <1616), Eng
   R.1   S.c
HALÉVY, Jacques (1799-1862), Fr
   R.1   S.c,1-11,18,24,42,44
HALFFTER JIMENEZ, Cristobal (1930-   ), Sp
   R.4
HALFFTER, Cristobal (1930-   ), Sp
   R.1   S.c,10
HALFFTER, Ernesto (1905-   ), Sp
   R.1   S.c,2,4,5,7-9,24
HALFFTER, Rodolfo (1900-   ), Sp
   R.1   S.5x,10,24,32,39
HALKET, James
            S.e
HALL, Carol (1936-   ), USA
   R.23   S.c
HALL, H. Foley (fl 1820-66), Eng
   R.44   S.e
HALL, Henry (c1656-1707), Eng
   R.1   S.8,10
HALL, James - pseud [ie James STANLEY] (1930-   ), USA
   R.4   S.13
HALL, John T. USA
            S.13
HALL, Pauline (1890-1969), Nor
   R.1   S.30,40,51,52
HALL, Ray - pseud [see FILLMORE, Henry]
HALL, Richard (1903-   ), Eng
   R.1   S.10
HALL, Robert Browne (1858-1907), USA
   R.30   S.54(328,46,60,65)
HALLA, V
            S.18
HALLAM, E. Percy (1887-1957), Eng
            S.c
HALLBERG, Bengt (1932-   ), Sweden
   R.1   S.40
HALLBERG, Björn Wilho (1938-   ), Sweden
   R.14   S.38
HALLE, Adam de la [see ADAM de la HALLE]
HALLÉN, Andreas (1846-1925), Sweden
   R.1   S.5x,56
HALLER, Edwin - pseud [see LAUTENSCLÄGER, Willi]

HALLER, Hans Peter (1929-   ), Ger
    R.1   S.c
HALLER, Hermann (1914-   ), Swiss
    R.1   S.c
HALLET, A. - Ritmische Studie (p)

HALLEY, Glen USA
            S.13
HALLNÄS, Hilding (1903-   ), Sweden
    R.1   S.c,5x,6,10,38,40,56
HALLSTROM, Ivar Christian (1826-1901), Sweden
    R.1   S.c,56
HALM, Anton (1789-1872), Aus
    R.8   S.c
HALSEY, Ernest
            S.e
HALSEY, Louis Arthur Owen (1922-   ), Eng
    R.1
HALTENBERGER, Bernhard (1748-1780), Ger
    R.1   S.c
HALVAN - Barcarolle in Canon
            S.21

HALVORSEN, Johan (1864-1935), Nor
    R.1   S.c,2-10,24,40,54(325)
HAMAL, Henri-Guillaume (1685-1752), S. Neth
    R.1   S.10
HAMAL, Jean-Noël, (1709-1778), S. Neth
    R.1   S.c,9
HAMBLEN, Bernard (1877-1962), USA
    R.23   S.e
HAMBRAUES, Bengt (1928-   ), Sweden
    R.1   S.c,9,10,38,40,56
HAMBURGER, Povl (1901-1972), Den
    R.1   S.33,57
HAMEL, Peter Michael (1947-   ), Ger
    R.4   S.c
HAMERIK, Asger (1843-1923), Den
    R.1   S.4,5
HAMERIK, Ebbe (1898-1951), Den
    R.1   S.40
HAMILTON, Iain (1922-   ), Scot
    R.1   S.c,9,10,24a
HAMILTON, Thomas (1946-   ), USA
    R.14   S.13
HAMLISCH, Marvin (1944-   ), USA
    R.19   S.9
HAMM, Charles Edward (1925-   ), USA
    R.1   S.10,13
HAMM, Johann Valentin (1811-1875), Ger
    R.3   S.54(343)

HAMMERSCHMIDT, Andreas (1611/12-1675), Aus
    R.1   S.c,2-4,5x,7,8,10
HAMMERSTROM - Part song
            S.5x
HAMMOND, Don (1917-   ), USA
    R.14   S.10,13
HAMMOND, William Gardiner (1874-1945), USA
    R.23   S.e
HAMONIC, Jean Marie (20th Cent)
            S.c
HAMPEL, Gunter (1937-   ), Ger
    R.4
HAMPTON, Calvin (1938-   ), USA
    R.14   S.10,13
HAMPTON, Robert (18??-1944), USA
    R.50   S.10
HAMURGER, Povl = HAMBURGER, Povl
HANBY, Benjamin Russell (1833-1867), USA
    R.50   S.10,24,47
HANCOCK, Gerre (1934-   ), USA
    R.19   S.12,13
HAND, Colin (1929-   ), USA
    R.14   S.10
HAND, Frederic (1947-   )

HANDBERG-JORGENSEN, Michael (d.1972), Den
            S.43
HANDEL, George Frideric (1685-1759), Ger/Eng
    R.1 S.c,1-11,18,19,21-28,33,42,43,53,54(322,30,37)
HANDL, Jacob [Gallus, Jacobus] (1550-1591), Slovenia
    R.1   S.c,2-8,10,11,15,16
HANDLON, James E.
            S.54(361)
HANDOSHKIN, Yvan [see KHANDOSHKIN, Ivan]
HANDY, William Christopher (1873-1958), USA
    R.1   S.c,9,10,54(315)
HANFF, Johann Nikolaus (1665-1711/12), Ger (see note)
    R.1   S.c,4,5x,7,8,10,53
HANISCH, Eduard (1908-   ), Ger
    R.4   S.c,20
HANLEY, James Frederick (1892-1942), USA
    R.23   S.10,24,54(332)
HANMER, Ronald Charles Douglas (1917-   ), Eng
    R.85   S.55
HANNA - My ain country
            S.e
HANNA, Stephen (1950-   ), USA
            S.13
HANNIKAIMEN, Ilmari (1892-1955), Fin
    R.1   S.c,5x,11,40

HANNIKAINEN, Arvo (1897-1942), Fin
   R.1   S.24
HANOUSEK, Karel (1902-   ), Cz
   R.14   S.24
HANRAY, Lawrence
            S.e
HANSEL, Walther

HANSEN, Adolf Johannes Waldenmar (1852-1911) Nor
   R.30   S.24
HANSEN, Erik
            S.54(338)
HANSEN, H. - Awakening
            S.5x
HANSON, Howard (1896-1981), USA
   R.1   S.c,2-5,7-13
HANSON, Raymond (1913-1976), Australia
   R.35   S.10,37
HANSON, Sten (1936-   ), Sweden
   R.30   S.56
HANSSEN, Johannes (1874-1967), Nor
   R.14   S.10
HANSSON, Stig (1900-1968), Sweden
   [pseud: Jules SYLVAIN] R.30   S.24,43
HANUŠ, Jan (1915-   ), Cz
   R.1   S.c,9,10,24a,31
HAQUINIUS, Johan Algot (1886-1966), Sweden
   R.1   S.5x,24,40
HARA, Hiroshi (1933-   ), Japan
   R.4   S.50
HARANT, Krystof (1564-1621), Cz
   R.1   S.c,5x,9,16
HARBISON, John (1938-   ), USA
   R.19   S.9,10,13,24a
HARDELOT, Guy d´ - pseud [ie Helen RHODES (née Guy)]
   (1858-1936), Fr   R.1   S.4,5x,10,24,43,44,52
HARDER, Egil (1917-   ), Den
   R.30   S.33
HARDIN, Louis Thomas (1916-   ), USA
   R.19   S.c
HARDING, James (d.1626), Eng
   R.1   S.c,10,16
HARDOUIN, Henri (1727-1808), Fr
   R.1
HARGREAVES - Watching the trains go by
            S.e
HARINGTON, Henry (1727-1816), Eng
   R.1   S.10,33
HARITO, E. - Crysanteme (vi & p)
            S.24

HARKNESS, Rebekah West (1915-   ), USA
    R.14   S.9,13,30,52
HARLING, William Franke (1887-1958), USA
    R.19   S.10,13
HARMAN, Carter (1918-   ), USA
    R.1   S.10,13
HARMON, Joel Jr (1773-1833), USA
    R.50   S.47
HARMONIC, Phil - pseud [ie Kenneth WERNER] (1949-   ),
    USA R.19   S.13
HARNEY, Benenjamin Robertson (1872-1938), USA
    R.59   S.10
HAROLD - A child's prayer
            S.e
HARPER, Edward (1941-   ), Eng
    R.1   S.c
HARREX, Patrick (1946-   ), Eng
    R.4
HARRIES, David (1933-   ), Wales
    R.1   S.c,10
HARRIS - Air on a shoestring; viva Vivaldi
            S.24a
HARRIS, Albert (1911-   ), USA
    R.19   S.10,13,24a
HARRIS, Arthur (1927-   ), USA
    R.19   S.10,13
HARRIS, Charles Kassel (1867-1930), USA
    R.23   S.10
HARRIS, Donald (1931-   ), USA
    R.19   S.10,13,24a
HARRIS, Roger (1940-   ), USA
    R.19   S.13
HARRIS, Ross (1945-   )

HARRIS, Roy (1898-1979), USA
    R.1   S.c,2-5,7-11,13,19,23-25,27
HARRIS, Russell (1914-   ), USA
    R.19   S.7,10,13
HARRIS, Sydney USA
            S.13
HARRIS, Victor (1869-1943), USA
    R.4   S.e
HARRIS, William Henry (1883-1973), Eng

    R.1   S.c,5,8
HARRISON, Annie Fortescue (Lady Arthur Hill)
    (1851-1944), Eng   R.7   S.10,19
HARRISON, John (1938-   )
            S.24a
HARRISON, Julius Alan (1885-1963), Eng
    R.1   S.c,1x,5x,24

HARRISON, Lou (1917-   ), USA
    R.1   S.7-10,13,24
HARSÁNYI, Tibor (1898-1954), Fr
    R.1   S.1-3,8,10
HART, Leen´t (1920-   ), Neth
    R.80   S.c
HARTEVELD, Julius Napoleon Wilhelm (1859-1927), Sweden
    R.1   S.5x
HARTIG, Heinz Friedrich (1907-1969), Ger
    R.14   S.10,32
HARTLEY, Gerald (1921-   ), USA
    R.19   S.8,13,21
HARTLEY, Harry - pseud [see FILLMORE, Henry]
HARTLEY, Lloyd Eng
    R.77   S.24
HARTLEY, Walter Sinclair (1927-   ), USA
    R.19   S.10,13,22
HARTLING, Carlos [see HAERTLING, Carlos]
HARTMAN, John (1830-1897)

HARTMANN - Facilita
              S.54(325)
HARTMANN, Emil (1836-1898), Den
    R.1   S.5x,24,35,57
HARTMANN, Emma Sophie Amalie (1807-1851), Den
    [pseud: Frederick H. PALMER] R.7   S.e
HARTMANN, Erich (1920-   ), Ger
    R.4   S.c
HARTMANN, Heinrich (c1580-1616), Ger
    R.1   S.c
HARTMANN, Johan Peter Emilius (1805-1900), Den
    R.1   S.c,4-8,24a,33,35,57
HARTMANN, Johann Ernst (1726-1793), Ger
    R.1
HARTMANN, Karl Amadeus (1905-1963), Ger
    R.1   S.c,7-10,24
HARTMANN, Pater [Paul] (1863-1914), Ger
    R.8
HARTMANN, Rolf (1928-   )
              S.c
HARTULARY-DARCKÉE, Ion (1886-1969), Fr
    R.14
HARTWAY, James John (1944-   ), USA
    R.19   S.13
HARTY, Hamilton (1879-1941), Ire
    R.1   S.c,1-6,10,24
HARUM - Light nights
              S.5x
HARUTUNYAN, Alexander Grigori (1920-   ),Arm
    R.1   S.c,10,18[Arutyunyan]

HARVEY, Jonathan (1939-   ), Eng
  R.1   S.c
HARVEY, Paul Milton (1935-   ), Eng
  R.80   S.22
HARWOOD, Basil (1859-1949), Eng
  R.1   S.c,8
HASELBÖCK, Hans (1928-   ), Aus
  R.1   S.10
HASHAGEN, Klaus (1924-   ), Ger
  R.1   S.c,10,32
HASKINS, Robert James (1937-   ), USA
  R.19   S.13
HASLAM, David (1940-   ), Eng
  R.80   S.c,10
HASLINDE, Paul Jobst (1886-   ), Ger
  R.3   S.24
HASLINGER, Tobias (1787-1842), Ger [publisher]
  R.1   S.c
HASPROIS [Haspre], Johannes Symonis (fl 1378-1428), Fr
  R.1   S.c,10,16
HASQUENOPH, Pierre (1922-   ), Fr
  R.4
HASSE, Johann Adolph (1699-1783), Ger
  R.1   S.c,4,5,7,8,10,23,24,28
HASSE, Nikolaus (c1617-1672), Ger
  R.1   S.c,10
HASSE, Peter (c1585-1640), Ger
  R.1   S.c,53
HASSELMANS, Alphonse (1845-1912), Fr
  R.1   S.c,10
HASSLER, Hans Leo (1562-1612), Ger
  R.1   S.c,2-11,14-16,18,32,53
HASSLER, Isaak (c1530-1591), Ger
  R.1
HÄSSLER, Johann Wilhelm (1747-1822), Ger
  R.1   S.c,3,5x,10
HASSLER, Kaspar (1562-1618), Ger
  R.1   S.c
HASTINGS, Thomas (1784-1872), USA
  R.1   S.e
HATHAWAY, Jane
           S.e
HATTON, John Liptrot (1808-1886), Eng
  R.1   S.c,10
HAUBENSTOCK-RAMATI, Roman (1919-   ), Aus
  R.1   S.c,10
HAUBIEL, Charles Troubridge (1892-1978), USA
  R.19   S.2,9,10,13,24a
HAUBLEIN, Ernst (1911-1971)
           S.c

HAUCOURT, Johannes (fl 1390-1410), Fr
    R.1   S.c,16[Acourt],c[D´Acourt]
HAUER, Josef Mathias (1883-1959), Aus
    R.1   S.c,7,10
HAUFRECHT, Herbert (1909-   ), USA
    R.19   S.10,13
HAUG, Halvor (1952-   )
                 S.24a
HAUG, Hans (1900-1967), Swiss
    R.1   S.10,32
HAUSER, Miska (1822-1887), Hun
    R.8   S.24
HAUSSMANN, Valentin (c1565-c1614), Ger
    R.1   S.c,2,3,5x,10,15,16
HAVELKA, Svatopluk (1925-   ), Cz
    R.1   S.c,31
HAWEL, Jan Wincenty (1936-   ), Pol
    R.4
HAWES, Jack Richards (1916-   ), Eng
    R.80   S.c
HAWKINS, George (1876-   ), Eng
    R.96   S.54(327,59)
HAWKINS, John (1944-   ), Can
    R.31
HAWLEY, Charles Beach (1858-1915), USA
    R.23   S.e
HAWLEY, Stanley (1887-1916), Eng
    R.3   S.e
HAWTHORNE, Alice - pseud [see WINNER, Septimus]
HAYAKAWA, Masaaki (1934-   ), Japan
    R.4   S.50
HAYASHI, Hikaru (1931-   ), Japan
    R.1   S.24,50
HAYDEN, Scott (1882-1915)

HAYDN, Franz Josef (1732-1809), Aus
    R.1   S.c,1-11,18,21-28,32,33,54(331)
HAYDN, Michael (1737-1806), Aus
    R.1   S.c,2,3,5-10,23,24
HAYE, De la (17th Cent) - French dances of the 17th
    Cent - Saraband   S.8
HAYES, Al - pseud [see FILLMORE, Henry]
HAYES, Philip (1738-1797), Eng
    R.1   S.c
HAYLES, Robert (d.1616)
                 S.16
HAYMAN, Richard Warren Joseph [pseud: M. E. DALY,
    Ray HOWARD, Richard SAVAGE] (1920-   ), USA
    R.23

HAYNE van GHIZEGHEM (c1445-c1472), Neth
   R.1   S.c,4,5x,10,15,16,41
HAYNES, Walter Battison (1859-1900), Eng
   R.39   S.10
HAYS, Doris Ernestine (1941-   ), USA
   R.19   S.13,30,52
HAYS, William Shakespeare (1837-1907), USA
   R.59   S.10,24
HAYSOM, Peter - pseud [ie Peter CRADDY]
   R.85   S.55
HAZEL, John (1865-1948), USA

HAZELL, Chris (1948-   ), Eng
             S.c
HEAD, Michael Dewar (1900-1976), Eng
   R.1   S.c,5x,6,8,10,25,27
HEADINGTON, Christopher (1930-   ), Eng
   R.1
HEALEY, Derek Edward (1936-   ), Eng
   R.14
HEANEY, Patrick (?-1911), Ire
   R.1
HEARD, Alan (1942-   ), Can
   R.31
HEATH - Widdicombe Fair
             S.e
HEATH, Bobby (1899-1952), USA
   R.23   S.10
HEATH, John (1608-1668), Eng
   R.1   S.c
HEATH, Lyman
             S.47
HEATON, W. - Praise
             S.54(350)
HEBDEN, John (fl 1740-50), Eng
   R.1   S.c
HEBERLE, Anton (18th Cent), Ger
   R.5   S.c
HECHTENBERG, Dieter
             S.c
HECKEL, Wolff (c1515-c1562), Ger
   R.1   S.c
HEDGCOCK, Walter William (1864-1932), Eng
   R.3   S.c
HEDGE, Edna Zema

HEDGES, Anthony (1931-   ), Eng
   R.1   S.c
HEDLEY - So he followed me
             S.e

HEDWALL, Lennart (1932-   ), Sweden
   R.14   S.40
HEENAN, Ashley (1925-   ), New Zealand
   R.1
HEER, Emil (1926-   ), Swiss
   R.4
HEER, Johannes (c1489-1553), Swiss [editor]
   R.1   S.c
HEEREN, Hans (1893-1964), Ger
   R.2   S.10
HEGAR, Friedrich (1841-1927), Swiss
   R.1   S.24

HEGDAL, Magne Gunnar (1944-   ), Nor
   R.80   S.40,51
HEIBERG, Johann Ludwig (1791-1860), Den
   R.30   S.e
HEIDEMANN, Wilhelm
          S.c
HEIDEN, Bernhard (1910-   ), USA
   R.1   S.10,13,22,24a
HEIDER, Werner (1930-   ), Ger
   R.1   S.c,10,24a
HEIFETZ, Robin Julian (1951-   ), USA
          S.13
HEIFMAN, Alexander

HEILLER, Anton (1923-1979), Aus
   R.1   S.c,10
HEILMANN, Harold (1924-   ), Ger
   R.1   S.c,24
HEILMER - Pontifical hymn
          S.5x
HEILNER, Irwin (1908-   ), USA
   R.19   S.10,13
HEIN, Silvio (1879-1928), USA
   R.23   S.10
HEIN-BADER - Er offenbart sich überall (v)
          S.c
HEINICHEN, Johann David (1683-1729), Ger
   R.1   S.c,10,24
HEININEN, Paavo Johannes (1938-   ), Fin
   R.1   S.c,40
HEINKE, Siegfried (1910-   ), Eng
          S.c
HEINRICH (signor Heinrich) (fl 1730)
          S.c
HEINRICH von Gundelfingen (15th Cent)
          S.c
HEINRICH von Laufenberg (13th Cent)
          S.c,16

HEINRICH von MEISSEN [see FRAUENLOB]
HEINRICH von MÜGLIN (14th Cent)
   R.5   S.c
HEINRICH von VELDEKE [see HENDRIK van VELDEKE]
HEINRICH, Anthony Philip (1781-1861), USA
   R.1   S.9,10,47
HEINRICHS, Wilhelm (1914-   )
             S.c
HEINSIUS, Ernst (fl 1760), Neth
   R.5   S.24
HEINTZ, James R. ?USA
             S.13
HEINTZ, Wolff (c1490-1552), Ger
   R.1   S.c,10
HEINTZE, Gustaf (1879-1946), Sweden
   R.30   S.56
HEINZ - Zwei dunkle Augen
             S.e
HEISE, Peter Arnold (1830-1879), Den
   R.1   S.c,4-8,10,11,33,35,40,57
HEISER, Wilhelm (1816-1897), Ger
   R.3   S.e
HEISINGER, Brent USA
             S.13
HEISS, John (1938-   ), USA
   R.19   S.10,13
HEKKING, Gérard (1879-1942), Fr
   R.4   S.5x
HELD, Johann Theobald (1770-1851), Boh
   R.5   S.5x
HELD, Wilbur C. (1914-   ), USA
   R.19   S.10,12,13
HELDEN, Daniel (1917-   ), Sweden
   R.68
HELDER, Bartholomäus (c1585-1635), Ger
   R.1   S.8,10
HELF, J. Fred
             S.13,24,54(345)
HELFMAN, Max (1901-1963), USA
   R.4
HELLENDAAL, Pieter (1721-1799), Neth
   R.1   S.c,24
HELLER, Kenneth (1949-   ), USA
             S.10,13
HELLER, Stephen (1813-1888), Fr
   R.1   S.c,5x,6,9,10,21
HELLERMANN, William (1939-   ), USA
   R.19   S.c,10,13
HELLINCK, Lupus (c1496-1541), Flem
   R.1   S.c,10,16

HELLMANN - Lore
            S.54(338)
HELLMESBERGER, Georg (1830-1852), Aus
    R.1   S.10
HELLMESBERGER, Joseph (1855-1907), Aus
    R.1   S.c,5x
HELLMUTH, Paul (1879-1919), Den
    R.30   S.5x
HELLSTRÖM, David Emanuel (1883-1965), Sweden
    R.30   S.5x
HELM, Everett Burton (1913-   ), USA
    R.1   S.5x,10,13,24
HELMER, Ch.
            S.54(352)
HELMONT, Adrien-Joseph van (1747-1830), S. Neth
    R.1   S.c
HELMONT, Charles-Joseph van (1715-1790), S. Neth
    R.1   S.c,10,53
HELMSCHROTT, Robert M. (1939-   ), Ger
    R.4   S.c
HELPS, Robert (1928-   ), USA
    R.1   S.9,10,13
HELSTED, Edvard (1816-1900), Den
    R.3   S.c,10
HELY, Cuthbert (fl 1620-48), Eng
    R.1   S.c
HELY-HUTCHINSON, Victor (1901-1947), Eng
    R.1   S.c,5x,6,10
HEMBERG, Eskil (1938-   ), Sweden
    R.1   S.c,56
HEMEL, Oscar van (1892-1981), Neth
    R.1   S.10,20,24
HEMERLING, Carlo (1903-1967), Swiss
    R.14
HEMERY, Valentine
            S.e
HEMING, Michael (1920-1942), Eng
    R.25   S.4
HEMINGWAY, Roger (1951-   ), Eng
            S.c
HEMMER, Eugene (1929-1977), USA
    R.19   S.13
HENDERSON, Ray (1896-1970), USA
    R.1   S.10,24
HENDERSON, Robert (1948-   ), USA
            S.10,13
HENDL, Walter (1917-   ), USA
    R.19   S.13
HENDRIK van VELDEKE (1140/50-<1210), Ger
    R.1

HENKEMANS, Hans (1913-   ), Neth
    R.1   S.8,10,24
HENKING, Bernard (1897-   ), Swiss
    R.4
HENLEY, William (1876-1957), Eng
    R.77   S.24
HENNAGIN, Michael (1936-   ), USA
    R.19   S.c,10,13
HENNEBERG, Albert (1901-   ), Sweden
    R.1   S.c,5x
HENNEBERG, Paul (1863-1929)

HENNEBERG, Richard (1853-1925), Ger
    R.3   S.11
HENNESSY - Home Canada, home
                 S.e
HENNINGS, Nancy USA
                 S.13
HENRI, Jacques
                 S.24
HENRICH - Adieu Grenade
                 S.e
HENRIKSON, Alice [pseud: Alice LEBEAU] (1906-   )
                 S.43
HENRION, Paul (1819-1901), Fr
    R.1   S.5x
HENRION, Richard (1854-1940), Ger
    R.4   S.10,54(326)
HENRIQUES, Fini Valdemar (1867-1940), Den
    R.1   S.4-8,10,11,24,35,40,57
HENRIQUES, Robert (1858-1914), Den
    R.3   S.e
HENRY V, King of England (1387-1422)

HENRY VI, King of England (1422-1453)
                 S.c,2,3,5x
HENRY VIII, King of England (1491-1547)
    R.1   S.c,5x,9,10,14,16
HENRY, H. F. - Faith of Our Fathers (see note)
                 S.5x
HENRY, John   .
                 S.e
HENRY, Leon

HENRY, Pierre (1927-   ), Fr
    R.1   S.c,9,10
HENRY, S. R. - pseud [see STERN, Henry]
HENSCHEL, George (1850-1934), Eng
    R.3   S.8,24
HENSEL, Fanny Cacilia [see MENDELSSOHN, Fanny]

HENSELT, Adolf von (1814-1889), Ger
    R.1   S.c,1x,5x,9,10,18
HENTSCHEL, Erwin (1889-1944), Ger
    R.4   S.24
HENZE, Hans Werner (1926-   ), Ger
    R.1   S.c,9,24,32,55
HEPPENER, Robert (1925-   ), Neth
    R.1   S.10
HERBECK, Johann Ritter von (1831-1877), Aus
    R.1   S.c,8
HERBERIGS, Robert (1886-1974), Bel
    R.1   S.7-9,36
HERBERT, Victor (1859-1924), USA
    R.1 S.c,1-4,5x,7-11,13,21,24,43,54(312,14,23)
HERBST, Johannes (1735-1812), USA
    R.8   S.8,10,47
HERDER, Ronald (1930-   ), USA
    R.19   S.10,13
HEREDIA, Pedro (d.1648), It
    R.1   S.15
HEREDIA, Sebastian Aguillera de
    [see AGUILLERA de HEREDIA, Sebastian]
HERITIER, Jean l´ [see L´HERITIER, Jean]
HERITTE-VIARDOT, Louis Pauline Marie (1841-1918), Fr
    R.7   S.10,30,52
HERMAN DAMEN (13th Cent)

HERMAN, A. - Angel´s dream
                S.54(313)
HERMAN, Jerry (1933-   ), USA
    R.1   S.c
HERMAN, Johann (16th Cent) (see note)
                S.c,10
HERMANN, Adolf - pseud [ie Constant HERMANT]
    (1823-1903), Fr   R.10   S.24
HERMANN, Hans (1870-1931), Ger
    R.3   S.e
HERMANN, Karl August (1851-1909) [S.18]
    = HEYMANN-RHEINECK, Karl August (1854-1922)
HERMANN, Monk of Salzburg [see MONK of SALZBURG]
HERMANN, Nicolaus (1500-1561), Ger (see note)
    R.1   S.16
HERMANN, Ralph J. (Reginald Hale) (1914-   ), USA
    R.23   S.22
HERMANNUS CONTRACTUS (1013-1054)
    R.1   S.c,10,16
HERMANSON, Åke (1923-   ), Sweden
    R.1   S.c,38,40,56
HERMANSSON, Christer (1943-   )
                S.c

HERMANSSON, Nils Bishop of Linkoping (14th Cent)
        S.c
HERMANT, Constant [see HERMAN, Adolf - pseud]
HERMITE, Maurice
        S.24
HERNANDEZ - Artistas en miniature; El Capitan de
   Lanceros   S.e
HERNÁNDEZ GONZALO, Gisela (1912-1971), Cuba
   R.1   S.30,52
HERNÁNDEZ LÓPEZ, Rhazes (1918-   ), Ven
   R.4
HERNANDEZ, Raphael (1895-1965), Puerto Rico [?]
   R.113   S.39
HEROLD, Johann Theodor (fl 1702), Ger
   R.5
HÉROLD, Ferdinand (1791-1833), Fr
   R.1   S.c,2-5,8-11,18,24
HERON, Henry (18th Cent), Eng
   R.5   S.c,53
HERRANDO, Joseph (c1700-c1765), Sp
   R.1   S.10,24
HERRARTE, Manuel (fl 1957), Guatemala
   R.56   S.10
HERRERA, Tomás de (fl 1611-20), Peru
   R.1   S.10
HERRICK, Joseph (1772-1807), USA

HERRMANN, Bernard (1911-1975), USA
   R.1   S.c,9,13
HERRMANN, Hugo (1896-1967), Ger
   R.1
HERRMANN, Thomas
        S.24
HERSCHEL, William (1738-1822), Eng
   R.1   S.c
HERSHFELD, David Grigorevich (1911-   )
        S.18
HERSTEIN, Peter
        S.10,13
HERTEL, Johann Christian (1699-1754), Ger
   R.1   S.10
HERTEL, Johann Wilhelm (1727-1789), Ger
   R.1   S.c,9,10
HERTER NORTON, Mary Dows (1892-   ), USA
   R.7   S.5x[Norton, M.D.H.]
HERTL, Frantisek (1906-   ), Cz
   R.14   S.31

HERVÉ - pseud [ie Florimond RONGÉ] (1825-1892), Fr
   R.1   S.c

HERVELOIS, Louis de Caix d'
  [see CAIX d'HERVELOIS, Louis de]
HERVEY, Arthur (1855-1922), Eng
  R.1   S.e
HERVIG, Richard (1917-   ), USA
  R.19   S.13,21
HERZ, Henri [Heinrich] (1803-1888), Ger
  R.1   S.c,10
HERZER, Rudolf (?-1914), Ger
  R.95   S.54(332,65)
HERZOGENBERG, Heinrich von (1843-1900), Aus
  R.1   S.c
HESDIN, Pierre Nicolle des Celliers de (d.1538), Fr
  R.1   S.8,10,14,15
HESELTINE, Philip Arnold [see WARLOCK, Peter - pseud]
HESPE, George William (1900-   ), Eng
  R.85   S.54(336),55
HESPOS, Hans-Joachim (1938-   ), Ger
  R.1
HESS - Domu-Home
               S.e
HESS, Ernst (1912-1968), Swiss
  R.1   S.24
HESS, Willy (1906-   ), Swiss
  R.1   S.5x
HESSE - My Lady Dainty
               S.54(344)
HESSE, Adolph Friedrich (1809-1863), Ger
  R.1   S.c
HESSE, Ernst Christian (1676-1762), Ger
  R.1   S.10
HESSE, Marjorie Anne (1911-   ), Australia
  R.7   S.52
HESSELBERG, Eyvind (1898-   ), Nor
  R.14   S.40
HESSEN, Bartholomeus (1518-1585), Pol
  R.5
HESSEN, Moritz Landgraf von
  [see MORITZ, Landgraf von Hessen-Kassel]
HESSENBERG, Kurt (1908-   ), Ger
  R.1   S.c,24
HÉTU, Jacques (1938-   ), Can
  R.14   S.10
HEUBERGER, Richard (1850-1914), Aus
  R.1   S.c,4,5x,10,24
HEUDELINNE, Louis (fl 1700-10), Fr
  R.1   S.c
HEUGEL, Johannes (c1500-1585), Ger
  R.1   S.c

HEUN, Hans [pseud: Larry LONES] (1920-   ), Ger
    R.4   S.c
HEURICH, Winfried

HEURTEUR, Guillaume le [see LE HEURTEUR, Guillaume]
HEUSER, Ernst (1863-1942), Ger
    R.4   S.c
HEUSSENSTAMM, George (1926-   ), USA
    R.19   S.10,13
HEUSSER, Hans (1892-1942), Swiss
    R.95   S.54(326)
HEUVAL, van den - Courage
             S.e
HEWITT, James (1770-1827), USA
    R.1   S.c,7,10,47
HEWITT, John Hill (1801-1890), USA
    R.1   S.47
HEWITT, Thomas James (1880-   ), Eng
    R.37   S.e
HEWITT-JONES, Tony (1926-   ), Eng
    R.14   S.c,10
HEYBURN, F - The Turtle Dove
             S.22
HEYKENS, Jonny the Elder (1884-   ), Ger
    R.3   S.c,24,54(358,62)
HEYMANN, A. - Ja, du bist mein
             S.e
HEYMANN-RHEINECK, Karl August (1854-1922), Ger
    R.2,3   S.18[Hermann, Karl August (1851-1909)]
HEYMANN, Werner Richard (1896-1961), Ger
    R.2   S.24,43
HEYNSIUS, Michael Ernst (18th Cent)

HIBBARD, William (1939-   ), USA
    R.19   S.10,13
HICKMANN, Esaias (1638-1691), Sp
             S.10
HICKS, J. W. (19th Cent), USA - The last hymn

HICKS, Marjorie Louise Kisbey (20th Cent), Can
             S.52
HIDALGO, Juan (1612/16-1685), Sp
    R.1   S.c,5x,7,10,16,39
HIDAS, Frigyes (1928-   ), Hun
    R.1   S.c,10,24
HIEBLER, Gelasius (1716-1780)
    R.5   S.c,10
HIEBNER, Armand (1898-   ), Swiss
    R.14

HIER, Ethel Glen (1889-1971), USA
   R.7
HIERRO, José del (1864-1933), Sp [?]
   R.9   S.24
HIGGINBOTTOM, Edward
         S.c
HIGGINS, Giles
         S.e
HIGO, Ichiro
         S.24a
HIGUET, Nestor

HILBER, Johann Baptist (1891-1967), Swiss
   R.1   S.c
HILDACH, Eugen (1849-1924), Ger
   R.2   S.1x,4,5x,10,24,43
HILDEGARD von Bingen (1098-1179), Ger
   R.1   S.c,30,52
HILDEMANN, Wolfgang (1925-   )
         S.c,20
HILDENBRAND, Siegfried (1917-   ), Swiss
   R.14
HILDERLEY, Jeriann (1937-   ), USA
         S.52
HILDRETH, R. E.
         S.54(332)
HILL, Alfred (1870-1960), Australia
   R.1   S.5-7,23,24a,29,37
HILL, Billy [see HILL, William J.]
HILL, Charles (1929-   )

HILL, Edward Burlingame (1872-1960), USA
   R.1   S.8,10,13
HILL, Lewis Eugene (1909-   ), Can
   R.14
HILL, Mr - The bird fancyers delight
         S.10
HILL, Richard V. (1942-   )
         S.10
HILL, Uri K. (1780-1844), USA
   R.1   S.10,47
HILL, Wilhelm (1838-1902), Ger
   R.2   S.24
HILL, William H. (1925-   )
         S.13
HILL, William J (1899-1940), USA
   R.23   S.5x,10
HILLEMACHER, Paul Joseph Guillaume (1852-1933), Fr
   R.1   S.1x,10

HILLER, Ferdinand (1811-1885), Ger
    R.1   S.c,10
HILLER, Johann Adam (1728-1804), Ger
    R.1   S.c
HILLER, Lejaren (1924-   ), USA
    R.1   S.9,10,13,24a
HILLER, Wilfried (1941-   ), Ger
              S.c
HILLERT, Richard Walter (1923-   ), USA
    R.19

HILMAR, František Matéj (1803-1881), Cz
    R.1   S.8
HILTON, John (i) (d.1608), Eng
    R.1   S.c,2,3,5x,7,8,14,16
HILTON, John (ii) (1599-1657), Eng
    R.1   S.c,2,3,5x,7,8,14
HIMMEL, Friedrich Heinrich (1765-1814), Ger
    R.1   S.c,2-4
HINDEMITH, Paul (1895-1963), Ger
    R.1   S.c,1-11,18-24
HINDLEY, Thomas
              S.54(349)
HINE, William (1687-1730), Eng
    R.1   S.c,53
HINGESTON, John (d.1688), Eng
    R.1   S.c,10,16
HINNER, Philipp Joseph (1754->1805), Ger
    R.1   S.c
HINTERLEITNER, Ferdinand Ignaz (1659-1710)

HINTZ, Ewaldt (d >c1666), Ger
    R.1   S.c
HINTZ, Jakob (1622-1702), Ger
    R.1   S.5x
HIPMAN, Sylvester (1893-   ), USSR
    R.4
HIRAI, Kozaburo [pseud: Yasuki HIRAI] (1910-   ),
    Japan   R.4   S.50
HIRAO, Kishio (1907-1953), Japan
    R.4
HIRAYOSHI, Takekuni (1936-   ), Japan
    R.4   S.50
HIRGSTÄTTER - Zwischen Marie und Sophie
              S.10
HIRNER, Teodor (1910-   ), Cz
    R.14   S.31
HIROSE, Ryohei (1930-   ), Japan
    R.4   S.50
HIROTA, Ryutaro (1892-1952), Japan
    R.36   S.24

HIRSCH, Hans Ludwig (1937-   ), Ger
   R.4   S.10
HIRSCH, Louis Achille (1881-1924), USA
   R.23   S.10,24
HIRSCH, Paul Adolf (1881-1951), Eng
   R.1   S.21
HIRSCHBERGER, Albericus (1709-1745), Ger
   R.5   S.c
HIRSCHFELDT, Ingrid (20th Cent), Ger
           S.c,52
HIRSH/HIRST - Boola, boola; Yale boola march
           S.54(317,66)
HIRTLER, Franz (1914-   )
           S.c
HITCHEN - La majeur
           S.54(339)
HIVELY, Wells (1902-1969), USA

   R.19   S.8,10,13
HJELT, August
           S.24
HLIBOVSKY, B. (1935-   )
           S.24a
HLOBIL, Emil (1901-   ) Cz
   R.1   S.c,5,10,22,24a,31
HO Chan-hao
           S.c,24
HO Lu-T´Ing
           S.c
HOBBS, Chistopher (1950-   ), USA
           S.13
HOBBS, Odell ?USA
           S.13
HOCHBRUCKER, Christian (1733->1799), Ger
   R.1   S.c
HOCHSTETTER - Noel
           S.e
HODDINOTT, Alun (1929-   ), Wales
   R.1   S.c,9,10,19,24a
HODEIR, André (1921-   ), Fr
   R.1   S.9,10
HODELL, Åke (1919-   ), Sweden
   R.30   S.40(92)
HODKINSON, Sydney Phillip (1934-   ), Can
   R.14   S.10,13,20,24a
HODSON, George Alexander (?-1863), Eng
   R.44   S.e
HØEBERG, Georg Valdemar (1872-1950), Den
   R.14   S.24,35,57
HOEDT, Georges Henri d´ (1885-1936), Bel
   R.25   S.36

HOELLER, Karl [see HOLLER, Karl]
HOELLREUTTER, Hans-Joachim (1915-   )

HOFER, Andreas (1629-1684), Aus
    R.1   S.10
HØFFDING, Finn (1899-   ), Den
    R.1   S.4,7,20,35,40,57
HOFFER, Johann Friedrich (1897-   )

HOFFER, Johann Jacob (1660-1737), Aus
    R.8   S.c,8
HÖFFER, Paul (1895-1949), Ger
    R.1   S.c,5x
HOFFERT, Paul (1943-   ), Can
    R.81   S.24a
HOFFMAN (19th Cent), USA - Ballade
             S.10
HOFFMAN, Edward
             S.10
HOFFMAN, Johann [No.IV in R.5] (fl 1800)
    R.5   S.c,8,10,24,32
HOFFMAN, Leopold (c1730-1793)
    R.5   S.8,10
HOFFMAN, Richard (1831-1909), USA
    R.1
HOFFMAN, Richard (1925-   ), USA
    R.14   S.10,13,24
HOFFMANN, Bruno (1913-   ), Ger
    R.1   S.c
HOFFMANN, Ernst Theodor Amadeus (1776-1822), Ger
    R.1   S.c,9,24a
HOFFMANN, Joachim (1788-1856)
             S.c
HOFFMANN, Melchior (c1685-1715), Ger (see note)
    R.1
HOFFMANN, Niels Frédéric (1943-   ), Ger
    R.4
HOFFMANN, Richard (1925-   ), Aus
    R.4
HOFFMEISTER, Franz Anton (1754-1812), Ger
    R.1   S.c,20,23,24
HOFHAIMER, Paul (1459-1537), Aus
    R.1   S.c,4,5,10,11,14-16,28,32,53
HOFMAN, Shlomo (1909-   ), Isr
    R.4   S.10
HOFMAN, Srdjan (1944-   ), Yug
             S.24a
HOFMANN, Heinrich Karl Johann (1842-1902), Ger
    R.1   S.10

HOFMANN, Josef (1876-1957), Pol
    R.1   S.c,10,19,21
HOFMANN, Leopold (1738-1793), Aus
    R.1   S.c,10
HOFMANN, Wolfgang (1922-   ), Ger
    R.4   S.c
HOFSTETTER, Romanus (d c1785), Ger
    R.8   S.c,10
HOGENHAVEN, Knud (1928-   ), Den
               S.40
HÖGNER, Friedrich (1897-   ), Ger
    R.14   S.c
HOHENZOLLERN, Prince Louis von
    [see LOUIS FERDINAND, Prince of Prussia]
HOHNE, Carl
               S.10
HOIBY, Lee (1926-   ), USA
    R.1   S.9,10,13
HOKANS, Henry

HOL, Rijk (1825-1904), Neth
    R.1   S.41
HOLAN ROVENSKÝ, Vaclav Karel (1644-1718), Cz
    R.1   S.c
HOLBORNE, Anthony (d.1602), Eng
    R.1   S.c,8,10,14-16,32,53
HOLBORNE, William (fl 1597), Eng
    R.1   S.c,10
HOLBROOK - Jesus lover of my soul
               S.e
HOLBROOKE, Josef (1878-1958), Eng

    R.1   S.c,2-5,19,20
HOLCOMBE, Henry (?1693-1750), Eng
    R.1   S.c
HOLDEN, Oliver (1765-1844), USA
    R.1   S.10,47
HOLDRIDGE, Lee (1944-   ), USA
    R.19   S.13,24a
HOLEWA, Hans (1905-   ), Sweden
    R.1   S.c,24a,38,40,56
HOLGER, Rolf (1903-1969), Nor
    R.30   S.c
HOLLAENDER, Friedrich (1896-1976), Ger
    R.1   S.10
HOLLAENDER, Victor (1866-1940), Ger
    R.1   S.e
HOLLAND, Dulcie (1913-   ), Australia
    R.7   S.29,52
HOLLAND, Jan Dawid (1746-1827), Pol
    R.1   S.c

HOLLAND, Theodore Samuel (1878-1947), Eng
    R.4   S.24
HOLLANDER, Bennoit (1853-1942), Neth
    R.3   S.24a
HOLLANDER, Lorin (1944-   ), USA
    R.19   S.10,13
HÖLLER, Karl (1907-   ), Ger
    R.1   S.c,5,10,23,24a
HOLLFELDER, Waldram (1924-   ), Ger
    R.4   S.c
HOLLIER, Donald Russel (1934-   ), Australia
    R.1   S.29
HOLLIGER, Heinz (1939-   ), Swiss
    R.1   S.c,10
HOLLINS, Alfred (1865-1942), Eng
    R.4   S.c,10
HOLLINSWORTH, Stanley (1924-   ), USA
    R.19   S.13
HOLLIS - Oh disclose thy lovely face
                 S.54(346)
HOLLIS, (17th Cent), Eng - John Blundeville's last
    farewell   S.c
HOLLMAN, Josef (1852-1927), Neth
    R.4   S.24
HOLLOWAY, John (fl 1835)
                 S.10,47
HOLLOWAY, Robin (1943-   ), Eng
    R.1   S.c,24a
HOLM, Peder (1923-   ), Den
    R.1   S.40
HOLMAN, Derek (1931-   ), Eng
    R.64
HOLMAN, George USA

HOLMBOE, Vagn (1909-   ), Den
    R.1   S.c,5-8,10,24,35,40
HOLMEK, Yngve Gunnar (1911-   ), Sweden [?]
    R.67   S.5x
HOLMES, Augusta (1847-1903), Fr
    R.1   S.c,5x,10,52
HOLMES, John (d.1629), Eng
    R.1   S.7,8,10,14,16
HOLMES, Paul (1923-   ), USA
    R.19   S.13
HOLMES, Robert L.
                 S.10,13
HOLMSEN, Borghild (1865-1938), Nor
    R.30   S.e
HOLOUBEK, Ladislav (1913-   ), Slovak
    R.1   S.5x,10,31

HOLOVSKI [see KOLOVSKI]
HOLST, Gustav (1874-1934), Eng
  R.1   S.c,1-11,23,24,54(343),55
HOLSTEIN, Jean-Paul (1939-   ), Fr
  R.80   S.c
HOLTEN, Bo (1948-   ), Den
  R.80   S.40
HOLYOKE, Samuel (1762-1820), USA
  R.1   S.10,47
HOLZ, R. E.
                 S.54(319,35,39)
HOLZBAUER, Ignaz (1711-1783), Aus
  R.1   S.c,10,24a
HÖLZEL, Gustave (1813-1883), Hun
  R.3   S.e
HOLZINGER, Benedikt (1747-1815), Ger
  R.5   S.c
HOLZMANN, Abraham (1874-1939), USA
  R.23   S.13,54(316,26,46,57)
HOLZNER, Anton (c1599-1635)
  R.1   S.c,10
HOMANN, Charles USA
                 S.7,10,47
HOMER, Sidney (1864-1953), USA
  R.1   S.10,13,24
HOMILIUS, Gottfried August (1714-1785), Ger
  R.1   S.c,8,10,53
HOMOLIAKA, Vadym Borysovych
  [see GOMOLYAKA, Vadym Borysovych]
HOMS, Joaquim (1906-   ), Sp
  R.1   S.10,24a
HONAUER, Leontzi (c1730-c1790), Alsatian
  R.1   S.5x
HONEGGER, Arthur (1892-1955), Swiss
  R.1   S.c,1-11,18-20,23,24,42
HONKANEN, Antero Terho (1941-   ), Fin
  R.80   S.40(89)
HONKY, Jams - pseud [see GUTZEIT, Erich]
HOOD, Boyde (1939-   ), USA
  R.14   S.13
HOOF, Jef van (1886-1959), Bel
  R.14   S.24a
HOOGHE, Clément d´ (1899-1951), Bel
  R.14
HOOK, James (1746-1827), Eng
  R.1   S.4,5x,6,8,10,24,42
HOOP, von - Etude in e (vi & p)
                 S.24
HOOPER, E. R. - Line pilot
                 S.54(338)

HOOPER, Edmund (c1553-1621), Eng
   R.1   S.c,8,10,14
HOOVER, Katherine (1937-   ), USA
   R.19   S.13,30,52
HOPE, Barbara Melville
   R.200   S.e
HOPE, Douglas - pseud [see WILSON, Hilda]
HOPE, Peter (20th Cent), Eng
           S.c
HOPE-TEMPLE, Mme A. Messager [see TEMPLE, Hope]
HOPKINS, Antony (1921-   ), Eng
   R.1   S.c,8,10,42
HOPKINS, James Frederick (1939-   ), USA
   R.19   S.10,13
HOPKINS, Jerome (1836-1898), USA
   R.1   S.10
HOPKINS, Kenyon
           S.9
HOPKINSON, Francis (1737-1791), USA
   R.1   S.8,10,47
HORI, Etsuko (1943-   ), Japan
   R.4   S.50
HORKÝ, Karel (1909-   ), Cz
   R.1   S.31
HORN, Charles Edward (1786-1849), Eng
   R.1   S.c,8
HORN, Johann Caspar (c1630-c1685), Aus
   R.1   S.10
HORN, Paul (1930-   ), USA
   R.19   S.c,13
HORNEMANN, Charles Frederick Emil (1840-1906), Den
   R.1   S.7,11,35,57
HORNEMANN, Johan Ole Emil (1809-1870), Den
   R.1   S.4,5x
HOROVITZ, Joseph (1926-   ), Eng
   R.1   S.c,19,21,55
HOROWITZ, Vladimir (1904-   ), Russia/USA
   R.1   S.c,10,13
HORROCKS, Amy Elsie (1867-   ), Eng
   R.7   S.e
HORSMAN, Edward (1873-1918), USA
   R.53   S.e
HORST, Anthon van der (1899-1965), Neth
   R.1   S.10
HORTENSE, Queen of Holland (Hortense de Beauharnais)
   (1783-1837) R.7   S.10[Beau.],52
HORTON, Philip, USA
   R.23   S.10
HORUSITZKY, Zoltán (1903-   ), Hun
   R.4

HORVATH, Andras Szkharosi (16th Cent)
            S.c
HORVÁTH, Jenő (1914-   ), Hun
   R.15
HORVATH, Josef Maria (1931-   ), Hun
   R.4   S.24
HORVIT, Michael (1932-   ), USA
   R.19   S.13
HORWOOD, Michael (1947-   ), USA
   R.19   S.13
HORZALKA, Johann (1798-1872)
            S.c
HOSCHNA, Karl (1877-1911), USA
   R.1   S.10
HOSKINS, William Barnes (1917-   ), USA
   R.19   S.13
HOSMER, Lucius (1870-1935), USA
   R.19   S.10,13,19,21
HOSSEIN, Andre Amine (1907-   )
            S.c,10
HOSTIA, Fra Pietro da
            S.c
HOTTETERRE, Jacques (1674-1763), Fr
   R.1   S.c,6,9,10
HOTTETERRE, Jean (i) (c1605-1690/92), Fr
   R.1   S.c
HOTTETERRE, Jean (iii) (d.1720), Fr
   R.1   S.c,9
HOTTETERRE, Louis (c1645/50-1716), Fr
   R.1   S.c,8,10
HOVALT, Lauritz (1885-1953), Den
            S.c
HOVE, Joachim van den (1567-1620), S. Neth
   R.1   S.c,10
HOVEY, Nilo (1906-   )
   R.200   S.19,21
HOVEY, Serge (1920-   ), USA
   R.19   S.13
HOVHANESS, Alan (1911-   ), USA
   R.1   S.c,4,5x,6,7,9,10,12,13,18-21,23,24,28
HOVHANESYAN, Edgar Sergey (1930-   ), Arm
   R.1   S.8,18
HOVLAND, Egil (1924-   ), Nor
   R.1   S.c,40,51
HOWARD, Joseph Edgar (1878-1961), USA
   R.23   S.10
HOWARD, Lesley John (1948-   ), Australia
   R.80   S.c
HOWARD, Ray - pseud [see HAYMAN, Richard Warren]

HOWARD, Rowland (19th Cent), USA

HOWARTH, Elgar (1935-   ), Eng
    R.1   S.c,55
HOWE, Hubert S. Jr. (1942-   ), USA
    R.19   S.13
HOWE, Julia Ward (1819-1910), USA (see note)
    R.53   S.e,54(314)
HOWE, Mary (1882-1964), USA
    R.19   S.5x,7,9,10,13,30,52
HOWELL, Thomas (1783-   ), Eng
    R.44
HOWELLS, Herbert (1892-1983), Eng
    R.1   S.c,2-6,8-10,20,23-25,27,55
HOWETT, Gregorio [see HUET, Gregorio]
HOY, Bonnee (1936-   ), USA
    R.19   S.9,10,13,30,52
HOYER, Karl (1891-1936), Ger
    R.2
HOYOUL, Balduin (1547/48-1594), S. Neth
    R.1   S.c,10,53
HOYSTRADT, John USA
                 S.11,13
HRABOVSKY, Leonid (1935-   ), USSR
    R.4   S.24a
HRACEK, Antonin (1722-1774), Cz
    R.18   S.c,32
HRAZCEK, Ireneus
                 S.10
HRISANIDE, Alexandru (1936-   ), Rum
    R.1   S.20[Haisanide]
HRISTIĆ, Stevan (1885-1958), Yug
    R.1   S.10,18,24
HRUŠOVSKÝ, Ivan (1927-   ), Slovak
    R.1
HSIAO-SHUSIEN - Chinese dream pictures (orch)
                 S.4
HSIEN HSING-HAI, Yellow River (1905-1945), China
    R.1   S.c
HSIN Hu-Kuang
                 S.c
HUARTE, Julian
                 S.c
HUBAY, Jeno (1858-1937), Hun
    R.1   S.c,1-8,10,18,24
HUBBELL, Raymond (1879-1954), USA
    R.23   S.10,24,54(350)
HUBEAU, Jean (1917-   ), Fr
    R.14   S.4,5,8,10,24

HUBENE - March du genie du cavalerie
         S.54(340)
HUBER, Ferdinand Fürchtegott (1791-1863), Swiss
   R.1
HUBER, Hans (1852-1921), Swiss
   R.1   S.c,8,24
HUBER, Klaus (1924-   ), Swiss
   R.1   S.c,10
HUBER, Nicolaus (1939-   ), Ger
   R.1   S.c
HUBER, Paul (1918-   ), Swiss
   R.14   S.c
HUBERTY - Sonnet de Ronsard
         S.e
HUDSON, Joseph A. (1952-   ), USA
   R.19   S.10,13,24a
HUDSON, Will (1908-   ), USA
   R.23   S.10
HÜE, Georges (1858-1948), Fr
   R.1   S.c,2-5,7,8,10
HUEBNER, Paul (1944-   )

HUERT, Pata - Mon coeur (vi & p)
         S.24
HUERTER, Charles (1885-   ), USA
   R.53   S.e
HUET, Gregorio (<1550-1616), Neth
   R.1   S.c,10,16,32
HUETE, Diego Fernandez de
   [see FERNANDEZ de HUETE, Diego]
HUFF, Will - pseud [see FILLMORE, Henry]
HUFFER, Fred (1879-   ), USA
         S.10,13
HUFFINE, G. H. USA
         S.10[Huffine, Will],13
HUFSCHMIDT, Wolfgang (1934-   ), Ger
   R.1   S.c
HUGARD, Monsieur (fl c1754)
   R.5   S.c
HUGARD, Pierre (fl 1744), Fr
   R.5   S.10,32
HUGGLER, John (1928-   ), USA
   R.19   S.10,13
HUGGS - Sussex by the sea [see WARD-HIGGS, W.]
HUGHES d´OISY (Le Conte de Bethune) (12th Cent)
         S.15
HUGHES - Clarion call; Salute to Buffalo; To your guard
         S.54(320,54,61)
HUGHES, Arwel (1909-   ), Wales
   R.4   S.5x

HUGHES, Eric (1924-   ), Eng
              S.19
HUGHES, Herbert (1882-1937), Ire
   R.4   S.c,4,10
HUGHES, Mark (1934-   ), USA
              S.13
HUGHES, Richard Samuel (1855-1893), Wales
   R.44   S.5x
HUGHES, Robert (1933-   ), USA
   R.19   S.13
HUGHES, Robert Watson (1912-   ), Australia
   R.1   S.29,37
HUGL, Anton (fl 1730)
   R.5   S.c
HUGLMANN, Joseph (1768-1839)
              S.c
HUGO von MONTFORT (1357-1423), Ger
   R.1   S.c
HUGON, Georges (1904-1982), Fr
   R.14   S.c,24a
HUHN, Bruno (1871-1950), USA
   R.23   S.5x,13
HULICK, Terry ?USA
              S.10,13
HULLAH, John (Pyke) (1812-1884), Eng
   R.1   S.e
HULLEBROECK, Emiel (1878-1965), Bel
   R.14   S.c
HÜLLMANDEL, Nicolas-Joseph (1756-1823), Alsatian
   R.1   S.24
HULSE, Camil van [see VAN HULSE, Camil]
HUMBERT, Jacqueline USA
              S.13
HUMBLE, Keith (1927-   ), Australia
   R.1   S.29,37
HUME, Alexander (1811-1859), Scotland
   R.44   S.e
HUME, James Ord (1864-1932), Eng
   R.85   S.54(315,39),55
HUME, Lionel
              S.e
HUME, Ruth
              S.30
HUME, Tobias (d.1645), Eng
   R.1   S.c,5x,10,14-16
HUMEL, Gerald (1931-   ), USA
   R.19   S.10,13,24
HUMFREY, Pelham (1647-1674), Eng
   R.1   S.c,5x,7,8,10

244 / Composers on Record

HUMMEL, Berthold (1925-   ), Ger
    R.14   S.c,24a
HUMMEL, Ferdinand (1855-1928), Ger (see note)
    R.1
HUMMEL, Johann Nepomuk (1778-1837), Ger
    R.1   S.c,2-11,18-21,23,24,28
HUMPERDINCK, Engelbert (1854-1921), Ger
    R.1   S.c,1-11,42
HUMPHREYS - Showcase five (brass quintet)
          S.10
HUMPHRIES, John (c1707-<c1740), Eng
    R.1
HUNDLEY, Richard (1931-   ), USA
    R.19   S.10,13,25,27
HUNSECKER, Ralph Blane (1914-   ), USA
    R.23   S.10[Blane]
HUNT, Donald Frederick (1930-   ), Eng
    R.14   S.c
HUNT, Eric (1903-1958), Eng
          S.c
HUNT, Jerry (1943-   ), USA
    R.19   S.13
HUNT, Oliver (1934-   ), Eng
          S.c
HUNT, Richard (1930-   ), Can
    R.31
HUNT, Thomas (fl c1600), Eng
    R.1   S.c,7,8,10,14,16
HÜNTEN, Franz (1793-1878), Ger
    R.1   S.10
HUNTER, Charles (1878-?1906), USA
    R.50   S.10
HUNTLEY, Helen - pseud [see VAN de VATE, Nancy Hayes]
HUNTLEY, William A.
          S.e
HUNTLEY-PARK - A memory
          S.e
HUPFELD, Herman (1894-1951), USA
    R.23   S.10
HURD, USA
          S.13
HURÉ, Jean (1877-1930), Fr
    R.1   S.c
HURFORD, Peter (1930-   ), Eng
    R.1   S.c
HURLEBUSCH, Conrad Friedrich (c1696-1765), Ger
    R.1   S.c,56
HURLEY, Alec
          S.e

HURLSTONE, William (1876-1906), Eng
   R.1   S.c,6,7
HURNIK, Ilja (1922-   ), Cz
   R.1   S.c,10,31
HURST, Michael (1925-   ), Australia
           S.29
HURT, Jaroslav (1914-   ), Cz
   R.18   S.31
HURTADO de XERES (fl 1500), Sp
   R.1   S.17
HURUM, Alf (1882-1972), Nor
   R.1   S.c,24a,51
HUSA, Karel (1921-   ), Cz
   R.1   S.9,10,13,20,22,24a
HUSADEL, Hans Felix [pseud: Lutz FRANKENSTEIN]
   (1897-1964), Ger   R.4,95   S.54(343,65)
HUS-DESFORGES, Pierre Louis (1773-1838), Fr
   R.1
HUSE, Peter (1938-   ), Can
   R.4
HUSEN, Friederich von [see FRIEDRICH von HUSEN]
HUSS, Henry Holden (1862-1953), USA
   R.1   S.13
HUSSONMOREL, V. - Rondel (vi & ce)
           S.24a
HUSTON, Thomas Scott (1916-   ), USA
   R.1   S.c,10,13,20
HUSZKA, Jeno (1875-1960), Hun
   R.4
HUTCHENS, Frank (1892-1965), Australia
   R.1   S.5,29
HUTCHESON, Jere (1938-   ), USA
   R.19   S.13
HUTCHINGS, Arthur (1906-   ), Eng
   R.1   S.c
HUTCHINS, Guy Starr (1905-   ), USA
   R.19   S.10,13
HUTCHINSON, Family (fl 1839-90), USA
   R.50   S.47
HUTCHINSON, J. J. - Eight dollars a day
           S.47
HUTCHINSON, Terry ?USA
           S.10,13
HUTCHINSON, William Marshall [pseud: Jos MEISSLER]
   (1854-1933), Eng   R.3   S.e
HUTCHISON, Warner (1930-   ), USA
   R.19   S.13
HÜTTENBRENNER, Anselm (1794-1868), Aus
   R.1   S.c

HUW, Robert Ap [see AP HUW, Robert]
HUYBRECHTS, Albert (1899-1938), Bel
   R.1   S.c,6,7,24,36,41
HUYGENS, Constantijn (1596-1687), Neth
   R.1   S.c,10
HUZELLA, Elek (1915-   ), Hun
   R.4   S.c,10,32
HVOSLEF [Saeverud], Ketil (1939-   ), Nor
              S.c,40
HWANG, Byongki (1936-   ), Korea

HYAMS, Ario S.

HYDE, Cicely (20th Cent), ?Eng
   R.7   S.24
HYDE, George, USA
              S.10,13
HYDE, Miriam Beatrice (1913-   ), Australia
   R.7   S.29,52
HYE-KNUDSEN, Johan (1896-   ), Den
   R.14   S.5x,57
HYMAN, Richard Roven (1927-   ), USA
   R.23   S.10
IACCHINI, Guiseppe Maria [see JACCHINI, Guiseppe Maria]
IANNACCONE, Anthony (1943-   ), USA
   R.19   S.9,10,13,22,24a
IBERT, Jacques (1890-1962), Fr
   R.1   S.c,1-11,18,22,24,32
ICHIYANAGI, Toshi (1933-   ), Japan
   R.1   S.10,24a,50
IEROM, Marcarie
              S.c
IFUKUBE, Akira (1914-   ), Japan
   R.14   S.24a,50
IGLESIAS, Angel
              S.c
IGLESIAS VILLOUD, Hector (1913-   ), Arg
   R.26   S.46
IKEBE, Shinichiro (1943-   ), Japan
   R.4   S.50
IKENOUCHI, Tomojiro (1906-   ), Japan
   R.1   S.18,24,50
ILEBORGH, Adam (fl c1448), Ger
   R.1   S.c,53
ILES, John Henry (1871-1951), Eng
   R.85   S.54(315)
ILGENFRITZ, McNair
              S.10
ILLIASCHENKO, André (1881-1954)
              S.c

ILLIN, Evžen (1924-   ), Cz
    R.18   S.31
ILYINSKY, Alexander Alexandrovich (1859-1920), Russia
    R.1   S.10,24a
IMBER, Naphtali Herz (1856-1909)
    R.200   S.e
IMBRIE, Andrew Welsh (1921-   ), USA
    R.1   S.8-10,13,20,24a
INDIA, Sigismondo d´ (c1582-<1629), It
    R.1   S.c,3,4,5x,8,10,28
INDRA, Youzas Stasevich (1918-1968), USSR
    R.14   S.18
INDY, Vincent d´ (1851-1931), Fr
    R.1   S.c,2-6,8-11,20,24
INFANTAS, Fernando de las (1534-c1610), Sp
    R.1   S.10,16,17
INFANTE, Manuel (1883-1958), Sp
    R.14   S.2,3,5,7,8,10,11,24
INGALLS, Jeremiah (1764-1838), USA
    R.1   S.10,47
INGEGNERI, Marco Antonio (c1547-1592), It
    R.1   S.c,2,4-8,10,14-16
INGENHOVEN, Clemens (1905-   )
                S.c
INGHAM - Adagio (vi & org)
                S.24a
INGHELBRECHT, Désiré-Emile (1880-1965), Fr
    R.1   S.c,2-4,10
INGLE, Charles - pseud [ie Auguste CHEVALIER]
    (?1863-1940)   R.200   S.e
INGLOTT, William (1554-1621), Eng
    R.1   S.c
INGRAHAM - All that I ask is love
                S.e
INGRAM, John - pseud [see MORGAN, Robert Orlando]
INNOCENZI, Carlo (1899-   ), It
    R.13   S.10,24
INSANGUINE, Giacomo (1728-1795), It
    R.1   S.c,53
INSULIS, Franco de [see GALLO, R.]
INZAURRAGA, Alejandro (1882-1956), Arg
    R.26   S.5x
IOANNIDIS, Yannis (1930-   ), Greece
    R.1   S.20[Joannides]
IONESCU, Constantin (1912-   ), Rum
    R.33   S.24
IPPOLITO, (16th Cent) - Canzon Sopra Susanna
                S.c
IPPOLITOV-IVANOV, Mikhail Mikhaylovich (1859-1935),
    Russia R.1   S.c,1-11,18

IRADIER [Yradier], Sebastián (1809-1865), Sp
R.1   S.4,10,19,24,54(348)
IRELAND, John (1879-1962), Eng
R.1   S.c,1-10,18-20,24-27,54(324),55
IRGENS, Sofie
               S.e
IRIGARAY, Carlos Albert
               S.c

IRINO, Yoshiro (1921-1980), Japan
R.1   S.24a,50
ISAAC, A. (16th Cent), Neth

ISAAC, Heinrich (c1450-1517), Neth
R.1   S.c,2-11,14-16,32,41,53
ISAACS, Edward (1881-1953), Eng
R.1   S.24
ISAACSON, Leonard Maxwell (1925-   ), USA
               S.13
ISELE, David Clark (1946-   ), USA
R.13   S.22
ISHAM [Isum], John (c1680-1726), Eng
R.1   S.c,10
ISHCHENKO, Yuri Yakovlyevich (1938-   )
               S.18,24a
ISHII, Kan (1921-   ), Japan
R.1   S.50
ISHII, Maki (1936-   ), Japan
R.1   S.10,24a,50
ISHIKETA, Mareo (1916-   ), Japan
R.4   S.50
ISKANDAROV, Alexei Iskandarovich (1906-   ), USSR
R.47   S.18
ISOLFSSON, Pall (1893-1974), Iceland
R.1   S.10,40
ISOUARD, Nicolas (1775-1818), Fr
R.1
ISOZ, Etienne (1905-   ), Hun
R.14   S.c
ISRAEL, Brian (1951-   ), USA
R.19   S.10,13
ISRAFIL-ZADE, M. - Elegiya

ISTCHENKO, J. - Little partita
               S.24a
IŠTVAN, Miloslav (1928-   ), Cz
R.1   S.c,10,31
ISUM, John [see ISHAM, John]
ITO, Hidenao (1933-   ), Japan
               S.50

ITOH, Eri (1968-   )
          S.24a
ITURBI, Jose (1895-1980), Sp
   R.1   S.10,13
IVANOV - Victory march
          S.5x
IVANOV, Georgi Nikolayevich (1924-   ), Bul
   R.14   S.18
IVANOV, Mikhail Mikhaylovich (1849-1927), Russia
   R.1   S.8,18
IVANOV, Yanis Andreyevich (1906-   ), Russia
   R.14   S.8,18,24
IVANOV-KRAMSKOY, Alexander Mikhailovich (1912-1973),
   USSR   R.47   S.10,18
IVANOV RADKEVICH, Nikolai Pavlovich (1904-1962), USSR
   R.14   S.54(361)
IVANOVICI, Iosif (?1845-1902), Rum
   R.1   S.c,5x,10,24,54(323)
IVANOVS, Janis (1906-   ), Lat
   R.1   S.24a
IVANSCHIZ, Amandus (fl mid 18th Cent), Aus
   R.1   S.c
IVES, Charles (1874-1954), USA
   R.1   S.c,2-13,18-20,23-28
IVES, Elam Jr. (1802-1864), USA
   R.53
IVES, Grayston (1948-   ), Eng
          S.c
IVES, Simon (1600-1662), Eng
   R.1   S.c,2,5x,7,10
IVEY, Jean Eichelberger (1923-   ), USA
   R.1   S.9,10,13,30,52
IZAMOV, Khairy (1922-   )
          S.18
JABLONSKY, Henryk (1915-   ), Ger
   R.4
JACCHINI, Giuseppe Maria (c1663-1727), It
   R.1   S.c,10,53
JACHET de MANTUA [see JACQUET of MANTUA]
JACHINO, Carlo (1887-1971), It
   R.1   S.5x
JACINTO, Frei (18th Cent), Port
   R.1   S.c,8,10,53
JACKSON, Francis (1917-   ), Eng
   R.1   S.c,10
JACKSON, George Knowil (1757-1822), USA
   R.1
JACKSON, John (d.1688), Eng
   R.1   S.5x,10

JACKSON, Nicholas Fane St. George (1934-   ), Eng
   R.64   S.c
JACKSON, William (1730-1803), Eng
   R.1   S.10
JACOB de SENLECHES (fl 1378-95), Fr
   R.1   S.c,10,16
JACOB le POLONAIS [see REYS, Jacob]
JACOB, Georges (1877-1950), Fr
   R.4
JACOB, Gordon Percival Septimus (1895-   ), Eng
   R.1   S.c,9,10,20,22,54(351),55
JACOB, Maxime (1906-1977), Fr
   R.1   S.c
JACOB, Vaclav Antonin (1685-1734)

JACOB, Werner (1938-   ), Ger
   R.4   S.c
JACOBI, Frederick (1891-1952), USA
   R.1   S.3,5,7-11,13,23,24
JACOBI, Michael (1618-1663), Ger
   R.1
JACOBI, Victor (1883-1921), Hun

   R.1   S.24
JACOBI, Wolfgang (1894-   ), Ger
   R.14   S.10,22
JACOBIDES, Stepan Vavrinec (17th Cent)

JACOBS, Al (1903-   ), USA
   R.23   S.10
JACOBS, Henry ?USA
         S.13
JACOBS-BOND, Carrie [see BOND, Carrie Jacobs]
JACOBSEN, Julius (1915-   ), Den
   R.30   S.c,5x,40
JACOPO da BOLOGNA (fl 1340-60), It
   R.1   S.c,3,4,5x,7,8,10,11,14,16
JACOPONE da TODI (c1230-1306), It
   R.1   S.c,8,14
JACOTIN, (fl 1st half 16th Cent), Flem
   R.1   S.c,7,10,14-16
JACQUENOD, Jean-Luc (1933-   )
         S.c
JACQUES de CAMBRAI [see JAQUE de CAMBRAI]
JACQUES-DALCROZE, Emile [see JAQUES-DALCROZE, Emile]
JACQUET de la GUERRE, Elizabeth-Claude (1666/67-1729), Fr
   R.1   S.c,3-5,30,52
JACQUET of MANTUA (1483-1559), Fr
   R.1   S.c,10,16
JADIN, Hyacinthe (1769-1802), Fr
   R.1

JADIN, Louis Emmanuel (1768-1853), Fr
R.1   S.c
JAEGER, David Trent (1947-   ), Can

JAEGER, Edmund
             S.10
JAEGGI, P. Oswald (1913-1963), Swiss
R.14   S.c
JAFFE, Stephen (1954-   )
             S.24a
JAKEWAY, Albert Henry (1893-   ), Eng
R.96   S.54(346,60,61,66)
JAKOBOWKSY, Edward - pseud [ie Edward BELVILLE]
(1858-   ), Eng   R.44,200   S.24
JAKUBENAS, Vladis (1904-   ), Lith
R.4
JAMBE de FER, Philibert (c1515-c1566), Fr
R.1   S.14,16
JAMES I, King of Scotland (1394-1437)
R.44   S.14
JAMES, Brother
[see title under BAIN, James Leith McBeth]
JAMES, Ifor (1931-   ), Eng
R.80   S.c,55
JAMES, John (d c1745), Eng
R.1   S.c,53
JAMES, Philip (1890-1975), USA
R.1   S.8-13
JAMES, Will (1896-   ), USA
R.23   S.10
JAMES, William Garnet (1895-1977), Australia
R.14   S.c,5x
JAN z LUBLINA (fl c1540), Pol
R.1   S.c,15,16,32
JANÁČEK, Bedřich (1920-   ), Sweden
R.14   S.c
JANÁČEK, Leoš (1854-1928), Cz
R.1   S.c,2-10,18,24,42
JANEQUIN, Clément (c1485-1558), Fr
R.1   S.c,2-11,14-16,53
JANIEWICZ, Feliks (1762-1848), Pol
R.1   S.c,8,10,18[Yaniewcz]
JANITSCH, Johann Gottlieb (1708-c1763), Silesia
R.1   S.c
JANNONE, René (1927-   )
             S.c
JAN of JENSTEJN [see MAISTRE JHAN]
JANOTHA, Nathalie (Marie Cecylia) (1856-1932), Pol
R.1   S.e

JANSA, Leopold (1795-1875), Boh
  R.1
JANSEN, Sigurd
              S.24a
JANSON, Alfred (1937-   ), Nor
  R.14   S.c,10,40,24a,51
JANSSEN, Hubert & Friedrich
              S.c
JANSSEN, Werner (1899-   ), USA
  R.1   S.2,13
JANSSENS, Peter (1934-   ), Ger
  R.4   S.c
JANSSENS, Robert (1939-   )
              S.c
JAPART, Jean (fl c1474-?1507), Flem
  R.1   S.c,16
JAQUE de CAMBRAI (fl c1260-80), Fr
  R.1   S.c,10
JAQUE, Rhené (Soeur Jacques-René) (1918-   ), Can
  R.81   S.30,52
JAQUES le VINIER, (fl 1240-60), Fr
  R.1
JAQUES-DALCROZE, Emile (1865-1950), Swiss
  R.1   S.24
JARDA, Tudor (1922-   ), Rum
  R.1
JÁRDÁNYI, Pál (1920-1966), Hun
  R.1   S.24
JARNACH, Philipp (1892-1982), Ger
  R.1   S.c,24
JÄRNEFELT, Armas (1869-1958), Sweden
  R.1   S.c,2-8,10,11,18,24,54(350)
JARNO, György (1868-1920), Hun
  R.8   S.c
JARNOVIC, Ivan [see GIORNOVICHI, Giovanni Mane]
JAROCH, Jiri (1920-   ), Cz
  R.1   S.31,24a
JARVIS, Charles - Rome! Thou art no more
              S.47
JARZEBSKI, Adam (d.1648/49), Pol
  R.1   S.c,8,10,16
JASUSHI, Akutagawa [see AKUTAGAWA, Yasushi]
JAUBERT, Maurice (1900-1940), Fr
  R.1   S.2-5,7,8
JAUFRE RUDEL [see RUDEL, Jaufre]
JAVALOYES, A. - El abanico
              S.54(311)
JEAN de LUBLIN [see JAN z LUBLINA]
JEAN de LIMBOURG [see JOHANNES de LYMBURGIA]

JEANJEAN, Paul (1874-1928), Fr
     R.105   S.10,19,21
JEEP, Johannes (1581/82-1640), Ger
     R.1   S.2,10,16
JEF, Maes (1905-   )

JEFFERYS, Charles (1807-1865), Eng
     R.44   S.10
JEFFES, Simon (1949-   ), Eng
                   S.c
JEFFREYS, George (c1610-1685), Eng
     R.1   S.c
JEFFRIES, Roy, Australia- Swagmans song
                   S.5x[Jeffreys]
JEHAN d´ESQUIRI (13th Cent)
                   S.c
JEHANNOT de l´ESCUREL (d.1304), Fr
     R.1   S.c,5x,8,10,14,16
JELESCU, Paul (1901-   ), Rum
     R.4
JELIC, Vincenz (1595-?1636), Aus
     R.1   S.c,10
JELINEK, Hanns (1901-1969), Aus
     R.1   S.c,8,10
JELINEK, Josef [see GELINEK Josef]
JELOBENSKY, Valery Viktorovich]
     [see ZHÉLOBINSKY, Valery Viktorovich]
JENEY, Zoltan (1943-   ), Hun
     R.1   S.c,10
JENKINS, Cyril (1885-1978), Wales
     R.85   S.10,55
JENKINS, Ella (1924-   ), USA
     R.23   S.52
JENKINS, Gordon Hill (1910-   ), USA
     R.23   S.9
JENKINS, John (1592-1678), Eng
     R.1   S.c,5x,8-10,14,16,24a
JENKINS, Joseph Willcox (1928-   ), USA
     R.19   S.10,13
JENKINSON, Ezra
                   S.24
JENKO, Davorin (1835-1914), Slovene
     R.1
JENNER, Gustav (1865-1920), Ger
     R.8   S.c
JENNI, Donald Martin (1937-   ), USA
     R.19   S.10,13
JENNINGS, Arthur B.
                   S.7,10,13

JENNY, Albert (1912-   ), Swiss
   R.14
JENSEN, Adolf (1837-1879), Ger
   R.1   S.c,2-5,7,25,27
JENSEN, Ludvig Irgens (1894-1969), Nor
   R.1   S.c,5x,8,10,18,24,51
JENSTEJN, Jan von [see MAISTRE JHAN]
JENTES, Harry (1897-1958), USA
   R.23   S.54(314)
JEPPESEN, Knud (1892-1974), Den
   R.1   S.c,8,35,40
JEPPESSON, Kerstin Maria (1948-   ), Sweden
   R.7   S.52
JEPSON, Harry Benjamin (1870-1952), USA
   R.19   S.12,13
JERABEK, Pavel (1948-   )
             S.c
JERAL, Wilhelm (1861-1935), Cz
   R.4   S.24
JEREA, Hilda (1916-   ), Rum
   R.7   S.52
JEREMIÁŠ, Bohuslav (1859-1918), Cz
   R.1   S.4
JEREMIÁŠ, Jaroslav (1889-1919), Cz
   R.1
JEREMIÁŠ, Otakar (1892-1962), Cz
   R.1   S.31
JERGENSON, Dale, USA
             S.13
JERGER, Wilhelm (1902-1978), Aus
   R.1   S.4,10
JEROME - My rose of the ghetto
             S.e
JEROME, Maurice Kraus (1893-   ), USA
   R.23   S.10,24
JERSILD, Jørgen (1913-   ), Den
   R.1   S.c,5x,2-4,18,35,40,57
JERUMS, Albert (1919-   ), Lat
   R.30
JESSEL, Franciszek (d.1838)

JESSEL, Leon (1871-1942), Ger
   R.1   S.c,1x,10,21,54(348,65)
JESSLER, Fritz (1924-   ), Ger
   R.4   S.c
JEUNE, Claude le [see LE JEUNE, Claude]
JEWELL, Fred (1875-1936), USA
   R.48   S.13[b 1876],54(328)
JEŽEK, Jaroslav (1906-1942), Cz
   R.1   S.c,5,6,24,31

JEZIERSKI, Kazimierz (fl early 18th Cent), Pol
   R.1   S.c
JIAN, E. Ke - Hung Hu vi concerto
          S.24a
JIANG, Zhong (1927-   )
          S.24a
JIE, Jiao - In the north-west plain
          S.24a
JIMÉNEZ MABARAK, Carlos (1916-   ), Mex
   R.14   S.c
JIMÉNEZ, Diego (17th Cent)
          S.c
JIMÉNEZ, Jerónimo [see GIMÉNEZ, Jerónimo]
JIMÉNEZ, José (16th Cent), Sp
   R.9   S.17,53
JIMÉNEZ, Miguel Bernal [see BERNAL Jiménez Miguel]
JIN, Yan Ping
          S.24a
JINDRA, Alfons - pseud [see LANGER, Alfons]
JINDŘICH - Sila kosilicku-my sweetheart
          S.e
JINDŘICH, Jindřich (1876-1967), Cz
   R.1   S.1x
JIRAK, Zdenek
          S.31
JIRÁSEK, Ivo (1920-   ), Cz
   R.14   S.10
JIRKO, Ivan (1926-1978), Cz
   R.1   S.31
JIROVEC, Adalbert [see GYROWETZ, Adalbert]
J. N. S. (19th Cent), USA - Oh, you must be a lover of
the Lord
JOACHIM, Davis (1949-   ), Can
   R.81
JOACHIM, Joseph (1831-1907), Hun
   R.1   S.c,9,10,23,24
JOACHIM, Otto (1910-   ), Can
   R.1   S.24
JOAN de SEGOVIA
          S.10
JOANNIDES, Jonnis [see IOANNIDIS, Yannis]
JOÃO IV, King of Portugal [see JOHN IV, King of Portugal]
JOBIM, Carlos Antonio (1927-   ), Brazil
   R.30   S.39
JOCELYN, Simeon (1746-1823), USA
   R.1   S.10,47
JOCHUM, Otto (1898-1969), Ger
   R.1   S.c
JOCOBSEN, Hans
          S.e

JÖDE, Fritz (1887-1970), Ger
    R.1   S.c
JOHANN ERNST, Prinz von Sachsen-Weimar (1696-1715)
    R.3
JOHANN RUDOLPH, Archduke of Aus
          S.10
JOHANN von BOPFINGEN (14th Cent)
          S.c
JOHANNES de LYMBURGIA (fl 1400-40), S. Neth
    R.1   S.c,10,16
JOHANNES de MERUCO (fl late 14th Cent), Fr
    R.1   S.c,10
JOHANNES de QUATRIS (fl mid 15th Cent)
    R.1
JOHANNESEN, Grant (1921-   ), USA
    R.1   S.10,13
JOHANSEN, David Monrad (1888-1974), Nor
    R.1   S.c,8,10,24a,51
JOHANSEN, Gunnar, (1906-   ), USA
    R.19   S.13
JOHANSEN, Svend Aaquist (1948-   ), Den
    R.14   S.40
JOHANSON, Sven-Eric (1919-   ), Sweden
    R.1   S.c,10,38,56
JOHANSSON, Bengt (1914-   ), Fin
    R.1   S.40
JOHN [João] IV, King of Portugal (1604-1656)
    R.1   S.2-4,8,10,11,14,16
JOHN of FORNSETE (d.1238/39), Eng
    R.1   S.1x,2-4,5x,11
JOHNER, Hans-Rudolf
          S.c
JOHNS - Where blooms the rose
          S.24a
JOHNS, Louis Edgar (1886-   ), USA
    R.53   S.13
JOHNSEN, Hallvard Olav (1916-   ), Nor
    R.1   S.c,51
JOHNSEN, Hinrich Philip (1717-1779), Ger
    R.1   S.c,56
JOHNSON, Bengt Emil (1936-   ), Sweden
    R.1   S.c,38,40,56
JOHNSON, Carl (1935-   )
          S.c
JOHNSON, Clair W. USA
          S.54(329)
JOHNSON, David N. (1922-   ), USA
    R.19   S.c,12,13
JOHNSON, Edward (fl 1572-1601), Eng
    R.1   S.7,8,10,16

JOHNSON, Francis (1792-1844), USA
  R.50   S.10,47
JOHNSON, Hall (1888-1970), USA
  R.1   S.10
JOHNSON, Harold McKinley (1899-1959), USA
  R.49   S.54(331)
JOHNSON, Hunter (1906-   ), USA
  R.1   S.7,8,10,13
JOHNSON, James Louis (J. J.) (1924-   ), USA
  R.1   S.10
JOHNSON, James Weldon (1871-1938), USA
  R.23   S.10,11,24
JOHNSON, John (fl 1579-94), Eng
  R.1   S.10,15,16,32
JOHNSON, John Rosamond (1873-1954), USA
  R.1   S.10,13,52[!]
JOHNSON, John St. Anthony, Eng
           S.2(425)
JOHNSON, Laurie (1927-   ), Eng
           S.c,9
JOHNSON, Robert (c1500-c1560), Eng
  R.1   S.c,14
JOHNSON, Robert (c1583-1633), Eng
  R.1   S.c,8,14,15,32,53
JOHNSON, Robert Sherlaw (1932-   ), Eng
  R.1   S.c,10
JOHNSON, Roger (1941-   ), USA
  R.19   S.10,13
JOHNSON, Romilly (1883-1929), USA
           S.13
JOHNSON, Roy Hamlin (1929-   ), USA
           S.13
JOHNSON-FARNABY - Alman for virginal
           S.15
JOHNSTON, Archibald (fl 1879)
           S.e
JOHNSTON, Benjamin Burwell (1926-   ), USA
  R.1   S.c,10,13
JOHNSTONE, Arthur Edward (1860-1944), USA
  R.4   S.13
JOHNSTONE, Maurice (1900-1976), Eng
  R.85   S.55
JOKINEN, Erkki (1941-   ), Fin
  R.1   S.40
JOLAS, Betsy (1926-   ), Fr
  R.1   S.c,10,30,52
JOLISCO - Danse indigène (p)
           S.24
JOLIVET, André (1905-1974), Fr
  R.1   S.5,6,8-10,18,20,22,24,32

258 / Composers on Record

JOLLES, Jerome, USA
            S.13
JOLY, Denis (1906-   ), Fr
    R.48   S.22
JOMMELLI, Niccolò (1714-1774), It
    R.1   S.c,18
JON NRODAL (1926-   ), Iceland

JON LEIFS [see LEIFS, Jon]
JONASSON, Emanuel
            S.c
JONCIÈRES, Victorin de - pseud [ie Felix Ludger
    ROSSIGNOL] (1839-1903), Fr   R.26
JONES, Bradwen
            S.5x
JONES, Charles (1910-   ), USA
    R.1   S.8,10,13,24a
JONES, Charles (1931-   ), USA
            S.13
JONES, Collier (1928-   ), USA
            S.10,13
JONES, Daniel (1912-   ), Wales
    R.1   S.c,5x
JONES, George Thaddeus (1917-   ), USA
    R.23   S.54(336,65)
JONES, Isham (1894-1956), USA
    R.23   S.10,24
JONES, J. Randolph (1910-   ), USA
            S.9,13
JONES, James

JONES, Jeffrey (1944-   ), USA
    R.19   S.10,13
JONES, Kelsey (1922-   ), Can
    R.1   S.10,24
JONES, Kenneth Victor (1924-   ), Eng
    R.14   S.c,24a
JONES, R. - Shaggy dog
            S.54(355)
JONES, Richard (d.1744), Eng
    R.1   S.c,8,10
JONES, Robert (fl 1597-1615), Eng
    R.1   S.c,2-5,7,8,10,14-16
JONES, Samuel (1935-   ), USA
    R.23   S.10,13
JONES, Sidney (1861-1946), Eng
    R.1   S.9,10,54(328)
JONES, Stan (1914-1963), USA
    R.23   S.10

JONES, William (1726-1800), Eng
 R.1   S.c
JONG, Marinus de (1891-   ), Bel
 R.1   S.36
JONGEN, Joseph (1873-1953), Bel
 R.1   S.c,2-5,7-10,18,24,36
JONGEN, Léon (1884-1969), Bel
 R.1   S.7,10,18,24a,36
JONGH, George de

JONSSON, Josef (1887-1969), Sweden
 R.30   S.56
JOPLIN, Scott (1868-1917), USA
 R.1   S.c,9,10,13,24a
JORA, Mihail (1891-1971), Russia
 R.1   S.10,18[Zhora],24
JORDA, Louis (1898-   ) - Romantic Mazurka
            S.24
JORDA, Luis G.
            S.8[1875-1900],24[b.1898]
JORDAN - Dost thou hear?
            S.5x
JORDAN - Sol a Sevilla
            S.54(356)
JORDAN, Alice Yost (1916-   ), USA
 R.7   S.52
JORDAN, H. - Fighting strength
            S.54(326)
JORDAN, Julian (fl 1884), USA
 R.53   S.e
JORDAN, Mrs. - pseud [ie Dorothea or Dora BLAND]
 (1762-1816), Ire   R.44   S.e
JORDAN, Sverre (1889-1972), Nor
 R.1   S.10
JORGE, Santos (1870-1941), Panama
 R.56   S.54(332)
JØRGENSEN, Erik (1912-   ), Den
 R.1   S.40
JORNS, Helge (1941-   )
            S.c,30
JOSEFSON, Jacob Axel (1818-1880), Sweden
 R.8   S.10
JOSEPH - Hebrew legend (vi & p)
            S.24
JOSEPH I, Emperor of Austria (1678-1711)
 R.1   S.c,10,24a
JOSEPHINE, Queen of Sweden and Norway (1807-1876)
 R.7   S.52
JOSEPHS, Wilfred (1927-   ), Eng
 R.1   S.55,24a

JOSEPHSON, Jacob Axel (1818-1880), Sweden
   R.3   S.56
JOSPE, Erwin - I believe [?]
           S.10,22
JOSQUIN DESPREZ (c1440-1521), Neth
   R.1   S.c,2-11,14-16,18,41,53
JOSTEN, Werner (1885-1963), USA
   R.1   S.7-10,13,24,25,27
JOUARD, Paul E. (1928-   ), USA
   R.19
JOUBERT, John (1927-   ), South Africa
   R.1   S.c,10,24a
JOURDAN, Johannes
           S.c
JOUVE, Ed
           S.e
JOUVY, Jules
           S.e
JOVICCHICH, Jovan
           S.18
JOYCE, Archibald
           S.54(348)
JOYE, Gilles (15th Cent)
   R.5   S.16
JUAN de LEON (15th Cent)

JUCHELKA, Miroslav (1922-   ), Cz
   R.14   S.31
JUDE, William Herbert (1851-   ), Eng
   R.44   S.e
JUDENKÜNIG, Hans (c1450-1526), Aus
   R.1   S.c,10,16,32
JUDGE, Jack (1878-1938), Eng
   R.4   S.10
JUHRE - Bethlehem
           S.c
JULARBO, Carl - pseud [ie Karl KARLSSON] (1893-1966),
   Sweden   R.30
JULEFF - I dreamt of you
           S.e
JULIA, Benito (fl 1750)
   R.5   S.c
JULIAN, Joseph (1948-   ), USA
   R.19   S.13
JULIEN, David (1914-   ),
           S.c
JULLIEN, Gilles (c1650-1703), Fr
   R.1   S.c,8,10,53
JUNCKER, August W. - I was dreaming (see note)
           S.10

JÜNEMANN, G. - Der Bruutschuss oder Der Hamburger
    Freischutz S.c
JUNG - Notre pere
            S.e
JUNG, Fridolin (fl 1572), Swiss
    R.5
JUNGK, Klaus (1916-   ), Ger
    R.14   S.c
JUNGMANN, Albert (1823-1892), Ger
    R.98   S.24
JUON, Paul (1872-1940), Russia
    R.1   S.c,1-3,10,24
JUOZAFAITIS, J. (1942-   )
            S.24a
JURAFSKY, Abraham (1906-   ), Arg
    R.26   S.46
JUREK, Wilhelm August (1870-1934), Aus
    R.3   S.10
JURGUTIS, V. (1930-   )
            S.24a
JURMANN, Walter (1903-   ), Aus
    R.3   S.24,43
JUROVSKÝ, Šimon (1912-1963), Slovak
    R.1   S.5x,6,24,31
JUSTINUS, Peter (18th Cent), Ger
    R.5
JUSTINUS à DESPONSATIONE BVM (d >1723), Ger
    R.1
JUZELIUNAS, Julius (1916-   ), Lith
    R.1   S.24
KABALEVSKY, Dmitry Borisovich (1904-   ), Russia
    R.1   S.c,4-10,18,20,24
KABELÁČ, Miloslav (1908-1979), Cz
    R.1   S.c,10,24a,31
KACHANAUSKAS, Alexandras (1882-1959)
            S.18
KAČINSKAS, Jeronimas (1907-   ), Lith
    R.4
KA DINZULU, Constance Magogo, Princess (1900-   ),
    South Africa   R.7   S.52
KADOMETSYEV, M. - Elegy (electronic)
            S.18
KADOSA, Pál (1903-1983), Hun
    R.1   S.c,9,10,24a
KADYROV, Gafur Kadyrovich (1917-   ), USSR
    R.47   S.18
KAELIN, Pierre (1913-   ), Swiss
    R.14
KAFENDA, Frico (1883-1963), Slovak
    R.1   S.31

KAGEL, Mauricio (1931-   ), Arg
  R.1   S.c,9,10,32,39,46
KAHN, Erich Itor (1905-1956), Ger
  R.14   S.10,13
KAHN [later CARNE], Gerald Friedmann
          S.44
KAHN, Gus (1886-1941), USA
  R.23   S.10,54(354)
KAHN, Percival Benedict (1880-1966), Eng
  R.14   S.1x,5x,24,44
KAHN, Roger Wolfe (1907-1962), USA
  R.23   S.24a
KAHNT, Moritz (1836-1904), Ger
  R.3   S.24
KAIRYUKSHTIS, V. (1931-   )
          S.18
KAISER [later KEYSER], Alfredo de
          S.e
KAISER-LINDEMANN, Wilhelm (1940-   )
          S.c
KAJONI, Janos [see CAIANU, Ioan]
KALABIS, Viktor (1923-   ), Cz
  R.1   S.c,10,20,24,31
KALACH, Jósef (1901-   ), Cz
  R.18   S.31
KALACHEVSKY, Mikhail (1851-   )
          S.18
KALAJIAN, Berge (1924-   ), USA
  R.23   S.c,13
KALAŠ, Julius (1902-1967), Cz
  R.1   S.31
KALASHNIKOV, Nicolay (fl c1700), Russia
  R.1   S.c
KALENSKY, Johan (d.1917), Cz
  R.3   S.10
KÁLIK, Václav (1891-1951), Cz
  R.1   S.5x,24a,31
KALINNIKOV, Vasily Sergeyevich (1866-1901), Russia
  R.1   S.c,1x,2-5,7-11,18
KALINNIKOV, Viktor Sergeyevich (1870-1927), Russia
  R.1   S.18
KALKBRENNER, Frederic (1785-1849), Ger
  R.1   S.c,10
KALLIWODA, Johann Wenzel (1801-1866), Boh
  R.1   S.c,1x,10,24a
KALLOSH, Shandor Ernestovich (1935-   )
          S.18
KALLSTENIUS, Edvin (1881-1967), Sweden
  R.1   S.5x,6,7,24,40,56

KÁLMÁN, Imre [Emmerich] (1882-1953), Hun
  R.1   S.c,1x,2-4,5x,9,10,24,42,43
KALMÁR, László (1931-   ), Hun
  R.1   S.c,10
KALNINŠ, Aldonis (1928-   ), Lat
  R.1   S.18[Kalnyn]
KALNINŠ, Alfreds (1879-1951), Lat
  R.1   S.c,18[Kalnyn],24
KALNINŠ, Imants (1941-   ), Lat
  R.1   S.18[Kalnyn, Amant]
KALNINŠ, Indulis (1918-   )
               S.18[Kalnyn]
KALOMIRIS, Manolis (1883-1962), Greece
  R.1   S.c,8,10,24
KALSONS, Romualds (1936-   ), Lat
  R.1   S.18,24
KALTHOFF, Ernst (1908-   ), Ger
  R.3   S.10
KALTNECKER, Hans

KALTNER, Franz (1721-1766)
               S.c
KAMEKE, Ernst-Ulrich von (1926-   ), Ger
  R.4   S.c
KAMIEŃSKI, Lucjan (1885-1964), Pol
  R.4
KAMIEŃSKI, Maciej (1734-1821), Pol
  R.1   S.c
KAMINISKY, Dimitri Romanovich (1907-   ), USSR
  R.14   S.18,24
KAMINISKY, Walter (1929-   ), USSR
  R.47   S.18
KAMINSKI, Heinrich (1886-1946), Ger
  R.1   S.c
KAMINSKI, Joseph (1903-1972), Isr
  R.1   S.c,10,24a
KAMMERER, Edvin (1938-   ), Den
               S.40
KÄMPF, Karl (1874-1950), Ger
  R.14   S.c,24
KANACHIAN, Barsagh (1888-1967), Arm

KANAI, Kikuku (1915-   ), Japan
               S.50
KANCHELI, Giya Alexandrovich (1935-   ), USSR
  R.1   S.18
KANDER, John (1927-   ), USA
  R.50   S.9
KANG, Sukhi (1934-   )

KANGRO, Raimo (1949-   ), Est
    R.58   S.24a
KANITZ, Ernst (1894-1978), Aus
    R.1   S.9,13,22,24a
KAŇKA, Jan Nepomuk (1772-1863), Cz
    R.1   S.5x
KANNE, Friedrich August (1778-1833), Aus
    R.1   S.c,28
KANTOR, Joseph (1930-   ), USA
    R.19   S.13
KAPELLER, Karl (1858-1918), Aus
    R.3   S.10
KAPER, Bronsilaw (1902-1983), USA
    R.1   S.10,24,43
KAPI-KRALIK, Jeno (1908-   )

KAPLAN, Nathan Ivan (1948-   )
                S.9,19,20
KAPLAN, Sol [see CHAPLIN, Saul]
KAPOYANU, Dumitru (1929-   )
                S.18,19[Kapoianu]
KAPP, Artur (1878-1952), Est
    R.1   S.18
KAPP, Eugen (1908-   ), Est
    R.1   S.18
KAPP, Villem (1913-1964), Est
    R.1   S.18
KAPPEG [S.54(367)] = KAPPEY, Jacob Adam
KAPPEL, Johannes (1855-1907), Est
    R.30a   S.18
KAPPELLER, Karl [see KAPELLER, Karl]
KAPPEY, Jacob Adam (1826-   ), Eng
    R.57   S.54(367)[Kappeg]
KAPR, Jan (1914-   ), Cz
    R.1   S.c,7,9,10,24a,31
KAPRÁL, Václav (1889-1947), Cz
    R.1   S.31
KAPRÁLOVÁ, Vítězslava (1915-1940), Cz
    R.1   S.31,52
KAPS, Hansjoachim (1942-   )
                S.c
KAPSBERGER, Johan Hieronymus (c1580-1651), Ger
    R.1   S.c
KARABIC, Ivan Fedor (1945-   )
                S.c
KARAM, Frederick (1926-   ), Can
    R.14   S.10
KARAS, Anton (1910-?1985), Aus (see note)
    R.62

KARASCHNARS - Hungarian romance (vi & orch)
          S.24a
KARATÏGIN, Vyacheslav Gavrilovich (1875-1925), Russia
     R.1
KARAYEV, Faradzh (1943-   )
          S.18
KARAYEV, Kara (1918-   ), USA
     R.1   S.8,9,18,24
KARDANOV, Hasan (1923-   ), USSR
     R.47   S.18
KARDOŠ, Dezider (1914-   ), Cz
     R.1   S.c,10,31
KAREL, Rudolph (1880-1945), Cz
     R.1   S.31
KAREVA, Hillar (1931-   ), Est
     R.58   S.24a
KARG-ELERT, Sigfrid (1877-1933), Ger
     R.1   S.c,2,5,7,8,10,11,19,20
KARGANOV, Gennadi Ossipovich
     [see KORGANOV, Gennadi Ossipovich]
KARGEL, Sixt (c1540-<1594),   Ger
     R.1   S.c,10,16,32
KARGES, Wilhelm (1613/14-1699), Ger
     R.1   S.c
KARIND, Alfred Edouardovich (1901-   ), Est
     R.13   S.18
KARJALAINEN, Ahti Eino (1907-   ), Fin
     R.14   S.40
KARK, Frederik (1869-   ), Ger [pseud: Fr. DANNENBERG,
     Charles DUFORT, E. ZEILBECK]   R.3   S.24
KARKOFF, Maurice (1927-   ), Sweden
     R.1   S.10,20,38,40,56
KARKOSCHKA, Erhard (1923-   ), Ger
     R.1   S.c
KARLINS, M. William (1932-   ), USA
     R.19   S.10,22
KARLOWICZ, Mieczyslaw (1876-1909), Pol
     R.1   S.c,5x,8,10,18,24
KARLSSON, Karl [see JULARBO, Carl - pseud]
KARLSPERKA, Daniel Karolides z (16th Cent)
          S.c
KARNITSKAYA, Nina Andreevna (1906-   ), USSR
     R.7   S.18,52
KARNOVICH, Yuri Larovich (1884-1941), Lith
     R.14   S.c,18,24
KAROLIDES, Daniel
          S.16
KÁROLYI, Pál (1934-   ), Hun
     R.1   S.c,10

KAROSAS, Juozas (1890-   ), Lith
    R.4   S.18,24
KARPIENIA, Joseph USA
            S.13
KARPILOWSKI, Daniel (1895-   ), Ukraine
    R.3   S.24
KARSEL, Kjell Mork (1947-   ), Nor
            S.40
KASATSCHENKO, Grigorii Alexeyevich (1858-1938), Russia
    R.47   S.e
KASATSCHENKO, Kaschin - Pan Sotkin
    = KASATSCHENKO, Grigorii Alexeyevich
KASCHUBEC, Erich (1899-   )
            S.24
KASEMETS, Udo (1919-   ), Can
    R.1   S.24
KAŠLÍK, Václav (1917-   ), Cz
    R.14   S.31
KASSERN, Tadeusz Zygfryd (1904-1957), Pol
    R.1
KASSIANOV, Alexander Alexandrovich (1891-   ), USSR
    R.14   S.18
KÄSSMAYER, Moritz (1831-1884), Aus
    R.25   S.c
KASTALSKY, Alexander Dmitriyevich (1856-1926), Russia
    R.1   S.c,8,10,11,18
KASTNER, Jean-Georges (1810-1867), Fr
    R.1   S.10,22
KATSCHER, Robert (1894-   ), Aus

    R.3   S.10
KATSKI, Antoni (1817-1899), Pol
    R.1
KATTNIGG, Rudolf (1895-1955), Aus
    R.1   S.c,10
KATZ, Erich (1900-1973), USA
    R.19   S.13
KATZ, Sigizmund Abramovich (1908-   ), USSR
    R.14   S.10
KAUDER, Hugo (1888-1972), USA
    R.14   S.4
KAUER, Ferdinand (1751-1831), Aus
    R.1   S.c
KAUFFMAN - In deiner Augen liegt all'mein Gluck
            S.10
KAUFFMANN - Introduce me
            S.54(334)
KAUFFMANN, Georg Friedrich (1679-1735), Ger
    R.1   S.c,5x,10,53
KAUFFMANN, Leo Justinus (1901-1944), Ger
    R.1   S.c,10

KAUFMANN, Armin (1902-1980), Rum
R.1   S.c,7,10
KAUFMANN, Jeffrey (1947-   )
             S.13,20
KAUFMANN, Walter (1907-   ), USA
R.1   S.10
KAUN, Hugo (1863-1932), Ger
R.1   S.e
KAURENTIUS, A. (15th Cent), Neth - Mij heeft een
   piperken   S.c
KAVYATSKAS - Piece (vi)
             S.24a
KAWASAKI, Masaru (1924-   ), Japan
             S.50
KAY, Donald (1933-   ), Australia
R.14   S.29
KAY, Hershy (1919-1981), USA
R.1   S.8-10,13
KAY, Norman (1929-   ), Eng
R.14
KAY, Ulysses (1917-   ), USA
R.1   S.c,8,10,13
KAYE, Buddy (1918-   ), USA
R.23   S.10
KAYN, Roland (1933-   ), Ger
R.1   S.c,10
KAYSER, Heinrich Ernst (1815-1888), Ger
R.2   S.c,24
KAYSER, Isfrid (1712-1771), Ger
R.1   S.c,10
KAYSER, Leif (1919-   ), Den
R.1   S.4,35,40,57
KAYSER, Philipp Christoph (1755-1823), Ger
R.1   S.c
KAZANDZHIEV, Vasil (1934-   ), Bul
R.1   S.20,24
KAZANECKI, Waldemar (1929-   )

KAZHAEVA, Tatiana Ibragimovna (1949-   ), USSR
             S.52
KAZHLAYEV, Murad (1931-   ), USSR
R.1   S.18
KAZURO, Stanislaw (1881-1961), Pol
R.1
KEARNEY, Peader (1883-1942), Ire
R.1
KEATS, Donald (1929-   ), USA
R.1   S.10,13
KEDROV, Nicolai Nicolaevich (1871-1940)
             S.c,10

KEE, Cor (1900-   ), Neth
    R.1   S.c
KEE, Piet (1927-   ), Neth
    R.1   S.c,10
KEEBLE, John (c1711-1786), Eng
    R.1   S.c
KEEL, James Frederick (1871-1950), Eng
    R.3   S.c,10
KEENEY, Wendell (1903-   ), USA
    R.19   S.13
KEETBAAS, Dirk (1921-   ), Can
    R.14
KEETMAN, Gunild (1904-   ), Ger
    R.4
KEEZER, Ronald (1940-   ), USA
    R.19   S.13
KEIGHLEY, Thomas (1869-   ), Eng
    R.85   S.55
KEISER, Robert - pseud [see KING, Robert A.]
KEISER, Reinhard (1674-1739), Ger
    R.1   S.c,5x,6,8-11
KELEMAN, Milko (1924-   ), Yug
    R.1   S.c,9,10,18
KÉLER, Béla (1820-1882), Hun
    R.1   S.c
KELKEL, Manfred (1929-   ), Ger
    R.14   S.c
KELLAM, Ian (1938-   )
                S.c
KELLAWAY, Roger (1939-   ), USA
    R.14   S.c,10,13
KELLER, Gottfried (d.1704), Ger
    R.1   S.c,10
KELLER, Homer (1915-   ), USA
    R.19   S.3,4,8,10,11,13,19-21
KELLER, Ludwig (1847-1930), Ger
    R.3   S.c
KELLER, Max (1770-1855), Ger
    R.2   S.c
KELLETTE, John William
                S.24
KELLEY, Edgar Stillman (1857-1944), USA
    R.1   S.10

KELLIE, Lawrence (1862-1932), Eng
    R.4   S.e
KELLNER, David (c1670-1748), Ger
    R.1   S.c,10
KELLNER, Johann Christoph (1736-1803), Ger
    R.1   S.c

KELLNER, Johann Peter (1705-1772), Ger
   R.1   S.c,10,53
KELLY, Bryan (1934-   ), Eng
   R.1   S.c,10,55
KELLY, Claude Arundale [see ARUNDALE, Claude - pseud]
KELLY, Columba

KELLY, Frederick Septimus (1881-1916), Australia
   R.1   S.10,24
KELLY, Georgia
            S.30
KELLY, Michael (1762-1826), Ire
   R.1   S.10
KELLY, Robert Emmet (1919-   ), USA
   R.19   S.8,10,13
KELLY, Thomas Alexander Erskine (1732-1781), Scot
   R.1   S.c
KELLY, Thomas C. (1917-   ), Ire
   R.40   S.10,49
KELLY, Walt (fl 1954), USA [poet]
            S.9
KELSO, Alice Anne (20th Cent), USA
            S.52
KELTERBORN, Rudolf (1931-   ), Swiss
   R.1   S.c,19,20,23
KEMP, Walter (1938-   ), Can
   R.14
KEMP, Winfred

KEMPFE, Hans Peter (1920-   )

KEMPIS, Nicolas [see A KEMPIS, Nicolas]
KEMPKENS, Arnold (1923-   )
            S.c
KEMPTER, Karl (1819-1871), Ger
   R.3   S.c
KENDZHAYEV, K (1939-   )
            S.18
KENEKE - Heroes all; W. Freeland Kendrick
            S.54(331,64)
KENEMAN, Fedor Fedorovich (1873-1937), USSR
   R.47
KENGYO, Joshizawa (1800-1872)
            S.24a
KENGYO, Mitsuzaki (d.1853)

KENGYO, Yatsuhashi (1614-1685)
            S.24a
KENINS, Talivaldis (1919-   ), Can
   R.1   S.24a

KENNAN, Kent Wheeler (1913-   ), USA
    R.1   S.4,5x,6,8,10,11,13,18
KENNAWAY, Lamont (1899-   ), Eng
    R.64,79   S.19,21
KENNEDY, Harry (fl 1880-1893)
             S.e
KENNEDY, Joseph J., USA
             S.10,13
KENNEDY, Sergeant Major
             S.10
KENNEDY-FRASER, Marjorie (1857-1930), Scot
    R.1   S.2-4,24a,52
KENNEY, H. Arthur (20th Cent), Eng
    R.85   S.55
KENNIS, Willem Gustave (1857-1923)
             S.24a
KENT, James (1918-   ), Can
    R.31
KENT, Walter (1911-   ), USA
    R.23   S.9,10
KENWARD, Maurice
             S.e
KEPITIS, Janis (1908-   ), Lat
    R.1   S.18,24,30
KEPPEL - Robin Adair
             S.e
KERCKHOVEN, Abraham van den (c1618-1701), Flem
    R.1   S.c,7,8,10,18,53
KEREKJARTO, Duci de (1900-1962)
             S.24
KERESELIDZE, Archil (1912-1971), USSR
    R.30a   S.18
KERKER, Gustav Adolph (1857-1923), USA
    R.1   S.24,54(315)
KERKOFF, Piet van den (1905-1968)
             S.c
KERLE, Jacobus de (1531/32-1591), S. Neth
    R.1   S.c,10,16
KERLL, Johann Kaspar (1627-1693), Ger
    R.1   S.c,8,10,53
KERN, Jerome (1885-1945), USA
    R.1   S.c,2-4,5x,9-11,13,24,54(339)
KERN, Kurt (1886-   ), Aus
    R.25   S.24
KERNICH, Fritz
             S.c
KERNOCHAN, Marshall Rutgers (1880-1955), USA
    R.19   S.10,13
KERR, Harrison (1897-1978), USA
    R.1   S.3,5x,8,10,13,20,24

KERR, Thomas H. Jr. USA
   R.19   S.10,13
KERRISON, Jan Eng
   R.77
KERSBERGEN, Jan Willem (1857-1927), Neth
   R.3   S.c
KERSTERS, Willem (1929-   ), Bel
   R.1   S.20,36
KERZKOWSKY, Joseph (1791-   )
            S.c
KESAYAN, Sergei (1918-   )
            S.18
KESSLER, Minuetta Schumiatcher (1914-   ), USA
   R.19   S.24a,30,52
KESSLER, Thomas (1937-   ), Swiss
   R.1   S.c,24a
KESSNER, Daniel Aaron (1946-   ), USA
   R.19   S.13
KETÈLBEY, Albert (1875-1959), Eng
   R.1   S.c,1-4,5x,9-11,24,54(315,17,34,53,66)
KETLAR, Jetvan
            S.24
KETTEN, Henri [pseud: VALERIO] (1848-1883), Fr
   R.3   S.24
KETTERER, Eugene (1831-1870), Fr
   R.3   S.c
KETTERING, Eunice Lea (1906-   ), USA
   R.7   S.52
KETTING, Otto (1935-   ), Neth
   R.1   S.10
KETTING, Piet (1904-   ), Neth
   R.4
KEULEN, Geert van (1943-   ), Neth
   R.25
KEURIS, Tristan (1946-   ), Neth
   R.4   S.24a
KEUTZENHOFF, Johann (fl 1557), Ger
   R.5   S.c,10
KEY, Francis Scott (1780-1843), USA (see note)
   R.53   S.e
KEYES, Nelson (1928-   ), USA
   R.19   S.10,13
KEYPER, Franz (c1756-1815), Neth
            S.c
KHABIBULLIN, Zagid (1910-   )
            S.18
KHACHATURIAN, Aram (1903-1978), Arm
   R.1   S.c,4-10,18-21,24
KHACHATURIAN, Karen (1920-   ), USA
   R.1   S.10,18,24,30

KHADOSHKIN, Ivan [see KHANDOSHKIN, Ivan]
KHAGAGORTYAN, Eduard (1930-   )
            S.18
KHAITBAYEV, S. - Concerto vi & orch
            S.18,24
KHAKHANOV, Dudar (1921-   )
            S.18
KHALMAMEDOV, Nury (1940-   ), USSR
    R.47   S.18[b.1910]
KHAMRAYEV, Ibragim (1916-   )
            S.18
KHANDOSHKIN, Ivan Yevstafyevich (1747-1804)
    R.1   S.10,18,23[Handoshkin],24
KHASANOV, Nabi (1913-   )
            S.18
KHODYASHEV, Viktor Alexandrovich (1917-   ), USSR
    R.14   S.18
KHODZHA-EINATOV, Leon Alexandrovich (1904-1955), USSR
    R.14   S.18
KHOLMINOV, Alexander Nikolayevich (1925-   ), Russia
    R.1   S.18
KHRENNIKOV, Tikhon Nikolayevich (1913-   ), Russia
    R.1   S.c,4,5,7,8,10,18,24a
KHRISTIC, Stevan [see HRISTIC, Stevan]
KHRISTOSKOV, Petr Khristov (1917-   ), Bul
    R.14   S.24a[Hristoskov]
KHUDOYAN, Adik (1921-   )
            S.10,18
KHUDOYAN, Ivan Gegamovich

KHYARMA, Miyna (1864-1941), USSR
            S.18,52
KIEFER, W. H.
            S.54(317,34)
KIEL, Alfredo
            S.24
KIELLAND, Olav (1901-   ), Nor
    R.14   S.c,10,51
KIENZL, Wilhelm (1857-1941), Aus
    R.1   S.c,1x,2-5,7,8,10,18
KIJIMA, Kiyohiko (1917-   ), Japan
    R.4
KIKTA, Valeri Grigoryevich (1941-   )
            S.18
KILADZE, Grigori Varfolomeyevich (1902-1962), USSR
    R.14   S.18
KILAR, Wojciech (1932-   ), Pol
    R.1
KILBURN, Paul (1936-   ), Can
    R.81

KILDARE, Dan
          S.e
KILLMAYER, Wilhelm (1927-   ), Ger
    R.1   S.c,10
KILPINEN, Yryö (1892-1959), Fin
    R.1   S.c,2-8,10,24,40
KIM, Earl (1920-   ), USA
    R.1   S.10,13
KIMBALL, Edward P.
          S.10
KIMBALL, Jacob (1761-1826), USA
    R.1   S.10,47

KINCL, Antonín (1898-   ), Cz
    R.18   S.31
KINDER, Ralph (1876-1952), USA
    R.19   S.12,13
KINDERMANN, Johann Erasmus (1616-1655), Ger
    R.1   S.c,10,53
KINEYA, Seihou (1914-   ), Japan
          S.50
KING, Frank [see KING, Pee Wee - pseud]
KING, Karl Lawrence (1891-1971), USA
    R.19   S.c,10,13,54(314,48)
KING, Larry (1932-   )
          S.c
KING, Oliver (1748-1818), USA

KING, Pee Wee - pseud [ie Frank KING] (1914-   ), USA
    R.61
KING, Reginald (1904-   ), Eng
    R.14   S.10,24
KING, Robert (fl 1676-1728), Eng
    R.1   S.c
KING, Robert A. (1862-1932), USA [pseud: Mary EARL,
    Robert KEISER, Mrs. RAVENHALL, R. A. WILSON]
    (1862-1932), USA   R.23   S.10,24[Earl]
KING, Wayne (1901-   ), USA
    R.23   S.10
KING, William (1624-1680), Eng
    R.1   S.c
KING, Wilton
          S.e
KINGMAN, Daniel C. (1924-   ), USA
    R.19   S.10,13
KINGO, Thomas (1634-1703), Den
          S.4,57
KINGSLEY, Gershon, (1928-   ), USA
    R.19   S.13
KINKEL, Charles (1832-   ), USA
    R.53   S.10,47

KINLEY - Anona
          S.e
KINLOCH, William (fl c1600), Scot
     R.1   S.c,16
KINSELLA, John (1932-   ), Ire
     R.30   S.13,49
KINT, Cor (1890-1944), Neth
     R.2   S.c
KINZE - Canzonetta (vi & p)
               S.24
KIR STEFAN, Domestikoes (15th Cent)
               S.c
KIRBYE, George (d.1634), Eng
     R.1   S.c,7,8,10,14,16
KIRCHGASSNER, Elisabeth Ger
               S.52
KIRCHHOFF, Gottfried (1685-1746), Ger
     R.1   S.5x
KIRCHNER, Leon (1919-   ), USA
     R.1   S.8-10,13,24
KIRCHNER, Theodor Fürchtegott (1823-1903), Ger
     R.1   S.c,10
KIRCULESCU, Nicolae (1903-   ), Rum
     R.4
KIREIKO, Vitali Dmitriyevich (1926-   ), USSR
     R.14   S.18
KIRIAC-GEORGESCU, Dumitri (1866-1928), Rum
     R.1
KIRK, H. - The penient
               S.54(349)
KIRK, Theron (1919-   ), USA
     R.19   S.13
KIRMAIR, Friedrich Joseph (c1770-1814)
     R.200   S.10
KIRMAN, Paul (20th Cent)
               S.c,24
KIRNBERGER, Johann Philipp (1721-1783), Ger
     R.1   S.c,53
KIRYUKOV, Leonti Petrovich (1895-1965), USSR
     R.47   S.18
KISIELEWSKY, Stefan (1911-   ), Pol
     R.14   S.18
KITAJIMA, Osamu

KITAZUME, Yayoi (1945-   ), Japan
               S.52
KITSON, Charles Herbert (1874-1944), Eng
     R.1   S.c
KITTEL, Caspar (1603-1639), Ger
     R.1   S.c

KITTEL, Johann Christian (1732-1809), Ger
   R.1   S.c
KITTERIDGE, Walter (1832 or 1834-1905), USA
   R.50   S.10,47
KIYOSE, Yasuji (1900-   ), Japan
   R.1   S.24,50
KJELLERUP, Christian (1889-1947), Den
          S.c
KJELLSBY, Erling (1901-1976), Nor
   R.14   S.51
KJERULF, Halfdan (1815-1868), Nor
   R.1   S.c,4,5x,10,11,18,33
KLABON, Krzystof (c1550-c1616), Pol
   R.1   S.c,16
KLAMI, Uuno (1900-1961), Fin
   R.1   S.c,24a,40
KLASEN, Willy (fl 1941)
          S.24
KLAUSMEYER, Peter Ballard (1942-   ), USA
   R.19   S.13
KLAUSNER, Joseph
          S.24a
KLAUSS, Noah (1901-1977), USA
   R.23
KLEBANOV, Dmitri Lvovich (1907-   ), USSR
   R.14   S.18

KLEBE, Giselher (1925-   ), Ger
   R.1   S.c,24
KLEBER, Henry (fl 1830), USA
   R.53   S.10
KLEBER, Leonhard (c1495-1556), Ger
   R.1   S.c,10,15,16,53
KLEFISCH, Walter (1910-   ), Ger
   R.14   S.c
KLEGA, Miroslav (1926-   ), Cz
   R.1   S.24a
KLEIN - Norges Hoitidsstund er kommt
          S.e
KLEIN, Bernhard (1793-1832), Ger
   R.1   S.c
KLEIN, John (1913-   ), USA
   R.19
KLEIN, Karl Heinz
          S.c
KLEIN, Lothar (1932-   ), USA
   R.14   S.10,13,22
KLEIN, Richard Rudolf (1921-   ), Ger
   R.14   S.c
KLEINKNECHT, Jakob Friedrich (1722-1794), Ger
   R.1   S.c

KLEINPAUL, Alfred
          S.e
KLEINSINGER, George (1914-1982), USA
   R.19   S.3,4,9,11,13,42
KLEM, O - Autumn winds are sighing
          S.e
KLEMM, Edward G.

KLEMPERER, Otto (1885-1973), Ger
   R.1   S.c,10
KLENAU, Paul August von (1883-1946), Den
   R.1   S.c,5x
KLENGEL, Julius (1859-1933), Ger
   R.1   S.c,18
KLENITSKIS, Abel Ruvimovich (1910-   ), USSR
   R.14   S.18
KLENOVSKI, Nikolay Semyonovich (1857-1915), Rus
   R.1   S.e
KLENZ, William (1915-   ), USA
   R.19   S.10,13,25,27
KLEPHTE - Vieille chanson
          S.e
KLERK, Albert de (1917-   ), Neth
   R.1   S.10
KLETZKI, Paul (1900-1973), Swiss
   R.1   S.24
KLIČKA, Josef (1855-1937), Cz
   R.2   S.c
KLIČKA, Václav (1882-1953), Cz
   R.1   S.c
KLICKMANN, F. Henri (1885-1966), USA
   R.23   S.22,24
KLÍMA, Alois (1905-   ), Cz

   R.18   S.31
KLING, Henri (1842-1918), Swiss
   R.1   S.10
KLOHR, John N. (1869-1956), USA
   R.23   S.c,10,13
KLOMP, Dick (1947-   )
          S.c
KLOP, Hendrik Teunis (1946-   ), Neth
   R.80   S.c
KLOSÉ, Hyacinthe Eléonore (1808-1880), Fr
   R.1   S.10
KLOVA, Vitautas Juliono (1926-   ), USSR
   R.14   S.18,24
KLUGE, Manfred (1928-1971), Ger
   R.4   S.c
KLUGHARDT, August (1847-1902), Ger
   R.1   S.c,8,21

KLUPSCH, Siegfried
        S.24
KLUSÁK, Jan (1934-   ), Cz
  R.1   S.c,10,24,31
KLYUCHAREV, Alexander Sergeyevich (1906-1972), USSR
  R.47   S.18
KNAB, Armin (1881-1951), Ger
  R.1   S.c,10
KNAEBEL, Simon (fl 1854), USA
  R.53   S.10,47
KNAPP, Phoebe Palmer (Mrs. Joseph F.) (1839-1908), USA
  R.7   S.e
KNEASS, Nelson (d.1869)
        S.24
KNECHT, Justin Heinrich (1752-1817), Ger
  R.1   S.10
KNEFFEL, Johann [see KNOFEL, Johann]
KNEISEL, Franz (1865-1926), Hun
  R.3   S.24
KNELLER, Andreas (1649-1724), Ger
  R.1   S.c,10,53
KNEUBUHL, John (1943-   ), USA
        S.13
KNEVEL, Andre (1950-   )
        S.c
KNIGHT, A. F. (19th Cent), USA - Post horn duetto (p)
        S.10,47
KNIGHT, Gerald (1908-1979), Eng
  R.80   S.c
KNIGHT, Jim USA
        S.13
KNIGHT, Joseph Philip (1812-1887), Eng
  R.3   S.e
KNIGHT, Morris (1933-   ), USA
  R.19   S.9,10,13,22
KNIPPER, Lev Konstantinovich (1898-1974), Russia
  R.1   S.c,10,11,18,24,54(319,36)
KNÍŽE, František Max (1784-1840), Boh
  R.1   S.5x
KNÖFEL, Johann (c1525->1617), Ger
  R.1   S.c
KNORR, Ernst-Lothar von (1896-1973), Ger
  R.1   S.24a
KNOSP, Gaston (1874-1942), Bel
  R.4   S.41
KNOX, Charles (1929-   ), USA
  R.19   S.13
KNUDOYAN, Adam (1921-   )
        S.c

KNUDSEN, Gunnar (1907-   ), Nor
    R.80   S.7,24
KNUDSEN, John Hye [see HYE-KNUDSEN, Johann]
KNUDSON, Thurston USA
            S.13
KNÜPFER, Sebastian (1633-1676), Ger
    R.1   S.c,10
KNUSSEN, Oliver (1952-   ), Eng
    R.1   S.c
KOBIAKIN, W. - Double variation (vi)
            S.24a
KOBIALKA, Daniel (1943-   )
            S.24a
KOBIERKOWICZ, Józef (fl c1730-51), Pol
    R.1   S.c
KOBIN, Otto
            S.24
KOBRICH, Johann Anton (fl 1753-78), Ger
    R.5   S.c
KOC, Marcelo (1918-   ), Arg
    R.26   S.46
KOCH, Erland von (1910-   ), Sweden
    R.1   S.c,5x,6,10,22,24,38,40,56
KOCH, Frederick (1924-   ), USA
    R.19   S.10,13
KOCH, Frierich (1862-1927), Ger
    R.1
KOCH, Jan (1929-   )

KOCH, Johannes Hermann Ernst (1918-   ), Ger
    R.14   S.c
KOCH, John (1928-   ), USA
    R.14   S.10,13,27
KOCH, Martin
            S.24a
KOCH, Sigurd von (1879-1919), Sweden
    R.3   S.56
KOCHAN, Günter (1930-   ), Ger
    R.1   S.8,24
KOCHANOVSKII Russia

KOCHETOW - The night is reigning
            S.e
KOCHUBEL, Yelizaveta Vasilevna (1822-1897)
            S.18
KOCHUROV, Yuri Vladimirovich (1907-1952), USSR
    R.14   S.18

KOCIAN, Jaroslav (1883-1950), Cz
    R.1   S.24

KOCSÁR, Miklós (1933-   ), Hun
    R.1   S.c,10
KOCSIS, Zoltán (1952-   ), Hun
    R.1   S.c
KOCŽWARA, František (c1750-1791), Boh
    R.1
KODÁLY, Zoltán (1882-1967), Hun
    R.1   S.c,2-11,18,23,24,28,42
KOEBERG, Frits Ehrhardt Adrian (1876-1961), Neth
    R.25   S.24a
KOECHLIN, Charles (1867-1950), Fr
    R.1   S.c,1-10,19,22,24a
KOELLREUTTER, Hans Joachim (1915-   ), Ger
    R.1   S.c
KOENEMAN, T. - When the king went forth to war, Op.7/6
                 S.e
KOENEMANN, Feodor (1873-1937), USSR
    R.4   S.1x,5x,10,18
KOENIG, Gottfried Michael (1926-   ), Ger
    R.1   S.10
KOENIG, H. - Post horn galop
                 S.54(350)
KOENNEMANN, Miloslav (1826-1879), Cz
    R.25
KOERPPEN, Alfred (1926-   ), Ger
    R.1   S.c
KOETSIER, Jan (1911-   ), Neth
    R.1   S.c,10
KOGOJ, Marij (1895-1956), Yug
    R.14   S.24a
KOHA, Jan Oskarovich (1929-   ), USSR
    R.14
KOHAUT, Josef (1738-?1793), Boh
    R.1   S.c
KOHAUT, Karl (1726-1784), Aus
    R.1   S.c,10,24,32
KOHLER, Ernesto (1849-1907), It
    R.3   S.c,10,24a
KÖHLER, Wolfgang (1923-   ), Ger
    R.4   S.c
KOHN, Karl (1926-   ), USA
    R.1   S.10,13,20
KOHOUT, Josef [see KOHAUT, Josef]
KOHOUTEK, Ctirad (1929-   ), Cz
    R.1   S.10
KOHS, Ellis Bonoff (1916-   ), USA
    R.1   S.5x,6-10,13,23,24
KOISHIBAYEV, Makalim (1926-   )
                 S.18

KOKA, Evgeni Konstantinovich (1893-1954), USSR
R.14   S.18
KÓKAI, Rezső (1906-1962), Hun
R.1   S.10,24
KOKHA, Jan Oskarovich (1929-   ), USSR
R.47   S.18
KOKHAN, Gunther (1930-   ), USSR
R.47   S.18
KOKINOS - Tsopanopulo (Shepherd song) (vi & p)
            S.24a
KOKKONEN, Joonas (1921-   ), Fin
R.1   S.c,10,18,40
KOKOITY, Aslan (1915-   )
            S.18,24
KOKOITY, Tatarkhan (1908-   )
            S.18
KOLB, Barbara (1939-   ), USA
R.7   S.10,13,30,52
KOLB, Carlmann (1703-1765), Ger
R.1   S.c,10,53
KOLBERG, Kåre (1936-   ), Nor
R.14   S.40,51
KOLER, Egolfus (16th Cent), Swiss
R.5
KOLESSA, Nikolai Filaretovich (1904-   ), USSR
R.14   S.18
KOLINSKI, Mieczyslaw (1901-   ), Can
R.1   S.9
KOLLO, Walter (1878-1940), Ger
R.1   S.c,5x
KOLMAN, Peter (1937-   ), Slovak
R.1   S.24,31
KOLODEZNIKOV, I. - Beyond the Ayansky mountain range
            S.18
KOLODUB, Lev Nikolaevich (1930-   ), USSR
R.7   S.c,18,52
KOLOSS, Itvan (1932-   )
            S.c
KOLOVSKY [?Holovski] - On the mountain, on the hill (v)
            S.10
KOMAIKO, William (1947-   ), USA
R.19   S.20
KOMAROVSKY, Gabriel (fl 1467), Boh
            S.5x
KOMITAS, Vartabed (1869-1935), Arm
R.1   S.9,10,18,24
KOMIVES, Janos (1932-   ), Fr
            S.c
KOMMA, Karl Michael (1913-   ), Ger
R.1   S.c,9

KOMOROUS, Rudolf (1931-   ), Cz
 R.1
KOMRAKOV, Herman Nikandrovich (1937-   )
          S.18
KOMZÁK, Karl (i) (1823-1893), Cz (see note)
 R.1,25   S.c,5x
KOMZAK, Karl (ii) (1850-1905), Cz (see note)
 R.1,25   S.c,3,10,54(325)
KOMZAK, Karl (iii) (1878-1924), Cz (see note)
 R.25
KONDO, Jo (1947-   ), Japan
 R.36   S.24a
KONDOR, Ernst
          S.24
KÖNIG - Da unten ist ruh
          S.e
KÖNIG, Wolfgang (1947-   )
          S.c
KÖNIGSBERGER, Josef
          S.24
KÖNIGSPERGER, Marianus (1708-1769), Ger
 R.1   S.c,53
KONINK, Servaas de (d.1717/18), Neth
 R.1   S.10
KONISHI, Nagako (1945-   ), Japan
          S.52
KONIUS, Julius [see KONYUS, Julius]
KONOJOVIC, Petar (1883-1970), Yug
 R.30   S.18
KONOYE, Hidemaro (1898-1973), Japan
 R.30
KONRAD von WÜRZBURG (d.1287), Ger
 R.1   S.c,16
KONSTANINESCU, Paul [see CONSTANINESCU, Paul]
KONSTANTINIDIS, Janis (1903-   ), Greece
 R.14   S.c,24
KONSTANTINOFF, Georgi

KONT, Paul (1920-   ), Aus
 R.69
KONTSKI, Anton [see KATSKI, Antoni]
KONVALINKA, Milos (1919-   ), Cz
 R.14   S.24a
KONYUS, Georgy Eduardovich (1862-1933), Russia
 R.1   S.c,18
KONYUS, Julius Eduardvich (1869-1942), Russia
 R.28   S.8,10,18,24
KOO, CHIH-JUNG

KOPELENT, Marek (1932-   ), Cz
    R.1   S.10,31
KOPETZKY, Wendelin (1844-1899), Aus
    R.95   S.54(324)
KOPF, Hermann - Mädchen, wach auf

KOPILOV, Alexander Alexandrovich (1854-1911), Russia
    R.1   S.24
KOPPEL, Herman David (1908-   ), Den
    R.1   S.c,5x,6,7,18,20,33,35,40,57[Christensen]
KOPPEL, Thomas Hermann (1944-   ), Den
    R.14   S.40
KOPŘIVA, Karl Blažej (1756-1785), Cz
    R.1   S.c,5x,10
KOPŘIVA, Václav Jan (1708-1789), Cz
    R.1   S.c,10
KOPYLOV, Alexander (1854-1911), Russia
    R.3   S.8,10
KOPYTMAN, Mark (1929-   ), Isr
    R.1   S.18
KORA, Toshio (1933-   ), Japan
    R.36   S.50
KORBAY, Ferenc (1846-1913), Hun
    R.15   S.c
KORD, Mira - pseud [see VORLOVA, Slavka]
KORDEN, Emilio - pseud [see LUBBE, Kurt
KORGANOV, Gennadi Ossipovich (1858-1890), Georgia
    R.28   S.c
KÖRLING, August (1842-1919), Sweden
    R.1   S.5x,11,43
KÖRLING, Felix (1864-1937), Sweden
    R.1
KORN, Peter Jona (1922-   ), USA
    R.1   S.c,10,13
KORNAUTH, Egon (1891-1959), Aus
    R.1   S.24
KORNGOLD, Erich Wolfgang (1897-1957), Aus
    R.1   S.c,1-10,24
KORÓLY - Fantaisie hongrois (vi & p)
              S.24
KORTE, Karl (1928-   ), USA
    R.1   S.10,13
KORTE, Oldrich Frantisek (1926-   ), Cz
    R.1   S.c,10,31
KORTES, Sergei Albertovich (1935-   )
              S.18
KÓSA, Gabor (1950-   )
              S.c

KÓSA, György (1897-   ), Hun
    R.1   S.c,9,18[KOSA, Derd],24[KOSA, D.]
KOS-ANATOLSKY, Anatoli Ossipovich (1909-   ), Ukraine
    R.80   S.18
KOSCHAT, Thomas (1845-1914), Ger
    R.3   S.5x,24
KOSCKI - Sendo Kawaiya - variations (vi & p)
                S.24
KOSENKO, Viktor Stepanovich (1896-1938), USSR
    R.25   S.18,24
KOSHA, Derd [S.18,24] = KÓSA, György
KOSHETZ, Nina Pavolova (1894-1965), USA
    R.25   S.52
KOSHKIN, Nikita (1956-   ), USSR
                S.c
KOSINS, Martin Scot (1947-   ), USA
                S.13
KOSLOFF, Hilarion
                S.24
KOSMA, Joseph (1905-1969), Hun
    R.1   S.8-10,24a,42
KOSS, Henning von (1855-1913), Ger
    R.3   S.e
KOSSE, Roberta (20th Cent), USA
    R.7   S.30,52
KOŠTÁL, Arnošt (1920-   ), Cz
    R.4
KOŠTÁL, Erno (1889-1957), Cz
    R.14   S.24
KOSTECK, Gregory (1937-   ), USA
    R.19   S.10,13,19,22
KOSTELANETZ, Andre (1901-1980), USA
    R.1   S.10,13
KOSTELETZKY, Viktor (1851-1899), Boh
    R.95
KOSTIAINEN, Pekka (1944-   ), Fin
    R.30   S.c
KOSUGI, Takehiva
                S.24a
KOSZEWSKI, Andrej (1922-   ), Pol
    R.4
KOTIK, Petr (1942-   ), USA
    R.19   S.13
KOTILAINEN, Otto (1868-1936), Fin
    R.4   S.4,5x
KOTLAR - Monte cristo (valse tzigane) (vi & p)
                S.24a
KOTOŃSKI, Wlodzimierz (1925-   ), Pol
    R.1   S.c,10

KOTSBATREVSKAYA (19th Cent), Russia
          S.52
KOTTAUN - Bullfighter's march
          S.54(317)
KOTTER, Hans (c1485-1541), Ger
     R.1   S.c,10,15,53
KOUGHELL, Arkadie (1898-   ), USA
     R.19   S.10,24a
KOUNTZ, Richard (1896-1950), USA
     R.19   S.10,13
KOUSSEVITSKY, Sergey (1874-1951), USA
     R.1   S.c,1,8,10,13,18
KOUTNIK, Tomas Norbert (1698-1775)
          S.5
KOUTZEN, Boris (1901-1966), USA
     R.19   S.7,9,10,13,24a
KOVAL, Marian Viktorovich (1907-1971), Russia
     R.1   S.5x,18
KOVALEVSKY, Maxime (1903-   )
          S.c
KOVAŘÍČEK, František (1924-   ), Cz
     R.1   S.20
KOVAŘOVIC, Karel (1862-1920), Cz
     R.1   S.4,5x,6,8,10
KOVÁTS, Varna (1920-   ), Hun
     R.4   S.10,32
KOVEN, Reginald de [see DE KOVEN, Reginald]
K.O.W.A [see ALMROTH, Knut O.W.]
KOWALSKI, Július (1912-   ), Cz
     R.1   S.10
KOWALSKI, Max (1882-1956), Ger
     R.1   S.3,5
KOX, Hans (1930-   ), Neth
     R.1   S.10,24
KOYAMA, Kiyoshige (1914-   ), Japan
     R.4   S.50
KOZELUCH, Johann Antonin (1738-1814), Boh
     R.1   S.5x,10,18
KOZELUCH, Leopold (1747-1818), Boh
     R.1   S.c,5,10,24
KOZHEVNIKOV, B. - March for solemn parade
          S.54(340)
KOZHEVNIKOVA, Ekaterina (1954-   ), USSR
          S.18,52
KOZINA, Marjan (1907-1966), Yug
     R.1   S.18
KOZINSKY, Petr Borisovich (1927-   )
          S.18
KOZLOVSKY, Alexey (1905-1977), USSR
     R.1   S.18

KOZLOWSKI, Józef (1757-1831), Pol
   R.1   S.c
KRAEHENBUEHL, David (1932-   ), USA
   R.19   S.8,10,13
KRAFFT, François-Joseph (1721-1795), S. Neth
   R.1
KRAFT, Anton (1749-1820), Aus
   R.1   S.c,3,11
KRAFT, K. - Speedway
          S.54(357)
KRAFT, Karl Joseph (1903-1978), Ger
   R.14   S.c
KRAFT, Leo (1922-   ), USA
   R.1   S.c,9,10,13
KRAFT, Nikolaus (1778-1820), Aus
   R.5   S.c
KRAFT, Robert
          S.24a
KRAFT, Walter (1905-1977), Ger
   R.1   S.c
KRAFT, William (1923-   ), USA
   R.19   S.c,9,10,13,24
KRAKAUER, Alexander (1866-1894), Aus
   R.3   S.5x,24
KRAKOV, Mikolaj z [see MIKOLAJ z KRAKOWA]
KRAL, Jan (1823-1909)

KRAL, Johan Nepomuk (1849-1896), Aus
   R.3   S.10,54(332)
KRAMER, Arthur Walter (1890-1969), USA
   R.1   S.c,10,13,24

KRAMER, Jonathan (1942-   ), USA
   R.80   S.13
KRAMER, Wilhem (1745-1799)
          S.24
KRAMS - Laddie o mine
          S.e
KRAMSKOY, Ivanov
          S.32
KRANNIG, Simon (1866-1891), Ger
   R.3   S.10
KRAPF, Gerhard (1924-   ), USA
   R.19   S.10,12
KRASATOV, A. (1936-   )
          S.24a
KRAUS, A. M. - Meadowbrook
          S.54(342)
KRAUS, Eberhard (1931-   ), Ger
   R.4   S.c

KRAUS, Joseph Martin (1756-1792), Ger
   R.1   S.c,9,10,23,24,56
KRAUS, Philip Charles (1918-   ), USA
   R.23   S.10,13
KRAUSE, Bernard

KRAUSE, Christian Gottfried (1719-1770), Ger
   R.1   S.c,10
KRAUSZ, Michael (1897-   ), Hun
   R.3
KRAUTER, Kilian (1708-1742), Ger
   R.5   S.c
KRAUTGARTNER, Karel (1922-   ), Cz
   R.18   S.31
KRAUZE, Zygmunt (1938-   ), Pol
   R.1   S.c,24a
KREBS, Helmut (1913-   ), Ger
   R.14   S.c
KREBS, Johann Ludwig (1713-1780), Ger
   R.1   S.c,8,10,18,24,53
KREEK, Kirillys (1889-1962), Est
   R.30a   S.18
KREICHY, Miroslav [see KREJČÍ, Miroslav]
KREICHY, Stanislav [see KREJČÍ, Stanislav]
KREIGER, Arthur (1945-   ), USA
           S.10,13
KREIN, Alexander Abramovich (1883-1951), Russia
   R.2   S.c,10,18,24
KREIN, Jascha (1874-1946)
           S.24a
KREIN, Michael (d.1966), Eng
           S.c
KREISING, Johann George (17th Cent), Ger
   R.8   S.c
KREISLER, Fritz (1875-1962), Aus
   R.1   S.c,2-11,18,22-24,32
KREJČÍ, Iša (1904-1968), Cz
   R.1   S.c,5,24a,31
KREJČÍ, Miroslav (1891-1964), Cz
   R.1   S.31,18[Kreichy]
KREJČÍ, Stanislav (1936-   ), Cz
           S.18[Kreichy]
KREJN, Alexander [see KREIN, Alexander]
KREK, Uros (1922-   ), Yug
   R.1   S.c,24a
KRELL, William H.
           S.10
KREMER, Gerard
           S.c

KREMER, Rudolf USA
        S.12,13
KREMSER, Eduard (1838-1914), Aus
  R.2   S.2-4,43
KREMSKI, Alain
        S.10
KRENEK, Ernst (1900-   ), USA
  R.1   S.c,1-3,6-12,18-20,23,24
KRENTZ, Arthur [S.20] = KREUTZ, Arthur
KRENZ, Jan (1926-   ), Pol
  R.4
KRESANEK, Jozef (1913-   ), Slovak
  R.1   S.5x,31
KRESS, Georg Adam (1744-1788)
        S.c
KRESTJANIN, Fedor (16th Cent)
        S.c
KRETSCHMER, Edmund (1830-1908), Ger
  R.8   S.5x,54(321)[Kretchmer]
KRETZSCHMAR, Gunther (1929-   )
        S.c
KRETZSCHMAR, Walter (1902-   ), Ger
  R.3   S.c
KREUDER, P. - 75 Millienen, ein Schlag
        S.54(355)
KREUGER, Karl (1894-1979), USA
        S.13
KREUTZ, Arthur (1906-   ), USA
  R.50   S.20[Krentz]
KREUTZENHOFF = KEUTZENHOFF, Johann
KREUTZER, Conradin (1780-1849), Ger
  R.1   S.c,1x,2-5,7-10,20,24,28,32
KREUTZER, Joseph (1778-1832), Ger
  R.106   S.c,24a
KREUTZER, Rodolphe (1766-1831), Fr
  R.1   S.c,10,24
KRICKA, Jaroslav (1882-1969), Cz
  R.1   S.1x,2,5,10,31
KRIEDEL, Johann Christoph (fl 1706), Boh
  R.5   S.5x,6,10
KRIEGER, Adam (1634-1666), Ger
  R.1   S.c,8-10,24
KRIEGER, Armando (1940-   ), Arg
  R.26   S.46
KRIEGER, Edino (1928-   ), Brazil
  R.14   S.24a
KRIEGER, Johann (1652-1735), Ger
  R.1   S.c,5x,6,8,10,53
KRIEGER, Johann Philipp (1649-1725), Ger
  R.1   S.c,2-5,8,10,11,24,53

KRIEKEN, Gerard Bartus van (1836-1913), Neth
R.3   S.c
KRIER, Georges
           S.10,54(352)
KRIER - El apache
           S.e
KRINITSYN, Yuri Nikolayevich (1947-   )
           S.18
KRIPS, Henry Joseph` (1914-   ), Australia
R.14   S.5x
KRIUKOV, Vladimir (1908-   ), USSR
R.14   S.c
KŘIVINKA, Gustav (1928-   ), Cz
R.1   S.24a,31
KŘÍŽHANOVSKÝ, Ivan Ivanovich (1867-1924)
           S.7
KŘÍŽKOVSKÝ, Pavel (1820-1885), Cz
R.1   S.1x
KRJUKOV, Vladimir (1902-1961), USSR
R.4   S.c
KROHN, Felix Julius Theofil (1898-   ), Fin
R.14   S.24
KRÖL, Bernhard (1920-   ), Ger
R.1   S.c,10
KRÖLL, George (1934-   ), Ger
R.1   S.c
KROLL, William (1901-1980), USA
R.1   S.3,5x,10,13,24
KROMMER, Franz (1759-1831), Cz
R.1   S.c,6-8,10,19-21
KRONSTEINER, Joseph (1910-   ), Aus
R.14   S.c
KRÖPFL, Francisco (1928-   ), Arg
R.26   S.46
KROPFREITER, Augustinus Franz (1936-   ), Aus
R.1   S.c
KROPIVNITSKY, Mark Lukich (1840-1910), Russia
R.47   S.18
KROYER, Hans Ernst (1798-1879), Den
           S.4,5x,11,33
KRUFFT, Nikolaus von (1779-1818), Aus
R.3   S.28
KRULL - Little orphan Annie
           S.e
KRUMLOVSKY, Jan (1719-1763), Boh
R.5   S.c,5x,10
KRUMM, Phillip (1941-   ), USA
R.19   S.13
KRUMPHOLTZ, Jean-Baptiste (1742-1790), Boh
R.1   S.c,5x,8,10

KRUPINSKI - Polish wedding Mazurka [S.10]
  = ?KURPINSKI, Karol Kazimierz
KRUSE, Werner (20th Cent)
            S.c
KRUYF, Ton de (1937-   ), Neth
  R.1   S.10
KRYCH, Czeslaw

KRYL, Bohumir (1875-1961)
            S.24
KRYUKOV, Vladimir Nikolayevich (1902-1960), Russia
  R.1   S.10,18
KUBELÍK, Jan (1880-1940), Cz
  R.1   S.5x,24
KUBELÍK, Rafael (1914-   ), Swiss
  R.1   S.10,24
KUBIK, Gail Thompson (1914-   ), USA
  R.1   S.c,9,10,13,19,21
KUBIK, Ladislav (1947-   )
            S.c,24a
KUBÍN, Rudolf (1909-1973), Cz
  R.1   S.20,31
KUBISCH, Christina (1948-   ), Ger
  R.7   S.30
KUBIZEK, Augustin (1918-   ), Aus
  R.14   S.c
KUČERA, Václav (1929-   ), Cz
  R.1   S.c,10,24a,31
KUCHAŘ, Jan Křtitel (1751-1829), Cz
  R.1   S.c,7,8
KUCHYNKA, Vojta (1871-   ), Cz
  R.3
KÜCKEN, Friedrich Wilhelm (1810-1882), Ger
  R.1   S.e
KUEN, Koo Kwok
            S.24a
KUFFNER, Joseph (1776-1856), Ger
  R.2   S.c,10,20
KUGELMANN, Johann (c1495-1542), Ger
  R.1   S.c,10,16
KUHLAU, Friedrich (1786-1832), Den
  R.1   S.c,3-10,24,35,57
KUHLENTHAL, Fred (1908-1943)
            S.c
KUHLO, Johannes (1856-1941)
  R.2s   S.c
KUHN, Max (1896-   ), Swiss
  R.4
KUHN, Siegfried (1893-1915), Ger
  R.3   S.c

KUHNAU, Johann (1660-1722), Ger
   R.1   S.c,2-5,8-11,53
KUHNE, Ferdinand
          S.5x
KÜHNEL, August (1645-c1700), Ger
   R.1   S.c,5x,6,10
KÜHNER, Vassili (1840-1911), Ger
   R.2   S.18
KUHNERT, Oskar (1897-1969)
          S.c
KUISMA, Rainer (1931-   ), Fin
   R.30   S.c,10,40
KUKUCK, Felicitas (1914-   ), Ger
   R.7   S.c,30,52
KULIEV, Ashir (1918-   ), USSR
   R.30a   S.18
KULIEV, Mamed (1936-   )
          S.18
KULLA, Hans (1910-1956), Ger
   R.4
KULLAK, Theodor (1818-1882), Ger
   R.1   S.10
KULSHETOV, Dmitri Mikailovich (1928-   )
          S.18
KUMMER, Friedrich August (1797-1879), Ger
   R.1   S.c
KUMMER, Kaspar (1795-1870), Ger
   R.3   S.c
KUMNER - Dearie
          S.e
KUN, Arpad (1894-   ), Hun
   R.3   S.24
KUN, Sha Han
          S.24a
KUNAD, Rainer (1936-   ), Ger
   R.14   S.24a
KUNC, Bozidar (1903-1964), Yug
   R.1   S.5x,10,24a
KUNC, Jan (1883-1976), Cz
   R.1   S.7,31
KUNGSBERGER, Urbanus (15th Cent), Ger
          S.c,10,16
KUNILEID - pseud [see SAEBELMANN, Alexander]
KUNKEL, Charles [pseud: Claude MELNOTTE] (1840-1923),
   USA R.53   S.10
KÜNNEKE, Eduard (1885-1953), Ger
   R.1   S.c,5x,10
KUNST, Jos (1936-   ), Neth
   R.4

KUNTZ - Faltvakten
          S.e
KUNZEN, Frederik Ludwig Aemilius (1761-1817), Ger
    R.1   S.57
KUO, Chih-jung
          S.c
KUPFERMAN, Meyer (1926-   ), USA
    R.1   S.8-10,13,20,24a
KUPKA, Karel (1927-   ), Cz
    R.1   S.31
KUPKOVIČ, Ladislav (1936-   ), Slovak
    R.1   S.c,24a,31
KÜPPER, Leo (1935-   ), Bel
    R.25
KUPREVICH, V. (1925-   )
          S.18
KUPRIYANOV, Vladislav Porfiryevich (1936-   )
          S.18
KURBANOV, Tulkum Umarovich (1936-   ), USSR
    R.47   S.18
KURKA, Robert (1921-1957), USA
    R.1   S.c,10,13
KURMANGAZY - Balbraun (vi & p); Sary-arka
          S.24
KURPIŃSKI, Karol Kazimierz (1785-1857), Pol
    R.1   S.c,19,[?S.10 - Krupinski]
KURTÁG, György (1926-   ), Hun
    R.1   S.c,24a
KURZ, Ivan (1947-   )
          S.24a
KURZ, Siegfried (1930-   ), Ger
    R.4
KURZBACH, Paul (1902-   ), Ger
    R.1
KUSAKAWA - Yuyake koyate; Edo no komoriuta
          S.32
KUSHELEV-BEZBORODKO, Grigori
          S.18
KUSHNAREV, Khristofer Stepanovich (1890-1960), USSR
    R.14   S.18
KUSS, Margarita Ivanova (1921-   ), USSR
    R.7   S.18,24,30,52
KUSSEL - Kameraden auf See
          S.54(335)
KUSSER, Johann Sigismund (1660-1727), Hun
    R.1   S.c
KUTAVICHYUS, B. (1932-   )
          S.18,24a
KUTSCHERA, Alois (1919-   ), Aus
    R.3   S.24

KUTZER, Ernst (1918-   ), Ger
  R.4   S.c
KUULA, Toivo (1883-1918), Fin
  R.1   S.c,5x,24a,40
KUULBERG, Mati (1947-   )
           S.18,24a
KUUSISTO, Ilkka Taneli (1933-   ), Fin
  R.4   S.40
KUUSISTO, Taneli (1905-   ), Fin
  R.1   S.c,40
KUZDO, Victor (1859-1966), Hun
  R.39   S.24
KUZHAMYAROV, Kuddus (1918-   ), USSR
  R.14   S.18
KUZNETSOV, Ivan (1919-   )
           S.18
KUZNIK, Jan Thomas (c1716-1786)
           S.10
KVANDAL, Johan (1919-   ), Nor
  R.1   S.c,24a,40,51
KVAPIL, Jaroslav (1892-1959), Cz
  R.1   S.31
KVARTIN, Savel
           S.c
KVECH, Otomar (1950-   ), Cz
  R.14   S.24a
KVERNADZE, Bidzina Alexandrovich (1928-   ), USSR
  R.1   S.18,24,52
KYES, M. (fl 1790), USA - Crucifixion

KYMLICKA, Milan (1936-   ), Can
  R.81
KYNASTON, Trent (1946-   ), USA
  R.19   S.10,13,22
KYOKU, Chideri No
           S.24a
KYROU (Chamass-Kyrou), Mireille (20th Cent), Greece
  R.7   S.52
KYRVER, Boris Voldemarovich (1917-   ), USSR
  R.14   S.18
LAANEPYLD, Nyeme (1913-   )
           S.18
LA BARBARA, Joan (1947-   ), USA
  R.19   S.13,30,52
LA BARRE, Joseph de [Chabanceau de la Barre]
  (1633-1678), Fr   R.1   S.c
LA BARRE, Michel de [Chabanceau de la Barre]
  (c1675-1743/44), Fr R.1   S.c,3,4,5x,8,10
LA BARRE, Pierre de
           S.32

LABARRE, Théodore (1805-1870), Fr
  R.1   S.c,10
L'ABBÉ, le fils [Joseph-Barnabé SAINT-SÉVIN]
  (1727-1803), Fr   R.1   S.2-5,24[Abbé]
LABITZKY, August (1832-1903), Boh
  R.1   S.24
LABITZKY, Joseph (1802-1881), Boh
  R.1   S.c
LABLER, Frantisek (1842-1863) [?]
          S.5x
LABRIC, Pierre

LABRIOLA, Pietro - Voga, voga

LABROCA, Mario (1896-1973), It
  R.1   S.4,5
LABUNSKI, Feliks Roderyk (1892-1979), USA
  R.1   S.10,13
LACALLE, Joseph M.
          S.c,10
LACAMBRA-MATÉO, F. - Chant du soir (Rêverie) (vi & p)
          S.24
LACERDA, Francisco (1869-1934), Port
  R.1
LACERDA, Osvaldo (1927-   ), Brazil
  R.1   S.c,10,32
LACERNA, Estacio de [see SERNA, Estacio de la]
LACHAPELLE, Guy (1931-   ), Can
  R.81
LACHENMANN, Helmut Friedrich (1935-   ), Ger
  R.30
LACHNER, Franz Paul (1803-1890), Ger
  R.1   S.c,10
LACHNER, Ignaz (1807-1895), Ger
  R.1   S.10
LACHNER, Simon
          S.46
LACHNER, Vinzenz (1811-1893), Ger
  R.1   S.c
LACHNITH, Ludwig Wenzel (1746-1820), Boh
  R.1   S.c,24
LACOMBE, Paul (1837-1927), Fr
  R.1   S.24
LÂCOME [Lâcome d'Estalenx], Paul Jean Jacques (1838-1920),
  Fr R.1
LACOSTE, Louis de (c1675-c1755), Fr
  R.1   S.4,5x
LA COUPELLE, Pierre de (13th Cent)
  R.5

LA COUR, Niels Jørgen (1944-   ), Den
  R.14
LA CROIX, Adrien de (17th Cent), Fr

LA CROIX, Antoine (1756-1806), Fr
  R.1   S.24
LA CROIX, Pierre [see PETRUS de CRUCE]
LACY, Steve - pseud [ie Steven LAKRITZ] (1934-   ), USA
  R.4   S.13
LACY, Thomas Alexander (1853-1931)

LADERMAN, Ezra (1924-   ), USA
  R.1   S.9,10,13,24a
LADMIRAULT, Paul (1877-1944), Fr
  R.1   S.24a
LADSCHECK, Max Leopold Henry (1889-   ), Ger
  R.14   S.24
LADYSLAW z GIELNIOWA (d.1505)
             S.c,16
L'AFFILARD, Michel (c1656-1708), Fr
  R.1   S.4,5x
LAFON, Henri
             S.24
LAFORGE, Frank (1879-1953), USA
  R.19   S.5x,10,11,13,24
LAGERCRANTZ, Th.
             S.e
LAGIDZE, Revaz Illyich (1921-   ), USSR
  R.1   S.18
LA GROTTE, Nicolas de (1530-c1600), Fr
  R.1   S.c,4,5x,8,10,11,14
LA GUERRE, Elisabeth
  [see JACQUET de LA GUERRE, Elizabeth-Claude]
LA HAYE - Orchésographie; Hexachord (lute)
             S.16
LAHUSEN, Christian (1886-1975), Ger
  R.14   S.c
LAIDLAW, Robert USA
             S.13
LAIRD of COLL [see MACLEAN, John Garve]
LAJTHA, László (1892-1963), Hun
  R.1   S.c,9,10
LAKE, Ian Thomson (1935-   ), Eng
  R.14   S.10
LAKE, Lawrence (1943-   ), Can

LAKE, Mayhew Lester (1879-1955), USA
  R.23   S.13,54(325,56)
LAKRITZ, Steven [see LACY, Steve - pseud]

LALANDE, Michel-Richard de (1657-1726), Fr
    R.1   S.c,4,5,8-10
LALLIET, Theodore (1837-1892)
             S.c
LALLOUETTE, Jean François (1651-1728), Fr
    R.1   S.c
LALO, Edouard (1823-1892), Fr
    R.1   S.c,1-11,18,24,42
LAM, Doming
             S.24a
LAMA, Gaetano (1886-   ), It
    R.10s   S.10,24
LAMARE - La passion
             S.1x
LA MAREILLE, X. - Ce que c'est que un drapeau
             S.e
LAMB - Cradle song
             S.5x
LAMB, John David (1935-   ), USA
    R.19   S.10,13,22
LAMB, Joseph Francis (1887-1960), USA
    R.1   S.10,24a
LAMB, Robert

LAMBE, Walter (15th Cent), Eng
    R.1   S.c,10,16
LAMBERT, Constant (1905-1951), Eng
    R.1   S.c,2-5,8,9,11
LAMBERT, Edward Frank (?-1925)
    R.3   S.e
LAMBERT, Louis - pseud [see GILMORE, Patrick Sarsfield]
LAMBERT, Michel (1610-1696), Fr
    R.1   S.c
LAMBERT de MONTE [see MONTE, Lambert de]
LAMBRANZI, Gregorio (18th Cent), It
    R.1   S.c
LAMBRO, Phillip (1935-   ), USA
    R.19   S.10,13
LA MONTAINE, John (1920-   ), USA
    R.1   S.7,10,12,13,24a,25,27
LAMORETTI, Pietro Maria (fl 1621), It
    R.5   S.c
LA MOTA, Antonio Duran de
             S.10
LAMOTE de GRIGNON (see note)
             S.54(354)
LAMPE, J. Bodewalt (1869-1929), USA
    R.23   S.54(321,22,25,31)
LAMPE, John Frederick (c1703-1751), Ger
    R.1   S.10

LAMPS - Unde Tom's cabin
        S.54(362)
LAMPUGNANI, Giovanni Battista (1706-1786), It
    R.1   S.c,10,25,27
LAMURAGLIA, Nicolás (1896-   ), Arg
    R.26   S.46
LANCASTER, H. - Lonely mill
        S.54(338)
LANCEN, Serge Jean (1922-   ), Fr
    R.14   S.c
LANCHBERY, John (1923-   ), Eng
    R.1   S.c,9
LANCIANI, Pierre (fl 1896-99), Bel
        S.1x
LANDGRAF von HESSEN
   [see MORITZ, Landgraf von Hessen-Kassel]
LANDI, Stefano (1586/87-1639), It
    R.1   S.8,10
LANDINI, Francesco (c1325-1397), It
    R.1   S.c,4,5x,7,8,10,11,14,16
LANDOWKSA, Wanda (1879-1959), Pol
    R.1   S.6,7,10,30,52

LANDOWSKI, Marcel (1915-   ), Fr
    R.1   S.c,5x,8,10
LANDRÉ, Guillaume (1905-1968), Neth
    R.1   S.4,10,20
LANDRY, Richard Miles (1938-   ), USA
    R.19   S.13
LANDSMAN, Simon (1888-1960)
        S.c
LANE, Burton (1912-   ), USA
    R.1   S.9
LANE, Gerald M., Eng
    R.44   S.24
LANE, Philip Thomas (1950-   ), Eng
    R.80   S.c
LANE, Richard (1933-   ), USA
    R.19   S.10,13,20
LANE-WILSON, Henry [see WILSON, Henry Lane]
LANES, Mathieu (1660-1725), Fr
        S.c,53
LANG, Craig Sellar (1891-1971), Eng
    R.14   S.c,13
LANG, Hans (1897-1968), Ger
    R.4
LANG, Hans (1908-   ), Aus
    R.4   S.c
LANG, Heinrich (1858-1919), Ger
    R.3   S.c

LANG, Hermann (1883-   ), Swiss
   R.14
LÁNG, István (1933-   ), Hun
   R.1   S.c,10,18,20,24a
LANG, Johann Georg (1722-1798), Ger
   R.1   S.c,24
LANG, Josephine (1815-1880), Ger
   R.1   S.c,30,52
LANG, Margaret Ruthven (1867-1972), USA
   R.7,14   S.10,13,52
LANG, Philip Emil Joseph (1911-   ), USA
   R.49   S.13[Lang, P.F.]
LANGA, Francisco Soto de [see SOTO de LANGA, Francisco]
LANGE, Daniel de (1841-1918), Neth
   R.3
LANGE, Gustav (1830-1889), Ger
   R.3   S.c,10,24
LANGE, Samuel de (1840-1911), Neth
   R.3   S.e
LANGE-MÜLLER, Peter Erasmus (1850-1926), Den
   R.1   S.c,4,5,7,8,10,11,24a,33,35,57
LANGENAU, Johann Leonhard von (15th Cent), Ger
   R.5   S.c,5x,11
LANGENUS, Gustave (1883-1957), USA
   R.14   S.20
LANGER, Alfons [pseud: Alfons JINDRA] (1908-   ), Cz
   R.4   S.31
LANGER, Gustav
             S.24

LANGEY, Otto (1851-1922), USA
   R.4
LANGFORD, Arthur (20th Cent), Eng
             S.c
LANGFORD, Gordon - pseud [ie Gordon COLMAN] (1930-   )
   Eng R.85   S.c,24a,55
LANGGAARD, Rued (1893-1952), Den
   R.1   S.c,24a,40
LANGLAIS, Jean (1907-   ), Fr
   R.1   S.5x,7-10
LANGLEY, Edith Thompson - Cinderella: All clear out of
   the park [?]
LANGLOIS, Théo (1909-   ), Bel
   R.14   S.20
LANGTON, Stephen (d.1228)

LANGWORTHY - Heavenly gales
             S.54(331)
LANIER, Nicholas (1588-1666), Eng
   R.1   S.c

LANIER, Sidney (1842-1881), USA
   R.1
LANNER, Joseph (1801-1843), Aus
   R.1   S.c,4,5,7,8,10,24
LANNOY, Heinrich Eduard Freiherr von (1787-1853), Aus
   R.2   S.c
LANSKY, Paul (1944-   ),USA
   R.19   S.10,13,24a
LANSVERYNS - Redis-moi toujours
          S.5x
LANTIER, Pierre Louis (1910-   ), Fr
   R.14   S.10,18,22
LANTINS, Arnold de (fl 1430), Franco-Flem
   R.1   S.c,3,4,5x,8,10,11,14,16,41
LANTINS, Hugo (fl 1420-30), Franco-Flem
   R.1   S.c,16
LANZA, Alcides (1929-   ), Arg
   R.1   S.46
LAPARRA, Raoul (1876-1943), Fr
   R.1   S.c,5,7,8,10,43
LAPHAM, Claude (1890-1957), USA
          S.1x,13
LAPICIDA, Erasmus (c1440-1547), Ger
   R.1   S.c,5x,10,16
LAPORTE, André (1931-   ), Bel
   R.14
LAPPI, Pietro (c1575-1630), It
   R.1   S.c,10
LARA, Augustín (1900-1970), Mex (see note)
   R.1   S.10,39
LARCHET, John Francis (1884-1967), Ire
   R.1   S.10,24,49
LAREN, Derek - pseud
   [see EPIN de GROOT, Else-Antonia van]
LARENTO, Jean
          S.24

LARGATO (16th Cent) - D'aquel fraire flaco
          S.c
LARICHEV, Yevgeni Dmitrievich (1934-   )
          S.18
LARMANJAT, Jacques (1878-1952), Fr [?]
   R.14   S.1x
LARRAÑAGA, José (d.1806), Sp
   R.104   S.c
LARREGLA, Carlos

LARREGLA, Joaquin (1865-1945), Sp
   R.3   S.5x,10
LARRUGA - Di mi Holanda, La reja
          S.e

LARSEN, Nils (1888-1937), Nor
  R.4   S.5x
LARSSON, Lars-Erik (1908-   ), Sweden
  R.1   S.c,4-8,10,19,24,38,40,56
LA RUE, Pierre de (c1460-1518), Flem
  R.1   S.c,4,8-11,14-16
LASALA, Angel E. (1914-   ), Arg
  R.26   S.10,32,46
LASANSKY, Julia Arg
           S.46
LASCEUX, Guillaume (1740-1829), Fr
  R.5   S.c,10,53
LASCH, Abe
           S.54(356)
LASERNA - El cordero perdido
           S.14
LASERNA, Blas de (1751-1816), Sp
  R.1   S.c,2,4,5,7,8,10,11,24,28
LASHWOOD - Fol the rol lol
           S.e
LAS INFANTAS, Fernando de
  [see INFANTAS, Ferdinand de las]
LASKA, Gustav (1847-1928), Boh [?]
  R.2   S.10
LASRY, Jacques (1918-   ), Fr
  R.14   S.c,9
LASS, Boris
           S.24
LASSEN, Eduard (1830-1904), Bel
  R.1   S.2-4,24
LASSON, Per (1859-1883), Nor
  R.3   S.c
LASSUS, Ferdinand de (c1560-1609), Ger
  R.1   S.c
LASSUS, Orlande de (1532-1594), Franco-Flem
  R.1   S.c,1-11,14-16,18,36,41
LASSUS, Rudolph de (c1563-1625), Ger
  R.1   S.c
LASZLO, Akos
           S.24
LASZLO, Alexander (1895-1970), USA
  R.19   S.7,10
LATANN, Karl (1840-1888), Ger
  R.3   S.54(327,38)
LATEEF, Yusef (1920-   ), USA
  R.19   S.10,13
LATHAM, William Peters (1917-   ), USA
  R.19   S.13
LATHIÈRE - La gitano
           S.54(329)

LATILLA, Gaetano (1711-1788), It
R.1   S.5x
LA TOMBELLE, Fernand de (1854-1928), Fr
R.1   S.2,3
LA TOUCHE, Edmond D.

LATOUR, Pierre (19th Cent), USA
           S.10
LATOUR, T. (fl 1815), Eng
           S.10
LATRE Petite, Jean de [see DE LATRE, Petit Jean]
LATROBE, Christian Ignatius (1758-1836), Eng
R.1   S.10
LATZELSBERGER, Josef (1849-1914), Aus
R.2   S.c
LAU, Heinz (1925-1975), Ger
R.1   S.c
LAUB, Ferdinand (1832-1875), Cz
R.1   S.24
LAUB, Thomas (1852-1927), Den
R.1   S.4,5x,33,35,57
LAUBER, Anne Marianne (1943-   ), Can
R.7   S.52
LAUBER, Joseph (1864-1952), Swiss
R.2   S.c
LAUCHERY, Albert (fl 1800)
           S.c
LAUDER, Harry Maclennan (1870-1950), Scot
R.1   S.54(314)
LAUDER, James (1535-1595), Scot
R.109   S.c
LAUDO - Ave mitis, ave pia (v)
           S.10
LAUGHTON, Gail
           S.30
LAUMENSKENE, E. (1880-   )
           S.18,24
LAURENCINI (17th Cent) [?see LORENZINI fl c1570-71]
LAURENDEAU, Louis Phillipe (1861-1916), Can
R.31   S.54(326)
LAURENTIUS de Florentia [see LORENZO de FIRENZE]
LAURENTIUS the ELDER (fl 1500)
           S.c,16
LAURENZI, Filiberto (1619/20->1651), It
R.1   S.10
LAURICELLA, Remo (1912-   ), Eng
R.14   S.24
LAURIDSEN, Laurids (1882-1946), Den
R.4   S.24a,33,57

LAURISHKUS, Max (1876-1929), Ger
   R.2   S.18
LAURO, Antonio (1917-   ), Ven
   R.14   S.c,10,18,32,39
LAURUSHAS, Vitautes Antano (1930-   ), USSR
   R.14   S.18,24a
LAUSCHNER - War songs of the boys in blue
          S.54(364)
LAUTENSCHLÄGER - Youth and vigor   ;
          S.54(367)
LAUTENSCHLÄGER, Willi (1880-1949), Ger
   [pseud: José ARMANDOLA, Edwin HALLER, A. NIPPON,
   Udo TURMER, James WANSON]
   R.4   S.24a[Armandola]
LAVAGNE, André (1913-   ), Fr
   R.14   S.4,5,8
LA VALLE, Deanne (20th Cent), USA
          S.52
LAVALLE, Paul (1908-   ), USA
   R.23   S.13,54(315,16,49)
LAVALLÉE, Calixa (1842-1891), Can
   R.1   S.9
LAVATER, Louis (1867-   ), Australia
   R.3   S.5x
LAVDAS, Antonis (1926-   )
          S.c
LAVIGNA, Vincenzo (1776-1836), It
   R.1   S.c
LAVIGNE, Ernest Tessier (dit) (1851-1909), Can
   R.31
LAVIGNE, Philibert de (fl 1739), Fr
   R.5   S.c,10
LAVILLA MUNARRIZ, Félix (1928-   ), Sp
   R.104   S.c,10,39
LAVIN, Carlos (1883-1962), Chile
   R.1   S.24
LA VIOLETTE, Wesley (1894-1978), USA
   R.19   S.7,10,13
LAVISTA, Mario (1943-   ), Mex
   R.4   S.24a
LAVOTTA, János (1764-1820), Hun
   R.1   S.5x
LAVOYE, Louis (1878-   ), Bel
   R.13   S.24a
LAVRY, Marc (1903-1967), Isr
   R.1   S.8,10,24
LAW, Andrew (1749-1821), USA
   R.50   S.10,47
LAWES, Henry (1596-1662), Eng
   R.1   S.c,5x,7,10,24,32

LAWES, William (1602-1645), Eng
   R.1   S.c,8-10
LAWRENCE, Harold (1906-   ), USA
   R.23   S.10,13
LAWSON, Malcolm Leonard (1849-   ), Eng
   R.44   S.e
LAYMAN, Pamela (20th Cent), USA
   R.7   S.13,24a,30,52
LAYOLLE, Francois de (1492-c1540), Fr
   R.1   S.c,10,16
LAYTON, Billy Jim (1924-   ), USA
   R.1   S.10,13,24
LAZÁR, Filip (1894-1936), Rum
   R.1   S.3,5x,10,24
LAZARE-LEVY, M. [see LEVY, Lazare]
LAZAREV, Eduard Leonidovich (1935-   ), USSR
   R.14   S.18
LAZARIN, (d.1653), Fr
   R.5   S.8,14
LAZAROF, Henri (1932-   ), USA
   R.1   S.9,10,13,23,24
LAZARUS, Daniel (1898-1964), Fr
   R.1   S.c,8,10
LAZARUS, Henry (1815-1895), Eng
   R.1   S.c
LAZZARI, Ferdinando Antonio (1678-1754), It
   R.1   S.c
LAZZARI, Sylvio (1857-1944), Fr
   R.2   S.c,5x,24a
LE, Yang Shan
            S.24a
LEA, William (1928-   ), Can

LEACH, Rowland (1885-   ), USA
   R.19   S.10,12,13
LEAF, Robert, USA
            S.10,13
LEAUMONT, Chevalier de (fl 1795-9), USA
            S.7,10,47
LEBARON, Alice Anne (1953-   ), USA
   R.7   S.30,52
LEBARRE, Theodore

LEBEAU, Alice - pseud [see HENRIKSON, Alice]
LEBÈGUE, Nicolas-Antoine (c1631-1702), Fr
   R.1   S.c,3,5,7,8,10,53
LEBEL, Firmin (d.1573), Fr
   R.1   S.2,3,5x
LE BLANC (18th Cent) - La chasse (vi & continuo)
   R.5   S.24a

LE BLANC - La complainte du desepere
        S.c
LE BLANC, Arthur (1906-   ), Can
  R.31   S.24
LE BLANC, Didier (fl 1578-84), Fr
  R.1   S.c

LE BORNE, Fernand (1862-1929), Bel
  R.2   S.c
LEBOW, Leonard Stanley (1929-   ), USA
  R.23   S.10,13
LEBRUN, Franziska (1756-1791), Ger
  R.1   S.c,24a,30,52
LEBRUN, Ludwig August (1752-1790), Ger
  R.1   S.c
LEBRUN, Paul Henri Josef (1861-1920), Bel
  R.3   S.41
LEBZELTER, Shipen

LE CAINE, Hugh (1914-   ), Can
  R.1   S.10
LE CAMUS, Sébastien (c1610-1677), Fr
  R.1   S.c
LECHNER, Leonhard (c1553-1606), Ger
  R.1   S.c,8,10,14-16
LECHTHALER, Josef (1891-1941), Aus
  R.2   S.c
LECLAIR, Jean-Marie [l'aîné] (1697-1764), Fr
  R.1   S.c,1-5,7-11,18,19,21,22,24
LECLAIR, Jean-Marie [le cadet] (1703-1777), Fr
  R.1
LECLERC, Michelle (1939-   ), Fr
        S.c,10,52
LECOCQ, Charles (1832-1918), Fr
  R.1   S.4,6-10,18,54(328)
LECOCQ, François (fl 1729), Fr
  R.5   S.c
LECOCQ, Maurice - pseud [see GOBBAERTS, Jean Louis]
LECUONA, Ernesto (1896-1963), Cuba
  R.1   S.c,4,5x,7-10,32,39
LEDENYOV, Roman (1930-   ) USSR
  R.1   S.18,23
LEDERER, Deszo (1858-   )
        S.24
LEDERER, Francis
        S.24a
LEDERER, Joseph (1733-1796), Ger
  R.1   S.c,53
LEDESMA, Dámaso (1868-1928), Sp
  R.1   S.10

LEDUC, Jacques (1932-   ), Bel
   R.1   S.c
LEDUC, Simon (<1748-1777), Fr
   R.1   S.c,24a
LEE, Dai-Keong (1915-   ), Hawaii
   R.14   S.4,9,13
LEE, Dorothy
             S.e
LEE, Eugene (1942-   ), Korea/USA
   R.19   S.13
LEE, Noel (1924-   ), USA
   R.19   S.10,13,24a
LEE, Norman (1895-   ), USA

   R.19   S.13
LEE, Sebastian (1805-1887), Ger
   R.1   S.c
LEE, Young Ja (1931-   ), Korea
             S.52
LEEDY, Douglas (1938-   ), USA
   R.19   S.13
LEEMANS, P. - March officielle
             S.54(341)
LEES, Benjamin (1924-   ), USA
   R.1   S.10,13,24a
LEESON, Joseph Frederick (c1806-1862), Scot
   R.44   S.e
LEETHERLAND, Thomas (fl 1599-1625), Eng
             S.c,10,16
LEEUW, Cornelius Janszoon de (c1613-c1662), Neth
   R.1   S.c
LEEUW, Reinbert de (1938-   ), Neth
   R.4
LEEUW, Ton de (1926-   ), Neth
   R.1   S.c,10
LeFANU, Nicola (1947-   ), Eng
   R.1   S.c,52
LEFÉBURE-WÉLY, Louis James Alfred (1817-1869), Fr
   R.2   S.c,10
LEFEBVRE, Charles Edouard (1843-1917), Fr
   R.1   S.c,8,10,21
LEFEBVRE, Claude (1931-   ), Fr
             S.c
LEFEBVRE, Jacques (17th Cent), Fr
   R.1   S.c,10
LEFEGUEUX, Francois (16th Cent)
             S.c
LEFEUVRE, Guy
             S.e
LEFÈVERE, Kamiel (1888-1972), Bel
   R.14   S.c

LEFÈVRE, Jean Xavier (1763-1829), Fr
   R.1   S.c,5x,6,19,20
LEFEVRE, Joseph
           S.4
LE FEVRE, Monsieur
           S.c
LEFFLOTH, Johann Matthias (1705-1731), Ger
   R.1   S.c,10,24a
LEFORT, Augustin (1852-   )
           S.24
LE GALLIENNE, Dorian (1915-1963), Australia
   R.1   S.c,10,29,37
LEGAY, Marcel
           S.e
LEGE, Gunter (1935-   ), Ger
   R.4
LEGINSKA, Ethel - pseud [ie Ethel LIGGINS] (1886-1970),
   Eng R.7   S.10,13,52
LEGLEY, Victor (1915-   ), Bel
   R.1   S.7,8,10,20,24,36
LEGNANI, Luigi (1790-1877), It
   R.1   S.c,10
LEGOUPIL, Jean (1945-   )
           S.c
LEGRAND, Michel (1932-   ), Fr
   R.1   S.c
LEGRANT, Guillaume (fl 1418-56), Fr
   R.1   S.c,16
LEGRANT, Johannes (fl c1420-40), Fr
   R.1   S.c,10,16
LEGRENZI, Giovanni (1626-1690), It
   R.1   S.c,2-5,7,8,10,11,24,25,27
LEGUERNEY, Jacques (1906-   ), Fr
   R.1   S.7,8,10,24,25,27
LEHÁR, Franz (1870-1948), Hun
   R.1   S.c,2-11,24,42,43,54(343,63)
LE HEURTEUR, Guillaume (fl 1530-45), Fr
   R.1   S.c,10,14,15
LEHMANN, Andreas
           S.c
LEHMANN, Hans-Ulrich (1937-   ), Swiss
   R.1   S.c,10,20
LEHMANN, Liza (1862-1918), Eng
   R.1   S.c,1-4,5x,10,52
LEHMBERG - El Puerto
           S.5x
LEHNER, Leo (1900-   ), Aus
   R.4   S.10
LEHNHARDT, Julius (1837-1913)

LEHRER, Thomas Andrew (1928-   ), USA
   R.23   S.9
LEHRNDORFER, Franz (1928-   ), Aus
   R.4   S.c
LEICH, Roland (1911-   ), USA
   R.19   S.13
LEICHTLING, Alan (1947-   ), USA
   R.19   S.9,13
LEIDESDORF, Maximilian Joseph (1787-1840), Aus
   [Publisher] R.1   S.c
LEIDING [Leyding], Georg Dietrich (1664-1710), Ger
   R.1   S.c,5x,10,53
LEIDZEN, Erik (1894-1962), USA
   R.19   S.10,13,54(318,20-22,31),55
LEIFS, Jón (1899-1968), Iceland
   R.1   S.c,10,40
LEIGH, Frank
               S.24
LEIGH, Mitch (1928-   ), USA
   R.1   S.10,13
LEIGH, Walter (1905-1942), Eng
   R.1   S.c,5
LEIGHTER - My lady Chlo
               S.e
LEIGHTHON, William (c1565-1622), Eng
   R.1   S.c
LEIGHTON, Kenneth (1929-   ), Eng
   R.1   S.c,10,24a
LEIMER, Kurt (1920-1974), Ger
   R.4   S.8
LEINBACH, Edward William (1823-1901), USA
   R.1   S.10,47
LEISRING, Volckmar (1588-1637), Ger
   R.1   S.7,10,14
LEITE, Antonio da Silva (1759-1833), Port
   R.3
LEIVISKA, Helvi Lemmiki (1902-   ), Fin
   R.7   S.52
LE JEUNE, Claude (c1528-1600), Fr
   R.1   S.c,2-11,14,16,32,53
LEJEUNE, Jacques (1940-   ), Fr
   R.4   S.c
LEKEU, Guillaume (1870-1894), Bel
   R.1   S.c,2-6,8-11,24,36,41
LELEN, Jean - La Chanson et la dance c1530
   [? see LUPI, Johannes]
LEMAIGRE, Edm
               S.c,10
LEMAIRE, Gaston Eugène (1854/55-1927/28), Fr (see note)
   R.4   S.24

LEMAIRE, Louis (1693/94-c1750), Fr
   R.1
LE MAISTRE, Matthaeus (c1505-<1577), Neth
   R.1   S.8
LEMAN, Albert Semyonovich (1915-   ), USSR
   R.14   S.18
LEMARE, Edwin Henry (1865-1934), Eng
   R.2   S.c,12,13,24
LEMARE, Jules
           S.10
LEMBA, Artur Gustavovich (1885-1963), USSR
   R.14   S.18,24a
LEMBCKE, Gustav Adolph (1844-1899), Den
   R.30   S.5x,33
LEMCKERT, Johann (1940-   ), Neth
   R.25   S.c
LEMELAND, Aubert (1932-   )
           S.c
LEMLIN, Lorenze (c1495->1549), Ger
   R.1   S.c,8,10,14,16
LEMMENS, Jaak Nikolaas (1823-1881), Bel
   R.1   S.c,10,41
LEMMIK, Heino (1931-   ), Est
   R.58   S.18
LEMON, Laura G. (1866-1924), Can
   R.7   S.10
LEMOYNE, Jean Baptiste (1751-1796), Fr
   R.1   S.10
LENDVAI, Erwin (1882-1949), Hun
   R.2   S.c,1
LENDVAY, Kamilló (1928-   ), Hun
   R.1   S.c,9,10
LENEL, Ludwig (1914-   ), Fr/USA
   R.19   S.10

LENGHAMER, Gaudentius (1699-1733)
   R.5   S.c
LENGSFELDER, Hans - pseud [Harry LENK, Hans FELDER,
   Günther BREHM] (1903-1979), USA
   R.4   S.9,13
LENK, Harry - pseud [see LENGSFELDER, Hans]
LENNARD, E.D. (Barret), Lady
           S.e
LENNON, John (1940-1980), Eng
   R.1   S.10
LENNOX - The dear home songs
           S.e
LENO - McGlochell's men
           S.e
LENOIR, Jean - pseud [see NEUBURGER, Jean]

LENORMAND, René (1846-1932), Fr
    R.3   S.1x
LENSKY, Alexander Stepanovich (1910-   ), USSR
    R.14   S.18
LENTON, John (17th Cent), Eng
    R.1   S.5x,7,10
LENTZ, Daniel (1942-   ), USA
    R.19   S.10,13
LENTZ, J. N. [?Nicholas] (fl 1761), Neth
    R.5   S.10
LENZ, F. - Concert mazurka (vi & p)
             S.24
LENZBERG - Hungarian rag
             S.54(333)
LEO, Leonardo (1694-1744), It
    R.1   S.c,5,8-10,24,28
LEON - Le vieux farceur
             S.e
LEON, Juane (16th Cent)
             S.14
LEON, Tania Justina (1944-), USA
    R.7   S.52
LEONARD, Clair (1901-   ), USA
    R.4   S.10,13
LEONARD, Harold
             S.24,19
LEONARD, Hubert (1819-1890), Bel
    R.1   S.24
LEONARDA, Sister Isabella (c1620-1700), It
    R.7   S.52
LEONARDO, Umberto (1954-   )
             S.24a
LEONCAVALLO, Ruggero (1857-1919), It
    R.1   S.c,1-11,18,24,34,42,44
LEONCHIK, Svetlana Gavrilovna (1939-   ), USSR
    R.7   S.18,52
LEONHARDT, Andreas (1866-   ), Aus
    R.3   S.10,54(311,41)
LEONI, Franco (1864-1949), It
    R.1   S.c
LÉONIN (fl c1163-90), Fr

    R.1   S.c,2-5,7,8,10,11,14,16,53
LEONTEV, Nikolai
             S.18
LEONTOVYCH, Mykola Dmytrovich (1877-1921), Russia
    R.1   S.c
LEOPOLD I, Emperor (1640-1705), Aus
    R.1   S.c,8,10,24a
LEOPOLD, Bohuslav (1888-1956), Cz
    R.18   S.31

LEOPOLDI, Hermann
        S.10
LEOPOLITA, Marcin (d.1589), Pol
  R.1   S.c,16,53
LEPIN, Anatoli Yakovlevich (1907-   ), USSR
  R.14   S.18
LEPKOJ
        S.5x
LEPLAE, Claire (20th Cent), Bel
        S.52
LEPLANC - pseud [see LOMBARDO, Carlo]
LEPNURM, Hugo (1914-   ), Est
  R.58   S.18,24
LE POLONAISE, Jacob [see REYS, Jacob]
LEPSÖE, Albert
        S.e
LEPSÖE, Christoffer (1859-1914), Nor
  R.30a   S.e
LERDAHL, Alfred (1943-   ), USA
  R.19   S.10,13,24a
LERICH, Pierre (20th Cent), Fr
        S.c
LERINCKX, Jos (1920-   ), Bel
  R.25
LE ROUX, Gaspard (d c1706), Fr
  R.1   S.c,9,10
LE ROUX, Maurice (1923-   ), Fr
  R.1   S.9
LEROUX, Xavier (1863-1919), Fr
  R.1   S.10,24
LE ROY, Adrien (c1520-1598), Fr
  R.1   S.c,5x,7,8,10,14,16
LE SAGE de RICHÉE, Philipp Franz (fl c1695), Ger
  R.1   S.c,32
LESCHETIZKY, Theodor (1830-1915), Pol
  R.1   S.5x,10
LESCUREL, Jehannot de [see JEHANNOT de l'ESCUREL]
LESEMANN, Frederick (1936-   ), USA
  R.19   S.10,13,20
LESLIE, Edgar (1885-1976), USA
  R.23   S.54(312,18)
LESLIE, Henry David (1822-1896), Eng
  R.1   S.5x,10,28
LESLIE-SMITH, Kenneth (1897-   )

LESSARD, John (1920-   ), USA
  R.1   S.9,10,13,24a
LESSEL, Franciszek (c1780-1838), Pol
  R.1   S.c
LESSO-VALERO, P - pseud [see PLESSOW, Erich]

L'ESTOCART, Paschal de (?1539->1584), Fr
   R.1   S.14,16
LE SUEUR, Jean-François (1760-1837), Fr
   R.1   S.c,8
LESUR, Daniel Jean Ives [see DANIEL LESUR, Jean Ives]
LETELIER, Alfonso (1912-   ), Chile
   R.1   S.8,10
LETHIÈRE, Charles
            S.19,21
LETONDAL, Arthur John (1869-1956), Can
   R.14
LETOREY - La fontaine de Carouet
            S.5x
LEUTJENS, Christopher
            S.24
LEVA, Enrico de (1867-1955), It
   R.2   S.e
LEVADÉ, Charles Gaston (1869-1948), Fr
   R.2   S.c,5x,10
LEVANT, Oscar (1906-1972), USA
   R.1   S.5x,11,13
LEVERIDGE, Richard (1670/71-1758), Eng
   R.1   S.5x
LEVEY, William Charles (1837-1894), Eng
   R.44   S.e
LEVI - Happy days
            S.54(331)
LEVI, Hermann (1839-1900), Ger
   R.1   S.e
LEVI, Natalia Nikolaevna (1901-1972), USSR
   R.7,14   S.18,52
LEVIEV, Minasai (1912-   ), USSR
   R.47   S.18
LEVINA, Zara Alexandrovna (1906/07-1976), USSR
   R.7,14   S.18,24a,52
LEVINAS, Michael (1949-   )
            S.c
LEVINE - No, no, I don't wish that (v)
            S.10
LE VINIER, Guillaume [see GUILLAUME li VINIER]
LEVISTER, Alonzo (fl 1953)
   R.200   S.9
LEVITCH, Leon (1927-   ), USA
   R.19   S.9,13,20,24a
LEVITIN, Yuri Abramovich (1912-   ), USSR
   R.4   S.18,24
LEVITZKI, Mischa (1898-1941), USA
   R.23   S.c,5x,10,13
LEVY, Alexandre (1864-1892), Brazil
   R.1   S.e

LEVY, Burt Jerome (1936-   ), USA
    R.19   S.10,13
LEVY, Frank (1930-   ), USA
    R.19   S.10,13,20
LEVY, John H.
                 S.24a
LEVY, Jules (1838-1903), Eng
    R.53
LÉVY, Lazare (1882-1964), Bel
    R.4   S.1x
LEVY, Marvin David (1932-   ), USA
    R.1   S.10,13
LEVY, Sarah (1908-   )
                 S.30
LEVY, Sol Paul (1881-1920), USA
    R.23   S.24
LEWALLEN, James C. (1926-   ), USA
    R.23   S.10
LEWANDOWSKI, Louis (1821-1894), Pol
    R.2   S.c
LEWENTHAL, Raymond (1926-   ), USA
    R.1   S.10
LEWER (fl 1800), USA
                 S.10,47
LEWICKI, Ernst (1863-1937), Ger
    R.2   S.10
LEWIN, David (1933-   ), USA
    R.4   S.10,13
LEWIN, Frank (1925-   ), USA
    R.19   S.13
LEWIN-RICHTER, Andres (1937-   ), Sp
    R.80   S.10,13
LEWIS, Al (1901-1967), USA
    R.23   S.10
LEWIS, John Aaron (1920-   ), USA
    R.1   S.9,10
LEWIS, Malcolm (1925-   ), USA
    R.19   S.10,13
LEWIS, Merills (1908-1980), USA
    R.25   S.13
LEWIS, Peter Tod (1932-   ), USA
    R.19   S.10,13
LEWIS, Robert Hall (1926-   ), USA
    R.1   S.10,13,24
LEWIS, Ted - pseud [see FRIEDMAN, Theodore Leopold]
LEWKOVITCH, Bernhard (1927-   ), Den
    R.1   S.8,33,40
LEY, Henry George (1887-1962), Eng
    R.1   S.c

LEYBACH, Ignace Xavier Joseph (1817-1891), Fr
   R.1   S.24
LEYDING, Georg Dietrich [see LEIDING, Georg Dietrich]
LEYDING, W. (1664-1710) [S.lx] = LEIDING, Georg Dietrich
L'HERITER, Jean (c1480->1552), Fr
   R.1   S.c,4,5,10
LHOTKA, Fran (1883-1962), Yug
   R.1   S.8,10,24a
LI, Zhong Han
           S.24a
LIADOV, Anatol [see LYADOV, Anatol]
LIAPUNOV, Sergei [see LYAPUNOV, Sergey Mikhaylovich]
LIBAEK, Sven Erik (1938-   ), Nor
   R.80   S.10,32
LIBAN, Jerzy (1464->1546), Pol
   R.1   S.c
LIBERATI, Alessandro (1847-1927), USA
   R.3
LICHFILD, Henry (fl 1613), Eng
   R.1   S.c,7,8,10,14
LICHNER, Heinrich (1829-1898), Ger
   R.3
LICHNOWSKY, Moritz von (1771-1837), Aus
   R.1
LIDDELL, Claire E. (20th Cent), Eng
   R.7   S.52
LIDDLE, Samuel (?1867-1951), Eng
           S.c,10
LIDGEY, C.A., Eng
   R.44   S.e
LIDHOLM, Ingvar (1921-   ), Sweden
   R.1   S.c,5x,6,10,38,40,56
LIDL, Václav (1922-   ), Cz
   R.14   S.10
LIDÓN, José (1746-1827), Sp
   R.1   S.c,10
LIE, Harald (1902-1942), Nor
   R.14   S.c,10
LIE, Sigurd (1871-1904), Nor
   R.1   S.c,5x,8,24
LIEBERMANN, Rolf (1910-   ), Swiss
   R.1   S.c,8-10,42
LIEBERSON, Goddard (1911-1977), USA
   R.19   S.9,10,13
LIEBERSON, Peter (1946-   ), USA
   R.19   S.10,13
LIEBESKIND, Joseph (1866-1916), Ger
   R.2   S.4,5
LIEBHOLD (18th Cent), Ger
   R.1   S.c

LIEBICH, Emmanuel (19th Cent)

LIEBIG - Zur Heimat
        S.5x
LIEBLING, Emil (1851-1914), Ger
  R.3   S.18
LIEFDE, Jan de (1814-1869)
        S.c
LIEGEOISE, Nicolas (16-17th Cent)
        S.c
LIENAS, Juan de (fl 1620-50), Mex
  R.1   S.10
LIER, Bertus van (1906-1972), Neth
  R.1   S.9,10
LIEURANCE, Thurlow Weed (1878-1963), USA
  R.1   S.2-4,5x,13,24
LIFCHITZ, Max (1948-   ), USA
  R.19
LIFTL, Franz J. (1864-1932), Aus
  R.3
LIGETI, György (1923-   ), Aus
  R.1   S.c,9,10
LIGGINS, Ethel [see LEGINSKA, Ethel - pseud]
LIGHT, Edward (c1747-c1832), Eng
  R.1
LIJNSCHOOTEN, Henk van (1928-   ), Neth
  R.4   S.10
LILBURN, Douglas (1915-   ), New Zealand
  R.1   S.c,24a
LILIUOKALANI, Queen of Hawaii [pseud: Mme Aorena]
  (1838-1917) R.7   S.c,5x,10,24,54(312)
LILIUS, Franciszek (d.1657), Pol
  R.1   S.c
LILJEFORS, Ingemar (1906-   ), Sweden
  R.30   S.56
LILJEFORS, Ruben (1871-1936), Sweden
  R.1   S.5x,40
LILLJEBJORN, H. (1797-1875)
        S.e
LIMBURGIA, Johannes de [see JOHANNES de LYMBURGIA]
LIN, Wu Hai
        S.24a
LINARES BECERRA, Luis (1887-   )

LINCILN, Henry J. [see SWEELEY, Charles C. - pseud]
LINCKE, Paul (1866-1946), Aus
  R.1   S.c,1x,4,5x,10,24,54(313,29,55)
LINDBERG, Helge Emanuel (1898-1973), Sweden
  R.30   S.43

LINDBERG, Oskar Frederik (1887-1955), Sweden
R.1   S.c,5x,6,40,56
LINDBLAD, Adolf Fredrik (1801-1878), Sweden
R.1   S.c,5x,10,56
LINDBLAD, Otto (1809-1864), Sweden
R.30   S.56
LINDBLAD, Rune (1923-   ), Sweden
R.30   S.40(92)
LINDE, Bo (1933-1970), Sweden
R.1   S.c,24a,40,56
LINDE, Hans-Martin (1930-   ), Swiss
R.1   S.c
LINDEMANN - Unter dem Grillenbanner (march)
           S.10,54(363)
LINDEMANN, Ole Andreas (1769-1857), Nor
R.1   S.c
LINDEMANN, Osmo (1929-   ), Fin
R.1   S.40(89)

LINDENFELD, Harris (1945-   ), USA
R.19   S.10,13
LINDHOLM, Inguar (1921-   ), Sweden

LINDLEY, Robert (1776-1855), Eng
R.1
LINDPAINTER, Peter Josef von (1791-1856), Ger
R.1   S.c
LINDSAY, G. O. - Raindrops
           S.5x
LINDTNER - Norge mit Norge
           S.e
LINEK, Georg Ignaz (1725-1791)
           S.c,4,5x,10,53
LINKE, Norbert (1933-   ), Ger
R.1   S.c,10,20,24a
LINLEY, Thomas (1733-1795), Eng
R.1   S.c
LINLEY, Thomas (1756-1778), Eng
R.1   S.c,10
LINLEY, William (1771-1835), Eng
R.1   S.c,10
LINN, Robert (1925-   ), USA
R.19   S.c,10,13,24a
LINTON, J. - Come pretty wenches [5x] = LENTON, John
LIONCOURT, Guy de (1885-1961), Fr
R.1   S.c
LIONNET, A. - Hymn d'amour
           S.e
LIOUBOFF - Prochela: L'amour passa
           S.24a

LIPATOV, Vasil Nikolayevich (1897-   )
                    S.18
LIPATTI, Dinu (1917-1950), Rum
    R.1   S.7,9,24a
LIPIŃSKI, Karol Józef (1790-1861), Pol
    R.1   S.18,24
LIPOVŠEK, Marijan (1910-   ), Yug
    R.1   S.24
LISBON, Kenneth [see DE VITO, Albert Kenneth]
LISHIN, Grigory Andreyevich (1854-1888), Russia
    R.3   S.10,18
LISITSIN Russia - Praise ye the name

LISLE, Rouget de [see ROUGET de LISLE]
LISLEY, John (16-17th Cent), Eng
    R.77   S.7,8,10,14
LISNYAI-SZABO, Gabour (1913-   ), Hun
             S.c
LISSENKO, Mikola Vitalyevych
    [see LYSENKO, Mikola Vitalyevych]
LISSMANN, Kurt (1902-1983), Ger
    R.2   S.c
LIST, Garrett (1943-   ), USA
    R.19   S.13
LIST, Kurt (1913-1970), USA

    R.14   S.10,13
LISZT, Franz (1811-1886), Hun
    R.1   S.c,1-11,18,23-28,43,54(333)
LITAIZE, Gaston Gilbert (1909-   ), Fr
    R.1   S.c,10
LITERES, Antonio (1673-1747), Sp
    R.1   S.c,5x,10,11,24
LITHGOW, A.F. - Invercargill
             S.54(334)
LITINSKY, Genrich Ilych (1901-   ), USSR
    R.14   S.18
LITOLFF, Henry Charles (1818-1891), Fr
    R.1   S.c,4,5x,6-11
LITSITE, P. (1889-   )
             S.18
LITSITIS, Janis (1913-   )
             S.18
LITTEL, Manuel Massotti
             S.39
LITZAU, Jan Barent (1822-1893), Neth
    R.3   S.c
LIUBOV, Timofeeva (20th Cent), USSR
             S.52
LJAPUNOW, Sergey Mikhaylovich
    [see LYAPUNOV, Sergey Mikhaylovich]

LLANSON, F. (1560-   )
                S.c,15,16
LLEÓ, Vincente (1870-1922), Sp
    R.1   S.9,10,39
LLOBET, Miguel (1878-1938), Sp
    R.1   S.c,10,32,39
LLORET, Jose Louis, Sp

LLOYD, Charles Francis (1852-   ), Eng
    R.44   S.e
LLOYD, Caroline Parkhurst (1924-   ), USA
    R.7   S.39,52
LLOYD, Charles Harford (1849-1919), Eng
    R.1   S.c,5x,19
LLOYD, E. - Song of the south
                S.e
LLOYD, George (1913-   ), Eng
    R.1   S.c
LLOYD, Richard (1933-   ), Eng
                S.c
LLOYD-WEBER, William Southcombe (1914-1982), Eng
    R.80   S.c
LLUSSA, Francisco (fl 1687-1738), Sp
    R.1   S.c,10,13,32,53
LLWYFO - Llongau Madog
                S.e
LOBEL, Michael

LOBKOVSKY, Abram Mikhailovich (1912-   ), USSR
    R.14   S.24a
LOBO, Alonso (c1555-1617), Sp
    R.1   S.c,16,17

LOCATELLI, Pietro Antonio (1695-1764), It
    R.1   S.c,2-11,18,24,32
LOCHTER, Jurgen

LOCKE, Matthew (1621/22-1677), Eng
    R.1   S.c,1-3,5,7-10,53
LOCKHART, Eugene (1891-1957), USA
    R.23   S.e
LOCKWOOD, Anna (1939-   ), New Zealand
    R.7   S.30,52
LOCKWOOD, Larry Paul (1943-   ), USA
    R.19   S.10,13
LOCKWOOD, Normand (1906-   ), USA
    R.1   S.8,10,12,13
LODER, Edward James (1813-1865), Eng
    R.1   S.e
LODGE, Thomas (d.1625), Eng
                S.c,16

LOEB, David (1939-   ), USA
    R.19
LOEB, John Jacob (1910-1970), USA
    R.23   S.10,13
LOEFFELHOLZ von COLBERG, Christoph (1572-1619), Ger
    [editor]   R.1   S.53
LOEFFLER, Charles Martin (1861-1935), USA
    R.1   S.3-5,7,8,10,11,13,23-25,27
LOEILLET, Jacques (1685-1748), Flem
    R.1   S.c,8,10
LOEILLET, Jean Baptiste (John of London) (1680-1730)
    Flem   R.1   S.c,5-10,18,22,24,32,53
LOEILLET, Jean Baptiste (Loeillet de Gant) (1688-c1720)
    Flem   R.1   S.c,8
LOEILLET, Jean-Baptiste (1653-1728), Flem (see note)
            S.c,3,4
LOESCH - Auf der Kirmes (v)
            S.10
LOESSER, Frank (1910-1969), USA (see note)
    R.1   S.9,10
LOEVENDIE, Theo (1930-   ), Neth
    R.80   S.20
LOEWE, Carl (1796-1869), Ger
    R.1   S.c,1-11,25-28
LOEWE, Frederick (1904-   ), USA
    R.1   S.c,9,10
LOEWE, Hilde (1895-1976) [pseud: Henry LOVE], Aus
    R.3   (see note)
LOEWE, Johann Jakob (1629-1703), Ger
    R.2   S.c
LÖFFELHOLZ, Christoph (1572-1619), Ger
    R.8   S.c,10,16
LOGAN, Frederick Knight (1871-1928), USA
    R.23   S.24
LOGAN, Wendell (1940-   ), USA
    R.19   S.13,24a
LOGAR, Mihovil (1902-   ), Yug
    R.14   S.24a
LOGE, Henri
            S.e
LOGER, A. - Le tout Paris March
            S.54(361)
LOGES, Karl Heinz
            S.10
LOGI, Graf von [see LOSY, Jan Antonin]
LOGOTHETIS, Anestis (1921-   ), Greece
    R.1   S.c
LOGROSCINO, Nicola Bonifacio (1698-1765/67), It
    R.1   S.8,10

LOGY, Johann Antonin [see LOSY, Jan Antonin]
LOHET, Simon (c1550-1611), S. Neth
    R.1   S.c,16,53
LOHMANN, Adolf (1935-   )
                S.c
LÖHNER, Johann (1645-1705), Ger
    R.1   S.7
LOHOEFER, Evelyn D. - pseud (1921-   ), USA
    R.7   S.30
LÖHR, Hermann (1871-1943), Eng
    R.1   S.5x,10,24
LOHR, Ina (1903-   ), Neth
    R.4
LOINAZ, E. - Himno invasor
                S.54(332)
LOKAY, Jakob (1752-   )
                S.c
LOKSHIN, Alexander Lazarevich (1920-   ), USSR
    R.14   S.c,18
LOLODUB, L. - Youth Suite

LOLOV, Vassil (1913-   )
                S.24a
LOMAKIN, Gavriil Yakimovich (1812-1885), Russia
    R.1   S.c,11
LOMBARD, Louis (1861-   ), It
    R.10   S.e
LOMBARDI, Luca (1945-   )
                S.c
LOMBARDO, Carlo [pseud: Léon BARD; LEPLANC] (1869-1959)
    It   R.4
LOMBARDO, Robert M. (1932-   ), USA
    R.19   S.10,13
LOMBIDA, Juan Andrés de (fl 1787), Sp
    R.9   S.c
LOMON, Ruth (1930-   ), USA
    R.7   S.52
LONATI, Carlo Ambrogio (c1645-c1710), It
    R.1   S.c,24a
LONDON, Edwin (1929-   ), USA
    R.19   S.10,13,23
LONES, Larry - pseud [see HEUN, Hans]
LONGÁS TORRES, Frederico (1893-1968), Sp
    R.4
LONGO, Alessandro (1864-1945), It
    R.1

LONGONE, Carol Perrenot
                S.10
LONGTIN, Michel (1946-   ), Can
    R.4

LONGUE, Georges (1900-   )
          S.24a
LONGUEVAL, Antoine de (fl 1507-1522), Fr
    R.1   S.c,10,16
LONQUE, Armand Josef (1908-   ), Bel
    R.14
LONQUE, Georges (1900-1967), Bel
    R.1   S.20,36
LOOS, Johann Karl (fl 1768), Boh
    R.5   S.5x[Karel Jan Loos (1725-1772)]
LOOSE, H. Detlev
          S.c
LOPATINSKY, Jaroslav (1871-1936), Ukraine
    R.3   S.18
LOPATNIKOFF, Nikolai (1903-1976), USA
    R.1   S.7,8,10,13,24
LOPE, Santiago (1871-1906)

LÓPEZ BUCHARDO, Carlos (1881-1948), Arg
    R.1   S.c,4,5,8,10,46
LÓPEZ BUCHARDO, Prospero (1883-1964), Arg
    R.26   S.46
LÓPEZ CAPILLAS, Francisco (c1615-1673), Mex
    R.1   S.10
LÓPEZ MORAGO, Estevao [see MORAGO, Estevao Lopes]
LÓPEZ TEJERA, Luis [pseud: Louis MARAVILLA] (1914-   )
    Sp R.4   S.10
LÓPEZ de VELASCO, Sebastián (d c1650), Sp
    R.1   S.c
LÓPEZ de la ROSA, Horacio (1933-   ), Arg
    R.26   S.46
LÓPEZ, Francis (1916-   ), Fr
    R.1   S.c
LÓPEZ JUARRANZ, Eduardo (1844-1897), Sp
    R.9   S.10
LÓPEZ, Miguel (1669-1723), Sp
    R.1   S.c,53
LÓPEZ-CHAVARRI y MARCO, Eduardo (1871-1970), Sp
    R.1   S.c,5x,10
LO PRESTI, Ronald (1933-   ), USA
    R.19   S.10,13
LOQUEVILLE, Richard (d.1418), Fr
    R.1   S.c,10
LORA, Antonio John (1899-1965), USA
    R.19   S.10,13
LORCA, Frederico García [see GARCÍA LORCA, Frederico]
LORD, Jon

LORENTZ, Johann (c1610-1689), Den
    R.1   S.10,53

LORENZI, Fabris Ausonio de (1861-   ), It
    R.52   S.e
LORENZINI [Laurencini] [Romanus, Laurenzinus]
    (fl c1570-71), It   R.1   S.c
LORENZITI, Antonio [Joseph Antoine] (fl 1740-1770), It
    R.5   S.10
LORENZO FERNÂNDEZ, Oscar (1897-1948), Brazil
    R.1   S.c,3-5,8,10,11,18,24,39
LORENZO da FIRENZE (d.1372/73), It
    R.1   S.c,10,16
LORENZO, Ange (1894-1971), USA
    R.23   S.24
LORET, Charles
               S.24
LORRAINE, William
               S.54(354)
LORTZING, Albert (1801-1851), Ger
    R.1   S.c,1-10,42
LOSCH, A. - Gee whiz
               S.54(328)
LOSEY, Frank H. (1872-1931), USA
    R.95   S.54(333)
LOSY [Logy, Logi], Jan Antonin (c1650-1721), Boh
    R.1   S.6,5x,32
LOTH, Louis Leslie (1888-1974), USA
    R.19   S.24
LOTHAR, Mark (1902-   ), Ger
    R.1   S.c,2-4
LOTHROP (19th Cent), USA - Fredonia March

LOTKA, Fran (1883-1962)
               S.18,24
LOTTER, Adolf - Slavonic scherzo
               S.5x
LOTTI, Antonio (c1667-1740), It
    R.1   S.c,1x,2-8,11,18,24
LOTTO, Izydor (1840 or 1844-1936), Pol
    R.1   S.24
LOUCHEUR, Raymond (1899-1979), Fr
    R.1   S.8,18,20,24a
LOUDOVÁ, Ivana (1941-   ), Cz
    R.1   S.c,30,52
LOUËL, Jean (1914-   ), Bel
    R.1   S.24a,36
LOUGHBOROUGH - Giles
               S.e
LOUGHBOROUGH, Raymond

LOUGHBOROUGH, William   USA
               S.13

LOUIS FERDINAND of PRUSSIA (1907-   )
    S.8
LOUIS FERDINAND, Prince of Prussia (1772-1806)
 R.1 S.c,7,8[Hohenzollern, Prince Louis von],10,24
LOUIS XIII (1601-1643), Fr
 R.1 S.8,10
LOURDOYS [see BRACONNIER, Jean]
LOUVIER, Alain (1945-   ), Fr
 R.80 S.c
LOVE, Henry - pseud [see LOEWE, Hilde]
LOVELOCK, William (1899-   ), Australia
 R.14 S.c,10,29
LØVENSKJOLD, Hermann Severin (1815-1870), Nor
 R.8 S.c,10,24
LOVER, Samuel (1797-1868), Ire
 R.1 S.e,47
LOVETT, Andrew (1962-   ), Eng
    S.c
LOVREGLIO, Donato (1841-1907), It
 R.10 S.c
LÖWE von EISENACH, Johann Jakob (1629-1703), Ger
 R.1 S.10
LOWRY, Robert (1826-1899), USA
 R.1 S.10
LOWTHIAN, Caroline (Mrs. Cyril A. Prescott) (c1860-   )
 Eng R.7 S.10
LOZZI, Michele F. (1876-1964)

LUALDI, Adriano (1885-1971), It
 R.1 S.4,5
LUBBE, Kurt (1888-   ), Ger [pseud: Emili KORDEN,
 Frank STAFFORD Frank] R.3 S.24
LÜBECK, Vincent (1654-1740), Ger
 R.1 S.c,5,7-11,24,53
LUBIN, Napoléon-Antoine [Léon de Saint Lubin]
 (1805-1850), Fr R.8 S.24[Saint-Lubin]
LUBLIN, Jan van [see JAN z LUBLINA]
LUBRICH, Fritz Jr. (1888-1971), Ger
 R.14 S.c
LUCA, Severo di (fl 1684-1701), It
 R.1 S.18[Lyuca]
LUCA, de - Dolce Madonna
    S.e
LUCANTONI, Giovanni (1825-1902), It
 R.8 S.24
LUCAS, Clarence (1866-1947), Can
 R.1

LUCAS, Leighton (1903-1982), Eng
   R.85   S.55
LUCCA, Chiara di (17th Cent)

LUCCHESI, Andrea (1741-1801), It
   R.1   S.c,24
LUCCHINETTI, Giovanni Bernardo (18th Cent)
          S.c,10
LUCE, J. - O salutaris
          S.e
LUCETT, Jean
          S.4
LUCHAS, Gabriel (fl c1500)
          S.8,10,13
LUCHENOK, Igor Mikhailovich (1938-   ), USSR
   R.47   S.18
LUCIANN - Serenade (orch)
          S.24
LUČIĆ, Franjo (1889-1972), Yug
   R.14   S.c
LUCIER, Alvin (1931-   ), USA
   R.19   S.10,13
LUCIUK, Juliusz (1927-   ), Pol
   R.1
LUCKÝ, Štěpán (1919-   ), Cz
   R.1   S.c,24a,31
LÜDERITZ, Wolfgang (1926-   ), Ger
   R.4   S.c
LUDERS, Gustav (1865-1913), USA
   R.1   S.10,54(351)
LUDEWIG, Wolfgang (1926-   ), Ger
   R.1   S.c
LUDIG, Michail Yakovlevich (1880-1958), Arg
   R.14
LUDOVIC, G. - pseud [see GOBBAERTS, Jean Louis]
LUDUC, Jacques (1932-   )

LUDWIG, Joachim [pseud: Lutz LUCKNER] (1933-   ), Ger
   R.4   S.c
LUDZASKY, Ludzasko [S.18] = LUZZASCHI, Luzzasco
LUENING, Otto (1900-   ), USA
   R.1   S.2,3,7,8,10,12,13,24,25
LUGGE, John (c1587->1647), Eng
   R.1   S.10
LUIGINI, Alexandre (1850-1906), Fr
   R.1   S.c,1,4,10,54(363)
LUKAČIĆ, Ivan (1587-1648), Croatian
   R.1   S.16
LUKAS of PRAGUE (fl 1490) - Christus humilitatis
   exemplum   S.5x

LUKÁŠ, Zdenek (1928-   ), Cz
  R.1   S.c,10,22,24a
LUKE, Ray (1926-   ), USA
  R.19   S.10,13
LULLY, Jean-Baptiste (1632-1687), Fr
  R.1   S.c,2-11,18,21-24,33,44
LUMBYE, Hans Christian (1810-1874), Den
  R.1   S.c,4-9,24,35,54(324),57
LUNA y CARNÉ, Pablo (1880-1942), Sp
  R.1   S.c,8-11,39,42
LUNDBERG, Fridolf Sweden

LUNDBERG, Lars Åke (1935-   ), Sweden
  R.30   S.c
LUNDBORG, Charles Erik (1948-   ), USA
  R.19   S.10,13
LUNDE, Lawson (1935-   ), USA
  R.19   S.13,22
LUNDKVIST, Erik (1940-   ), Sweden
  R.30   S.c,40
LUNDQUIST, Torbjörn (1920-   ), Sweden
  R.14   S.c,10,24a,40,56
LUNDSTEN, Ralph (1936-   ), Sweden
  R.14   S.38,40,56
LUNDVIK, Hildor (1885-1951), Sweden
  R.30   S.5x,56
LUNETTA, Stanley G. (1937-   ), USA
  R.4
LUNGUL, Semen Vasilyevich (1927-   )
             S.18
LUNTU S. - Chorus
             S.18
LUPI SECOND, Didier (16th Cent), Fr
  R.1   S.c
LUPI, Johannes (c1506-1539), Franco-Flem
  R.1   S.16,10[Lelen, Jean]
LUPO, Thomas (d.1628), Eng
  R.1   S.c,10,16,24a
LURANO [Luprano], Filippo de (c1475->1520), It
  R.1   S.c,10
LUSCINIUS, Othmar (c1478-1537), Ger
  R.1   S.16
LUTHER, Martin (1483-1546), Ger
  R.1   S.c,2-5,10,16
LÜTHOLD, Ernest (1904-1966), Swiss
  R.95
LUTOSLAWSKI, Witold (1913-   ), Pol
  R.1   S.c,8-10,18-20
LUTSTSY, L. [S.18] = LUZZI, Luigi

LUTYENS, Elisabeth (1906-1983), Eng
    R.1   S.c,10,20,30,52
LUTZOW - Olympische Hymne
            S.54(347)
LUYTON, Charles (1556-1620), Neth
    R.2   S.c,10,16,53
LUZ, Ernest
            S.24
LUZZASCHI, Luzzasco (?1545-1607), It
    R.1   S.c,5x,8,10,14,16,18[Ludzasky],53
LUZZATTI, Arturo (1875-1959), Arg
    R.26   S.46
LUZZI, Luigi (1828-1876), It
    R.8   S.5x,18[Lutstsy],24
LVOV, Alexy Fyodorovich (1798-1870), Russia
    R.1   S.10,54(316)
LVOV-KOMPANEETS, David Lvovich (1918-   )

*** LVOVSKY, Alexis (1799-1871) (see note)
LVOVSKY, Grigor Fiodorovich (1830-1894), Russia
    R.28   S.5x,10,11 (see note)
LYADOV, Anatol Konsayantinovich (1855-1914), Russia
    R.1
LYAPUNOV, Sergey Mikhaylovich (1859-1924), Russia
    R.1   S.c,5,7,8,10,18,24
LYATOSHINSKY, Boris Mikolayovich (1895-1968), Ukraine
    R.1   S.18,24
LYATTE, Alexander (1860-1948)
            S.18
LYATTE, Raimond (1931-   )
            S.18
LYBBERT, Donald (1923-   ), USA
    R.1   S.10,13
LYLLOFF, Bent (1930-   ), Den
    R.30   S.10,40
LYMAN - Mother in Ireland
            S.e
LYMBURGIA, Johannes de [see JOHANNES de LYMBURGIA]
LYNE, Peter (1946-   ), Sweden
    R.68   S.c,40
LYNTON, Everett - pseud [see WRIGHT, Lawrence]
LYON, James (1735-1794), USA
    R.86   S.10,47
LYON, James (1872-1949), Eng
    R.4   S.c
LYON, M. (fl 1979), USA - Suite, low brass
            S.13
LYRA, Abdao
            S.24a

LYRA, Carlinhos (1933-   ), Brazil
   R.67   S.39
LYSBERG, Charles-Samuel
  [see BOVY-LYSBERG, Charles Samuel]
LYSENKO, Mykola Vitalyevych (1842-1912), Ukraine
   R.1   S.8,9,18,24,42
LYSTE, H. P.
             S.e
LYTLE, Cecil
             S.10
LYTTON, Henry (1865-1936)

LYUDIG, Mikhkel (1880-1958)
             S.18
LYUDKEVYCH, Stanislav Pylypovych (1879-1979), USSR
   R.1   S.18
LYUTOSLAVSKI, Witold [see LUTOSLAWSKI, Witold]
MA Yao-Hsien
             S.c,24a
MAASE, Wilhelm (?1850-1932), Ger
   R.3   S.e
MAASZ, Gerhard (1906-   ), Ger
   R.14   S.c
MAAYANI, Ami (1936-   ), Isr
   R.1   S.c,10,24a
McAFEE, Donald (1935-   ), USA
   R.19   S.10,13
MacALLISTER, Forrest L.
             S.54(326)
MACALUSO, Vincenzo
             S.10,32
McAMIS, Hugh (1899-1942), USA
             S.10,12,13
McARTHUR, Edwin (1907-   ), USA
   R.23   S.10,13
McBAIN, David (1901-   ),Eng
   R.49   S.54(342,55)
MACBETH, Allan (1856-1910), Scot
   R.8   S.24
McBETH, William Francis (1933-   ), USA
   R.19   S.10
McBRIDE, Robert (1911-   ), USA
   R.1   S.3-5,7,8,10,11,13,24
McCABE, John (1939-   ), Eng
   R.1   S.c,10,32
McCALL, J. Petter - pseud
             S.10[McCall, J.B.]
McCARTHY, Henry (fl 1865), USA
   R.53   S.10

McCARTY, Patrick (1928-   ), USA
    R.19   S.13
McCAULEY, William Alexander (1917-   ), Can
    R.14   S.10
McCLELLAN, Randall (1938-   ), USA
                S.13
McCORMICK, Peter Dodds [see AMICUS - pseud]
McCOY, Earl E. (1884-1934), USA
    R.49   S.c,54(338)
MacCUNN, Hamish (1868-1916), Scot
    R.1   S.c
MacDERMID, James G. (1875-1960), USA
    R.4
McDERMOT, Arthur Terence Galt (1929-   ), Can
    R.31   S.c,9,10
McDONALD, (19th Cent), USA - Musical snuff box waltzes

McDONALD, Harl (1899-1955), USA
    R.19   S.2-6,8-10,13
McDONALD, Ian (1937-   ), New Zealand

MacDOUGALL, Robert (1941-   ), USA
    R.19   S.10,13
MacDOWELL, Edward (1860-1908), USA
    R.1   S.c,1-11,18,20-22,24,26,27,54(328)
MACE, Thomas (1612/13-?1706), Eng
    R.1   S.c,10,32
MACERO, Ted (1925-   ), USA
    R.19   S.10
McEWEN, Sir John Blackwood (1868-1948), Scot
    R.1   S.c
MACFARREN, Sir George Alexander (1813-1887), Eng
    R.1   S.e
MACFAYDEN, Alexander (1876-1936), USA
    R.23   S.e
McGEOCH, Daisy
                S.e
McGIBBON, William (c1690-1756), Scot
    R.1   S.c
McGILL, Josephine (1877-1919), USA
    R.53,200   S.c,10,13
MACGIMSEY, Robert (1898-1979), USA
    R.23   S.c,10,13
McGRANAHAN - Sometime we'll understand
                S.e
McGRANAHAN, James (1840-1907), USA
    R.1   S.10
McGRATH, Joseph (1889-1968), USA
    R.19   S.12,13

MacGREGOR, Laurie (1951-   ), USA
   R.19   S.30,52
MÁCHA, Otmar (1922-   ), Cz
   R.1   S.c,31
MACHADO, Manuel (c1590-1646), Port
   R.1   S.c,17
MACHADO - Leyenda de la petenera; Viva Castilla
          S.10,39

MACHAUT, Guillaume de (c1300-1377), Fr
   R.1   S.c,2-6,8-11,14-16,32,53
MACHAVARIANI, Alexey Davidovich (1913-   ), USSR
   R.1   S.8,10,18,24
MÂCHE, François-Bernard (1935-   ), Fr
   R.1   S.c,10
MACHL, Tadeusz (1922-   ), Pol
   R.4
MACHO, Gustav
          S.24
McHUGH, James Francis (1894-1969), USA
   R.1   S.10,24a
MACHY, Sieur de (fl 1685-92), Fr
   R.1   S.c
MACIAS - La ronda; El primer jefe
          S.54(351,53)
MACIEJEWSKI, Roman (1910-   ), Pol
   R.1   S.c
MACINELLI, Luigi (1848-1921), It
   R.93   S.54(325,34)
MacINNIS, Donald (1923-   ), USA
   R.19
MACK - Story of the Rose
          S.e
MACK, David
          S.9
MACK, Edward (d.1882), USA
   R.200
MACKAY, Eugene USA
          S.13
McKAY, George Frederick (1899-1970), USA
   R.19   S.13
McKAY, Neil (1924-   ), Can
   R.14   S.10,13
MACKEBEN, Theo (1897-1953), Ger
   R.1   S.5x
MACKENZIE, Sir Alexander (1847-1935), Eng
   R.1   S.c,24
MACKENZIE, Gordon - pseud [ie William SMITH] (1878-1948)
   Eng R.96   S.54(336,54,65)
MACKENZIE, Jack H. (1930-   ), USA
   R.19   S.10,13

MACKERRAS, Charles (1925-   ), USA
   R.4
McKIE, Sir William (1901-   ), Australia
   R.1   S.c,10
McKINLEY, Carl (1895-1966), USA
   R.19   S.12,13
McKINLEY, William, Thomas (1939-   ), USA
   R.19   S.13
McKUEN, Rod (1933-   ), USA
   R.19   S.9,13
McLEAN, Barton (1938-   ), USA
   R.19   S.9,10,13
MACLEAN, John Garves (Laird of Coll) (b c1580), Scot
   R.109   S.c
McLEAN, Priscilla (1942-   ), USA
   R.19   S.10,13,52
MacLEAN, T. Ross (1904-   ), USA
   R.23
MACLEOD, Jennifer Helen (1941-   ), New Zealand
   R.7   S.30,52
McLEOD, John (1934-   ), Scot
          S.c
McLIN, Lena [née Johnson] (20th Cent), USA
   R.7   S.13,52
McMILLAN, Ann (1923-   ), USA
   R.19   S.10,13,30,52
MacMILLAN, Sir Ernest (1893-1973), Can
   R.1   S.9,10
MACMILLEN, Francis (1885-   )
   R.3   S.24
McMOON, Cosme
          S.10
MACMURROUGH, Dermot (1872-1943)
          S.24
MACNAB (19th Cent), Fr
          S.5x
McNALLY - The lass of Richmond Hill
          S.e
MACONCHY, Elizabeth (1907-   ), Eng
   R.1   S.c,2,10,20,24a,28,30,49,52
McPEEK, Benjamin D. (1934-1981), Can
   R.14
McPHEE, Colin (1901-1964), Can
   R.1   S.c,10,13
MACQUE, Giovanni de (?1548/50-1614), Flem
   R.1   S.c,16,53
McREARY, John (1932-   ), USA
          S.c
MACY, J. C. - Good night little girl
          S.e

MADDEN, Edward (1877-1952), USA (see note)
R.23   S.13
MADDEN, Richard (see note)
          S.10
MADENSKY, Eduard (1877-1923)
          S.c
MADER, Clarence (1904-1971), USA
R.19   S.10,13
MADERNA, Bruno (1920-1973), It
R.1   S.c,10,24a
MADETOJA, Leevi (1887-1947), Fin
R.1   S.c,5x,40
MADI, T. Brazil - Cançao dos olhos tristes (song of sad
eyes)   S.39
MADISON, Carolyn (20th Cent), USA
          S.13,30,52
MADLSEDER, Nonnosus (1730-1797), Ger
R.1   S.8
MADRID, Juan Fernández de (fl 1480), Sp
R.1   S.16
MADRIGAL GIL, Delfino (1923-   )
          S.c

MADRIGUERA, Enrique (1902-1973), Sp
R.9   S.10
MADRIGUERA, Paquita (1900-   ), Sp
R.9   S.c,10,30,32,52
MADRUGARA - Pelo amor
          S.e
MADSEN, Trygve (1940-   ), Nor
R.80   S.c,51
MADURO, Charles (1883-1947), USA
R.23   S.10
MAE, Thomas

MAES, Jeff (1905-   ), Bel
R.1   S.c,23,24a,36
MAFFEIS, Daniele (1901-1966)
          S.c
MAGALHÃES, Felipe de (c1571-1652), Port
R.1
MAGE Pierre du [see DUMAGE, Pierre]
MAGEAU, Mary Magdalen (Sister) (1934-   ), USA
R.7   S.30
MÄGI, Ester (1922-   ), Est
R.58   S.24,30
MAGINE, Frank (1888-   )
          S.24
MAGISTER GOSLENUS EPISCOPUS SUESSIONIS (12th Cent)

MAGNAN - Concerto for baritone horn
          S.10
MAGNARD, Albéric (1865-1914), Fr
   R.1   S.c,2,8,10,24
MAGNAU - Boheme
          S.e
MAGNE, Michel (1930-   ), Fr
   R.4
MAGNUSSON, Sverker (1943-   ), Sweden
          S.40
MAGOGO KA DINIZULU, Constance, Princess
   [see KA DINIZULU, Constance Magogo]
MAGOMAYEV, Abdul Muslim Magometovic (1885-1937),
   Azerbajan   R.8   S.18
MAHAUT, Antoine (c1720-c1785), Neth
   R.1   S.10,24
MAHLE, Ernst (1909-   ), Brazil
   R.4   S.24a
MAHLER, Alma Maria (née Schindler) (1879-1964), Aus
   R.7   S.52
MAHLER, Gustav (1860-1911), Aus
   R.1   S.c,1-11,18,24-28
MAHU, A. (fl early 16th Cent) - Songs of the Lansquenet
          S.5x
MAHU, Stephan (c1490-?1541)
   R.1   S.c,10,14,16
MAIBORODA, Georgi Illarionovich (1913-   ), USSR
   R.14   S.18
MAICHELBECK, Franz Anton (1702-1750), Ger
   R.1   S.c,10
MAIG - Anacreontica, Sp
          S.c
MAIGUASHCA, Mesías (1938-   ), Ecuador
   R.1
MAILLARD, Jean (fl c1538-70), Fr
   R.1   S.5x
MAILLART, Aimé (1817-1871), Fr
   R.1   S.c,2-5,10
MAILMAN, Martin (1932-   ), USA
   R.19   S.10,13
MAINARDI, Enrico (1897-1976), It
   R.1   S.c,10
MAINERIO, Giorgio (c1535-1582), It
   R.1   S.c,10,32
MAIS, Chester L. (1936-   ), USA
   R.19   S.13
MAISTRAL, Mario - Ajacciu bellu

MAISTRE JHAN (c1485-c1545), Fr
   R.1   S.c,5x[Jan of Jentstein],10

MAISTRE, Matthaus le [see LE MAISTRE, Matthaeus]
MAIWALD, Dirk (1950-   )
          S.c
MAJO, Gian Francesco de (1732-1770), It
    R.1   S.c
MAKACHINAS, Teisutis (1938-   )
          S.18
MAKAROV, Pavel Semenovich
          S.10
MAKAROVA, Nina Vladimirovna (1908-1976), Russia
    R.7   S.10,18,24,30,52
MAKHA, Otmar (1922-   )
          S.18
MAKINO, Yutaka (1930-   ), Japan
    R.4   S.50
MAKLAKIEWICZ, Jan Adam (1899-1954), Pol
    R.1
MAKOSZA, Edward

MAKSIMOV, Khristofor Trofimovich (1917-   )
          S.18
MALARTIN, Erkki Gustaf

MALASHKIN, Leonid Dmitriyevich (1842-1902), Russia
    R.10   S.c,5x,10,18
MALÁT, Jan (1843-1915), Cz
    R.1   S.5x,6,8,10
MALATS, Joaquín (1872-1912), Sp
    R.9   S.c,5x,8,10,18,32
MALAWSKI, Artur (1904-1957), Pol
    R.1
MALCHINGER (Malchier) (fl 1512-13)
          S.10
MALCOLM, George (1917-   ), Eng
    R.1   S.c,10
MALDERE, Pierre Van (1729-1768), S. Neth
    R.1   S.c,9,10,24a
MALDEREN, Edward van
          S.24
MALDONADO, Carlos (1948-   ), USA
          S.39
MALDONADO, Raoul (20th Cent)
          S.c
MALDYBAYEV, Abdylas (1906-   ), USSR
    R.14   S.18
MALEC, Ivo (1925-   ), Yug
    R.1   S.c,10
MALENFANT, Anna (1905-   ), Can
    R.31   S.30

MALENGREAU, Paul (1887-1959), Bel
   R.1   S.7,10
MALEVZZI, Cristofano [see MALVEZZI, Christofano]
MALFETTI, Paolo (1856-   ), It
   R.10s   S.e
MALIBRAN, Maria Felicia (1808-1836), Sp
   R.1   S.10,30,52
MALIPIERO, Francesco (1824-1887), It
   R.8
MALIPIERO, Gian Francesco (1882-1973), It
   R.1   S.c,1-8,10,11,18,23,24
MALIPIERO, Riccardo (1914-   ), It
   R.1
MALLING - Spejling
          S.e
MALLINSON, Albert James (1870-1946), Eng
   R.2   S.10
MALMFORS, Åke (1918-1951), Sweden
   R.30   S.40,56
MALMLÖF-FORSSLING, Carin (1916-   ), Sweden
   R.7   S.40,52
MALOT - Cruel mystère
          S.e
MALOTTE, Albert Hay (1895-1964), USA
   R.19   S.3,4,5x,10,13
MALOVEC, Jozef (1933-   ), Slovak
   R.1   S.c,10,24a,31
MALVEZZI, Christofano (1547-1599), It
   R.1   S.c,10,16,53
MALZ, Heinrich (1870-   ), Ger
   R.3   S.c
MAMANGAKIS, Nicos (1929-   ), Greece
   R.1
MAMEDOV, Ibranim (1928-   ), USSR
   R.47   S.18,24
MAMISASHVILY, Nodar (1930-   ), USSR
   R.47   S.18
MAMIYA, Michio (1929-   ), Japan
   R.1   S.24,50
MAMLOK, Ursula (1928-   ), USA
   R.19   S.10,13,28,30,52
MAMYEDEV, Nariam (1927-   )
          S.18[under Bakikhanov, Tofik]
MANALT, Francisco (c1710-1759), Sp
   R.1   S.c,24a
MANA-ZUCCA, Ki-Lu (Auguste-Zuckerman) (1887-1981), USA
   R.7   S.22,24a,30,52
MANCHICOURT, Pierre de (c1510-1564), Neth
   R.1   S.c,10,14,16

MANCIA, Luigi.(c1660->1708), It
   R.1   S.c
MANCINELLI, Luigi (1848-1921), It
   R.1   S.2-5,10
MANCINI, Curzio (1550/53->1608), It
   R.1
MANCINI, Francesco (1672-1737),It
   R.1   S.c,8,10,24
MANCINI, Henry (1924-   ), USA
   R.1   S.9,24
MANCINUS, Thomas (1550-1611/12), Ger
   R.1   S.c
MANDENO - La Partida
             S.e
MANEN, Christian
             S.20
MANÉN, Juan (1883-1971), Sp
   R.1   S.5x,10,18,24,32,39
MANENTE, Giuseppe (1868-1941), It
   R.3   S.54(341)
MANERI, (20th Cent), It - Salve Regina (org)
             S.c
MANESCAU - Au son des cloches
             S.e
MANEVICH, Alexander Mendelevich (1908-   ), USSR
   R.14   S.10,19,21
MANFREDINI, Francesco Onofrio (1684-1762), It
   R.1   S.c,6-10,18,24
MANFREDINI, Vincenzo (1737-1799), It
   R.1   S.c
MANGOLD, Carl Amand (1813-1889), Ger [?]
   R.1   S.5x
MANGOLT, Burk (15th Cent)
   R.1
MANGON, Johannes (c1525-1578), S. Neth
   R.1   S.c,10,14,16
MANICA-JOTAS - Si fuera un aeroplane
             S.e
MANKELL, Henning (1868-1930), Sweden
   R.1   S.24a,40
MANN, Arthur Henry (1850-1929), Eng
   R.1   S.c
MANN, Leslie (1923-1977), Can
   R.4
MANN, Robert (1920-   ), USA
   R.19   S.13
MANNEKE, Daniël (1939-   ), Neth
   R.1   S.c
MANNING - Women's way
             S.e

MANNING, Kathleen Lockhart (1890-1951), USA
   R.19   S.10,13,30,52
MANNINO, Franco (1924-   ), It
   R.1   S.9,18,24a
MANSE
              S.e
MANSURYAN, Tigran (1939-   ), Arm
   R.1   S.18,24
MANTEGAZZI, Johann Baptist (1889-1958), Swiss
   R.4   S.5x
MANTIA, Simone (1873-1953), USA
   R.49   S.10
MANTICHY, Enrique Gonzales (1912-   )
              S.18
MANTOVA, Rossii [see ROSSINO MANTOVANO]
MANTOVANO, Alberto [see RIPA, Alberto da]
MANTOVANO, Rossino [see ROSSINO MANTOVANO]
MANTUA, Guglielmo (1538-1587), It
              S.c
MANTZAROS, Nicolaos (1795-1872), Greece
   R.1   S.54(330)
MANYKIN-NEVSTRUEV, Nikolai Alexander (1869-   ), Russia
   R.47   S.5x,11[Nevstruev],18
MANZ, Paul (1919-   ), USA
   R.19   S.12,13
MANZIA, Luigi [see MANCIA, Luigi]
MANZIARLY, Marcelle de (1899-   ), Fr
   R.1   S.c,5x,10,52
MANZOLO, Domenico (fl 1623-39), It
   R.1   S.2-4,5x,8,11
MANZONI, Giacomo (1932-   ), It
   R.1   S.c,10
MAO Yuan
              S.c,24a
MAPELLI, Luigi (1855-1913), It
   R.8   S.c
MAQUIA - Tout comme les autres
              S.e
MAQUIS, G. - Ma jolie
              S.e
MARAGNO, Virtú (1928-   ), Arg
   R.26   S.46
MARAIS, Marin (1656-1728), Fr
   R.1   S.c,2-10,18,23,24
MARAZZOLI, Marco (c1602-1662), It
   R.1
MARBE, Myriam (1931-   ), Rum
   R.7   S.20,30,52
MARBECK, John [see MERBECKE, John]

MARC, Thomas (fl 1720-35), Fr
R.1   S.c
MARCABRU (fl 1128-50), Gascony
R.1   S.c,8,10,14,16
MARCADANTE

MARCADE, Nicolas (16th Cent)
             S.c
MARCEAU, V. - pseud [ie Marceau VERSCHUEREN]
             S.10
MARCELLO, Alessandro (1684-1750), It
R.1   S.c,5-10,18,24,32
MARCELLO, Benedetto (1686-1739), It
R.1   S.c,2-11,18,21,24,25,28,53
MARCHAND, Joseph (1673-1747), Fr
R.16   S.c
MARCHAND, Louis (1669-1732), Fr
R.1   S.c,3,4,5x,7-10,53
MARCHANT, Arthur William (1850-1921), Eng
R.39   S.10
MARCHANT, Sir Stanley (1883-1949), Eng
R.1
MARCHESELLI, Domenico (17th Cent)
             S.24
MARCHESI, Salvatore (1822-1908), It
R.1   S.c,5x,10
MARCHETTI, Filippo (1831-1902), It
R.1   S.c,24
MARCLAND, Patrick (1944-   )
             S.c
MARCO, Leonard
             S.24a
MARCO, Sano (1898-1970), USA
R.23   S.24
MARCO, Tomás (1942-   ), Sp
R.1   S.c
MARCOS, Manuel (20th Cent), Brazil

MARCOTTE, Don
             S.10
MARCUS, Sol (1912-1976), USA
R.23   S.10
MARCZEWSKI, Lucjan (1879-1935), Pol
R.4
MARDIROSIAN, Haig USA
             S.12,13
MARECHAL - Machine gun guards
             S.54(339)
MARELLA, Giovanni Battista (fl 1753-63), It
R.5   S.c,10,32

MARELLY - Chargez
           S.e
MAREN, Roger ?USA
           S.13
MARENCO, Romualdo (1841-1907), It
    R.1   S.24
MARENZIO, Luca (1553/54-1599), It
    R.1   S.c,2-5,7,8,10,11,14-16,18
MARESCHALL, Samuel (1554-1640), Swiss
    R.1   S.c
MARESCOTTI, André-François (1902-   ), Swiss
    R.1   S.c,4,5,8,10,18
MARESCOTTI, Ercole Arturo (1866-1928), It
    R.10   S.4
MAREZ OYENS, Tera de (1932-   ), Neth
    R.1   S.c,30,52
MARGETSON, E. J. - Tommy lad
           S.e
MARGIS, Alfred (1874-   )
           S.24
MARGOLA, Franco (1908-   ), It
    R.1   S.8,10
MARGUERITE d'AUTRICHE (1480-1530) [Notenbücher]
           S.c,14,52
MARGUSTE, Anti (1931-   ), USSR
    R.30   S.18
MARGUTTI - Canzone appassionata
           S.24
MARI, G. - serenade badine
           S.24a
MARI, Pierrette (1929-   ), Fr
    R.7   S.c
MARIA, Antônio - pseud [ie Antonio Maria Araujo de
    MORAIS] (1921-1964), Brazil
    R.67   S.39
MARIANI, Angelo (1821-1873), It
    R.8   S.24
MARIC, Ljubica (1909-   ), Yug
    R.7   S.52
MARIE ANTOINETTE, Queen of France (1755-1793)
    R.7   S.5x,30
MARIE de BOURGOGNE (15th Cent)
           S.c,10,16,30
MARIE, E. A. [S.54(337)] = MARIO, E. A.
           S.54(337)
MARIE, Gabriel [pseud: GABRIEL-MARIE] (1852-1928), Fr
    R.2   S.10,22,24 [Gabriel-Marie] (see note)
MARIE, Jean-Etienne (1917-   ), Fr
    R.1

MARIETTI, G.
          S.e
MARÍN, José (?1618/19-1699), Sp
  R.1   S.c,5x,10,16,39
MARÍN, Rafael (1862-   ), Sp
  R.106
MARINI, Biagio (c1587-1663), It
  R.1   S.c,2,4,5x,7,8,10,16,24
MARINIER, Paul
          S.e,24[Marrinier]
MARINOV, Ivan (1928-   ), Bul
  R.1   S.18

MARINUZZI, Gino Sr. (1882-1945), It
  R.1   S.4,5x,8,54(363)
MARIO, E. A. - pseud [ie Giovanni GAETA] (1884-   ), It
  R.10   S.18,54(337)[Marie, E. A.]
MARION, Sander van (1938-   )
          S.c
MARISCHAL, Louis (1928-   )
          S.c,24a
MARKAITIS, Bruno (1922-   ), USA
  R.19   S.13,24
MARKEVITCH, Igor (1912-1983), It
  R.1   S.c,3-5
MARKOV, Albert Alexandrovich (1933-   ), USA
          S.13,18,24
MARKOVITCH, Ivan (1929-   ), Yug
          S.22
MARKS, Florence Mary
          S.24,30
MARLIANI, Marco Aurelio (1805-1849), It
  R.1   S.10
MARLING, Henri - pseud [see SCHUTT, Eduard]
MARLY, Anna Fr
          S.10,30
MARÓS, Miklós (1943-   ), Hun
  R.4   S.10,40
MAROS, Rudolf (1917-   ), Hun
  R.1   S.c,9,10
MAROT de CASERTA [see ANTHONELLO de CASERTA]
MAROTO, Sebastian (1930-   )
          S.c,32
MARPURG, Friedrich Wilhelm (1718-1795), Ger
  R.1   S.4,5
MARQUÉS y GARCÍA, Pedro Miguel (1843-1925), Sp
  R.1   S.10
MARQUES, Juan (1582-1658)
          S.16
MARQUINA, Pascual (1873-   ), Sp
  R.9   S.10,39

MARRACO y FERRER, José (1835-1913), Sp
  R.1
MARRINER, P. [S.24] = MARINIER, Paul
MARROQUIN, Jose Sabre (1910-   )
          S.24
MARSAGLIA, V. A. - Pas du cygne (vi & p)
          S.24
MARSCHNER, Heinrich August (1795-1861), Ger
  R.1   S.c,2-5,7,8,10,42
MARSCHNER, Wolfgang (1926-   ), Ger
  R.4   S.24a
MARSELHA, Folquet de [see FOLQUET de MARSEILLE]
MARSH, Roger (1949-   )
          S.c
MARSHALL - The liberator; Ransomed
          S.54(337,51)
MARSHALL, Arthur Owen (1881-1956), USA
  R.50   S.10
MARSHALL, Charles (1857-1927)

          S.5x,10,24
MARSHALL, Frank (1883-   ), USA
          S.10,13
MARSHALL, Jack (1921-   ), USA
  R.14   S.22
MARSHALL, Philip (1921-   ), Eng
          S.c
MARSICK, Armand Louis Joseph (1877-1959), Bel
  R.1   S.8,36
MARSICK, Martin Pierre Joseph (1848-1924), Bel
  R.1   S.18,24
MARSON, George (c1573-1632), Eng
  R.1   S.7,8,10,14,16
MARTEAU, Henri (1874-1934), Fr
  R.3   S.24a
MARTELLI, Henri (1895-   ), Fr
  R.1   S.c,8
MARTENS, Charles (1866-1921), Bel
  R.76   S.c
MARTI, Heinz (1934-   ), Swiss
  R.1   S.c
MARTÍ, José (1500-1565), Sp
          S.17
MARTÍ, José (1719-1763), Sp
  R.5   S.c
MARTIN Codax [see CODAX, Martin]
MARTÍN y COLL, Antonio (18th Cent), Sp
  R.9   S.c,10,32,53
MARTÍN y SOLER, Vincente (1754-1806), Sp
  R.1   S.c

MARTIN - Flashing glory
             S.54(327)
MARTIN, Antonio (17th Cent)
             S.c
MARTIN, Cora
             S.10,30
MARTIN, David (1907-1975), USA
   R.23   S.9
MARTIN, David L. (1926-   ), USA
   R.14   S.13
MARTIN, E ?USA - Evensong
             S.5x,13
MARTIN, Easthope (1887-1925), Eng
   R.200   S.10,24
MARTIN, Emile (1914-   ), Fr
   R.14   S.c,9,10
MARTIN, Frank (1890-1974), Swiss
   R.1   S.c,4-10,23,24,42
MARTIN, Freddy (1906-   ), USA
   R.61   S.10
MARTIN, Hugh (1914-   ), USA
   R.19   S.9
MARTIN, Louis (fl 1550)
             S.c
MARTIN, Nicolas (1498-1566), Fr
   R.1   S.c,8

MARTIN, Richard (1570-1618), Eng
   R.5   S.c
MARTIN, Roberta Evelyn
             S.10,30
MARTINET, Jean-Louis (1912-   ), Fr
   R.1
MARTINEZ VALLS, Rafael (1887-1946)
             S.10
MARTINEZ ZARATE, George (1923-   )
             S.c
MARTINEZ, Marianne von (1744-1812), Aus
   R.1   S.30,52
MARTINI, Giovanni Battista (1706-1784), It
   R.1   S.c,2-6,8,10,18,22,24,32,53
MARTINI, Johann Paul Aegidius (1741-1816), Ger
   R.1   S.c,1-8,10,18,24,25,27
MARTINI, Johannes (c1440-1497/98), Flem
   R.1   S.c,10
MARTINO, Donald (1931-   ), USA
   R.1   S.10,13,19,21,24
MARTINON, Jean (1910-1976), Fr
   R.1   S.c,10,24
MARTINS, Francisco (c1620-1680), Port
   R.1

MARTINS, Joseph

MARTINS, Maria de Lourdes (1926-   ), Port
    R.7   S.52
MARTINŮ, Bohuslav (1890-1959), Cz
    R.1   S.c,2-5,7-10,18,19,21,23,24
MARTIRANO, Salvatore (1927-   ), USA
    R.1   . S.9,10,13
MARTTINEN, Tauno (1912-   ), Fin
    R.1   S.c,40
MARTUCCI, Giuseppe (1856-1909), It
    R.1   S.c,1-5,8-10,23
MARTY, Georges Eugène (1860-1908), Fr
    R.3   S.19,21
MARUTA, Shozo (?1938-   ), Japan
    R.36   S.50
MARVEL, Robert (1918-   ), USA
             S.4,13
MARX, Joseph (1882-1964), Aus
    R.1   S.1x,2-8,10,18,28
MARX, Karl (1897-   ), Ger
    R.1   S.c
MARY (19th Cent) - Rosebud quickstep
             S.30
MARZIALS, Theophilus Julius Henry (1850-1920), Eng
    R.57   S.e
MARZIS, Pasqualino de (fl 1750)
    R.5   S.c
MASCAGNI, Pietro (1863-1945), It
    R.1   S.c,1-11,18,24,28,42,44,54(318,19)
MASCHERA, Florentio (c1540-c1584), It
    R.1   S.c,8,10,14-16,53
MASCHERONI, Angelo (1855-1905), It

    R.1   S.c,24
MASCHERONI, Vittorio (1895-   ), It
    R.10s   S.10
MASCITTI, Michele (1663/64-1760), It
    R.1   S.c,10,24a
MAŠEK, Václav Vincenc (1755-1831), Boh
    R.1   S.c
MASETTI, Enzo (1893-1961), It
    R.10   S.5x,18[Mazetti]
MASINI, Antonio (1639-1678), It
    R.1
MASINI, Francesco (1804-1863), It
    R.3
MASINI, Laurentius [see LORENZO da FIRENZE]
MASON, Daniel Gregory (1873-1953), USA
    R.1   S.3-5,7-11,13,19,20,24

MASON, Jack (1906-1965), USA
  R.23   S.10
MASON, John [of Chichester] (d.1548), Eng
  R.1   S.c
MASON, Lowell (1792-1872), USA
  R.10   S.c,5x,10,47
MASON, William (1829-1908), USA
  R.10   S.10
MASSA, Juan Bautista (1885-1938), Arg
  R.56   S.5x,10
MASSAINO, Tiburtio (<1550-c1609), It
  R.1   S.c,10,15,16
MASSANA, Antonio (1890-1966), Sp
  R.1   S.42
MASSÉ, Victor (1822-1884), Fr
  R.1   S.c,4,10
MASSENET, Jules (1842-1912), Fr
  R.1   S.c,1-11,18,21,23,24,28,32,34
MASSENGALE, John
           S.47
MASSIS, Amable (1893-   ), Fr
  R.14   S.c,10
MASSON, Askell (1953-   ), Iceland
           S.40
MASSON-KIEK, F. - En relisant vos lettres - valse lent
  (orch)   S.24
MASSOUDIEH, Mohammad Taghi (1927-   ), Iran
  R.80   S.c
MASSUMOTO, Kikuko (1937-   ), Japan
  R.7   S.30
MASTERS, Joe
           S.9
MASTERS, Stanley Smith - pseud [see SIEBERT, Edrich]
MA SY-TSUN (1912-   )
           S.18
MATA, Eduardo (1942-   ), Mex
  R.4   S.24a
MATCHAVARIANI, Alexey Davidovich
  [see MACHAVARIANI, Alexey Davidovich]
MATÉJ, Jósef (1922-   ), Cz

  R.1   S.10,20,24a,31
MATELART, Ioanne (<1538-1607), It
  R.1   S.c,10,32
MATHE, Edouard (1863-1936)
           S.24
MATHER, Bruce (1939-   ), Can
  R.1   S.22
MATHES, Willy [see WILDMAN, Charles - pseud]
MATHESON, Johann (1681-1764), Ger
           S.c,2,7,10,53

MATHEUS de PEROUSE [see MATTEO de PERUGIA]
MATHEWS, Artie (1888-1959), USA
   R.50   S.10
MATHEWS, Max V. (1926-   ), USA
   R.19   S.10,13
MATHEWS, Thomas (1915-   ), USA
              S.12,13
MATHEWS, William (1950-   ), USA
              S.13
MATHEY, Paul (1909-   ), Swiss
   R.41
MATHIAS, William James (1934-   ), Wales
   R.1   S.c,9,10,55
MATHIESON, Muir (1911-1975), Eng
   R.1   S.9
MATHIEU, André René (1929-1968), Can
   R.14   S.4,24
MATHIEU, Rodolphe (1896-1962), Can
   R.14   S.24
MATIEGKA, Wenzel Thomas (1773-1830), Aus
   R.1   S.c,5x,8,10
MATIELLI, Giovanni Antonio (c1733-1805), It
   R.8   S.3-5,10
MATINSKY, Mikhail Alexeyevich (1750-c1825), Russia
   R.1   S.c,18
MATOS RODRIGUEZ, Gherardo Hernau (?-1948)
              S.5x,10,24[Rodriguez]
MATS, Rudolf (1901-   )
              S.18
MATSON - Australia
              S.e
MATSUDAIRA, Yori-Aki (1931-   ), Japan
   R.1   S.c,10,50
MATSUDAIRA, Yoritsune (1907-   ), Japan
   R.1   S.50
MATSUMOTO, Masao [pseud: Kazuyoshi MATSUMOTO] (1915-   )
   Japan   R.36   S.50
MATSUMOTO, Taminosuke (1914-   ), Japan
   R.36   S.50
MATSUMURA, Teizo (1929-   ), Japan
   R.1   S.50
MATSUSHITA, Shin'ichi (1922-   ), Japan
   R.4   S.50
MATT, Albert E. Eng - Fame & Glory
              S.54(325)
MATTEI, Tito (1841-1914), It
   R.8   S.5x,24

MATTEIS, Nicola (d ?1707), It
   R.1   S.c,8,10

MATTEO da PERUGIA [Perouse] (d c1418), It
   R.1   S.c,3,4,5x,8,10,14,16
MATTES, Willy [see WILDMAN, Charles]
MATTHES, Rene (1897-1967), Swiss
   R.14
MATTHESON, Johann, (1681-1764), Ger
   R.1   S.c,3-6,14,18,24
MATTHEWS, David (1942-   ), USA
   R.60
MATTHEWS, Thomas (1915-   ), USA
             S.10,12,13
MATTHUS, Siegfried (1934-   ), Ger
   R.14   S.24a
MATTIESEN, Emil (1875-1939), Ger
   R.8   S.c
MATTON, Roger (1929-   ), Can
   R.1   S.10
MATTULLATH, Alice (20th Cent), ?USA
   R.7   S.24,30
MATUSKA, Janko (1821-1877), Cz
   R.18   S.5x,24
MATUSZCZAK, Bernadetta (1937-   ), Pol
   R.7   S.52
MATVEYEV, Mikhail Alexandrovich (1912-   ), USSR
   R.14   S.18
MATVEYEVNA, Novella (1934-   ), USSR
   R.7   S.52
MATYS, Jiří (1927-   ), Cz
   R.14   S.24a
MATYS, Josef (1851-1937), Cz
   R.4   S.10
MAUD, Constance (19th Cent), USA
   R.53   S.e
MAUDUIT, Jacques (1557-1627), Fr
   R.1   S.c,2-5,7,8,10,11,14-16
MAUERSBERGER, Erhard (1903-   ), Ger
   R.4
MAUERSBERGER, Rudolf (1889-1971), Ger
   R.1   S.c,24a
MAUL, Octavio
             S.10,24a
MAULDIN, Michael (1947-   ), USA
   R.19   S.13
MAUNDER, John Henry (1858-1920), Eng
   R.1   S.c
MAURAGE - La China
             S.1x
MAURER, Ludwig (1789-1878), Ger
   R.1   S.c,10

MAURICA, Santiago de (17th Cent), Sp

MAURICE, Paule (1910-1967), Fr
   R.7   S.c,10,22,30,52
MAURO-COTTONE, (20th Cent), It

MAURY, Lowndes (1911-1975), USA
   R.19   S.10,13,24
MAVISAKALYAN, M. - Sonata (vi & p)
            S.24a
MAW, Nicholas (1935-   ), Eng
   R.1   S.c,9,10
MAXFIELD, Richard (1927-1969), USA
   R.1   S.9,10,13
MAXIM, Abraham (1773-1829), USA
            S.10,47
MAXWELL - The singer
            S.e
MAXWELL GEDDES, John (1941-   ), Scot
            S.c
MAXWELL, Michael Somerset Cullen (1921-   ), Eng [?]
   R.80   S.8
MAXWELL, Robert (1921-   ), USA
   R.23   S.10
MAXWELL-DAVIES, Peter [see DAVIES, Peter Maxwell]
MAXYLEWICZ, Wincenty (1685-1745), Pol
   R.1   S.c
MAY - Il est un chant d'amour

MAY, Frederick (1911-   ), Ire
   R.1   S.10,49
MAY, Hans (1886-1958), Aus
   R.4   S.10
MAYA, Eusebio (18th Cent)

MAYA, Raphael (1898-   ), Colombia
            S.39
MAYBRICK, Michael [see ADAMS, Stephen - pseud]
MAYER, Charles (1799-1862), Ger
   R.1
MAYER, Johann (19th Cent) - Schnofler-Tanz
            S.c,10
MAYER, John (1930-   ), India
   R.1   S.c
MAYER, William (1925-   ), USA
   R.19   S.10,13
MAYERL, Billy (1902-1959), USA
   R.1   S.c
MAYNARD, John (1577->1614), Eng
   R.1   S.c

MAYONE, Ascanio (c1565-1627), It
   R.1   S.c,53
MAYR, Johannes Simone (1763-1845), Ger
   R.1   S.c,9,10
MAYR, Rathart (1737-1805)
   R.200   S.c
MAYR, Rupert Ignaz (1646-1712), Ger
   R.1   S.c,10
MAYS, Walter (1941-   ), USA
   R.19   S.10,13,22
MAYSEDER, Joseph (1789-1863), Aus
   R.1   S.c
MAYUZUMI, Toshiro (1929-   ), Japan
   R.1   S.c,9,10,50
MAZA, Regino Sainz de la [see SAINZ de la MAZA, Regino]
MAZAEV, Arkadi Nikolayevich (1909-   ), USSR
   R.14   S.18
MAZAS, Jacques-Féréol (1782-1849), Fr
   R.1   S.c,24a
MAZELLIER, Jules (1879-1959), Fr
   R.14   S.4,10,19,20
MAZETTI, Enzo [S.18] = MASETTI, Enzo

MAZIJK, R. van (1934-   )
            S.c
MAZOUROVA, Jarmila (1941-   ), Cz
   R.7   S.52
MAZUEL, Michel (1603-1676), Fr
   R.1   S.8
MAZUREK, Bohdan (20th Cent)
            S.c,10
MAZZA, Giuseppe (1806-1885), It
   R.3
MAZZOCCHI, Domenico (1592-1665), It
   R.1   S.c
MAZZOCCHI, Virgilio (1597-1646), It
   R.1
MAZZOLA, Guerino (1947-   ),
            S.c
MEACHEM, Frank W.
            S.c,10,54(312)
MEALE - Sonny
            S.e
MEALE, Richard (1932-   ), Australia
   R.1   S.29,37
MEAUX, Etienne de [see ETIENNE de MEAUX]
MECCIA - Il mondo
            S.10
MECHEM, Kirke (1925-   ), USA
   R.19   S.10,13

MÉCHURA, Leopold Eugen (1804-1870), Boh
   R.1
MECK, Joseph (1690-1758), Ger
   R.1   S.c,8
MEDEIROS, Alfredo de
             S.c
MEDEK, Tilo (1940-   ), Ger
   R.1   S.c
MEDER, Johann Gabriel (fl c1755-1800), Ger
   R.1
MEDER, Johann Valentin (1649-1719), Ger
   R.1   S.c
MEDIAVILLA - Mi tierra [see also MUZA y MEDIAVILLA]
             S.39
MEDINŠ [Medyn], Janis (1890-1966), Lat
   R.1   S.9,10,18,24
MEDINŚ [Medyn], Jazeps (1877-1947), Lat
   R.1   S.18,24
MEDINŚ [Medyn], Jekabs (1885-1971), Lat
   R.1   S.18,20,24
MEDTNER, Nikolai [see METNER, Nikolai]
MEEK, Kenneth (1908-1976), Can
   R.14   S.10
MEESTER, Louis de (1904-   ), Bel
   R.1   S.36
MÉFANO, Paul (1937-   ), Fr
   R.1   S.c
MEGEVAND, Denise (20th Cent), Fr
   R.7   S.52
MEGLI, Domenico Maria [see MELLI, Domenico Maria]
MEGLIO, Vincenzo de (1825-1883), It
   R.10   S.24
MEHDEN - Flora
             S.54(327)
MEHLER, Friedrich (1896-1981), Sweden
   R.14   S.40
MÉHUL, Etienne-Nicolas (1763-1817), Fr
   R.1   S.c,1x,2-5,7,8,10,11,22,23
MEIEN, Vadim Alexandrovich (1911-   )
             S.18
MEIER, Daniel (1934-   )
             S.c
MEIER, Ernst (1905-   )
             S.18
MEIER, Jost (1939-   )

MEIER, Pius (1896-   )
             S.c
MEIJER, Axel (1940-   ), Neth

MEINECKE, Christopher (1782-1850)
   R.200   S.10
MEISEL, Will (1897-1967), Ger
   R.14   S.10,24
MEISSEN, Heinrich von [see FRAUENLOB]
MEISSER - Grenadier du Caucase
           S.54(330)
MEISSLER, Jos - pseud [see HUTCHINSON, William Marshall]
MEISTER ALEXANDER [See ALEXANDER, Meister]
MEISTER POPPE (13th Cent), Swiss
   R.5
MEISTER, F. - Erwinn fantaisie (cl & p)
           S.10,19
MEISTER, Karl [pseud: AXOLOTL] (1903-   ), Ger
   R.4
MEITUS, Yuli Sergeyevich (1903-   ), USSR
   R.14   S.18,24a
MEKEEL, Joyce (1931-   ), USA
   R.19   S.10,13,24a,52
MEL, Rinaldo del (c1554-c1598), Flem
   R.1   S.16
MELANI, Jacopo (1623-1676), It
   R.1
MELARTIN, Erkki (1875-1937), Fin
   R.1   S.1x,10,18,24,40
MELBY, John (1941-   ), USA
   R.19   S.10,13
MELCHERT, J. - Raslende Solv, Brusende Bolge (vi & p)
           S.24
MELFI, Mario (1905-   )
           S.24
MELGAZ, Diogo Dias (1638-1700), Port
   R.1
MELICHAR, Alois (1896-1976), Aus
   R.14   S.10
MELIKIAN, Grachik (1913-1942)
           S.24a
MELIKIAN, Spiridon Avetisi (1880-   ), Arm
   R.200   S.10
MELIKOV, Arif (1933-   ), USSR
   R.1   S.18,24a
MELIKYAN, Romanus Hovakimi (1883-1935), Arm
   R.1   S.18
MELL, Davis (1604-1662), Eng
   R.1   S.c
MELL, Gertrud Maria (1947-   ), Sweden
   R.7   S.52
MELLERS, Wilfrid (1914-   ), Eng
   R.1

MELLI, Domenico Maria (17th Cent), It
    R.1   S.c
MELLI, Pietro Paolo (fl 1612-20), It
    R.1   S.c,10,16
MELLING - Patriotic hymn
            S.e
MELLISH, Colonel R. (c1777-1817)
            S.e
MELLNÄS, Arne (1933-   ), Sweden
    R.1   S.10,38,40,56
MELNGAILIS, Emilis (1874-1954), Lat
    R.1   S.18
MELNIK, The Lute player of (18th Cent)
            S.5x
MELNOTTE, Claude - pseud [see KUNKEL, Charles]
MELROSE, Walter (1889-   ), USA
    R.23   S.10
MELUZZI - Salvatore (1813-1897), It
    R.10   S.e
MELVILL, David (17th Cent), Eng

MELVILLE, G. J. Whyte
            S.e
MENA, Gabriel (fl 1511-16), Sp
    R.1   S.[Gabriel],c,5x,10,14,16,39
MENALT [Menault], Gabriel (d.1687), Sp
    R.1   S.c,53
MENASCE, Jacques de (1905-1960), USA
    R.1   S.c,8,9,13,23,24
MENCEL of KOLSDORF (fl 1605), Boh
            S.5x
MENDANCA, Jobim
            S.32
MENDELSSOHN, Fanny (1805-1847), Ger
    R.1   S.c,10,24a,25,30,52[Hensel]
MENDELSSOHN, Alfred (1910-1966), Rum
    R.1   S.7,8,10,18,24
MENDELSSOHN, Arnold (1855-1933), Ger
    R.1
MENDELSSOHN, Felix (1809-1847), Ger
    R.1   S.c,1-11,18-28,32,54(312,15,25)
MENDELSSOHN, Ludwig (1858-1921), Ger
    R.3   S.10
MENDES, Manuel (c1547-1605), Port
    R.1
MENDES, Sergio (1941-   ), Brazil
    R.4   S.39
MENDEZ, Rafael (1906-   ), USA
    R.61

MENDIGALIEV, N. (1921-   )
          S.24a
MENDONÇA, Newton (1927-1960), Brazil
    R.67   S.39
MENDOZA y CORTEZ, Quirino (1862-1957), Mex
    R.4   S.10
MENDOZA-NAVA, Jaime (1925-   ), Bolivia
    R.1   S.10,39
MENEGALI (18-19th Cent)
    R.5   S.8,10
MENEGHETTI - Canzone del Grappa
          S.54(318)
MENENDEZ, Pedro (1906-   )
          S.8
MENESCAL, Roberto (1937-   ), Brazil
    R.67   S.39 (see note under Bôscoli)
MENGELBERG, Karel (1902-   ), Neth
    R.4
MENGELBERG, Rudolf (1892-1959), Neth
    R.1   S.7
MENICHETTI, François (1892-   ), Fr
          S.10
MENNIN, Peter (1923-1983), USA
    R.1   S.c,8,10,13,24a
MENNINI, Louis (1920-   ), USA
    R.19   S.7,10,13
MENOTTI, Gian Carlo (1911-   ), It
    R.1   S.c,3-11,13,18,24,42
MENSCHICK, Wolfram
          S.c
MENTER, Sophie (1846-1918), Ger

    R.7
MENZEL, Franz
          S.24
MERBECKE [Marbeck], John (c1510-c1585), Eng
    R.1   S.c,2-5,7,8,16
MERCADANTE, Giuseppe Saverio Raffaele (1795-1870), It
    R.1   S.c,8,10,24
MERCER, John H. (1909-1976), USA
    R.23   S.10
MERCHI, Joseph Bernard (c1730-1793), It
    R.1   S.c
MERCKER, Matthias (fl 1600-22), Neth
    R.1
MERCURE, Jean (17th Cent), Fr
          S.c
MERCURE, Pierre (1927-1966), Can
    R.1   S.10
MEREDITH - Sursum corda: The lord is my shepherd
          S.e

MERETTA, Leonard V. (1915-   ), USA
R.23   S.54(342)
MERGEL, Tony

MERGNER, Adam Fredrich Christoph (1818-1891), Ger
R.25
MERIDA, M. - Isa palmera
        S.39
MERIKANTO, Aarre (1893-1958), Fin
R.1   S.c,9,24a,40
MERIKANTO, Oskar (1868-1924), Fin
R.1   S.c,5x,18,24,40
MERILÄINEN, Usko (1930-   ), Fin
R.1   S.c,40,24a
MERKEL, Gustav Adolf (1827-1885), Ger
R.1   S.c,18
MERKER, Mathaus (fl 1618-22), Neth
R.21   S.c
MERKLER, Andro
        S.24
MERKUR, Jacob Louis (1895-   ), USA
R.23   S.24
MERMOUD, Robert (1912-   ), Swiss
R.14   S.c
MEROFF - pseud [see RILLE, Laurent Francois Anatole de]
MERRICK, Frank (1886-1981), Eng
R.1   S.8
MERSENNE, Marin (1588-1648), Fr
R.1   S.c,2,5x,10
MERTEL, Elias (c1561-1626), Ger
R.1   S.c,10,16,32
MERTENS, Jos (1834-1901), Bel
R.3   S.c
MERTZ, Joseph Kasper (1806-1856), Hun
R.15   S.c,10
MERUCO, Johannes de [see JOHANNES de MERUCO]
MERULA, Tarquinio (1594/95-1665), It
R.1   S.8,10,18,24,53
MERULO, Claudio (1533-1604), It
R.1   S.c,5x,8,10,14,16,53
MESA, Manuel (16-17th Cent)
        S.c
MESANGEAU, René (d.1638), Fr
R.1   S.c
MESOMEDES (2nd Cent), Greece
R.1   S.2-4,5x,10
MESQUIDA
        S.32
MESQUITA, Carlos de (1864-1953), Brazil
R.56   S.24

MESQUITA, José Joaquím Emirico Lôbo de (1730/45-1805),
    Brazil   R.1
MESSAGER, André (1853-1929), Fr
    R.1   S.c,1-5,7-10,19,21,42,54(323)
MESSAGER, Mme [see TEMPLE, Hope - pseud]
MESSAUS, Guillaume (1589-1640), Flem
    R.1   S.c
MESSER, Donald (1909-1973), Can
    R.31
MESSIAEN, Olivier (1908-   ), Fr
    R.1   S.c,4-10,18-21,24,27,28
MESSLINGER, Karl (1902-1973)
               S.c
MESSNER, Joseph (1893-1969), Aus
    R.1   S.c
MESTDAGH, Karel (1850-1924), Bel
    R.3   S.41
MESTRES, Antonio (18th Cent)
               S.c
MESTRES-QUADRENY, Josep (1929-   ), Sp
    R.1   S.10
META, Sy USA

METALLA, G. - Sharpshooter's March
               S.54(355)
METAYER, M. - Dans une humble étable

METCALF, John W. (?1856-1926), USA
    R.53,200   S.5x,10,24,28
MÉTÉHEN, Jacques (1903-   ), Fr
    R.14   S.24a
METHVEN, Agnes Florence (fl 1916), USA
               S.e
METNER [Medtner], Nikolay Karlovich (1880-1951), Russia
    R.1   S.c,1-7,9-11,18,24,28
MÉTRA, Jules Louis Olivier (1830-1889), Fr
    R.1   S.c
METRAL, Pierre (1936-   )
               S.c,24a
METSCH, Placidus (1700-1778), Ger
    R.5   S.c
METSCHNABL, Paul Josef (1910-   )
               S.c
MEULEMANS, Arthur (1884-1966), Bel
    R.1   S.8,10,36
MEUMANE [S.54 (332)] = NEUMANE, Antonio
MEUNIER, M. J. - Ave Maria
               S.1x
MEYER von SCHAUENSEE, Franz Joseph Leonti (1720-1789),
    Swiss   R.1   S.c

MEYER, Ernst Hermann (1905-   ), Ger
    R.1   S.23,24
MEYER, Gregor (>1510-1576), Swiss
    R.2   S.c,10,16
MEYER, Hannes (1939-   )
               S.c
MEYER, Joseph (1894-   ), USA
    R.23   S.24a
MEYER, Krzysztof (1943-   ), Pol
    R.1   S.c,24a
MEYER, Phillippe-Jacques (1737-1819), Alsatian
    R.1   S.8
MEYER, Sigtenhorst

MEYER-HELMUND, Erik (1861-1932), Russia
    R.3   S.c,1x,5x,10,24
MEYERBEER, Giacomo (1791-1864), Ger
    R.1   S.c,1-11,18,20,34,4254(315,21,25,32)
MEYERS, Billy (1894-   ), USA
    R.23   S.10
MEYERS, Emerson (1910-   ), USA
    R.19   S.13
MEYERS, Lois (20th Cent), USA
               S.52
MEYNAUD, Michel (1950-   )
               S.c,24a
MEYSEL - Der Kellermeister
               S.e
MEYTUS, Yuly Sergeyevich (1903-   ), Russia
    R.1   S.2-4,5x,11
MEZANGEAU, René [see MESANGEAU, René]
MEZZACAPO, Edouardo (fl 1887-1911), It
    R.106   S.24
MIAGI, Ester Kustovna (1922-   ), USSR
    R.7   S.18[Myagi],52
MIASKOVSKY, Nikolai Yokovlevich
    [see MYASKOVSKY, Nikolai Yokovlevich]
MÍČA, František Adam (1746-1811), Cz
    R.1   S.c,10,24
MÍČA, František Antonín Václav (1694-1744), Cz
    R.1   S.c,4,5,18
MICHA, Octave (1879-   )
               S.24a
MICHAEL, Christian (c1593-1637), Ger
    R.1   S.c,53
MICHAEL, David Moritz (1751-1827), USA
    R.1   S.8,10,47
MICHAEL, Frank (1943-   ), Ger
    R.4   S.c

MICHAELIS, Theodor (1831-1887), Ger
   R.3   S.54(327,62)
MICHAILOW, Maxim (1895-1971), USSR
   R.4   S.24
MICHALSKY, Donal Ray (1928-1975), USA
   R.19   S.10,13
MICHÉ - Valse bluette (vi & p)
            S.24a
MICHEELSEN, Hans Friedrich (1902-1973), Ger
   R.2   S.c,7,8,10
MICHEL, Guillaume (fl 1636-56), Fr
   R.1   S.8
MICHEL, Jean Christian

MICHEL, Josef (1928-   ), Ger
   R.4   S.c
MICHEL, Marius - pseud [see MISSA, Edmund]
MICHEL, Paul-Baudouin (1930-   ), Bel
   R.4   S.c,24a
MICHEL, Wilfried (1940-   )
            S.c
MICHELENA - A la luze la luna
            S.44
MICHELET, Michel (1894-   ), USA
   R.19   S.9,13
MICHELI - Reverie (vi & p); Serenata (vi & p)
            S.24
MICHI, Orazio (1594/95-1641), It
   R.1
MICHIELS, Gustav (1845-   )
   R.3   S.24
MICHL, Ferdinand (1723-1754), Ger
   R.1   S.c
MICHL, Gilbert (1750-1828)
            S.c
MICHL, Joseph Willibald (1745-1816), Ger
   R.1   S.c
MICHNA, Adam Václav (c1600-1676), Cz
   R.1   S.c,5x,7
MICO, Richard (c1590-1661), Eng
   R.1   S.c,10,16
MIDDELEER, Jean de (1908-   ), Bel
   R.14
MIDDELSCHULTE, Wilhelm (1863-1943), Ger
   R.2   S.10
MIDDLETON, John (1944-   ), Eng
            S.c
MIDDLETON, Owen (1941-   ), USA
   R.23   S.c

MIEG, Peter (1906-   ), Swiss
    R.1   S.c,4,24a
MIELCZEWSKI, Marcin (d.1651), Pol
    R.1   S.5x,6,8-10,16,24
MIEREANU, Costin (1943-   ), Rum
    R.14   S.20
MIERISCH-LOWITZ - The Swanee river bend
             S.e
MIESSNER - Hearing
             S.e
MIGLIAVACCA, Luciano (1919-   )
             S.c
MIGNONE, Francisco (1897-1980), Brazil
    R.1   S.c,3-8,10,11,24,32
MIGOT, Georges Elbert (1891-1976), Fr
    R.1   S.c,1,4,5,19,24
MIGRANYAN, Emma (1940-   ), USSR
             S.52
MIGUEZ, Leopoldo (1850-1902), Brazil
    R.1   S.c,10
MIHALOVICI, Marcel (1898-   ), Rum
    R.1   S.c,2,3,8,10,20,24
MIHÁLY, András (1917-   ), Hun
    R.1   S.c,10,24
MIHULE, Jiri (1907-   ), Cz
             S.31
MIKHAILOV, A. - Melodies of the Volga
             S.18
MIKHAILOV, N. - Spring is beautiful in my homeland
             S.18
MIKHOTIN, V. - I was attracted by your grief
             S.18
MIKI, Minoru (1930-   ), Japan
    R.1   S.10,50
MIKKELSEN - Sunbeam
             S.5x
MIKOLAJ z CHRZANOWA (c1485-c1555)
             S.c,16
MIKOLAJ z KRAKOWA [Nicolaus Cracoviensis] (16th Cent),
    Pol R.1   S.c,10,16,18,53
MIKOLAJ z RADOMIA
             S.c,16
MIKULA, Zdenko (1916-   ), Cz
    R.14   S.c,31
MILÁN, Luis de (c1500-c1561),Sp
    R.1   S.c,2-8,10,11,14-18,32,39,53
MILANDRE, Louis-Toussaint (1770-   ), Fr
    R.8   S.c,7,10,24
MILANES (de Milanes) (17th Cent)
             S.c,10

MILANESI, Negri
          S.32
MILANO, Francesco [see FRANCESCO CANOVA da MILANO]
MILANUZZI, Carlo de (d c1647), It
   R.1   S.c,2-4,5x
MILARTE, Jacobus de (16th Cent)
          S.c,10,16,17,32,39
MILBURN, Ellsworth (1938-   ), USA
   R.19   S.10,13
MILCINSKY, Daniel Alois Frantisek (1732-1808), Cz
   R.18   S.c
MILES, C. Austin [pseud: A. A. PAYN, G. W. PAYN]
   (1868-1946), USA   R.23   S.10
MILES, Percy Hilder
          S.24
MILETIC, Miroslav (1925-   ), Yug
   R.14   S.24a
MILFORD, Robin (1903-1959), Eng
   R.1   S.c,10
MILHAUD, Darius (1892-1974), Fr
   R.1   S.c,1-11,18-20,22-24,26,27,32
MILLÁN, Francisco (16th Cent), Sp
   R.1   S.17
MILLÁN, Lopez Monis
          S.9
MILLÁN, Rafael (1893-   ), Sp

MILLARD, Harrison (1830-1895), USA
   R.10   S.10
MILLER - Hail to the Prince
          S.54(328,30)
MILLER, Charles (1899-   ), USA
   R.19   S.10,13,24
MILLER, Edward (1735-1807), Eng
   R.1
MILLER, Edward Jay (1930-   ), USA
   R.19   S.10,13
MILLER, George J. (ii) (1853-   ), Eng
   R.49   S.54(364)
MILLER, Jacques (1900-   ), USA
   R.19   S.13
MILLER, L. B. - Abraham Lincoln's funeral march
          S.47
MILLER, Malloy (1918-1981), USA
   R.19   S.10,13
MILLER, W. B. (19th Cent), USA - The girl I left behind
   me   S.10,47
MILLET, Luis (1867-1941), Sp
   R.9

MILLÖCKER, Carl (1842-1899), Aus
R.1   S.c,1x,2-10,42,43,54(328)
MILLOT - Louis XIV
              S.54(339)
MILLOT, Nicolas (fl 1556-86), Fr
R.1   S.c
MILLS, Charles (1914-1982), USA
R.1   S.10,13
MILLS, Frederick Allen (Kerry) (1869-1948), USA
R.23   S.10,54(314)
MILLS, Irving (1894-   ), USA
R.23   S.10
MILNE, Dennis (20th Cent)
              S.c
MILNER, Anthony (1925-   ), Eng
R.1   S.c
MILNER, Arthur Frederick (1894-1972), Eng
R.4
MILOJEVÍC, Miloje (1884-1946), Yug
R.42,200   S.24[Miloieritsch, M.D.]
MILSTEIN, Nathan (1904-   ), USA
R.1   S.c,24
MILTON, John (c1563-1647), Eng
R.1   S.c,7,8,10,14
MILVEDEN, Ingmar (1920-   ), Sweden
R.30   S.56
MILWID, Antoni (18th Cent), Pol
R.1   S.c
MIMAROĞLU, Ilhan Kemaleddin (1926-   ), Turkey
R.1   S.c,9,10,13,24
MING, Hu Hui
              S.24a
MING, Zhang Jiah
              S.24a
MING-XIN, Du (1928-   )
              S.24a
MINGUS, Charles (1922-1979), USA
R.1   S.10
MINISCALCHI, Guglielmo (fl 1622-30), It
R.1   S.c,3,4,5x,8
MINKUS, Léon (1826-1917), Aus
R.1   S.5x,7-10,18,24
MINORET, Guillaume (c1650-1717), Fr
R.1   S.8,10
MIRA BAI (1498-1547), India
              S.52
MIRANDA, Ronaldo
              S.24a
MIRAVAL, Raimon de [see RAIMON de MIRAVAL]

MIROGLIO, Francis (1924-   ), Fr
   R.1
MIRON, Issachar (1920-   ), Isr
   R.1   S.9,10
MIROSHNIKOV, O. - Scherzo (bassoon)
         S.10
MIRSHAKAR, Zarrina Mirsaidovna (1947-   ), USSR
         S.24a,52
MIRZA-ZADE, Khaiyam (1935-   ), USSR
   R.47   S.18
MIRZOEV, Musa (1933-   ), USSR
   R.47   S.18,24
MIRZOYEN, Edvard Mikaeli (1921-   ), Arm
   R.1   S.18,24a
MISEK, Adolf (1875-1955)

MISKOV, Sextus (1857-1928), Den
   R.30   S.5x
MISÓN, Luis (d.1766), Sp
   R.1   S.c
MISRAKI, Paul (1908-   ), Fr
   R.14   S.24

MISSA, Edmund [pseud: Marius MICHEL] (1861-1910), Fr
   R.3   S.e
MISSAL, Joshua M. (1915-   ), USA
   R.19
MISSUD, Jean Marie (1852-1941), Fr
   R.49
MISTAK, Alvin Frank (1930-   ), USA
   R.14   S.22
MISTOWSKI, Alfred (1872-   ), Eng
   R.37   S.24
MITCHELL, Ian Douglas (1926-   ), USA
         S.13
MITCHELL, Lyndol (1923-1964), USA
   R.19   S.10,13
MITERAN, Alain (20th Cent)
         S.c
MITREA-CELERIANU, Mihai (1935-   ), Rum
   R.4
MITSUKURI, Shukichi (1895-1971), Japan
   R.1   S.24,50
MITTANTIER, (fl 1536-47), Fr
   R.1   S.c
MITTERER, Ignaz Martin (1850-1924), Aus
   R.2   S.c,2,3
MITTERMAYR, Georg (1950-   )
         S.c
MITUSHIN, Alexander Sergeevich (1888-   )
         S.10

MIYAGI, Michio (1894-1956), Japan
 R.1   S.10,18,24
MIYAKE, Haruna (1942-   ), Japan
 R.4   S.50,52
MIYASHITA, Shuretsu (1909-   ), Japan
 R.36   S.24a
MIYOSHI, Akira (1933-   ), Japan
 R.1   S.10,24,50
MIZERIT, Klaro (1914-   ), It
 R.81
MIZUNO, Shuko (1934-   ), Japan
 R.1   S.50
MJASKOWSKY, Nikolai [see MYASKOVSKY, Nikolay]
MLYNARSKI, Emil (1870-1935), Pol
 R.1   S.24
MOBACH, Elke (1836-1898), Neth
 R.3   S.c
MODENA, Julio de [see SEGNI, Julio]
MODERNE, Jacques (16th Cent), Fr
 R.1   S.c,10,16
MODR, Antonín (1898-   ), Cz
 R.14   S.5x,31
MOERAN, Ernest John (1894-1950), Eng
 R.1   S.c,3-5,8-10,24,27
MOESCHINGER, Albert (1897-   ), Swiss
 R.1   S.c,4,5,8,10,24
MOEVS, Robert (1921-   ), USA
 R.1   S.10,13
MOHAUPT, Richard (1904-1957), Ger

 R.1   S.8-10,13,42
MOHLER, Philipp (1908-   ), Ger
 R.1
MOHR J. - Air varié (cl & p)
 R.105   S.20,54(311)
MOHRIG, Ludwig-Gunter

MÖHRING, Ferdinand (1816-1887), Ger
 R.30a   S.e
MOIR, Frank Lewis (1852-1902), Eng
 R.3
MOISY, Heinz von
     S.c
MOKRANJAC, Stevan (1856-1914), Serbian
 R.1   S.c
MOKROUSOV, Boris (1909-1968), USSR
 R.14   S.5x
MOL, Willem de [see DE MOL, Willem]
MOLARSKY, Delmar ?USA
     S.3,4,13

MOLCHANOV, Kirill Vladimirovich (1922-   ), Russia
   R.1   S.18
MOLDOBASANOV, Kaly (1929-   ), USSR
   R.47   S.18
MOLDOVAN, Mihai (1937-   ), Rum
   R.4
MOLEIRO, Moises (1905-   ), Ven
   R.4
MOLINARO, Simone (c1565-1615), It
   R.1   S.c,5x,8,10,16,32
MOLINEAUX, Allen Walter (1950-   ), USA
   R.19   S.13
MOLINO, Francesco (c1775-1847), It
   R.3   S.c,10
MOLINS, P. des (14th Cent), Fr
   R.1   S.c,3,5x,8,10,11
MOLIQUE, Wilhelm Bernhard (1802-1869), Ger
   R.1   S.c,10
MOLITOR, Valentin (1637-1713), Swiss
   R.1   S.c
MOLLEDA, José Muñoz [see MUÑOZ MOLLEDA, José]
MOLLENDORF, Julius (1821-1895), Ger
   R.3   S.54(348)
MOLLENDORF, Willy von (1907-   )
             S.c
MOLLER, Friedrich
             S.10
MOLLER, John Christopher (1755-1803), USA
   R.1   S.7,8,10,47
MOLLIER, Louis de (c1615-1688), Fr
   R.1   S.c
MOLLOY, James (1837-1909), Eng
   R.57   S.c,5x,10,24
MOLTER, Johan Melchior (1696-1765), Ger
   R.1   S.c,10,19-21
MOLTKE, Graf Kuno (?-1923)

   R.3   S.10,54(330)
MOMPOU, Federico (1893-   ), Sp
   R.1   S.c,1,4-10,18,24,32,39
MONACHUS, Guillelmus [see GUILLELMUS MONACHUS]
MONACO, James V. (1885-1945), USA
   R.23   S.e
MONARI, Bartolomeo (fl 1670-80), It
   R.23   S.c,53
MONASTERIO, Jesús (1836-1903), Sp
   R.1   S.18,24
MONASYPOV, Almaz (1925-   )
             S.18
MONCAYO GARCÍA, José Pablo (1912-1958), Mex
   R.1   S.8,10,18,39

MONCKTON, Lionel [pseud: Leslie MAYNE] (1861-1924), Eng
    R.1   S.54(313,51)
MONDÉJAR, Alonso de (fl 1502-05), Sp
    R.1   S.5x,10,14,39
MONDELLO, Nuncio (1929-   ), USA
                S.13
MONDONVILLE, Jean Joseph Cassanea de (1711-1772), Fr
    R.1   S.5x,9,22,24
MONFERRATO, Natale (c1603-1685), It
    R.1
MONFRED, Avenir H. de (1903-   ), Fr
    R.14   S.c,24a
MONIOT d'ARRAS (fl 1213-39), Fr
    R.1   S.c,5x,7,10,14,16,32
MONIOT de PARIS (13th Cent), Fr
    R.1   S.c,10
MONIUSZKO, Stanislaw (1819-1872), Pol
    R.1   S.c,2-10,18,24,42
MONK of Montaudon [SEE Montaudon, Monk of]
MONK of SALZBURG (14th Cent), Ger
    R.1   S.c
MONK, Edwin George (1819-1900), Eng
    R.1   S.c
MONK, Meredith (1942-   ), USA
    R.19   S.c,9,13,30,52
MONK, William Henry (1823-1889), Eng
    R.1   S.c,5x,10,24,54(311)
MONN, Mathias Georg (1717-1750), Aus
    R.1   S.c,10,24
MONNET - Le Fanion de la Legion
                S.54(326)
MONNIKENDAM, Marius (1896-1977), Neth
    R.1   S.c,10
MONNOT, Marguerite Angele (1903-1961), Fr
    R.7   S.c,9,30,52
MONOD, Jacques Louis (1927-   ), Fr
    R.1   S.10,13
MONRAD JOHANSEN, David [see JOHANSEN, David Monrad]
MONRO, George (d.1731), Eng
    R.5   S.c,5x,10,26-28
MONROE, Ervin USA
                S.10,13
MONSIGNY, Pierre-Alexandre (1729-1817), Fr
    R.1   S.c,2,4,5,10,24,28
MONT, Henri du [see DU MONT, Henri]
MONTAG, Ludwig (1906-   )
                S.c
MONTANI, Pietro (1885-1967), It
    R.14   S.c,4,5

MONTARIN (fl 1710-27)
   R.5
MONTAUDON, Monk of (12th Cent)
            S.10,16,39
MONTAVANI - Impromptu serenade (vi & p)
            S.7,22,24
MONTBRUN, Raymond Gallois
   [see GALLOIS-MONTBRUNN, Raymond]
MONTE, Lambert de (17th Cent)
            S.c
MONTE, Philippe de (1521-1603), Flem
   R.1   S.c,7,8,10,14-16,39,53
MONTÉCLAIR, Michel Pignolet de (1667-1737), Fr
   R.1   S.c,1-5,10,11,24a
MONTEHUS - Chants des jeunes gardes
            S.5x
MONTEMEZZI, Italo (1875-1952), It
   R.1   S.c,2-4,6,9,42
MONTERDE, B. Bautista (fl 1924), Sp - La virgen de la
   Macarena   R.200
MONTERREY, E. - The chink of gold
            S.47
MONTEVERDI, Claudio (1567-1643), It
   R.1   S.c,1-11,14-16,18,24,26-28,42
MONTGOMERY, James Louis (1943-   ), Can

MONTI, Vittorio (1868-1922), It
   R.1   S.c,10,24
MONTORIO, Daniel

MONTSALVATGE, Xavier (1912-   ), Sp
   R.14   S.c,8,10,24a,32,39
MONZA, Carlo (c1735-1801), It
   R.1   S.c
MONZINI, Bernardo (16-17th Cent)
            S.c
MOODY, James (1925-   ), USA
   R.4   S.c,10,13
MOONEY, Harold (1917-   ), USA
   R.23   S.10
MOÓR, Emanuel (1863-1931), Hun
   R.1   S.10,24a
MOOR, Karel (1873-1945), Cz
   R.1   S.5x
MOORE - Varsity march
            S.54(363)
MOORE, Carman (1939-   ), USA
   R.19   S.10,13
MOORE, Dorothy Rudd (1940-   ), USA
   R.7   S.30,52[Rudd]

MOORE, Douglas Stewart (1893-1969), USA
   R.1   S.c,7-10,13,19,21,25,27,42
MOORE, Glen Richard (1941-   ), USA
   R.23   S.13
MOORE, Graham Ponsonby (1859-1916), Australia
   R.3   S.c
MOORE, Philip John (1943-   ), Eng
   R.80   S.c
MOORE, Raymond

MOORE, Thomas (1779-1852), Ire
   R.1   S.10,24
MOORE, Thomas (1933-   ), USA
   R.19   S.13
MOORE, Undine Smith (1906-   ), USA
   R.19   S.10,13,30,52
MOORS, Hezekiah (1775-1814), USA
   R.50   S.10,47
MORAES, Vinicius de (1913-1980), Brazil
   R.67   S.39
MORAGO, Estêvão Lopes (c1575->1630), Sp
   R.1   S.10,13
MORAIS, Antônio Maria Araujo de
   [see MARIA, Antônio - pseud]
MORALEDA - La gran revista; Manoletin

MORALES, Abdulio (1916-   )

MORALES, Cristóbal de (c1500-1553), Sp
   R.1   S.c,5x,7-11,14-16,18,32,53
MORAN, Robert (1937-   ), USA
   R.1   S.c,13
MORAND, P. - Trepak
             S.54(361)
MORANDI, Giovanni (1777-1856), It
   R.8   S.c
MORANDO, Luis
             S.10
MORATA, Ginés de (16th Cent), Sp
   R.1   S.c,8,10,14-16
MORATH, Max
             S.10
MORAWETZ, Oskar (1917-   ), Cz
   R.1   S.10,24
MORDASOVA, Maria (20th Cent), USSR
             S.52
MOREAU, L. - Coeur Solitaire
             S.e
MOREIRA, António Leal (1758-1819), Port
   R.1   S.10

MOREL CAMPOS, Juan (1857-1896), Puerto Rico
    R.9   S.9,4,5x,11
MOREL, Francois d´Assise (1926-   ), Can
    R.1   S.10
MORELENBAUM, Henrique
                S.24a
MORENO TORROBA, Federico (1891-1982), Sp
    R.1   S.c,2,3,5-10,18,32,39,42
MORENO, Joan (16th Cent)
                S.10,13,30
MORENO MANZANO, Salvador (1916-   ), Mex
    R.22   S.c
MORERA, Enrique (1865-1942), Sp
    R.1   S.10
MORET, Ernest
                S.5x,10
MORET, Niel - pseud [ie Charles N. DANIELS] (1878-1943)
    USA R.50   S.54(331,35,50,56)
MORETON, H. R. - Medallion march [S.54 (342)]
    = ? MORTIMER, Harry
MORETTO, Nelly (1925-   ), Arg
    R.26   S.46,52
MOREY, Florence

MORGAN, David Sydney (1933-   ), Eng
    R.14   S.c,24a
MORGAN, Harold
                S.24
MORGAN, Justin (1747-1798), USA
    R.1   S.10,47
MORGAN, Mary Hannah [see BRAHE, May - pseud]
MORGAN, Robert Orlando (1865-1956), Eng [pseud: John
    INGRAM; VALÈRE]   R.3   S.43
MORGAN, Robert P. (1934-   ), USA
    R.19   S.13
MORGAN, Thomas (fl 1691-99), Ire
    R.1
MORGAN, Virginia
                S.30
MORGAN, Wilfred
                S.e
MORGENSTERN, Sam   USA
                S.10,13
MORHANGE, Charles-Henri-Valentin
    [see ALKAN, C. H. V. - pseud]
MORICONI, August (1844-1907), It
    R.3   S.5x
MORILLO, Roberto García (1911-   ), Arg
    R.14   S.5x

MORIN, Jean-Baptiste (1677-1754), Fr
   R.1   S.c,8-10,42
MORINI, Erica (1904-   ), Aus
   R.4
MORITZ, Edvard (1891-   ), USA
   R.14   S.22
MORITZ, Landgraf von Hessen-Kassel (1572-1632), Ger
   R.1   S.c,10,16,32
MORLACCHI, Francesco (1784-1841), It
   R.1   S.c,10
MORLACCHI, Pietro (fl 1843-50), It
   R.10s   S.10
MORLAYE, Guillaume (c1510->1558), Fr
   R.1   S.c
MORLEY, Angela (20th Cent), Eng
           S.52
MORLEY, Charles - pseud [see BEHR, Franz]
MORLEY, Thomas (1557/58-1602), Eng
   R.1   S.c,1-11,14-16,18,22,27,28,32,33
MORNABLE, Antoine (fl 1530-53), Fr
   R.1   S.10,16
MORNINGTON, Garret Wesley (1735-1781), Ire
   R.1
MORO, Vicente
           S.10
MOROI, Makoto (1930-   ), Japan
   R.1   S.24a,50
MOROI, Saburo (1903-1977), Japan
   R.1   S.50
MOROSS, Jerome (1913-1983), USA
   R.1   S.9,10,13
MORRILL, Dexter (1938-   ), USA
   R.19   S.10,13
MORRIS, Franklin (1920-   ), USA
   R.19   S.13
MORRIS, Harold (1890-1964), USA
   R.1   S.10,13
MORRIS, Robert Daniel (1943-   ), USA
   R.19   S.10,13
MORRIS, S. E. - Kilties march
           S.54(336)
MORRISON, Charles Summer (?1860-1933), USA
   R.3   S.13,24
MORRISSEY, John J. (1906-   ), USA
   R.19   S.10,13
MORSE - Catch of the season
           S.e
MORSE - Up the street; Yankee boys in blue
           S.54(363,67)

MORSE, Anna J.
                S.10
MORSE, Robert G. (1931-   ), USA
                S.10,13
MORSE, Theodore (1873-1924), USA
    R.23   S.e
MORTARI, Virgilio (1902-   ), It
    R.1   S.c,24
MORTARO, Antonio (fl 1587-1610), It
    R.1   S.c
MORTELMANS, Lodewijk (1868-1952), Bel
    R.1   S.c,36
MORTENSEN, Carl (1832-1893)
                S.c
MORTENSEN, Finn (1922-   ), Nor
    R.1   S.c,5x,10,40,51
MORTENSEN, Otto (1907-   ), Den
    R.1   S.18,33,35,40,57
MORTENSON, Kai (1908-   ), Den
    R.30   S.10,24
MORTHENSON, Jan Wilhelm (1940-   ), Sweden
    R.1   S.c,38,40,56
MORTIFEE, Ann (1947-   ), Can
    R.81   S.52
MORTIMER, Fred (1880-1953), Eng
    R.85   S.55
MORTIMER, Harry (1902-   ), Eng
    R.85   S.54(339)
MORTIN, Antonio (17th Cent)

MORTON, Ferdinand Joseph (Jelly Roll) (1885-1941), USA
    R.1   S.9,10
MORTON, Lawrence (1942-   ), USA
    R.19   S.10,13
MORTON, Robert (c1430-1476), Eng
    R.1   S.c,4,5x,10,15,16
MORYL, Richard (1929-   ), USA
    R.19   S.c,9,10,13
MORZANIS [see GORZANIS ?]
                S.c
MOSCA, Luigi (1775-1824), It
    R.1   S.c
MOSCHELES, Ignaz (1794-1870), Ger
    R.1   S.c,8-10,20,24a
MOSEL, Ignaz Franz von (1772-1844), Aus
    R.1   S.c
MOSER, Roland (1943-   ), Swiss
    R.4   S.c
MOSSOLOV, Alexander (1900-1973), Russia
    R.1   S.2-5,8,10,11

MOSONYI, Mihaly - pseud [ie Michael BRAND] (1815-1870),
    Hun R.1   S.c,10
MOSS - Somewhere in Connemara (vi & p)
           S.24a
MOSS, Katie (1881-   ), Eng
    R.7   S.c,30
MOSS, Lawrence Kenneth (1927-   ), USA
    R.14   S.c,10,13,22,24
MOSSEL, Max (1871-1929), Neth
    R.4   S.24a
MOSSMAN, Ted (1914-   ), USA
    R.19   S.10
MOSSMAYER, Johann Baptist (c1765-c1835)
           S.c
MOSTO, Giovanni Battista (<1550-1596), It
    R.1   S.c,10
MOSTRAS, Konstantin Georgievich (1886-1965), Russia
    R.1   S.18,24
MOSZKOWSKI, Moritz (1854-1925), Pol
    R.1   S.c,1-10,18,21,24,54(355)
MOSZUMAŃSKA-NAZAR, Krystyna (1924-   ), Ger
    R.1   S.c,20,30,52
MOTOORI, Nagayo
           S.24a
MOTT - Nada
           S.e
MOTT, David Howard (1945-   ), USA
    R.19   S.13
MOTTA, Jose Vianna de [see VIANNA da MOTTA, Jose]
MOTTE, Diether de la (1928-   ), Ger
    R.1
MOTTL, Felix (1856-1911), Aus
    R.1   S.c
MOTTU, Alexandre (1883-1943), Swiss
    R.8   S.c
MOTZAN, Otto (1880-1937), USA
    R.23   S.e
MOULAERT, Pierre (1907-1967), Bel
    R.1   S.c,36
MOULAERT, Raymond (1875-1962), Bel
    R.1   S.36
MOULD, Warren (1933-   ), Can
    R.81
MOULINIÉ, Etienne (c1600->1669), Fr
    R.1   S.c,8,13
MOULU, Pierre (c1480-c1550), Flem
    R.1   S.c,10,16
MOUNT, William Sydney (1807-1868), USA
    R.50   S.9

MOUNTAIN, H. A. - Defence march
              S.54(322)
MOUQUET, Jules (1867-1946), Fr
  R.4   S.10
MOURANT, Walter (1910-   ), USA
  R.19   S.10,13,19
MOURAVIEFF, Léon (1905-   ), Fr
  R.4   S.c,10
MOURET, Jean Joseph (1682-1738), Fr
  R.1   S.c,2-6,8-10,24,32
MOUTON, Charles (1626->1699), Fr
  R.1   S.c,8,10
MOUTON, Jean (c1459-1522), Fr
  R.1   S.c,4,5,7,8,10,14-16,41
MOY, Louis de (fl 1631)
  R.5   S.c
MOYA - pseud [see VICARS, Harold]
MOYLE, William Edward (fl 1940-50), Eng
  R.85   S.55
MOYREAU, [?Christophe] (fl 1754), Fr
  R.5   S.c
MOYZES, Alexander (1906-   ), Slovak
  R.1   S.c,5x,6-8,24,31
MOYZES, Mikuláš (1872-1944), Slovak
  R.1   S.5x,6
MOZART, Franz Xavier (1791-1844), Aus

  R.1   S.c,24a
MOZART, Leopold (1719-1787), Aus
  R.1   S.c,2-6,8-10,18,24
MOZART, Wolfgang Amadeus (1756-1791), Aus
  R.1   S.c,1-11,18-28,32-34,42,43,54(341)
MÓŽI, Aladar (1923-   ), Cz
  R.14   S.24a
MÓŽI, Julius (1908-   ), Cz
  R.18   S.31
MOZZANI, Luigi (1869-   ), It
  R.10   S.5x
MSHVELIDZE, Shalva Mikhaylovich (1904-   ), USSR
  R.1   S.18
MUCHITSKY, Lukian (18-19th Cent)

MUCZYNSKI, Robert (1929-   ), USA
  R.19   S.10,13,20,22
MUDARRA, Alonso (c1510-1580), Sp
  R.1   S.c,3,4,5x,6-8,10,11,14-17,28,32,53
MUDD, Thomas (c1560->1619), Eng
  R.1   S.c
MUDDE, Willem (1909-   ), Neth
  R.4   S.c

MUDGE, Richard (1718-1763), Eng
   R.1   S.c,10
MUELLER, Charles (19th Cent), USA
              S.10,47
MUELLER, Frederick A. (1921-   ), USA
   R.19   S.13
MUFFAT, Georg (1653-1704), Ger
   R.1   S.c,8-10,24,53
MUFFAT, Gottlieb (1690-1770), Ger
   R.1   S.c,2,5,8,53
MUGNONE, Leopoldo (1858-1941), It
   R.1
MUGUERZA - Tristes amores
              S.e
MÜHLBERGER, Karl (1857-1944), Aus
   R.4   S.10
MÜHLING, August (1786-1847), Neth
   R.2   S.10
MUIR, Lewis F. (1884-1950), USA
   R.23   S.10
MUKHAMEDZHANOV, Sydykh (1924-   ), USSR
   R.47   S.18,24
MUKHATOV, Velimuhamed (1916-   ), USSR
   R.14   S.18
MUL, Jan (1911-1971), Neth
   R.1   S.10
MULDER, Klaas (1930-   )
              S.c
MULÈ, Giuseppe (1885-1951), It
   R.1   S.4,5,54(341)
MULET, Henri (1878-1967), Fr
   R.1   S.c,4,5x,8,10
MULHAUSEN, Ferdinand (1864-1944)

              S.18
MÜLLER, Adolf (1801-1886), Ger
   R.1   S.c
MULLER, Ernst
              S.c
MULLER, George Gottfried (1762-1821), USA
   R.1   S.8,10,47
MÜLLER, Frederick [see MUELLER, Frederick]
MULLER, Johann Peter
              S.9
*** MÜLLER, Karl Franz (1808-1855) (see note)
MÜLLER, Karl Franz (1922-   ), Aus
   R.69   S.c
MÜLLER, Marianus (1724-1780), Ger
              S.c
MULLER, P. - Banater Jux polka; Errinerung an schone
   Stunden   S.54(314,25)

MULLER, Rudolf (1889-1961), Ger
   R.4   S.c
MULLER-MEDEK, Tilo

MULLER-ZURICH, Paul (1898-   ), Swiss
   R.1   S.c,7,8,10,23,24
MULSO, Edward
               S.10
MULYAR, Alexander Borisovich (1922-   )
               S.18,24
MUMFORD, Jeffrey (1955-   ), USA
   R.19   S.24a
MUMMA, Gordon (1935-   ), USA
   R.1   S.10,13
MÜNCH, Gerhart (1907-   ), Ger
   R.3   S.24a
MUNDAY, J. - New Topia
               S.47
MUNDY, John (c1555-1630), Eng
   R.1   S.c,1x,2,3,5,7,8,10,14-16
MUNDY, William (c1529-1591), Eng
   R.1   S.c,5,8,10
MUNKITTRICJ, Richard Li [see TALBOT, Howard - pseud]
MUNNINCKX, Guillielmus (fl 1600)
               S.c
MUNOT, Felicien (fl 1924), Fr
   R.200
MUÑOZ MOLLEDA, José (1905-   ), Sp
   R.1   S.c,9,10,32
MUÑOZ, Garcia (16th Cent)
               S.c,8,16,17
MUNROW, David (1942-1976), Eng
   R.1   S.c,9
MUNROW, George
               S.33
MUNSON, Amos (fl 1790), USA

MUNSON, Lawrence (1878-1950), USA
   R.19
MÜNSTER, Joseph Joachim Benedict (1694->1751), Ger
   R.1   S.c
MUNTZ-BERGER, Joseph (1769-1844), Ger
   R.5
MURADELI, Vano (1908-1970), Russia
   R.1   S.18
MURATORI, G. - Amore (T´amo perche sei bella)
               S.24
MURAVLEV, Alexei (1924-   ), USSR
   R.14   S.10,24

MURCIA, Santiago de (17-18th Cent), Sp
   R.9   S.c,10,32
MURDOCH, Marjolijn (1943-   ), Neth
   R.7   S.52
MUREAU, Gilles (d.1512)
   R.5   S.c,8,10,14-16
MURET, Marc-Antoine de (1526-1585), Fr
   R.1   S.c
MURGIER, Jacques (1912-   ), Fr
   R.14   S.c
MURILLA - Pastora
            S.5x
MUROV, Askold Fedorovich (1928-   ), USSR
   R.47   S.18
MURRAY, Alan (1890-   ), Eng
   R.77   S.c,5x,13,55(330)
MURRAY, Bain (1926-   ), USA
   R.14   S.10,13
MURRAY, Edward
            S.e
MURRAY, James R. (1842-   ), USA
   R.53
MURRAY, Sonny (1937-   ), USA
   R.1   S.10
MURRIA, Santiago de (16-17th Cent)
            S.17
MURRILL, Herbert (1909-1952), Eng
   R.1   S.c,7,10,53
MURRIN, Jacobus (15th Cent), Fr
   R.1   S.c
MURSCHHAUSER, Franz Xavier (1663-1738), Ger
   R.1   S.c,7,10,53
MURTULA, Giovanni (1881-1954), It
            S.c,10
MUSCHEL, Georgy [see MUSHEL, Georgy]
MUSET, Colin (fl c1200-50), Fr
   R.1   S.c,8,10,16
MUSGRAVE, Thea (1928-   ), Scot
   R.1   S.c,9,10,20,24,32,52
MUSHEL, Georgy (1909-   ), USSR
   R.1   S.c,10,18
MUSICESCU, Gavriil (1847-1903), Rum
   R.1   S.c
MUSIL, Frantisek (1852-1908), Cz
   R.25   S.c
MUSIN, Ovide (1854-1929), Bel
   R.8   S.24

MUSINS, Kappan (1921-   )
            S.18

MUSORGSKY, Modest Petrovich (1839-1881), Russia
    R.1   S.c,1-11,18,22,24,28,32,42
MUSSER, Clair
                 S.8,13
MUSSI - Babilonce
                 S.54(314)
MUSSI, Giulio (fl 1619-25), It
    R.8   S.c
MÜTHEL, Johann Gottfried (1728-1788), Ger
    R.1   S.c,9,10
MUTHSPIEL, Kurt
                 S.c
MUTHUSWAMY DIKSHITAR (1776-1835), India

MUTII, Nicola (16th Cent) [editor]

MUZA y MEDIAVILLA - Gitana mia [see also MEDIAVILLA]

MUZAFAROV, Mansur Akhmetovich (1902-1966), USSR
    R.47   S.18,24
MYAGY, Ester Kustovna [see MIAGI, Ester Kustovna]
MYASKOVSKY, Nikolai Yokovlevich (1881-1950), Russia
    R.1   S.c,3-5,7-11,18,24
MYASNIKOV - My soul doth magnify the Lord
                 S.10
MYDDLETON
                 S.54(324,37,49,53,55)
MYERS, Robert (1941-   ), USA
    R.19   S.10,13
MYERS, Sherman
                 S.10
MYERS, Theldon (1927-   ), USA
    R.19   S.13
MYGRANT, W. S. USA - My Maryland (march)
                 S.13,54(344)
MYHRE, Milford USA
                 S.13
MYLIUS, Johann Daniel (1584/85-c1628), Ger
    R.1   S.c,4,5x
MYRBERG, F. M. - Aftonstamning; For lange se'n den
    gamlavison S.e
MYRONOFF - Caprice
                 S.5x
MYROW, Frederic (1939-   ), USA
    R.19   S.10,13,24
MYSLIVEČEK, Josef (1737-1781), Cz
    R.1   S.c,4,5x,6,9,10,18,24a
NABAŽAS, Jonas (1907-   ), Lith
    R.4   S.18

NABOKOV, Nicolas (1903-1978), USA
   R.1   S.9,10,13
NACHÉZ, Tividar (1859-1930), Hun
   R.2   S.1x,5x,24
NACHO, Tata - pseud [see FERNÁNDEZ ESPERÓN, Ignacio]
NADAUD, Gustave (1820-1893), Fr
   R.3   S.e
NADENENKO, Fedor Nikolayevich (1902-1964), USSR
   R.25   S.18
NADERMAN, François-Joseph (1781-1835), Fr
   R.1   S.c,10
NADEZHIN, Boris Borisovich (1905-   ), USSR
   R.14   S.18
NAGAI, Kazunori
            S.10
NAGASAWA, Katsutoshi (1923-   ), Japan
            S.50
NAGATOMI, Masayuki (1932-   ), Japan
   R.36   S.50
NAGEL, Robert (1924-   ), USA
   R.19   S.10,13
NÄGELI, Hans Georg (1773-1836), Swiss
   R.1   S.c
NAGINSKI, Charles (1909-1940), USA
   R.19   S.3,5x,10,11,13
NAGOVITSIN, Vyacheslav Lavrentovich (1939-   )
            S.18
NAICH, Hubert (c1513-<1546), S. Neth
   R.1   S.c
NAIRNE, Caroline Oliphant, Baroness (1766-1845), Scot
   R.77   S.e
NAISSOO, Uno (1928-   ), Est
   R.30   S.18
NAJERA, Edmund (1936-   ), USA
   R.19   S.13
NAKADA, Yoshinao (1923-   ), Japan
   R.1   S.c,10,50
NAKAMURA, Sawako (1931-   ), Japan
   R.36   S.50
NAKAMURA, Toroh (1911-   )
            S.24a
NAKANOSHIMA, Kin-ichi (1904-   ), Japan
   R.36   S.50
NAKHABIN, Vladimir Nikolayevich (1910-   ), USSR
   R.14   S.18
NALBANDION, K. (fl 1925), Ethiopia
            S.54(325)
NANCARROW, Conlon (1912-   ), USA
   R.1   S.9,10,13

NANDOR - Oszi Levelet
    S.24a
NANINO, Giovanni Bernardino (c1560-1623), It
 R.1
NANINO, Giovanni Maria (1543/44-1607), It
 R.1   S.c,2-5,7,8,10,11,13,14,16,18
NANTERMI, Orazio (b c1550), It
 R.1   S.c,53
NAPOLEÃO, Arthur (1845-1925), Brazil
 R.56   S.24a
NAPOLETANO, Daniele (1872-1943), It
 R.8   S.18,24
NAPOLI, Gennaro (1881-1943), It
 R.8   S.8,10
NAPOLI, Jacopo (1911-), It
 R.1   S.24
NÁPRAVNÍK, Eduard (1839-1916), Cz
 R.1   S.1-5,7,8,10,18,24a
NARDELLA, Evemero (1879-), It
 R.10s S.e
NARDINI, Pietro (1722-1793), It
 R.1   S.c,2,3,5,6,10,18,24
NARDIS, Camillo de (1857-1951), It
 R.2   S.8,9
NARES, James (1715-1783), Eng
 R.1   S.c,10
NARITA - Hamabe no uta; Kazoe uta
    S.32
NARVÁEZ, Luys de (fl 1530-50), Sp
 R.1   S.c,3,5x,7,10,14-17,32,39,53
NASALLI - March de la Vittoria
    S.54(340)
NASCO, Jan [Giovanni] (c1510-1561), Flem
 R.1   S.c,8,10,14
NASH, D. E. - Minuet in D; A sleepy tune (vi & p)
    S.24
NASHE, Thomas (17th Cent), Eng
    S.c,16
NASIDZE, Sulkhan Ivanovich (1927-), USSR
 R.1   S.18,24a
NASSAAN, W. - Connecticut march
    S.54(321)
NASSARRE, Pablo (d.1730), Sp
 R.1   S.c,53
NAT, Yves (1890-1956), Fr
 R.1   S.18
NATAL, Nanette

NATRA, Sergiu (1924-), Isr
 R.1   S.10

NATVIG, Candace
        S.52
NAU, Stephen (c1600-1661), Fr
  R.1
NAUDOT, F. - Masonic songs
        S.5x
NAUDOT, Jacques-Christoph (c1690-1762), Fr
  R.1   S.c,4,6-10
NAUMAN, Johan Gottlieb (1741-1801), Ger
  R.1   S.c,7,8,10,33,56
NAUMANN - Erster Marsch des Regiments von Kalckstein
        S.10
NAUMANN, Joel USA
        S.13,24a
NAUMANN, Siegfried (1919-   ), Sweden

  R.1   S.c,38,40,56
NAUSS, Johann Xaver (c1690-1764), Ger
  R.1   S.c
NAUWACH, Johann (c1595-c1630), Ger
  R.1   S.c
NAUYALIS, Yuozas (1869-1934), Lith
  R.2   S.18,24a
NAVARRO, Enrique Sp

NAVARRO, Juan (c1530-1580), Sp
  R.1   S.c,1,17
NAVAS, Juan de (fl 1659-1709), Sp
  R.1   S.c
NAVRÁTIL, František (1732-1802), Cz
  R.18   S.c
NAYLOR - Irish pieces
        S.5x
NAYLOR, Bernard (1907-   ), Eng
  R.1   S.c,10,19
NAYLOR, Edward (1867-1934), Eng
  R.1   S.c
NAZARETH, Ernesto (1863-1934), Brazil
  R.1   S.c
NAZIROVA, Elmira Mirza Riza (1928-   ), USSR
  R.7   S.18,52
NEAGA - Elegy (vi & p)
        S.24
NEAR, Gerald (1942-   ), USA
  R.19   S.10,12,13
NEAT, John [see RAY, Lillian - pseud]
NEBRA, Manuel Blasco de [see BLASCO de NEBRA, Manuel]
NECHEPORENKO, Pavel Ivanovich (1916-)
        S.18
NECKE, Hermann (1850-1912), Ger
  R.10s

NEDBAL, Oskar (1874-1930), Cz
    R.1   S.c,4,5x,9,10,24
NEEDHAM, Alicia Adelaide (née Montgomery) (1875-   ),
    Ire R.7   S.e
NEEF, Wilhelm (1916-   ), Ger
    R.14   S.24a
NEEFE, Christian Gottlob (1748-1798), Ger
    R.1   S.c,10,24
NEES, Staf (1901-1965), Bel
    R.1   S.c
NEES, Vic (1936-   ), Bel
    R.80
NEEVE, Robert Jan de (1943-   ), Neth

NEGLIA, Francesco Paolo (1874-1932), It
    R.1   S.4,5,23,24
NEGREA, Martian (1893-1973), Rum
    R.1   S.8,10
NEGRI, Cesare (c1535->1604), It
    R.1   S.c,8,10,14-16,32
NEGRI, Marc Antonio (d.1621), It
    R.1   S.c

NEIDHARDT von REUENTAL (c1180->1237), Ger
    R.1   S.c,7,8,10,14-16
NEIKRUG, Marc (1946-   ), USA
    R.19   S.13
NEJEDLÝ, Vít (1912-1945), Cz
    R.1   S.c,5,24,31
NEKES, Franz (1844-1914), Ger
    R.2   S.2,4
NELHAM, Edmund (d.1646), Eng
    R.5
NELHÝBEL, Václav (1919-   ), USA
    R.1   S.c,9,10,13
NELMAN, Edward T.
                   S.10
NELSON, Leon
                   S.12,13
NELSON, Oliver E. (1932-1975), USA
    R.19   S.9,13
NELSON, Ronald (1929-   ), USA
    R.19   S.10,13
NELSON, Sydney (1800-1862), Eng
    R.1   S.10,24
NEMEROVSKY, Alexandre (1859-   )
                   S.24
NEMES - Die Sprode
                   S.e
NEMESCU, Octavian (1940-   ), Rum
    R.14   S.20

NEMTIN, Alexander Pavlovich (1936-   )
             S.18
NENNA, Pomponio (c1550-<1613), It
   R.1   S.c,10
NEPOMUCENO, Alberto (1864-1920), Brazil
   R.1   S.c,10,39
NERI, Massimilano (?1615-1666), It
   R.1   S.c,10
NÉRINI, Emile (1882-1967), Fr
   R.4   S.5x
NERO, Peter Bernard (1924-   ), USA
   R.19   S.10,13
NERUDA, Franz (1843-1915), Moravia
   R.1   S.24
NERUDA, Johann Baptiste Georg (c1707-c1780), Cz
   R.1   S.c,10
NESBET, John (d ?1488), Eng
   R.1   S.c,10,16
NESLE, Blondel de [see BLONDEL de NESLE]
NESSLER, Viktor (1841-1890), Ger
   R.1   S.c,1x,4,5x
NESTICO, Samuel Louis (1924-   ), USA
   R.23   S.c,10,13,22
NESTROY, Johann Nepomuk (1801-1862), Aus
   R.1   S.c
NÉSVERA, Josef (1842-1914), Cz
   R.1   S.24
NETZER, Ephraim Israel
             S.10

NEUBAUER, Franz Christoph (c1760-1795), Boh
   R.1   S.3,4,10,11
NEUBURGER, Jean [pseud: Jean LENOIR] (1891-1975), Fr
   R.4   S.10,24a
NEUENDORFF, Adolph (1843-1897), Ger
   R.2   S.10,24a
NEUHAUS, Hermann
             S.c
NEUKOMM, Sigismund (1778-1858), Aus
   R.1   S.c
NEULAT - Jonas, le vieux sonneur
             S.e
NEUMAIER, Ferdinand
             S.c
NEUMANE [Neumann], Antonio (1818-1871), Ecuador
   R.97   S.54(332 - Meumane)
NEUMANN, Anton (18th Cent)
             S.10
NEUMANN, Emil (1836-1922), Ger
   R.3   S.e

NEUMANN, František (1874-1919), Ger
  R.3
NEUMANN, Mathieu (1867-1928), Ger
  R.2   S.c
NEUMANN, Richard (1914-   ), USA
  R.19   S.13
NEUMANN, Věroslav (1931-   ), Cz
  R.1   S.31
NEUMARK, Georg (1621-1681), Ger
  R.1   S.c,2,10
NEUMAYER, Fritz (1900-1983), Ger
  R.14   S.c
NEUPARTH, Julio (1863-   ), Port
          S.e
NEUPERT, Edmund (1842-1888), Nor
  R.3   S.8
NEUSIDLER, Hans (c1508-1563), Ger
  R.1   S.c,5x,8,10,14-16,18,32,53
NEUSIDLER, Melchior (1531-1591), Ger
  R.1   S.c,10,16
NEVILLE, Paul (20th Cent)
          S.c
NEVIN, Ethelbert (1862-1901), USA
  R.1   S.c,1x,2-4,5x,10,12,18,23,24,28,54(344,53)
NEVIN, Gordon Balch (1892-1943), USA
  R.19   S.c,12,13
NEVSTRUEV [see MANYKIN-NEVSTRUEV, Nikolai Alexandrovich]
NEVYADOMSKI, Stanislav (1859-1936)
          S.18
NEWARK, William (c1450-1509), Eng
  R.1   S.c
NEWBURY, Kent A. (1925-   ), USA
  R.19   S.10,13
NEWELL, Robert (1940-   ), USA
  R.19   S.13
NEWLIN, Dika (1923-   ), USA

  R.1   S.10,13,30,52
NEWMAN, (fl c1583), Eng
  R.1   S.c,8,10,14-16,53
NEWMAN, Alfred (1901-1970), USA
  R.1   S.c,9,10
NEWMAN, Anthony (1941-   ), USA
  R.19   S.10,12,13,24a
NEWSOM, Hugh Raymond (1891-1978), USA
  R.19   S.13
NEWSOME, Roy (1930-   ), Eng
  R.85   S.55
NEWTON, Ernest
          S.e

NIBELLE, Henri-Jules-Joseph (1883-1967), Fr
   R.14   S.c
NICCOLÒ da PERUGIA (14th Cent), It
   R.1   S.c
NICHELMANN, Christoph (1717-1761/62), Ger
   R.1   S.c
NICHOL, J. USA - The summer of Timothy Once
          S.13
NICHOLAS - Music Box
          S.10
NICHOLAS, John Morgan (1895-1963), Eng
   R.14   S.10
NICHOLL, Joseph Weston (1876-1925), Eng
   R.85   S.55
NICHOLLS, Horatio - pseud [see WRIGHT, Lawrence]
NICHOLSON, Charles (1795-1837), Eng
   R.1
NICHOLSON, Richard (d c1639), Eng
   R.1   S.c,7,8,10,14,16
NICHOLSON, Sydney Hugo (1875-1947), Eng
   R.1   S.c
NICHOLSON, William
          S.47
NICK, Edmund (1891-1974), Ger
   R.1   S.c
NICKLASS-KEMPNER, Siegfried (1849-1928), Ger
   R.3   S.24
NICODÉ, Jean Louis (1853-1919), Ger
   R.1   S.8,10
NICOLAI - Troost, Bloemke
          S.e
NICOLAI, Johann Michael (1629-1685), Ger
   R.1   S.c
NICOLAI, Otto (1810-1849), Ger
   R.1   S.c,2-11,18,24,42,54(343)
NICOLAI, Philipp (1556-1608), Ger
   R.1   S.c,3,26
NICOLAS de la GROTTE [see LA GROTTE, Nicolas]
NICOLAS, Rene (20th Cent)
          S.c
NICOLAU, Antonio (1858-1933), Sp
   R.1   S.1-3,5x,6,8
NICOLAUS CRACOVIENSIS [see MIKOLAJ z KRAKOWA]

NICOLINI, Giuseppe (1762-1842), It
   R.1   S.c
NICOLO, Isouard - Jaconde (opera) [see ISOUARD, Nicolas]
NICOLSON, Richard [see NICHOLSON, Richard]
NICTO - Teresita mia
          S.e

NICULESCO, Stefan (1927-   ), Rum
   R.1
NIEDERBERGER, Max (fl 1922-5), Ger

NIEDERMEYER, Louis (1802-1861), Swiss
   R.1   S.c,43
NIEDHART von REUENTHAL [see NEIDHART von REUENTHAL]
NIEDLINGER - Sweet Miss Mary
          S.e
NIEHAUS, Manfred (1933-   ), Ger
   R.1   S.c
NIEL, E. A. - Erika (Marschlied)
          S.10
NIELAND, Hermus Jacobus Josephus (1910-   ), Neth
   R.25   S.c
NIELAND, Jan (1903-1963), Neth
   R.14   S.c
NIELSON, Carl (1865-1931), Den
   R.1   S.c,2-10,18,19,21,24,26,27,33,35,57
NIELSON, Hans (c1580-c1626), Den
   R.1   S.14
NIELSON, Ludvig (1906-   ), Nor
   R.1   S.c,40
NIELSON, Svend (1937-   ), Den
   R.14   S.40
NIELSON, Tage (1929-   ), Den
   R.1   S.40
NIEMAN, Alfred Abbe (1913-   ), Eng
   R.14   S.10
NIEMANN, Walter (1876-1953), Ger
   R.4   S.1x
NIEMCZYK, Waclaw (1907-   ), Pol
   R.14   S.24a
NIETO, Miguel (1844-1915), Sp
   R.1   S.39
NIEUWENHOVE, Ernest Aflons van [pseud: Ernest d´AGRÈVES]
   (1880-1968) R.25   S.c
NIEWIADOMSKI, Stanislaw (1859-1936), Pol
   R.1   S.10
NIGG, Serge (1924-   ), Fr
   R.1   S.c,10,24
NIGHTINGALE, James (1948-   ), USA
   R.19   S.13
NIGRINO, Nicolo (15-16th Cent)
   R.5   S.5x,8,10,14,18
NIKIPROWETZKY, Tolia (1916-   ), Fr
   R.1
NIKODEM, Bedrich (1909-   ), Cz
   R.18   S.31

NIKOLAIS, Alwin (1912-   ), USA
    R.19   S.13
NIKOLAYEV, Alexey Alexandrovich (1931-   ), USSR
    R.1   S.18,24
NIKOLAYEVA, Tatyana Petrovna (1924-   ), USSR
    R.1   S.7,8,18,30,52
NIKOLSKAYA, O. - To heroes of Azerbaijan
                S.54(361)
NIKOLSKY, Yuri Sergeyevich (1895-1962), USSR
    R.14   S.18
NILES, John Jacob (1892-1980), USA
    R.19   S.5x,10,13
NILOVIC, Janko (1941-   )

NILSON, Leo (1939-   ), Sweden
    R.4   S.56
NILSSON, Bo (1937-   ), Sweden
    R.1   S.c,10,38,40,56
NILSSON, Torsten (1920-   ), Sweden
    R.1   S.c,38,40,56
NIN, Anaïs (1903-1977), Cuba
    R.25
NIN, Joaquín (1879-1949), Cuba
    R.1   S.c,1-8,10,18,22,24,27,28,39
NIN-CULMELL, Joaquín María (1908-   ), Cuba
    R.1   S.c,7,10,13,32,39
NINGER, Ferenc (18th Cent)
                S.c
NINOT le PETIT (d.1501/02), Fr
    R.1   S.c,10,16
NINOV - Sonata (vi & p)
                S.24
NIPPON, A. - pseud [see LAUTENSCHLÄGER, Willi]
NIREELA, D. - Rainbow division
                S.54(351)
NISHIYAMA, Tokumoichi (fl 1868-90), Japan

NISLE, Johann Wilhelm Friedrich (1768-1839), Ger
    R.1   S.10
NISLE, Johannes (1735-1788), Ger
    R.1   S.24a
NISSIMOV, Nissim (1909-1951), Isr
    R.14
NITKE - Madrigal of May
                S.e
NITZSCHE, Jack (1937-   ) USA
    R.23   S.c
NIVERS, Guillaume Gabriel (c1632-1714), Fr
    R.1   S.c,10,53

NIXON, Roger (1921-   ), USA
    R.19   S.5x,6-10,13
NIYAZY, Taki Zulfugarovich (1912-   ), USSR
    R.14   S.18
NJURLING, Sten [pseud: Igor BORGANOFF, Fred WINTER]
    (1892-1945), Sweden
    R.30[Winter] S.43,10[Borganoff],24[Winter]
NOA, Peter
                S.c
NOBLE, Ramon
                S.10
NOBLE, Ray (1903-1978), Eng
    R.1   S.10
NOBLE, Thomas Tertius (1867-1953), Eng
    R.1
NOBRE, Marlos (1939-   ), Brazil
    R.1
NOBUTOKI, Kiyoshi (1887-1965), Japan
    R.1   S.50
NOCETI, Jean
                S.24
NOCETI, M. - Waltz in F (vi & p)
                S.24
NODA, R. - Improvisation
                S.22
NODA, Teruyuki (1940-   ), Japan
    R.4   S.c,10,24a,50
NODARI, Giovanni Paolo (d >1620), It
    R.1   S.c
NOEHREN, Robert (1910-   ), USA
    R.1   S.10,12,13
NOEREN, J. M. - Slow March, Midnight!
                S.10
NOGERO, Francisco di
                S.e
NOGINSKY, Charles (1909-1940)

NOLA, Giovanni Dvomenico del Giovane da (1510/20-1592),
    It R.1   S.c,7,8,10,14,16
NOLINSKY, Nikolai Mihailovich (1886-1966), USSR
    R.14   S.18
NONO, Luigi (1924-   ), It
    R.1   S.c,9,10,20
NOON, David (1946-   ), USA
    R.19   S.13
NOORDT, Anthoni van (d.1675), Neth
    R.1   S.c,8,10,16,53
NOORDT, Sybrand van (d.1705), Neth
    R.1   S.10

NORBY, Erik (1936-   ), Den
    R.14   S.c,40
NORCOMBE, Daniel (i) (1576-<1626), Eng - With Angels
    Face   R.1 S.c,7,8,14
NORCOMBE, Daniel (ii) (fl 1602-47), Eng - Division on
    a Ground for Viola da gamba & lute (see note)
    R.1   S.1x,2-4,5x
NORDAL, Jon (1926-   ), Iceland
    R.4
NORDBO, Jens
                S.33
NORDENSTROM, Gladys (1924-   ), USA
    R.19   ‘ S.c,13,30,52
NORDGREN, Pehr Henrik (1944-   ), Fin
    R.1   S.c,40
NORDHEIM, Arne (1931-   ), Nor
    R.1   S.c,10,40,51
NORDLAND - Barndomsminde
                S.e
NORDLANDER, Bert Carsten [pseud: Bert CARSTEN]
    (1905-   ) S.43
NORDOFF, Paul (1909-1977), USA
    R.1   S.10,13,25,27
NORDQVIST, Gustav (1886-1949), Sweden
    R.1   S.c,5x,10,18,24,43,56
NORDRAAK, Rikard (1842-1866), Nor
    R.1   S.54(345)
NOREN - Vintervisa; Konungars konung
                S.e
NØRGÅRD, Johannes (1916-1977), Den
    R.30
NØRGÅRD, Per (1932-   ), Den
    R.1   S.c,9,10,40
NØRHOLM, Ib (1931-   ), Den
    R.1   S.c,24a
NORLEN, Helmer

NORMAN - The bullfrog (orch)
                S.10
NORMAN, Ludvig (1831-1885), Sweden
    R.30   S.56
NORMAN, Ruth (1927-   ), USA
    R.7   S.13,30,52
NORMAN, Theodore (1912-   ), USA
    R.19   S.13
NORMET, Leopold Tarmovich (1922-   ), USSR
    R.14   S.18
NÖRMIGER, August (c1560-1613), Ger
    R.1   S.c,10,16,53

NORODOM, King of Cambodia
           S.10
NORRIS, Ralph (d >1576)
           S.14
NORTH - My black haired Mary
           S.e
NORTH, Alex (1910-   ), USA
   R.1   S.8-10,13
NORTH, Michael (1902-   )
           S.5x
NORTH, Roger (1926-   ), Eng
   R.4   S.c
NORTHRUP, Theo Havemager (fl 1906/07), USA
   R.200   S.10
NORTON, Caroline Elizabeth Sarah (?1808-1877), Eng
   R.7   S.e (see note)
NORTON, Frederic (1869-1946), Eng
   R.1   S.24a
NORTON, Mary Dows Herter [see HERTER NORTON, Mary Dows]
NORTON, Spencer (1909-   ), USA
   R.19   S.4,10,13
NORWORTH, Jack (1879-1959), USA
   R.23   S.10
NOSKOWSKI, Zygmunt (1846-1909), Pol
   R.1   S.c,5x,18
NOTARI, Angelo (1566-1663), It
   R.1   S.c
NOTKER (c840-c912), Swiss
   R.1   S.c,16
NOTTARA, Constantin (1890-1951), Rum
   R.33   S.24a
NOUGUÈS, Jean (1876-1932), Fr
   R.3
NOVÁČEK, Ottokar (1866-1900), Hun
   R.1   S.c,4,5x,10,18,24
NOVÁK, Jan (1921-   ), Cz
   R.1   S.10,18,31
NOVÁK, Milan (1927-   ), Cz
   R.14   S.31
NOVÁK, Vitézslav (1870-1949), Cz
   R.1   S.c,1x,4-10,24
NOVARO, Michele (1822-1885), It
   R.3
NOVELLA, Guilhem Augier (1185-1240)
           S.c,16
NOVELLO, Franko (1929-   )
           S.24
NOVELLO, Ivor (1893-1951), Eng
   R.4   S.10

NOVICH, Clara Kora

NOVIKOV, Anatoli Grigorevich (1896-   ), Russia
  R.1   S.5x,10,18
NOVOTNÁ - Song
          S.5x
NOVOTNÝ, Franz Nikolaus (1743-1773), Boh
  R.1   S.c
NOVOTNÝ, Jaroslav (1886-1918), Cz
  R.1   S.5x
NOWAK, Lionel (1911-   ), USA
  R.19   S.10,13
NOWOWIEJSKI, Feliks (1877-1946), Pol
  R.1   S.c,5x
NOYON, Joseph (1888-   ), Fr - Il est né le divin enfant [?]
NUCIUS, Johannes (c1556-1620), Ger
  R.1   S.c,10
NUDERA, Adalbert (fl 1796), Boh
  R.5

NUFFEL, Jules van (1883-1953), Bel
  R.1   S.10
NUMMI, Seppo (1932-1981), Fin
  R.1   S.c,40
NUÑES GARCÍA, José Mauricio
  [see GARCÍA, José Mauricio Nuñes]
ÑUÑEZ NIETO, José
          S.10
NUNLIST, Juli (1916-   ), USA
  R.19   S.10,13,30,52
NUNÓ, Jaime (1824-1908), Sp
  R.1   S.54(332)
NUROCK, Kirk (1948-   ), USA
  R.19   S.13
NURYMOV, Chary (1941-   )
          S.18
NUSSIO, Otmar (1902-   ), It
  R.1   S.10,24a
NUTILE, Emanuele (1862-1932), It
  R.10s   S.c,10,44
NUTTING - Sing, sing birds on the wing
          S.e
NYAGA, Georgi Stepanovich (1922-   )
          S.18,24
NYAGA, Stepan Timofeyovich (1900-1951)
          S.18
NYAZI, Taki (1912-   )
          S.8
NYBLOM, Carl Goren (1867-1920), Sweden
  R.30   S.43

NYQUIST, Roger Thomas (1934-   ), USA
    R.19   S.12,13
NYSTEDT, Knut (1915-   ), Nor
    R.1   S.c,10,18,20,40,51
NYSTROEM, Gösta (1890-1966), Sweden
    R.1   S.c,5-10,23,38,40,56
N.Z. CRACOVIENSIS (16th Cent), Pol
    R.1
OAK, Kil Sung (1942-   ), Korea/USA
    R.19   S.10,13
OAKLAND, Ben (1907-1979), USA
    R.23   S.10
OBERMEYER, C. - Mein Heimatland
                S.e
OBERMULLER, Johann Joseph Adam (1701-1769)
                S.c
OBERSON, Rene (1945-   )
                S.c
OBERTHÜR, Charles (1819-1895), Ger
    R.10   S.c
OBOUKOV, Nicolas [see OBUKHOV, Nikolay]
OBOUSSIER, Robert (1900-1957), Swiss
    R.1   S.4,5,7,8,10
OBRADORS, Fernando (1897-1945), Sp
    R.9   S.c,5x,8,10,24,39
OBRADOVIĆ, Alexandar (1927-   ), Yug
    R.1   S.20
OBRECHT, Jacob (c1450-1505), Neth
    R.1   S.c,2-11,14-16,21,22,32,41,53
O´BRIEN Eugene (1945-   ), USA
    R.14   S.13
O´BRIEN, Vincent (1870-1948), Ire
    R.4
OBROVSKÁ, Jana (1930-   ), Cz
    R.18   S.10,30,32,52
OBRY - St Hubertusmesse
                S.c
OBUKHOV, Nikolay (1892-1954), Russia
    R.1   S.2,3[Oboukhov]
OCAMPO, Mauricio Cardozo
                S.32
OČENÁŠ, Andrej (1911-   ), Slovak
    R.1   S.c,5x,24,31
OCHOA - El tamborilero; Nostalgia
                S.e
OCHS, Siegfried (1858-1929), Ger
    R.1   S.c,10
OCHSENKUN, Sebastian (1521-1574), Ger
    R.1   S.c,10,16,32

OCKEGHEM, Johannes (c1410-1497), Franco-Flem
R.1   S.c,2-5,7-11,14-16,41
O´CONNOR, Frederick
             S.10
O´CONNOR-MORRIS, Geoffrey (1886-1964), Ire
R.14   S.10
ODAGESCU-TUTUIANU, Irina (1937-   ), Rum
R.7   S.30,24a,52
ODAK, Krsto (1888-1965), Yug
R.14   S.24a
ODAKA, Atsutada (1944-   ), Japan
R.36   S.50
ODAKA, Hisatada (1911-1951), Japan
R.4
ODENCRANTS, Gerhard (1888-1967), Sweden
             S.56
ODDONE SULLI-RAO, Elisabetta (1878-1972) [pseud: ELIOD]
It R.7
ODINAYEV, Abdulfatakh (1938-   )
             S.18
O´DONELL, Charley
             S.10
O´DONELL, Rudolf P.
             S.54(336)
ODSTRČIL, Karel (1930-   ), Cz
R.14   S.10,22
OESTEN, Theodor (1813-1870), Ger
R.3
OEVERING, Rynoldus Popma van
[see POPMA van OEVERING, Rynoldus]
OFFENBACH, Jacques (1819-1880), Ger
R.1   S.c,1-11,18,22,24,42,43,54(314)
O´GALLAGHER, Eamonn (1906-   ), Ire
R.40   S.49

O´GALLAGHER, Liam
             S.10
OGANESYAN, Edgar [see HOVHANESYAN, Edgar]
OGAREW, Michael von (1857-   )
             S.24
OGDON, John (1937-   ), Eng
R.1   S.10
OGDON, Wilbur (1921-   ), USA
R.19   S.10,13
OGERMANN, Claus (1930-   )
             S.24a
OGG, R. - Rousseau march
             S.54(353)
OGIŃSKI, Michal Kleofas (1765-1833), Pol
R.1   S.c,7,8,10,18

OGURA, Roh (1916-   ), Japan
   R.4   S.24a,50
OGURI, Hiroshi (1918-   ), Japan
   R.36   S.c,50
O´HAGAN, Betsy - pseud [see WRIGHT, Lawrence]
OHANA, Maurice (1914-   ), Fr
   R.1   S.c,8-10,32
O´HARA, Geoffrey (1882-1967), Can
   R.23   S.10,12,24,54(347)
OHKI, Masao (1901-1971), Japan
   R.4   S.50
OIKONOMOPOULOS, Eleni N. (1912-   ), Greece
   R.7   S.52
OJA, Edward (1905-1950), Est
   R.58   S.24a
OKEOVER, John (>1590-c1663), Eng
   R.1   S.c,10,16
OKI, Hideko (1919-   ), Japan
   R.36   S.50
OKOLO-KULAKS, Alexandre

OKUMURA, Hajime (1925-   ), Japan
   R.4   S.50
OKUNEV, Boris Petrovich (1946-   )
           S.18
OKUNEV, Herman Grigorevich (1931-   ), USSR
   R.47   S.18
OLAGNIER, Marguerite (1844-1906), Fr
   R.7   S.5x,30
OLAGUE, Bartolomeo de (17th Cent), Sp
           S.c
OLAH, Tiberiu (1928-   ), Rum
   R.1   S.20
OLAN, David (1948-   ), USA
           S.13,24a
OLÄNDER, Per August (1824-1886), Sweden
   R.1   S.c
OLCOTT, Chauncey (1858-1932), USA
   R.23   S.10,24
OLDHAM, Arthur (1926-   ), Eng
   R.1   S.c,8,10
OLDROYD, George (1886-1956), Eng
   R.4   S.c
OLEY, Johann Christoph (1738-1789), Ger
   R.1   S.c
OLIVEIRA, Babi de (20th Cent), Brazil
           S.10,52
OLIVER y ASTORGA, Juan (1733/34-1830), Sp
   R.1

OLIVER, Henry Kemble (1800-1885), USA
R.50   S.47
OLIVER, Herbert Eng
R.37   S.e
OLIVER, Stephen (1950-   ), Eng
R.4   S.c
OLIVERI, Dino
            S.10
OLIVEROS, Pauline (1932-   ), USA
R.1   S.10,13,30,52
OLIVIER, Johannes (14th Cent), Fr
R.1   S.c
OLIVIERI - Schon ist's bei den Soldat
    ·   S.54(354)
OLIVIERI, Alessio (1830-1867), It
R.8   S.44
OLIVIERO, Gaetano Nino (1920-   ), It
R.14
OLKUSNIK, Joachim (1927-   ), Pol
R.4   S.24a
OLNICK, Harvey (1917-   ), Can
R.31   S.10
OLOVNIKOV, Vladimir (1919-   ), USSR
R.14   S.18
OLSEN - Sunset song
            S.5x
OLSEN, Poul Rousing (1922-   ), Den
R.1   S.c,24a
OLSEN, Sparre (1903-   ), Nor
R.1   S.c,10,51
OLSSON, Hjort-Anders Sweden

OLSSON, Otto (1879-1964), Sweden
R.1   S.c,40,56
OLSSON-FÖLLINGER, Göran (1886-1969), Sweden
R.30   S.24
OLTER, Marcus (17th Cent)
            S.c,10,53
O MANSSO, Lasse (1931-   ), Sweden

ONDŘIČEK, František (1857-1922), Cz
R.1   S.18,24
ONDŘIČEK, Johann (d.1742), Boh
R.5   S.24
O'NEILL, Charles (1882-1964), Can
R.4   S.54(317)
ONO, C. - Yoimachigusa (vi & p)
            S.24a
ONO, Mamoru (1915-   ), Japan
            S.50

ONOFRIO - Danza Mascherata (p)

ONSLOW, Georges (1784-1853), Fr
  R.1   S.c,1,8-10,24a
OPENSHAW, John (1880-   ), Eng
  R.37   S.24
OPHOVEN, Hermann (1914-   ), Ger
  R.4   S.c
OPPEL, A. - Watching the purple sunset
             S.10,18
OPRAEM, Gilbert Michl (1750-1828)
             S.24
OPSTAL, A. Van (1895-1970)
             S.c
ORAM, Daphne Blake (1925-   ), Eng
  R.7   S.52
ORANSKY, Viktor Alexandrovich (1899-1953), USSR
  R.14   S.18
ORBAN, Marcel (1884-1958), Fr
  R.14   S.5x
ØRBECK, Anne-Marie (1911-   ), Nor
  R.7   S.c,30,52
ORBELYAN, Konstantin Agaparonovich (1928-   ), USSR
  R.14   S.18
ORBÓN, Julián (1925-   ), Cuba
  R.1   S.c,7,8,10,32,39
ORD, Boris (1897-1961), Eng
  R.1   S.c
ORDWAY, John P. (fl 1840), USA
  R.53,200   S.e
OREFICE, Giacomo (1865-1922), It
  R.1   S.8
OREJÓN - La gitana celosa
             S.e
OREJÓN y APARICIO, José de (1706-1765), Peru
  R.1   S.10
ORELLANA, Gilberto (c1948-   )
             S.39
OREM, Preston Ware (1865-1938), USA
  R.4   S.13
ORFF, Carl (1895-1982), Ger
  R.1   S.c,7-10,18,42
ORGAD, Ben-Zion (1926-   ), Isr
  R.1
ORGAS, Annibale (c1585-1629), It
  R.1   S.c
Ó RIADA, Seán (1931-1971), Ire
  R.40   S.49
ORION - Curfew song
             S.e

ORLINSKI, Heinz Bernard (1928-   ), USA
    R.4   S.c
ORLOB, Harold F. (1883-   ), USA
    R.23   S.10
ORMINSKI, Stanislaw

ORNSTEIN, Leo (1892-   ), USA
    R.19   S.c,9,10,24a
OROLOGIO, Alessandro (c1550-?1633), It
    R.1   S.c
ORR, Buxton (1924-   ), Eng
    R.85   S.55
ORR, Charles Wilfred (1893-1976), Eng
    R.1
ORR, Robin (1909-   ), Scot
    R.1   S.c,4,10,24
ORREGO-SALAS, Juan (1919-   ), Chile
    R.1   S.4,10,20,22,39
ORSO, Francesco d´ - pseud [see BEHR, Franz]
ORTEGA, Francisco (16th Cent)
                 S.c,10,16
ORTH, Charles J.
                 S.5x,10,54(334)
ORTH, Ph. - Eyes of blue
                 S.e
ORTHEL, Leon (1905-   ), Neth
    R.30   S.7,10
ORTIZ, Alfredo (1946-   )

ORTIZ, Diego (c1510-c1570), Sp
    R.1   S.c,3,4,5x,8-11,14-16,18,32,53
ORTMANS, René (1863-   ), Fr
    R.37   S.8,24
ORTO, Marbrianus de (c1460-c1529), Fr
    R.1   S.16
ORTON, Richard (1940-   ), Eng
    R.1   S.10
OSAWA, Kazuko (1926-   ), Japan
    R.7   S.52
OSBORNE, Nat (1878-1954), USA
    R.23   S.e
OSBORNE, Willson (1906-   ), USA
    R.19   S.10,13,19
OSER, Hans (1895-1951), Swiss
    R.3
OSGOOD - Heaven at the end of the road
                 S.e
OSGOOD, Hubert Albert Jack (1919-1979), Eng
    R.85   S.55

OSIANDER, Lucas (1534-1604), Ger
    R.1   S.c,10,16
OSKKER, O. - Verlangen (vi & p)
                 S.24a
OSMA - Ay del ay

OSOKIN, Mikhail Alexeyevich (1903-   ), USSR
    R.14   S.18
OSSER, William

OSSORGIN, Michail (1887-1950)

OSSORGIN, Nicolas (1924-   )

OSSORGIN, Sergei (1926-   )

OSTEN-SAGEN, Maximilian Ernestovich
                 S.18
OSTERLING, Eric (1926-   ), USA
    R.19   S.13
OSTERMAYER, Georg (d.1572), Ger
    R.5
OSTOVAR, Houchang
                 S.c
OSTRČIL, Otakar (1879-1935), Cz
    R.1   S.c,5,24
OSTROVSKY, Fredy (1922-   )
                 S.7,10,18,24
OSWALD von WOLKENSTEIN (c1377-1445), South Tyrol
    R.1   S.c,8-10,14,16
OSWALD, Enrique (1852-1931), Brazil
    R.3   S.24a
OSWALD, James (1711-1769), Scot
    R.1   S.10
OSWALT, Curtis W.

OTAKA, Hisatada (1911-1951), Japan
    R.4   S.50
OTEO, Alfonso Esparza (1896-   )
                 S.5x,24
OTHEGRAVEN, August von (1864-1946), Ger
    R.2   S.c,5x
OTHMAYR, Caspar (1515-1553), Ger
    R.1   S.c,5x,8,10,11,14,16
OTSA, Harry (1926-   ), Est
    R.58   S.18
OTT, Hans (d.1546), Ger
    R.1   S.14
OTT, Lorenz Justinian (1748-1805), Ger
    R.1   S.c

OTTE, Hans (1926-   ), Ger
  R.1   S.c,10
OTTEN, Hans [pseud: Alexander RULAND] (1905-1942), Ger
  R.4   S.33
OTTERLOO, Willem van (1907-1978), Neth
  R.1   S.10
OTTO, Luigi

OTTO, Valerius (1579->1612), Ger
  R.1   S.5x
OUBRADOUS, Fernand (1903-   ), Fr
  R.1   S.4,5x,8,19
OUDRID y SEGURA, Cristóbal (1825-1877), Sp
  R.1   S.32
OUSELEY, Frederick Arthur Gore (1825-1889), Eng
  R.1   S.c,8,10
OUZOUNOFF, Daniel

OVALLE, Jaime (1894-1955), Brazil
  R.14   S.8,10,11,32,39
OVANES, Alan [see HOVHANESS, Alan]
OVCHINNIKOV, Evgeni Ivanovich (1903-1965), USSR
  R.14   S.18
OVCHINNIKOV, Vyacheslav Alexandrovich (1936-   )
  R.62   S.9,18,24
OVERHOFF, Kurt (1902-   ), Aus
  R.14   S.c
OVERTON, Hall (1920-1972), USA
  R.1   S.9,10,13,23
OVEZOV, Dangater (1911-   ), USSR
  R.14   S.18 [under Meitus]
*** OVSIANIKO-KULIKOVSKII, Nikolai Dmitrievich
  (1768-1846) (see note)   S.10
OVTCHINNIKOV, Viacheslav Alexandrovich (1936-   ), USSR
  R.14   S.9,18,24
OVUNTS, Gagik (1930-   )
             S.18
OWEN, Alan (1930-   ), Eng

OWEN, Blythe (1898-   ), USA
  R.19   S.12,13
OWEN, David (1720-1749)

OWEN, Elwyn
             S.24
OWEN, Harold (1931-   )
  R.19   S.10,13
OWEN, John [called Ap Galslyn], Wales
             S.e

OWEN, Morfydd (1891-1918), Wales
   R.7   S.c,5x,7
OWEN, Richard (1922-   ), USA
   R.19   S.10,13
OWENS, Harry
          S.10
OXINAGA, Joaquín de (fl 1740-54), Sp
   R.104   S.c,10,39,53
OXLEY, Harrison (1933-   ), Eng
   R.80   S.c
OXTOBY, Charles (1912-   )

OYA, Eduard (1905-1950)
          S.18
OYSTERMAYRE, Johann (16th Cent)
   R.5   S.15,16
OZOLINŠ, Janis Adolfovich (1908-   ), USSR
   R.14   S.18
PAAP, Wouter (1908-1981), Neth
   R.1   S.10
PABLO, Luis de (1930-   ), Sp
   R.1   S.c
PABST, Paul (1854-1897), Ger
   R.8   S.c
PACCHIAROTTI, Gasparo (1740-1821), It [singer]
   R.1   (see note)
PACCHIEROTTI, Ubaldo (187?-1916), It (see note)
   R.10   S.24
PACELLI, Asprilio (1570-1623), It
   R.1   S.c,16
PACH, Walter (1905-1977), Aus
   R.4   S.c
PACHELBEL, Johann (1653-1706), Ger
   R.1   S.c,2-11,18,24,32,53
PACHELBEL, Wilhelm Hieronymus (1686-1764), Ger
   R.1   S.c,53
PACHERKEVICH, Tadeus (1916-   )
          S.18
PACINI, Giovanni (1796-1867), It
   R.1   S.e
PACIORKIEWICZ, Tadeusz (1916-   ), Pol
   R.1   S.c
PACIUS, Fredrik (1809-1891), Fin
   R.1   S.e
PACK, Beulah Frances (1896-1971), USA
   R.7   S.52
PACOLINI, Giovanni (fl 1590), It
   R.5   S.c,10
PADBRUÉ, Cornelis Thymanszoon (c1592-1670), S. Neth
   R.1

PADEREWSKI, Ignacy Jan (1860-1941), Pol
   R.1   S.c,1-11,18,24
PADILLA, José (1889-1960), Sp
   R.1   S.c,5x,10,34
PADILLA, Juan Gutiérrez de (c1590-1664), Mex
   R.1   S.10
PADILLE, Antoine (1944-   )

PÁDIVÝ, Karol (1908-1965), Cz
   R.18   S.31
PADOVANO, Annibale (1527-1575), It
   R.1   S.c,16,53
PADOVETZ, Johann (1800-1873), Aus
   R.106
PADUREANO - Eyes of sin (Sund Ochi Adinci ca un pacat)
   (vi & p)   S.24
PAEMURRU, Elze Janova [see AARNE, Els - pseud]
PAER, Ferdinando (1771-1839), It
   R.1   S.c,2,10
PAGANETTI, C. - Meditation (vi & p); Scherzo (vi & p)
             S.24
PAGANINI, Niccolo (1782-1840), It
   R.1   S.c,2-11,18,23,24,32,54(349)
PAGANS, Don L.
             S.e
PAGE, Arthur James (1846-   )
             S.e
PAGGI, Le Chevalier Giovanni (19th Cent), It
             S.c
PAGIN, André Noël (1721->1785), Fr
   R.1   S.5x,24
PAIN - Kaiser and God; Eva; Airs
             S.e,5x
PAINE, John Knowles (1839-1906), USA
   R.1   S.c,3,4,8,10-12,47
PAINE, Thomas (1737-1809), USA
             S.10
PAISIBLE, James (d.1721), Fr/Eng
   R.1   S.c
PAISIELLO, Giovanni (1740-1816), It
   R.1   S.c,3-5,7-11,18,26,27,42
PAISNER, Ben (1912-   )
             S.21
PAIVA, Heliodoro de (d.1552), Port
   R.29   S.32
PAIX, Jakob (1556->1623), Ger
   R.1   S.c,10,16,53
PAIXÃO, da - Luar do sertajo
             S.5x[Paxao, Da]

PAK EN DEN (1909-   ), Korea
            S.18
PAKALNIS, Juozas (1912-1948), Lith
    R.4   S.18,24
PAKETURAS, Vatslovas (1928-   )
            S.18
PAKHMUTOVA, Alexandra Nikolayevna (1929-   ), USSR
   ˙R.1   S.10,18,52
PALACIO, Carlos (1911-   ), USSR
    R.14   S.18
PALACIOS - A Granada
            S.e
PALADILHE, Emil (1844-1926), Fr
    R.1   S.c,4,7,8,10,11,27,34
PALAFUTI (fl 1780), It - Elevatione (see note)
    R.5   S.c
PALASZ, Eduard
            S.24a
PALAU BOIX, Manuel (1893-1967), Sp
    R.1   S.c,5,7,8,10,32
PÁLENÍČEK, Jósef (1914-   ), Cz
    R.1   S.18,24a,31
PALERO, Francisco Fernandez
    [see FERNANDEZ PALERO, Francisco]
PALESTRINA, Giovanni da (1525/26-1594), It
    R.1   S.c,1-11,14-16,18,53
PALIASHVILI, Zakary Petrovich (1871-1933), Russia
    R.1   S.c,8,18
PALICOT, Georges
            S.e
PALIGON, Marcin (16-17th Cent), Pol
    R.1   S.c
PÁLKA, Dušan (1909-   ), Cz
    R.18   S.31
PALL, Isolfsson (1893-   ), Iceland

PALLA, Hynek (1837-1896), Cz
    R.18   S.5x
PALLAVICINO, Carlo (d.1688), It
    R.1   S.10
PALLESI - Noi (v)
            S.10
PALM - Partsong
            S.5x
PALMA, John (fl 1757), USA
    R.53   S.10,12,47
PALMAY, Ilka (1864-1945)
    R.3
PALMER (c1800), Aus - Waltz in E
            S.c

PALMER, Charles (1935-   )

PALMER, Courtlandt (1872-   ), USA
   R.3   S.12,13
PALMER, Frederik - pseud
[see HARTMANN, Emma Sophie Amalie]
PALMER, Jane Hetherington (1952-   ), Eng
   R.7   S.52
PALMER, K. - Galopade
           S.54(328)
PALMER, Robert (1915-   ), USA
   R.1   S.7,8,10,13,20,24a
PALMER, Rudolph (1952-   ), USA
           S.13
PALMGREN, Selim (1878-1951), Fin

   R.1   S.c,1-8,24,40
PÁLÓCZI HORVÁTH, Ádám (1760-1820), Hun
   R.1
PALOMARES, Juan de (c1573-<1609), Sp
   R.1   S.16
PALOMBO, Paul (1937-   ), USA
   R.19   S.10,13
PALOMERO - Princesita (v)
           S.39
PALOMINO, José (1755-1810), Sp
   R.1   S.10
PALONI - Non guardarmi cosi
           S.e
PÁLSSON, Páll (1928-   ), Iceland
   R.1   S.c,40
PALTANAVICHYUS, Vitautas (1924-   )
           S.18
PALUSELLI, Stefan (1748-1805), Aus
   R.1   S.8
PAMER, Michael (1782-1827)
           S.c,10
PAMINGER, Leonhard (1495-1567), Ger
   R.1   S.c,10,16
PANCHENKO, Semen Viktorovich
           S.10
PANELLA, Frank (1878-1953), USA
   R.49   S.10,13,54(347)
PANELLA, Louis
           S.24
PANIAGUA, Gregorio
           S.c
PANIN, Piotr (1936-   )
           S.c
PANIZZA, Ettore (1875-1967), Arg
   R.1   S.8,24

PANIZZA, Giacomo (1803/04-1860), It
   R.3   S.c
PANNE, Wim van der (1930-   )
             S.c
PANNY, Joseph (1794-1838), Aus
   R.1   S.c
PANOFKA, Heinrich (1807-1887), Silesia
   R.1   S.18
PANSERON, Auguste Mathieu (1796-1859), Fr
   R.1   S.10
PANTRIRU, Grigore
             S.c
PANTSCHENKO, Sergei (1867-1912)

PANUFNIK, Andrzej (1914-   ), Pol
   R.1   S.c,7-10,24a
PANULA, Jorma Juhani (1930-   ), Fin
   R.14   S.c
PAOLO de FIRENZE (d.1419), It
   R.1   S.4,5x
PAOLO, Gian (fl 1570) [see CIMA, Giovanni Paolo]
PAPAIOANNOU, Yannis Andreou (1911-   ), Greece
   R.1   S.24
PAPALE, Henry

PAPANDOPULO, Boris (1906-   ), Yug
   R.14   S.24a
PAPAPOSTOLU, Dimitrios
             S.c
PAPAVOINE, (c1720-1793), Fr
   R.1   S.c
PAPINEAU-COUTURE, Jean (1916-   ), Can
   R.1   S.8,10,24
PAPINI, Guido (1847-1912), It
   R.1   S.24
PAPORISZ, Yoram (1940-   ), Isr
   R.14   S.10
PAPP, Lajos (1935-   ), Hun
   R.1   S.c,10
PAPPE, Hans Georg (1935-   )
             S.c
PAPPERT, Walter (1936-   ), Ger
   R.4   S.c
PÂQUE, Désiré (1867-1939), Bel
   R.1   S.c
PAQUINO, Giovanni Saello del
             S.10
PAR, C. F. (see note)
             S.5x

PARABOSCO, Girolamo (c1524-1557), It
   R.1   S.c,16,53
PARADIES, Pietro Domenico (1707-1791), It
   R.1   S.c,2-8,10,11,18,24
PARADIS, Maria Theresia von (1759-1824), Aus
   R.1   S.c,2-5,7,8,10,18,24,30,52
PARAY, Paul (1886-1979), Fr
   R.1   S.9,24
PARCHAM, Andrew (17th Cent), Eng
   R.5   S.c,10
PARDAVE - The Nightingale
           S.5x
PAREDES, Carlos Portugal

PAREE, Paul - pseud [see WRIGHT, Lawrence]
PARELLI, Attilio [really PAPARELLA] (1874-1944), It
   R.4   S.24
PARGA - Alhambra (guitar)
           S.5x
PARIBENI, Giulio Cesare (1881-1964), It
   R.14   S.4
PARÍK, Ivan (1936-   ), Slovak
   R.1   S.31
PARISH ALVARS, Elias (1808-1849), Eng
   R.1   S.c,10
PARISIENSIS, Albertus (12th Cent)
           S.39
PARISOTTI, Alessandro (1853-1913), It
   R.3

PARK, Edna Rosalind (19th Cent), USA
   R.7   S.e
PARKER, Alice (1925-   ), USA
   R.7   S.30,52
PARKER, Clifton (1905-   ), Eng
   R.4   S.4
PARKER, Horatio William (1863-1919), USA
   R.1   S.8,10,12,13,54(322,59)
PARKER, Martin (17th Cent)
           S.c
PARKER, Mary Lou - Do you know him?
           S.10,30
PARKHURST, Mrs. E. A. (fl 1864), USA
   R.200   S.10
PARKS, James A. (c1863-1945), USA
           S.13
PARKYNS, Beatrice (née Crawford) (19th Cent), Eng
   R.7   S.30
PARMA, Nicolo (fl 1575-1613), It
   R.1   S.c,32

PARMEGIANI, Bernard (1927-   ), Fr
    R.14   S.c,10,24
PARPINELLI, Santino
                 S.24a
PARRATT, Sir Walter (1841-1924), Eng
    R.1
PARRIS, Robert (1924-   ), USA
    R.19   S.10,13
PARROTT, Ian (1916-   ), Eng
    R.1   S.c,10
PARRY - Soldiers of the King
                 S.54(356)
PARRY, D. D. - Bugail Hafod y Cwm
                 S.e
PARRY, Hubert (1848-1918), Eng
    R.1   S.c,2-10,26-28
PARRY, John (c1710-1782), Wales
    R.1   S.c,10
PARRY, Joseph (1841-1903), Wales (see note)
    R.1   S.8,10
PARRY, Roland (1897-   ), USA
    R.19   S.10,13
PARSADANYAN, Boris (1925-   )
                 S.18,24a
PARSCH, Arnošt (1936-   ), Cz
    R.1   S.c,10
PARSLEY, Osbert (1511-1585), Eng
    R.1   S.c
PARSONS, John (c1575-1623), Eng
    R.1   S.14
PARSONS, Robert (c1530-1570), Eng
    R.1   S.c,8,10,16
PÄRT, Arvo (1935-   ), Est
    R.1   S.c,24a
PARTCH, Harry (1901-1974), USA (see note)
    R.1   S.8-10,13

PARTICHELA, F. A. - Jarabe tapatio (Mexican hat dance)
                 S.10
PARTOS, Oedoen (1907-1977), Isr
    R.1   S.10,23,24
PARTRIDGE - Coronation bells
                 S.54(321)
PARTSKHALADZE, Merib (1924-   )
                 S.18,24a
PARVIAINEN, Jarmo (1927-   ), Fin
                 S.c,40
PASCAL, Claude René Georges (1921-   ), Fr
    R.1   S.c,8,10,18,22,24
PASCANU, Alexandru (1920-   ), Rum
    R.14

PASCHA, Edmund (1714-1772), Slovak
R.18   S.c
PASCHKEVITSCH, Vassili Alexeyevich (1742-1797), Russia
R.30   S.c,18
PASCULLI, Antonio (1842-1924), It
            S.c
PASHKALOV, Viktor Nikandrovich (1841-1885), Russia
R.28   S.18
PASQUALI, Niccolo (c1718-1757), It
R.1   S.c
PASQUINI, Bernado (1637-1710), It
R.1   S.c,2-11,18,24,32,53
PASQUINI, Ercole (17th Cent), It
R.1   S.5
PASSEREAU, Pierre (fl 1509-47), Fr
R.1   S.c,7,8,10,14-16,22
PASSY, Edmond (1789-1870), Sweden
R.30   S.56
PASTERNACK - Taps
            S.e
PASTERWIZ, Georg von (1730-1803), Aus
R.1   S.c
PASTRANA, Pedro de (c1480->1559), Sp
R.1   S.c,10,16
PASQUALI, Niccolo (c1718-1757), It
R.1   S.c
PATA, Huert [see PATAKY, Hubert]
PATACHICH, Iván (1922-   ), Hun
R.1   S.c,10,22
PATÁKY, Hubert (1892-1953), Ger
R.14   S.24
PATAVINO, Francesco (c1497-1556), It
            S.c
PATERNA - Quien te llama
            S.e
PATERSON, Wilma (1944-   ), Eng
R.7   S.c
PATHIE, Rogier (c1510->1565), Franco-Flem
R.1   S.c
PATIÑO, Carlos (d.1675), Sp
R.1   S.1,10,16,39
PATRIQUIN, Donald

PATSIUS, Friedrich (1809-1891)
            S.18
PATTERSON, Paul (1947-   ), Eng
R.1   S.c,55
PATTI, Adelina (Adela Juana Maria) (1843-1919), It
R.7   S.e,52

PAUER, Jiří (1919-   ), Cz
  R.1   S.c,10,18,24
PAUER, Max (1866-1945), Ger
  R.1   S.c
PAUL, Berthold (1948-   )
          S.c
PAUL, David (1948-   )

PAUL, Ernst Julius (1907-1979), Aus
  R.4
PAUL, Gerhard (1935-   ), Ger
  R.4   S.c
PAULI, Maurus (1747-1786), Ger
          S.c
PAULIN, Gaston (fl 1898-1910), Fr
  R.200   S.10
PAULL, E. T. (1858-1924), USA
  R.23   S.54(314,15)
PAULLI, Holger Simon (1810-1891), Den
  R.1   S.c,33,57
PAULOWICZ - Habe Mitlied mit mir! - Zigeunerlied
          S.24a
PAULS, Raimond (1936-   )
          S.18
PAULSEN, Hellmut (1909-   ), Ger
  R.3   S.5x
PAULSON, Gustaf (1898-1966), Sweden
  R.1   S.10,56
PAULUS de BRODA (15-16th Cent), Boh
  R.8   S.10,16
PAUMANN, Conrad (c1410-1473), Ger
  R.1   S.c,2-4,8,10,11,14-16,53
PAUMGARTNER, (15th Cent) [see BAUMGARTNER]
PAUMGARTNER, Bernhard (1887-1971), Aus
  R.1   S.c
PAUS, Jakob Valerian
          S.c
PAVCIC, Josip (1870-1949), Yug
  R.8   S.10
PAVESI, Stefano (1779-1850), It
  R.1   S.c
PAX, Karl Ed (1802-1867)
  R.3   S.e
PAXÃO, da [see PAIXÃO, da]
PAXSON, Theodore (fl 1940), USA
  R.200   S.10
PAYER, Hieronymous (1787-1845), Aus
  R.10   S.c,10
PAYET, Carlos (1944-   )
          S.c

PAYN, A. A./G. G. - pseud [see MILES, C. Austin]
PAYNE - Punjaub march
                S.54(351)
PAYNE, Anthony (1936-   ), Eng
    R.1   S.c
PAZ, Juan Carlos (1901-1972), Arg
    R.1   S.5x,46
PAZELLER, Jakob (1869-1959), Aus
    R.4   S.c
PAZTHORY - Im Volkston
                S.5x
PEARCE [Piers, Pierce], Edward (c1560-?1613), Eng
    R.1   S.c,16
PEARSALL, Robert Lucas [?pseud: G. BERTHOLD] (1795-1856)
    Eng (see note)   R.1   S.c,1x,e[Berthold]
PEARSON, Leslie
                S.10
PECCI, Tomaso (c1576-1606), It
    R.1   S.c
PECELIUS, Johann Christoph [see PEZEL, Johann Christoph]
PECHED - Andulko Safarova
                S.54(313)
PECHOTSCH, Raimund
                S.24
PECK, Russell (1945-   ), USA
    R.19   S.13
PEČKE, Karel (1890-   ), Cz
    R.18   S.31
PECKING, H. - Radio march
                S.54(351)
PÉCOUR, Louis Guillaume (?1651-1729), Fr
    R.1   S.c
PEDERSEN, Paul Richard (1935-   ), Can
    R.4
PEDERSON, Gunnar Moller (1943-   ), Den
    R.80   S.40
PEDERSON, Jens Wilhelm (1939-   ), Den
    R.14   S.40
PEDERSØN, Mogens (c1583-1623), Den
    R.1   S.c,4,5,35,57
PEDRELL, Carlos (1878-1941), Uruguay
    R.1   S.c,8,10,11,32
PEDRELL, Felipe (1841-1922), Sp
    R.1   S.1,2
PEDRO da ESPERANCA [see ESPERANCA, Pedro de]
PEDRO de CRISTO (c1545-1618)
                S.10,16
PEDROLLO, Arrigo (1878-1964), It
    R.1   S.10

PEDROTTI, Carlo (1817-1893), It
    R.1   S.1-4
PEEK, Richard Maurice (1927-   ), USA
    R.19   S.12,13
PEEL, Graham (1877-1937), Eng
    R.4   S.c,5x,10
PEELE, George (16th Cent)
                 S.c,10,16
PEELEMANS - Sonatine
                 S.32
PEERSON, Martin (1571/73-1651), Eng
    R.1   S.c,2-5,7,8,10,11,14-16,53
PEETERS, Flor (1903-   ), Bel
    R.1   S.c,8-10
PEIKO, Nikolai Ivanovich [see PEYKO, Nikolai Ivanovich]
PEIRE CARDENAL (?1180-?1278), Fr
    R.1   S.c,10,16,17,39
PEIROL (?1160->1221), Fr
    R.1   S.c,8,14
PEISHE, Gerre [S.18] = GUERRA PEIXE, Cesar
PEJMAN, Ahmad (1935-   ), Iran
    R.80   S.c
PEKIEL, Bartlomiej (d c1670), Pol
    R.1   S.c,16
PELAJA, Giovanni Francesco (16th Cent), It
    R.5   S.c
PELEMANS, Willem (1901-   ), Bel
    R.1   S.36
PELHAM, Peter Jr. (b.1721), Eng
    R.53   S.10,47
PÉLISSIER, H. G. (1874-1913)
                 S.e
PELISSIER, Victor (c1740-c1820), Fr/USA
    R.1   S.10,47
PELLEGRINI, Domenico (17th Cent), It
    R.8   S.c
PELLEGRINI, Vincenzo (d c1631), It
    R.1   S.c,53
PELLETIER, Frédéric (1870-1944), Can
    R.8
PELOQUIN, Charles Alexander (1918-   ), USA
    R.19
PELUSI, Mario (1851-   ), USA
                 S.13
PEMBERTON, Carlos (1932-   ), Arg
    R.26   S.46
PEÑA - El carbon

PEÑALOSA, Francisco de (c1470-1528), Sp
    R.1   S.8,10,14,16,39

PENBERTHY, James (1917-   ), Australia
R.1   S.29,37
PENCERDD GWALIA [see THOMAS, John]
PENDERECKI, Krzystof (1933-   ), Pol
R.1   S.c,9,10,18,20,24

PENELLA, Manuel (1880-   ), Sp
R.200   S.10,39
PENN, Arthur A. (1875-1941), Eng/USA
R.19   S.10,24
PENN, William Albert (1943-   ), USA
R.19   S.10,13
PENN, William H.
             S.e
PENNARIO, Leonard (1924-   ), USA
R.19   S.13
PENNINO - Pe´cche
             S.44
PENTE, Emilio (1860-1929), It
R.8   S.24
PENTLAND, Barbara (1912-   ), Can
R.1   S.24,30,52
PEPE, Carmine USA
             S.13,24a
PEPETER - Toreador
             S.e
PÉPIN, Clermont (1926-   ), Can
R.1   S.10
PEPPING, Ernst (1901-1981), Ger
R.1   S.c,7,8,10
PEPUSCH, Johann Christoph (1667-1752), Ger
R.1   S.c,3-6,8-11,24,42
PERAGALLO, Mario (1910-   ), It
R.1   S.10
PERANDA, Marco Gioseppe (c1625-1675), It
R.1   S.c
PERANDREU, José (17th Cent), Sp
R.1   S.10,53
PERAZA, Francisco de (1564-1598), Sp
R.1   S.c,10,15,16,17,53
PERCEVAL, Julio (1903-1963), Arg
R.14   S.10,39,46
PERDUCET, G. (fl 1913), Fr - La berceuse du violineux;
Noel   S.e
PEREIRA, Diana Maria (1932-   ), Sri Lanka/Den
R.7   S.52
PEREIRA, Geraldo (1918-1955), Brazil
R.67   S.39
PERELLI - The happy morning waits
             S.e

PERERA, Ronald (1941-   ), USA
    R.19   S.13
PEREZ, Amador
                S.54(351)
PEREZ, David (1711-1778), It
    R.1   S.8,10
PEREZ BOCANEGRA, Juan (17th Cent)
                S.10
PEREZ FREIRE, Osman [see FREIRE, Osman Perez]
PEREZ SORIANO, Augustin (1846-1907), Sp
    R.104   S.c,34[Soriano]
PERGAMENT, Moses (1893-1977), Sweden
    R.1   S.c,6,9,10,24,40,56
PERGAMENT, Ruvim (1906-1965), USSR
    R.1   S.18
PERGOLESI, Giovanni Battista (1710-1736), It
    R.1   S.c,2-4,6-11,18,24-28,42
PERGOLESI, Nina [see note under CIAMPI, Vincenzo]
PERI, Jacopo (1561-1633), It
    R.1   S.c,1-10,18,42
PERICHON, Jean (16th Cent), Fr
    R.5   S.16
PÉRILHOU, Albert (1846-1936), Fr
    R.4   S.10
PERINO FIORENTINO (1523-1552), It
    R.1   S.5x,6,8,10,14
PERISSAS, Madeleine (20th Cent), Fr
    R.7   S.5x,30,52
PERKIN, Helen (1909-   ), Eng
    R.7   S.30,52
PERKINS, Frank (1908-   ), USA
    R.23   S.10,13
PERKINS, John MacIvor (1935-   ), USA
    R.19   S.10,13
PERKINS, William Oscar (1831-1902), USA
    R.53   S.e
PERKINS, William (1941-   ), USA
    R.19   S.13
PERKOWSKI, Piotr (1901-   ), Pol
    R.8   S.24a
PERLE, George (1915-   ), USA
    R.1   S.c,5x,8,10,13,19,24
PERLEA, Jonel (1900-1970), Rum
    R.1
PERLMAN, George USA
                S.10,13
PERLONGO, Daniel James (1942-   ), USA
    R.19
PERNAMBUCO, João (1883-1947)
                S.c,10,32

PERNE, Heinz (1930-   )
          S.c
PERONNET, Amelie [pseud: Léon BERNOUX] (c1831-1903), Fr
     R.7   S.e
PEROSI, Lorenzo (1872-1956), It
     R.1   S.c,2-4,5x,8-10
PEROSI, Marziano (1875-1959), It
     R.14   S.3,4
PÉROTIN (fl c1200), Fr
     R.1   S.c,2,3,5-8,10,11,14-16,18,53
PERRAULT, Michel (1925-   ), Can
     R.14   S.24
PERRICHON, Julien [Jean] (1566-c1600), Fr
     R.1   S.10
PERRIN d´ANGICOURT (fl 1245-70), Fr
     R.1   S.c,2-5,8,10,11,14,16
PERRIN, Jean (1920-   ), Swiss
     R.4
PERRINET [Perinetus, Prunet] (14-15th Cent), Fr
     R.1   S.c
PERRINS - At the end of a beautiful day
          S.e
PERRUCHOT, Lazare (1852-1930), Fr
          S.7
PERRY, Julia (1924-1979), USA
     R.1   S.10,13,30,52
PERRY, T. - Warbler´s serenade
          S.54(364)
PERSEN, John (1941-   ), Nor
          S.c,40
PERSICHETTI, Vincent (1915-   ), USA
     R.1   S.c,8-10,12,13,22,24a,25,27,28
PERSICO, Mario (1892-1977), It
     R.4   S.10
PERSLEY, George W.
          S.10
PERSSON, Bo Anders (1937-   )
          S.c
PERT, Morris (1947-   ), Scot
     R.4   S.c
PERTI, Giacomo Antonio (1661-1756), It
     R.1   S.c,10
PERUGIA, Matteo da [see MATTEO da PERUGIA]
PERUSIO, Matteo da [see MATTEO da PERUGIA]
PERUSSO, Mario (1936-   ), Arg
     R.26   S.46
PER VINGE [see VINGE, Per]
PESCETTI, Giovanni Battista (c1704-1766), It
     R.1   S.c,2,3,5x,10,18,53

PESCHIN, Gregor (c1500->1547), Boh
R.1
PESENTI, Martino (c1600-c1648), It
R.1   S.c,16
PESENTI, Michele (c1470->1524), It
R.1   S.10,14-16
PESKIN, Vladimir Amenevich (1906-   )
             S.18
PESORI, Stefano (17th Cent), It
R.1   S.c
PESSARD, Emile (1843-1917), Fr
R.1   S.4,5x,10,11,27
PESTALOZZA, Alberto (1851-1934), It
R.3   S.c,10
PETER von BLOIS
             S.c,16
PETER, Johann Friedrich (1746-1813), USA
R.1   S.4,7,9,10,47
PETER, Simon (1743-1819), USA
R.1   S.8,10,47
PETERS - Jolly coppersmith
             S.54(335)
PETERS, Gordon

PETERS, J. - Strömt herbei; Rheinlied
             S.e
PETERS, William Cummings (1805-1866), USA
R.1
PETERSEN, David (17th Cent)
R.1   S.24
PETERSEN, Nils Holger (1946-   )., Den
             S.40
PETERSEN, Wilhelm (1890-1957), Ger
R.14   S.c,24a
PETERSON, Theodore USA
             S.13
PETERSON, Wayne (1927-   ), USA
R.19   S.10,13
PETERSON-BERGER, Wilhelm (1867-1942), Sweden
R.1   S.c,5-10,24,40,43,56
PETHER, Henry E.
             S.10
PETIT - Salut à 85e
             S.54(354)
PETIT, Adrien [see COCLICO, Andrianus Petit]
PETIT, Pierre Yves (1922-   ), Fr
R.14   S.c,10,32
PETIT JEHAN, Claude (d.1589), Fr
R.1   S.7

PETR, Zdeněk (1919-   ), Cz
    R.18   S.31
PETRA-BASACOPOL, Carmen (1926-   ), Rum
    R.7   S.24a,30,52
PETRALI, Vincenzo Antonio (1832-1889), It
    R.8   S.c,53
PETRASSI, Goffredo (1904-   ), It
    R.1   S.c,5,8,10,24a,32
PETRAUSKAS, Mikas (1873-1937), Lith
    R.4   S.18
PETRELLA, Errico (1813-1877), It
    R.1
PETRENKO, Mickail (1902-1967)
                S.10
PETRIĆ, Ivo (1931-   ),Yug
    R.1   S.24a
PETRIDIS, Petros (1892-1977), Greece
    R.1
PETRIE, Henry W. (1857-1925), USA
    R.23   S.10,24
PETRINI, Francesco (1744-1819), It
    R.1   S.10
PETROBELLI, Francesco (d.1695), It
    R.1
PETROS, Frater [see PETRUS, Frater]
PETROV, Andrey Pavlovich (1930-   ), USSR
    R.1   S.c,18,24a
PETROV, N. - Do not believe child
                S.18
PETROVA KRUPKOVA, Elena (1929-   ), Cz
    R.7   S.c,52
PETROVICS, Emil (1930-   ), Hun
    R.1   S.c,9,10
PETRUCCI, Ottaviano (1466-1539), It
    R.1   S.c,8
PETRUS de CRUCE [Pierre de la Croix] (fl c1290)
    R.1   S.c,5x,10,14,16
PETRUS, Frater (15-16th Cent), It
    R.8   S.c
PETRŽELKA, Vilém (1889-1967), Cz
    R.1   S.5x,6,24a,31
PETSCHNIKOFF, Alexander (1873-1949)
    R.4   S.24a
PETTERSSON, Allan (1911-1980), Sweden
    R.1   S.c,9,10,24a,38,40,56
PETZOLD, Johannes (1912-   ), Ger
    R.4   S.c
PETZOLDT, Johann Christoph [see PEZEL, Johann Christoph]
PEUERL, Paul (c1570->1625), Ger
    R.1   S.c,8,10,16

PEVERNAGE, Andreas (1543-1591), Flem
R.1   S.c
PEYKO, Nikolay Ivanovich (1916-   ), USSR
R.1   S.7,8,10,18,24
PEYROT, Fernande (1888-   ), Swiss
R.7   S.30,52
PEYTON, Malcolm C. (1932-   ), USA
R.19   S.24a
PEZ, Johan Christoph (1664-1716), Ger
R.1   S.c,10
PEZEL [Pecelius], Johann Christoph (1639-1694), Ger
R.1   S.c,2-6,8-11
PEZOLD, Christian (1677-1733), Ger
R.1   S.c
PFEIFFER, Georges Jean (1835-1908), Fr
R.1   S.e
PFEIFFER, Hubert (1891-1932), Ger
R.3   S.c
PFEIFFER, Johann (1697-1761), Ger
R.1   S.3,4,5x
PFEIFFER, John (1920-   ), USA
R.19   S.10,13
PFEIL, Heinrich (1835-1899), Ger
R.3   S.e
PFENDNER, Heinrich (c1590-c1631), Ger
R.1   S.c
PFEYLL, Baltsaro Antonio
          S.c,53
PFIFFNER, Ernst (1922-   ), Swiss
R.4
PFISTER, Hugo (1914-1969), Swiss
R.1   S.c
PFITZNER, Hans (1869-1949), Ger
R.1   S.c,1-11,20,24,28
PFLÜGER, Hans Georg (1944-   ), Ger
R.4   S.c
PFOHL, Ferdinand (1862-1949), Ger
R.4   S.e
PHALÈSE, Pierre (c1510-1573/76), Neth
R.1   S.c,10,16

PHELPS - On morning land
          S.e
PHILE, Philip (c1734-1793), USA
R.53   S.10,47
PHILIDOR, Andre [l'aîné] (c1647-1730), Fr
R.1   S.c,8,10
PHILIDOR, Anne (1681-1728), Fr
R.1   S.c,10
PHILIDOR, François (1689-1717/18), Fr
R.1   S.6

PHILIDOR, François André (1726-1795), Fr
   R.1   S.c,5x
PHILIDOR, Jacques [le Cadet] (1657-1708), Fr
   R.1
PHILIDOR, Pierre (1681-1731), Fr
   R.1   S.2-4,10
PHILIPP, Franz (1890-1972), Ger
   R.1   S.c
PHILIPP, Isidore (1863-1958), Fr
   R.1   S.2,5x,10
PHILIPPART, Renée (1905-　　　), Fr
   R.7   S.52
PHILIPPE de VITRY [see VITRY, Philippe de]
PHILIPPE the CHANCELLOR, (c1160-1236), Fr
   R.1   S.c
PHILIPPENKO, Arkady Dmitrovich (1912-　　　)
          S.8
PHILIPPINE, Charlotte, Princess of Prussia
          S.10,52
PHILIPPOT, Michel Paul (1925-　　　), Fr
   R.1   S.c,10,52
PHILIPPUS ROYLLART [see ROYLLART, Philippus]
PHILIPS, Peter (1560/61-1628), Eng
   R.1   S.c,2-5,7,8,10,11,14,16,32,53
PHILIPS, Sir Thomas
          S.10
PHILLIPS, Barre (1934-　　　), USA
   R.19   S.13
PHILLIPS, Burrill (1907-　　　), USA
   R.1   S.3,4,5x,8,10-13,24a
PHILLIPS, Gerald
          S.24
PHILLIPS, Linda (20th Cent), Australia
   R.7   S.24a,52
PHILLIPS, Montague Fawcett (1885-1969), Eng
   R.1   S.c
PHILLIPS, Peter (1930-　　　), USA
   R.1   S.c,10,13
PHILLIPS, R. - Garden of memory
          S.e
PHILLIPS, Walter Alison (1864-　　　),
   R.200   S.10
PIAGGIO, Celestino (1886-1931), Arg
   R.26   S.46
PIANELLI, Antonio de (1747-1803), It
   R.10s   S.24
PIANI, Giovani Antonio [Desplanes, Jean Antoine]
   (1678->1757), It   R.1   S.c,2,5x,8,10,24

PIANNELLI - Villanelle (ce)
                S.lx
PIANTADOSI, Al (1884-1955), USA
    R.23   S.10
PIANTONI, Louis (1885-1958), It
    R.3
PIASTRO, Josef Borissoff (1889-   ), USA
    R.14   S.24
PIATTI, Alfredo Carlo (1822-1901), It
    R.1   S.c
PIAZANZA, Domenico de (15th Cent)
                S.17
PIAZZA, Gaetano (18th Cent), It
    R.5   S.c,10,53
PICARD [Pycard] (fl c1410), Fr
    R.1   S.c
PICCHI, Ermanno (1811-1856), It
    R.3
PICCHI, Giovanni (fl 1600-25), It
    R.1   S.c,10,16
PICCHI, Sylvano (1922-   ), Arg
    R.26   S.46
PICCI-MANTIA - Fantasia original (baritone horn)
                S.10
PICCININI, Alessandro (1566-c1638), It
    R.1   S.c,10,32
PICCINNI, Niccolò (1728-1800), It
    R.1   S.c,2,8,10,18,25,27
PICCIONI, Giovanni (c1550->1619), It
    R.1   S.10,14
PICCOLINI - Au Maroc
                S.e
PICCOLOMINI, Marietta (1834-1899), It
    R.1   S.e
PÍCHA, František (1893-1964), Cz
    R.1   S.5x,24a,31
PICHAUD, Marie-Claire
                S.30
PICHAUREAU, Claude (1940-   )
                S.c
PICHE, Bernard Paul (1908-   ), Can
    R.31
PICHL, Václav (1741-1805), Cz
    R.1   S.5x,10
PICHLER, L.
                S.c
PICINETTI, Felice Marie (17-18th Cent)
    R.5
PICK, Richard Samuel Burns (1915-   ), USA
    R.19   S.13,32

PICK-MANGIAGALLI, Riccardo (1882-1949), It
R.1   S.1-6,8,10,24a
PICKER, Tobias (1954-   ), USA
R.19   S.13,24a
PICO - La leggerezza (p)

PICON - Mantilla
           S.5x
PICON, A. - Diabolero; Two grotesques
           S.54(323)
PIECHLER, Arthur (1896-1974), Ger
R.14   S.c
PIEFKE, Gottfried (1817-1884), Ger
R.3   S.10,54(324)
PIELTAIN, Dieudonne-Pascal (1754-1833), Bel
R.1   S.c,24
PIER, George - pseud [see PIRCKMAYER, Georg]
PIERACCINI, Mario (1877-   ), It
R.3   S.10
PIERCE, Alexandra (1934-   ), USA
R.19   S.13,52
PIERCE, Edward [see PEARCE, Edward]
PIERCE, John Robinson (1910-   ) USA
R.30   S.10,13
PIEREKEN de la COUPELE (fl 1240-60), Fr
           S.10,16
PIERNÉ, Gabriel (1863-1937), Fr
R.1   S.c,1-11,18-22,24,54(341)
PIERNÉ, Paul (1874-1952), Fr
R.14   S.6,10,18,22
PIERNIK, Zdzislaw (1937-   ), Pol
           S.c
PIERO, Magister (fl 1340-50), It
R.1   S.8,10,14,16
PIERPONT, James S. (1822-1893)

PIERRE de CORBIE (d >1195), Fr
R.1   S.c,10
PIERRE de MOLINS (fl ?1190-1220), Fr
R.1   S.c,4,10,14,53
PIERRE de la Croix [see PETRUS de CRUCE]
PIERS, Edward [see PEARCE, Edward]
PIETERSZOON = SWEELINCK, Jan Pieterszoon
PIÉTON, Loyset (fl 1530-45)
R.1   S.c,14
PIETRAGRUA, Carl [see GRUA, Carlo Luigi Pietro]
PIETRI, Giuseppe (1886-1946), It
R.8   S.3,4,5x,10
PIETRO - Lontan da te
           S.e

PIETROBONO (c1417-1497), It
   R.1   S.c
PIETROWSKI, Karol (fl c1790-1800), Pol
   R.1   S.c
PIGARELLI - La Montanara (v)
          S.10
PIJPER, Willem (1894-1947), Neth
   R.1   S.7-10,24
PIKE, Eleanor Baxter Franklin (1890-c1973), Eng
   R.7,37   S.24[Franklin-Pike],30
PIKET, Frederick (1903-1974), USA
   R.19   S.10,13
PILIS, Heda (1925-   ), Yug
   R.7   S.52
PILKINGTON, Francis (c1570-1638), Eng
   R.1   S.c,1x,2-5,7,8,10,11,14-16,32
PILLIN, Boris (1941-   ), USA
   R.14   S.9,10,13,19
PILLNEY, Karl Hermann (1896-   ), Ger
   R.1   S.c
PILOTTI, Giuseppe (1784-1838), It
   R.8   S.c
PILSS, Karl (1902-   ), Aus
   R.14   S.5x,10
PIMSLEUR, Solomon (1900-1962), USA
   R.19   S.10,13
PINCHARD, Max (1928-   ), Fr
   R.14   S.c
PING, Jin Yan

          S.24a
PING, Zhang Jing

          S.24a
PINGAULT - Johnny Palmer
          S.5x
PINI-CORSI, Antonio (1858-1918), It
   R.1   S.44
PINKARD, Maceo (1897-1962), USA
   R.23   S.24
PINKHAM, Daniel (1923-   ), USA
   R.1   S.c,10,12,13,24,25,27
PINO, Carmelo (1934-   )

PIŇOS, Alois (1925-   ), Cz
   R.1   S.10
PINOZZI, Carlo - pseud [see ROTHSTEIN, James]
PINSUTI, Ciro (1829-1888), It
   R.1   S.10,24
PINTO - La vraie
          S.54(364)

PINTO, Alejandro (1922-   ), Arg
    R.26   S.46
PINTO, George Frederic (1785-1806), Eng
    R.1   S.c
PINTO, Octavio (1890-1950), Brazil
    R.14   S.8,10,39
PINZON URREA, Jesus (1928-   ), Colombia
    R.14   S.10,39
PIOT, Julien (1850-1923), Fr
    R.3   S.24

PIPELARE, Matthaeus (c1450-c1515), Neth
    R.1   S.c,4,5x,16,41
PIPKOV, Lyubomir (1904-1974), Bul
    R.1   S.c,10,20,24
PIPO, Antonio Ruiz [see RUIZ PIPO, Antonio]
PIPO, Filippo Amadei [see AMADEI, Filippo]
PIPPING, Ernst

PIQUET - Pour l'oublier
            S.e
PIRANDELLI - Amor amor

PIRCKMAYER, Georg [pseud: George PIER] (1918-1977), Aus
    R.4
PIRENNE, Maurice Maria (1928-   ), Neth
    R.80   S.c
PIRES de CAMPOS, Lina (20th Cent), Brazil
                S.52
PIRON, Armand John (1888-1943), USA
    R.23   S.10
PIROYE, Charles (1668/72-1717/30), Fr
    R.1   S.10,53
PIROZZI - L'urdemo sole (v)
                S.10
PIRUMOV, Alexander Ivanovich (1930-   ), USSR
    R.14   S.18
PISADOR, Diego (1509/10->1557), Sp
    R.1   S.c,2-4,5x,8,10,11,14,16,32,39
PISENDEL, Johann Georg (1687-1755), Ger
    R.1   S.c,10,24
PISK, Paul Amadeus (1893-   ), USA
    R.1   S.10,13,19,21
PISTOLETA (1150-1200)
                S.c
PISTON, Walter (1894-1976), USA
    R.1   S.c,2-5,7-13,18,20,21,23,24
PITFIELD, Thomas Baron (1903-   ), Eng
    R.1   S.c
PITONI, Giuseppe Ottavio (1657-1743), It
    R.1   S.c,2,5x,10

PITSCH, Karl Franz (1786-1858), Boh
R.8   S.c
PITT, Percy (1869-1932), Eng
R.1   S.e
PITTALUGA, Gustavo (1906-   ), Sp
R.14   S.2,3,5,7,8,10,39
PITTAWAY, Rudolph USA
             S.13
PIXIS, Johann Peter (1788-1874), Ger
R.1   S.c,10,24a
PIZZETTI, Ildebrando (1880-1968), It
R.1   S.c,1-11,24
PIZZETTI, Odoardo (1853-1926), It
R.10s   S.e
PIZZINI, Carlo Alberto (1905-   ), It
R.1   S.3-6,8
PIZZIONI, Giovanni [see PICCIONI, Giovanni]

PIZZONI, C. - Duo degli occhi lucenti [S.5x]
   = PIZZIONI, Giovanni
PJATS, Richo (1899-   ), Est
R.4   S.18
PLÁ, Juan Bautista
             S.10
PLACHY, Wenzel (1785-1858), Cz
R.10s   S.c
PLAIN, Gerald (1940-   ), USA
R.19   S.13
PLAKIDIS, P. (1947-   )
             S.18
PLANCON, Jean [see PLANSON, Jean]
PLANEL, Robert (1908-   ), Fr
R.10s   S.c,10
PLANQUETTE, Robert (1848-1903), Fr
R.1   S.c,4,7-10,42,54(319)
PLANSON, Jean (c1559->1612), Fr
R.1   S.c,10,14,16
PLANYAVSKY, Peter Felix (1947-   ), Aus
R.1   S.c
PLATER, D. J.
             S.54(341)
PLATTI, Giovanni Benedetto (c1700-1763), Aus
R.1   S.c,3,5,7-11,18,22,24
PLATTNER, Augustin (fl 1613-24), Ger
R.1   S.c
PLAUTZIUS, Gabriel (1580-1641), Slovene
R.1   S.c
PLAVEC, Josef (1905-   ), Cz
R.18   S.31
PLAYFORD, John (1623-1686), Eng [publisher]
R.1   S.c

PLAZA ALFONZO, Eduardo (1911-   ), Ven
    R.4
PLAZA ALFONZO, Juan Bautista (1898-1965), Ven
    R.4
PLESKOW, Raoul (1931-   ), USA
    R.19   S.10,13,24a
PLESSIS, Hubert du (1922-   ), South Africa
    R.4
PLESSOW, Eric (1899-   ), Ger [pseud: LESSO-VALERO,
    Manuel ESTVILLA, Ewald WALTER, Edward WILLS]
    R.3   S.43
PLEYEL, Ignace Joseph (1757-1831), Aus
    R.1   S.c,8-10,23,24
PLICHTA, Jan (1898-   ), Cz
    R.18   S.31
PLOG, Anthony (1947-   ), USA
    R.19   S.10
PLUMB, EDWARD H.
            S.5x
PLUMHOF, Heinrich (1836-1914), Swiss
    R.3
PLUMMER, John (c1410-c1484), Eng
    R.1   S.c
PLUMSTEAD, Mary Frost (1905-1980), Eng
    R.7   S.c
PLUNKETT, Mert W. - Canadian Army marching song: We're
    on our way S.5x,54(365)
POCCI, Franz Graf von (1807-1876),Ger
    R.1   S.c
POCHON, Alfred (1878-1959), USA
    R.19   S.24a
POCKH, Karl

POCKRISS, Lee J. (1927-   ), USA
    R.23   S.9
PODBIELSKI, Jan (fl 1650)
    R.5   S.c,10,16,53
PODELSKY, Gennadi Vyacheslavovich (1927-   )
            S.18
PODÉŠT, Ludvik (1921-1968), Cz
    R.1   S.31
PODEŠTA, A. - Soy Criollo
            S.54(357)
PODESVA, Jaromír (1927-   ), Cz
    R.1   S.24,31
PODKOVIUROV, Petr Petrovich (1910-   ), USSR
    R.14   S.18,24
POENITZ, Franz [pseud: Franc. BENIZZO] (1850-1913), Ger
    R.3   S.c,5x

POERTNER, Hermann
        S.c
POGGIS - Amor; Laura (vi & p)
        S.24
POGLIETTI, Alessandro (d.1683),It
  R.1   S.c,10,53
POHLE, David (1624-1695), Ger
  R.1   S.c
POISE, Jean Alexander Ferdinand (1828-1892), Fr
  R.1   S.e
POISSL, Johan Nepomuk (1783-1865), Ger
  R.1   S.c
POISTER, Arthur W. (1898-1980), USA
        S.12,13
POITEVIN, Guillaume (1646-1706), Fr
  R.1
POKORNY, Franz Xaver (1729-1794), Boh
  R.1   S.c,10,19-21,24a
POLA, Edward (1907-   ), USA
  R.23   S.10
POLAK, Jakub [see REYS, Jakob]
POLDINI, Ede (1869-1957), Hun
  R.1   S.c,4,5x,18,24
POLDOWSKI - pseud [see WIENIAWSKA, Irene Regine]
POLERO - Romance
        S.c
POLGÁR, Tibor (1907-   ), Hun
  R.4   S.24
POLIAKIN, F. - Le canari (concert-polka); Marche des
  petits tambours (vi & p)   S.24
POLIAKIN, Miron (1895-1941) (see note)
        S.c
POLIN, Claire (1926-   ), USA
  R.19   S.10,13,30,52
POLLA, W. C. (1876-1939), USA
  R.23   S.10
POLLACK, Lew (1895-1946), USA
  R.23   S.24
POLLAROLO, Carlo Francesco (c1653-1723), It
  R.1   S.53
POLLEDRO, Giovanni Battista (1781-1853), It
  R.1   S.8,10
POLLINI, Francesco (1762-1846), It
  R.1   S.24a
POLLOCK, Robert Emil (1946-   ), USA
  R.19   S.10,13
POLOLÁNÍK, Zdeněk (1935-   ), Cz
  R.1   S.20,31
POLSON, Arthur (1934-   ), Can
  R.4   S.24

POLYAKOV, Valeri Leonidovich (1913-1970), USSR
 R.14 S.18
POLYANICHENKO, Alexander Alexandrovich (1895-1968), USSR
 R.47 S.18
POMBO, Rafael (1833-1912), Colombia
    S.39
POMPER, Albert (1862-1917), Neth
 R.3 S.c
PONC, Miroslav (1902-1976), Cz
 R.1 S.4
PONCE, Juan (c1480->1521), Sp
 R.1   S.c,8,10,14,16,32
PONCE, Manuel María (1882-1948), Mex
 R.1   S.c,5x,7,8,10,15,18,24,39
PONCHIELLI, Amilcare (1834-1886), It
 R.1   S.c,1-11,18,28,42-44,54(322,28)
POND - Shoulder arms
    S.54(355)
PONGRÁCZ, Zoltán (1912-), Hun
 R.1 S.10
PONIATOWSKI, József (1816-1873), Pol
 R.1 S.e
PONIRIDIS, Georgios (1892-), Greece
 R.14 S.10
PONSE, Luctor (1914-), Neth
 R.1 S.10
PONT, Jacques du (c1500->1564), Fr
 R.1 S.15
POOL, Geoffrey (20th Cent)
    S.c
POOL, Philip (d.1762)
 R.5 S.c
POOS, Heinrich (1928-), Ger
 R.4 S.c
POOT, Marcel (1901-), Bel
 R.1   S.4,5,7,8,10,18,20,22,24,36
POPE - Kitchener's boys
    S.e
PÖPEL, Thomas (fl 1542), Ger
 R.5
POPMA van OEVERING, Rynoldus (1692-1782), Neth
 R.1
POPOV, Gavriil Nikolayevitch (1904-1972), Russia
 R.1   S.4,18,24
POPOVICI, Doru (1932-), Rum
 R.14 S.c
POPOVICI, Timotei (1870-1950), Rum
 R.1 S.20
POPP, Wilhelm [pseud: Henry ALBERT] (1828-1903), Ger
 R.3 S.10

POPPE [Boppe], Meister
              S.c
POPPER, David (1843-1913), Aus
   R.1   S.c,1x,2-4,5x,9,10,18,24
POPPLEWELL, Richard John (1935-   ), Eng
   R.80   S.c
POPY, Francis [pseud: Henry STAZ] (1874-1928), Fr
   R.3   S.c,3,24
PORCAIRAGUES, Azalais de [see AZALAIS de PORCAIRAGUES]
PORCELIJN, David (1947-   ), Neth
   R.4
PORPORA, Nicola (1686-1768), It
   R.1   S.c,2-7,10,11,18,22,24,53
PORRET, Julien (1896-   )

PORRINO, Ennio (1910-1959), It
   R.1   S.3,4,10
PORTA, Costanzo (1528/29-1601), It
   R.1   S.8,10,14
PORTA, Ercole (1585-1630), It
   R.1
PORTA, Francesco della [see DELLA PORTA, Francesco]
PORTER, Ambrose Probert (1885-1971), Eng
   R.77   S.c
PORTER, Cole (1891-1964), USA
   R.1   S.c,4,9-11,24,33
PORTER, Quincy (1897-1966), USA
   R.1   S.2,3,5,6,8-13,18,20,24
PORTER, Walter (c1595-1659), Eng
   R.1   S.c
PORTINARO, Francesco (c1520->1578), It
   R.1   S.c
PORTNOFF, Mischa (1901-   ), USA
   R.14   S.10,13
PORTO ALEGRE, W. S.   Brazil - Sinfonia da vitoria
              S.5x,6
PORTOGALLO, Marcos [see PORTUGAL, Marcos Antonio]
PORTUGAL, Marcos Antonio da Fonseca (1762-1830), Port
   R.1   S.c,10
PORUMBESCO, Ciprian (1853-1883), Rum
   R.1   S.18,24
POSADAS - Noche feliz
              S.39,44
POSCA, George - Zweifelnder Wunsch
              S.e

POSCH, Isaac (d.1622/23), Aus
   R.1   S.10,16
POSER, Hans (1917-1970), Ger
   R.1

POSFORD, Benjamin George Ashwell (1906-   ), Eng
   R.1
POSPÍŠIL, Juraj (1931-   ), Slovak
   R.1   S.31
POSS, Georg (c1570->1633), Ger
   R.1   S.c
POSSE, Wilhelm (1852-1925), Ger
   R.1   S.c
POST, Max
           S.24a
POSTON, Elizabeth (1905-   ), Eng
   R.1   S.c,30,52
POTHOLT, Jacobus (1726-1782), Neth
   R.5   S.c
POTTER, Archibald James (1918-1980), Ire
   R.1   S.10,19,49
POTTER, Philip Cipriani Hamby (1792-1871), Eng
   R.8   S.24
POTTER, Sophie
           S.e
POTULOV, Nikolai (1810-1873), Russia
   R.3   S.c
POULENC, Francis (1899-1963), Fr
   R.1   S.c,1-11,18-21,24-28,42
POULTON, George
           S.47
POUND, Ezra (1885-1972), USA
   R.1   S.9,13
POURNY, Charles (fl 1872)
   R.200   S.e
POUSSEUR, Henri (1929-   ), Bel
   R.1   S.c,10,20,24
POVILAITIS, Leonas (1927-   )
           S.18
POWELL, James Baden (1843-1931)
   R.3   S.c
POWELL, John (1882-1963), USA
   R.1   S.7-11,13,24
POWELL, Maud (1868-1920), USA
   R.8   S.24
POWELL, Mel (1923-   ), USA
   R.1   S.c,9,10,13,20,24
POWELL, Morgan (1938-   ), USA
   R.19   S.13
POWELL, Roger USA
           S.13
POWELL, Thomas James (1897-1965), Wales
   R.85   S.55,54(361)
POWER, Henry Baynton
           S.e

POWER, Leonel (d.1445), Eng
  R.1   S.c,8,10,14,16
POWER, Teobaldo (1848-1884), Sp
  R.9   S.10
POZAJIC, Mladen (1905-1979), Yug
  R.14   S.c
POZDRO, John Walter (1923-   ), USA
  R.19   S.10,13
POZZOLI, Ettore (1873-1957), It
  R.1   S.c
POZZOLO, Bartolomeo (1849-1927), It
  R.10   S.e
PRADO, José de Almeida (1943-   ), Brazil
  R.1   S.10
PRAETORIUS, Hieronymus (1560-1629), Ger
  R.1   S.c
PRAETORIUS, Jacob (1586-1651), Ger
  R.1   S.5,10,53
PRAETORIUS, Michael (1569/73-1621), Ger
  R.1   S.c,2-4,6-11,14-16,18,22,24,32,53
PRAEGER, Heinrich Aloys (1783-1854), Ger
  R.8   S.c
PRAGUE, Lukas of [see LUKAS of PRAGUE]
PRATELLA, Francesco Balilla (1880-1955), It
  R.1   S.c,1x
PRATESI, Mira [see SULPIZI, Mira]
PRATI, Alessio (1750-1788), It
  R.1
PRATS, Rodrigo (fl 1941), Cuba - Maria's song [?]
               S.24
PRATT, Charles E. (1841-1902), USA
               S.10
PRATT, Paul USA
               S.10
PRAUNSPERGER, Marian (1681-1761), Ger
  R.5   S.c
PRAUS, Arnost (1873-1907), Cz
  R.18   S.5x
PRAVECEK, Jindrich (1909-   ), Cz
  R.18   S.31
PREDIERI, Giovanni Battista (fl 1730-55), It
  R.1   S.c
PREDIERI, Luca Antonio (1688-1767), It
  R.1   S.18,24
PREGER, Leo (1907-1965), Fr
  R.4   S.2,4,5x,10
PREHN, Ernst (1892-   ), Den
  R.13   S.24
PREIS, Ferdinand
               S.10

PREISSLER, Jos. [see BOLDI, Giuseppe - pseud]
PREMRU, Raymond Eugene (1934-   ), USA
   R.80   S.c
PRENDERGAST, William (1868-1933), Eng
            S.c
PRENTZL (17th Cent)
   R.5   S.c,10
PREOBRAJENSKO, Vera Nicolaevna (1926-   ), USA
   R.7   S.52
PRESS, Jacques (1903-   ), USA
   R.19   S.10,13
PRESSEL, Gustav Adolf (1827-1890), Ger
   R.3   S.e
PRESSER, William Henry (1916-   ), USA
   R.19   S.10,13
PRESSMAN, Samuel
            S.24
PRESTI, Ida (1924-1967), Fr
   R.7   S.c,10,30,32,52
PRESTON, Simon (1938-   ), Eng
   R.1   S.c
PRESTON, Thomas (d >1559), Eng
   R.1   S.c,8,53
PRETI, Alfonso (fl 1586-92), It
   R.8   S.c
PREVIN, André (1929-   ), USA
   R.1   S.c,10,13,32
PRÉVOST, André (1934-   ), Can
   R.1   S.c,5x,10,24
PREZA CASTRO, Velino M. (1866-1944), Mex
   R.22   S.54(318,19,26,38)
PRICE, Florence Beatrice (1888-1953), USA
   R.7   S.30
PRICE, Richard Maldwyn (1890-1952), Wales
   R.85,96   S.54(365)
PRIESING, Dorothy Jean (née McLemore) (1910-   ), USA
   R.7   S.52
PRIGOZHIN, Lyutsian Abramovich (1926-   ), USSR
   R.14   S.24a
PŘÍHODA, Váša (1900-1960), Cz
   R.1   S.5x,24
PRINCE, Charles A. (fl 1905-26), USA
            S.24, 45(311,17,18)
PRINCE, Robert (1929-   ), USA
   R.19   S.9,10,13
PRINCE-JOSEPH, Bruce (1925-   ), USA
            S.10,12,13
PRINCIPE, Remy (1889-   ), It
   R.14   S.5x,24

PRING, Joseph (1776-1842), USA
   R.25   S.10
PRINS Gustaf [see GUSTAF, Prince]
PRINZ, Alfred (1930-   ), Aus
   R.80   S.c,20
PRINZ, J. A. - Albumbatt (vi & p)
              S.24a
PRINZ, Jean Baptist (d c1742)

              S.c
PRIOLI, Giovanni [see PRIULI, Giovanni]
PRITCHARD, Arthur John (1908-   ), Eng
   R.14   S.c
PRITCHARD, Robert (1929-   ), USA [?]
   R.4   S.13
PRITCHARD, Rowland Hugh
              S.10
PRIULI, Giovanni (c1575-1629), It
   R.1   S.c
PRIXNER, Sebastian (1744-1799), Ger
   R.5   S.c
PROCACCINI, Teresa (1934-   ), It
   R.7   S.30,52
PROCH, Heinrich (1809-1878), Aus
   R.8   S.c,1x,2-4,5x,10,18
PROCTER, Leland (1914-   ), USA
   R.19   S.10,13
PRODROMIDÈS, Jean (1927-   ), Fr
   R.14   S.c
PROFETA, Laurentiu (1925-   ), Rum
   R.1
PROHASKA, Karl (1869-1927), Aus
   R.1   S.24
PROHASKA, Miljenko (1925-   ), Yug
   R.42   S.10
PROKOFIEV, Sergey (1891-1953), Russia
   R.1   S.c,1-11,18-21,23,24,42
PROSKE, Erwin Hero (1925-   ), Ger
   R.4   S.c
PROSNAK, Karol M.

PROSTAKOFF, Joseph (1911-   ), USA
   R.19   S.10,13
PROTHEROE, Daniel (1866-1934), Wales
   R.1   S.e
PROTO, Frank (1941-   ), USA
   R.19   S.13,24a
PROTOPSALTUL, Eustatie de la Punta
   [see EUSTATIE de la PUTNA]
PROULX, Anita Can

PROVAZNÍK, Anatol (1887-1950), Cz
   R.14   S.24,31
PROVENZALE, Francesco (c1626-1704), It
   R.1
PROVINCIALI, Emilio (fl 1898), Fr
   R.200   S.24
PROVOST, Heinz (1891-   )
             S.c,10,24
PRUDEN, Larry (1925-   ), New Zealand
   R.1
PRUME, François Hubert (1816-1849)
   R.3   S.24
PRUNET [see PERRINET]
PRYOR, Arthur (1870-1942), USA
   R.23   S.10,54(314,21,28,34,36,65)

PRZYBLSKI, Bronislaw Kazinierz (1943-   )

PTASZYNSKA, Marta (1943-   ), It
   R.7   S.30
PUCCINI, Domenico (1772-1815), It
   R.1   S.c,10
PUCCINI, Giacomo (1858-1924), It
   R.1   S.c,1-11,18,24,28,34,42,43,54(316,33)
PUCCIO - La lettera
             S.e
PUCHTLER, Wilhelm Maria (1848-1881), Ger
   R.3   S.c
PUCITTA, Vincenzo (1778-1861), It
   R.1   S.c
PUGET, Loisa (1810-1889), Fr
   R.7
PUGHE-EVANS, David (1866-1897), Wales
             S.5x
PUGLIANI, Francesco (18th Cent)
             S.c
PUGNACCI - Il guitano re
             S.34
PUGNANI - La Capriciosa (p)
   R.1
PUGNANI, Gaetano (1731-1798), It
   R.1   S.c,2-6,8,10,24
PUGNI, Cesare (1802-1870), It
   R.1   S.c,10,24
PUGNO, Raoul (1852-1914), Fr
   R.1
PUIG, Michel (1930-   ), Fr
   R.4
PUJOL VILLARUBÍ, Emilio (1886-   ), Sp
   R.1   S.c,10,39

PUJOL, Juan (c1573-1626), Sp
   R.1   S.c,15,17,32
PUKST, Grigori Konstantinovich (1900-1960), USSR
   R.14   S.18
PULIASCHI, Giovanni Domenico (17th Cent), It
   R.1   S.c
PULITI, Gabriello (c1575-1641/44), It
   R.1   S.c
PUNTO, Giovanni (1746-1803), Boh
   R.1   S.c,5x,10,24
PURCELL, Daniel (d.1717), Eng
   R.1   S.c,5,8,10
PURCELL, Edward Cockrane
             S.2-4,5x,10
PURCELL, Henry (1659-1695), Eng
   R.1   S.c,1-11,18,22,24-28,32,42,53
PURDY, William T. (1882-1918), USA
   R.23   S.54(347)
PURSELL, William (1926-   ), USA
   R.19   S.13
PURSWELL, Patrick (1939-   ), USA
   R.19   S.13
PURVIS, Richard Irven (1915-   )
   R.19   S.8,9,12,13
PUTRA, Alfredo
             S.18
PUTSCHE, Thomas (1929-   ), USA
   R.19   S.13
PYART, Arvo (1935-   )
             S.18
PYCARD [see PICARD]
PYGOTT, Richard (16th Cent), Eng
   R.1   S.c,16
PYKINI (fl ?1370), Fr
   R.1   S.c
PYLKKÄNEN, Tauno (1918-1980), Fin
   R.1   S.40
QIN, Youg Cheng
             S.24a
QUADRIS, Johannes de [see JOHANNES de QUADRIS]
QUAGLIA, Agostino (1744-1823), It
   R.8   S.c
QUAGLIATI, Paolo (c1555-1628), It
   R.1   S.8,10,15
QUAN, Liu Chun
             S.24a
QUANTZ, Johann Joachim (1697-1773), Ger
   R.1   S.c,2-10,18,24
QUARANTA, Francesco (1848-1897), It
   R.3

QUARANTINO, Pascual (1904-   ), Arg
  R.26   S.46
QUARLES, Charles (d c1727), Eng
  R.1   S.c,53
QUATRIS, Johannes de [see JOHANNES de QUADRIS]
QUEDRON (16-17th Cent) - Airs de Cour
          S.10
QUEEN, John
          S.10
QUEILLE, A. - Je ne pleurais
          S.e
QUELDRYK, (fl c1400), Eng
  R.1   S.16
QUENES de BÉTHUNE [see CONON de BÉTHUNE]
QUENTIN - Soldier's honeymoon
          S.e
QUENTIN, Bertin (d ?1767), Fr
  R.1   S.c,10
QUENTIN, Jean-Baptiste (fl 1718-c1750), Fr
  R.1   S.c,9
QUERFURTH, Franz (fl 1751), Aus
  R.5   S.c
QUESNEL, Joseph (1746-1809), Can
  R.1   S.9
QUESTENBURG, Johann Adam (1678-1752)
          S.c
QUET, L. - Petite pièce (cl)
          S.10
QUILTER, Roger (1877-1953), Eng
  R.1   S.c,1-5,7-11,24,26-28
QUINE
          S.32
QUINET, Fernand (1898-1971), Bel
  R.1   S.36
QUINET, Marcel (1915-   ), Bel
  R.1   S.36,24a
QUINN - Serenata (vi & p); Souvenir de Venise (vi & p)
          S.24
QUINTANAR, Héctor (1936-   ), Mex
  R.1   S.10,24a,39
QUINTERO - En el mundo
          S.54(324)
QUINTERO MUÑOZ, Juan
          S.c,10
QUINTÓN, José Ignacio (1881-1925), Puerto Rico
  R.56
QUIRKE, Raymond - Your voice
          S.e
QUIROGA, Manuel (1892-1961), Sp
  R.14   S.24

RAAIJMAKERS, Dick (1930-   )
        S.10
RAASTED, Niels Otto (1888-1966), Den
  R.14   S.5x,6-8,10
RÄÄTS, Jaan (1932-   ), Est
  R.1   S.c,24
RABAUD, Henri (1873-1949), Fr
  R.1   S.c,1-6,8,10,19-22

RABE, Folke (1935-   ), Sweden
  R.1   S.c,38,40,56
RABEY, Rene (1878-   )
        S.5x,24
RABSCH, Edgar (1892-   ), Ger
  R.8   S.c[b.1928]
RAČIUNAS, Antanas Ionovich (1905-   ), USSR
  R.14   S.18
RACK, Jeanette
        S.5x
RACQUET [Raquet], Charles (1597-1664), Fr
  R.1   S.c,10,53
RÁCZ, Aladár (1886-1958), Hun
  R.8   S.10
RACZKOWSKI, Feliks (1906-   )

RADCLIFFE, Philip (1905-   ), Eng
  R.1   S.c
RADECK, Ferdinand (1828-1903), Ger
  R.3   S.10
RADECKE, Robert (1830-1911), Ger
  R.3   S.5x,10
RADERMACHER, Friedrich (1924-   ), Ger
  R.4   S.c
RADESCA di FOGGIA, Enrico (d.1625), It
  R.1   S.c
RADIĆ, Dušan (1929-   ), Yug
  R.1   S.18
RADOMIA, Mikolaj z [see MIKOLAJ z RADOMIA]
RADZIWILL, Maciej (?1751-1800), Pol
  R.1
RAFF, Joachim (1822-1882), Swiss
  R.1   S.c,2-5,8-10,18,24
RAFFMAN, Relly (1921-   ), USA
  R.19   S.13
RAHBARI, Ali (1948-   ), Iran
  R.80   S.c
RAICHL, Miroslav (1930-   ), Cz
  R.14   S.31
RAICK, Dieudonné (1703-1764), S. Neth
  R.1   S.c,53

RAIDACH - Desire
               S.e
RAIMBAUT de VAQUEIRAS (d.1207), Fr
   R.1   S.c,2-4,5x,8,10,11,14-16
RAIMON de MIRAVAL (fl 1180-1215), Fr
   R.1   S.c,16
RAIMUND, Ferdinand (1790-1836), Aus
   R.1   S.e
RAINGER, Ralph (1901-1942), USA
   R.1   S.10,24
RAINIER, Priaulx (1903-   ), South Africa
   R.1   S.c,5,10,30,52
RAIRIGH, Max

RAISON, André (<1650-1719),Fr
   R.1   S.c,8,10,18,53
RAITH, G. - Fliegerparade
               S.54(327)
RAITIO, Väinö (1891-1945), Fin
   R.1   S.40
RAITŠJEV, Alexander (1922-   ), Bul
   R.8   S.18
RAJIČIČ, Stanojlo (1910-   ), Yug
   R.14   S.24a
RAK, Stepan (1945-   )
               S.c
RAKHIMOV, Hamid (1927-   )
               S.18
RAKHMADIEV, Erkegali (1932-   ), USSR
   R.47   S.18
RAKHMANINOV, Sergey (1873-1943), Russia
   R.1   S.c,1-11,18,23,24,28,32,42,43
RAKOV, Nikolay Petrovich (1908-   ), Russia
   R.1   S.c,5,7-10,18,20,24
RAKSIN, David (1912-   ), USA
   R.19   S.9,10,13
RALEIGH, Stewart W. (1940-   ), USA
   R.80   S.10,13
RALF, Einar Christian (1888-1971), Sweden
   R.25   S.5x
RALF-DRIFFILL, W. [see DRIFFILL, W. Ralph]
RAMANS, Gedert (1927-   ), USSR
               S.18
RAMEAU, Jean-Philippe (1683-1764), Fr
   R.1   S.c,1-11,18,21-24,28,32,42
RAMEY, Phillip (1939-   ), USA
   R.19   S.13
RAMIN, Günter (1898-1956), Ger
   R.1

RAMIN, Sid (1924-   ), USA
    R.23
RAMIREZ, Ariel (1921-   ), Arg
    R.30   S.39
RAMOS, Juan Jose (20th Cent)
                S.24a
RAMOS, Miguel

RAMOS, Silvano R.
                S.10
RAMOVŠ, Primož (1921-   ), Yug
    R.1   S.18,24a
RAMRATH, Konrad (1880-   ), Ger
    R.10s   S.e
RAMSEY, Basil (1929-   ), Eng
    R.64
RAMSEY, Gordon (1926-   ), USA
                S.13,24a
RAMSEY, Robert (fl 1612-44), Eng
    R.1   S.c
RAMSÖE, Wilhelm (1837-1895), Den
    R.3   S.c,40

RAN, Shulamit (1949-   ), Isr
    R.1   S.10,30,52
RANDEL, Andreas (1806-1864), Sweden
    R.111   S.56
RANDALL, James (1929-   ), USA
    R.1   S.10,13,24
RANDALL, William (d ?1604), Eng
    R.1   S.c,10,16
RANDALU, Ivalo (1936-   )
                S.18
RANDEGGER, Alberto (1832-1911), It
    R.30a   S.e
RANDEGGER, Alberto Iginio (1880-1918), It
    R.8   S.24
RANDEL, Andreas (1806-1864), Sweden
    R.1   S.56
RANGSTRÖM, Ture (1884-1947), Sweden
    R.1   S.4-10,18,24a,40,43
RANISH, John Frederick (1692/93-1777), Eng
    R.1   S.c
RÁNKI, György (1907-   ), Hun
    R.1   S.c,9,10,18
RANSE, Marc de (1881-1951), Fr
    R.14   S.c
RANTA, Sulho (1901-1960), Fin
    R.14   S.c
RANZATO, Virgilio (1883-1937), Fr
    R.8   S.24

RAPÉE, Ernö (1891-1945), Hun
   R.8   S.24
RAPF, Kurt (1922-   ), Aus
   R.4   S.c,24a
RAPH, Alan (1933-   ), USA
   R.23
RAPHAEL, Günter (1903-1960), Ger
   R.1   S.c,24a
RAPHLING, Sam (1910-   ), USA
   R.19   S.7,9,10,13
RAPPAPORT, Moshe (1903-   ), Isr
   R.14   S.10
RAQUET, Charles [see RACQUET, Charles]
RARIG, John (1912-   ), USA
           S.13
RASBACH, Oscar (1888-1975), USA
   R.19   S.5x,10,13,33
RASCH, Hugo (1873-   ), Ger
   R.3   S.4
RASCH, Kurt (1902-   ), Ger
   R.14   S.7
RASCHER, Sigurd (1907-   ), USA
   R.1   S.10,22
RASELIUS, Andrease (c1563-1602), Ger
   R.1   S.c,10,16
RASI, Francesco (1574->1620), It
   R.1   S.c,2-4,5x,10
RASKIN - Laura (excerpt)
           S.5x

RASMUSSEN, Karl Aage (1947-   ), Den
   R.30   S.40
RASMUSSEN, Peter (1838-1913), Den
   R.111   S.40
RASSE, François (1873-1955), Bel
   R.1   S.8,9,24,36
RATCLIFFE, Philip (20th Cent), Eng
           S.c
RATHAUS, Karol (1895-1954), USA
   R.1   S.8,10,13,20,24
RATHBONE, Christopher Bruce (1947-   ), Eng
   R.80   S.c
RATHBURN, Eldon Davis (1916-   ), Can
   R.14
RATHGEBER, Johann Valentin (1682-1750), Ger
   R.1   S.c,5x,8,10,53
RATNER, Leonard (1916-   ), USA
   R.1   S.7-9,13
RATTENBACH, Augusto Benjamín (1927-   ), Arg
   R.26   S.46

RAUBUCH, Erhard (1909-   )
        S.c
RAUCH, Andreas (1592-1656), Aus
  R.1   S.c
RAUCH, Hans
        S.c
RAUDONIKIS, Algimantas (1934-   ),
        S.18
RAUKHVERGER, Mikhail Rafailovich (1901-   ), USSR
  R.14   S.18
RAUPP, Jan (1928-   ), Cz
  R.4   S.24a
RAUSCHER, Andreas (d.1702), Ger
  R.5   S.c
RAUTAVAARA, Einojuhani (1928-   ), Fin
  R.1   S.c,10,24a,40
RAUTIO, Erkki (1931-   ), Fin
  R.4   S.c
RAUTIO, Matti (1922-   ), Fin
  R.1   S.40
RAUTIO, Roine (1934-1961)
        S.18,24
RAVANELLO, Oreste (1871-1938), It
  R.8   S.c
RAVEL, Maurice (1875-1937), Fr
  R.1   S.c,1-11,18-22,24-28,32,33,42
RAVENHALL, Mrs. - pseud [see KING, Robert A.]
RAVENSCROFT, Thomas (c1582-c1635), Eng
  R.1   S.c,5x,8,10,11,14-16
RAVICH, Matvei Borisovich (1923-   )
        S.18
RAVINA, Jean Henri (1818-1906), Fr
  R.3
RAVINI, E. - Serenade (Sans les étoiles) (vi & p)
        S.24
RAWSTHORNE, Alan (1905-1971), Eng

  R.1   S.3-5,7-10,18-20,24,32
RAWSTHORNE, Noel (1929-   ), Eng
  R.1   S.c
RAXACH, Enrique (1932-   ), Neth
  R.1   S.c,10
RAY, Lillian - pseud [ie John NEAT] (?-1949)
        S.24,43
RAYKI, György (1921-   ), Hun
  R.4   S.10
RAYMOND, Fred (1900-1954), Ger
  R.1   S.c,5x
RAYMOND, Lewis (1908-1965), USA
  R.19   S.10,13

RAYNAL, L. - La valse du Cliquot
        S.e
RAYNER, A. - The enchanted garden; A woolly tale
        S.54(324,66)
RAZECK, Antonin (1852-1929)
        S.c
RAZORENOV, Sergei Alexeyevich (1909-   ), USSR
  R.47   S.18
RAZZA, de - Come Il Fuoco
        S.54(320)
RAZZI, Giovanni (1531-1611), It
  R.1   S.c
REA, John (1944-   ), Can
  R.31
READ, Daniel (1757-1836), USA
  R.1   S.10,47
READ, Gardner (1913-   ), USA
  R.1   S.8,10,12,13
READING, John (c1645-1692), Eng
  R.1   S.24
REAH, Ronald Eng
        S.c
REALI, Giovanni (fl 1727), It
  R.5
REBEL, Jean-Féry (1666-1747), Fr
  R.1   S.c,10,24
REBEL, François (1701-1775), Fr
  R.1
REBER, Henri (1807-1880), Fr
  R.1
REBIKOV, Vladimir Ivanovich (1866-1920), Russia
  R.1   S.2,3,5x,18
REBOUD, Rene-Marie
        S.10
REBULL, Teresa (20th Cent), Sp
        S.52
RECHBERGER, Hermann (1947-   ), Fin
  R.30   S.40(89)
RECHKUNOV, M. - The sea (v)
        S.18
RECK, David (1935-   ), USA
  R.19   S.13
RECKLING, August (1843-1922), Ger
  R.95   S.54(364)
RECLI, Giulia (1890-   ), It
  R.14
REDA, Siegfried (1916-1968), Ger
  R.1   S.c,10
REDCLIFFE, Frederick J. [see CARTER, Stanley - pseud]

REDEL, Martin Christoph (1947-   ), Ger
   R.1   S.c
REDFORD, John (d.1547), Eng
   R.1   S.c,7,8,10,14,16,53
REDOLFI, Michel (1951-   )
           S.c
REED - Band plays
           S.54(314)
REED, Alfred (1921-   ), USA
   R.19   S.c,13,21
REED, Herbert Owen (1910-   ), USA
   R.19   S.8,10,13
REESEN, Emil (1887-1964), Den
   R.14   S.4,5x,8,10,33
REESEN, N. J. - F. D. F. March
           S.5x
REEVE, William (1757-1815), Eng
   R.1   S.e
REEVES, David Wallace (1838-1900), USA
   R.53   S.10,54(319,32,40,54)
REFICE, Licinio (1883-1954), It
   R.1   S.c,3-5,8-10,18
REGAMEY, Constantin (1907-1982), Swiss
   R.1   S.8,10,24
REGER, Max (1873-1916), Ger
   R.1   S.c,1-11,18-21,23,24,26,27
REGGIO, Pietro Paulo Melli de
           S.32
REGIS, Johannes (c1430-c1485), Neth
   R.1   S.c,16
REGNART, François (fl 1579), Fr
   R.1   S.7,8,14,16
REGNART, Jacob (c1540-1599), S. Neth
   R.1   S.c,10,15,16
*** REGNART, Jacob François (1530-1600) (see note)
REGNAULT, Joseph (fl 1679-84), S. Neth
   R.5
REGNAULT, Pierre [see SANDRIN]
REGNER, Hermann (1928-   ), Ger [?]
   R.95   S.c
REGNEY, Noel USA
           S.10,13
REGO, I de C - White Clouds
           S.5x
REGTEREN-ALTENA, Lucas van Neth

REHFELD, Fabian (1842-1920), Ger
   R.3   S.24
REHM, Gerhard (1926-   )
           S.c

REHS, Evelyn
              S.24a
REIBEL, Guy (1936-   ), Fr
   R.4   S.c
REICH, Steve (1936-   ), USA
   R.1   S.c,9,10,13,24
REICHA [Rejcha], Antoine (1770-1836), Cz
   R.1   S.c,5-10,20
REICHA, Joseph (1752-1795), Cz
   R.1   S.c,10,24a
REICHARDT, Alexander (1825-1885), Fr
   R.3   S.e
REICHARDT, Johann Friedrich (1752-1814), Ger
   R.1   S.c,5x,7,10,24
REICHARDT, Louise (1779-1826), Ger
   R.1   S.30,52
REICHE, Eugen
              S.c
REICHE, Gottfried (1667-1734), Ger
   R.1   S.c,8,10
REICHEL, Bernard (1901-   ), Swiss
   R.1   S.c,7,10
REICHERT, James (1932-   ), USA
   R.19   S.13
REIDARSON, Per (1879-1954), Nor
   R.14   S.43
REIF, Paul (1910-1978), USA
   R.19   S.9,10,13,20,27
REILICH, Gabriel (1630/39-1677), Transylvania
   R.1
REIMAN, Villem Madisovich (1906-   ), USSR
   R.14   S.18
REIMANN, Aribert (1936-   ), Ger
   R.1   S.c
REIMANN, Heinrich (1850-1906), Ger
   R.1
REIN, Walter (1893-1955), Ger
   R.1   S.c
REINAGLE, Alexander (1756-1809), USA
   R.1   S.7,9,10,47
REINCKEN, Johann Adam (1623-1722), Ger
   R.1   S.c,5x,6,10,53
REINECKE, Carl (1824-1910), Ger
   R.1   S.c,9,10
REINER, Jacob (<1560-1606), Ger
   R.1   S.c,10
REINER, Karel (1910-1979), Cz
   R.1   S.10,20,24a,31
REINGOLD, Janis (1882-1938)
              S.18

REINHARDT, Heinrich (1865-1922), Aus
R.3   S.e
REINHOLD, Hugo (1854-1935), Aus
R.8   S.10
REINHOLD, Otto (1899-1965), Ger
R.1   S.23
REINKEN, Johann Adam [see REINCKEN, Johann Adam]
REINMAR von BRENNENBERG (d <1276), Ger
R.1   S.c,16
REINMAR von HAGENAU (fl 1185-1205)
R.1
REINTHALER, Karl Martin (1822-1896), Ger
R.1   S.c
REIS - Wo du hinghest = RIES, Franz
REIS, Gaspar dos [see GASPAR DOS REIS]
REIS, Dilermando (1916-   ), Brazil
R.67   S.c
REISER, Violet (1905 or 1915-   ), USA
R.7   S.52
REISSIGER, Carl Gottlieb (1798-1859), Ger
R.1   S.c,4,24a,54(343,67)
REISSIGER, Friedrich August (1809-1883), Ger
R.30   S.e
REITER, Albert (1905-   ), Aus
R.14   S.24a
REIZENSTEIN, Franz (1911-1968), Ger
R.1   S.c,5,9,24
REJCHA, Antoine/Joseph [see REICHA, Antoine/Joseph]
REKAI, Miklos (1906-1961), Hun
R.15
REKASHYUS, Antanas (1928-   )
             S.18
REMACHA, Fernando (1898-   ), Sp
R.1   S.10
REMENKOV, Stefan Nikolov (1923-   ), Bul
R.14   S.24a
REMONDI, Roberto (1851-1928), It
R.3   S.c
RENARD - L'enfant dormira bientôt
             S.5x
RENARD, Felix
             S.24
RENAUD, Albert (1855-   ), Fr
R.3   S.c
RENAUD, Emiliano (1875-1932), Can
R.31
RENAULD (17th Cent) - Aimons, buvons nuit et jour
R.5   S.4,5x
RENDINE, Furio
             S.10

RENES, N. (16th Cent), Fr
    R.5   S.3,4,5x,8,10,14,15
RENIÉ, Henriette (1875-1956), Fr
    R.14   S.1-4,10,30,52
RENNER, Joseph Jr (1868-1934), Ger
    R.2   S.10
RENNES, Catharina van (1858-1940), Neth
    R.8   S.e
RENÖ, Seress
                S.24
RENOSTO, Paolo (1935-   ), It
    R.1   S.39
RENOTTE, Hubert (1704-1745), S. Neth
    R.1
RENWICK, Wilke Richard (1921-   ), USA
    R.23   S.10,13
REPNIKOV, Albin (1932-   )
                S.18
RESINARIUS, Balthasar (c1485-1544), Ger
    R.1   S.c,2,8,10,16
RESKE - Amor segrets (vi & p)
                S.24
RESPIGHI, Elsa (nee Olivier Sangiacomo) (1894-   ), It
    R.7   S.52
RESPIGHI, Ottorini (1879-1936), It
    R.1   S.c,1-11,18,24
RESTA, Natale (fl 1748), It
    R.1   S.5x
RETTIG - Desir
                S.e
REUBKE, Julius (1834-1858), Ger
    R.1   S.c,4,5x,7-10
REUBKE, Otto (1842-1913), Ger
    R.1   S.c
REUCHSEL, Eugène (1900-   ), Fr
    R.8   S.c
REUENTAL, Neidhart von [see NEIDHART von REUENTAL]
REUSNER, Esaias (d.1660-80), Ger
    R.1   S.c,4,5,7,10,32
REUSSNER, Andreas (17th Cent)

REUTER, Florizel von (1890-   ), USA
    R.14   S.24
REUTER, Fritz (1896-1963), Ger
    R.1   S.24
REUTTER, Hermann. (1900-   ), Ger
    R.14   S.c,22
REUTTER, Johann Adam Joseph Karl Georg (1708-1772), Aus
    R.1   S.c,10,53

REVELI, I. - Diavoli Rossi
        S.54(323)
REVUELTAS, Silvestre (1899-1940), Mex
  R.1   S.c,5x,8-10,24,39
REVUTSKY, Levko Mykolayevich (1889-1977), Ukraine
  R.1   S.8,18,24
REY, Louis Charles Joseph (1738-1811), Fr
  R.1   S.21
REYER, Ernest (1823-1909), Fr
  R.1   S.c,2-5,7,8,11
REYNOLDS, Jeffrey (1943-   ), USA
        S.10,13
REYNOLDS, Roger (1934-   ), USA
  R.1   S.9,10,13
REYNOLDS, Verne (1926-   ), USA
  R.19   S.10,13
REYS, Jakub [Jacob le Polonaise] (c1540-c1605), Pol
  R.1   S.7,10,16,53
REZ - Croix de Lorraine
        S.54(321)
ŘEZÁČ Ivan (1924-1977), Cz
  R.1   S.c,31
REZNIČEK, Emil Nikolaus von (1860-1945), Aus
  R.1   S.c,2-8,10,11,24a
REZNIKOV, Nikolai Panteleimonovich
        S.10
RHAU, Georg (1488-1548), Ger
  R.1   S.8,10,14,16
RHEINBERGER, Joseph (1839-1901), Ger
  R.1   S.c,1-4,7,9,10,24a
RHENÉ-BATON, pseud [ie René BATON] (1879-1940), Fr
  R.8   S.c
RHODE, Erich (1870-1950), Ger
  R.2   S.c
RHODE, Max [pseud: G. ROYER], (1884-1945), Ger
  R.95
RHODES, Helen [see HARDELOT, Guy d´ - pseud]
RHODES, Phillip (1940-   ), USA
  R.14   S.9,10,13,24,27,28
RHOMER - More in sorrow than anger
        S.e
RHUDYAR, Dane [S.8] = RUDHYAR, Dane
RHYNE, H. E. - pseud [see SAUVEPLANE, Henri Emile]
RHYS-WILLIAMS, Elspeth (1938-   )
        S.8,30
RIADIS, Emilios (?1886-1935), Greece
  R.1   S.8
RIBÁRI, Antal (1924-   ), Hun
  R.1   S.c,9,24a
RIBAYAZ Lucas-Ruiz de [see RUIZ de RIBAYEZ, Lucas]

RIBBLE, M. H.   USA - Bennet´s triumphal
                S.13
RIBEIRO, Lambert
                S.24a
RIBERA, Antonio de (16th Cent), Sp
    R.1   S.c,8,10,14,16,39
RICARDO do NASCIMIENTO, Alfredo
                S.39
RICCARDI - Amor mio
                S.44
RICCI, Frederico (1809-1877), It
    R.1   S.c,10,28
RICCI, Luigi (1805-1859), It
    R.1   S.c,10
RICCIO, Giovanni Battista (fl 1609-21) It
    R.1   S.c
RICCIOTTI, Carlo (c1681-1756), It
    R.1   S.c,5x,10
RICCIUS, August Ferdinand (1819-1886), Ger [?]
    R.3   S.5x
RICE, Gitz Ingraham (1891-1947), Can
    R.31   S.24
RICH, Gladys (1892-   ), USA
    R.19   S.10,13,30
RICH, Louis
                S.24
RICHAFORT, Jean (c1480-c1547), Flem
    R.1   S.c,10,16
RICHARD I, Coeur de Lion (1157-1199), Eng
    R.1   S.c,2-4,5x,8,10,11,14,16
RICHARD, Balthazar (c1600->1660), S. Neth
    R.1   S.c
RICHARD, Edmund (1926-   ), USA
                S.13
RICHARD, Etienne (c1621-1669), Fr
    R.1   S.c,53
RICHARDS - Namur
                S.54(344)
RICHARDS, David - Cymru fach
                S.5x[Richards, E.]
RICHARDS, Henry Brinley (1819-1885), Wales
    R.1   S.c,24,54(329)
RICHARDS, Stephen (1935-   ), USA
    R.19   S.13
RICHARDSON, Alan (1904-1978), Scot
    R.1   S.10,19,21,24
RICHARDSON, Clive (1909-   ), Eng
    R.80   S.c,4,5x
RICHARDSON, Ferdinand (c1558-1618), Eng
    R.1   S.c,16

RICHARDSON, Harriette Slack   USA
              S.12,13
RICHARDSON, T. - Mary (vi & p)
              S.24
RICHART de SEMILLI (12-13th Cent), Fr
   R.1   S.16
RICHARTZ, Willy (1900-1972), Ger
   R.14   S.c,24
RICHÉE, Le Sage de [see LE SAGE de RICHÉE, Philipp Franz]
RICHEPIN, Tiarko Francois (1884-   ), Fr
   R.14   S.24
RICHMOND, Dolly [pseud]
              S.10
RICHMOND, Legh (1772-1827), Eng
   R.57   S.8
RICHTER, Ernst Friedrich (1808-1879), Ger
   R.1   S.c
RICHTER, Ferdinand Tobias (1651-1711), Aus
   R.1   S.5,8,10,53
RICHTER, Franz Xaver (1709-1789), Ger
   R.1   S.3-5,8-11,24
RICHTER, Johann Christian (1689-1744), Ger
   R.5   S.c
RICHTER, Marga (1926-   ), USA
   R.19   S.10,13,23,30,52
RICKETTS, Frederick Joseph

   [see ALFORD, Kenneth J. - pseud]
RICO, J. - Primo Bachio (vi & p)
              S.24
RIDER, Ambros (1771-1855)

RIDIL, Christian
              S.c
ŘIDKÝ, Jaroslav (1897-1956), Cz
   R.1   S.c,5,24,31
RIDOUT, Alan (1934-   ), Eng
   R.1   S.c
RIDOUT, Godfrey (1918-1984), Can
   R.1
RIEDE, Erich (1903-   ), Ger
   R.14   S.c
RIEDEL, Carl (1827-1888), Ger
   R.1   S.c
RIEDEL, Georg (1934-   ), Sweden
   R.30   S.40
RIEDER, Ambrosius (1771-1855), Aus
   R.3   S.c
RIEDING, O. - Concerto in G (allegro moderato)
              S.24a

RIEDL, Johann Bartholomäus (1720-1771), Ger
   R.1   S.c
RIEDL, Josef Anton (1927-   ), Ger
   R.1   S.c
RIEDLBAUCH, Václav (1947-   ), Cz
   R.14   S.c
RIEGER, Gottfried (1764-1855), Moravia
   R.1   S.c
RIEGGER, Wallingford (1885-1961), USA
   R.1   S.c,2-5,7-13,24
RIEGO, Teresa del [see DEL RIEGO, Teresa]
RIEHM, Ranier (1941-   ), Ger
   R.14   S.10
RIENER, Mark

RIEPE, Russell (1945-   ), USA
   R.19   S.13
RIERA, Rodrigo (1923-   )
             S.10,32
RIES, Ferdinand (1784-1838), Ger
   R.1   S.c,5x,10,18,20,24a
RIES, Franz (1846-1932), Ger
   R.1   S.c,5x,10,24
RIETI, Vittorio (1898-   ), It
   R.1   S.c,5,6,8-11,13,18,25,24a,27
RIETZ, Julius (1812-1877), Ger
   R.1   S.c,10
RIGAI, Amiram (1933-   ), Isr
             S.10
RIGHINI, Vincenzo (1756-1812), It
   R.1   S.c
RIGLER, Franz Paul (1747/48-1796), Aus
   R.1   S.c

RIISAGER, Knudage (1897-1974), Den
   R.1   S.3-5,7-10,18,24,33,35,40,57
RIK, J. - Erinnerung (vi & p)
             S.24a
RIKER, Franklin (1876-   ), USA
   R.43   S.e
RILEY, Dennis (1943-   ), USA
   R.1   S.10,13
RILEY, Terry (1935-   ), USA
   R.1   S.c,9,13
RILLÉ, Laurent François Anatole de [pseud: MÉROFF]
   (1828-1915), Fr   R.3   S.e
RIMINI, Vincenzo da [see VINCENZO da RIMINI]
RIMMER, Drake Eng
   R.85,96   S.55
RIMMER, John (1939-   ), New Zealand

RIMMER, William (1862-1936), Eng
   R.85   S.54(315,31,43,51),55
RIMONTE, Pedro (c1570->1618), Sp
   R.1   S.c,14,17
RIMSKY-KORSAKOV, Nikolay (1844-1908), Russia
   R.1   S.c,1-11,18-21,24,28,42,43,54(321,22)
RINALDO di CAPUA (c1705-c1780), It
   R.1   S.c,9,26(29)
RINCK, Johann Christian Heinrich (1770-1846), Ger
   R.1   S.c,10
RING, Oluf (1884-1946), Den
   R.30   S.4,5x,33,35
RING-HAGER [see HAGER, Ring]
RINGSDORF - L´oeuvre devine
              S.e
RIOS, Felipe de los (d.1801)

RIOTTE, Philipp Jakob (1766-1856), Ger
   R.1   S.c
RIPA, Alberto da (c1500-1551), It
   R.1   S.c,10,14
RIPPERT, Jean-Jacques (fl 1696-1725), Fr
   [supposed composer] R.1   S.c
RIQUIER, Guiraut (c1230-c1300), Fr
   R.1   S.c,4,5x,8,10,14,16
RISCHE, Quirin (1903-   ), Ger
   R.3   S.c
RISI, de - Intermezzo notturno

RISSET, Jean Claude (1938-   ), Fr
   R.1   S.c,10
RISSI - II carretiere del Vomero (v)
              S.10
RISSLAND, Rudolf (1868-1960)

RITCHIE, John (1920-   )
              S.20
RITHIELE - Unsere Marine
              S.54(363)
RITTER - Sun of my soul

              S.e
RITTER, August (c1760-c1820)
              S.c
RITTER, August Gottfried (1811-1885), Ger
   R.2   S.c,10
RITTER, Christian (1645/50-<1717), Ger
   R.1   S.c,5x,10,53,56
RIVAFRECHA, Martín de (d.1528), Sp
   R.1   S.c,10,14-17

RIVERA, Antonio de (fl 1514)
            S.17
RIVIER, Jean (1896-   ), Fr
    R.1   S.c,4-6,8-10,18,19,22
RIVILIS, Pavel Borisovich (1936-   ),
            S.18,24
RIVULO, Francziscus de (fl 1560-66), Neth
    R.1   S.c
RIZOL, Mykola Ivanovych (1919-   ), USSR
    R.47
RIZZI, O. Bernardino (1891-1968), It
    R.14   S.10
RIZZO, Joe (1917-   ), USA
    R.23   S.10
ROBAUDI, Vincenzo (1819-1882), It
    R.3   S.e,24a
ROBB, John Donald (1892-   ), USA
    R.1   S.9,10,13,24a
ROBERDAY, François (1624-1680), Fr
    R.1   S.c,9,10,53
ROBERT, Camille (fl 1918), Fr - Quand Madelon
    R.200
ROBERT, Lucie (1936-   ), Fr
    R.7   S.22,52
ROBERT, Pierre (c1618-1699), Fr
    R.1   S.c
ROBERTI, Robert - pseud [see VOLLSTEDT, Robert]
ROBERTON, Sir Hugh (1874-1952), Scot
    R.4   S.4
ROBERTS - Topsy turvy
            S.e
ROBERTS, Arthur - electronic music
ROBERTS, Charles Luckeyth (?1887-1968), USA
    R.1   S.10,24a
ROBERTS, Gertrud Hermine Kuenzel (1906-   ), USA
    R.7   S.30,52
ROBERTS, Jeremy Dale
            S.24
ROBERTS, Lee S. (1884-1949), USA
    R.23   S.10,24
ROBERTS, Megan [see GHIRARDO, Megan Roberts]
ROBERTS, Myron (1912-   ), USA
    R.19   S.10,12,13
ROBERTS, Osborne (1879-c1942), Wales
    R.37   S.5x
ROBERTSON - Violin d´amour (vi & p)
            S.24

ROBERTSON - Jean upon the uplands
            S.e

ROBERTSON, Donna Lou Nagey (1935-   ), USA
   R.7   S.30
ROBERTSON, Leroy (1896-1971), USA
   R.19   S.c,10,13
ROBEY - The Mormon's Song
          S.e
ROBIN, Leo (1900-   ), USA
   R.23   S.24
ROBINET de la MAGDALAINE [Rubinus] (1415-1478), Fr
   R.1   S.c,8,14
ROBINSON, Avery (1878-1965), USA
   R.23   S.10,13
ROBINSON, Christopher (1936-   ), Eng
          S.c
ROBINSON, Earl (1910-   )., USA
   R.19   S.4,10,11,13
ROBINSON, Edward (1905-1970), USA
   R.19   S.11,13
ROBINSON, J. Russel (1892-1963), USA
   R.23   S.10
ROBINSON, John (c1812-1844), Ire
   R.1   S.c
ROBINSON, Joseph (1816-1898), Ire
   R.1   S.10,19
ROBINSON, Richard (1923-   ), USA
   R.19   S.13
ROBINSON, Thomas (fl 1589-1609), Eng
   R.1   S.c,10,16,24,32
ROBISON (fl 1810), USA - Fiducia
          S.10,47
ROBLEDO, Julian
          S.24
ROBLEDO, Melchor (c1520-<1587), Sp
   R.1   S.c,10,14,16
ROBLES, José García (?-1910), Sp
   R.10   S.e
ROBLES, Marisa (1937-   ), Sp,
   R.1   S.c,39,52
ROBSON, Jean-Jacques (1723-1785), S. Neth
   R.1   S.c,53
ROBYN, Alfred George (1860-1935), USA
   R.23   S.e
ROCCA, Lodovic (1895-   ), It
   R.1   S.3-5,11
ROCHA, Francisco Gomes da (d.1808), Brazil
   R.1
ROCHBERG, George (1918-   ), USA
   R.1   S.c,9,10,13,24,32
ROCHE, Gustav
          S.c,24

ROCHEROLLE, Eugénie Katherine (née Ricau) (1936-   )
    USA   R.7   S.52
RÖCKEL, Joseph Leopold (1838-1923), Ger
    R.1   S.e
ROCKSTRO, William Smith (1823-1895), Eng
    R.3
RODAMILANS, Angel

RODBY, John Leonard (1944-   ), USA
    R.19   S.9,13,22,24a
RODE, Alfredo (1905-   )
    S.24
RODE, Pierre (1774-1830), Fr
    R.1   S.c,10,24
RODEN, Robert - Difference of Opinions

RODGERS, J. H. [= ROGERS, James Hotchkiss]
RODGERS, Mary (1931-   ), USA
    R.19   S.9
RODGERS, Richard (1902-1979), USA
    R.1   S.c,4,9,10,24a,54(330)
RODNEY, Paul
    R.44   S.e
RODOLPHE de FENIS [see RUDOLF von FENIS-NEUENBERG]
RODOREDA, J. Virolai

RODRIGO, Joaquín (1901-   ), Sp
    R.1   S.c,5x,7-10,18,24,32,39
RODRIGUE, Nicole (1943-   ), Can
    R.7   S.52
RODRIGUES COELHO, Manuel (c1555-c1635), Port
    R.1   S.c,10,53
RODRIGUEZ, Felipe (1759-1814), Sp
    R.8   S.c,5x,8,10,39
RODRIGUEZ, G.H. Matos [see MATOS RODRIGUEZ, G. H.]
RODRIGUEZ, Jorge (17-18th Cent), Sp
    S.c,10
RODRIGUEZ, Juan (fl 1460-1503), Sp
    R.5   S.39
RODRIGUEZ, Ricardo (1879-1951), Arg
    R.26   S.46
RODRIGUEZ, Robert Xavier (1946-   ), USA
    R.19   S.10,13,22,24a
RODRIGUEZ, Vincente (d.1760), Sp
    R.1   S.8,10
RODWELL, George Herbert Bonaparte (1800-1852), Eng
    R.25   S.e
ROE, Eileen Betty (1930-   ), Eng
    R.7   S.30,52

ROECK, Gustave Adolphe de (1892-1966), Bel
   R.25   S.54(315)
ROECKEL, Joseph Leopold [see ROCKEL, Joseph Leopold]
ROEFS, Benedict E. (19th Cent), USA

ROELSTRAETE, Herman (1925-   ), Bel
   R.1
ROEMHELD, Heinz (1901-   ), USA
   R.23   S.10
ROESELING, Kaspar (1894-1960), Ger
   R.4
ROESER, Valentin (c1735-1782), Ger
   R.1   S.c
ROESGEN-CHAMPION, Marguerite Sara [pseud: Jean DELYSSE]
   (1894-1976), Swiss R.7   S.4-6,8,24,30,52
ROESSEL - Wo du hingehst
              S.1x
ROESSINGER - Nuvole blanche
              S.e
ROGATIS, Pascual de [see DE ROGATIS, Pascual]
ROGALSKI, Theodor (1901-1954), Rum
   R.1   S.10
ROGER, Victor (1853-1903), Fr
   R.1   S.e
ROGER-DUCASSE, Jean (1873-1954), Fr
   R.1   S.c,2,10
ROGER-HENRICHSEN, Borge (1915-   ), Den
   R.30   S.57
ROGERS, Alex
              S.10
ROGERS, Benjamin (1614-1698), Eng
   R.1   S.c,10
ROGERS, Bernard (1893-1968), USA
   R.1   S.c,3,4,8,10,11,13
ROGERS, James Hotchkiss (1857-1940), USA
   R.23   S.5x,10,24
ROGERS, Kenneth - pseud [see DE VITO, Albert Kenneth]
ROGERS, Melville Reuben ?USA
              S.13
ROGERS, Walter B. (1865-1939)

ROGERS, William Keith (1921-   ), Can
   R.4
ROGERT, Ditlev Ludwig (1742-1813), Den
   R.30a   S.5x,33
ROGET, Clair Nicolas (fl 1739)
              S.c
ROGET, Henriette Puig (1910-   ), Fr
   R.14   S.10,52

ROGG, Lionel (1936-   ), Swiss
    R.14
ROGIER, Philippe (c1561-1596), Flem
    R.1   S.10
ROGISTER, Jean (1879-1964), Bel
    R.1   S.24,36
ROGNIONO (16-17th Cent) - Anchor che col partire
            S.14
ROGNONI TAEGGIO, Francesco (d <1626), It
    R.1   S.c,16

ROGNONI TAEGGIO, Giovanni Domenico (d <1626), It
    R.1   S.c,16
ROGNONI, Riccardo (d.1619/20), It
    R.1   S.c
ROGOZINNIKOV, V. Russia

ROGUSKI, Gustaw (1839-1921), Pol
    R.3
ROHACZEWSKI, Andrej (fl c1620), Pol
    R.1   S.c,16,53
ROHE, Robert Kenneth (1916-   ), USA
    R.19   S.10,13
ROHLAND, Peter
            S.c
ROHWER, Jens (1914-   ), Ger
    R.1   S.c
ROIG, Gonzalo (1890-1970), Cuba
    R.4   S.9,10
ROIKJER, Kjell (1901-   ), Den
    R.14   S.40
ROJO, Jesus Villa
            S.10
ROLAND, M. - Parademarsch der Langen Kerls
            S.54(348)
ROLAND, Marc (1894-   ), Ger
    R.14   S.c,10
ROLAND-MANUEL (1891-1966), Fr
    R.1   S.8,10,18
ROLDÁN, Amadeo (1900-1939), Cuba
    R.1   S.8,10,18,32,39
ROLF, Irving
            S.24
ROLIN de VAUX
            S.c
ROLLA, Alessandro (1757-1841), It
    R.1   S.5,9-11,19,23,24a
ROLLA, Antonio (1798-1837), It
    R.10   S.24a
ROLLAND - Lamento (trumpet)
            S.10

RÖLLIG, Karl Leopold (d.1804), Aus
    R.1   S.10
ROLLIN, Robert (1947-   ), USA
    R.19   S.10,13
ROLLINAT, Maurice (1853-1903)
    R.200   S.5x
ROLÓN, José (1883-1945), Mex
    R.1   S.10,24
ROLT, Bernard (1874-   ) - Our waltz [?]
    R.200   S.10
ROMA, Caro (1866-   ), USA
    R.43   S.e
ROMAN, Johan Helmich (1694-1758), Sweden
    R.1   S.c,4,5,7,9,10,24,33,56
ROMAN, Juan (15th Cent), Sp
    R.9   S.c,17
ROMANI (17th Cent) [see LORENZINI]

ROMANI, Romano (1881-1934), It
    R.10,10s   S.e
ROMANINI, Antonio (17th Cent)
    R.5   S.c,53
ROMANIO, Giuseppe (17th Cent)
              S.c
ROMANO, Enrico (1877-   ), It
    R.10   S.e
ROMANOWSKI, Otto Fin
              S.40(89)
ROMANUS, Laurenzinus [see LORENZINI]
ROMBERG, Bernhard Heinrich (1767-1841), Ger
    R.1   S.c,10
ROMBERG, Sigmund (1887-1951), Hun
    R.1   S.2-4,9-11,24,43,54(328)
ROME, Harold (1908-   ), USA
    R.1   S.9
ROMERO, Celedonio (1917-   ), Sp
    R.80   S.c,10,39
ROMERO, Mateo (1575/76-1647), Neth
    R.1   S.c,10,14,16,17,39
ROMERO, Ricardo
              S.32
ROMERO, Vicente
              S.10
ROMILLI - Rosa; Marietta
              S.e
ROMMEL, Kurt (1926-   ), Ger
    R.4   S.c
ROMO, Jesus

RONALD, Landon (1873-1938), Eng
    R.1   S.2-4,5x,10,24

RONAN, John Edward (1894-1962), Can
     R.31
RONCAL, S. - February third
                 S.54(326)
RONCALLI, Conte Ludovico de (17th Cent), It
     R.1   S.c,4,5x,8-10,32
RONGÉ, Florimond [see HERVÉ - pseud]
RONSHEIM, John (1927-   ), USA
     R.19   S.10,13,24
RONTANI, Raffaello (d.1622), It
     R.1   S.c,8,10
RÖNTGEN, Julius (1855-1932), Ger
     R.1   S.c,8,10,41
ROONEY - Only for you
                 S.e
ROOS, Robert de (1907-1976), Neth
     R.1   S.10
ROOSEVELT, Willard (1918-   ), USA
                 S.13
ROOT, Frederick Woodman (1846-1916), USA
     R.3
ROOT, George Frederick [pseud: G. F. Wurzel] (1820-1895)
     USA R.1   S.10,47
ROOTHAM, Cyril (1875-1938), Eng

     R.1   S.c
ROPARTZ, Joseph Guy (1864-1955), Fr
     R.1   S.1,2,8-10,18,24
ROPE, Arturi (1903-   ), Fin [?]
     R.14   S.5x
ROPEK, Jiří (1922-   ), Cz
     R.1   S.10
ROPP, J. B. - Canto per te (vi & p)
                 S.24
ROQUÉ ALSINA, Carlos (1941-   ), Arg
     R.4   S.39
ROQUELLAY (16th Cent)
     R.5   S.c
ROQUES, J.

RORE, Cipriano de (1515/16-1565), Flem
     R.1   S.c,5x,8,10,11,14,16
ROREM, Ned (1923-   ), USA
     R.1   S.8-10,13,19,20,24a,25-28
RORICH, Karl (1869-1941), Ger
     R.4   S.c
ROSA, Salvatore (1615-1673), It
     R.1   S.5x,7,8,10,28
ROSAS, Juventino (1868-1894), Mex
     R.1   S.c,10,54(348)

ROSE, Barry (1934-   ), Eng
    R.1   S.c
ROSE, Bernard (1916-   ), Eng
    R.1   S.c,10
ROSE, Cyrille (1830-1902/03), Fr
    R.105   S.19
ROSE, David (1919-   ), USA
    R.23   S.10
ROSE, Fred (1897-1954), USA
    R.23   S.24
ROSE, Gordon
                 S.10
ROSE, Gregory
                 S.10
ROSE, Peter de [see DE ROSE, Peter]
ROSEINGRAVE, Thomas (1688-1766), Eng
    R.1   S.c,8-10,53
ROSELL, Lars-Erik (1944-   ), Sweden
    R.4   S.40
ROSELLI, Francesco [see ROUSSEL, François]
ROSEN, Jerome (1921-   ), USA
    R.1   S.10,13,19,21,24a
ROSENBERG, Hilding (1892-   ), Sweden
    R.1   S.c,4-10,24,38,40,56
ROSENBERG, Wolf (1915-   ), Ger
    R.4   S.10
ROSENBLATT, Jean-Joseph (1923-   )
                 S.c
ROSENBLOOM, Sydney (1889-1967), Scot
    R.14   S.24
ROSENBLUTH, Leo (1904-   ), Sweden
    R.30   S.40,56
ROSENBOOM, David (1947-   ), USA
    R.19   S.13
ROSENFELD, Gerhard (1931-   ), Ger
    R.1   S.24
ROSENFELD, Leopold (1850-1909), Den
    R.30
ROSENFELD, Monroe H.
                 S.10
ROSENKRANZ, Václav Josef (1797-1861), Cz
    R.18   S.5x
ROSENMAN, Leonard (1924-   ), USA
    R.1   S.9,10,13,24a
ROSENMÜLLER, Johann (c1619-1684), Ger
    R.1   S.c,2-5,7-11,24,32
ROSENTHAL, Moriz (1862-1946), Aus
    R.4
ROSENTHAL, Paul (1942-   )
                 S.24a

ROSENWALD, Helmuth (1929-   ), Est
    R.58   S.18
ROSENWEIG, Florence
    R.7   S.24,30
ROSER, Franz de Paula (1779-1830), Aus
    R.1   S.c
ROSETTI, Antonio (c1750-1792), Boh
    R.1   S.c,8,9,18
ROSIER, Carl (1640-1725), Neth
    R.1   S.c,10
ROSIERS, André (fl 1634-72), Fr
    R.1   S.8
ROSILLO - La granjera de Arles

ROSKOVSZKY, Pantaleon (1734-1789)
    R.15   S.c,9
ROSLAVETS, Nikolay Andreyevich (1881-1944), Ukraine
    R.1   S.c
RÖSLER, Jan Josef (1771-1813), Boh
    R.1   S.c
ROS-MARBA, Antoni (1937-   )
                S.24a
ROSOWSKY, Solomon (1878-1962), Lat
    R.4
ROSS, A. - Chant du rossignol (vi & p)
                S.24
ROSS, Richard (1914-1954), USA
                S.12,13
ROSS, Robert de

ROSS, Walter Beghtol (1936-   ), USA
    R.19   S.10,13
ROSSE, Frederick (1867-1940), Eng
    R.1
ROSSEAU, Norbert (1907-1975), Bel
    R.1   S.24a,36
ROSSELLI, Francesco [see ROUSSEL, François]
ROSSELLINI, Renzo (1908-1982), It
    R.1   S.8,18,24
ROSSETER, Philip (1567/68-1623), Eng
    R.1   S.c,7,8,10,14-16,27,28,32
ROSSI - E se domani
                S.10
*** ROSSI, Francesco (1627-c1700) or (b c1645)
                S.4,18   (see note)
ROSSI, Luigi (c1597-1653), It
    R.1   S.c,8-10,24
ROSSI, Michelangelo (1601/02-1656), It
    R.1   S.c,2-5,10,11,18,53

ROSSI, Salamone (1570-c1630), It
   R.1   S.9,10,14,16,24
ROSSIGNOL, Felix Ludger
   [see JONCIÈRES, Victorin de - pseud]
ROSSINI, Gioachino (1792-1868), It
   R.1   S.c,1-11,18-21,23-28,34,42,43,54(314,28)
ROSSINO MANTOVANO (fl 1505-11), It
   R.1   S.10,16
RÖSSLER, Ernst Karl (1909-1980), Ger
   R.14   S.c
ROSSLER, Franz [Frantisek Antonin] [see ROSETTI, Antonio]
ROSSUM, Frederik van (1939-   ), Bel
   R.1   S.c,24a
ROSTROPOVICH, Mstislav (1927-   ), USSR
   R.1   S.18
ROTA, Nino (1911-1979), It
   R.1   S.c,9,10
ROTENBUCHER, Erasmus (c1525-1586), Ger
   R.1   S.c
ROTH, Daniel (1942-   ), Fr
   R.14   S.c
ROTHSCHILD, Matilde, Baronne Willy de (1832-1924), Fr
   R.3
ROTHSTEIN, James [pseud: Carlo PINOZZI] (1871-   ), Ger
             S.10
ROTOLI, Augusto (1847-1904), It
   R.10   S.c,10,34,44
ROTTA, Antonio (c1495-1549), It
   R.1   S.c
ROTTER - Baby-Lied

ROTTER, Fritz (1900-   ), USA
   R.4   S.10
ROTTIERS, Jef (1904-   ), Bel
   R.25
ROUCAIROL, Joseph - Hommage et Louange à Dieu
             S.c
ROUGET de LISLE, Claude-Joseph (1760-1836), Fr
   R.1   S.c,1x,10,54(342)
ROUGNON, Paul (1846-1934), Fr
   R.3   S.e
ROUS, Fred   Can

ROUSE, Christopher (1949-   ), USA
   R.19   S.13
ROUSSAKIS, Nicolas (1934-   ), USA
   R.19   S.10,13
ROUSSEAU, Jean-Jacques (1712-1778), Fr
   R.1   S.c,2-5,9,11,42

ROUSSEAU, Jean-Marie (d.1784), Fr
   R.1   S.c
ROUSSEAU, L. Julien
            S.24
ROUSSEAU, Marcel Samuel [see SAMUEL-ROUSSEAU, Marcel]
ROUSSEAU, Norbert = ROSSEAU, Norbert
ROUSSEAU, Samuel (1853-1904), Fr
   R.3   S.24
ROUSSEL, Albert (1869-1937), Fr
   R.1   S.c,1-11,18,23-27
ROUSSEL [Rosselli], François (c1510->1577), Fr
   R.1   S.c,5x,8,10,14,32
ROUX, Gaspard le [see LE ROUX, Gaspard]
ROVENSKY, Vaclav Karel Holan
   [see HOLAN ROVENSKY, Vaclav Karel]
RÖVENSTRUNCK, Barnhard (1920-   ), Ger
   R.14
ROVETTA, Giovanni (c1595-1668), It
   R.1   S.c
ROVICS, Howard (1936-   ), USA
   R.19   S.10,13
ROVIGO, Francesco (1541/42-1597), It
   R.1   S.c,53
ROVSING OLSEN, Poul (1922-   ), Den
   R.4
ROWLAND - Blaenwern
            S.54(316)
ROWLEY, Alec (1892-1958), Eng
   R.1   S.c
ROXAS, Emanuele de (1827-1891), It
   R.3   S.e
ROXBURGH, Edwin (1937-   ), Eng
   R.1   S.c
ROXBURY, Ronald (1946-   ), USA
   R.19   S.13
ROY - How do I love thee
            S.5x
ROY, Adrien le [see LE ROY, Adrian]
ROY, Alphonse (1906-   ), Swiss
   R.4
ROY, Klaus George (1924-   ), USA
   R.19   S.10,13
ROYER, Joseph-Nicolas-Pancrace (c1705-1755), Fr
   R.1   S.c,10
ROYER, G. - pseud [see RHODE, Max]
ROYLLART, Philippus (14th Cent), Fr
   R.1   S.c,10
ROZDOLSKY, D. - Sontse Zakhodyti

ROZHDESTVENSKY, Vsevolod Petrovich (1918-   ), USSR
   R.14   S.18
ROZHOV, A. - Anthology of tropes for Easter
           S.10
RÓZMANN, Ákos (1939-   ), Sweden
   R.30   S.40
RÓZSA, Miklós (1907-   ), USA
   R.1   S.c,4,5x,6-10,13,20,21,24
ROZSAVÖLGI, Mark R. (1790-1848), Hun
   R.3
RÓZYCKI, Jacek (d.1697), Pol
   R.1   S.c
RÓZYCKI, Ludomir (1884-1953), Pol
   R.1   S.c,24
ROZZI - Moto perpetuo
           S.5x
RUBASHEVSKY, Vladimir (1931-   )
           S.24a
RUBBEN, Hermannjosef (1928-   )
           S.c
RUBBRA, Edmund (1901-   ), Eng
   R.1   S.c,4,5,7-10,24,55
RUBENS, Paul Alfred (1875-1917), Eng
   R.1   S.c,24
RUBIN, Marcel (1905-   ), Aus
   R.14   S.c,24a
RUBIN, Vladimir Ilich (1924-   ), USSR
   R.14   S.18
RUBINO, Cesare (fl 17th Cent)
           S.8
RUBINOFF, David (1897-   ), USA
   R.61   S.24
RUBINSTEIN, Anton (1829-1894), Russia
   R.1   S.c,1-11,18,21,23,24,28,34,44
RUBINSTEIN, Beryl (1898-1952), USA
   R.19   S.5,8,10,11,13
RUBINUS [see ROBINET de la MAGDALAINE]
RUBRECHT - Samum
           S.54(354)
RÜCKAUF, Anton (1855-1903), Boh
   R.3   S.e
RUCKER - Cancion andalusa

RUDEL, Jaufre (12th Cent), Fr
   R.1   S.c,4,5x,8,10,14,16
RUDENYI, Jan (d.1914)
           S.24
RUDHYAR, Dane (1895-   ), USA
   R.1   S.9,10,13,8[Rhudyar]

RUDIN, Andrew (1939-   ), USA
   R.19   S.9,13
RUDING, Karl
            S.c
RÜDINGER, Gottfried (1886-1946), Ger
   R.1   S.c
RUDNICK, Wilhelm (1850-1927), Pol
   R.39   S.c
RUDNIK, Eugeniusz (1933-   )
            S.c,10
RUDOLF von FENIS-NEUENBERG (12th Cent), Ger
   R.1   S.c,16
RUDOLPH, Archduke of Austria (1788-1831)
   R.1   S.c,10,19,20
RUDZIŃSKI, Zbigniew (1935-   ), Pol
   R.4
RUDZIŃSKY, Witold (1913-   ), Pol
   R.1   S.c
RUE, Le Grand (c 1600)
            S.c
RUE, Pierre de la [see LA RUE, Pierre de]
RUEFF, Jeanine (1922-   ), Fr
   R.7   S.20,22,30,52
RUFFLES, Edgar Thomas (1903-   ), Eng
   R.37,96   S.54(321)
RUFFO, Vincenzo (c1508-1587), It
   R.1   S.c,8,10,14
RÜGEN, Wîzlaw von [see WÎZLAW III von RÜGEN]
RUGER, Morris Hutchins (1902-   ), USA
   R.19   S.13
RUGGERI, Roger (1939-   ), USA
            S.c
RUGGI, Francesco (1826-1901), It
   R.3   S.e
RUGGIERI, Giovanni Maria (fl 1690-1720), It
   R.1   S.c,8-10,24
RUGGIERO, Giuseppe
            S.10,22
RUGGLES, Carl (1876-1971), USA
   R.1   S.c,2,3,8,10,13
RUIZ de LUNA
            S.10
RUIZ de RIBAYAZ, Lucas (17th Cent), Sp
   R.1   S.c,10,17,32
RUIZ-PIPO, Antonio (1934-   ), Sp
            S.c,10,39
RULAND, Alexander - pseud [see OTTEN, Hans]
RULOFFS, Bartolomeus (1741-1801), Neth
   R.1   S.c

RUMEAU, Gaston (20th Cent)
          S.1
RUMELANT, Meister (13th Cent), Ger
          S.2-4,5x,8,10,11,14,16
RUMMEL, Josef (1818-1880), Ger
  R.3
RUNCU, Ion Popescu (1901-1975)
          S.c
RUNG, Frederick (1854-1914), Den
  R.1   S.5x
RUNG, Henrik (1807-1871), Den
  R.3   S.4,33,35,57
RUNGIS, Rene
          S.10,22
RÚNÓLFSSON, Karl Ottó (1900-1970), Iceland
  R.1   S.5x
RUNOV, V. - Capital march
          S.54(318)
RUNSWICK, Daryl (1946-   )
          S.c
RUNZINSKY, Vitold (1913-   )
          S.18
RUOHOMAKI, Jukka Fin
          S.40(89)
RUPES, Georges - Pastorale languedoçienne

RUPP, Carl (1892-   ), USA
  R.23   S.24
RUPPE, Christian Friedrich (1753-1826), Neth
  R.1   S.c
RUPPE, Friedrich Christian (1771-1834), Neth
  R.1
RUPPEL, Paul Ernst (1913-   ), Ger
  R.4   S.c
RUSCONI, Gerardo (1922-1974), It
  R.14   S.10
RUSH, Loren (1935-   ), USA
  R.19   S.c,13
RUSINEIN
          S.5x
RUSSEL, Oswald (1930-   )
          S.c
RUSSELL, Armand (1932-   ), USA
  R.23
RUSSELL, George (1923-   ), USA
  R.1   S.10,13
RUSSELL, George Alexander (1880-1953), USA
  R.19   S.3,8,10,12,13
RUSSELL, Henry (1812-1900), Eng
  R.1   S.9

RUSSELL, James J.
        S.24
RUSSELL, Kennedy (1883-   )

RUSSELL, Sydney King
        S.10
RUSSELL, Welford (c1901-1975), Can
  R.81   S.10
RUSSELL, William (1777-1813), Eng
  R.1
RUSSELL, William (1905-   ), USA
  R.19   S.3,5x,10,13
RUSSO, John (1943-   ), USA
  R.19   S.10
RUSSO, N. - Torre del lago Puccini

        S.5x
RUSSO, William Joseph (1928-   ), USA
  R.19   S.c,10,13,24a
RUSSOTTO - Hatikvah
        S.e
RUST - Faithful and bold
        S.54(325)
RUST, Friedrich Wilhelm (1739-1796), Ger
  R.1   S.c,8-10,23,24
RUTA, Gilda, Countesse (Cagnazzi) (1853/56-1932), It
  R.7   S.52
RUTHSTRÖM, Julius (1877-1944), Sweden
  R.1   S.24
RUTINI, Giovanni Marco [Giovanni Placido]
  (1723-1797), It   R.1   S.3-5,10
RUTKOWSKY, Antoni Wincenty (1859-1886), Pol
  R.1   S.18
RUTTER, John (1943-   ), Eng
        S.c
RUYNEMAN, Daniel (1886-1963), Neth
  R.1   S.10,24
RUZHITSKY, Lyudomir (1884-1953)
        S.18
RUZICKA, Peter (1948-   ), Ger
  R.1   S.c
RYABOV, Alexei Lantelemonovich (1899-1955), USSR
  R.47
RYAETS, Jan (1932-   ), USSR
  R.47   S.18
RYAN, Thomas USA
        S.13
RYAUZOV, Sergei Nikolayevich (1905-   ), USSR
  R.47   S.18
RYBA, Jakub Jan (1765-1815), Cz
  R.1   S.c,8

RYBALCHENKO, Vsevolod Petrovich (1904-   ), USSR
   R.14   S.18
RYBRANT, Stig (1916-   ), Sweden
   R.30   S.56
RYCHLIK, Jan (1916-1964), Cz
   R.1   S.10,31
RYCHNOVSKY, Jiri (c1545-c1616)
            S.c,16
RYDER, Thomas Philander (1836-1887), USA
   R.53   S.10,47
RYDMAN, Kari (1936-   ), Fin
   R.1   S.39
RYE - Normandy march
            S.54(345)
RYELANDT, Joseph (1870-1965), Bel
   R.4
RYKHLIK, Jan (1916-   )
            S.18
RYMAL, Grant V.
            S.10
RYSBYE, (16th Cent), Eng
            S.c,10
RYTERBAND, Roman (1914-   ), USA
   R.19   S.9,13,24a
RYGAARD, Georg (1894-1921), Den
   R.30a   S.4,33
RZAYEV, Azer Guseinovich (1930-   ), USSR
   R.14   S.18,24
RZEWSKI, Frederic (1938-   ), USA
   R.1   S.c,9,10,13
SAAR, Louis Victor (1868-1937), Neth
   R.1   S.24
SAAR, Mart (1882-1963), Est
   R.1   S.18
SAARUNY, E. (1894-   )
            S.18
SAATKULOV, Dada-Ali (1917-   )
            S.18
SABAANOV, Yaikhel (1929-   )

SABADINI, Bernardo
            S.32
SABAINO - Te solo
            S.e
SABARICH, Raymond (1909-   )
            S.8-10
SABATA, Victor de [see DE SABATA, Victor]
SABATHIL, Ferdinand (1852-1937), Cz
   R.4   S.e

SABBATINI, Galeazzo (1597-1662), It
   R.1   S.c
SABICIAS, pseud [ie Augustin CASTELLON]
          S.10
SABIO, Alfonso el [see ALFONSO el SABIO]
SABITOV, Nariman (1925-1971), USSR
   R.47   S.18,24
SABO, Ferents [see SZABÓ, Ferenc]
SABOLY, Nicolas (1614-1675), Fr
   R.1   S.c,8,10
SABRE MARROQUÍN, José (1910-   ), Mex
   R.56   S.10
SABZANOV, Yaikel (1929-   )
          S.18
SACCHI, Virgilio (1857-1910), It [?]
   R.10   S.5x
SACCHINI, Antonio Maria Gasparo (1730-1786), It
   R.1   S.c,2-5,8,10
SACCO, John Charles (1905-   ), USA
   R.19   S.5x,10,13
SACCO, Peter (1928-   ), USA
   R.19   S.10,13
SACHNOWSKY, G. - The clock
          S.e
SACHS, Hans (1494-1576), Ger
   R.1   S.c,10,14-16
SACHS, Julius (1830-1880), Ger
   R.39   S.e
SACHSE, Ernst
          S.c
SACHSEN-WEIMAR, Anna Amalie von
   [see Anna AMALIE, Duchess of Saxe-Weimar]
SACHSEN-WEIMER, Johann-Ernest von
          S.10
SACRATI, Francesco (1605-1650), It
   R.1   S.10
SADAN - Serenade to spring (vi & p)
          S.24
SADERO, Geni - pseud [see SCARPA, Eugenia]
SADLER, Helmut (1921-   ), Ger
   R.4   S.c
SADYKOV, Talib (1907-   ), USSR
   R.47   S.18[under Glier, R. M.]
SAEBELMANN, Alexander [pseud: KUNILEID] (1845-1875)
   R.3   S.18
SAEGUSA, Shigeaki (1942-   ), Japan
   R.4
SAELLO del PAQUINO, Giovanni

SAENGER, Gustav (1865-1935), USA
  R.23   S.24
SAENZ, Pedro (1915-   ), Arg
  R.4
SAEVERUD, Harald (1897-   ), Nor
  R.1   S.c,4-6,8,10,51
SAEVERUD, Ketil (1939-   ), Nor
  R.1   S.51
SAFRONI - Imperial echoes
           S.54(333)
SAGAEV, Dimiter Konstaninov (1915-   ), Bul
  R.14   S.24a
SAGE de RICHÉE, Philipp Franz le
  [see LE SAGE de RICHÉE, Philipp Franz]
SAGI-BARBA, Emilio (1875-   ), Sp

  R.55   S.e
SAGRERAS, Casparos Julio (1867-   ), Arg
           S.c,10,32,39
SAHL, Michael (1934-   ), USA
  R.19   S.9,10,13,24
SAHLBERG(-KNOOP), Sanja (d.1968), Sweden
           S.43
SAIDAMINOVA, Dilorom (1943-   ), USSR
  R.7   S.18,52
SAIDASHEV, Salikh (1900-1954), USSR
  R.14   S.18
SAIFI, Dzhalil (1932-   )
           S.18
SAIFIDDINOV, Sharofiddin (1929-   ), USSR
  R.14   S.18
SAIGUN, Akmed Adnan (1907-   ), USSR
  R.47   S.18
SAINE, A. - L´exile (vi & p)
           S.24a
SAINT CLAIR, Floyd J. (1871-1942), USA [?]
  R.23   S.54(312)
SAINT DENIS - Le balcon, Op.42 (vi & p)
           S.24a
SAINT-GEORGES, Joseph Boulogne Chevalier de (c1739-1799)
  Fr R.1   S.c,9,24
SAINT GERMAIN, Comte de (d.1784)
  R.1
SAINT-GODRIC (d.1170)
           S.c,10
SAINT-LUBIN, Léon de [see LUBIN, Napoléon-Antoine-Eugène]
SAINT-LUC, Jacques de (1616-c1684), Fr
  R.1   S.c,8,10,24
SAINT-MARCOUX, Micheline Coulombe (1938-   ), Can
  R.4

SAINT-MARTIN, Léonce de (1886-1954), Fr
   R.10s   S.c
SAINT-SAËNS, Camille (1835-1921), Fr
   R.1   S.c,1-11,18-21,23,24,42,54(322)
SAINT VICTOR, Adam de [see ADAM de SAINT VICTOR]
SAINTE-COLOMBE, (d.1691-1701), Fr
   R.1   S.c,10
SAINTON, Prosper (1813-1890), Fr
   R.1   S.9,24
SAINTON-DOLBY, Charlotte Helen (1821-1885), Eng
   R.1   S.e
SÁINZ de la MAZA, Eduardo (1903-   )
            S.32,39
SÁINZ de la MAZA, Regino (1897-   ), Sp
   R.9   S.10,32,39
SAIRT, Louis
            S.10
SAK - Dance of the wood nymphs
            S.54(322)
SAKELARIDES - That good old time
            S.1x
SAKER, George Morton (1874-   ), Eng
   R.77   S.e
SAKHAROV, Lev Nikolayevich (1902-   )
            S.18
SAKHNOVSKY, Yuri Sergeyevich (1866-1930), Russia
   R.47   S.5x,18
SALA, Oskar (1910-   ), Ger
   R.8   S.c,10
SALADIN, Louis (17th Cent)
   R.5   S.c
SALAMAN, Charles Kensington (1814-1901), Eng
   R.8   S.e
SALAMON - Extase

SALAVERDE, Bartolome de Selma
   [see SELMA y SALAVERDE, Bartolome de]
SALAZAR, Antonio (c1950-   ), USA
            S.39
SALAZAR, Diego José de (d.1709), Sp
   R.1   S.c
SALBERT, Dieter
            S.c
SALEM, Bernard von
            S.16,53
SALEMA - Choruses
            S.5x
SALEN, Sven (1890-1969), Sweden
            S.10,43

SALESKI, Gdal (1888-1966), USA [?]
  R.4   S.24
SALIERI, Antonio (1750-1825), It
  R.1   S.c,5x,10,24
SALIEV, Fazyl (1914-   )
            S.18
SALIKHOV, Enmark (1934-   )
            S.18
SALINAS, J. - Crépusculo espagñol (guitar)
            S.32
SALISBURY (16th Cent)
            S.c
SALLINEN, Aulis (1935-   ), Fin
  R.1   S.c,9,10,18,24,40
SALMANOV, Vadim Nikolayevich (1912-1978), Russia
  R.1   S.18,24
SALMENHAARA, Erkki (1941-   ), Fin
  R.1   S.c,10,40
SALMHOFER, Franz (1900-1975), Aus
  R.1   S.c
SALMON, Jacques (fl 1571-86), Fr
  R.1   S.8
SALOMÉ, Theodore Césare (1834-1896), Fr
  R.10   S.c
SALOMON, Joseph-François (1649-1732), Fr
  R.1
SALOMON, Siegfried (1885-1962), Den
  R.1   S.5x,57
SALONEN, Sulo (1899-1976), Fin

  R.1   S.c,40
SALTER, Mary Elizabeth (Mrs. Sumner) (née Turner)
  (1856-1938), USA   R.7
SALTER, Timothy (1942-   ), Eng
  R.64   S.c
SALULINI, Paolo (1709-1780), It
  R.8   S.c
SALUSTRI, Carlo Albert [pseud: TRILUSSA] (1873-   )
  R.200   S.10
SALVATORE, Giovanni (d ?1688), It
  R.1   S.c,53
SALVEY, Thomas
            S.c
SALVI, Matteo (1816-1887), It
  R.3   S.10
SALZEDO, Carlos (1885-1961), Fr
  R.1   S.3,5,7,8,10,13,18
SALZEDO, Leonard (1921-   ), Eng
  R.1   S.c,10
SALZMAN, Eric (1933-   ), USA
  R.1   S.9,13,32

SAMAN, René (fl 1610-31), Fr
R.1   S.c
SAMARAS, Spyridon (?1863-1917), Greece
R.1   S.e
SAMAZEUILH, Gustave (1877-1967), Fr
R.1   S.c,2-5,10,24
SAMINSKY, Lazare (1882-1959), USA
R.1   S.10,13,24a
SAMMARTINI, Giovanni Battista (1700/01-1775), It
R.1   S.c,2-5,8-10,18,23,24
SAMMARTINI, Giuseppe (1695-1750), It
R.1   S.c,1-8,10,24
SAMMONS, Albert (1886-1957), Eng
R.1   S.24
SAMPLE, Steve
             S.10
SAMPSON, Peggi (1912-   ), Scot
R.4   S.52
SAMSON, Joseph (1888-1957), Fr
R.14   S.c,7,8
SAMSON-FRANCOIS (1924-1970), Fr
R.1   S.8
SAMTER, Alice (1908-   ), Ger
R.7   S.c,30,52
SAMUEL, Gerhard (1924-   ), USA
R.1   S.13
SAMUEL-ROUSSEAU, Marcel (1882-1955), Fr
R.1   S.c,5x,18
SAMUELS, Homer (1889-   ), USA
R.43   S.e
SAMUELSON, Laura Byers (20th Cent), USA
             S.52
SANADZE, Eduard (1938-   )
             S.18
SANCAN, Pierre (1916-   ), Fr
R.14   S.10,18

SANCEDO - El mar sin playas
             S.e
SANCES, Giovanni Felice (c1600-1679), It
R.1   S.c
SÁNCHEZ - Christus factus est
             S.16
SÁNCHEZ de FUENTES, Eduardo (1874-1944), Cuba
R.1   S.32,44
SÁNCHEZ, Blas (20th Cent)
             S.c
SANCTA MARÍA, Tomás de [see SANTA MARÍA, Tomás de]
SANDBY, Hermann (1881-1965), Den
R.1   S.5x

SANDELL, Lina (1832-1903), Sweden
R.7   S.52
SANDERS, Erl
           S.24
SANDERS, John Derek (1933-   ), Eng
R.80   S.c
SANDERS, Robert Levine (1906-1974), USA
R.1   S.8-10,13
SANDERSON, James (1769-1841), Eng
R.57,200   S.10
SANDERSON, Wilfred Ernest (1878-1935), Eng
R.37   S.c,5x,10,24,28
SANDI, Luis (1905-   ), Mex
R.1   S.8,10,39
SANDOVAL, A. C.
           S.24a
SANDOVAL, Miguel (1903-1953), USA
R.19   S.7,10,13
SANDRIN [Regnault, Pierre] (c1490->1561), Fr
R.1   S.c,8,10,14-16,53
SANDSTRÖM, Carl Israel (1824-1880), Sweden
R.111   S.e
SANDSTRÖM, Sven-David (1942-   ), Sweden
R.1   S.c,40,56
SANDVOLD, Arild Edvin (1895-   ), Nor
R.14   S.c,40
SANDYS, M. L. - Marston
           S.54(342)
SANFORD - Lincoln Centennial
           S.54(338)
SANGSTER, John ?USA
           S.13
SANJUAN, Pedro (1886-1976), USA
R.19   S.10,39
SANKEY, Ira David (1840-1908), USA
R.50   S.e
SAN MIGUEL, Mariano (c1880-1935), Sp
R.105   S.39
SAN SEBASTIAN - Dolor
           S.5x
SAN SEBASTIAN, Padre José Antonio de
   [see DONOSTIA, José Antonio de]
SANSEVERINO, Benedetto (fl 1620-22), It

R.1   S.c
SANTA CRUZ, Antonio de (17th Cent)
           S.c
SANTA CRUZ, Domingo (1899-   ), Chile
R.1   S.8,10,24a
SANTA MARÍA, Tomás de (d.1570), Sp
R.1   S.c,3,4,5x,8,10,14-18,32,39,53

SANTANA, Carlos (1947-   ), USA
    R.25   S.39
SANTERRE, Pierre (d <1567), Fr
    R.1   S.14
SANTINI, Fortunato (1778-1861), It
    R.1   S.c
SANTINI, Prospero (fl 1591-1614), It
    R.1
SANTLEY, Charles [pseud: Ralph BETTERTON] (1834-1922)
    Eng R.1   S.e
SANTLY, Joseph H. (1886-1962), USA
    R.23   S.24
SANTO ELIAS, Manuel de (18th Cent)
                S.c,10
SANTOLIQUIDO, Francesco (1883-1971), It
    R.1   S.c,10
SANTORO, Cláudio (1919-   ), Brazil
    R.1   S.c,8,18,24a
SANTÓRSOLA, Guido (1904-   ), Uruguay
    R.1   S.c,8,10,32
SANTOS, (José Manuel) Joly Braga [see BRAGA SANTOS, Joly]
SANTOS, José Joaquím dos (c1747-1801), Sp
    R.1   S.8,10
SANZ, Gaspar (17-18th Cent), Sp
    R.1   S.c,3,5x,8,10,17,18,32,39
SAO MARCOS, M. - O mar
                S.32
SAPAYEV, Erik Nikitich (1932-1963)
                S.18
SAPERSTEIN, David (1948-   ), USA
    R.19   S.10,13
SAPTEFRATI, Liana Alexandria (1947-   ), Rum
    R.7   S.30,52
SARACINI, Claudio (1586->1649), It
    R.1   S.c,10
SÁRAI, Tibor (1919-   ), Hun
    R.1   S.c,9,24
SARASATE, Pablo (1844-1908), Sp
    R.1   S.c,2-10,18,24,39
SARBECK - Tendrement
                S.5x
SARCHIZOV, Sergiu (1924-   ), Rum
    R.33   S.24a
SARDINHA, Annibal Augesto [see GARÔTO - pseud]
SARGENT, Paul (1910-   ), USA
    R.19   S.10,13
SÁRI, József (1935-   ), Hun
    R.14   S.c
SARIAN, Ghazar [see SARYAN, Ghazar]

SARJEANT, J. - Watchman! What of the night
          S.5x
SARK, Einar Traerup (1921-   ), Den
   R.30   S.40
SÁRKÖZY, István (1920-   ), Hun
   R.1   S.c,9,10,19,24a
SARMANTO, Heikki (1939-   ), Fin
   R.30   S.c
SARO - Melodias de invierno (vi & p)
          S.24a
SAROYAN, Aram (1943-   )
          S.10
SARRO, Domenico Natale (1679-1744), It
   R.1   S.c,8,10
SARTI, Giuseppe (1729-1802), It
   R.1   S.c,4-11,25,27
SARTORIO, Antonio (1630-1680), It
   R.1   S.c,2,3,5x
SARTORIUS, Johann (1712-1787), Rum
   R.33
SARTORIUS, Thomas (1577-1637)
   R.5   S.5,11
SÁRY, László (1940-   ), Hun
   R.1   S.c,10
SARYAN, Ghazar (1920-   ), Arm
   R.1   S.10,18,24a
SAS, Andrés (1900-1967), Peru
   R.1   S.c,10,11,24,39
SASHINA, Elena = SHASHINA, Elizaveta
SASNAUSKAS, Cheslovas (1867-1916), Russia
   R.47   S.18
SASONKIN, Manus
          S.8
SATIE, Erik (1866-1925), Fr
   R.1   S.c,1-11,18,24-28,32,42
SATO, Shin (1938-   ), Japan
   R.36   S.50
SATOH, Keijiro (1927-   ), Japan
   R.4   S.50
ŠATRA, Antonín (1901-   ), Cz
   R.14   S.5,6,24a,31
SATS, Illya Alexandrovich (1875-1912)
          S.18
SATTLER, Hermann [pseud: Joe GARWIN] (1921-   ), USA
   R.4   S.10
SATUREN, David Haskell (1939-   ), USA
   R.80   S.13
SATYAN, Ashot Movsesovich (1906-1958), USSR
   R.14   S.18

SAU, Olev (1929-   ), Est
   R.58   S.18
SAUCE, Angel (1911-   ), Ven
   R.14
SAUCEDO, Victor (1937-   ), USA
   R.19   S.13
SAUER, Emil von (1862-1942), Ger
   R.1   S.c,1x,5x,18
SAUER, František (1912-   ), Cz
             S.31
SAUGUET, Henri (1901-   ), Fr
   R.1   S.c,4-6,8-10,18,27,32
SAUMELL ROBREDO, Manuel (1817-1870), Cuba
   R.1   S.8,10,32
SAURET, Emile (1852-1920), Fr
   R.1   S.24
SAUTER, Edward Ernest (1914-   ), USA
   R.19   S.13
SAUVEPLANE, Henri Emile [pseud: H. E. RHYNE] (1892-   )
   Fr R.3   S.3-5,8,24
SAUX, Gaston

SAVAGE, Richard - pseud [see HAYMAN, Richard Warren]
SAVAGE, William (1720-1789), Eng
   R.1   S.10
SAVELYEV, Boris Vladimirovich (1896-1966), USSR
   R.14   S.18,24
SAVERY, Finn (1933-   ), Den
   R.14   S.40
SAVILE, Jeremy (fl 1651-65), Eng
   R.1   S.10,16
SAVINO, Domenico (1882-1973), USA
   R.19   S.10,39
SAVIO, Isaias (1900-   ), Brazil
   R.80   S.c,5x,10,32
SAVOURET, Alain Louis Camille (1942-   ), Fr
   R.80   S.c
SAXE, Serge
             S.10
SAXLEHNER, Andor
             S.e
SAYGUN, Ahmet Adnan (1907-   ), Turkey
   R.1   S.c
SAYLOR, Bruce Stuart (1946-   ), USA
   R.19   S.13
SAYVE, Lambert de (1548/49-1614), Flem
   R.1   S.c
SCACCHI, Marco (c1600-1681/87), It
   R.1   S.16

SCALANO - Ballerina (p)

SCALETTI, Carla (1956-   ), USA
   R.7   S.10,30,52
SCANDELLO, Antonio (1517-1580), It
   R.1   S.c,5,7,8,10,11,14-16

SCARLATESCU, Ioan (1872-1922), Rum
   R.4   S.c,4,5x,24
SCARLATTI, Alessandro (1660-1725), It
   R.1   S.c,1-11,18,24-28,32,42,53
SCARLATTI, Domenico (1685-1757), It
   R.1   S.c,1-6,8-11,18,22,24,32,42,53
SCARLATTI, Pietro Filippo (1679-1750), It
   R.1   S.10
SCARMOLIN, Anthony Louis (1890-1969), USA
   R.4
SCARPA, Eugenia [pseud: Geni SADERO] (1886-1961), It
   R.8   S.10[Sadero]
SCASSERRA - Elegie (vi & p)
                S.24
SCAVARDA, Donald (1928-   ), USA
   R.19   S.10,13,19,21
SCELSI, Giacinto (1905-   ), It
   R.1   S.c,10,24a
SCHAAL, Herbert (1940-   )
                S.c
SCHACHT, Theodor (1748-1823), Ger
   R.1   S.c,10,20
SCHAEFER - The sandman
                S.e
SCHAEFER, Myron (1908-1965), Can
   R.31   S.10
SCHAEFER, Theodor (1904-1969), Cz
   R.1
SCHAEFFER, Pierre (1910-   ), Fr
   R.1   S.c,10
SCHAERER, Melchior (fl 1602)
   R.5   S.16
SCHAEUBLE, Hans (1906-   ), Swiss
   R.1   S.20
SCHAFER - Das Pfafflein
                S.e
SCHAFER, Raymond Murray (1933-   ), Can
   R.1   S.10
SCHAFFER - Aftonen
                S.e
SCHÄFFER, Boguslaw (1929-   ), Pol
   R.1   S.c
SCHAFFRATH, Christoph (1709-1763), Ger
   R.1   S.c,10

SCHALE, Christian Friedrich (1713-1800), Ger
   R.1   S.10,32
SCHANTL, Josef Aus

SCHAPER, Heinz-Christian (1927-   ), Ger
   R.4
SCHAPOSHNIKOV, Adrian [see SHAPOSHNIKOV, Adrian]
SCHARLI, Ruth (1929-   ), Swiss
   R.7   S.c,52
SCHARRES, Charles (1888-   )

SCHARWENKA, Franz Xaver (1850-1924), Ger
   R.1   S.c,9,10,24

SCHARWENKA, Philipp (1847-1917), Ger
   R.1   S.c,10
SCHAT, Peter (1935-   ), Neth
   R.1   S.10,24a
SCHATTE - Severo Torelli
            S.e
SCHAUSS-FLAKE, Magdalene (1921-   ), Ger
   R.7   S.c,52
SCHEBECK, T. - Violinens sang (vi & p)
            S.24
SCHEIBE, Johann Adolph (1708-1776), Ger
   R.1   S.c
SCHEIDEGGER, Daniel (1956-   )
            S.c
SCHEIDEMANN, Heinrich (c1595-1663), Ger
   R.1   S.c,5x,10,53
SCHEIDLER, Christian Gottlieb (?1752-?1814), Ger
   R.3   S.c,,10,24a,32
SCHEIDT, Samuel (1587-1654), Ger
   R.1   S.c,2-11,18,32,53
SCHEIN, Johann Herman (1586-1630), Ger
   R.1   S.c,2-11,15,16,18,32,53
SCHELB, Josef (1894-   ), Ger
   R.4
SCHELBECK, J. - Canzona del violino (vi & p)
            S.24
SCHELLE, Johann (1648-1701), Ger
   R.1   S.c
SCHELLING, Ernest (1876-1939), USA
   R.1   S.c,1-3,11,13,18,24
SCHEMELLI, Georg Christian (c1676-1762), Ger
   R.1   S.8
SCHEMPER, Raúl Arg
            S.46
SCHENCK, Johannes (1660-1712), Ger
   R.1   S.c,10

SCHENK, Johann Baptist (1753-1836), Aus
   R.1   S.c,32
SCHEPERS, Boudewijn (d.1781)
            S.8
SCHEPERS, Geleyn (fl 1660) (see note)
   R.5   S.8
SCHERBACHEV, Vladimir

SCHERCHEN-HSIAO, Tona (1938-   ), Swiss
   R.7   S.30,52
SCHERER, N. (fl c1770-90), Ger
   R.1
SCHERER, Sebastian Anton (1631-1712), Ger
   R.1   S.c,8,10,53
SCHERTZINGER, Victor (1890-1941), USA
   R.23   S.10,24
SCHERZER, Adolf (1815-1864), Ger
   R.95   S.54(315)
SCHEU, Archie W.
            S.10

SCHEURER, Rolf (1918-   ), USA
            S.c
SCHIASSI, Gaetano Maria (1698-1754), It
   R.1   S.c,3-5,11
SCHIAVETTO, Giulio (16th Cent), Croatia
   R.1   S.16
SCHIBLER, Armin (1920-   ), Swiss
   R.1   S.5,7,9,19,23,24
SCHICK
            S.5x
SCHICKELE, Peter (1935-   ), USA
   R.1   S.10,13
SCHICKHARDT, Johann Christian (c1682-1762), Ger
   R.1   S.c,5,11
SCHIEDERMAYER, Johann Baptiste (1779-1840), Ger
   R.3   S.c
SCHIEDLER, Christian Gottlieb (c1752-1815)

SCHIEFERDECKER, Johann Christian (1679-1732), Ger
   R.1   S.10,53
SCHIERBECK, Poul (1888-1949), Den
   R.1   S.5x,6-8,10,40
SCHIERI, Fritz (1922-   ), Ger
   R.4
SCHIEVE, Catherine (20th Cent), USA
            S.52
SCHIFRIN, Lalo (1932-   ), USA
   R.1   S.9,10,13
SCHILDERMAYR, Johann Baptiste
   = SCHIEDERMAYER, Johann Baptiste

SCHILDKNECHT, Björn Albert (1905-1946), Sweden
R.30   S.24
SCHILDT, Melchior (1592/93-1667), Ger
R.1   S.c,5x,10,53
SCHILLING, Hans Ludwig (1927-   ), Ger
R.1   S.c,20
SCHILLINGS, Max von (1868-1933), Ger
R.1   S.c,1-4,5x,8,10
SCHIMBRACZKY, Johannes (fl 1635-48), Slovak
R.1   S.c[Scimbracky]
SCHINDLER, Allen (1944-   ), USA
R.19   S.10,13
SCHINDLER, Kurt (1882-1938), USA
R.1   S.24
SCHIPA, Tito (1888-1965), It
R.1   S.5x
SCHIPA-HUA - Cubanita
          S.34
SCHIPPERS, Leen
          S.c
SCHISKE, Karl (1916-1969), Aus
R.1   S.20,24a
SCHLEIFFARTH, George M. (d.1921)
R.200   S.e
SCHLESINGER, Martin (1751-1818), Boh
R.5   S.24
SCHLETT, Joseph (c1763-1836), Ger

R.5   S.10
SCHLICK, Arnolt (c1460->1521), Boh
R.1   S.c,6,10,14,16,18,32,53
SCHLICK, Johann Conrad (c1759-c1825), Ger
R.5   S.c,10
SCHMALSTICH, Clemens (1880-1960), Ger
R.14   S.c,5x,24
SCHMELTZER, A. E. (c1630-1680) [S.5x]
   = SCHMELZER, Johann Heinrich
SCHMELZER [von EHRENRUFF], Johann Heinrich (c1620-1680)
   Aus R.1   S.c,2,4,5,10,24
SCHMID, Bernhard (i) (1535-1592), Alsace
R.1   S.c,5,10,16,53
SCHMID, Bernhard (ii) (1567-<1625), Alsace
R.1   S.1x,2-5,53
SCHMID, Heinrich Kaspar (1874-1953), Ger
R.1   S.c
SCHMID, Johann C.
          S.24
SCHMID, K. N. (1923-   )
          S.c
SCHMID, Wilhelm F.
          S.c

SCHMIDEK, Kurt (1919-   ), Aus
    R.14   S.19,24
SCHMIDSEDER, Ludwig [pseud: Louis FABRO] (1904-1971)
    Aus   R.2   S.5x,10,33
SCHMIDT - Blue-white march
                S.54(316)
SCHMIDT, Eric (1907-   ), Swiss
    R.14   S.c

SCHMIDT, Franz (1874-1939), Aus
    R.1   S.c,4,5,7-10,19,20,24
SCHMIDT, H. - Abenlied
                S.5x
SCHMIDT, Hans [pseud: SCHMIDT-MANNHEIM] (1931-   ), Ger
    R.4   S.c
SCHMIDT, Harvey (1929-   ), USA
    R.23   S.9
SCHMIDT, Hugo Wolfram (1903-   ), Ger
    R.4
SCHMIDT, William Joseph (1926-   ), USA
    R.19   S.9,10,12,13,19,22
SCHMIDT-MANNHEIM - pseud [see SCHMIDT, Hans]
SCHMIT, Camille (1908-1976), Bel
    R.1   S.24,36
SCHMITT - Dionysiaques
                S.54(323)
SCHMITT, Florent (1870-1958), Fr
    R.1   S.c,1-5,8-10,18,21,22,24
SCHMITT, R. - Einzug der Flieger
                S.54(324)
SCHMITZ-GOHR, Else (1901-   ), Ger
    R.7   S.52
SCHMOLL, Friedrich (d.1792), Ger
    R.5   S.c,24
SCHMÜGEL, Johann Christoph (1727-1798), Ger
    R.1   S.c
SCHMUTZER - Frankonia march
                S.54(327)
SCHNABEL, Artur (1882-1951), Aus
    R.1   S.7,8,10,24a
SCHNABEL, Joseph Ignaz (1767-1831), Ger
    R.1   S.c,5x
SCHNAUBELT, Fred (1910-   ), Cz
    R.4   S.c
SCHNEBEL, Dieter (1930-   ), Ger
    R.1   S.c,10
SCHNEIDER, Conrad Michael (1673-1752), Ger
    R.1   S.c,10
SCHNEIDER, Franz (1737-1812), Aus
    R.25   S.c

SCHNEIDER, Georg Abraham (1770-1839), Ger
   R.1   S.c
SCHNEIDER, Gisbert

SCHNEIDER, Johann (1702-1788), Ger
   R.1   S.c,10
SCHNEIDER, Martin Gotthard
            S.c
SCHNEIDER, Urs Peter (1939-   ), Swiss
   R.4   S.c
SCHNEIDER-TRNAVSKÝ, Mikuláš (1881-1958), Slovak
   R.1   S.8,10,31
SCHNELL, Johann Jacob (1687-1754), Neth
   R.25   S.c
SCHNITTKE, Alfred [see SHNITKE, Alfred]
SCHNITZER, Franz (1740-1785), Ger
   R.1   S.c
SCHNITZER, Magnus (1755-1827)
            S.c
SCHNYDER von WARTENSEE, Xaver (1786-1868), Swiss
   R.1   S.c,8,10
SCHOBERLECHNER, Franz (1797-1843), Aus
   R.1   S.c
SCHOBERT, Johann (c1735-1767), Silesia
   R.1   S.c,3-5,9,10,24
SCHOEBEL, Elmer (1896-   ), USA
   R.23   S.10
SCHOECK, Othmar (1886-1957), Swiss
   R.1   S.4,5,7,9,10,18,20,24,26
SCHOEFFER, Peter (c1475-1547), Ger
   R.1   S.8
SCHOELL, Helmut (1911-   )
            S.c
SCHOEMAKER, Maurice (1890-1964), Bel
   R.1   S.36
SCHOENBERG, Arnold (1874-1951), Aus
   R.1   S.c,2-12,18,20,21,24,28,32,42
SCHOENBERGER, Malvin
            S.10
SCHOENDORFF, Philipp (c1565-1617), S. Neth
   R.1   S.c
SCHOENFIELD, Paul (1947-   ), USA
            S.13
SCHOFFER, Nicolas (1912-   )
            S.c
SCHOFFER, Peter [see SCHOEFFER, Peter]
SCHOLEFIELD, Clement Cotterill (1839-1904), Eng
   R.44   S.c,10
SCHOLLUM, Robert (1913-   ), Aus
   R.1   S.24a

SCHOLZ, Bernhard (1835-1916), Ger
  R.1
SCHOLZ, Viktor (1935-   )
        S.c
SCHOLZE, Johann Sigismond [see SPERONTES]
SCHÖNBACH, Dieter (1931-   ), Ger
  R.1   S.c
SCHÖNBERG, Stig Gustav (1933-   ), Sweden
  R.1   S.c,56
SCHÖNFELD, Johann Philipp (1742-1790), Alsace
  R.1
SCHÖNFELDER, Jorg (15th Cent), Ger [?]
  R.5   S.c
SCHÖNHERR, Max. (1903-   ), Aus
  R.1   S.10
SCHÖNSTEDT, Arno (1913-   ), Ger
  R.30
SCHONTHAL, Ruth E. (1924-   ), USA
  R.7   S.30,52
SCHOOLCRAFT, Luke
        S.24
SCHOOP, Paul (1909-1976), USA
  R.19   S.7,10,13
SCHOP, Johann (d.1667), Ger
  R.1   S.2,10
SCHRADER, Mogens (d.1934), Den
        S.4,33,43
SCHRADER, Rudolf (1863-1936), Ger
  R.4   S.e
SCHRAMM, Harold (1935-1971), USA
  R.19   S.10,13
SCHRAMMEL, Johann (1850-1893), Aus
  R.1   S.c,10
SCHRAMMEL, Josef (1852-1895), Aus
  R.2   S.c,54(366)
SCHRECK, Gustav (1849-1918), Ger
  R.3
SCHREIBER, Hans (1912-1969), Den
  R.30   S.57
SCHREIBER, Josef (1900-   ), Cz
  R.18   S.31
SCHREIER-BOTTERO, Josef
        S.24,31
SCHREINER, Alexander (1901-   ), USA
  R.23   S.10,12,13
SCHREINER, Hermann L. (fl 1865), USA
  R.53   S.10,47
SCHREKER, Franz (1878-1934), Aus
  R.1   S.c,1-4,24a

SCHREY, Wilhelm (1915-1967)
        S.c
SCHRÖDER - Deutschlands Ruhm
        S.54(323)
SCHRÖDER, Friedrich (1910-1972), Swiss (see note)
  R.1   S.c
SCHRÖDER, Hanning (1896-   ), Ger
  R.14   S.c
SCHRÖDER, Hermann (1843-1909), Ger (see note)
  R.1   S.8,10
SCHRÖDER, Karl (1848-1935), Ger
  R.3
SCHROEDER - Ave Marie klare
        S.16
SCHROEDER, Edward Wendell
        S.24
SCHROEDER, Hermann (1904-   ), Ger (see note)
  R.1   S.c,8,10
SCHROETER, Johann Samuel (c1752-1788), Ger
  R.1   S.c
SCHROETER, Leonhard (c1532-c1601), Ger
  R.1   S.c,4,10,14-16
SCHUBACK, Peter (1947-   ), Sweden
  R.68   S.c
SCHUBART, Christian Friedrich Daniel (1739-1791), Ger
  R.1   S.c
SCHUBEL, Max (1932-   ), USA
  R.19   S.9,10,13,24a
SCHUBERT, Franz (François) (1808-1878), Ger
  R.1   S.c,4,5x,10,24
SCHUBERT, Franz (1797-1828), Aus
  R.1   S.c,1-11,18-28,32,33,42,43
SCHUBERT, Heino (1928-   ), Ger
  R.4   S.c
SCHUBERT, Heinz (1908-1945), Ger
  R.4   S.5,7,24
SCHUBERT, Josef (1757-1837), Ger
  R.1   S.c
SCHUBERT, Manfred (1937-   ), Ger
  R.4   S.24a
SCHUBIGER, Anselm (1815-1888), Swiss
  R.1   S.c
SCHUËCKER, Edmund (1860-1911), Ger
  R.1   S.c
SCHUETKY, Franz Joseph [see SCHUTKY, Franz Joseph]
SCHULÉ, Bernard Emmanuel (1909-   ), USA
  R.14   S.10,13
SCHULHOFF, Ervín (1894-1942), Cz
  R.1   S.c,2,5,10,24

SCHULHOFF, Julius (1825-1898), Cz
   R.2   S.c
SCHULHOFF, O. - Pizzicato Polka, Op.9/2
             S.10
SCHULLER, Gunther (1925-   ), USA
   R.1   S.9,10,13,18,20
SCHULTHEISS, Benedict (1653-1693), Ger
   R.1   S.c
SCHULTHESS, Walter (1894-1971), Swiss
   R.1   S.5
SCHULTZ - Yo te amo
             S.e
SCHULTZ, Herbert
             S.c
*** SCHULTZ, Johann Christian (1582-1653) (see note)
SCHULTZ, Johannes (1582-1653), Ger
   R.1   S.c,14
SCHULTZ, Svend Simon (1913-   ), Den
   R.1   S.3-5,8,10,35,40,57
SCHULTZ, Wolfgang Andreas (1948-   )
             S.c
*** SCHULTZE, Johann Christian (1606-1683) (see note)
SCHULTZE, Johann Christoph (c1733-1813), Ger
   R.5   S.c,10
SCHULTZE, Norbert (1911-   ), Ger
   R.1   S.c
SCHULZ, Johann Abraham Peter (1747-1800), Ger
   R.1   S.c,2,5-7,10
SCHULZ, Johann Philipp Christian (1773-1827), Ger
   R.1   S.c,10
SCHULZ-EVLER, Andrei (1854-1905), Pol
   R.3   S.10
SCHULZE, Klaus (1947-   )
             S.c
SCHULZE, Richard (1928-   ), USA
   R.3   S.c
SCHUMACHER, Paul (1848-1891), Ger
   R.3   S.24
SCHUMACHER, Richard (1860-1932), Ger
   R.3   S.e
SCHUMAN, William (1910-   ), USA
   R.1   S.3-11,13,24
SCHUMANN, Camillo (1872-1946), Ger
   R.2   S.c
SCHUMANN, Clara (née Wieck) (1819-1896), Ger
   R.1   S.4,5,7-11,24,52
SCHUMANN, Valentin (16th Cent)

SCHUMANN, Walter (1913-1958), USA
   R.19   S.10,13

SCHUMMAN, Robert (1810-1856), Ger
R.1   S.c,1-11,18-28,32,33,34
SCHURMANN, Gerard (1928-   ), Eng
R.1   S.c,10,26,27
SCHUSTER, Ignaz (1813-1869), Ger
           S.c
SCHÜTKY, Franz Joseph (1817-1893), Ger
R.3   S.8,10[Schuetky]
SCHÜTT, Eduard [pseud: Henri MARLING, Arnolde CLAIRLIE]
    (1856-1933), Ger   R.3   S.c,1x,10,24
SCHÜTZ, Heinrich (1585-1672), Ger
R.1   S.c,2-11,18,24,33
SCHUURMANN, Melchert
           S.24
SCHUYT, Cornelis (1557-1616), Neth
R.1   S.8,10,14
SCHUYT, Nico (1922-   ), Neth
R.1   S.10
SCHWAB, Siegfried (20th Cent)
           S.32
SCHWAEN, Kurt (1909-   ), Ger
R.1   S.c
SCHWANTNER, Joseph (1943-   ), USA
R.19   S.10,13,24a
SCHWARTZ, Arthur (1900-   ), USA
R.1   S.9,10
SCHWARTZ, Elliott (1936-   ),USA
R.1   S.10,13,20,24
SCHWARTZ, Paul (1907-   ), Aus
R.14   S.10,13
SCHWARTZENDORF, Johann Paul Aegidius
    [see MARTINI, Johann Paul Aegidius]
SCHWARZ, Gerhard (1902-   ), Ger
R.1   S.c
SCHWARZ, Jean (1939-   )
           S.c
SCHWARZ-SCHILLING, Reinhard (1904-   ), Ger
R.14   S.c,24a
SCHWEIZER, Rolf (1936-   )
           S.c
SCHYTTE, Ludvig (1848-1909), Den
R.1   S.24
SCIAMARELLA, Valdo (1924-   ), Arg
R.26   S.10,39,46
SCIANNI, Joseph (1928-   ), USA
R.19   S.10,13
SCIARRINO, Salvatore (1947-   ), It
R.1   S.24a
SCIORTINO, Patrice (1922-   )
           S.c

SCKRONX, Gherardus [see SCRONX, Gerard]
SCMIDT, Ole (1928-   ), Den
   R.30   S.40
SCOTO - Petite toukinoise
              S.54(349)
SCOTSON-CLARK - Angels Chorus
              S.5x
SCOTT - Haere ra
              S.5x
SCOTT, Alicia Ann [see SCOTT, Lady John Douglas]
SCOTT, Clara H. (19th Cent), USA
   R.7   S.10,30
SCOTT, Cyril Meir (1879-1970), Eng
   R.1   S.c,1-10,18,21,24
SCOTT, Francis George (1880-1958), Scot
   R.1
SCOTT, James Sylvester (1886-1938), USA
   R.1   S.9,10,24a
SCOTT, Lady John Douglas (née Alicia Ann Spottiswoode)
   (1810-1900), Scot
   R.7   S.c,5x,8,10,24,52
SCOTT, Maurice
              S.10
SCOTT, Raymond - pseud [see WARNOW, Harry]
SCOTT, Thomas Jefferson (1912-1961), USA
   R.19   S.10,13
SCOTT-GATTY, Alfred (1847-1919), Eng
   R.39   S.e
SCOTTI, William (1895-   ), USA
   R.23   S.10
SCOTTO - Angelina
              S.e
SCOTTO, Girolamo (c1505-1572), It
   R.1   S.10
SCOTTO, Paolo (fl 1510), It
              S.c,10
SCOTTO, Vincent (1878-1952), Fr
   R.1   S.c,10,24a
SCOVILLE, Margaret (1944-   ), USA
   R.19   S.13,52
SCRIABIN, Alexander (1872-1915), Russia
   R.1   S.c,1-11,18,24,32
SCRIABIN, Julian (1908-1919) [sic]
              S.c
SCRONX, Gérard (17th Cent), Neth
   R.1   S.c,10,16,53
SCUDERI, Gaspari (1889-1962), It
   R.14   S.10
SCUDERI, Salvatore (1845-1927), It
   R.3   S.e

SCULL, H. - Trombones to the fore
              S.54(361)
SCULTHORPE, Peter (1929-   ), Australia
   R.1   S.c,10,24,29,37
SEALY, Helen Douglas Eng
   R.7   S.24,30
SEALY, Ray (1945-   ), Can
              S.c
SEARLE, Humphrey (1915-1982), Eng
   R.1   S.c,8-10,20
SEAVER, Blanche Ebert (1891-   ), USA
   R.19   S.10,13,52
SEBASTIAN z FELSZTYNA (c1480->1543), Pol
   R.1   S.c
SEBASTIAN, John (1915-1980), USA
   R.14   S.10,13
ŠEBOR, Karel Richard (1843-1903), Boh
   R.8   S.10

SECCHI, Antonio (1761-1833), It
   R.5   S.5x,8
SECCHI, Benedetto (1831-1883), It
   R.3   S.44
SECHTER, Simon (1788-1867), Aus
   R.1   S.c,10
SECKENDORFF, Karl Siegmund (1744-1785), Ger
   R.1   S.10,24
SECUNDA, Sholom (1894-1974), USA
   R.19   S.10,13
SEDANO (16th Cent)
              S.14
SEDANO, Carlos (?-1978)
              S.24a
SEDULIUS (c 1450)
              S.c
SEEGER, Charles Louis (1886-1979), USA
   R.19   S.24a
SEEGER, Ruth Crawford [see CRAWFORD, Ruth]
SEGARRA, Ireneu (1917-   ), Sp
   R.4
SEGER [Seeger], Joseph (1716-1782), Boh
   R.1   S.c,5x,8,10,53
SEGERSTAM, Leif (1944-   ), Fin
   R.1   S.c,9,24a,40
SEGNI, Jiulio (Giulio da Modena) (1498-1561), It
   R.1   S.c,16,53
SEGOND, Pierre (1913-   ), Swiss
   R.1   S.c
SEGOVIA, Andrés (1893-   ), Sp
   R.1   S.c,8,10,32,39

SEGOVIA, Juan de (15-16th Cent)
        S.17,53
SEHLBACH, Erich (1898-   ), Ger
  R.1   S.c
SEHLING, Josef Antonín (1710-1756), Boh
  R.1
SEIBER, Mátyás (1905-1960), Eng
  R.1   S.c,4,7,8,10,19,20,23,24a,32
SEIDEL, Jan (1908-   ), Cz
  R.1   S.4,7,8,31
SEIDLER-WINKLER, Bruno (1880-1960), Ger
  R.4   S.24
SEIFEN, Wolfgang (1956-   )
        S.c
SEIFERT, Adolf (1902-1945)
        S.c
SEIFERT, Anton
        S.10
SEIKILOS (1st Cent AD] - Epitaph
        S.5x,10
SEILER, Edward (1911-1952), USA [author]
  R.23   S.10
SEISMIT-DODA, Albano
        S.34
SEITZ, Ernest Joseph (1892-1978), Can

  R.31   S.19[Sertz],21,24
SEITZ, Friedrich (1848-1918), Ger
  R.10s   S.8,24
SEITZ, Roland Forrest (1867-1946), USA
  R.49   S.13,54(349,54)
SEIXAS, Carlos de (1704-1742), Port
  R.1   S.c,8-10,18,53
SÉJAN, Nicolas (1745-1819), Fr
  R.1   S.c
SELBY, William (?1738-1798), USA
  R.1   S.c,10,12,47
SELESSES, Jacopinus [see JACOB de SENLECHES]
SELETSKY, Harold (1927-   ), USA
  R.14   S.13
SELF, William (1906-   ), USA
        S.8,10,13
SELIG, Robert (1939-   ), USA
  R.19   S.10,13
SELLARS, G. - At the portals of the palace
        S.54(314)
SELLE, Thomas (1599-1663), Ger
  R.1   S.c
SELLENICK, Adolphe Valentin (c1816-1893), Fr
  R.49   S.54(318,40)

SELLICK - Songs of love and death (cl)
          S.20
SELMA y SALAVERDE, Bartolomé de (fl 1638), Sp
    R.1   S.c,9,10,17
SELMAR, Johan Peter (1844-1910), Nor
    R.1   S.30
SEMEGEN, Daria (1946-   ), USA
    R.19   S.10,13,24a,30,52
SEMENOFF, Ivan (1917-   ), Fr
    R.14   S.7,8,10,24
SEMENYAKO, Yuri Vladimirovich (1925-   ), USSR
    R.47   S.18
SEMENZATO, Domingo (20th Cent)
             S.c
SEMILLI, Richarde [see RICHART de SEMILLI]
SEMLER-COLLERY, Jules (1876-   ), Fr
    R.49   S.10
SEMMLER, Alexander (1900-1977), USA
    R.19   S.10,13
SEMPRINI, Albert
             S.10
SENAILLÉ, Jean Baptiste (c1688-1730), Fr
    R.1   S.c,4,5,7,8,10,18,24,54(334)
SENDT, Willy (1907-1952), Ger
    R.2   S.c
SENEDAT, Andre

SENEE, Henri
             S.10
SENFL, Ludwig (c1486-1542/43), Swiss
    R.1   S.c,3-5,7-11,14-16,24,53
SENGER, Hugo von (1832/35-1892), Ger

    R.3
SENKYR, Augustin (18th Cent)

SENLECHES, Jacob de [see JACOB de SENLECHES]
SEPP, Ilmar (1931-1958)
             S.18
SEPPILLI, Armando (1860-1931), It
    R.3   S.10
SEQUIER, Jose (1907-   )
             S.20
SEREBRIER, José (1938-   ), Uruguay
    R.1   S.10,13,39
SEREMETEV - song [S.5x]
    = SHEREMETEV, Boris Sergeyevich [?]
SERINI, Giovanni Battista (b c1710), It (see note)
    R.8   S.4,5x
SERLY, Tibor (1901-1978), USA
    R.1   S.6,7,9,10,13,24

SERMILA, Jarmo Kalevi (1939-   ), Fin
R.80   S.40
SERMISY, Claudin de (c1490-1562), Fr
R.1   S.c,2-5,7,8,10,11,14-16,24,32,53
SERNA, Eustacio de la (c1570->1616), Peru
R.1   S.10,16,53
SEROCKI, Kazimierz (1922-1981), Pol
R.1   S.c,10,18
SEROV, Alexander Nikolayevich (1820-1871), Russia
R.1   S.2,3,5x,8,10,18
SERPETTE, Gaston (1846-1904), Fr
R.1   S.e
SERRA, Joaquin (1907-   )
            S.8,10
SERRA, Luis María (1942-   ), Arg
R.26   S.46
SERRADELL SEVILLA, Narciso (1843-1910), Mex
R.22   S.5x,10,24
SERRANO REDONNET, Ana (1914-   ), Arg
R.26   S.46
SERRANO SIMEON, Jose (1873-1941), Sp
R.1   S.1x,2,3,8-10,39,42
SERRANO y BERTO, L. - Donde estás corazón? (v)

SERRANO y RUIZ, Emilio (1850-1939), Sp
R.1   S.24
SERRANO, Blas (c1770-   )
            S.8,10,39
SERRATOS, Ramon
            S.10,24
SERVAIS, Adrien François (1807-1886), Bel
R.1   S.9
SERVIN, Jean (c1530-1596), Fr
R.1   S.14,16
SESSIONS, Roger (1896-   ), USA
R.1   S.c,6-13,24
SETE, Bola - pseud [ie Djalmi de ANDRADE] (1923-   )
Brazil   R.67   S.32
SETER, Mordecai (1916-   ), Isr

R.1   S.20
ŠEVČÍK, Otakar (1852-1934), Cz
R.1   S.8,24
SÉVERAC, Déodat de (1872-1921), Fr
R.1   S.c,1-8,10
SEVERI, Francesco (d.1630), It
R.1   S.c
SEVERO di LUCA, Antonio [see LUCA, Severo di]
SEYBOLD, Arthur (1868-1948), Ger
R.2   S.c,24a

SEYDLER, Anton
        S.e
SEYFERT, Johann Caspar (?1697-1767), Ger
  R.1   S.10
SEYFRIED, Erhard

SEYMER, John William (1890-1964), Sweden
  R.14   S.c,5x,56
SGAMBATI, Giovanni (1841-1914), It
  R.1   S.c,2,3,5x,9,10,18,24
SGRIZZI, Luciano (1910-   ), It
  R.1   S.9
SHACKLEFORD, Rudolph Owens (1944-   ), USA
  R.19   S.10,13
SHADWELL, Nancy (20th Cent), USA
        S.10,13,30,52
SHAFFER, Sherwood (1934-   ), USA
  R.19   S.13
SHAHAN, Paul (1923-   ), USA
  R.19   S.10,13
SHAIMARDANOVA, Shakhida (1938-   ), USSR
  R.7   S.18,52
SHAKHIDY, Ziyadullo (1914-   ), USSR
  R.14   S.18
SHAKHOBOV, Fazlitdin (1911-   )
        S.18
SHALITT - Eili Eili
        S.5x
SHALLENBERG, Robert (1930-   ), USA
  R.14   S.10,13
SHAMO, Igor Naumovich (1925-   ), USSR
  R.14   S.18,24
SHAND, Ernest (1868-1924), Eng
  R.106   S.10
SHANKAR, Ravi (1920-   ), India
  R.1   S.c,9,10,24
SHANNON, James Royce (1881-1946), USA
  R.23   S.10,24
SHANTYR, Grigori Alexandrovich (1923-   ), USSR
  R.14   S.18
SHAPERO, Harold (1920-   ), USA
  R.1   S.7-10,13
SHAPEY, Ralph (1921-   ), USA
  R.1   S.9,10,13,24
SHAPIRO, Solomon Borisovich (1909-1967)
        S.18
SHAPLEIGH, Bertram Lincoln (1871-1940), USA
  R.19   S.13,24a
SHAPORIN, Yury Alexandrovich (1887-1966), Russia
  R.1   S.5,7,8,10,18,42

SHAPOSHNIKOV, Adrian Grigoryevich (1887/88-1967), Russia
R.1   S.7,8,10,18
SHAPOSHNIKOV, Ilya Kalustovich (1896-1953), USSR
R.14   S.18
SHARKEZY, Istvan (1920-   )
             S.18
SHARLIN, William (1920-   ), USA
R.19   S.13
SHARPE, Anna Wright (1914-   ), USA
R.7   S.24,30
SHARPE, Evelyn
             S.e
SHARPE, Herbert Francis (1861-   ), Eng
R.39   S.e
SHASHINA, Elizaveta Sergeyevna (19th Cent), Russia
             S.10,18,52a
SHATIN, Judith Allen (1949-   ), USA
R.19   S.52 [Allen]
SHATTUCK, Charles F.
             S.e
SHAUAN, Aziz el (1916-   )
             S.18
SHAUGHNESSY, Robert Michael (1925-   ), USA
R.19   S.10,13,24a
SHAVERZASHVILI, Alexander Vasilyevich (1919-   ), USSR
R.14   S.18,24
SHAW, Christopher (1924-   ), Eng
R.1   S.c,10
SHAW, Clifford (1911-1976), USA
R.19   S.10,13
SHAW, David T. (fl 1814), USA
R.53   S.10,54(351)
SHAW, Geoffrey (1911-   ), Eng
             S.c
SHAW, Geoffrey Turton (1879-1943), Eng
R.4
SHAW, Martin (1875-1958), Eng
R.1   S.c,5x,10
SHAW, Oliver (1779-1848), USA
R.1   S.10,47
SHCHEDRIN, Rodion Konstantinovich (1932-   ), USSR
R.1   S.9,10,18,24
SHCHERBACHOV, Vladimir Vladimirovich (1889-1952), Russia
R.1   S.10,18
SHEA, M. - Notre Dame victory march
             S.54(345,63)
SHEBALIN, Vissarion Yakovlevich (1902-1963), Russia
R.1   S.10,18,24
SHEELES, John (1688-1761), Eng
R.5   S.c

SHEFTER, Bert Abram (1904-   ), USA
   R.23   S.10
SHEIBLER, Truvor Karlovich (1900-1960), USSR
   R.14
SHEINFELD, David (1906-   ), USA
   R.19   S.10,13
SHEKHTER, Boris Semyonovich (1900-1961), Russia
   R.1   S.18

SHELBYE, William (d >1561), Eng
   R.1   S.10,16,53
SHELDON, Earl (1915-1977), USA
   R.23   S.13
SHELLEY, Harry Rowe (1858-1947), USA
   R.8   S.10-12
SHELTON, James H. (1912-1975), USA
   R.23   S.9
SHENDEREV, Georgi Grigorevich (1937-   )
              S.18
SHEPARD, R. N. ?USA - Shepard's tones (electronic)
              S.10,13
SHEPHERD, Arthur (1880-1958), USA
   R.1   S.7,9,10,12,13
SHEPPARD, John (c1515-c1559/60), Eng
   R.1   S.c,10,14-16
SHER, Veniamin Josifovich (1900-1962)
              S.18,24
SHERARD, James (1666-1738), Eng
   R.1
SHEREMETIEV, Alexander Dmitriyevich (1859-1931), Russia
   R.47   S.11   (see note)
SHEREMETIEV, Boris Sergeyevich (1822-1906)
              S.10,18,5x[Seremetev]
SHERIFF, Noam (1935-   ), Isr
   R.1   S.c
SHERLAW JOHNSON, Robert [see JOHNSON, Robert Sherlaw]
SHERLY, Joseph (fl 1621), Eng
   R.1   S.c
SHERMAN, Allan (1924-1974)
   R.23
SHERMAN, Robert William (1921-   ), USA
   R.19   S.10,13
SHERWIN, William Fisk (1826-1888), USA
   R.53   S.10
SHERYNGHAM, (fl c1500) Eng
   R.1   S.c
SHEVCHENKO, Viktor Vladimirovich (1936-   )
              S.5x,18
SHIBATA, Minao (1916-   ), Japan
   R.1   S.50

SHIBUYA, Takucho (1930-   ), Japan
    R.36   S.50
SHIELD, William (1748-1829), Eng
    R.1   S.c,9,10,25,27
SHIELDS, Alice Ferree (1943-   ), USA
    R.7   S.10,13,30,52
SHIELDS, Ren (1868-1913), USA
    R.23   S.10
SHIFRIN, Lalo
                S.10
SHIFRIN, Seymour (1926-1979), USA
    R.1   S.c,10,13,24
SHILKRET, Jack (1896-1964), USA
    R.8   S.10
SHILKRET, Nathaniel (1895-   ), USA

    R.19   S.10,13,24a
SHILOVSKY, Konstantin Stepanovich (1849-1893)
                S.18
SHIMANOVSKY, Karol [S.18] = SZYMANOWSKI, Carol
SHIMIZU, Osamu (1911-   ), Japan
    R.1   S.50
SHIMKUS, Stasis (1887-1943), USSR
    R.47   S.18,24a
SHIMONOVSKAYA, M. [S.18] = SZYMANOWSKA, Maria Agata
SHIMOYAMA, Hifumi (1930-   ), Japan
    R.4   S.50
SHINOHARA, Makoto (1931-   ), Tokyo
    R.1   S.c,50
SHIRLEY, Lilian - pseud [see WRIGHT, Lawrence]
SHIROKOV, Vyacheslav Nikolayevich
                S.18
SHISHAKOV, Yuri Nikolayevich (1925-   ), USSR
    R.14   S.10
SHISHIDO, Matsuo (1929-   ), Japan
    R.4   S.50
SHISHOV, Ivan Petrovich (1888-1947), USSR
    R.14   S.18
SHLETSER, I. - Concert étude for p, Op.1/2
                S.18
SHNITKE, Alfred Garriyevich (1934-   ), USSR
    R.1   S.c,18,24
SHNORALY, N. - Song of sunrise
                S.24a
SHOEMAKER, Maurice (1890-   )

SHORT, Thomas V. (1856-1931)

SHOSTAKOVICH, Dmitriy (1906-1975), Russia
    R.1   S.c,2-11,18,20,24

SHREINER - Waltz (cl)
        S.20
SHTEYNBERG [Steinberg], Maximilian Oseyevich (1883-1946)
    Russia   R.1   S.4,18
SHTOGARENKO, Andriy Yakovlevich (1902-   ), Ukraine
    R.1   S.18,24
SHUBANOV, A. - Aria (vi & p)
        S.24
SHUBAYEV - Romance (vi & p)
        S.24
SHULMAN, Alan (1915-   ), USA
    R.19   S.10,13,24
SHUMWAY, Nehemiah (fl 1793), USA
    R.53   S.47
SHURE, Ralph Deane (1885-   ), USA
    R.19   S.10,13
SHVARTSMAN, Izrail Abramovich (1924-   )
        S.18
SHVEDOV, Konstatin Nikolaievich (1886-   ), USSR
    R.14   S.10
SHYARNAS, Tadas (1933-   )
        S.18

SIBBING, Robert (1929-   ), USA
    R.19   S.13
SIBELIUS, Jean (1865-1957), Fin
    R.1   S.c,1-11,18,24,26-28,40,43,54(326)
SIBELLA, Gabriele
        S.10
SICART MARJEVOLS, Bernart (13th Cent)
        S.c
SICHER, Fridolin (1490-1546), Swiss
    R.1   S.c,10,11,16,53
SICHINSKY, Denis Vladimirovich (1865-1909), Russia
    R.47   S.18
SICILIANI, Jose (1910-   ), Arg
        S.8,10
SIDELNIKOV, Nikolay Nikolayevich (1930-   ), USSR
    R.1   S.18
SIEBENKÄS, Johann (1714-1781), Ger
    R.1   S.c
SIEBERT, Edrich - pseud [ie Stanley Smith MASTERS]
    (1903-   ), Eng
    R.85   S.54(348,50,59,60,64),55
SIECZYNSKY, Rudolf (1879-1952), Aus
    R.4   S.c,5x,10,24
SIEDE - Lippe Detmold Marsch
        S.54(338)
SIEFERT [Sivert], Paul (1586-1666), Ger
    R.1   S.c,10,53

SIEGEL, Paul (1914-   ), USA
   R.14   S.7,10,13
SIEGEN - New Year greetings
             S.54(345)
SIEGL, Otto, (1896-1978), Aus
   R.1   S.c
SIEGMEISTER, Elie (1909-   ), USA
   R.1   S.3-5,8-10,13,20,24
SIEMONEIT, Hans Rudolf (1927-   ), Ger
   R.4   S.c
SIENNICKI, Edmund John (1920-   ), Ger
   R.23   S.20,21
SIEPRAVSKI, Pavel (c1780)
             S.c
SIESS, Johannes (d ?<1534), Ger
   R.1   S.10,16
SIESSMAYR, Herkulan (1761-1832)
             S.c
SIFLER, Paul J. (1911-   ), USA
   R.19   S.c,9,10,13
SIGEFRID, Cornelius (c1550-c1605), Ger
   R.1   S.16
SIGNAC (<1600->1630), Fr
   R.1   S.14,16
SIGNORELLI, Frank (1901-   ), USA
   R.23   S.10
SIGTENHORST-MEYER, Bernhard van den (1888-1953), Neth
   R.1   S.10
SIGURBJÖRNSSON, Thorkell (1938-   ), Iceland
   R.1   S.40
SIKHRA, Andrey Osipovich (c1773-1850), Russia
   R.1   S.c
SIKORA, Elzbieta (1945-   ), Pol
   R.7   S.c,52
SIKORSKI, Kazimierz (1895-   ), Pol
   R.1
SIKORSKI, Klement (1910-   )
             S.20
SIKORSKI, Tomasz (1939-   ), Pol
   R.1
SILBERMAN, Benedict (1901-1971), Neth
   R.25
SILBERTA, Rhea (1900-1959), USA
   R.7   S.e
SILCHER, Friedrich (1789-1860), Ger
   R.1   S.c,1x,4,5x,9,10,19
SILÉSU, Lao (1883-1953), It
   R.8   S.10,24
SILSBEE, Ann L. (1930-   ), USA
   R.7   S.52

SILVA PEREIRA, Antonio Claudio da (18th Cent)
          S.10
SILVA TEIXEIRA - The duck (O pato)
          S.32
SILVA, David Poll da (1834-1875), Fr
   R.3   S.5x,10
SILVA, Francisco Manuel da (1795-1865), Brazil
   R.1   S.39
SILVA, Giulio (1875-   ), USA
   R.14   S.7,9
SILVA, João Cordeiro da (c1735-c1808), Port
   R.1   S.8,10
SILVANSKY, Nikolai Joslovich (1915-   )
          S.18
SILVER, Charles (1868-1949), Fr
   R.4
SILVERI - Senza te (v - Beniamino Gigli)
          S.10
SILVERMAN, Faye-Ellen (1947-   ), USA
   R.7   S.52
SILVERMAN, Stanley (1938-   ), USA
   R.19   S.9,10,13
SILVERS, Louis (1889-1954), USA
   R.23   S.10
SILVESTRI, Giuseppe (1841-1921), It
   R.10   S.5x,24
SILVESTROV, Valentin Vasilyevich (1937-   ), USSR
   R.1
SIMAI, Pavol (1930-   ), Cz
          S.31
SIMBRACKY, Jan [see SCHIMBRACZKY, Johannes]
SIMBRIGER, Heinrich (1903-   )
          S.c,24
SIMM, Yuhan Janovich (1885-1959), Est
   R.4   S.18
SIMMES, William (fl 1607-16), Eng

   R.1   S.c,10,16
SIMON, Anton (1850-1916), Fr
   R.1   S.c,10,24
SIMON, Frank (1889-1967), USA
   R.49   S.10,13,54(366)
SIMON, Hermann (1896-1948), Ger
   R.4   S.c
SIMON, Johann Kaspar (1701-1776), Ger
   R.1   S.c,5x,6-8,10
SIMON, Louise Marie [see ARRIEU, Claude - pseud]
SIMON, Nat (1900-1979), USA
   R.23   S.10
SIMON, Rudolf
          S.e

SIMON, Simon (?c1735->1780), Fr
R.1   S.c
SIMON, W. - Kurfurst
             S.54(336)
SIMONDS, Bruce (1895-   ), USA
R.19   S.8,10,12,13
SIMONELLI, Matteo (>1618-1696), It
R.1   S.c,10
SIMONETI, Achille (1857-1928), It
R.1   S.4,5x,24
SIMONIS, Jean-Marie (1931-   ), Bel
R.4   S.c
SIMONS, Gardell
             S.10,13
SIMONS, Moisés (1888-1944) Cuba
R.56   S.10,24
SIMONS, Netty (1913-   ), USA
R.19   S.9,10,13,30,52
SIMOVICH, Roman Apollonovich (1901-   ), USSR
R.14   S.18
SIMPSON - One little dream of love
             S.e
SIMPSON, Christopher (c1605-1669), Eng
R.1   S.c,2,3,5x
SIMPSON, Dudley USA
             S.13
SIMPSON, Nellie
             S.e
SIMPSON, Robert (1921-   ), Eng
R.1   S.c,9,19
SIMPSON, Thomas (1582->1630), Eng
R.1   S.c,10,16
SIMS, Albert Ernest - March of the R.A.F. Association
R.49,77   S.5x
SIMS, Ezra (1928-   ), USA
R.1   S.10,13
SIMSON, Harold Fraser [see FRASER-SIMSON, Harold]
SINATRA, Ray (1904-1980), USA
R.19   S.10
SINCLAIR, John (1790-1857), Eng
R.44   S.47
SINDICI, Orestes (1837-1904), Colombia
R.56(vol.1,p.227)   S.54(332)

SINDING, Christian (1856-1941), Nor
R.1   S.c,1-8,10,11,18,24
SINGELÉE, Jean Baptiste (1812-1875), Bel
R.25   S.24
SINGER, Andre (1907-   ), USA
R.19   S.13

SINGER, Lawrence (1940-   ), USA
          S.13
SINGER, Louis C. (1912-1966), USA
    R.23   S.10
SINIGAGLIA, Leone (1868-1944), It
    R.1   S.c,1x,4,5,8,24
SINISALO, Helmer-Rayner (1920-   ), USSR
    R.1   S.18
SINK, Kuldar (1942-   ), Est
    R.1   S.18,24a
SINOPOLI, Antonio (1878-   ), Arg
              S.10,32,39
SINOPOLI, Giuseppe (1946-   ), It
    R.1
SIOLY, Johann (1843-1911), Aus
    R.3   S.c
SIPILÄ, Eero (1918-1972), Fin
    R.1   S.40
SIQUEIRA, Baptista (1906-   ), Brazil
    R.4   S.24a
SIQUEIRA, José (1907-   ), Brazil
    R.1   S.8,24a
SIRERA
              S.5x,32
SIRET, Nicholas (1663-1754), Fr
    R.1   S.8,10
SIROONI, Alice (20th Cent), USA
    R.7   S.30
SITSKY, Larry (1934-   ), Australia
    R.1   S.c,29
SITT, Hans (1850-1922), Boh
    R.1   S.c,10,24
SITTARD, Alfred (1878-1942), Ger
    R.4   S.1x
SIVERT, Paulus [see SIEFERT, Paul]
SIVORI, Camillo (1815-1894), It
    R.1   S.24
SIZOV, Nikolai Ivanovich (1886-1962), USSR
    R.47   S.18
SJAPORIN, Jurig [see SHAPORIN, Yury]
SJÖBERG, Birger (1885-1929), Sweden
    R.30   S.33
SJÖBERG, Carl (1861-1900), Sweden
    R.30   S.c,24,43,56
SJÖBERG, Svante Leonard (1873-1935), Sweden
    R.4   S.1x,5x,10
SJÖGREN, Emil (1853-1918), Sweden
    R.1   S.4-7,10,24,40,43,56
SKALKOTTAS, Nikolaos (1904-1949), Greece
    R.1   S.c,8-10,24

SKELLY, Alan (fl 1954), USA
          S.10,13
SKELLY, Joseph P. (c1853-1895)
    R.200   S.10
ŠKERJANC, Lucijan Marija (1900-1973), Yug
    R.1   S.c
SKILES - Cyrano de Bergerac
          S.5x
SKILTON, Charles Sanford (1868-1941), USA
    R.1   S.4,5x,8,11,13
SKINNER - Amsterdam Kongress
          S.54(313)
SKINNER, C. - Let songs abound
          S.54(337)
SKOLAUDE, Walter (1919-   )

SKÖLD, Bengt-Goran (1936-   )
          S.c
SKÖLD, Sven (1899-1956), Sweden
    R.14   S.c,5x,24
SKORIK, Miroslav Mikhailovich (1938-   ), USSR
    R.47   S.c,18,24a
SKORNICKA, Joseph E. (1902-   ), USA
    R.19   S.54(334,48)
SKORULSKY, Mikhail Adamovich (1887-1950), USSR
    R.14   S.18
SKORZENY, Fritz (1900-1965), Aus
    R.14   S.24
SKOUEN, Synne (1950-   ), Nor
    R.7   S.52
SKRIVAN, H. - Czechs are fine people
          S.5x
SKRIVANEK, Tomas (18th Cent)

ŠKROUP, František Jan (1801-1862), Cz
    R.1   S.1x,4,6,24
ŠKROUP, Jan Nepomuk (1811-1892), Boh
    R.1   S.5x
SKROWACZEWSKI, Stanislaw (1923-   ), USA
    R.1   S.10,13
SKULTE, Adolfs (1909-   ), Lat
    R.1   S.18,24
ŠKVOR, František (1898-   ), Cz
    R.14   S.5x,31
SLATER, David Dick (1869-1942), Can
    R.31   S.e
SLATER, Edward [pseud: Odoardo BARRI] (1844-1920)
    R.200   S.e
SLATER, Gordon Archibald (1896-1979), Eng
    R.37   S.c

SLAUGHTER, A. Walter (1860-1908), Eng
R.3   S.e
SLAVENSKI, Josip (1896-1955), Yug
R.1   S.8,9,24
SLAVICKÝ, Klement (1910-   ), Cz
R.1   S.5x,8,18,20,24,31
SLAVÍK, Jósef (1806-1833), Cz
R.1   S.c,4,5,24
SLAVINSKY, Yevgeni Vikentevich (1897-   )
           S.18
SLAWSON, Wayne (1932-   ), USA
R.19   S.10,13
SLOGEDAL, Bjarne (1927-   ), Nor

SLONIMSKY, Nicolas (1894-   ), USA
R.1   S.9,13
SLONIMSKY, Sergey Mikhaylovich (1932-   ), USSR
R.1   S.18,23
SLONOV, Mikhail Akimovich (1869-1930), USSR
R.47   S.18
SLUKA, Luboš (1928-   ), Cz
R.14   S.c,24a,31
SLY, Allan Bernard (1907-   ), Eng/USA [?]
R.37   S.13
SMALLEY, Denis Arthur (1946-   ), New Zealand
R.80   S.c
SMALLS, Charlie
           S.9
SMAREGLIA, Antonio (1854-1929), It
R.1
SMART, George (1776-1867), Eng
R.1   S.c
SMART, Henry Thomas (1813-1879), Eng
R.1   S.c
SMATEK, Miloš (1895-   ), Cz
R.14   S.31
SMERT, Richard (fl 1428-77), Eng
R.1   S.10,14,16
SMETÁČEK, Václav (1906-   ), Cz
R.1   S.5x[Smetacek, R.],31
SMETANA, Bedřich (1824-1884), Cz
R.1   S.c,1-11,18,24,42,54(314)
SMILEY, Pril (1943-   ), USA
R.19   S.c,10,13,30,52
SMIRNOV, I. - Bogorodice vsech carice
           S.c
SMIRNOV, Kuma Alexeyevich (1917-1963), USSR
R.47   S.18
SMIRNOV, L. (1932-   )
           S.24a

SMIRNOV, Mikhail Dmitrievich (1929-   )
            S.18
SMIRNOVA, T. - Sonata Poem (vi & p)
            S.24a
SMIRNOVA SOLODCHENKOVA, Tatiana Georgievna (1940-   )
   USSR   R.7 S.52
SMIT, Leo (1900-1943), Neth
   R.1   S.4,10,13
SMITH (19th Cent), USA - Home quickstep

SMITH BRINDLE, Reginald (1917-   ), Eng
   R.1   S.c,10,32
SMITH, Alice Mary (1839-1884), Eng
   R.1   S.10,30,52
SMITH, C. W. - When my dear lady sleeps
            S.e,54(356)
SMITH, C. R. - Secrets (v)
            S.10
SMITH, Chris (1879-1949), USA [?]
   R.23   S.10
SMITH, Claude T. (1932-   ), USA
   R.19   S.13
SMITH, Clay (1877-1930), USA
   R.23
SMITH, Edwin - pseud [see BEHR, Franz]
SMITH, F. S. Breville
            S.e
SMITH, George M. (1912-   ), USA
   R.23
SMITH, Glenn - Mood music
            S.22
SMITH, Gregg (1931-   ), USA
   R.19   S.9,13
SMITH, Hale (1925-   ), USA
   R.1   S.10,13,28
SMITH, John Christopher (1712-1795), Ger
   R.1   S.c,3,5,7,10,11
SMITH, John Stafford (1750-1836), Eng
   R.1   S.10
SMITH, Julia (1911-   ), USA
   R.1   S.9,10,13,30,52
SMITH, Kenneth Leslie
            S.c,24
SMITH, Ladonna Carol (1951-   ), USA
   R.7   S.30,52
SMITH, Leland (1925-   ), USA
   R.1   S.10,13,24
SMITH, Leo (1881-1952), Can
   R.4

SMITH, Leonard Bingley (1915-   ), USA
  R.23   S.54(315,24,30)
SMITH, Margit (20th Cent), USA
               S.30,52
SMITH, Paul Joseph (1906-   ), USA
  R.23   S.9
SMITH, Peter Melville (1943-   )
               S.c
SMITH, Richard Burney ?USA
               S.12,13
SMITH, Robert (c1648-c1675), Eng
  R.1   S.5x,7,10
SMITH, Russell (1927-   ), USA
  R.19   S.7,8,10,13,23
SMITH, Stuart (1948-   ), USA
  R.19   S.13
SMITH, Sydney (1839-1889), Eng
  R.1   S.c,10
SMITH, Walter (1887-   )
               S.24
SMITH, Walter Milton (1890-1937)

SMITH, William [see MACKENZIE, Gordon - pseud]
SMITH, William (1603-1645), Eng
  R.1   S.16
SMITH, William (1924-   )

SMITH, William O. (1926-   ), USA
  R.1   S.9,10,13,19-21,24
SMOKER, Paul, USA
               S.10,13
SMOLENSKY, Stepan Vasilyevich (1848-1909), Russia
  R.1   S.c,10
SMOLKA, Jaroslav (1933-   ), Cz
  R.1
SMOLSKY, Dmitri Bronislavovich (1937-   ), USSR
  R.47   S.18
SMYTH, Ethel (1858-1944), Eng
  R.1   S.c,3,5,11,30,52
SMYTH, William (c1550-1600) - Preces and responses
  = SMITH, William (1603-1645) (see note)
SMYTHE, Thomas (16-17th Cent), Eng
               S.c
SNOW, David Jason (1954-   ), USA
  R.19   S.13
SNYDER, Ted (1881-1965), USA
  R.23   S.10
SOBRINHO, Salles F.
               S.1x

SOCOR, Matei (1908-   ), Rum
  R.33   S.24a
SODDU, U. - La madre e il figlio (cantata)
          S.4
SÖDERBERG, Wilhelm Theodor (1845-1922), Sweden
  R.111   S.e
SÖDERHOLM, Vlademar (1909-   ), Sweden
  R.14   S.c,10,56
SODERINI, Agostino (16-17th Cent), It
  R.1   S.16,53
SØDERLIND, Ragnar (1945-   ), Nor
  R.14   S.c,40,51
SÖDERLUNDH, Bror Axel (Lille Bror) (1912-1957), Sweden
  R.14   S.10,40,56
SÖDERMAN, Johann August (1832-1876), Sweden
  R.1   S.c,4,5,8,24,43,56
SÖDERSTEN, Gunno (1920-   ), Sweden
  R.14   S.40,56
SOHN - Erzherzog-Albrecht Marsch
         S.10
SOJO, Vicente Emilio (1887-1974), Ven
  R.1   S.c,10,32
SOKALSKY, Pyotr Petrovich (1832-1887), Ukraine
  R.1   S.18
SOKOL, Thomas (1929-   ), USA
         S.13
SOKOLA, Miloš (1913-1976), Cz
  R.1   S.31
SOKOLOV, Nikolay Alexandrovich (1859-1922), Russia
  R.1   S.18
SOKOLOV, Vladimir Timofeyevich (1830-1890)
         S.18
SOKOLOVSKY, Nestor Fedorovich (1902-1950)
         S.18
SOLA, Andrés de (1634-1696), Sp
  R.1   S.c,10,53
SOLAGE, (fl 1370-90), Fr
  R.1   S.c,10,16
SOLAL, Martial (1927-   ), Fr
  R.1   S.c
SOLER, Antonio (1729-1783), Sp
  R.1   S.c,2-6,9-11,18,24,32,39
SOLER, José (1935-   ), Sp
  R.1   S.c,10
SOLIVA, Carlo Evasio (1792-1851), It
  R.1
SOLLBERGER, Harvey (1938-   ), USA (see note)
  R.1   S.10,13,24a
SOLMAN, Alfred (1868-1937), USA
  R.23   S.10

SOLODUKHO, Yakov Semenovich (1911-   ), USSR
  R.14   S.18
SOLOMON, Mirrie Irma (Mirrie Irma Hill) (1892/93-   )
  Australia R.7   S.52
SOLOVYOV, Dimitri
          S.c
SOLOVYOV-SEDOY, Vasily Pavlovich (1907-1979), Russia
  R.1   S.10,18
SOLTANS, N. - Trinklied
          S.e
SOLWAY, Maurice (1908-   )
          S.24a
SOMERS, D. - Savoy hunting medley
          S.54(354)
SOMERS, Harry Stuart (1925-   ), Can
  R.1   S.10,24
SOMERSET, Henry Richard Charles (1849-1932), Eng
  R.10s,44   S.e   (see note)
SOMERVELL, Arthur (1863-1937), Eng
  R.1   S.c,4-6
SOMERVILLE, Stephen

SOMIS, Giovanni Battista (1686-1763), It
  R.1   S.8
SOMMA, Bonaventura (1893-1960), It
  R.14   S.4,5x

SOMMER - Jugend; Ganz leise
          S.e
SOMMER, Johann (d.1627), Ger
  R.1   S.c,10,16
SOMMER, Vladimír (1921-   ), Cz
  R.1   S.10,24,31
SOMMERFELDT, Øistein (1919-   ), Nor
  R.14   S.c,40,51
SOMMERLATTE, Ulrich [pseud Oliver STAAL] (1914-   ), Ger
  R.4   S.c
SOMMERVILLE - When spring returns
          S.e
SONDHEIM, Stephen (1930-   ), USA
  R.1   S.9,10
SONNINEN, Ahti (1914-   ), Fin
  R.1   S.8,10,40
SONNTAG, Gottfried (1846-1921), Ger
  R.3   S.10
SØNSTEVOLD, Gunnar (1912-   ), Nor
  R.1   S.40,51
SØNSTEVOLD, Maj (1917-   ), Nor
  R.7,38   S.40,51,52
SOPHRONIUS, Patriarch of Jerusalem (c560-c638)
          S.c,16

SOPRONI, József (1930-   ), Hun
   R.1   S.9,10,24
SOR, Fernando (1778-1839), Sp
   R.1   S.c,1x,4-11,18,32,39
SORABJI, Kaikhosru Shapurji [Leon DUDLEY] (1892-   )
   Eng R.1   S.c
SORBI, J. B. [see SOURSBY]
SÖRENSON, Torsten Napoleon (1908-   ), Sweden
   R.14   S.c,40,56
SORGE, Georg Andreas (1703-1778), Ger
   R.1   S.c,10,53
SORIANO, Alberto (1915-   ), Uruguay
   R.14   S.24a
SORIANO, Francesco (1548/49-1621), It
   R.1   S.c,8,14,16
SORIANO, Perez [see PEREZ SORIANO, Augustin]
SORO BARRIGA, Enrique (1884-1954), Chile
   R.1   S.8,10,24
SOROZABAL, Pablo (1887-   ), Sp
   R.4
SORTES (fl 14th Cent)

SOSTOA, Padre Manuel de (b.1749), Sp
   R.104   S.c
SOTHCOTT, John
             S.c,10
SOTO de LANGA, Francisco (1534-1619), Sp (see note)
   R.1   S.c,10,15,16,39,53
*** SOTO de LANGA, Pedro Francisco (1534-1619) (see note)
SOTO, Francisco de (c1500-1563), Sp (see note)
   R.8
SOTO, Pedro de (fl 1591), Sp (see note)
             S.10,53

SOUCI - A rose, a kiss
             S.44
SOULIAERT, Carolus (16th Cent), Neth
   R.5   S.c,16
SOURIS, André (1890-1970), Bel
   R.1   S.23,24
SOURSBY [Sourbi] (fl 1430-60), Eng
   R.1   S.24
SOUSA CARVALHO, João de [see CARVALHO, João de Sousa]
SOUSA, John Philip (1854-1932), USA
   R.1   S.c,2-4,5x,9-11,21,54
SOUSA, Oswaldo
             S.10
SOUSTER, Tim (1943-   ), Eng
   R.1   S.c
SOUTHAM, Ann (1937-   ), Can
   R.7   S.24a,30,52

SOUTHAM, T. W. (1900-   ), Eng
        S.c
SOUTHERS, Leroy William (1941-   ), USA
  R.19   S.12,13
SOUTHGATE, Dorothy (1889-1946), Eng
  R.7   S.24,30
SOUTHGATE, E. D. - The butterfly (vi & org)
        S.24
SOUTHGATE, Elsie Eng
  R.7   S.24,30
SOUTHGATE, F. S. - Dance of the elves; Pleading;
  Rêve d´amour (vi & org)   S.24
SOUTHGATE, S. - Inspiration (vi & org)
        S.24
SOUTULLO, Reveriano (1884-1932), Sp
  R.200   S.c,8-10
SOWA, Jakub (d.1600)
        S.c,16
SOWANDE, Fela (1905-   ), Nigeria
  R.1   S.c,9,10
SOWERBY, Leo (1895-1968), USA
  R.1   S.c,2-5,7-13,23
SPADI, Giovanni Battista (17th Cent), It
  R.8   S.c
SPALDING, Albert (1888-1953), USA
  R.19   S.2,3,5x,13,24
SPARROW, Frederick W.
        S.e
SPEAIGHT, Joseph (1868-1947), Eng
  R.37   S.1x
SPEAKS, Oley (1874-1948), USA
  R.19   S.5x,9,10,24,43
SPECHTSART, Hugo (c1285-1359/60), Ger
  R.1
SPEER, Daniel (1636-1707), Ger
  R.1   S.c,5x,9,10,18
SPEETH, S.D. ?USA - Theme & variations (electronic)
        S.10,13
SPEKTOR, Mira J. (20th Cent), USA
        S.52

SPELMAN, Timothy (1891-1970), USA
  R.1   S.8,9,13
SPENA, Lita (1904-   ), Arg
  R.26   S.46
SPENCER - Me neenyah
        S.e
SPENCER, Herbert (1878-1944), USA
  R.23   S.24
SPENCER, Willamette (1932-   ), USA
  R.7   S.30,52

SPENDIARYAN, Alexander Afanasii (1871-1928), Arm
   R.1   S.10,18,24
SPERANZA, Alessandro (c1728-1797), It
   R.1
SPERATUS, Julius

SPERGER, Johannes [?Matthias] (1750-1812), Ger
   R.1   S.c,10
SPERONTES [Johann Sigismond SCHOLZE] (1705-1750), Ger
   R.1   S.c
SPERVOGEL (12-13th Cent), Ger
   R.1   S.c
SPETH, Johannes (1664-c1720), Ger
   R.1   S.c,10,53
SPEUY, Henderick (c1575-1625), Neth
   R.1   S.c,10,16,53
SPIEGEL, Laurie (1945-   ), USA
   R.19   S.13,30,52
SPIEGELMAN, Joel (1933-   ), USA
   R.19   S.10,13
SPIER, Larry (1901-1956), USA
   R.23   S.24
SPIES, Claudio (1925-   ), USA
   R.1   S.10,13
SPIES, Ernst (fl 1884)
   R.200   S.24
SPIESS, Meinrad (1683-1761), Ger
   R.1   S.c
SPILKA - Koupim ja si (I will buy)
            S.1x
SPILLING, Willy (1909-1965), Ger
   R.4   S.c
SPILLMAN, Robert (1935-   ), USA
            S.13
SPILMAN, J. E. - Flow gently sweet Afton
            S.e
SPINACINO, Francesco (fl 1507), It
   R.1   S.5x,10,14,16,32
SPINAROVA, Vera (20th Cent), Cz
            S.52
SPINDLER, Fritz (1817-1905), Ger
   R.3
SPIRIDION (1615-1685), Ger
   R.1   S.c
SPISAK, Michal (1914-1965), Pol
   R.1   S.c,18
SPITZMÜLLER, Alexander (1894-1962), Aus
   R.1   S.5x,8
SPOFFORTH, Reginald (1768/70-1827), Eng
   R.1   S.c,10

SPOHR, Louis (1784-1859), Ger
    R.1   S.c,2-5,7-11,18-21,24,54(330)
SPOLIANSKY, Mischa (1898-   ), Ger
    R.4   S.c,10,24
SPONTINI, Gasparo (1774-1851), It
    R.1   S.c,1-10,28,42
SPRATLAN, Lewis (1940-   ), USA
    R.19   S.10,13
SPRONGL, Norbert (1892-1983), Aus
    R.14   S.c,10,24a
SPROSS, Charles Gilbert (1876-1961), USA
    R.19   S.5x,10,13
SQUIRE, Hope (19th Cent), Eng
               S.52
SQUIRE, William Henry (1871-1963), Eng
    R.1   S.c,5x,10,24
ŠRÁMEK, Vladimir (1923-   ), Cz
    R.14
SREBOTNJAK, Alojz (1931-   ), Yug
    R.4
SRNKA, Jiří (1907-1982), Cz
    R.14   S.24,31
ŚROM, Karel (1904-   ), Cz
    R.1   S.31
STAAL, Oliver - pseud [see SOMMERLATTE, Ulrich]
STABILE, Annibale (c1535-1595), It
    R.1   S.c,16
STACEY - Adieu
               S.e
STACHOWICZ, Damian (1658-1699), Pol
    R.1   S.c
STACHOWICZ, Damian (d.1729)
    = ?TORZYNSKI, Damian (1673-1729) (see note)
STADEN, Johann (1581-1634), Ger
    R.1   S.c,10,15,16,24
STADEN, Sigmund Theophil (1607-1655), Ger
    R.1   S.c
STADLER, Anton (1753-1812), Aus
    R.1   S.c,10
STADLER, Maximilian (1748-1833), Aus
    R.1   S.c
STADLMAIR, Hans (1929-   )
               S.c,24
STADLMAYR, Johann (c1575-1648), Ger
    R.1   S.16
STAEMPFLI, Edward (1908-   ), Swiss
    R.1
STAES, Godefroid (18th Cent)
    R.5   S.c,24a
STAFFORD, Frank - pseud [see LUBBE, Kurt]

STAHEL, Johann (16th Cent), Ger
  R.1   S.10,14
STAHLBERY, Heinz
          S.24a
STAHMER, Klaus Hinrich (1941-   )
          S.c
STAHULJAK, Juraj (1901-   ), Yug
  R.14   S.24a
STAIGERS, Charles Delaware (1899-1950), USA
  R.49   S.54(318)
STAINER, C

STAINER, Sir John (1840-1901), Eng
  R.1   S.c,1-10,24
STALDER, Joseph Franz Xaver Dominik (1725-1765), Swiss
  R.1   S.c
STALLAERT, Alphonse (1920-   ), Neth
  R.14   S.8
STALVEY, Dorrance (1930-   ), USA
  R.19   S.10,13
STAM, George (1905-   ), Neth
  R.14   S.c
STAMITZ, Anton (1750-1789/1809), Boh (see note)
  R.1   S.c,24a
STAMITZ, Johann Wenzel Anton(1717-1757), Boh
  R.1   S.4,5,7,9,19,21,24
STAMITZ, Karl Philipp (1745-1801), Ger
  R.1   S.c,1-11,19,20,23,24
STANCHINSKY, Alexey Vladimirovich (1888-1914), Russia
  R.1   S.1x
STANEKAITE-LAUMYANSKENE, Elena Ionovna (1880-)
  Russia R.7   S.52
STANFORD, Charles Villiers (1852-1924), Eng
  R.1   S.c,1-8,19,20,24,26-28
STANGE, Max (1856-1932), Ger
  R.3
STANISLAS, A. - Marianne
          S.e
STANISLAV, Josef (1897-1971), Cz
  R.1   S.31,24a
STANKOVYCH, Yevhen (1942-)
          S.24a
STANLEY, James [see HALL, James - pseud]
STANLEY, John (1712-1786), Eng
  R.1   S.c,8-10,18,21,53
STANLEY, L. R. - The Contemptibles
          S.54(321)
STARER, Robert (1924-),USA
  R.1   S.7-10,13,19,20,23,24

STARK, Richard (1923-   ), ?USA
            S.8,10,13,21
STARKE - With sword and lance; My regiment
            S.54(344,66)
STAROKADOMSKY, Mihail Leonidovich (1901-1954), Russia
    R.14   S.c,10,21
STAROMIEYSKI, J. (fl c1740), Pol
    R.1   S.c
STAROROUSSKY - Many years
            S.10
STARR - Little Alabama coon

STARZER, Joseph (1726/27-1787), Aus
    R.1   S.c,10
STASNEY, Ludwig (1823-1883), Cz
    R.10
STATHAM, Heathcote Dicken (1889-1973), Eng
    R.1   S.c
STATKOWSKI, Roman (1859-1925), Pol
    R.1   S.c,18,24
STAVENHAGEN, Bernhard (1862-1914), Ger
    R.2   S.c,5x
STAZ, Henry - pseud [see POPY, Francis]
STEADMAN-ALLEN, Raymond Victor (1922-   ), Eng
    R.85   S.55
STEANE, Bruce Harry Dennis (1866-   ), Eng
    R.44   S.24
STEARNS, Peter Pindar (1931-   ), USA
    R.19   S.10,13
STEBBINS, George Waring (1869-1930), USA
    R.53   S.12,13
STECHER, Marianus
            S.10
STECKEL - Sun-down sea
            S.e
ŠTĚDROŇ, Vladimír (1900-1982), Cz
    R.1   S.10,31
STEED, Graham (1913-   ), Eng
    R.80   S.c
STEENBERG, Julius (1830-1911), Sweden
    R.30   S.e
STEENWIECK, Gisbert (d.1679), Ger
    R.1   S.c,10,53
STEFANI, Giovanni (fl 1618-26), It
    R.1   S.c
STEFFANI, Agostino (1654-1728), It
    R.1   S.c,2,4,5x,8,10,11,24,28
STEFFANI, Josef Antonin [see STEPAN, Josef Antonin]
STEFFE, William (c1830-1890), USA
    R.50   S.10

STEFFEN, Wolfgang - pseud [Eberhardt WOLFGANG]
   (1923-   ), Ger   R.4
STEFFENS, Johann (c1560-1616), Ger
   R.1   S.c
STEFFENS, Walter (1934-   ), Ger
   R.14   S.24a
STEGGALL, Charles (1826-1905), Eng
   R.8   S.c
STEHL, George
               S.24

STEHLE, J. Gustave Eduard (1839-1915), Ger
   R.3   S.e
STEHMAN, Jacques (1912-1975), Bel
   R.1   S.c,8,9,36
STEIBELT, Daniel (1765-1823), Ger
   R.1   S.c,10
STEIGLEDER, Johann Ulrich (1593-1635), Ger
   R.1   S.c,6,8,10
STEIGLER, Karl

STEIN, Herman (1915-   ), USA
   R.14   S.10,13
STEIN, Leon (1910-   ), USA
   R.1   S.8,10,13,22,24
STEINBACH, Emil (1849-1919), Ger
   R.1   S.e
STEINBECK, Heinrich (1884-1967), Ger
   R.95   S.54(352)
STEINBERG, Maximilian Oseyevich
   [see SHTEYNBERG, Maximilian Oseyevich]
STEINER, Gitta Hana (1932-   ), USA
   R.7   S.30
STEINER, Johann Ludwig (1688-1761), Swiss
   R.1   S.c
STEINER, Max (1888-1971), USA
   R.1   S.5x,9,10
STEINERT, Alexander Lang (1900-1982), USA
   R.8   S.20
STEINKUHLER, Emil
               S.c
STEINMETZ - Concerto for horn in D major
   R.5   S.10
STEKKE, Léon (1905-   ), Bel
   R.14   S.20
STELLA, Domenico (1881-   ), It
   R.10   S.10
STELLA, Scipione (?1559-1610/30), It
   R.1   S.c
STELZMULLER, Vinzenz (19th Cent), Aus
               S.c,10

STENHAMMAR, Per Ulrik (1829-1875), Sweden
   R.30   S.56
STENHAMMAR, Wilhelm (1871-1927), Sweden
   R.1   S.c,2-10,18,24,40,43,56
STENIUS, Torsten Harald (1918-1964), Sweden
   R.30a
STENSON - Prayer perfect
           S.e
ŠTĚPÁN - Kdyz jsem-on my way
           S.e
ŠTĚPÁN [Steffani], Josef Antonin (1726-1797), Boh
   R.1   S.c,18
STEPANYAN, Haro Levoni (1897-1966), Arm
   R.1
STEPHAN, Rudolf (1887-1915), Ger
   R.1   S.c,4,7,24a
STEPHEN, Val
           S.10
STEPHENS, Evan (fl 1899), USA
   R.200   S.10
STEPHENS, Ward (1869-1940), USA
   R.23   S.e
STEPHENSON, Joseph (1723-1810), USA
           S.10
STEPHENSON, Thomas Wilkinson (?1855-1936)
   R.200   S.e
STEPOVOY, Jakov Stepanovich (1883-1921), Russia
   R.47   S.18
STEPTOE, Roger Guy (1953-   ), Eng
   R.80   S.c
STERKEL, Johann Franz Xavier (1750-1817), Ger
   R.1   S.c,8,10
STERN, Henry [pseud: S. R. HENRY] (1874-1966), USA
   R.23   S.54(349,62)
STERN, Hermann (1912-   )

STERN, Joseph W. (1870-1934), USA
   R.59   S.10
STERN, Leo (1862-1904), Eng
   R.1   S.10
STERN, Robert (1934-   ), USA
   R.19   S.10,13
STERNBERG, Constantin Ivanovich von (1852-1924), Russia
   R.3
STERNBERG, Hans (1910-   ), Ger
   R.4
STERNEFELD, Daniel (1905-   ), Bel
   R.1   S.c
STERNHOLD - Fêtes tziganes
           S.10,24a

STERNWALD, Jiří (1910-   ), Cz
   R.18   S.31
STERRY, J. A. - She sweetly sleeps
              S.47
STETZENKO, Kyril Fedorovich (1882-1922), Ukraine
   R.47   S.10,18
STEUERMANN, Eduard (1892-1964), Ger
   R.4   S.24a
STEVENS, Bernard (1916-1983), Eng
   R.1   S.8,24
STEVENS, Everett ?USA
              S.13
STEVENS, Halsey (1908-   ), USA
   R.1   S.c,8,10,13,19,22,24a
STEVENS, John USA
              S.13
STEVENS, Leith (1909-1970), USA
   R.62   S.9
STEVENS, Noel ?USA
              S.13
STEVENS, Richard John Samuel (1757-1837), Eng
   R.1   S.5x,10
STEVENS, Thomas (1938-   ), USA
              S.13

STEVENSON, John Andrew (1761-1833), Ire
   R.1   S.24
STEWART, Charles Hylton (1884-1932), Eng (see note)
   R.1.5   S.c,10
STEWART, Haldane Campbell (1868-1942), Eng (see note)
   R.37
STEWART, James E.
              S.e
STEWART, Ora Pate (1910-   ), USA
   R.23   S.30,52
STEWART, Redd - The Tennessee waltz
              S.10
STEWART, Richard (1910-1971), Eng

STEWART, Richard (1918-   ), USA
              S.c
STEWART, Richard (1942-   )
              S.c
STEWART, Robert (1918-   ), USA
   R.19   S.13
STEWART, Robert Prescott (1825-1894), Ire
   R.1   S.10,24
STEWART, W. - Trumpet tune in 17th Cent style
              S.54(362)
STIBILJ, Milan (1929-   ), Yug
   R.4   S.24a

STICH, Johann Wenzel [see PUNTO, Giovanni]
STIEGLER, Karl (1876-1932), Aus
   R.3
STIERLIN-VALLON, Henri (1887-1952), Swiss
   R.4
STILL, Robert (1910-1971), Eng
   R.1   S.9,23
STILL, William Grant (1895-1978), USA
   R.1   S.c,3-5,7-11,13,24
STILLMAN, Mitya (1892-1936), USA
   R.19   S.10,13
STILLMAN-KELLY, Edgar (1857-1944), USA
   R.4   S.28
STILMAN-LASANSKY, Julia (1935 or 1938-   ), Arg
   R.7   S.30
STIRLING, Ian (20th Cent), Eng
   R.64   S.c
STIX, Carl (? -1909)
   R.200   S.10
STOBAEUS, Johann (1580-1646), Ger
   R.1   S.c
STOCK, David Frederick (1939-   ), USA
   R.19   S.10,13,20
STOCK, Frederick (1872-1942), USA
   R.1   S.2,10
STOCK, George Chadwick
           S.e
STOCKEM, Johannes [see STOKEM, Johannes de]
STOCKHAUSEN, Karlheinz (1928-   ), Ger
   R.1   S.c,9,10,24a
STOCKMEIER, Wolfgang (1931-   ), Ger
   R.14   S.c
STOELZEL, Gottfried [see STOLZEL, Gottfried Henrich]
STOESSEL, Albert (1894-1943), USA
   R.1   S.13,24
STOIA, Achim (1910-   ), Rum
   R.14   S.8
STOIKOV, Todor (1932-   )
           S.24a
STOJANOFF, Wesselin [see STOYANOV, Vesselin]
STOJANOVIC, Petar Lazar (1877-1957), Yug
   R.14   S.24a
STOJOWSKI, Zygmunt (1870-1946), Pol
   R.1   S.1-4,10,13
STOKEM, Johannes de (c1445->1501), Neth
   R.1   S.c,10,14,16
STOKES, Eric (1930-   ), USA
   R.19   S.13
STOLCER-SLAVENSKI [see SLAVENSKI, Josip]

STOLTZE, Robert H. (1910-   ), USA
    R.19
STOLTZER, Thomas (c1480-1526), Ger
    R.1   S.c,9,10,14,16
STOLYPIN, Dmitri Arkadevich (1818-1893)
               S.18
STOLZ, Robert (1880-1975), Aus
    R.1   S.5x,9,10,24
STOLZEL, Gottfried Henrich (1690-1749), Ger
    R.1   S.c,8,10,53
STOMIUS, Johannes (1502-1562), Ger
    R.1   S.c
STONE, David (1922-   )
               S.10,24
STONE, Robert (1516-1613), Eng
    R.1   S.16
STORACE, Bernardo (17th Cent), It
    R.1   S.c,10
STORACE, Stephen (1762-1796), Eng
    R.1   S.10,26,27,53
STÖRL, Johann Georg Christian (1675-1719), Ger
    R.1   S.c
STORM, Charles (1877-1965)

STÖRMER (fl 1730) - Sonata vi & continuo in F major
    R.5
STORNELLO - E la mia dama

STOTHART, Herbert (1885-1949), USA
    R.1   S.10
STOUGHTON, Roy Spalding (1884-1953), USA
    R.23   S.12,13
STOUT, Alan (1932-   ), USA
    R.19   S.10,13
STOYANOV, Vesselin (1902-1969), Bul
    R.1   S.c,24
STRACHAN - Colonel Donovan
               S.54(320)
STRACHEY, Jack (fl 1948-49), Eng
               S.10,24a,54(360)
STRADELLA, Alessandro (1644-1682), It
    R.1   S.c,2,4-6,8-10,18,24,25,28,43
STRAESSER, Joep (1934-   ), Neth
    R.1   S.10
STRAIGHT, Willard (1930-   ), USA
    R.19   S.10,13
STRAKOSCH, Moritz (1825-1887), Boh
    R.8   S.10,47
STRALOCH, Robert Gordon of (fl 1629), Scot
    R.54   S.5x

STRANDBERG, Newton (1921-   ), USA
   R.19   S.10,13
STRANG, Gerald (1908-   ), USA
   R.1   S.3,10,13,20
STRANGE, Allen (1943-   ), USA
   R.19   S.13,24
STRANGE, Paul

STRANSKY, Josef (1872-1936), Cz
   R.1   S.24
STRASSBURG - Lost
             S.5x
STRATEGIER, Herman (1912-   ), Neth
   R.1   S.c
STRATTNER, Georg Christoph (c1644-1704), Ger
   R.1   S.10
STRAUBE, Karl (1873-1950), Ger
   R.1
STRAUBE, Rudolf (1717-c1780), Ger
   R.1   S.c,10,32
STRAUS, Hugo
             S.24
STRAUS, Oscar (1870-1954), Aus
   R.1   S.c,2-4,5x,9,10,24,54(319)
STRAUSS, Eduard (1835-1916), Aus
   R.1   S.c,2-5,7,8,10
STRAUSS, Franz (1822-1905), Ger
   R.1   S.c,10
STRAUSS, Johann (i) (1804-1849), Aus
   R.1   S.c,2-11
STRAUSS, Johann (ii) (1825-1899), Aus
   R.1   S.c,1-11,18,21,24,43,54(316,38)
STRAUSS, Johann (iii) (1866-1939), Aus
   R.1   S.3,5
STRAUSS, Josef (1827-1870), Aus
   R.1   S.c,2,3,5-8,10,11
STRAUSS, Richard (1864-1949), Aus
   R.1   S.c,1-10,18-21,23-28,42,43
STRAUSS-KÖNIG, Richard (1930-   ), Ger
   R.4   S.c
STRAVINSKI, Igor (1882-1971), Russia
   R.1   S.c,1-11,18-21,23,24,42
STRAVINSKY, Soulima (1910-   ), USA
   R.14   S.13
STREABBOG - pseud [see GOBBAERTS, Jean Louis]
STREBEL, Arnold (1879-1949), Ger
   R.3   S.c
STRECKE, Gerhard Werner (1890-1968), Ger
   R.14   S.c

STRECKER, Heinrich (1893-   ), Aus
  R.4   S.10,24
STREET, Allan (20th Cent), Eng
  R.85   S.55
STREET, Arlene Anderson (1933-   ), Can
            S.52
STREET, Tison (1943-   ), USA
  R.19   S.10,13
STREICHER, Theodor (1874-1940), Aus
  R.1
STREIFF, Peter (1944-   ), Swiss
  R.4   S.c
STRELETZKI, Anton - pseud [see BURNAND, Arthur Bransby]
STREMMEL - Einst war die Welt um mich her
            S.c
STRENGTHFEILD, Thomas (fl 1657), Eng
  R.1   S.c
STRENS, Jules (1892-1971), Bel
  R.25
STRICKLAND, Lily Teresa (1887-1958), USA
  R.19   S.10,13,30,52
STRICKLAND, William (1914-   ), USA
  R.4   S.13
STRIEBEL, Martin
            S.c
STRIGGIO, Alessandro (c1540-1592), It
  R.1   S.c,10,14,16
STRILKO, Anthony (1931-   ), USA
  R.19   S.13
STRINGARI, Antonio (fl 1505-14), It
  R.1   S.c
STRINGFIELD, Lamar Edwin (1897-1959), USA
  R.1   S.2,8,11,13
STRNIŠTÉ, Jiři (1914-   ), Cz
  R.18   S.31
STROE, Aurel (1932-   ), Rum
  R.4
STROGERS, Nicholas (fl 1560-75), Eng
  R.1   S.c,10,16
STROHBACH, Siegfried (1929-   ), Ger
  R.4   S.c
STROHMEYER, Alois (1822-1890), Aus
            S.c
STROKINE, Mikhail Porfirevich (1832-1887)
            S.10
STROMBERG, John (1853-1902), USA
  R.50   S.10
STRØMHOLM, Folke (1941-   ), Nor
  R.14   S.40,51

STRONG, George Templeton (1856-1948), USA
    R.1   S.10,13
STRONG, Joseph (1729-1803), USA

STROUD, Richard (1929-   ), USA
    R.19   S.13
STROUSE, Charles (1928-   ), USA
    R.1   S.9
STROZZI, Barbara (1619-?1664), It
    R.1   S.c,4,5x,30,52
STRUNGK, Delphin (1600/01-1694), Ger
    R.1   S.c,10,53
STRUZENEGGER, Richard (1905-   )

STUART, Leslie - pseud [see BARRETT, Thomas Augustine]
STUBLEY, Simon (18th Cent), Eng
             S.c
STUCKEN, Frank van der (1858-1929), USA
    R.1   S.5x
STUCKENSCHMIDT, Hanns Heinz (1901-   ), Ger
    R.1   S.c
STUDENKA - To Mother
             S.5x
STUDER, Hans (1911-   ), Swiss
    R.4
STULTS, Robert Morrison (1862-1933), USA
    R.53   S.10
STUMPF, Carl (1848-1936), Ger
    R.1   S.10
STUNTZ, Joseph Hartmann (1793-1859), Swiss
    R.1   S.c
STUPCANU, Teodor (1861-1930?)
             S.c
STURCHIO - L´entrata trionfale in glorizia
             S.54(337,40)
STURESTEP, Voldemar (1909-   )
             S.24
STURGEON, N.[?Nicholas] (d.1454), Eng
    R.1   S.10,14
STÜRMER, Bruno (1892-1958), Ger
    R.1   S.c
STURMS, Arnolds (1912-   ), Lat

STURZENEGGER, Richard (1905-1976), Swiss
    R.1   S.24
STUTSCHEWSKY, Joachim (1891-1982), Isr
    R.1   S.8,10,20
STYNE, Jule (1905-   ), USA
    R.1   S.9,10

STYRCHA, Alexei Geogievich (1919-   )
           S.18
SUBOTNIK, Morton (1933-   ), USA
   R.1   S.9,10,13
SUCHANEK, Frantisek (18th Cent)
   R.5
SUCHER, Josef (1843-1908), Aus
   R.1   S.e
SUCHOŇ, Eugen (1908-   ), Slovak
   R.1   S.c,5x,6,8-10,18,24,31,42
SUCHONY - Wine festival (v)
           S.10
SUCK, Charles J. (fl 1780), Eng
   R.1   S.c
SÜDA, Peeter (1883-1920), Est
   R.58   S.18[Suida]
SUDDS, William F. (1843-1920), USA
   R.3,98   S.10
SUDER, Joseph (1892-1980), Ger
   R.14   S.c
SUDERBERG, Robert (1936-   ), USA
   R.19   S.10,13
SUDZUKI, Ivao (1932-   )
           S.18
SUESSE, Dana (1911-1983), USA
   R.19   S.10,11,13,52
SUEYOSHI, Yasuo (1937-   ), Japan
   R.36   S.50
SUFFERN, Carlos (1905-   ), Arg
   R.26   S.5x,46
SUGANO, Hirokazu (1923-   ), Japan
   R.4   S.50
SUGÁR, Rezső (1919-   ), Hun
   R.1   S.9,24
SUGIYAMA, Haseo (1889-1952), Japan
           S.24
SUIDA, Peeter [see SÜDA, Peeter]
SUK, Josef (1874-1935), Cz
   R.1   S.c,1-11,18,24
SUK, Václav (1861-1933), Russia
   R.1   S.4
SUKEGAWA, Toshiya (1930-   ), Japan
   R.36   S.50
ŠULEK, Stjepan (1914-   ), Yug
   R.4   S.24a
SULLIVA - Thou art passing hence

SULLIVAN, Arthur (1842-1900), Eng
   R.1   S.c,1-10,24,28,42,54(329,47)

SULLIVAN, Dan J. (1875-1948), USA
R.23   S.10

SULLY - Sombre woods
S.e

SULPIZI, Mira (Pratesi) (1923-   ), It
R.7   S.30,52

SULYOK, Imre (1912-   ), Hun
R.14   S.c,10

SULZER, Balduin (1932-   ), Aus
R.4   S.24a

SULZER, Joseph (1850-1926), Aus
R.8   S.10,24

SUMERA, Lepo (1950-   ), Est
R.58   S.24a

SUMMARTE, Richard de (17th Cent)
S.c

SUMNER, Jezeniah USA
S.10,47

SUMSION, Herbert (1899-   ), Eng
R.1   S.c,10

SUN I- ch´iang
S.c

SUNDERLAND, Raymond (1921-1977)
S.c

SUNDSTRØM, Andy (1940-   ), Den
R.30   S.40

SUPPÉ, Franz (1819-1895), Aus
R.1   S.c,1-6,8-11,18,22,54(323,26,35)

SURDIN, Morris (1914-   ), Can
R.14   S.10

SUREAU, Hughes (16th Cent)
S.14

SURIANI, Albert (1920-   )

SURIANO, Francesco [see SORIANO, Francesco]

SURINACH, Carlos (1915-   ), USA
R.1   S.c,8-10,13,24,39

SURZYŃSKI, Józef (1851-1919), Pol
R.3

SURZYNSKI, Mieczyslaw (1866-1924), Pol
R.1   S.c

SUSATO, Tylman (?c1500-1561/64), It
R.1   S.7,8,10,14,16,17,53

SUSAY [Suzoy], Johannes (fl c1380), Fr
R.1   S.c,5x

SÜSSMAYR, Franz Xaver (1766-1803), Aus
R.1   S.c,10

SUST, Jiri (1919-   ), Cz
S.31

SUTCLIFFE, James (1929-   ), USA
    R.19   S.10,13
SUTER, Hermann (1870-1926), Swiss
    R.1   S.c,8
SUTER, Robert (1919-   ), Swiss
    R.1   S.c,24
SUTERMEISTER, Heinrich (1910-   ), Swiss
    R.1   S.c,4,8,10,20
SUTHERLAND, Margaret (1897-   ), Australia
    R.1   S.5,20,29,30,37,52
SUTTER, Ignace de (c1600)
                 S.c
SUTTER, Jules Toussaint de (1889-1959), Bel
    R.25   S.36
SUTTON, Harry O.

                 S.10
SUZOY, Johannes [see SUSAY, Johannes]
SUZUKI, Tadashi (1934-   ), Japan
    R.36   S.50
SVEDBOM, Vilhelm (1843-1904), Sweden
    R.1   S.c,5x,10,56
SVEDLUND, Karl-Erik (1906-1974)
    R.30   S.c
SVEINSSON, Atli Heimir (1938-   ), Iceland
    R.1   S.c,40
SVENDSEN, Johan (1840-1911), Norway
    R.1   S.c,2-10,18,24a,57
SVESHNIKOV, Alexander Vasilyevich (1890-   ), USSR
    R.1   S.5x,18
SVETLANOV, Evegny (1928-   ), USSR
    R.1   S.c,18,24a
SVIRIDOV, Georgi Vasilevich (1915-   ), USSR
    R.1   S.c,5x,9,18,24
SWAN, M. L. - Hightower (attrib)
                 S.47
SWAN, Timothy (1758-1842), USA
    R.1   S.10,47
SWANN, Donald (1923-   ), Eng
    R.4   S.9,10
SWANN, Frederick Lewis (1931-   ), USA
    R.64   S.c
SWANSON, Howard (1907-1978), USA
    R.1   S.c,6-8,10,13
SWAYNE, Giles Oliver Cairnes (1946-   ), Eng
    R.80   S.10
SWEELEY, Charles C. - pseud [ie Henry J. LINCILN], USA
                 S.13,54(352)
SWEELINCK, Dirck Janszoon (1591-1652), Neth
    R.1   S.c,3-5,8,9

SWEELINCK, Jan Pieterszoon (1562-1621), Neth
    R.1   S.c,2,6,7,10,11,14-16,18,41,53
SWEENEY, Eric (1948-   ), Ire
    R.40   S.49
SWEET, Milo Allison (1899-   ), USA
    R.23   S.54(326)
SWICKARD, Ralph (1922-   ), USA
    R.19   S.10,13
SWIESZNIKOW, Anatol

SWIFT, Kay (Mrs. Paul WARBURG) (1905-   ), USA
    R.7   S.30
SWIFT, Richard (1927-   ), USA
    R.1   S.10,13,24a
SWING, Raymond Gram (1887-   ), USA
    R.19   S.13,24,32
SYDEMAN, William (1928-   ), USA
    R.1   S.10,13,20,24,32
SYLVA, George Gard (1896-1950)
           S.24
SYLVA, Johann Elias de (1716-1797)
           S.8

SYLVA, de - Memory lane
           S.e
SYLVAIN, Jules - pseud [see HANSSON, Stig]
SYLVIANO, Rene (1903-   ), It
    R.62   S.24
SYMIANE - Lina
           S.e
SYMONDS, Norman Alec (1920-   ), Can
    R.31
SYROKHVATOV, Valeri Gennadievich (1935-   )
           S.18
SZABADOS, Gyorgy
           S.9
SZABELSKI, Boleslaw (1896-1979), Pol
    R.1   S.c
SZABÓ, Ferenc (1902-1969), Hun
    R.1   S.c,8-10,18,24[Sabo]
SZADEK, Thomaz (d.1612), Pol
    R.1   S.c,16
SZALAY, Josephe de (1800-1860)
           S.c
SZALONEK, Witold (1927-   ), Pol
    R.1   S.c
SZALOWSKI, Antoni (1907-1973), Pol
    R.1   S.10,19,21
SZAMOTUL, Waclaw z (c1524-1560), Pol
    R.1   S.2,4,8,10,11,14,16

SZARZYŃSKI, Stanislaw Sylwester (fl 1692-1713), Pol
  R.1   S.c,8,10,24a
SZATHMÁRY, Zsigmond (1939-   ), Hun
  R.4   S.c
SZCZENIOWSKI, Boleslaw (1898-   ), Can
  R.14
SZÉKELY, Endre (1912-   ), Hun
  R.1   S.c,9,10
SZELÉNYI, István (1904-1972), Hun
  R.1   S.24
SZELIGOWSKI, Tadeusz (1896-1963), Pol
  R.1   S.c,8
SZEPETHNEKI, Janos (16th Cent)
           S.14
SZERVÁNZSKY, Endre (1911-1977), Hun
  R.1   S.c,9,10,19
SZMIDT, Rogeriusz Vincenty (1933-   )
           S.c
SZOKOLAY, Sándor (1931-   ), Hun
  R.1   S.c,9,10
SZŐLLŐSY, Andras (1921-   ), Hun
  R.1   S.c,9,10
SZONYI, Ersebet (1924-   ), Hun
  R.1   S.c,10,30,52
SZOPOWICZ, Henryk
           S.5x,24
SZOPSKI, Felician (1865-1939), Pol
  R.4
SZULC, Józef Zygmunt (1875-1956), Fr
  R.1   S.1x,4,5x,10,24
SZYMANOWSKA, Maria Agata (1789-1831), Pol
  R.1   S.c,10,18[Shim.],30,52
SZYMANOWSKI, Karol (1882-1937), Pol
  R.1   S.c,1x,2-8,10,11,24
TABOUROT, Jehan - pseud [see ARBEAU, Thoinot]
TABUYO, J. - Mi pobre reja
           S.1x
TACHISKO, Oles [see TCHISHKO, Oles Semenovich]
TACKETT, Fred (1945-   ), USA
           S.10,13
TADOLINI, Giovanni (?1789-1872), It
  R.1   S.10
TAEGGIO, Giovanni Domenico
  [see ROGNONI TAEGGIO, Giovanni Domenico]
TAEYE, Alex de (1898-   ), Bel
  R.25   S.24a
TAFALLA, Pedro de (17th Cent)
           S.16
TAFFANEL, Claude Paul (1844-1908), Fr
  R.1   S.c,1x,4,5x,6,7,10

TAG, Christian Gotthilf (1735-1811), Ger
   R.1   S.c
TAGLIAFERRI, Ernesto (1891-1937), It
   R.4   S.5x,10,18
TAGLIAFICO, Joseph Dieudonne (1821-1900), Fr
   R.1   S.e
TAGORE, Rabindranath (1861-1941), India
   R.1   S.18
TAHOURDIN, Peter (1928-   ), Australia
            S.29
TAICHKOV, A. - Dostojno jest
            S.c
TAILLEFERRE, Germaine (1892-1983), Fr
   R.1   S.c,2,6-8,10,18,20,24,30,52
TAIRA, Yoshihisa (1938-   ), Japan
            S.c
TAJČEVIĆ, Marko (1900-   ), Yug
   R.1   S.c
TAKACS, Jeno von (1902-   ), USA
   R.14   S.24a
TAKAHASHI, Yuji (1938-   ), Japan
   R.1   S.10,24a,50
TAKATA, Saburo (1913-   ), Japan
   R.1   S.10,24a,50
TAKAYAMA, Minoru

TAKEMITSU, Toru (1930-   ), Japan
   R.1   S.c,9,10,24a,50
TAKI, Rentaro (1879-1903), Japan
   R.1   S.24,32
TAKTAKISHVILI, Otar Vasilyevich (1924-   ), USSR
   R.1   S.c,8,10,18,24
TAKTAKISHVILI, Shalva Mikhailovich (1900-1965), USSR
   R.1   S.18
TAL, Josef (1910-   ), Isr
   R.1
TAL, Marjo (1915-   ), Neth
   R.7   S.52
TALBOT, Howard - pseud [ie Richard Li MUNKITTRICJ]
   (1869-1928), Eng   R.3
TALEXY, Adrien (1820-1881), Fr
   R.3   S.10,47
TALLAT-KELPŠA, Juozas (1889-1949), Lith
   R.1   S.18
TALLIS, Thomas (c1505-1585), Eng
   R.1   S.c,2,4,5,7-10,14-16,53
TALMA, Louise (1906-   ), USA
   R.1   S.10,13,30,52
TALMI, Yoav (1943-   ), Isr
   R.80   S.10

TALTABULL BALAGUER, Cristóbal (1888-1964), Sp
  R.9   S.10
TAMAS, Gregory Aloisius
          S.9
TAMBA, Akira (1932-   ), Japan
  R.36
TAMBERG, Eino (1930-   ), Est
  R.1   S.c,18
TAMBERT, Otto (1833-1903)
          S.11
TAMKIN, David (1906-1975), USA
  R.19   S.9
TAMULYUNAS, P. (1919-   )
          S.18
TANAKA, Toshimitsu (1927-   ), Japan
  R.4   S.50
TANENBAUM, Elias (1924-   ), USA
  R.19   S.9,10,13
TANEV, Alexander (1928-   ), Bul
  R.1   S.c
TANEYEV, Sergey Ivanovich (1856-1915), Russia
  R.1   S.c,5,7-10,18,20,23,24
TANG, Jordan Cho-Tung (1948-   ), USA
  R.19
TANGUAY, Georges-Emile (1893-1964), Can
  R.31   S.24
TANNER, Peter (1936-   ), USA
  R.19   S.13
TANNHÄUSER (c1205-c1270), Ger
  R.1   S.c
TANSMAN, Alexander (1897-   ), Fr
  R.1   S.c,2-11,20,24,32
TANTI - Serenade
          S.e
TAPISSIER, Johannes (c1370-<1410), Fr
  R.1   S.16
TAPRAY, Jean-Francois (1738-c1819), Fr
  R.1   S.9,10,24
TARANOV, Gleb Pavlovich (1904-   ), USSR
  R.14   S.18
TĂRANU, Cornel (1934-   ), Rum
  R.4
TARDITI, Giovanni (1875-1935), It [?]
  R.4,10   S.54(363)
TARDOS, Béla (1910-1966), Hun
  R.1   S.c,9,10,24a
TARENGHI, Mario (1870-1938), It
  R.8   S.24
TARIVERDIEV, Mikael Leonovich (1931-   ), USSR
  R.47   S.18

TARNAY, Alajos (1870-1933), Hun
   R.15   S.5x
TARP, Svend Erik (1908-   ), Den
   R.1   S.4,5,7,8,24,33,35
TARRAGÓ, Graciano
             S.10,32
TARRANT - One world, one smile
             S.e
TÁRREGA, Francisco (1852-1909), Sp
   R.1   S.c,2-10,18,24a,32,39
TARTINI, Giuseppe (1692-1770), It
   R.1   S.c,1-11,18,22,24
TARVER, James L. (1916-   ), USA
   R.24   S.54(319)
TASHJIAN, Charmian B. (1950-   ), USA

             S.52
TASKIN, Henri-Joseph (1779-1852), Fr
   R.1   S.c
TASSIN (13th Cent)
             S.16
TASSO, Giovanni Maria (fl 1559-90), It
   R.5   S.c
TATE, Arthur Frank [pseud: Frank FOTHERGILL] (1880-1950)
   Eng R.37   S.c,10,24
TATE, Phyllis (1911-   ), Eng
   R.1   S.c,6,19-21,30,52,55
TAUB, Bruce J. H. (1948-   ), USA
   R.19   S.13
TAUBE, Evert (1889-1976), Sweden
   R.4
TAUBER, Richard (1891-1948), Aus
   R.1   S.c,10
TAUBERT, Carl Gottfried Wilhelm (1811-1891), Ger
   R.1   S.c,4,5x,10
TAUBERT, Whilhelm (1811-1891), Ger
   R.3   S.c
TAURIELLO, Antonio (1931-   ), Arg
   R.1   S.c,10,19,46
TAUSIG, Carl (1841-1871), Pol
   R.1   S.c,9,10
TAUSINGER, Jan (1921-1980), Cz
   R.1   S.c,10,24a
TAUSKY, Vilem (1910-   ), Cz
   R.80   S.c
TAUSSIG, Elyakim
             S.24a
TAVARES, Hekel (1896-1969), Brazil
   R.55   S.8-10,24,39
TAVARES, Mario (1928-   ), Brazil
   R.14   S.24a

TAVENER, John Kenneth (1944-   ), Eng
  R.1   S.c,9
TAVERNER, John (c1490-1545), Eng
  R.1   S.c,3-5,8-11,14,16
TAVONI, Francesco
             S.4,5x
TAYLOR - Ten thousand men of Harvard
             S.54(360)
TAYLOR, C. - Intermezzo
             S.54(334)
TAYLOR, Colin (1881-1973), South Africa
  R.4
TAYLOR, Daniel (d.1643), Eng
  R.1
TAYLOR, Dub USA
             S.13
TAYLOR, Franklin (1843-1919), Eng
  R.1   S.10
TAYLOR, John Siebert (1869-1948)

TAYLOR, Joseph Deems (1885-1966), USA
  R.1   S.1-5,8-11,13
TAYLOR, Master (16th Cent)
             S.c,53
TAYLOR, Raynor (1747-1825), Eng/USA
  R.1   S.7,10,24a,47
TAYLOR, Richard B. (1768-1813), Eng - Quick Step [?]
  R.57   S.10
TAYLOR, Silas (1624-1678), Eng
  R.1   S.c,10
TAYLOR, Tell - Down by the Old Mill Stream
             S.10
TCHAIKOVSKY, André (1935-   ), Pol
  R.80   S.20
TCHAIKOVSKY, Boris [see CHAYKOVSKY, Boris]
TCHAIKOVSKY, Pyotr Ilyich (1840-1893), Russia
  R.1   S.c,1-11,18-24,28,32,33,42,43,54(324)
TCHEMBERDZHIE, Nicholas (1903-   )
             S.5,7
TCHEREPIN, Ivan (1943-   ), USA
  R.4
TCHEREPNIN, Alexander (1899-1977), Russia
  R.1   S.c,2,3,5,8,9,18,22,24
TCHEREPNIN, Nicolay (1873-1945), Russia
  R.1   S.c,2,4,5,7,8,18
TCHESNOKOV, Pavel Grigoryevich
  [see CHESNOKOV, Pavel Grigoryevich]
TCHISHKO, Oles Semyonovich
  [see CHISHKO, Oles Semyonovich]

TCHONKUSROV, P. (1930-   )
          S.24a
TECHELMANN, Franz Matthias (c1649-1714), Aus
     R.1   S.c,53
TEGNER, Alice Charlotte (née Sandström) (1864-1943)
     Sweden   R.7   S.52
TEIKE, Carl (1864-1922), Ger
     R.1   S.10,54(321,29,46)
TEIXEIRA, Nicanor
          S.c
TEJADA - La perjura
          S.e
TEJEDA, Eduardo (1923-   ), Arg
     R.26   S.46
TEJERA ABANADES - Brisas malagueñas
          S.7,10
TEJERA FRANCO - Aires (Gallegos) & Rondena
          S.7,10
TEJERA, Lopez
          S.9
TEJON, Rev. Jose I
          S.10
TEKELIEV, Alexander

TELEMAN, Georg Philipp (1681-1767), Ger
     R.1   S.c,2-11,18-22,24,28,53,32
TELESFOR, S. - Hungarian song
          S.24
TELLAMN, Heinrich - pseud [see DECOURCELLE, Paul]
TELLEZ, Hernando Colombia
          S.39
TEML, Jiri (1935-   )
          S.24a
TEMPLE, Hope (Mme. Messager) - pseud [ie Dotie DAVIES]
     (1859-1938), Eng   R.7   S.e
TEMPLETON, Alec Andrew (1909-1963), Wales/USA
     R.19   S.8-11,13,19,21
TENAGLIA, Francesco Antonio (17th Cent), It
     R.8   S.5x,22,24
TENAGLIA, Raffaele (1884-   ), It
     R.3
TENNET, H. M. - If winter comes
          S.e
TENNEY, James (1934-   ), USA
     R.19   S.10,13
TEODARAKIS, Mikis [see THEODORAKIS, Mikis]
TERAMO, Antonio Zacar da [see ZACAR]
TE RANGI-PAI (20th Cent), New Zealand
          S.52

TERENTIEV, Boris Mikailovich (1913-   ), USSR
   R.14   S.18
TER-GEVONDIAN, Anushaven Grigorievich (1887-1961), USSR
   R.14   S.18
TERKELSEN, Søren (?1590-1656/57), Den
   R.30   S.57
TER-OSIPOV, Yuri Grigorevich (1933-   )
              S.18,24a
TERPERLYUK, P. - Fantasy (vi & orch)
              S.24
TERRENI, Bonaventura (18th Cent)
              S.10,53
TERRY, Richard Runciman (1865-1938), Eng
   R.1   S.c
TER-TATEVOSYAN, Hovhannes Gurgeni (1926-   ), Arm
   R.1   S.18
TERTERYAN, Avet (1929-   ), Arm
   R.1   S.18
TERTRE, Etienne du [see DU TERTRE, Estienne]
TERZI, Benevuto (1892-   )

TERZI, Giovanni Antonio (c1580-1620), It
   R.1   S.c,10,32
TERZIÁN, Alicia (1936-   ), Arg
   R.26   S.24a,46,52
TERZIANI - Hostias et preces
              S.e
TESSARINI, Carlo (c1690->1766), It
   R.1   S.c,10
TESSIER, Charles (fl c1600), Fr
   R.1   S.3,5,10,11,14,16
*** TESSIER, George (Charles Guillaume?) (16th Cent)
   (see note)
TESSIER, Guillaume (fl c1582), Fr
   R.1   S.c
TESSIER, Roger (1939-   ), Fr

   R.14   S.c
TESTO - Chitarrata Abruzzese
              S.34
TEUGLIN, Hans (16th Cent), Ger
   R.5   S.c
TEXIDOR DALMAU, Jaime
              S.10,54(313)
TEYBER, Anton (1756-1822), Aus
   R.1   S.c,24
THADEWALT, Herman (1827-1909), Ger
   R.3   S.c
THALBEN-BALL, George (1896-   ), Eng
   R.1   S.c

THALBERG, Sigismond (1812-1871), Aus
   R.1   S.c,9,10,18
THAYER, M.C. - Children's Prayer (see note)
          S.10
THAYER, Pat - Snowbird (see note)
          S.5x
THAYER, Whitney Eugene (1838-1889), USA
   R.1   S.10
THAYER, William Armour (1874-1933), USA
   R.19   S.13
THEILE, Johann (1646-1724), Ger
   R.1   S.c
THEISS, August (1870-   ), Ger [?]
   R.3   S.54(312)
THEMMEN, Ivana Marburger (1935-   ), USA
   R.7   S.13,30,52
THEODORAKIS, Mikis (1925-   ), Greece
   R.1   S.c,9,18,24,32
THÉRÉSA - pseud [ie Emma Eugenie Rose VALLADON]
   (1837-1913), Fr (see note) R.7,10s   S.52
THERESE, Princess of Saxe-Altenburg & Sweden (1836-1914)
   R.7   S.52
THEUMSER - Real swing march
          S.54(351)
THIBAULT de COURVILLE
   [see COURVILLE, Joachim Thibault de]
THIBAUT de BLAISON (d >1229), Fr
   R.1   S.c
THIBAUT IV, King of Navarre (1201-1253)
   R.1   S.c,2,3,8,10,14-16
THIEL, Carl (1862-1939), Ger
   R.2   S.c
THIEL, Jörn (1921-   ), Ger
   R.4   S.c
THIEL, Olof [pseud: Jacques ARMAND] (1892-1976), Sweden
   R.30a   S.43
THIELMAN, Ronald (1936-   ), USA
   R.23
THIELMANN, Per
          S.24
THIEME, Karl (1909-   ), Ger
   R.14   S.c
THILDE, Jean

          S.10
THILMAN, Johannes Paul (1906-1973), Ger
   R.1   S.c,24a
THIMAN, Eric Harding (1900-1975), Eng
   R.1   S.c
THIMMIG, Leslie (1943-   ), USA
   R.19   S.10,13

THIRIET, Maurice (1906-1972), Fr
    R.1   S.5x,7,8,10
THOMA, Annette (née Schenk) (1886-1974), Ger
    R.7   S.c,52
THOMA, Wolfgang (20th Cent), Ger
             S.c
THOMAS, Ambroise (1811-1896), Fr
    R.1   S.c,2-11,18,24,34,42,43,54(351)
THOMAS, Andre
             S.4
THOMAS, Andrew (1939-   ), USA
    R.19   S.13
THOMAS, Arthur Goring (1850-1892), Eng
    R.1   S.c,5x
THOMAS, Christopher (1894-   ), USA
    R.19   S.13
THOMAS, David Vaughn (1873-1934), Wales
    R.3   S.5x,7
THOMAS, John Rogers (1829-1896), USA
    R.3   S.e
THOMAS, John [Gwalia PENCERDD] (1826-1913), Wales
    R.1   S.c,5x,8,10,24
THOMAS, Kurt (1904-1973), Ger
    R.1   S.c,2
THOMAS, Lester - pseud [see BARRETT, Thomas Augustine]
THOMAS, Mansel (1909-   ), Wales
    R.1   S.c,5x
THOMAS, Max - pseud [see YODER, Paul]
THOMAS-MIFUNE, Werner (1941-   )
             S.c
THOME, Diane (1942-   ), USA
    R.7   S.30,52
THOMÉ, Francis (1850-1909), Fr
    R.1   S.5x,10,24
THOMELIN, Jacques-Denis (c1640-1693), Fr
    R.1   S.c[Tomelin],32,53
THOMMESSEN, Olav Anton (1946-   ), Nor
    R.38   S.24a,40,51
THOMPSON - If I forget
             S.e
THOMPSON - Lonely Hawaii (vi & p)
             S.24a
THOMPSON, Alma [pseud: Alma Bazel ANDROZZO] (1912-   )
    USA R.23   S.10
THOMPSON, Leland ?USA
             S.10,13
THOMPSON, Randall (1899-   ), USA
    R.1   S.c,4-11,13
THOMPSON, Van Denman (1890-1969), USA
    R.19   S.12,13

THOMPSON, Will Lamartine (1847-1909), USA
        S.10
THOMSEN, Christian
        S.33
THOMSEN, Knud Vad (1905-1971), Den
    R.30   S.33,57
THOMSON, David Cleghorn (1900-1980), Scot
    R.37   S.c
THOMSON, Virgil (1896-   ), USA
    R.1   S.c,4-10,12,13,21,24-27
THÓRARINSSON, Leifur (1934-   ), Iceland,
    R.1   S.c,24a,40
THORESEN, Lasse (1949-   ), Nor
        S.40
THORILD - Song of the smallholder
        S.5x
THORKELL, Sigurbjornsson (1938-   ), Nor

THORNE, Francis (1922-   ), USA
    R.1   S.c,9,10
THORNTON, James (1861-1938), USA
    R.23   S.10
THORPE DAVIE, Cedric (1913-1983), Scot
    R.1   S.c,8
THRANE, Waldemar (1790-1828), Nor
    R.1   S.c,10,24a
THUILLE, Ludwig (1861-1907), Ger
    R.1   S.1x,10
THUILLIER, Edmund
        S.24
THURBAN - Americana; Farmyard caprice
        S.54(313,26)
THYBO, Lief (1922-   ), Den
    R.1   S.c,8
THYRESTAM, Gunnar Olaf (1900-   ), Sweden
    R.14   S.40,56
TIBBITS, George (1933-   ), Australia
    R.1   S.29
TIBURTINO, Giuliano (c1510-1569), It
    R.1   S.c
TICCIATI, Francesco (1893-1949), It
    R.8   S.4,5x
TICHENOR, Trebor Jay
        S.10
TICHÝ, František Antonín (1898-   ), Cz
    R.18   S.31
TICHÝ, Rudolf (?-1926), Aus
    R.3   S.24
TIERNEY, Harry (1890-1965), USA
    R.1   S.10,24a

TIERSOT, Julien (1857-1936), Fr
  R.1   S.4,5x
TIESSEN, Heinz (1887-1971), Ger
  R.1   S.c,1x,7,24
TIGRANYAN, Armen Tigran (1879-1950), Arm
  R.1   S.9,18,42
TIGRANIAN, Vartan Armenovich (1906-   ), USSR
  R.14   S.18
TIKOTSKY, Evgeny Karlovich (1893-1970), Russia
  R.1   S.18
TILKINS, Felix [see CARYLL, Ivan - pseud]
TILBURG, Frans van (1933-   )
          S.c
TILLING, Erik (1908-   ), Sweden
          S.43
TILLIS, Frederick Charles (1930-   ), USA
  R.19   S.10,13
TIMM, Kenneth (1934-   ), USA
  R.19   S.10,13
TIMOSHENKO, Alexander Borisovich (1946-   )
          S.18
TINCTORIS, Johannes de (c1435-?1511), Flem
  R.1   S.c,9,16,53
TINEL, Edgar (1854-1912), Bel
  R.1   S.10
TINEL, Emiel Jozef (1885-1972), Bel
  R.14   S.8
TING SHAN-TE
          S.c
TINÓDI, Sebestyén [Lantos] (c1505-1556), Hun
  R.1   S.c
TIOMKIN, Dimitri (1894-1979), USA
  R.1   S.c,4,9,10
TIPPET, Michael, (1905-   ), Eng
  R.1   S.c,5,7-10,24,27,28
TIRINDELLI, Pier Adolfo (1858-1937), It
  R.8   S.c,10,24
TISCHHAUSER, Franz (1921-   ), Swiss
  R.4
TISDALE, William (16th Cent.), Eng
  R.1   S.10,16
TISHCHENKO, Boris Ivanovich (1939-   ), USSR
  R.1   S.10,18,24a
TISNÉ, Antoine (1932-   ), Fr
  R.1   S.c
TISSERAND, F. J. (15th Cent) - Grâces soient rendues
          S.7
TISSOT, Mireille (20th Cent), Fr
          S.c,52

TITCOMB, Everett (1884-1968), USA
    R.19   S.8,10,12,13
TITELOUZE, Jehan (1562/63-1633), Fr
    R.1   S.c,4,5,8,10,11,16,53
TITL, Anton Emil (1809-1882), Boh
    R.1   S.24,54(336)
TITOV - Romance (vla & p)
                S.23
TITOV, Alexander Fedorovich
                S.18
TITOV, Nikolay Alexeyevich (1800-1875), Russia
    R.1   S.18
TITOV, Nikolay Sergeyevich (1798-1843), Russia
    R.1   S.18
TITOV, Vasilii Polikarpovich (c1650-c1715), Russia
    R.1
TITTA, Ettore (1875-1956)
                S.34
TITTEL, Ernest (1910-1969), Aus
    R.1   S.c
TITTLE, John Steven

TITTO - Nazareth
                S.e
TJEKNAVORIAN, Loris (1937-   ), Iran
                S.c
TLENDIEV, N. - Armandy Kiyal (vi & p)
                S.24
TOBANI, Theodore Moses (1855-1933), USA
    R.3   S.24,54(312,24,46)
TOBIAS, Charles (1898-1970), USA
    R.23   S.24
TOBIAS, Rudolf (1873-1918), Est
    R.30   S.18
TOBLER, Johann Heinrich (1777-1838)
    R.3
TOCH, Ernst (1897-1964), Aus
    R.1   S.c,3-11,13,23,24
TODA, Kunio (1915-   ), Japan
    R.4   S.24a,50
TODD, James
                S.10
TODUTĂ, Sigismund (1908-   ), Rum
    R.1
TOEBOSCH, Louis (1916-   ), Neth
    R.1   S.10
TOENSING, Richard (1940-   ), USA
    R.19   S.10,13
TOESCHI, Carl Joseph (1731-1788), Ger
    R.1   S.c,24

TOESCHI, Johann Baptist Christoph (1735-1800), It
   R.1   S.10[Giovanni Batista]
TOFFT, Alfred (1865-1931), Den
   R.8   S.4,5x
TOGNARELLI, Umberto Den
            S.43
TOHNO, Kyoko (1968-   )
            S.24a
TOKAREV, Averi Matveyvich (1918-   )
            S.18
TOLAR, Jan Krtitel (17th Cent), Boh
   R.1   S.c,5x,10,16

TOLDRA, Eduardo (1895-1962), Catalan
   R.1   S.1x,10,24a,39
TOLLEFSEN, Augusta (18??-1955)

TOLLETT, Thomas (d ?1696), Ire [?]
   R.1   S.5x
TOLLIUS, Jan (c1550->1603), Neth
   R.1   S.8,10,14
TOLOZA, Guiraut de [see GUIRAUT d´ESPANHA de TOLOZA]
TOMÁŠEK, Jaroslav (1896-   ), Cz
   R.18   S.31
TOMÁŠEK, Vaclav Jan Křtitel (1774-1850), Boh
   R.1   S.c,5x,7,10,24
TOMASI, Henri (1901-1971), Fr
   R.1   S.c,2,4,5,7,8,10,18-20,22,24a
TOMASINI, Alois Luigi (1741-1808), It
   R.1   S.c,8,23,24
TOMBELLE, Ferdinand de la
   [see LA TOMBELLE, Ferdinand de]
TOMELIN, Joseph [see THOMELIN, Jacques-Denis]
TOMEONI, Florido (1755-1820), It [?]
   R.1   S.5x
TOMER, William Gould
            S.24
TOMKINS, Thomas (1572-1656), Eng
   R.1   S.c,5-10,14-16,18,24,53
TOMLINSON, Ernest (1924-   ), Eng
   R.1   S.c,24,55
TOMLINSON, Kellom (18th Cent), Eng
   R.1   S.c
TOMMASINI, Vincenzo (1878-1950), It
   R.1   S.2-5,10,11
TONINI, Aldo
            S.24a
TON-THAT-TIET (1933-   )
            S.c
TÖPFER, Johann Gottlob (1791-1870), Ger
   R.1   S.c

TOPHAM, William (fl 1701-9), Eng
  R.1   S.c,10
TOPOLSKI, Zlatko (1914-   )
           S.24a
TORADZE, David Alexandrovich (1922-   ), USSR
  R.1   S.18
TORCH, Sydney (1908-   ), Eng
  R.77   S.24
TORELLI, Giacomo (1608-1678), It (see note)
  R.1   S.c
TORELLI, Giuseppe (1658-1709), It
  R.1   S.c,3-5,7-11,18,24,25,27,28,32
TORMIS, Velio (1930-   ), Est
  R.1   S.18
TORNQUIST, Folke (1899-   ), Sweden
           S.43
TÖRNUDD, Axel Olof (1874-1923), Fin
  R.3   S.5x
TORRÁ - Sardana (vilandrau) (p)
           S.10
TORRÁ, Celia (1889-1962), Arg
  R.26   S.46
TORRE, Francisco de la (fl 1483-1504), Sp
  R.1   S.c,2,4,5x,8,10,14-17,39
TORRE, Jerónimo de la (c1620-1695), Sp
  R.9   S.53
TORREGROSA, Tomás Lopez (1868-1913)

TORREJÓN y VELASCO, Tomás de (1644-1728), Peru
  R.1   S.10
TORRENS - Dreams
           S.e
TORRENTES, Andrés de (c1510-1580), Sp
  R.1   S.10,16,17
TORRES, Eduardo (1872-1934), Sp
  R.3   S.c,5x
TORRES, Juan de (fl 1653-83), Sp
  R.9   S.16
TORRI, Pietro (c1650-1737), It
  R.1   S.c
TORRIJOS, Diego de (c1640-1691), Sp
  R.1   S.10,17,53
TORROBA, Federico [see MORENO TORROBA, Frederico]
TORTELIER, Paul (1914-   ), Fr
  R.1   S.c,5x,10,18
TORTORELLI - Ave Maria
           S.10[Tortorella]
TORZYNSKI, Damian (1673-1729)
  (see note under Stachowicz)

TOSAR, Héctor (1923-   ), Uruguay
    R.1   S.10,39
TOSCO, Virgilio Arg
              S.46
TOSELLI, Enrico (1883-1926), It
    R.1   S.c,4,5x,10,24,28,43
TOSTI, Francesco Paolo (1846-1916), It
    R.1   S.1x,4,5x,10,18,24,28,34,43
TOTZKE, Irenaus (1932-   )
              S.c
TOUCHE, Edmond D. La [see LA TOUCHE, Edmond D.]
TOUCHEMOULIN, Joseph (1727-1801), Fr
    R.1   S.c
TOUMA, Habib Hassin (1934-   ), Arab
    R.1   S.10
TOURNEMIRE, Charles (1870-1939), Fr
    R.1   S.c,2,4,9,10
TOURNHOUT, Gerard de [see TURNHOUT, Gerard de]
TOURNIER, Franz Andre (1923-   ), Fr
              S.22
TOURNIER, Marcel-Lucien (1879-1951), Fr
    R.14   S.c,7,8,10,18,24a
TOURS, Berthold (1838-1897), Eng
    R.1   S.c,10
TOURS, Frank E. (1877-1963), Eng/USA
    R.4   S.5x,10,13,43
TOVAČOVSKÝ-FÖRCHTGOTT, Arnošt (1825-1874), Cz [?]
    R.18   S.5x
TOVEY, Donald Francis (1875-1940), Eng
    R.1   S.20
TOWER, Joan (1938-   ), USA
    R.19   S.10,13,30,52
TOWNER, Ralph USA
              S.13
TOWNSEND, Pearl Dea Etta [Nataile Townsend]
    [Madame Lawrence] (1886-   )
    R.7   S.18,24,30
TOYAMA, Michiko (1912-   ), Japan
    R.7   S.9,30,52
TOYAMA, Yuzo (1931-   ), Japan
    R.14   S.18,24,50
TOYE, Geoffrey (1889-1942), Eng
    R.1   S.c,4
TRABACI, Giovanni Maria (c1575-1647), It
    R.1   S.c,5x,10,11,16,53
TRACK, Gerhard (1934-   ), USA
    R.19   S.12,13
TRÄDER, Willi (1920-   ), Ger
    R.4   S.c

TRAETTA, Tommaso (1727-1779), It
  R.1   S.c,8,10
TRANOVSKÝ, Juraj (1592-1637), Cz
  R.1   S.c
TRANSLATEUR, Siegfried (1875-1944), Ger
  R.4   S.c
TRAPP, Max (1887-1971), Ger
  R.1   S.7
TRAPP, Willy (1923-   )
           S.c
TRAUTSCH, Leonhard (1693-1762), Ger
  R.1   S.c
TRAVERS, John (c1703-1758), Eng
  R.1   S.c,10,53
TRAVIS, Roy Elihu (1922-   ), USA
  R.19   S.7,9,10,13,24a
TREBILCO, Leonard [see DUNCAN, Trevor - pseud]
TREBOR (fl 1390-1410), ?Fr
  R.1   S.c
TREDE, Yngve Jan (1933-   ), Den
  R.30   S.40
TREDINNICK, Noel Howard (1949-   ), Eng
  R.80   S.c,13
TREHARNE, Bryceson (1879-1948), Wales
  R.4
TREJADA, de [see DE TREJADA]
TRELAWNY - My heart is with the old folk
           S.e
TREMAIN, Ronald (1923-   ), New Zealand
  R.4
TREMBLAY, George (1911-   ), USA
  R.1   S.10,13
TREMBLAY, Gilles (1932-   ), Can
  R.1
TRÉMISOT, Edouard (1874-1952), Fr
  R.4   S.34
TREMOIS, Marcel
           S.10
TRENET, Charles (1913-   ), Fr
  R.4   S.10
TRENT, Anthony - pseud [see CLARKE, Rebecca]
TRENTINAGLIA, Erardo (1889-1950), It
  R.8   S.5x
TREVALSA, Joan (fl 1910)
  R.200   S.10
TREVATHAN, Charles E. (fl 1896)
  R.200   S.10
TREVOR - When its apple blossom time in Normandy
           S.e

TREXLER, Georg (1903-1979), Ger
   R.1   S.c
TRIANA, Juan de (fl 1478-83), Sp
   R.1   S.c,10,17
TRIEBENSEE, Josef (1772-1846), Boh
   R.1   S.c
TRIESTE, Robert USA
            S.13
TRIGGS, Harold (1900-   ), USA
   R.19   S.5x,10,13,24
TRILLER, Valentin (d.1573), Ger
   R.1
TRILUSSA - pseud [see SALUSTRI, Carlo Alberto]
TRIM - Serenade de Magali
            S.e
TRIMARCHI, Rocco (1861-   ), It
   R.10   S.c,10,44
TRIMBLE, Lester (1923-   ), USA
   R.1   S.10,13,21,28
TRINONETTI - Madrigal (vi & p)
            S.24a
TRIOLET - Berceuse
            S.e
TRIOLIN - Lipkowska waltz
            S.e
TRITONIUS, Petrus (c1465-c1525), Aus
   R.1
TRNEČEK, Hanuš (1858-1914), Boh
   R.1   S.10
TRODING - Janteblick
            S.e
TROFEO, Ruggier (c1550-1614), It
   R.1   S.10,16,53
TROGAN, Roland (1933-   ), USA
   R.19   S.9,10,13,24a
TROIANI, Gaetano (1873-1942), Arg
   R.9   S.3,4,5x
TROJAHN, Manfred (1949-   )
            S.c
TROJAN TURNOVSKÝ, Jan (c1550-c1595), Cz
   R.1   S.5x
TROJAN, Václav (1907-   ), Cz
   R.1   S.c,24,31
TROJANSKY - Let joy abide you
            S.e
TROMBLY, Preston (1945-   ), USA
   R.19   S.10,13
TROMBONCINO, Bartolomeo (c1470-c1535), It
   R.1   S.c,5x,8,10,14-16,24

TROMMER, Jack (1905-   )
              S.c
TROOSTWYCK, Hendrika (19-20th Cent), Neth
    R.7   S.24
TROTÈRE, Henry (1855-1912), Eng
    R.44
TROTSYUK, Bogdan Jakoblevich (1931-   )
              S.18
TROWBRIDGE, Luther (1892-   ), USA
    R.14   S.10,13
TRUAX, Barry Douglas (1947-   ), Can
    R.31
TRUHLAR, Jan (1928-   )
              S.10,32
TRUNK, Richard (1879-1968), Ger
    R.1   S.c,5x,8,10
TRYTHALL, Harry Gilbert (1930-   ), USA
    R.19   S.10,13
TRYTHALL, Richard (1939-   ), USA
    R.19   S.10,13
TSCHESNOKOV, Pavel Grigoryevich
    [see CHESNOKOV, Pavel Grigoryevich]
TSCHISCHKO, Oles Semyonovich
    [see CHISHKO, Oles Semyonovich]
TSEGLYAR, Yakov Semalovich (1912-   )
              S.18
TSEKHLIN, Rut (1926-   )
              S.18
TSFASMAN, Alexander Naumovich (1906-1971), USSR
    R.14   S.54(342)
TSINTSADZE, Sulkhan Fyodorovich (1925-   ), USSR
    R.1   S.8,18,23,24
TSU-CHIANG WU (20th Cent)
              S.c
TSVETAEV, Mikhail Alexeyevich (1907-   )
              S.18
TSYTOVICH, Vladimir (1931-   )
              S.18,23
TUBIN, Eduard (1905-1982), Est
    R.1   S.c,18,24a
TUČAPSKY, Antonín (1928-   ), Cz
    R.80   S.c
TUCCI, Terig
              S.10
TUCKER, Gregory (1908-1971), USA
    R.19   S.3,5x,13
TUCKER, Henry (fl 1862), USA
    R.53   S.10
TUCKFIELD - Underneath the mango tree
              S.e

TUDE - For king and country
              S.e
TUDOR, David (1926-   ), USA
   R.19   S.13
TUFTS, John (1689-1750), USA
   R.1   S.10
TUFTS, Paul (1924-   ), USA
              S.13
TUKKER, C. A. (1938-   )
              S.c
TULEBAYEV, Mukan Tulebaevich (1913-1960), USSR
   R.14   S.18
TULEYEV, Askar (1920-1962)
              S.18
TULINDBERG, Erik (1761-1814), Fin
   R.1   S.10
TULL, Fisher Aubrey (1934-   ), USA
   R.19   S.10,13
TULOU, Jean-Louis (1786-1865), Fr
   R.1   S.10
TŮMA, Fratišek Ignác Antonín (1704-1774), Cz
   R.1   S.c,5x,9
TUNBRIDGE (19th cent) - Virginia
              S.c
TUNDER, Franz (1614-1667), Ger
   R.1   S.c,5x,10,53
TUOTILO (d.915)
   R.1   S.c,16
TUPINAMBA, Marcelo - pseud [ie Fernando LOBO]
   (1889-1953), Brazil R.67   S.1x
TURBA-WINKEL - German marching songs
              S.10
TURCHANINOV, Pyotr Ivanovich (1779-1856), Ukraine
   R.1   S.c,10
TURCO, Giovanni del [see DEL TURCO, Giovanni]
TURECEK, Eduard (1899-   )
              S.24
TURENKOV, Alexei Evlampievich (1886-1958), USSR
   R.14   S.18
TURETZKY, Bertram (1933-   ), USA
   R.19   S.13
TURGES, Edmund (b c1450), Eng
   R.1   S.c
TURINA, Joaquín (1882-1949), Sp
   R.1   S.c,1-11,18,23,24,25,27,32,39
TURINI, Ferdinando Gasparo
   [see TURRINI, Ferdinando Gasparo]
TURINI, Francesco (c1589-1656), It
   R.1   S.c,10,24

TÜRK, Daniel Gottlob (1750-1813), Ger
   R.1   S.c
TURK, Roy (1892-1934), USA
   R.23   S.24
TURLE, James (1802-1882), Eng
   R.1   S.c
TURLET - French national defile
           S.54(327)
TÜRMER, Udo - pseud [see LAUTENSCHLÄGER, Willi]
TURNER, Charles (1921-   ), USA
   R.19   S.10,13,24
TURNER, Frank (1896-   )

TURNER, Mildred Cozzens (Mrs. Huntington) (1897-   )
   USA   R.7   S.52
TURNER, Robert Comrie (1920-   ), Can
   R.31   S.24
TURNER, William (1651-1740), Eng
   R.1   S.8,10
TURNHOUT, Gérard de (c1520-1580), Flem
   R.1   S.c,8,10,14,16
TURNOUT, Jan-Jacob van (c1545->1618), Flem
   R.1   S.c
TURNOVSKY, Jan Trojan [see TROJAN TURNOVSKÝ, Jan]
TUROK, Paul (1929-   ), USA
   R.19   S.10,13
TURPIN, Thomas Million (c1873-1922), USA
   R.50   S.10,22
TURRINI, Ferdinando Gasparo (1749-1812), It
   R.8   S.5
TURSKI, Zbigniew (1908-1979), Pol
   R.1   S.24
TURVEY SCHETKY, Carol
           S.e
TURYSHEV, Oleg
           S.18
TUTHILL, Burnet Corwin (1888-   ), USA
   R.23   S.8,10,13,19,20,22
TUTILLON, [see TUOTILO]
TÜZÜN, Ferit (1929-1977), Turkey
   R.1   S.c
TVEITT, Geirr (1908-   ), Nor
   R.1   S.c,7,40,24,51
TWARDOWSKI, Romuald (1930-   ), Pol
   R.1
TWINKLE, Kate van - pseud [see VANNAH, Kate]
TWOREK, Wandy (1913-   ), Den
   R.80   S.5x,24
TYAN-KHUA, Liu (1895-1932), China
           S.18,52

TYE, Christopher (1505-?1572), Eng
  R.1   S.c,2,5,9,10,14,16,53
TYERS, William H. (1876-1924), USA
  R.23   S.54(311)
TYLE, Ted - Whodunit
          S.22
TYRMAND, Eta Moiseyevna (1917-   ), USSR
          S.18,52
TYSON, Mildred Lund (1901-   ), USA
  R.19   S.10,13,30,52
TYULIN, Yury Nikolayevich (1893-   ), USSR
  R.1   S.18
TYURIO, Seki
          S.18
TYURNPU, Konstantin (1865-1927)
          S.18
TZINTSADZE, Sulkhan Fyodorovich
  [see TSINTSADZE, Sulkhan Fyodorovich]
TZVETANOV, Tzvetant (1931-   ), Bul
  R.4
UBER, David Albert (1921-   ), USA
  R.19   S.c
UCCELLINI, Marco (c1603-c1680), It
  R.5   S.c,24a
UFFORD, Rev. E. S. (19th Cent) - Throw out the lifeline
          S.10
UGARTE, Floro Manuel (1884-1975), Arg
  R.1   S.5,8,10,24,46
UHL, Afred (1909-   ), Aus
  R.1   S.c,10,19,20,23
UHLÍŘ, Jan (1894-   ), Cz
  R.18   S.31
ULEHLA, Ludmila (1923-   ), USA
  R.19   S.10,13,30,52
ULLRICH, Josef (1911-   ), Cz
  R.18   S.31
UMLAUF, Michael (1781-1842), Aus
  R.1   S.c
UMSTATT, Joseph (1711-1762), Aus
  R.1   S.c
UNG, Chinary (1942-   ), USA
  R.19   S.10,13
UNGER, Hermann (1886-1958), Ger
  R.1   S.c,24a
UNGÖR, Osman Zeki (1880-1958), Turkey
  R.1
UNGVARY, Tamas (1936-   ), Hun
  R.80   S.40
UNVERZAGTE, Der (13th Cent), Ger
  R.1   S.c,5x,14,16

URAY, Ernst Ludwig (1906-   ), Aus
    R.14   S.24
URBAKH, Samuil Yulievich (1908-1969), USSR
    R.14   S.18
URBAN, Stepan (1913-   )
    R.14   S.32
URBANEC, Bartolomej (1918-   ), Cz
    R.18   S.31
URBANEC, Rudolf (1907-   ), Cz
    R.18   S.31
URBANNER, Erich (1936-   ), Aus
    R.1   S.c,10,24a
URIBE HOLGUÍN, Guillermo (1880-1971), Colombia
    R.1   S.3,11,24a
URREDA [Wreede], Johannes (15th Cent), Sp
    R.1   S.c,16,17
USANDIZAGA, José María (1887-1915), Sp
    R.1   S.8-10,39,42
USIGLIO,Emilio (1841-1910), It
    R.1   S.e
USMANBAS, Ilhan (1921-   ), Turkey
    R.1   S.10
USPENSKY, Vladislav Alexandrovich (1937-   )
                S.18
USPER, Francesco (<1570-1641), It
    R.1   S.c
USSACHEVSKY, Vladimir (1911-   ), Russia/USA
    R.1   S.8-10,13
USTVOLSKAYA, Galina Ivanova (1919-   ), USSR
    R.1   S.18,52
UTEN, Eugeen Emil Karel (1919-   ), Bel
    R.25
UTKIN, Valentin Fedorovich (1904-   )
                S.18,54(357)
UTTINI, Francesco Antonio Baldassare (1723-1795), It
    R.1   S.c,10,56
UY, Paul (1932-   )
                S.c
UYTTENHOVE, Pieter Franz (1874-1923), Bel
    R.25   S.41
VACCAI, Nicola (1790-1848), It
    R.1   S.c,10
VACCHERAS, Beltrame [see VAQUERAS, Bertrandus]
VACEK, Karel Václev (1908-1982), Cz
    R.18   .   S.31
VACEK, Miloš (1928-   ), Cz
    R.18   S.31
VACH, Ferdinand (1860-1939), Cz [?]
    R.18   S.5x

VACHON, Pierre (1731-1803), Fr
   R.1   S.7,10
VAČKÁŘ, Dalibor Cyril (1906-   ), Cz
   R.1   S.20,24a,31
VAČKÁŘ, Tomáš (1945-1963), Cz
   R.1
VAČKÁŘ, Václav (1881-1954), Cz
   R.1   S.31
VADO, Juan del (fl 1635-75), Sp
   R.1   S.c,10,53
VAET, Jacobus (c1529-1567), Neth
   R.1   S.c,10
VAGA y PALACIO, Aurelio

VAGGIONE, Horacio (1940-   ), Arg
   R.26   S.46
VAGNER, Genrikh Matusovich (1922-   ), USSR
   R.1   S.18
VAILLANT, Jehan (fl ?1360-90), Fr
   R.1   S.10,16
VAIN, Evald (1915-1970)
   R.58   S.18
VAINBERG, Moyssey Samuilovich
   [see VAYNBERG, Moyssey Samuilovich]
VAINIUNAS, Stasis Andriaus (1909-   ), USSR
   R.14   S.18,24
VAISBURD, Jakob Isayevich (1928-   )
               S.18
VALADON, Emma Eugene Rose [see THÉRÉSA - pseud]
VALDAUF, Karel (1913-   ), Cz
   R.18   S.31
VALDERRÁBANO, Enríquez de (16th Cent), Sp
   R.1   S.c,4,5x,10,11,14,16,17,32,33,53
VALDÉS, Gilberto (1905-   ), Cuba
   R.9   S.18
VALDEZ, Charles Robert
               S.18,24
VALDEZ FRAGA, P.
               S.24a
VALE, Francisco (1869-1906), Brazil (see note)
   R.56
VÁLEK, Jiři (1923-   ), Cz
   R.14   S.c,24a,31
VALEN, Fartein (1887-1952), Nor
   R.1   S.c,5x,6-8,10,24,40,51
VALENCIANO, Miguel Marti (17th Cent)
               S.c,10,16,39
VALENSIN, Georges (1844-   )
               S.5x,24

VALENTE, Antonio (fl 1565-80), It
   R.1   S.c,10,16,53
VALENTE, Nicola (1881-1946), It
   R.8   S.44
VALENTE, Vincenzo (1855-1921), It
   R.3   S.e
VALENTI COSTA, Pedro (1905-   ), Arg
   R.26   S.46
VALENTINE, Robert (c1680-c1735), Eng
   R.1   S.c,8,10
VALENTINE, Thomas (1790-1878), Eng
   R.44
VALENTINI, Giovanni (1582/83-1649), It
   R.1   S.c
VALENTINI, Giuseppe (c1680->1759), It
   R.1   S.c,2,3,5,6,8,10,18,24
VALERA, Maria Esteband de
   [see ESTEBAND de VALERA, Marie]
VALÈRE - pseud [see MORGAN, Robert Orlando]
VALERI, Gaetano (1760-1822), It
   R.1   S.c
VALERIO - psued [see KETTEN, Henri]
VALERIUS, Adriaen (c1575-1625), Neth (see note)
   R.1   S.c,10,14,54(324)
VALESCO - Ojas tapatios [see also VELASCOS]
            S.e
VALIULLIN, Allagiar (1924-   )
            S.18
VALIULLIN, Khusnulla (1914-   )
            S.18,24
VALKARE, Gunnar (1943-   ), Sweden
   R.30   S.56
VALLADON, Emma Eugénie Rose [see THÉRÉSA - pseud]
VALLE - Stein
            S.54(358)
VALLE, Francisco L. - Ao pe da fogueira (Preludio XV)
   arr vi & p, Heifetz (see note under Vale)
            S.c,5x,10,23,24
VALLE, Pietro della [see DELLA VALLE, Pietro]
VALLERAND, Jean (1915-   ), Can
   R.1   S.24
VALLET, Nichlas (c1583->1642), Fr
   R.1   S.c,10,16
VALLINI - Sempre amarti
            S.e
VALLS, Francisco (1665-1747), Sp
   R.1   S.c
VALLS, Rafael Martinez [see MARTINEZ VALLS, Rafael]
VALLS GORINA, Manuel (1920-   ), Sp
   R.14   S.24a

VALOIS, Philippe (1734-1775)
                    S.c
VALTON, Peter
              S.47
VALVERDE, Joaquín (1846-1910), Sp
   R.1   S.1x,4,5x,8,10,39
VANAGAITIS, Antanas (1890-1949), Lith
   R.4
VAN ALSTYNE, Egbert Anson (1882-1951), USA
   R.23   S.10
VAN APPLEDORN, Mary Jeanne (1927-   ), USA
   R.7   S.13,30,52
VAN BERCHAM, Jaquet [see BERCHEM, Jacquet de]
VAN BIENE, Auguste [see BIENE, August van]
VAN BOSKERCK, Francis Saltus
              S.10
VAN CAMPENHAUT, François [see CAMPENHOUT, François van]
VANCEA, Zeno (1900-   ), Rum
   R.1
VAN DELDEN, Lex [see DELDEN, Lex Van]
VANDELLE, Romuald (1895-   ), Fr
   R.14
VAN den GHEYN, Matthias (1721-1785), Flem
   R.1   S.c,1x,2-4,5x,8,18,41,53
VAN den HOVE, Joachim [see HOVE, Joachim van den]
VAN den KERCKHOVEN, Abraham
   [see KERCKHOVEN, Abraham van den]
VANDERCOOK, Hale Ascher (1864-1949), USA
   R.49   S.54(367)
VANDERMAESBRUGGE, Max (1933-   ), Bel
   R.4
VANDERPOOL, Frederick William (1877-1947), USA
   R.23   S.e
VANDERSLOAT - Dreamy Hawaii (vi & p)
              S.24
VANDERSLOOT, Carl D. USA
              S.13,54(328)
VAN der STUCKEN, Frank Valentin (1858-1929), USA
   R.3
VAN der VELDEN, Renier [see VELDEN, Renier van der]
VANDERWATER - The Penitent
              S.e
VAN de VATE, Nancy Hayes [pseud: Helen HUNTLEY]
   (1930-   ), USA   R.7   S.52
VAN DIEREN, Bernard [see DIEREN, Bernard van]
VÁNDOR, Sándor (1901-1945), Hun
   R.1
VAN EYCK, Jacob [see EYCK, Jacob van]
VAN GOENS [see GOENS, Daniel van]

VAN HAGEN, Peter Albrecht
    [see HAGEN, Peter Albrecht van]
VANHAL, Johann Baptist (1739-1813), Cz
    R.1   S.c,5x,7,10,19,23,24a,32
VAN HELMONT, Charles-Joseph
    [see HELMONT, Charles-Joseph van]
VAN HERZEEL - Het dierbaar ouderhuis
          S.e
VAN HEUSEN, James - pseud [see BABCOCK, Edward Chester]
VAN HOEK, Jan Anton (1936-   )

VAN HULSE, Camil (1897-   ), USA
    R.19   S.10,12,13
VANHURA, Ceslav (1667-1736), Cz
          S.c
VANIER, Jeannine (1929-   ), Can
    R.7   S.10,30
VANIS - Magic of love
          S.54(339)
VAN LIER, Bertus [see LIER, Bertus van]
VAN MALDERE, Pierre [see MALDERE, Pierre van]
VANNAH, Kate [pseud: Kate van TWINKLE] (1855-1933), USA
    R.7   S.e
VAN NIEUWENHOVE, Ernest Alfons
    [see NIEUWENHOVE, Ernest Alfons van]
VAN NOORDT, Anthoni [see NOORDT, Anthoni van]
VAN NUFFEL, Jules [see NUFFEL, Jules van]
VAN OVERBEEK, Coos

VAN ROSSUM, Frederic [see ROSSUM, Frederick van]
VAN SOLDT, Suzanne (16-17th Cent)
          S.c
VANTOURA, Suzanne Haik (1912-   ), Fr
    R.7   S.c,52[Haik]
VANURA, Ceslav (1694-1736), Cz
    R.1
VAN VACTOR, David (1906-   ), USA
    R.19   S.9,10,13
VAN VEELEN, Paul (1939-   ), Neth
    R.80   S.10,13
VAN WEERBEKE, Gaspar [see WEERBEKE, Gaspar van]
VAN WICHEL, Philippus [see WICHEL, Philippus van]
VAN WILDER, Philip [see WILDER, Philip van]
VAQUEIRAS, Raimbault de [see RAIMBAULT de VAQUEIRAS]
VAQUERAS, Bertrandus (c1450-c1507)
    R.1   S.c
VARDELL, Charles Gildersleeve Jr. (1893-1962), USA
    R.19   S.3,5x,10,11,13
VARDI, Emanuel (1917-   ), USA
    R.19   S.10,13

VAREL - Ah luna
        S.44
VARELAS, Sovet Afanasevich (1923-   )
        S.18
VARELLA CID, Sergio de (1935-   ), Port
    R.4   S.18
VARÈSE, Edgard (1883-1965), Fr
    R.1   S.c,3-6,8-11,13
VARGA, Ruben (1928-   ), Isr
    R.4   S.10,24
VARGAS, Eva (1937-   ), Ger
    R.4   S.c,30,52
VARGUES, Felicien (fl 1896-1904), Fr
        S.e
VARLAMOV, Alexander Egarovich (1801-1848), Russia
    R.1   S.c,5x,10,18
VARNEY, Louis (1844-1908), Fr
    R.1   S.c,18,42
VARONA - O cuanto sufro; Dame un beso
        S.e
VAROTER, Francesco [see ANA, Francesco d´]
VAROTTI, Albino (1925-   ), It
    R.14   S.10
VARVOGLIS, Mario (1885-1967), Greece
    R.1   S.8,24
VASILENKO, Sergey Nikiforovich (1872-1956), Russia
    R.1   S.5x,7,9,10,18,20
VASILEV, Fedor Semenovich (1920-   ), USSR
    R.47   S.18

VASQUEZ, Juan (c1510-c1560), Sp
    R.1   S.c,2-4,5x,8,10,11,14,16,17,32,39
VASSEUR, Léon (1844-1917), Fr
    R.1
VASSILENKO, Sergey Nikiforovich
    [see VASILENKO, Sergey Nikiforovich]
VAUDRY, A. (19th Cent), Fr
        S.5x
VAUGHAN THOMAS, M. (20th Cent), Wales
        S.c
VAUGHAN WILLIAMS, Ralph (1872-1958), Eng
    R.1   S.c,1-11,18,19,23-28,54(354,27,50),55
VAUGHAN, Clifford (1893-   ), USA
    R.19   S.13
VAUGHAN, Rodger (1932-   ), USA
    R.19   S.13
VAUTOR, Thomas (fl 1600-20), Eng
    R.1   S.c,1x,2,3,5,7,8,10,11,14,16,32
VAVRINECZ, Béla (1925-   ), Hun
    R.14

VAYNBERG, Moyssey Samuilovich (1919-   ), USSR
   R.1   S.c,8,10,18,24
VAZQUEZ, Juan [see VASQUEZ, Juan]
VAZZANA, Anthony E. (1922-   ), USA
   R.19   S.13,24a
VECCHI, Orazio (1550-1605), It
   R.1   S.c,5-11,14-16,18,32,42
*** VECCHI, Orazio Orfeo (1540?-1604?) (see note)
VECCHIA, Wolfgango della (1923-   )
              S.c
VECSEY, Franz von (1893-1935), Hun
   R.9   S.5x,10,18,24a
VEDEL, Artemiy Lukyanovich (c1772-1808), Russia
   R.47   S.c,10
VEDRO, Adu (1890-1944), Est
   R.4   S.18
VEGA - Cancion de amor
              S.e
VEGA, Aurelio de la (1925-   ), USA
   R.1   S.8,10,24a
VEGGIO, Claudio Maria (b ?c1510), It
   R.1   S.16
VEIGA OLIVEIRA, Sofia Helena da (20th Cent), Brazil
              S.52
VEJVANOWSKÝ, Pavel Jósef (c1633/39-c1693), Moravia
   R.1   S.c,5x,9,10,24a
VELASCOS - Ojas tapatios [see also VALESCO]
              S.e
VELAZQUEZ, Higinio (1926-   ), Mex
              S.10
VELDEN, Renier van der (1910-   ), Bel
   R.,20,30   S.c
VELLERE, Lucie (1896-1966), Bel
   R.7   S.c,30,52
VELLONES, Pierre (Rousseau) (1889-1939), Fr
   R.4   S.c,4,5

VELLUTI, Giovanni Battista (1781-1861), It [composer?]
   R.1   S.c
VELT, Jacob M. (fl 1943), Sweden [editor?]
   R.200   S.24
VENETO, Francesco [see ANA, Francesco d´]
VENEZIANO, Gaetano (1656-1716), It [?]
   R.1   S.5x
VENT, Jan [see WENT, Johann]
VENTADORN, Bernart de [see BERNART de VENTADORN]
VENTO, Ivo de (c1543-1575), Ger
   R.1   S.c,10,16
VENTO, Mattia (1735-1776), It [?]
   R.1   S.5x

VENTURA, José (1818-1875), Sp
  R.3
VENTURINI, Francesco (c1675-1745), Ger
  R.1   S.c
VENZANO, Luigi (1814-1878), It
  R.10   S.c
VEPRIK, Alexander Moiseyevich (1899-1958), USSR
  R.1   S.18
VERACINI, Francesco Maria (1690-1768), It
  R.1   S.c,1x,2-5,7-11,18,23-25,27
VERARDI, Carlo (16th Cent), Sp
           S.c,10,17
VERAY, Amaury Puerto Rico

VERBESSELT, August Frans (1919-   ), Bel
  R.14
VERBONNET, Johannes [see GHISELIN, Johannes]
VERBRUGGHEN, Henri (1873-1934), Bel
  R.1   S.24
VERCOE, Barry Lloyd (1937-   ), USA
  R.19   S.10,13
VERCOE, Elizabeth (1941-   ), USA
  R.7   S.30,52
VERDALLE, Gabriel (fl 1898)
  R.200   S.c
VERDELOT, Philippe (?1470/80-<1552), Neth
  R.1   S.c,8,10,14,16,18
VERDI, Giuseppe (1813-1901), It
  R.1 S.c,1-11,18,19,24,26,28,34,42,43,54(311,13,14,25)
VERDIER, Pierre (1627-1706), Fr
  R.1   S.c
VERDONCK, Cornelis (1563-1625), Flem
  R.1   S.c
VERDONCK, Jean (16-17th Cent)
           S.16
VEREMANS, Renaat (1894-1969), Bel
  R.14   S.c
VERESS, Sándor (1907-   ), Swiss
  R.1   S.c,5,24
VERGER, P. Maillard
           S.8,14
VERGINE - Vieni sul mar
           S.5x

VERHEUL, W. P. (1913-   )
           S.c
VERHEY, Theodore H. H. (1848-1929), Neth
  R.3   S.19,21
VERHOEVEN, Arthur Hendrik (1889-1958), Bel
  R.25   S.c

VERIKIVSKY, Mykhaylo (1896-1962), Ukraine
   R.1   S.18
VERLAIN (14th Cent), It

VERMEIREN, Jef (1904-   ), Bel
   R.25
VERMEULEN, Matthijs (1888-1967), Neth
   R.1   S.10,24a
VERMONT, Pierre (d.1532), Fr
   R.1   S.10,16
VERMULST, Jan

VERNON, Joseph (c1739-1782), Eng
   R.1   S.5x,8
VERNOR, F. Dudleigh (1892-1974), USA
   R.23   S.10
VEROLI, Donato di [see DI VEROLI, Donato]
VERRALL, John (1908-   ), USA
   R.1   S.8-10,13
VERSCHRAEGEN, Gabriël (1919-1981), Bel
   R.25   S.c
VERSCHUEREN, Marceau [see MARCEAU, V. - pseud]
VERSTOVSKY, Alexey Nikolayevich (1799-1862), Russia
   R.1   S.c,5x,18,23
VERT, Juan (1890-1931)
             S.c,8,10,39
VERYKIVSKYI, Mikhailo Ivanovych (1896-1962)

VESELOV, Vadim Fedorovich (1931-   ), USSR
   R.47   S.18
VESI, Simone (c1610->1667), It
   R.1   S.c
VESSELLA, Alessandro (1860-1929), It
   R.8   S.5x,54(340)
VESSELLA, M. - Pasadena day
             S.54(348)
VETTER, Daniel (1657/58-1721), Ger
   R.1   S.8,10
VETTER, Michael (1943-   ), Ger
   R.1   S.c
VETTIK, Tuudur (1898-   ), Est
   R.58   S.18
VÉZINA, Joseph (1849-1924), Can
   R.1
VIADANA, Lodovici (c1560-1627), It
   R.1   S.c,2-6,8,10,14-16,18,24a
VIAERA, Fredericas (fl 1563-64)

VIANNA da MOTTA, José (1868-1948), Port
   R.1   S.c,18

VIANNA, Frutuoso (1896-1976), Brazil
    R.14   S.c,5x,10
VIANO, A. - Purple moon (v)
            S.18
VIARDOT-GARCIA, Pauline (1821-1910), Fr
    R.8   S.10,30,52
VIBERT, Mathieu (1920-   ), Swiss
    R.4
VICARS, Harold [pseud: MOYA] (d.1922), Eng
    R.23   S.10,24
VICENTINO, Nicola (1511-c1576), It
    R.1   S.9
VICKERY - Rays of sunshine
            S.54(351)
VICTORIA, Tomás Luis de (1548-1611), Sp
    R.1   S.c,1x,2-11,14-16,18,39
VICTORY, Gerard (1921-   ), Ire
    R.1   S.c,49
VIDAL, Paul Antonin (1863-1931), Fr
    R.1   S.10
VIDAL, Peire (fl c1175-c1210), Fr
    R.1   S.8,10,14,16
VIDE, Jacobus (fl 1410-1433), Franco-Flem
    R.1
VIELGORSKY, Mikhail Yurevich (1794-1866), Russia
    R.47   S.18
VIERDANCK, Johann (c1605-1646), Ger
    R.1   S.c
VIERLING, Johann Gottfried (1750-1813), Ger
    R.1   S.c
VIERNE, Louis (1870-1937), Fr
    R.1   S.c,1-5,7-10
VIERU, Anatol (1926-   ), Rum
    R.33
VIEUXTEMPS, Henry (1820-1881), Bel
    R.1   S.c,1-7,10,18,24,41
VIGNAS, Jose [S.18] = VIÑAS, José
VIGUERIE, Bernard (c1761-1819), Fr
    R.1   S.10
VIJFWINKEL, Wim
            S.c
VILA, Gabriel

VILA, Pedro [see ALBERCH VILA, Pere]
VILAR, Francisco (d.1770), Sp
    R.1   S.c
VILBOA, Konstantin Petrovich (1817-1882), Russia
            S.10,18
VILCHES (fl 15-16th Cent), Sp
            S.8,10,14,16,17,39

VILDANOV, Rumil (1939-   )
        S.18
VILEC, Michal (1902-   ), Slovak
  R.1   S.31
VILKOMIRSKY, Kazimir (1900-   ), Pol
        S.18
VILLA, Pedro (1517-1582), Sp
        S.c
VILLA, Ricardo (1873-1935), Sp
  R.3
VILLA-LOBOS, Heitor (1887-1959), Brazil
  R.1   S.c,1-11,18,19,22-24,28,32,39
VILLALAR, Andrés de (c1530->1593), Sp
  R.1   S.16
VILLANEUVA, Felipe (1862-1893)
        S.24a
VILLASENOR, Jesus (1936-   )

VILLENEUVE, Charles A. (1930-   ), Can

VILLETTE, Pierre/Paul (20th Cent), Fr
        S.c
VILLIERS, P. [?Pierre] de (fl 1532-50), Fr
  R.1   S.15
VIÑALS, Fray Esteban (b.1780), Sp
  R.9   S.c
VIÑAS, José (1823-1888), Sp
  R.9   S.c,18,32
VINAVER, Chemjo (1900-   ), Isr
  R.14   S.c
VINCENET, Johannes (c1400-79), Fr
  R.1
VINCENT, (d c1650), Fr
  R.1   S.c
VINCENT, John (1902-1977), USA
  R.1   S.8,9,13
VINCENT, Thomas (c1720-1783), Eng
  R.1   S.c
VINCENZO da RIMINI (14th Cent), It
  R.1   S.c,3-4,5x,8,11,14,53
VINCI, Leonardo (c1690-1730), It
  R.1   S.c,3,4,8,10,11,19,21
VINCI, Pietro (c1535-1584), It
  R.1   S.c
VINCI-WALN - Sonata no.1 [S.19]
  = VINCI, Leonardo, arr Waln
VINCK, (20th Cent) - Chant a Ventadour (guitar)
        S.c
VINCZE, Imre (1926-1969), Hun
  R.1

VINDERS, Jheronimus [Hieronymus] (fl 1510-50), Flem
            S.10,16
VINET, Michel Raymond (1950-   ), Can
    R.81
VINGE, Per (1858-1935), Nor

    R.30]   S.e
VINIER, Guillaume li [see GUILLAUME li VINIER]
VINOGRADOV, Vasili Ivanovich (1874-1948), Russia
    R.47   S.10,18
VINTER, Gilbert (1909-1969), Eng
    R.85   S.c,9,54(323),55
VINTER, Yulo Alexandrovich (1924-   ), USSR
    R.47   S.18
VIOLA, Anselmo (1738-1798), Catalan
    R.9   S.c,10
VIOLETTE, Andrew USA
            S.13
VIOLETTE, Wesley la [see LA VIOLETTE, Wesley]
VIOTTA, Johannes Josephus (1814-1859), Neth
    R.1   S.41
VIOTTI, Giovanni Battista (1755-1824), It
    R.1   S.c,1,2,6,8-10,18,24
VIPLER, Vlastislav Antonín (1903-   ), Cz
    R.18   S.31
VIRGILI, Lavinio (1902-1976), It
    R.14   S.c
VIRGILIANO, Aurelio (16th Cent)
            S.c
VIRGILIO, Renato (1881-   ), It
    R.52   S.e
VIRU, Valdeko (1921-   )
            S.18
VISÉE, Robert (17-18th Cent), Fr
    R.1   S.c,3-5,7,8,10,18,32
VÏSHNEGRADSKY [Vysh., Wysch.], Ivan Alexandrovich
    (1893-1979), Russia R.1   S.3,4
VISKI, János (1906-1961), Hun
    R.1   S.10,24
VISOTSKY, Mikhail Timofeyevich (1791-1837), Russia
    R.1   S.10,32
VITALI, Filippo (c1590-1653), It
    R.1   S.c
VITALI, Giovanni Battista (1632-1692), It
    R.1   S.c,8,10,24
VITALI, Tomaso Antonio (1663-1745), It
    R.1   S.c,2-5,7,8,10,11,18,24
VITALINI, Alberico (1921-   ), It
    R.14   S.8,10
VITÁSEK, Jan August (1770-1839), Boh
    R.1   S.c,5x

VITEZSLAV, Novak (1870-1949)
S.24a
VITO, Edward USA
S.10,13
VITO-DELVAUX, Berthe di (1915-   ), Bel
R.7   S.30,52
VITOLS, Jazeps (1863-1948), Lat
R.1   S.18[Witols],24
VITOLYN, Jan Ottovich
S.10
VITONE, Nicola (1913-   )
S.c

VITRY, Philippe de (1291-1361), Fr
R.1   S.c,10,16
VITTADINI, Franco (1884-1948), It
R.1   S.8
VITTORI, Loreto (1600-1670), It
R.1
VITTORIA, Mario (1911-   ), Fr
R.14   S.c,24a
VIVADO ORSINI, Ida (1916-   ), Chile
R.7   S.52
VIVALDI, Antonio (1678-1741), It
R.1   S.c,1-11,18,21-24,26,27,32
VIVANCO, Sebastian de (c1551-1622), Sp
R.1   S.c,16,17
VIVARINO, Innocentio (c1575-1626), It
R.1   S.c
VIVES, Amadeo (1871-1932), Sp
R.1   S.c,1,5x,8-10,39,42
VIVIANI, Giovanni Buonaventura (1638-c1693), It
R.1   S.c,10,24
VLADIGEROV, Alexander (1933-   ), Bul
R.14   S.24a
VLADIGEROV, Pancho (1899-1978), Bul
R.1   S.1,4-8,10,18,24
VLASOV, Alexander Kondratevich (1911-   ), USSR
R.47   S.18
VLASSOV, Vladimir Alexandrovich (1903-   ), USSR
R.1   S.c,10,24
VLIET, Herman van (1941-   )
S.c
VLIJMEN, Jan van (1935-   ), Neth
R.1   S.10,24a
VOCHT, Lodewijk de (1887-1977), Bel
R.1   S.7,24
VODICKA, Vaclav [see WODICZKA, Wenceslaus]
VODNANSKY, Jan Campanus [see CAMPANUS, Jan]
VODRAZKA, Jaroslav (1930-   ), Cz
R.18   S.c

VODRÁŽKA, Karel (1904-   ), Cz
    R.18   S.31
VOEGELI, Don USA
                 S.13
VOELCKEL, Samuel (c1560->1617), Ger
    R.1   S.c
VOELKER, G. - A hunt in the Black Forest (orch)
                 S.10
VOGEL, Johann Christoph (1756-1788), Ger
    R.1   S.c,8,10,24a
VOGEL, Wladimir (1896-1984), Swiss
    R.1   S.c,24a
VOGELWEIDE, Walther von der
    [see WALTHER von der VOGELWEIDE]
VOGL, Erwin [see ERWIN, Ralph - pseud]
VOGL, Georg (1725-1761)
                 S.c
VOGL, Johann Michael (1768-1840), Aus
    R.1   S.c

VOGLEIN - Old Viennese dance (vi & p)
                 S.24
VOGLER, Georg Joseph (1749-1814), Ger (see note)
    R.1   S.c,2,10,24
VOGRICH, Max Wilhelm (1852-1916), Ger
    R.3   S.24
VOGT, Hans (1911-   ), Ger
    R.1   S.c
VOGTL, Hans (1909-   ), Swiss
    R.14
VOICU, Ion (1925-   ), Rum
    R.1   S.24
VOIGHT, John USA
                 S.13
VOIGT, G. Bernhard
                 S.24
VOIGTLÄNDER, Gabriel (c1596-1643), Ger
    R.1   S.c
VOIS, Alewijn Pietersz de (c1607-1667), Neth
    R.25
VOIS, Pieter Alewijnsz de (c1581-1654), Neth
    R.25   S.c
VOIT, Hans (16th Cent), Ger
    R.5   S.10,14,16
VOITA, Johann Ignaz Franz (18th Cent)
    R.5
VOJTECH, Jirovec (1763-1850)
                 S.24a
VOKOS, Georg (1915-   )
                 S.c

VOLKMANN, Robert (1815-1883), Ger
   R.1   S.c,9,10,24
VOLKONSKY, Andrey Mikhaylovich (1933-   ), USSR
   R.1
VOLKOV, K. (1943-   )
          S.24a
VOLLENWEIDER, Hans (1918-   ), Swiss
   R.14   S.c
VOLLERTHUN, Georg (1876-1945), Ger
   R.4
VOLLINGER, William (1945-   ), USA
   R.19   S.13
VOLLRATH, Carl Paul (1931-   ), USA
   R.19   S.13
VOLLSTEDT, Robert [pseud: Robert ROBERTI] (1854-1919)
   Ger   R.3
VOLNEY, Ivan - pseud [see VÏSCHNEGRADSKY, Ivan]
VOLOSHINOV, Viktor Vladimirovich (1905-1960), USSR
   R.47   S.18,24
VOLPI, Adamo (1903-   ), It
          S.c
VOMÁČKA, Boleslav (1887-1965), Cz
   R.1   S.31,24a
VONDRACKOVA, Helena (20th Cent), Cz
          S.52
VON TILZER, Albert (1873-1956), USA
   R.1   S.10
VON TILZER, Harry (1872-1946), USA
   R.1   S.10,54(321)
VOORMOLEN, Alexander (1895-1980), Neth
   R.1   S.c,7,8,10
VOŘÍŠEK, Jan Václav [Jan Hugo] (1791-1825), Boh
   R.1   S.c,4,6,7,9,10,24
VORISOFF, Alexander
          S.10
VORLOVÁ, Slávka (née Johnova) [pseud: Mira KORD]
   (1894-1973), Cz   R.7   S.24a,52
VOROTNIKOV, S. - The thief forgiven
          S.10
VORREI - Could I? (vi & p)
          S.24
VOS, Frans

VOSS, Friedrich (1930-   ), Ger
   R.1
VOSTŘAK, Zbynék (1920-   ), Cz
   R.1   S.9,10,31
VOUILLEMIN, Sylvain (1910-   ), Bel
   R.14

VOUSDEN, Valentine
            S.47
VOYS, de la (fl 17th Cent)
            S.8
VRÁNA, František (1914-   ), Cz
    R.14   S.c,22
VRANICKY, Paul [see WRANITZKY, Paul]
VREDEMAN, Jacob (c1564-1621), Neth
    R.1
VREDENBURG, Max (1904-   ), Neth
    R.4
VREULS, Victor (1876-1944), Bel
    R.4
VRIEND, Jan (1938-   ), Neth
    R.4
VRIES, Hendrik de (1857-1929), Neth
    R.25   S.c
VRIES, Klaas de (1944-   ), Neth
            S.c
VUATAZ, Roger (1898-   ), Swiss
    R.1   S.8
VUILDRE, Philipp van (16th Cent), Neth

VUILLEMENT - Hornpipe (p)
            S.10
VUILLERMOZ, Emile (1878-1960), Fr
    R.1   S.c,1
VUJICSICS, Tihamér (1929-1976), Hun
    R.15
VULPIUS, Melchior (c1570-1615), Ger
    R.1   S.c,2,4,8,10,14-16
VYCPÁLEK, Ladislav (1882-1969), Cz
    R.1   S.4,5,9,10,23,24,31
VYEYEVO, Lembit (1926-   )
            S.18
VYMER, Isidor Ilych (1906-   )
            S.18
VYRK, Enn (1905-   )
            S.18
VYSHNEGRADSKY, Ivan Alexandrovich
    [see VÏSHNEGRADSKY, Ivan Alexandrovich]
WAAGSTEIN, Joen (1879-1949), Faroe Islands
    R.30   S.33
WACHOVSKI, Gerd
            S.c
WACLAW, Szamotul [see SZAMOTUL, Waclaw z]
WADA, Norihiko (1932-   ), Japan
    R.36   S.50
WADDINGTON, Sydney Reine (1869-1953), Eng
    R.4

WADE, James (1930-   ), USA
   R.19   S.9,13
WADE, John Francis (?1711-1786), USA
   R.200   S.10
WADELY, Frederick William (1882-   ), Eng
   R.37   S.c
WADHAM - Come to me
             S.e
WAELRANT, Hubert (1516/17-1595), Flem
   R.1   S.c,8,10,16,41
WAGEMANS, Peter Jan (1952-   ), Neth
   R.80   S.c
WAGENAAR, Bernard (1894-1971), USA
   R.1   S.2,8-10,13
WAGENAAR, Diderik - pseud [ie J. D. Haakma WAGENAAR]
   (1946-   ), Neth   R.25
WAGENAAR, Johan (1862-1941), Neth
   R.1   S.6-8,10,41
WAGENSEIL, Georg Christoph (1715-1777), Aus
   R.1   S.c,3-5,10,18
WAGNER - Death of Custer
             S.54(322)
WAGNER, George Gottfried (1698-1756), Ger
   R.1   S.c,5x,10
WAGNER, Gotthard (1678-1738), Ger
   R.1   S.c
WAGNER, Heinrich Matusowiṭsch [see VAGNER, Genrikh M.]
WAGNER, Joseph Franz (1856-1908), Aus
   R.1   S.c,5x,10,54(362)
WAGNER, Joseph Frederick (1900-1974), USA
   R.19   S.9,10,12,13,24
WAGNER, Richard (1813-1883), Ger
   (see note under Baermann)
   R.1   S.c,1-11,18,19,21,24-28,34,42,43,54
WAGNER, Siegfried (1869-1930), Ger
   R.1   S.c,4,5,24
WAGNER, Werner (1927-   ), Arg
   R.26   S.46
WAGNER-RÉGENY, Rudolf (1903-1969), Ger
   R.1   S.c
WAGNES, Eduard (1863-1936), Aus
   R.4   S.10
WAILLY, Paul de (1854-1933), Fr
   R.8   S.8,10
WAINBERG, Moisse Samuilovich
   [see VAYNBERG, Moisse Samuilovich]
WAINWRIGHT, Mary Lee Sellers (1913-   ), USA
   R.23   S.30
WAINWRIGHT, Richard (1757-1825), Eng
   R.1   S.5x

WAISSEL, Matthäus (c1535/40-1602), Neth
   R.1   S.c,5x,8,10,14,16,53
WAKEFIELD - O, Canada march on
              S.e
WAKEFIELD, Charles C. - pseud
  [see CADMAN, Charles Wakefield]
WAKLEY - You gave me comfort
              S.e
WALACIŃSKI, Adam (1928-   ), Pol
   R.4
WALCH, Johann Heinrich (1776-1855), Ger
   R.3   S.10
WALCHA, Helmut (1907-   ), Ger
   R.1   S.c,8,10
WALDEN, Stanley (1932-   ), USA
   R.19   S.10,13
WALDER, Johann Jakob (1750-1817), Swiss
   R.1   S.c
WALDO, Elisabeth (1923-   ), USA
   R.7   S.30,52
WALDTEUFEL, Emil (1837-1915), Ger
   R.1   S.c,2-10,24,54(313,23,56)
WALHOUT = WAELRANT [?]
              S.16
WALKER - Marine's hymn
              S.54(342)
WALKER, Ernest (1870-1949), Eng
   R.1   S.c
WALKER, George (1922-   ), USA
   R.1   S.c,10,13
WALKER, Louise (20th Cent), Aus
   R.7   S.c,10,30,52
WALKER, Richard (1912-   ), USA
   R.19   S.13
WALKER, Robert (1946-   ), Eng
              S.c
WALKER, Timothy (1943-   ), South Africa
              S.c,10
WALLACE, J. C. (19th Cent), USA - We are coming from
  the cotton fields (v)
WALLACE, William (1860-1940), Scot
   R.1   S.5x
WALLACE, William Vincent (1812-1865), Ire
   R.1   S.c,1-5,7,8,10,24
WALLER, Jack (1886-   ), Eng
   R.37   S.24
WALLIN, Bengt-Arne (1926-   ), Sweden
   R.4   S.40
WALLIS, Cedric (20th Cent), Eng
              S.c

WALLISER, Christoph Thomas (1568-1648), Alsace
R.21
WALLOWITCH, John (1930-   ), USA
R.23   S.13
WALMISLEY, Thomas Attwood (1814-1856), Eng
R.1   S.c,7,8
WALMISLEY, Thomas Forbes (1783-1866), Eng
R.1   S.10
WALOND, William (c1725-1770), Eng
R.1   S.c,10,53
WALSINGHAM, Thomas (14-15th Cent), Eng [theorist, hist-
rian]   S.c
WALTER of CHÂTILLON (c1135-c1190), Fr
R.1   S.c,14,16
WALTER, Arnold (1902-1973), Can

R.1   S.10
WALTER, Bruno (1876-1962), Ger
R.1   S.c
WALTER, Ewald - pseud [see PLESSOW, Erich]
WALTER, Johann (1496-1570), Ger
R.1   S.8,10,14-16,32
WALTER, Thomas (1696-1725), USA
R.1   S.10
WALTER-BEHRENS - Romance (vi & p)
            S.24
WALTERS, Gareth (1928-   ), Eng
R.80   S.c
WALTERS, Harold L. (1918-   ), USA
R.19   S.13
WALTHER von der VOGELWEIDE (c1170-c1230), Ger
R.1   S.2-4,8,10,11,14-16
WALTHER, Johann Gottfried (1684-1748), Ger
R.1   S.c,2,4,6-10,18,53
WALTHER, Johann Jakob (c1650-1717), Ger
R.1   S.6,24
WALTHER, Johann [see WALTER, Johann]
WALTHEW, Richard Henry (1872-1951), Eng
R.14   S.3-5,23
WALTON, James G.
            S.5x,10
WALTON, Kenneth (1904-   ), USA
R.19   S.13
WALTON, William Turner (1902-1983), Eng
R.1   S.c,2-11,23,24,28,32,42
WALWORTH, Charles
            S.10
WALZEL, Leopold Mathias (1902-1970), Aus
R.4
WAMBACH, Emile Xaver (1854-1924), Bel
R.3

WANGEMANN, Otto Carl (1848-1914), Ger
   R.3   S.24
WANHAL, Johann Baptist [see VANHAL, Johann Baptist]
WANNENMACHER, Johannes (c1485-1551), Swiss
   R.1   S.c,16
WANNING, Johannes (1537-1603), Ger
   R.1   S.c
WAŃSKI, Jan (1762->1821), Pol
   R.1   S.c
WANSON, James - pseud [see LAUTENSCHLÄGER, Willi]
WARD, Charles B. (1865-1917), USA
   R.23   S.54(314)
WARD, David - An abstract
             S.22
WARD, John (1571-1638), Eng
   R.1   S.c,1x,2,3,5,8,10,14,16
WARD, Robert (1917-   ), USA
   R.1   S.7-10,13,24a,27
WARD, Samuel Augustus (1848-1903), USA
   R.53   S.10
WARD, William Reed (1918-   ), USA
   R.19   S.13

WARD-HIGGS, W. - Sussex by the sea
             S.54(359)
WARD-STEINMAN, David (1936-   )
   R.1   S.10,13,19
WARDEN, David
             S.47
WARE, Harriet (1877-1962), USA
   R.19   S.13
WARE, Helen (1887-1962), USA
   R.7   S.24,30
WARFIELD, Gerald Alexander (1940-   ), USA
   R.19   S.13
WARING, Fred (1900-   ), USA
   R.23   S.10
WARLOCK, Peter - pseud [ie Philip Arnold HESELTINE]
   (1894-1930), Eng   R.1   S.c,1-11,24-28
WARLOP - Tempete sur les cordes (cl quartet)
             S.21
WARNER, Harry Waldo (1874-1945), Eng
   R.4   S.5x,24
WARNER, Richard Lyman (1908-   ), USA
             S.12,13
WARNKEN - Treue zu Kaiser und Reich
             S.54(361)
WARNOW, Harry [pseud: Raymond SCOTT], (1909-   ), USA
   R.23   S.11,13
WARRACK, Guy (1900-   ), Scot
   R.1   S.5x

WARREN, Elinor Remick (1905/06-   ), USA
    R.19   S.9,13,30,52
WARREN, George William (1828-1902), USA
    R.53   S.10
WARREN, Harry (1893-1981), USA
    R.1   S.10,24
WASHBURN, Robert (1928-   ), USA
    R.19   S.13
WASNER, Franz (fl 1950) [editor?]
    R.200   S.10
WASSENAAR, Unico Graf van (1692-1766), Neth
    R.25   S.c
WASSMUTH, Johann (d.1766)
              S.c
WATANABE, Urato (1909-   ), Japan
    R.4,36   S.50
WATERS, James (1930-   ), USA
    R.19   S.10,13
WATERSON, James (1834-1893)
              S.c
WATHAY, Ferenc (16th Cent)
              S.c
WATKINS, David Nigel (1938-   ), Eng
    R.80   S.c,10,13
WATKINS, Michael Blake (20th Cent), Eng
              S.c
WATKINSON, Percy Gerd (1918-   ), Ger
    R.4
WATSON - The Vicar of Bray

WATSON, Anthony (1933-   )

WATSON, Walter Robert (1933-   ), USA
    R.14   S.10,13
WATSON, William Michael (1840-1889), Eng
    R.3   S.c
WATTERS, Clarence USA
              S.12,13
WATTS, John (1930-   ), USA
    R.19   S.10,13
WATTS, Wintter (1884-1962), USA
    R.4
WAXMAN, Donald (1925-   ), USA
    R.19   S.13
WAXMAN, Ernest (1918-   ), USA
              S.13
WAXMAN, Franz (1906-1967), USA
    R.1   S.9,10,13,24
WAYDITCH, Gabriel von (1888-1969), USA
    R.19   S.13

WAYNE, Mabel (1904-   ), USA
　　R.23　　　　S.24,30
WEAIT,ᵃ Christopher Robert Irving (1939-   ), Eng
　　R.80　　　　S.10
WEATHERLY, Frederic Edward (1848-1929), Eng
　　R.57　　　　S.10
WEAVER, John (1937-   ), USA
　　R.19　　　　S.10,12,13
WEAVER, Powell (1890-1951), USA
　　R.19　　　　S.10,12,13
WEBB, George James (1803-1887), USA
　　R.3　　　　S.10
WEBBE, Samuel (i) (1740-1816), Eng
　　R.1　　　　S.c,10
WEBBE, Samuel (ii) (c1770-1843), Eng
　　R.1　　　　S.c
WEBBER, Amherst (1867-1946), Eng
　　R.4　　　　S.10
WEBBER, Lloyd (1914-   )
　　　　　　　　S.c,9
WEBBER, Russel
　　　　　　　　S.24a
WEBER, Alain (1930-   ), Fr
　　R.14　　　　S.c
WEBER, Bedřich Diviś (1766-1842), Boh
　　R.1　　　　S.c,10
WEBER, Ben Brian (1916-1979), USA
　　R.19　　　　S.7,8,10,13,23,24a,25,27
WEBER, Bernhard (1912-1974), Ger
　　R.4　　　　S.c
WEBER, Bernhard Anselm (1764-1821), Ger (see note)
　　R.1　　　　S.2,5x
WEBER, Carl Maria von (1786-1826), Ger
　　R.1
S.c,1-11,18,19,21,22,24,32,42,54(321,25,27,34)
WEBER, Franz (1805-1876), Ger
　　R.98　　　　S.c
WEBER, Friedrich Dionys (1766-1842), Boh
　　R.2
WEBER, Gustave (1845-1887), Swiss
　　R.3
WEBER, Hans (1917-   )
　　　　　　　　S.c
WEBER, Heinrich (1901-   ), Ger
　　R.14　　　　S.c
WEBER, Heinrich (19th Cent), USA

WEBER, Ludwig (1891-1947), Ger
　　R.1　　　　S.c
WEBER, Reinhold (1927-   ), Ger
　　R.4　　　　S.c

WEBERN, Anton (1883-1945), Aus
R.1   S.c,3-10,18,24,28
WEBSTER, Joseph Philbrick (1819-1875), USA
R.1   S.10,47
WEBSTER, Maurice (fl 1621-36), Eng
R.1   S.c
WEBSTER, Michael (1944-   ), USA
             S.13
WECK, Johann (c1495-1536), Ger
R.1   S.c,10,16,53
WECKER, Georg Caspar (1632-1695), Ger
R.1   S.c
WECKERLIN, Jean-Baptiste (1821-1910), Fr
R.1   S.c,4,9,10,18,24a,53
WECKMANN, Matthias (c1619-1674), Ger
R.1   S.c,6-8,10,18
WEDEL, Artemi Lukyanovich
[see VEDEL, Artemi Lukyanovich]
WEELDEN, Jan van (1917-   )
             S.c
WEELKES, Thomas (1576-1623), Eng
R.1   S.c,1x,2-11,14-16,53
WEERBEKE, Gaspar van (c1445->1517), Neth
R.1   S.c,8,14-16
WEGE, Paul (1890-   ), Ger
R.3   S.c
WEHLE, Peter (1914-   ), Aus
R.4   S.10
WEHRLE, Heinz (1921-   ), Swiss
R.80   S.c
WEICHENBERGER, Johann Georg (1676-1740), Aus
R.1
WEIDENAAR, Reynold (1945-   ), USA
R.19   S.13
WEIGEL, Eugene John (1910-   ), USA
R.19   S.8,10,13
WEIGL, Joseph (1766-1846), Ger
R.1   S.c
WEIGL, Karl (1881-1949), Aus
R.1   S.8-10,23,28
WEIGL, Vally (1889-1982), USA
R.7   S.10,30,52
WEIJLAND, Willem (1909-1947)

             S.c
WEIL, Oscar (1840-1921), USA
R.53
WEILAND, Frits (1933-   ), Neth
R.25
WEILAND, Johann Julius (d.1663), Ger
R.25   S.c

WEILL, Kurt (1900-1950), Ger
    R.1   S.c,1x,2-10,18,24,42
WEINBERG, Henry (1931-   ), USA
    R.1   S.10,13
WEINBERG, Jacob (1879-1956), USA
    R.4   S.24a
WEINBERG, Moysey Samuilovich
    [see VAYNBERG, Moysey Samuilovich]
WEINBERGER, Bernard
                 S.22
WEINBERGER, Jaromír (1896-1967), Cz
    R.1   S.c,1-5,7,8,10,11,24
WEINER, Lawrence (1932-   ), USA
    R.23
WEINER, Lazar (1897-1982), USA
    R.19   S.13
WEINER, Leó (1885-1960), Hun
    R.1   S.c,6-10,18,19,24
WEINER, Stanley Milton (1925-   ), USA
    R.19   S.10,13,18,24
WEINGARTNER, Felix (1863-1942), Aus
    R.1   S.c,1x,2-5,8,24a
WEINZIERL, Franz Xaver (1757-1833)
                 S.c
WEINZWEIG, John (1913-   ), Can
    R.1   S.10,24
WEIS, Fleming (1898-   ), Den
    R.1   S.5x,7,19,35,40,57
WEIS, Karel (1862-1944), Cz
    R.1   S.8,10
WEISGALL, Hugo (1912-   ), USA
    R.1   S.9,10,13
WEISGARBER, Elliot (1919-   ), USA
    R.19   S.13
WEISMANN, Julius (1879-1950), Ger
    R.1   S.c
WEISMANN, Wilhelm (1900-   ), Ger
    R.1   S.10
WEISS - Rosen von gestern
                 S.1x
WEISS, Adolph (1891-1971), USA
    R.1   S.2,3,10,13,19,23
WEISS, Ewald (1906-   ), Ger
    R.4   S.c
WEISS, Franz (1778-1830), Aus
    R.3   S.c
WEISS, Harald
                 S.c
WEISS, Helen L. (1920-1948), USA
    R.7   S.10,13,30,52

WEISS, Silvius Leopold (1686-1750), Ger
R.1   S.c,2,5,7-10,18,32
WEISS, Urban (16th Cent)
             S.c
WEISS, Willoughby Hunter (1820-1867), Eng
R.57   S.c,5x
WEITZ, Guy (1883-1970)
             S.c
WELANDER, Waldemar (1899-   ), Sweden
R.14   S.10
WELCHER, Dan Edward (1948-   ), USA
R.19   S.10,13
WELDON - Gate city
             S.54(328)
WELDON, Alfred Frederick (1862-1914), USA
             S.10,13
WELDON, John (1676-1736), Eng
R.1   S.c,10
WELIN, Karl-Erik (1934-   ), Sweden
R.1   S.c,10,38,40,56
WELLESZ, Egon (1885-1974), Aus
R.1   S.c,7,10,24,42
WELSH - Home Guards march
             S.54(332)
WELSH, Wilmer Hayden (1932-   ), USA
R.19   S.12,13
WELTE, Paul [S.11] = WHITE, Paul (1895-1973)
WELTZELL, Jorg (16th Cent)
             S.c
WENDEL, Martin (1925-   ), Swiss
R.14   S.24a
WENDS, A - Lufthansa march
             S.54(339)
WENINGER, Leopold (1879-1940), Ger
R.4   S.24
WENKEL, Johann Friedrich Wilhelm (1734-?1792), Ger
R.1   S.10
WENNERBERG, Gunnar (1817-1901), Sweden
R.1   S.c,5x,10,33,40,43,56
WENRICH, Percy (1887-1952), USA
R.1   S.10
WENT, Johann (1745-1801), Boh
R.1   S.c,10
WENZEL, Eberhard (1896-1982), Ger
R.14   S.c
WERDER, Felix (1922-   ), Australia
R.1   S.24a,29,37
WERDIN, Eberhard (1911-   ), Ger
R.14   S.c

WERIKOWSKY, Michail (1896-1962), Ukraine
    R.4   S.c
WERLÉ, Floyd (1929-   ), USA
    R.19   S.13
WERLE, Frederick (1914-   ), USA
           S.10,13
WERLE, Heinrich (1887-1955), Ger
    R.4   S.8
WERLE, Lars Johan (1926-   ), Sweden
    R.1   S.c,10,38,40,56
WERNER, Fritz Eugen Heinrich (1898-1977), Ger
    R.14   S.c,10
WERNER, Gregor Joseph (1693-1766), Aus
    R.1   S.c,9,10
WERNER, Heinrich (1800-1833), Ger
    R.2   S.5x,10
WERNER, Jean-Jacques (1935-   ), Fr
    R.14   S.c
WERNER, Kenneth [see HARMONIC, Phil - pseud]
WERNER, Sven Erik (1937-   ), Den
    R.80   S.40
WERNICK, Richard (1934-   ), USA
    R.19   S.c,10,24a
WERNICKE, Israel Gottlieb (1755-1836), Den
    R.30   S.c
WERRECORE, Matthias Hermann (d >1574), Flem
    R.1
WERSTOVSKY, Alexey Nikolayevich
    [see VERSTOVSKY, Alexey Nikolayevich]
WERT, Giaches de (1535-1596), Neth
    R.1   S.c,5x,7,9,10,14,16
WERZLAU, Joachim (1913-   ), Ger
    R.4
WESLEY, Charles (1757-1834), Eng
    R.1   S.c,8
WESLEY, Garret Colley [see MORNINGTON, Garret Wesley]
WESLEY, John (1703-1791), Eng
    R.1
WESLEY, Samuel (1766-1837), Eng
    R.1   S.c,5,7,8,10
WESLEY, Samuel Sebastian (1810-1876), Eng
    R.1   S.c,1x,5-10
WESLEY-SMITH, Martin (1945-   ), Australia
    R.1   S.29
WEST, Elisha (1756-18??), USA
    R.50   S.47
WEST, John Ebenezer (1863-1929), Eng
    R.1   S.c
WESTENDORF, Thomas Paine (1848-1923), USA
    R.53   S.10,24

WESTERGAARD, Peter (1931-   ), USA
   R.1   S.10,13
WESTERGAARD, Svend (1922-   ), Den
   R.1   S.40
WESTERING, Paul Christiaan van (1911-   ), Neth
   R.14   S.c
WESTERMAN, Gerhart von (1894-1963), Ger
   R.14   S.c,24
WESTERVELT - Red and blue
              S.54(351)
WESTHOFF, Johann Paul von (1656-1705), Ger
   R.5   S.c
WESTPHAL, Frank (1889-1948), USA
   R.23   S.24
WESTRUP, Jack Allan (1904-1975), Eng
   R.4
WETZ, Richard (1875-1935), Ger
   R.1   S.c
WETZEL, Justus Hermann (1879-1973), Ger
   R.1
WEVERS, Harold (1949-   ), Can

WEYSE, Christoph Ernst Friedrich (1774-1842), Den
   R.1   S.4-8,33,35,57
WHEAR, Paul William (1925-   ), USA
   R.19   S.9
WHITE (fl 1810), USA - Power
              S.10,47
WHITE LAFITTE, José (1836-1918), Cuba
   R.1   S.10
WHITE, Alice Mary
              S.30
WHITE, B. F. - Anthem on the Saviour; Morning trumpet
              S.47
WHITE, Charles Albert (1832-1892), USA
   R.53   S.10
WHITE, Clarence Cameron (1880-1960), USA
   R.1   S.10,13,18,24
WHITE, Donald (1921-   ), USA
   R.19   S.10,13
WHITE, E. - The Roundabout
              S.5x
WHITE, John (1936-   )
              S.10
WHITE, John David (1931-   ), USA
   R.19   S.9,10,13
WHITE, José Silvestre de los Dolores (1839-1918)
              S.24a
WHITE, Matthew (fl 1600-30), Eng
   R.1   S.5x,7,10

WHITE, Maud Valérie (1855-1937), Eng
   R.1   S.c,5x,30
WHITE, Michael (1931-   ), USA
   R.19   S.13
WHITE, Paul Taylor (1895-1973), USA
   R.19   S.4,5x,10,11,13,24a
WHITE, Peter Gilbert (1937-   ), Eng
   R.80   S.c
WHITE, Robert (c1538-1574), Eng
   R.1   S.c,8,10,14,16,53
WHITE, Roy E.

WHITE, Ruth Eden (1925-   ), USA
   R.19   S.9,10,13,30,52
WHITE, William Carter (1886-   ), USA
   R.49   S.54(354)
WHITEHEAD, Gillian (1941-   ), New Zealand
   R.7   S.30,52
WHITELOCKE, Bulstrode (1605-1675)
              S.c
WHITFORD, Homer P. (1892-   ), USA
   R.19   S.12,13
WHITHORNE, Emerson (1884-1958), USA
   R.1   S.13
WHITING, George Elbridge (1840-1923), USA
   R.1   S.10
WHITING, Richard (1891-1938), USA
   R.1   S.10,24
WHITLOCK, Percy (1903-1946), Eng
   R.1   S.c,8,10
WHITLOCK, Peter
              S.10
WHITNEY - Mosquitos on parade
              S.54(344)
WHITNEY, Maurice C. (1909-   ), USA
   R.19   S.5x,22,54(360)
WHITNEY, Robert (1904-   ), USA
   R.1   S.10,13
WHITTAKER, Howard (1922-   ), USA
   R.19   S.10,13
WHITTAKER, William Gillies (1876-1944), Eng
   R.1   S.c
WHITTEMORE, Thomas (1800-1861)
              S.24
WHITTENBERG, Charles (1927-   ), USA
   R.1   S.c,10,13,19,21
WHITTER, Mark (1964-   ), Eng
              S.c
WHYTE, Robert [see WHITE, Robert]

WHYTHORNE, Thomas (1528-1596), Eng
   R.1   S.c,10,14,16
WIBLÉ, Michel (1923-   ), Swiss
   R.4
WICHEL, Philippus van (fl 1641), S. Neth
   R.5   S.c
WICHMANN, Hermann (1824-1905), USA
   R.98   S.5x
WICK - The witness
           S.e
WICKENS, Dennis John (1926-   ), Eng
   R.14   S.c
WICKS, Allan (1923-   ), Eng
   R.1   S.c
WICKS, Camilla (1928-   ), USA
   R.7   S.24,30
WIDDOES, Lawrence (1932-   ), USA
   R.19   S.10,13
WIDE, Erich - pseud [see WIDESTEDT, Ragnar]

WIDEEN, Ivar (1871-1951), Sweden
   R.30   S.56
WIDERKEHR, Jacques Christian Michel (1759-1823), Alsace
   R.1   S.c
WIDESTEDT, Ragnar (1887-1954) [pseud: Erich WIDE],
   Sweden   S.43
WIDMANN, Erasmus (1572-1634), Ger
   R.1   S.c,8,10,14,16,32
WIDMER, Ernst (1927-   ), Swiss
   R.14   S.24a
WIDOR, Charles-Marie (1844-1937), Fr
   R.1   S.1-10,18,19,24,32
WIECHOWICZ, Stanislaw (1893-1963), Pol
   R.1
WIECK, Clara [see SCHUMANN, Clara]
WIEDEMANN, Josef (Franz?) (1828-1919), Aus
   R.95   S.10
WIEDERMANN, Bedřich Antonín (1883-1951), Cz
   R.1   S.c
WIEDOEFT, Rudy (1893-1940), USA
   R.23   S.10,22
WIENER, Jean (1896-   ), Fr
   R.1   S.c,8,9,18
WIENIAWSKA, Irene Regine [pseud: POLDOWSKI] (1880-1932)
   Eng R.7   S.10,24,52
WIENIAWSKI, Adam Tadeusz (1879-1950), Pol
   R.1   S.5x
WIENIAWSKI, Henryk (1835-1880), Pol
   R.1   S.c,2-11,18,24
WIERUSZOWSKI, Lili (1900-   ), Ger
   R.7

WIESLANDER, Ignvar Axel Otto (1917-1963), Sweden
   R.14   S.40
WIGGLESWORTH, Frank (1918-   ), USA
   R.1   S.10,13
WIGTHORPE, William (?1579-c1610), Eng
   R.1   S.c,16
WIHTOL, Yazep [see VITOLS, Jazeps]
WIJDEVELD, Wolfgang (1910-   ), Neth
   R.14   S.24
WIKANDER, David (1884-1955), Sweden
   R.14   S.c,5x,56
WIKLUND, Adolf (1879-1950), Sweden
   R.1   S.c,5,7,10,40,56
WIKMANSON, Johan (1753-1800), Sweden
   R.1   S.c,10,56
WILBYE, John (1574-1638), Eng
   R.1   S.c,1x,2-5,7-11,14-16
WILCOCK, Anthea (20th Cent), Eng
          S.52
WILCZYNSKI - Nur dir will ich gehoren

WILD, Eric Lees (1910-   ), Can
   R.31
WILDBERGER, Jacques (1922-   ), Swiss
   R.1   S.c
WILDER, Alec (1907-1980), USA

   R.1   S.c,8-11,13
WILDER, F. - Invalid Corps
          S.47
WILDER, Philip van (c1500-1553), Flem
   R.1   S.c,10,32
WILDING-WHITE, Raymond (1922-   ), USA
   R.19   S.10,13
WILDMAN, Charles - pseud [ie Willy MATHES] (1916-   )
   Sweden   R.30   S.10
WILDMANN, Erasmus (1572-1634)
          S.c
WILENSKY, Moshe (1910-   ), Isr
          S.10
WILHELMINA, Sophie Frederike (Princess of Prussia,
   Markgrafin von Bayreuth) (1709-1758)
   R.7   S.8,10
WILHELMJ, August (1845-1908), Ger
   R.1   S.24
WILHITE, Monte (1898-1961), USA
   R.23   S.24
WILKES, John Bernard (1785-1869)

WILKINSON (fl ?1579-96), Eng (see note)
   R.1

WILKINSON, Marc (1929-   ), Australia
    R.1   S.9
WILKINSON [Wylkynson], Robert (c1450-c1515)
    R.1   S.c,16
WILKINSON, Scott (1922-   ), USA
    R.19   S.13
WILKOMIRSKI, Kazimierz (1900-   ), Pol
    R.30
WILL, Justinus (1675-1747)
                S.c
WILLAERT, Adrian (c1490-1562), Flem
    R.1   S.c,3,4,6-11,14-16,18,32,36,41,53
WILLAN, Healey (1880-1968), Eng
    R.1   S.c,7,8,10,24
WILLAUME, Gabriel (1873-   )
                S.24
WILLCOCK, Anthea (20th Cent), Eng
                S.c
WILLCOCKS, Sir David (1919-   ), 'Eng
    R.80   S.c
WILLCOCKS, George Henry (1899-1962), Eng
    R.85   S.55
WILLE, Rudolf (fl 1939), Aus
    R.200   S.4
WILLEMETZ, Albert (1888-1965)
                S.c
WILLIAMS - Blue devils march; Gathering of the clans
                S.54(316,28)
WILLIAMS - Jealous Lover
                S.10
WILLIAMS, A. - Guards; patrol
                S.54(330)
WILLIAMS, Alberto (1862-1952), Arg

    R.1   S.5x,8,10,24,46
WILLIAMS, Bert [Egbert Austin] (1874-1922), USA
    R.50   S.10
WILLIAMS, Charles (1893-   ), Eng
    R.1   S.c,10
WILLIAMS, Clifton (1923-1976), USA
    R.19   S.10,13,54(325)
WILLIAMS, David H. (1919-   ), USA
    R.19   S.10
WILLIAMS, David McKay (1887-1978), USA
    R.19   S.7,10,13
WILLIAMS, Ernest S. (1881-1947), USA
    R.49   S.54(359)
WILLIAMS, Gene - pseud [see WRIGHT, Lawrence]
WILLIAMS, Gerrard (1888-1947), Eng
                S.c

WILLIAMS, Grace (1906-1977), Wales
   R.1   S.c,6,10,30,52
WILLIAMS, Harry (1879-1922), USA
   R.23   S.10,54(335)
WILLIAMS, Hiram Hank Sr. (1923-1952), USA
   R.23   S.21
WILLIAMS, J. - The trumpet
             S.47
WILLIAMS, Jan (1946-   ), USA
             S.10,13
WILLIAMS, John Gerrard (1888-1947), Eng
   R.4   S.c
WILLIAMS, John Towner (1932-   ), USA
   R.1   S.c,10,13
WILLIAMS, Mary Lou (1910-1981), USA
   R.1   S.10,30,52
WILLIAMS, Meirion (1901-   ), Wales
   R.80   S.5x,7
WILLIAMS, Owen (1877-   ), Wales
   R.37   S.5x
WILLIAMS, William (d <1701), Eng
   R.1   S.c,10
WILLIAMS, William Sydney Gwynn (1896-   ), Eng
   R.14   S.28
WILLIAMSON, Malcolm (1931-   ), Australia
   R.1   S.c,9,10,24a,29,37
WILLINGHAM, Jerry ?USA
             S.13
WILLIS (c1730) - Here Tom, here's a health
             S.10
WILLS, Arthur (1926-   ), Eng
   R.1   S.c
WILLS, Edward - pseud [see PLESSOW, Eric]
WILLSON, Meredith (1902-   ), USA
   R.1   S.9
WILM, Peter Nicolai von (1834-1911), Ger
   R.1   S.24a
WILSON, A. - Connemara
             S.e
WILSON, Charles Mills (1931-   ), Can
   R.31
WILSON, Donald M. (1937-   ), USA
   R.19   S.13
WILSON, Eugene ?USA
             S.13
WILSON, Galen (1926-   ), USA
   R.19   S.13
WILSON, George Balch (1927-   ), USA
   R.19   S.10,13

WILSON, Harry Robert (1901-1968), USA
    R.19   S.13
WILSON, Henry James Lane

WILSON, Hilda (Matilda Ellen Wilson) [pseud: Douglas
    HOPE] (1860-1918), Eng   R.7
WILSON, James (1922-   ), Ire
    R.1   S.c,49
WILSON, John (1595-1674), Eng
    R.1   S.c,5x,8,10,11,16
WILSON, Leonard (1911-1963), Can
    R.81
WILSON, Olly (1937-   ), USA
    R.1   S.c,10,13
WILSON, R. A. - pseud [see KING, Robert A.]
WILSON, Ransom (1951-   )

WILSON, Richard (1941-   ), USA
    R.19   S.10,13,24
WILSON, Sandy (1924-   ), Eng
    R.1   S.9
WILSON, Thomas (1927-   ), Scot
    R.1   S.c,55
WILSON, Walter
                S.10
WILTON, Charles Henry (1761-   ), Eng
    R.1   S.8,10,24
WINDSOR - Alpine echoes
                S.54(312)
WINGHAM, Thomas (1846-1893), Eng
    R.3   S.c
WINHAM, Godfrey (1934-1975), USA
    R.19   S.13
WINKHLER, Charles Angelus von (1796-1845)
                S.c
WINNER, Septimus [pseud: Alice HAWTHORNE] (1827-1902)
    USA R.1   S.10,24,47
WINSON - Four flags march; Wake up England
                S.54(327,64)
WINSOR, Philip (1938-   ), USA
    R.19   S.10,13
WINSTANLEY, Gerald (17th Cent)
                S.c
WINTELROY, Jan van (16th Cent)
    R.5
WINTER, A. - Martial moments
                S.54(342)

WINTER, Aubrey
                S.54(358)

WINTER, F. - Olympia fanfare
S.54(347)
WINTER, Fred - pseud [see NJURLING, Sten]
WINTER, Gloria Frances [Sister Miriam Therese WINTER]
(1938-   ), USA   R.23   S.30,52
WINTER, Peter (1754-1825), Ger
R.1   S.c,10,19,21
WINTERFIELD, Max - pseud [see GILBERT, Jean]
WINTERNITZ, Felix (1872-1948)
S.24
WITNI, Monica (20th Cent), USA
R.7   S.52
WIPO, (c995-c1050)
R.1   S.c,15,16
WIREN, Dag (1905-   ), Sweden
R.1   S.c,4-8,10,24,38,40,56
WIRTH, Carl Anton (1912-   ), USA
R.19   S.10,13,22
WISCHNEGRADSKY, Ivan Alexandrovich
[see VÏSHNEGRADSKY, Ivan Alexandrovich]
WISE, James Waterman USA
S.13
WISE, Michael (c1647-1687), Eng
R.1   S.c,5x,7,10
WISHART, Peter (1921-   ), Eng
R.1   S.c,10
WISHART, Trevor (1946-   ), Eng
S.c
WISSMER, Pierre (1915-   ), Fr
R.48   S.c
WISZNIEWSKI, Zbigniew (1922-   ), Pol
R.1   S.c
WITHEFELDE (17th Cent) - The English hunt's up
S.16
WITKIN, Beatrice (1916-   ), USA
R.19   S.13,24a,30,52
WITKOWSKI, Georges (1867-1943), Fr
R.1   S.1-3,5
WITT, de - Irish Regiment
S.54(334)
WITT, Christian Friedrich (c1660-1716), Ger
R.3
WITT, Fred
S.c
WITT, Friedrich (1770-1836), Ger
R.1   S.c,10
WITTASSEK, Johann Nepomuk [see VITASEK, Jan August]
WITTE, Gerd (1927-   )

WITTGENSTEIN, Paul (1887-1961), Aus
   R.1   S.10
WITTINGER, Robert (1945-   ), Hun
   R.1   S.c,24a
WITTMER, Eberhard Ludwig (1905-   ), Ger
   R.4   S.c
WITTY, J. - The country of dreams
           S.e
WÎZLAV III von RÜGEN (1265/68-1325), Ger
   R.1   S.c,2-4,5x,8,10,11,14-16
WLADIGEROFF, Pancho [see VLADIGEROV, Pancho]
WODICZKA, Wenceslaus (?1715/20-1774)
           S.24a
WOELDERINK, Egbert (1914-   )
           S.c
WOELFL, Joseph [see WOLFL, Joseph]
WOESTIJNE, David van de (1915-1979), Bel
   R.1   S.24,36
WOHLGEMUTH, Gerhard (1920-   ), Ger
   R.1   S.24
WOHLMUTH, Janoes (1653-1724)

WOJTA, Johann Ignaz Franz
   [see VOITA, Johann Ignaz Franz]
WOLDIN, Judd (fl 1973)
           S.9
WOLEY, John

WOLF, Cornelis de (1880-1935), Neth
   R.3   S.c
WOLF, Ernst Wilhelm (1735-1792), Ger
   R.1   S.24
WOLF, Hugo (1860-1903), Aus
   R.1   S.c,1-11,18,23-28,33,42,43
WOLF-COHEN, Veronika (1944-   ), Isr
           S.52
WOLF-FERRARI, Ermanno (1876-1948), It
   R.1   S.c,1-11,24a,25,27,42
WOLFE, Jacques (1896-1973), USA
   R.19   S.5x,10,13
WOLFE, Stanley (1924-   ), USA
   R.19   S.10,13
WOLFF, Albert (1884-1970), Fr
   R.1   S.c,8
WOLFF, Bernhard (1835-1906), Ger
   R.3
WOLFF, Christian (1934-   ), USA
   R.1   S.c,9,10,12,13,24
WOLFF, Erich (1874-1913), Aus
   R.3   S.5,9

WOLFF, Henry USA
       S.13
WOLFGANG, Eberhardt - pseud [see STEFFEN, Wolfgang]
WÖLFL, Joseph (1773-1812), Aus
   R.1   S.c,9
WOLFRAM von ESCHENBACH (fl c1170-1220), Ger
   R.1   S.c
WOLKENSTEIN, Oswald von [see OSWALD von WALKENSTEIN]
WOLKI, Konrad (1904-   ), Ger
       S.c
WOLL, Erna (1917-   ), Ger
   R.7   S.52
WOLLE, Peter (1792-1871), USA
   R.1   S.10,47
WOLLEB, Johann Jakob (1613-1667), Swiss
   R.1
WOLLENHAUPT, Hermann Adolf (1827-1865), Ger
   R.3
WOLPE, Stefan (1902-1972), USA
   R.1   S.c,8-10,13,24
WOLSTENHOLME, William (1865-1931), Eng
   R.3   S.c,24
WOLSY, E. - Into thy hands
       S.54(334)
WOLTERS, Gottfried (1910-   ), Ger
   R.1   S.c
WONDRATSCHEK, Francesco (1730-1780),
       S.7,10
WONRICH - Come, be my rainbow [e] = WENRICH, Percy
WOOD, Abraham (1732-1804), USA
   R.50   S.47
WOOD, Arthur (1875-1953), Eng
   R.85   S.5x,55
WOOD, Charles (1866-1926), Ire
   R.1   S.c,5,7,8,10
WOOD, F. C. - Antioch
       S.47
WOOD, Haydn (1882-1959), Eng
   R.1   S.c,5x,24,54(339,60)
WOOD, Henry (1869-1944), Eng
   R.1   S.c,10,11
WOOD, Hugh (1932-   ), Eng
   R.1   S.c,10,24a
WOOD, Joseph Roberts (1915-   ), USA
   R.19   S.10,13
WOOD, William Frank (1935-   ), USA
   R.19   S.13,24a
WOODALL, A. - Serenade (fl & p)
       S.5x

WOODBURY, Arthur (1930-   ), USA
   R.4
WOODBURY, Isaac Baker (1819-1858), USA
   R.1   S.10
WOODCOCK, Clement (fl c1575), Eng
   R.1   S.c
WOODCOCK, Robert (18th Cent), Eng
   R.1   S.c,10
WOODFORDE-FINDEN, Amy (1860-1919), Eng
   R.1   S.c,10,24,28,30,52

WOODHOUSE, Charles (1879-1939), Eng
   R.4   S.54(353,57)
WOODHOUSE, S. - A morning song
            S.54(344)
WOODS - Valse phantastique

WOODS, Clarence
            S.10,24a
WOODS, Harvey J. (1874-1933)

WOODS, John J. (1849-1934), New Zealand
   R.1
WOODSON, Thomas (d >1605), Eng
   R.1   S.c
WOOLFENDEN, Guy Anthony (1937-   ), Eng
   R.80   S.c
WOOLLEN, Russell (1923-   ), USA
   R.19   S.c,10,13
WORDEN, Wilfred
            S.24a
WORDSWORTH, William (1908-   ), Eng
   R.1   S.c,23
WORISCHEK, Jan Vaclav [Jan Hugo]
   [see VOŘÍŠEK, Jan Václav]
WORK, Henry Clay (1832-1884), USA
   R.1   S.9,10,24
WORK, John Wesley (1901-1967), USA
   R.1   S.10,13
WORK, Julian C. (1910-   ), USA
   R.19   S.10,13
WORLEY, John C. USA
            S.22
WORTH, Amy (1888-1967), USA
   R.19   S.5x,10,28,30
WORTH, Bobby (1921-   ), USA
   R.23   S.10
WORTMANN, Hartmut
            S.c
WOTJA, Jan Ignaz [see WOJTA, Johann Ignaz Franz]

WOWK, Bohdan E.

WOYTOWICZ, Boleslaw (1899-1980), Pol
R.1
WRANITZKY, Anton (1761-1820), Cz
R.1   S.c,5x,23
WRANITZKY, Paul (1756-1808), Cz
R.1   S.c,5x,10
WREEDE, Johannes [see URREDA, Jan]
WRIGHT - Dainty lady
             S.54(322)
WRIGHT, Denis (1895-1967), Eng
R.85   S.54(321),55
WRIGHT, Frank Joseph Henry (1901-1970), Australia
R.85,96   S.54(366),55
WRIGHT, Kenneth Anthony (1899-1975), Eng
R.85   S.55

WRIGHT, Lawrence (1888-1964), Eng [pseud: Victor
    AMBROISE, Kathleen CAVANAGH, Everett LYNTON,
    Betsy O'HAGEN, Horatio NICHOLLS, Shirley LILIAN,
    Paul PAREE, Gene WILLIAMS]
R.1   S.24,54(341)
WRIGHT, Maurice (1949-   ), USA
R.19   S.10,13
WRIGHT, Nannie Louise (1879-   ), USA
R.7
WRIGHT, Robert Craig (1914-   ), USA
R.23   S.c,10
WRIGHT, Searle (1918-   ), USA
             S.10,12,13
WRIGHT, Thomas (16th Cent) - Nesciens mater
R.200   S.c,10,16
WRIGHTON, W. T. (1816-1880), Eng
R.57   S.5x
WUENSCH, Gerhard Joseph (1925-   ), Can
R.31
WULSTAN, David (1937-   ), Eng
R.80   S.10
WUNDERER, Anton (1850-1906), Aus
R.3
WUNDERLICH, Hans-Joachim (1918-   ), Ger
R.4   S.c
WUORINEN, Charles (1938-   ), USA.
R.1   S.9,10,13,24
WURMAN, Hans G. (1922-   ), USA
R.23   S.10
WURTZLER, Astrid von (1925-   ), USA
R.14   S.13
WÜRZ, Richard (1885-1965), Ger
R.1   S.c

WURZBURG, Konrad von [see KONRAD von WURZBURG]
WURZEL, G. F. - pseud [see ROOT, George Frederick]
WÜSTHOFF, Klaus (1922-   ), Ger
    R.4   S.c
WU TSU-CHIANG
              S.c
WUYTACK, Jos (1935-   ), Bel
    R.25
WYATT, Thomas (16-17th Cent) - Blame not my lute
              S.c
WYBICKIEGO - Polish national anthem (see note)
              S.54(350)
WYKES, Robert Arthur (1926-   ), USA
    R.19   S.9,13
WYLIE, Betty Jane (see note)
              S.52
WYLIE, Ruth Shaw (1916-   ), USA
    R.19   S.10,13,30,52
WYLKYNSON, Robert [see WILKINSON, Robert]
WYMAN, Addison P. (1832-1872), USA
    R.3,53
WYNER, Yehudi (1929-   ), USA
    R.1   S.10,13,24
WYNNE, David (1900-1983), Wales
    R.1   S.c,10
WYSCHNEGRADSKI, Ivan Alexandrovich
    [see VÏSHNEGRADSKY, Ivan Alexandrovich]
WYSSENBACH, Rudolf (16th Cent), Swiss
    R.1
WYSZOMIRSKI, Stanley W.
              S.24a
WYTON, Alec (1921-   ), USA
    R.1   S.12,13
WYTTENBACH, Jürg (1935-   ), Swiss
    R.1   S.c,24a
XANTOPOULOS, Timotheus

XARABA, Diego (17th Cent)
              S.10,53
XENAKIS, Iannis (1922-   ), Fr
    R.1   S.c,9,10,24a
XENOPOL, Margareta (1892-   ), Rum
    R.7   S.52
XIMÉNEZ, José (1601-1672), Sp
    R.1   S.c,10,16
YAKHIN, Rustem (1921-   ), USSR
    R.14   S.18
YAKOVLEV, Mikhail Lukyanovich (1798-1869), Russia
    R.1   S.18

YAKOVLEV, Vladimir Adrianovich (1930-   )
          S.18
YAMADA, Kosaku (1886-1965), Japan
    R.1   S.5x,18,24,32
YAMASHTA, Stomu (1947-   ), Japan
    R.25
YAMPILOV, Baudordza Bazorovich (1916-   ), USSR
    R.14   S.18
YANADA, Tadashi (1885-1959)
          S.24a
YANCHENKO, Oleg Grigorevich (1939-   )
          S.18
YANG CHEN-WEI
          S.c
YANIEWICZ, Felix [see JANIEWICZ, Feliks]
YANNATOS, James (1929-   ), USA
    R.19   S.13
YARDEN, Elie (1923-   ), USA
    R.19   S.10,13
YARDUMIAN, Richard (1917-   ), USA
    R.1   S.c,8-10,13,24
YAREMIN, Igor Alexandrovich (1916-   ),
          S.18
YARGON, Jan (1928-   )
          S.18
YARNOLD, Benjamin (d.1787), USA
    R.53   S.7,10,47
YAROVINSKY, Boris Lvovich (1922-   ), USSR
    R.14   S.18
YARULLIN, Farid Zagudoullovich (1914-1945), USSR
    R.14   S.18
YASHIRO, Akio (1929-   ), Japan
    R.4   S.50
YAZHENBSKY, Adam (1590-1648)
          S.18
YEARSLY, Claude Blakesley
          S.24
YEGIAZARYAN, Grigori (1908-   ), USSR
    R.47   S.18
YEKMALYAN, M.
          S.24a
YELLEN, Jack (1892-   ), USA
    R.23   S.24
YENIKEYEV, Renat (1937-   )
          S.18
YEPES, Narciso (1927-   ), Sp
    R.1   S.c,10,32
YERMAK, Romuald Boleslavovich (1931-   ), USSR
    R.47   S.18

YESAULOV, N. - Melancholy waltz (harp)
        S.18
YESHANOV, Godel Simkhovich (1922-   ),
        S.18
YEVDOKIMOV, Yuri
        S.18
YEVLAKHOV, Orest Alexandrovich (1912-   ), USSR
  R.47   S.18,24a
YIP-FAT, Richard Tsang
        S.24a
YLVISAKER, John Carl (1937-   ), USA
  R.23   S.13
YOCOH, Yoquijiro (1929-   ), Japan
        S.c,32
YODER, Paul [pseud: Max THOMAS] (1908-   ), USA
  R.49   S.54(339)
YODLING - Fritz's serenade
        S.e
YON, Pietro Alessandro 1886-1943), It
  R.4   S.c,10,12,13
YONGE, Nicholas (d.1619), Eng
  R.1   S.16
YORKE, Peter (1902-1966), Eng
  R.85   S.54(325),55
YOSHIOKA, Emmett Genne (1944-   ), USA
  R.19   S.22
YOSSIFOV, Alexander (1940-   )
        S.24a
YOULL, Henry (fl 1608), Eng
  R.1   S.5x,10,16
YOUMANS, Vincent (1898-1946), USA
  R.1   S.c,9,10,24a,54(345)
YOUNG - Beacon march; Tournament march
        S.54(315,61)
YOUNG, Anthony (fl 1744), Eng
  R.5   S.5x
YOUNG, Douglas (1947-   ), Eng
  R.1   S.c
YOUNG, Gordon Ellsworth (1919-   ), USA
  R.23   S.22
YOUNG, Jane Corner (1915-   ), USA
  R.19   S.10,13,30,52
YOUNG, Nicholas [see YONGE, Nicholas]
YOUNG, Ruth
        S.30
YOUNG, Victor (1900-1956), USA
  R.1   S.c,9,10
YOUNG, William, (d.1662), Eng
  R.1   S.c

YOUROVSKY - Joking march
          S.10
YOUSE, Glad Robinson (1898-   ), USA
    R.19   S.30,52
YRADIER, Sebastian [see IRADIER, Sebastian]
YSAŸE, Eugène (1858-1931), Bel
    R.1   S.c,3,5,8-11,18,24,41
YSAŸE, Théophile (1865-1918), Bel
    R.1
YTTREHUS, Rolv (1926-   ), USA
    R.19   S.10,13
YUASA, Joji (1929-   ), Japan
    R.1   S.24a,50
YUDAKOV, Solomon Alexandrovich (1916-   ), USSR
    R.14   S.18
YUIZE, Shin-ichi (1923-   ), Japan
    R.36   S.50
YUN, Isang (1917-   ), South Korea
    R.1   S.c,9,10,24
YUOZAPAITIS, V. (1936-   )
          S.18
YUPANQUI, Atahualpa - pseud [ie Mario CHAVERO]
    (1911-   ), Arg   R.30   S.c
YURASOVSKY, Alexander Ivanovich (1890-1924)
          S.18
YURGUTIS, Vitautas (1930-   )
          S.18
YURISALU, Heino Arturovich (1930-   ), USSR
    R.47   S.18
YUROVSKY, Vladimir Mikhailovich (1915-   ), USSR
    R.14   S.18
YURYAN, Andrei (1856-1922)
          S.18
YUST - Tampame
          S.e
YUSUPOV, Matniyaz (1925-   )
          S.18
YUYAMA, Akira (1932-   ), Japan
    R.4   S.50
YUZELYUNAS, Julius (1916-   )
          S.18
YVAIN, Maurice (1891-1965), Fr
    R.1   S.c,5x,18
ZABEL, Albert Heinrich (1834-1910), Russia
    R.1   S.c,10
ZABOROV, Grigori
          S.24a
ZABRACK, Harold Allen (1928-   ), USA
    R.19   S.13

ZACAR [Zacharias, Zachara, Zacharie] (14-15th Cent), It
   R.1   S.c   (see note)
ZACH, Jan (1699-1773), Cz
   R.1   S.c,5x,24a,53
ZACHAREWITSCH, Michael (1879-1953), USSR
   R.4   S.24
ZACHER, Gerd (1929-   ), Ger
   R.4   S.10
ZACHOW, Friedrich Wilhelm (1663-1712), Ger
   R.1   S.c,10,53
ZACK, Victor (1854-1939), Aus
   R.4
ZACZ, Jan (1699-1773), Boh
           S.c
ZADOR, Dezider Yevgenevich (1912-   ), USSR
   R.47   S.18
ZADOR, Eugen (1894-1977), USA
   R.23
ZÁDOR, Jenő (1894-1977), USA
   R.1   S.10,11,13
ZAGATTI, Francesco (17th Cent)
           S.c

ZAGORSKY, Vasili Geogievich (1926-   ), USSR
   R.14   S.18,24a
ZAIMONT, Judith Lang (1945-   ), USA
   R.19   S.13,30,52
ZAIMOV, Khailik (1914-   ), USSR
   R.4   S.18,24
ZAIRA, Mordecai [see ZEIRA, Mordecai]
ZAITZEV - Taste and see
           S.10
ZAJAC - Five miniatures
           S.22
ZAJACZEK, Roman W. (1927-   )
           S.c
ZAJDA, Edward M. (1941-   ), ?USA
           S.13
ZAKARYAN, Karo Oganesovich (1895-1967), USSR
   R.14   S.18
ZAKIROV, Dani (1914-   ), USSR
   R.47   S.18
ZALEUCUS (19th Cent) - The giraffe waltz

ZALITIS, Janis (1884-1943), Lat
   R.47   S.18
ZAMACIOS - Escencia chula
           S.e
ZAMBONA, Hans Georg (1928-   )
           S.24a

ZÁMEČNÍK, Evžen (1939-   ), Cz
  R.14   S.c,24a
ZAMECNIK, J. S. (1872-1953), USA
  R.23   S.13,24,54(311)
ZAMFIR, Gheorghe (20th Cent)
              S.c
ZAMFIRESCU, Radu (1927-   )
              S.c
ZAMKOCHIAN, Berj USA
              S.12,13
ZANDONAI, Riccardo (1883-1944), It
  R.1   S.c,1-8,10,18,24,42
ZANELLA, Amilcar (1873-1949), It
  R.1
ZANETTI, Gasparo (fl 1626-45), It
  R.1   S.c,8,10,16
ZANGIUS, Nikolaus (c1570-c1618), Ger
  R.1   S.c,8,14-16
ZANI, Andrea (1696-1757), It
  R.1
ZANINELLI, Luigi (1932-   ), USA
  R.19   S.10,13
ZANNETTI, Francesco (1737-1788), It
  R.1   S.c,10
ZANNETTI, Gasparo [see ZANETTI, Gasparo]
ZANOTTI, Camillo (c1545-1591), It
  R.1   S.c
ZAPATA - A la luna
              S.e
ZAPATEADO - El padrino de el nene
              S.e
ZARDINI, Terenzio
              S.c
ZARDO, Napoleone (1858-1913), It
  R.52   S.44
ZAREBSKI, Juliusz (1854-1885), Pol
  R.1   S.24
ZAREMBA, Vladislav Ivanovich (1833-1902), Ukraine
  R.1   S.18
ZAREVUTIUS, Zacharias (fl c1649-65), Slovak
  R.1   S.c
ZARINŠ, Margers (1910-   ), Lat
  R.1   S.18
ZARLINO, Gioseffo (1517-1590), It
  R.1   S.16
ZARZYCKI, Alexander (1834-1895), Pol
  R.1   S.5x,10,18,24
ZATMAN, Andrew (1945-   ), USA
  R.19   S.13

ZAVALA y ARRAMBARI, Cleto (1847-1912), Sp
R.104   S.10
ZAVALISHINA, Maria Semyonovna (1903-   ), USSR
R.7   S.18,52
ZAVATERI, Lorenzo Gaetano (1690-1764), It
R.1   S.24
ZAVIS, Magister
             S.5x
ZAY, William Henri (1869-   ), USA
R.53   S.e
ZAYDE, Jascha

ZAYOUX - Alsace-Lorraine march
             S.54(312)
ZAZANJIEV, V. - Fugue (vi & p)
             S.24a
ZBINDEN, Julien-François (1917-   ), Swiss
R.1   S.c,10
ZDANIUS, Jonas

ZEBEL, Albert

ZEBROWSKI, Marcin Józef (fl 1748-65), Pol
R.1   S.c
ZECH, Chrysogonus (1728-1804)
             S.c
ZECHIEL, Ernest ?USA
             S.10,12,13
ZECHLIN, Ruth (1926-   ), Ger
R.7   S.30,52
ZEDOR, Jeno

ZEHLE, Wilhelm (1876-1956)
             S.54(313,61,65)
ZEHM, Friedrich (1923-   ), Ger
R.1   S.c

ZEIDLER, Jozef (d c1809)
             S.c
ZEIDMAN, Boris Isaakovich (1908-   ), USSR
R.14   S.18
ZEIGER, Yukhan (1897-1969), Est
             S.18
ZEILBECKE, E. - pseud [see KARK, Frederik]
ZEILER, Gallus (1705-1755), Ger
R.1   S.c
ZEINALLY, Assaf (1909-1932), USSR
R.14   S.18
ZEIRA, Mordecai (1905-   ), Isr
R.25   S.10

ZEISL, Eric (1905-1959), USA
   R.1   S.7,13,23,24
ZEITLIN, Denis Jay (1938-   )

ZELECHOWSKI, Piotr (fl c1650), Pol
   R.1   S.c,16,53
ZELENKA, Jan Dismas (1679-1745), Cz
   R.1   S.c,5x,10,24a
ZELEŃSKI, Wladyslaw (1837-1921), Pol
   R.1   S.c,5x,18
ŽELEZNÝ, Lubomir (1925-1979), Cz
   R.14   S.24,31
ZELJENKA, Ilja (1932-   ), Slovak
   R.1   S.c,24,31
ZELLBELL, Ferdinand (1719-1780), Sweden
   R.1   S.c,56
ZELLER, Carl (1842-1898), Aus
   R.1   S.c,2-5,7,8,10,24
ZELTER, Carl Friedrich (1758-1832), Ger
   R.1   S.c,8,10,23,28
ZEMACHSON, Arnold (1892-   ), USA
            S.2,12,13
ZEMLINKSY, Alexander (1871-1942), Aus
   R.1   S.c,1x
ZENDER, Hans (1936-   ), Ger
   R.1   S.c
ZENER, Johannes (1903-   )

ZENGER, Max (1837-1911), Ger
   R.3   S.c
ZERKOVITZ, Bela
            S.24
ZESSO, Giovanni Battista (16th Cent), It
   R.1   S.c,10
ZHELEKHOVSKY, Piotr [see ZELECHOWSKI, Piotr]
ZHELOBINSKY, Valery Viktorovich (1913-1946), Russia
   R.1   S.4,5x[Jelobensky],10,11
ZHI, Du Zhao
            S.24a
ZHI, Li Huan
            S.24a
ZHIGAITAS, Rimvidas [see ZIGAITAS, Rimuydas]
ZHIGANOV, Nazib Gayazovich (1911-   ), USSR
   R.14   S.18
ZHILINSKY, Arvid (1905-   ), USSR
   R.47   S.18
ZHIRKOV, Mark Nikolayevich (1892-1951), USSR
   R.47   S.18
ZHIVOTOV, Alexey Semyonovich (1904-1964), Russia
   R.1   S.18

ZHORA, Mikhail [S.18] = JORA, Mihail
ZHUBANOV, Ahmet Kuyanovich (1906-1968), USSR
    R.47   S.18
ZHUBANOVA, Gaziza Akhmetovna (1927-   ), USSR
    R.47   S.18   (see note)
ZHUKOVSKY, German Leontyevich (1913-   ), USSR
    R.1   S.18
ZHUMBAYEV, E. (1941-   )
                S.18
ZIANI, Marc´ Antonio (c1653-1715), It
    R.1   S.c,10
ZIANI, Pietro Andrea (c1616-1684), It
    R.1   S.c,10
ZICH, Jaroslav (1912-   ), Cz
    R.1   S.5,23
ZICH, Otakar (1879-1934), Cz
    R.1   S.4,5,7
ZIEHRER, Carl Michael (1843-1922), Aus
    R.1   S.c,4,5x,10
ZIELINSKI, Mikolaj (fl 1611), Pol
    R.1   S.2,4,5x,8,10,11,14,16
ZIERITZ, Grete von (1899-   ), Aus
    R.7   S.52
ZIFRIN, Marilyn Jane (1926-   ), USA
    R.19   S.13,30,52
ZIGAITIS, Rimuydas Dionizas (1933-   )
                S.18[Zhigaitas]
ZILCH, Josef (1928-   )
                S.c
ZILCHER, Hermann (1881-1948), Ger
    R.4
ZILLIG, Winfried (1905-1963), Ger
    R.1   S.c
ZILLINGER, Erwin (1893-1974), Ger
    R.4
ZIMBALIST, Efrem (1889-1985), USA (see note)
    R.1   S.3-5,7,11,13,18,23,24
ZIMBALIST, Efrem Jr (1923-   ), USA
                S.13
ZIMMER, Jan (1926-   ), Slovak
    R.1   S.5x,31
ZIMMERMAN, Charles A. (1861-1916)
    R.49   S.10,54(313)
ZIMMERMANN, Antal (18th Cent)

ZIMMERMANN, Anton (?1741-1781), Aus
    R.1   S.c,8(218),24a
ZIMMERMANN, Bernard Alois (1918-1970), Ger
    R.1   S.c,10,24a

ZIMMERMANN, Heinz Werner (1930-   ), Ger
   R.1   S.c
ZIMMERMANN, Josef (20th Cent)
            S.c
ZIMMERMANN, Louis (1873-1954), Neth
   R.14   S.24
ZINGARELLI, Niccolò Antonio (1752-1837), It
   R.1   S.c
ZINGER, Grigori Solomonovich (1913-   )
            S.18
ZINNEN, J. A. (1827-1898), Luxembourg

ZINOS, Fredrick (1942-   ), USA
            S.13
ZINZADZE, Sulkhan [see TSINTSADZE, Sulkhan]
ZIPOLI, Domenico (1688-1726), It
   R.1   S.c,4,5,8,10,11,18,24a,53
ZIPP, Friedrich (1914-   ), Ger
   R.1   S.c
ZIRLER, Stephan (c1518-1568), Ger
   R.1   S.16
ZITO, V. - La cumparsita
            S.24a
ZIV, Mikhail Pavlovich (1921-   ), USSR
   R.14   S.18
ZLATEV-CHERKIN, Georgi Dimitrov (1905-   ), Bul
   R.14   S.18,24
ZLATOV, Semen Vladimirovich (1893-1970), USSR
   R.14   S.18
ZNATOKOV, Yuri Vladimirovich (1926-   ), USSR
   R.47   S.18
ZNOSKO-BOROWSKY, Alexander Fedorovich (1908-   ) USSR
   R.47   S.18,24
ZOCARINI, Matteo (18th Cent)
            S.c
ZOILO, Annibale (c1537-1592), It
   R.1   S.32
ZOLL, Paul (1907-   ), Ger
   R.14   S.c
ZOLLER - The nightingale
            S.24a
ZOLLER, Alfred Hans
            S.c
ZÖLLNER, Carl Friedrich (1800-1860), Ger
   R.1   S.c,10
ZOLOTAREV, Vladislav Andreyevich (1943-   )
            S.18
ZOLOTUKHIN, Vladimir Maksovich (1936-   ), USSR
   R.47   S.18

ZONN, Paul (1938-   ), USA
            S.10,13
ZOOB, David B.
            S.54(326)
ZORBELEY, Hans Rudolf
            S.c
ZORITA, Nicasio (c1545-c1593), Sp
    R.1   S.16
ZORZI, Juan Carlos (1935-   ), Arg
    R.4   S.c
ZOUBEK, Karol (1902-1959)
            S.24
ZSOLT, Durko (1934-   ), Hun
    R.95   S.19
ZSOLT, Nándor (1887-1936), Hun
    R.1   S.24
ZUBELDIA, Emiliana de (1948-   ), Sp
    R.7   S.52
ZUBILLAGA, Luis (1928-   ), Arg
    R.26   S.46
ZUBITSKY, N. (1953-   )
            S.24a
ZUBIZARRETA y ARANA, Victor de (1899-1970), Sp
    R.104   S.5x
ZUCCALMAGLIO, Anton Wilhelm Florentin (1803-1869), Ger
    R.3
ZUCCHINI, Gregorio (c1540-c1616), It
    R.1   S.10
ZUCKERMAN, Mark (1948-   ), USA
    R.19   S.10,13
ZUCKERMANN, Augusta [see MANA-ZUCCA, Ki-Lu]
ZUCKERT, Leon (1904-   ), USSR
    R.4
ZULEHNER, Carl (c1770->1830), Ger
    R.5   S.5x
ZULFUGAROV, Oktai (1929-   ), USSR
    R.47   S.18
ZULUETA, de - Adore te devote
            S.e
ZUMAYA, Manuel de (c1678-1756), Mex
    R.1   S.10
ZUMBROICH, Eberhard Maria (1933-   )
            S.c
ZUMPE, Herman (1850-1903), Ger
    R.1
ZUMSTEEG, Johann Rudolf (1760-1802), Ger
    R.1   S.c,10
ZUNDEL, John (1815-1882), Ger
    R.53   S.c

ZUPKO, Ramon (1932-   ), USA
    R.19   S.13
ZUR, Menachem (1942-   ), Isr
    R.80   S.10,13
ZVANEPOL, Jan (1936-   )
              S.c

ZVART, Dirk Janszoon (1917-   )
              S.c
ZVARTI, Jan (1877-1937)
              S.c
ZVARTI, Willem Hendrick (1925-   )
              S.c
ZVETKOFF, P. - Lied aus der unteren Schenke
              S.c
ZVONAŘ, Jósef Leopold (1824-1865), Cz
    R.1   S.c
ZWIERZCHOWSKI, Matteuz (c1713-1768), Pol
    R.1   S.c
ZWILICH, Ellen Taaffe (1939-   ), USA
    R.7   S.30,52
ZWINGLI, Ulrich (1484-1531), Swiss
    R.1   S.c,10,16
ZYRYANOV, Vasili Aleyevich (1936-   )
              S.18
ZYWNY, Wojciech (1756-1842), Pol
    R.1

ABBÉ - Aria, chasse & minuetto (Columbia DFX 199)
S.5x has this record under L´ABBÉ, le fils
(1727-1803) whereas S.24 attributes it to George
Joseph Vogler (1749-1814)

ALIPRANDI, Bernardo (1710-1785)
ALIPRANDI, Paul (20th Cent)
 - Esquises pyrénéennes; Fantasia
S.24 attributes these pieces to the 18th Century
Aliprandi, whereas S.24a attributes them to the 20th
Century Aliprandi.

ALLITSEN, Francis (1849-1912)
   R.1:   ALLITSEN [Bumpus], Mary Francis. "ALLITSEN"
             was a pseud.
   R.7:   ALLITSEN, Frances (Mary Frances Bumpus).
   R.44:   ALLITSEN, Frances. Mention is made of her
             sister Emma Allitsen.
   R.82:   ALLITSEN, Frances Mary Frances Bumpus
   R.88:   ALLITSEN, Francis - pseud [ie Mary Francis
             Bumpus].
   R.88:   ALLITSEN, Francis. See ALLITSEN (Frances)
             pseud.
   R.108: ALLITSEN, Frances (née Mary Frances Bumpus)
Questions arising from the above:
   1. Both R.1 and R.88 give "Francis" as one of her
      christian names, yet this is the male version.
   2. If "Allitsen" was a pseudonym did her sister
      Emma use it also?

ANDREA di GIOVANNI - Sotto candido vel
ANDREAS de FLORENTIA - Non più doglie ebbe Dido
S.16 has entries for both the above names. According
to R.1 they are one and the same person.

*** ANDRIESSEN, Hedrick (1913-   )
This name appears in the Bielefelder catalogue. The
works listed under it are by Hendrik Andriessen
(1892-1981)

ANFOSSI, Pasquale (1727-1797)
This composer appears in S.5x but the reference is to
a recording of Mozart's "Un bacio di mano" (K.541)
which Mozart wrote for Anfossi's opera "Le gelosie
fortunate".

AYRTON - Allegrament (arr hps - H. Casadesus)
This may be an original composition by Henri
Casadesus (1879-1947). See the article about the
Casadesus family in R.1.

BACH, Johannes (1604-1673)
- Ach was soll ich Sünder machen.
This entry appears in S.10 with the note that
although the record gives J. S. Bach as the composer
it was actually composed by the above. However,
according to R.1 only three pieces by this member of
the Bach family are extant, non of which has the
above title. The Johann Sebastian Bach thematic
catalogue lists two pieces with this title: BWV.259
and BWV.770. In R.1 the latter is described as
"doubtful".

BACH, Vincent (1890-1976) - Hungarian Melodies
According to R.70 "Hungarian Melodies" was "compiled,
edited and published" by Vincent Bach. Composition
is not mentioned. Vincent Bach is principally
remembered as a brass instrument maker.

BACHOFEN/BACKOFEN
S.10 has the entry:
  Backofen, Johann Gottlieb Heinrich
  - Concertante, F major for basset horn & harp with
    cello accompaniment.
In R.88 this piece is attributed to:
  Backofen, Johann Geog Heinrich (1768-1839)
Bielefelder has the entry:
  Bachofen, Johann Gottlieb Heinrich (1768-1839)
  - Sonate für Harfe, Bassetthorn und Violoncello
  - Viele verachten die edele Musik
The first piece is presumably the same as above.
The second piece is by:
  Johann Caspar Bachofen (1695-1755)
Presumably the name Johann Gottlieb Heinrich
Bachofen/Backofen is a fiction.

BAERMANN, Heinrich (1784-1847) - Adagio for cl & p

This piece was at one time attributed to Richard
Wagner. It is in fact an arrangement of part of
Baermann´s string quartet, Op.23. See R.88.

BALLANTINE, James - Castles in the air
R.87: Composer unknown; words by James Ballantine.

BANNISTER, John
 - The tempest: Come unto these yellow sands
R.1 states that it is not always possible to be sure
whether certain pieces are by the father (c1625-1679)
or by the son (d.?1725). Both were named John
Bannister.

BARBAUD, Pierre
 R.1: "date of birth undisclosed".
 R.4: b.1925.
 R.14: b.1911.

BARCLAY, Martin
 R.3 states that Martin Barclay was a pseudonym used
by Frederick Austin. However, R.88 has entries for
both names with no indication that the former is a
pseudonym used by the latter.

BARKER, George
 - Masonic March
BARKER, George Arthur
 - Where are the friends of my youth?
 - The white squall
 - Irish emigrant
Several sources confuse these two names. As far as I
know they were not the same person.

BASSI, Luigi (1766-1825) [singer]
BASSI, Luigi (1833-1871) [clarinet virtuoso]
 R.89 and several other sources confuse these
 two people.

BAUER, Marion
 Date of birth: R.1: 15 August 1897
     R.6, R.7, R.19: 15 August 1887.

BEAULIEU, Lambert de - Balet comique de la Royne.
 Fétis claimed that he composed the vocal music to
 Beaujoyeux´s "Balet comique de la Royne", though

Mersènne attributed it to Girard de Beaulieu. R.1
seems to lean towards the latter, which would make
Lambert de Beaulieu just a singer.

BERBERIAN, Cathy
Date of birth: R.1: 4 July 1928.
             R.6,7,82: 4 July 1925.

BERGMAN, Stefan
- Celestial song, Op.2/1; Polka caprice, Op.1/3.
Around 1942 Eileen Joyce recorded these piano pieces.
These titles appear in R.90 under Stefan Bergmann.
Is this the same person as the pianist Stevan Bergmann
(1903-   )?

BERNAL, José (16th Cent) - Ave, sanctissimum corpus
BERNAL GONZAL, Francisco (16th Cent) - Navego en hondo
mar
These two entries appear in S.16. However according
to R.1 and R.9 they are the same person. R.1 gives
his first name as "?José" whereas R.9 gives it as
"Francisco?"

BESOYAN, Rick (1924-1970)
R.1, published 1980, makes no reference to the
composer´s death.

BINDER, Carl (1816-1860)
Carl Binder composed the well-known overture to
Offenbach´s "Orphée aux Enfers".

*** BORNE, François Ferdinand de (1862-1929)
This hybrid name appears in the Bielefelder catalogue.
It is a combination of:
    1. François Borne (1840-1920)
    2. Fernand le Borne (1862-1929)
The piece listed under this hybrid name - "Fantaisie
brillante on themes from Bizet´s Carmen" is by #1.

BOSCÔLI, Ronaldo (1929-   ) - Barquino
According to R.67 Boscôli wrote only the words to the
song "Barquinho"; the music being composed by Roberto
Menescal.

BOTTACCIARI, Ugo/Luigi (1879-   )
R.10 gives his christian name as "Ugo", whereas R.93
calls him "Luigi".

BROSCHI, Carlo [pseud: FARINELLI] (1705-1782) [singer]
Listed in the Bielefelder catalogue as composer of the
opera "Idaspe". This opera was composed by his
brother Riccardo Broschi (1703-1756).

BUCKY, Frida Sarsen (1883/84-1974)
Her orbituary appeared in the New York Times, Tuesday
8 Oct. 1974. It stated that she "died Wednesday aged
91".

BURIAN, Karel (1870-1924) [singer]
The Gramophone Classical Catalogue (December 1978) has
this Czech tenor as the composer of the piece
"American Suite". This piece was composed by Emil
Frantisek Burian (1904-1959).

CAMBINI, Giuseppe Maria (1746-1825).
According to R.1 Fétis mistakenly gave Cambini's
forenames as Giovanni Giuseppe. Some current
catalogues are still using this incorrect information.

*** CAPIROLA, Giovanni Paolo (1474-1547)
This hybrid name appears is Croucher. It is a
combination of:
    1. Vincenzo Capirola (1474->1548)
    2. Giovanni Paolo Caprioli (d ?c1627).

CARRION, Miguel Ramos (1845-1915)
In S.39 Carrion is given as the composer of the
zarzuela "La bruja". However, according to R.93
Carrion was the librettist and Ruperto Chapi was the
composer.

*** CASTILLO, Dario (mid 16th Cent)
This hybrid name appears in S.24 and stems from an
incorrectly labeled recording. It is a combination
of:
    1. Dario Castello
    2. Diego del Castillo.
The piece listed under this hybrid name - "Sonata
concertante (1629)" - is by #1.

*** CASTRO, Juan de (1540?-1600)
This hybrid name appears in Bielefelder and Croucher.
It is a combination of:
    1. Jean de Castro (c1540-c1600), S. Neth
    2. Juan Blas de Castro (c1560-1631), Sp
In addition, S.17 and the Gramophone Classical Cata-
logue attribute "Angelus Domini ad Pastores ait" to
#2. According to R.1 it is by #1 and was published in
Denkmaler rheinischer Musik, xvii (Dusseldorf, 1974).

CEBALLOS, Francisco de (fl 1554-71)
CEBALLOS, Rodrigo de (c1530-1591)
According to R.1 Eslava attributed several of Rodrigo
de Ceballos´ works to Francisco de Ceballos. R.1 goes
on to say that no works by Francisco de Ceballos are
known to survive.

CIAMPI, Vincenzo (?1719-1762)
S.10 has an entry "Pergolesi, Nina. See Ciampi, Nina".
This is a reference to the song "Tre giorni son che
Nina" whose authorship "remains uproved". It has been
attributed to Giovanni Battista Pergolesi and to
Vincenzo Ciampi. See Musical Times xl (1899), 241 and
xc (1949), 432.

*** CLÉMENT, Charles François (1780-1842)
This hybrid name appears in the Bielefelder catalogue.
It is a combination of:
    1. Charles-François Clément (c1720-c1782)
    2. François Clément (1780-1842).
The titles listed under this hybrid name are
attributed in R.5 to #1.

CONRADI, Johann Gottfried (fl 1724)
 - Suites for lute in A minor and C major.
Current catalogues attribute recordings with these
titles to a variety of composers having the surname
Conradi. Bielefelder has tried:
    1. Johann Gottfried Conradi (1820-1896)
    2. *** Johann Gottfried Conradi (?-1700).
#2 is a hybrid, combining #1 with Johann Georg Conradi
(d.1699). A more likely candidate is Johann Gottfried
Conradi who was a lutenist in Frankfurt in 1724.

COSTANTINI, Alessandro (1709?-1795)
This name appears in the Bielefelder catalogue with
the motet "Pastores loquebantur" attributed to it.
The Music Library of the University of Toronto has the
same recording under Alessandro Costantini
(c1581-1657).

CRESCENZO
S.10 attributes the song "Guardann´a luna" to
Constantino de Crescenzo whereas R.52 attributes it to
Vincenzo de Crescenzo.

CZERNY, Joseph (1785-1842) [publisher]
The works listed in the Bielefelder catalogue under
this name are by Carl Czerny (1791-1857).

*** DALZA, Esteban (16th Cent), Sp
This hybrid name appears in the Gramophone Classical
Catalogue. It is a combination of:
    1. Joan Ambrosio Dalza (fl 1508)
    2. Esteban Daza (fl 1575).

DAVIDE de BERGAMO, (Padre) Felice Moretti (1791-1842)
Both the Bielefelder and Diapason catalogues give his

dates as (1791-1863). They may be confusing him with
the Italian tenor Giovanni Davide (1790-1864).

DECRUCK, Maurice (1896-1954)
He composed a number of works jointly with his wife
Fernando Breilh. See R.7,48.

DICKSON, Ellen [pseud: DOLORES] (1819-1878)
Both R.7 and R.44 give her christian name as Ellen.
However, the entry in R.88 is:
 DOLORES, pseud [ie Elizabeth Dickson].
R.88 also has an entry for Elizabeth Dickson with no
mention of the pseudonym Dolores.

ECKHARDT-GRAMATTÉ, Sophie-Carmen (1899-1974)
Reference sources published prior to 1981 (e.g.
R.1,2,6,7,12) give her date of birth as Jan 6 1902.
Mr Lorne Watson of Brandon, Manitoba, informs me that
this is incorrect. Mr. Watson knew her for several
years and wrote the article about her that appears in
R.81. He told me that the composer's mother falsified
the date of birth to enable her daughter to enter the
Paris Conservatory. The correct date of birth is
6 Jan 1899.

EDMUNDSON, Garth
Dates vary: S.13: (1900-   )
             R.19: (1895-   )
Gramophone Classical Catalogue: (1900-1971).

EDSON, Lewis
S.10 has the titles "Refuge" and "Greenfield" listed
under Lewis Edson Jr. However, S.47 attributes
"Refuge" to Lewis Edson Jr. and "Greenfield" to Lewis
Edson Sr.

ELWYN-EDWARDS, Dilys (20th Cent)
The Gramophone Classical Catalogue (Sept 1979) insists
that this composer is a man, giving her the christian
name of David. See R.83.

FARMER, Henry (1819-1891)
R.90 has the entry:
   Farmer, Henry (1882-   ) - The Empress Quadrille.
This is incorrect. Henry George Farmer (1882-1965)
was a musicologist (see R.1). The Empress Quadrille
was composed by Henry Farmer (1819-1891). See R.88.

FARRANDINI
In a footnote in S.5, p.815 mention is made of a
Farrandini who set Metastasio's libretto "Catone in
Utica" in 1753. This appears to be a misprint as
according to R.93 in 1753 "Catone in Utica" was set by
Giovanni Ferrandini (c1710-1791).

FISHBURN, Chrisopher (fl 1678-98)
The catch "Fie, nay prithee John" generally attributed
to Henry Purcell has been ascribed to Fishburn. See
R.24, p.414.

FROSINI
The entry in S.10 is:
   Frosini and/or Arban: Carnival of Venice (arr
   Camarata)" (trumpet).
Jean Baptiste Arban (1825-1889) is described in R.1 as
the founder of modern trumpet playing and goes on to
say that his setting of "The Carnival of Venice" was
the cornettist's solo piece par excellence during his
and the next two or three generations.

GAILLARD, Marius François (1900-1973)
R.1, published 1980, makes no reference to the
composer's death. He died 23 July 1973.

GAVEAUX, G. L'aîné
R.1 states that the work attributed to this composer -
"Nouvelle Méthode pour le flageolot, suivie de petits
airs" - is probably by Simon Gaveaux (b.1759).

GENTILI, Giorgio (?c1669->1731)
The only recording of music by Gentili seems to be in
the form of an arrangement by Johann Gottfried Walther
(1684-1748): Gentili: Concerto, A major, Allegro
   (arr Walther, L.130).

GERSTER, Ottmar (1897-1969)
R.1, published 1980, makes no reference to the
composer's death some 11 years prior to publication.

*** GIGOUT, Eugène (1797-1828)
This name appears in the Bielefelder catalogue. The
piece under this name is by Eugène Gigout (1844-1925).

GILBERT, Robert
The piece listed under this name in S.10 - "Nocturne"
- is by Henry Franklin Belknap Gilbert (1868-1928).
See S.13.

GREENWOOD, John A.
R.85 has no dates. R.96 has "date of birth not for
publication" and notes that his name appeared in a
directory of band trainers published in 1895.

*** GROBE, Charles (1839-   )
This name appears in S.24 and R.53. But the book
referenced in R.53 (Moore, J. W. Appendix to
Encyclopedia of Music. Boston: Oliver Ditson, 1875)
mentions only Charles Grobe (1817-1880) who happened
to arrive in the USA in 1839. Presumably this is the
origin of the above name-date combination.

HANNFF, Johann Nikolause (1665-1711/12)
Older references (eg R.1.5, R.3) give his dates as
(1630-1706).

HENRY, H. F.
S.5x gives him as the composer of "Faith of our
Fathers". This may be only an arrangement.

HERMAN, Johann (16th Cent)
For some reason catalogues often attribute the
Lutheran hymn "Lobt Gott, ihr Christen alle gleich" to
Johann Hermann. Both R.1 and R.12 state that both
text and music are by Nicolaus Herman (1500-1561).

HOFFMANN, Melchior (c1685-1715)
Bach cantatas BWV.53 and BWV.189 have been ascribed to
this composer. See R.1.

HOWE, Julia Ward (1819-1910)
Early recordings give her as composer of "The Battle
Hymn of the Republic". However she supplied only the
words; the music being an arrangement of the air "John
Brown's body" by William Steffe. See R.87.

HUMMEL, Ferdinand (1855-1928)
The Library of Congress card (77-762513) for the
recording of Emmy Destinn singing various songs
origionally recorded 1905-11 attributes the song

"Hallelujah" to Johann Nepomuk Hummel (1778-1837).
This would appear to be incorrect as his thematic
catalogue does not mention any work with this title.
On the other hand a song with this title was composed
by Ferdinand Hummel (1855-1928). See his Op.73 in the
work list in R.12.

JUNCKER, August W.
According to R.91 the song "I was dreaming" comes from
the opera "Ma mie rosette" by A. W. Juncker. However
R.93 has no entry for a composer with this name and
gives the composer of opera "Ma mie rosette" as Paul
Jean Lâcombe d´Estalenx (1838-1920).

KARAS, Anton (1910-?1985)
Anton Karas composed the music for the film "The Third
Man". His orbituary appeared in Canadian newspapers
11 Jan 1985.

KEY, Francis Scott (1780-1843)
Listed in early recordings as the composer of the
music to "The Star-Spangled Banner". However, R.1
states that he wrote only the words using a melody by
the English composer John Stafford Smith (1750-1836).

KOMZÀK, Karel (1823-1893) R.1,2,2s, 18,25
KOMZAK, Karel (1850-1905) R.1,2,2s,3,18,25
KOMZAK, Karel (1878-1924) R.   2s,3   25
Not only did the three generations of the Komzak

family share the same christian name but they also
composed similar types of music. The confusion is
increased by the fact that some reference sources
mention only two out of the three. The omission of #3
from R.18 is puzzling considering the amount of space
devoted to #1 and #2 and the fact that it is a Czech
publication. The omission of #3 from R.1 is easier to
explain: the articles in R.1 are merely condensations
of the articles in R.18. The entries in the Bielefelder catalogue are equally confusing. From 1962 to
1971 Bielefelder mentions only #1. With the 1972
edition a strange change took place: #3 made his
appearance and the works listed for ten years under #1
were moved to #2. R.32 is incorrect when it states
that #1 is unrelated to #2 and #3.

LAMOTE de GRIGNON
This could be either:
    1. Juan Lamote de Grignon (1872-1949)
    2. Ricardo Lamote de Grignon y Ribas (1899-1962).
They were father and son and both served as conductor

of La Banda Municipal de Barcelona, which is the band
playing in the recording.

LARA, Augustín (1900-1970)
R.1 is incorrect in stating he died in 1969. His
orbituary appeared in the New York Times, 7 November
1970. He died 6/7 November 1970.

LEMAIRE, Caston Eugène
R.2: b.1854
R.3: b.1855
Committed suicide December 1927, body found in River
Seine 8 January 1928.

LOEILLET, Jean-Baptiste (1653-1728)
This name does not appear on the Loeillet family tree
published in R.1. Considering the confusion surrounding the identity of the various members of this family
this is not surprising.

LOESSER, Frank (1910-1969)
R.1, published 1980, makes no reference to the
composers death.

LOEWE, Hilde [pseud: Henry LOVE] (1895-1976)
She is remembered for her song "Das alte Lied". Her
name does not appear in any of the usual reference
sources on women composers. R.3 has an entry for her
but without dates. Her orbituary appeared in Musik-
handel July 1976, p.220. It states that she died in
London 15 May 1976 and would have been 81 on 8 July
1976.

*** LVOVSKY, Alexis (1799-1871)
This hybrid name appears in S.11. It is a combination
of:

    1. LVOV, Alexey Fyodorovich (1798-1870)
    2. LVOVSKI, Grigor Fyodorovich (1830-1894).
Both composers are in R.28, both composed church
music. S.10 also confuses these composers.

MADDEN, Edward (1877-1952)
MADDEN, Richard
 - Symphonic variations on a theme by Purcell.
S.13 attributes this piece to Edward, S.10 attributes
it to Richard. From Edward Madden's work list in R.23
I would think that he was not the composer of this
piece.

MARIE, Gabriel [?pseud: Jean GABRIEL-MARIE] (1852-1928)
Some confusion surrounds this composer. R.2 treats
the composer as a man but Aaron Cohen includes the
name in his international Encyclopedia of Women Comp-
sers (R.7). R.7 is probably incorrect as the only
reference given is R.89. The entry in R.89 is
"Gabriel Marie" which R.7 has interpreted as a surname
followed by a christian name. Hence the entry in R.7:
"GABRIEL, Marie. R.2 makes no mention of any pseudonym, whereas the entry in R.3 is:
    MARIE, Jean Marie [pseud: Jean GABRIEL-MARIE,
    G. MARGIERI, Jean REX].

*** MÜLLER, Karl Franz (1808-1855)
This name appears in the Bielefelder catalogue. The
piece listed under this name - "Variationen uber ein
Thema von Bach" - is by Karl Franz Müller (1822-1978).
See work list in R.69.

NORCOMBE, Daniel (ii) (fl 1602-47)
- Division on a ground for viola da gamba & lute
S.1x, 2-4,5x attribute this piece to Daniel Norcombe
(i) (1576-<1626). R.1 states that is probably by
Daniel (ii).

NORTON, Caroline Elizabeth Sarah (née Sheridan)
(1808/09-1877)
NORTON, Hon. Mrs (Lady W. Stirling-Maxwell (1809-1877)
R.7 contains the above entries. They are no doubt one
and the same person.

*** OVSIANIKO-KULIKOVSKII, Nikolai Dmitrievich
(1768-1846)
This name was invented by the Russian violinist
Mikhail Goldstein as part of a hoax to decieve the
Soviet Music Publishing House. See R.6, xvii.

PACCHIAROTTI, Giuseppe (1740-1821)
The above was a soprano castrato. "L'Albatro", one of
the two titles listed under this name in S.24, is an
opera by Ubaldo Pacchiarotti.

PACCHIAROTTI, Ubaldo
Year of birth R.3: 1874 (1877?)
             R.10: 1877
             R.93: 1875

PALAFUTTI (fl 1780), It
R.5 has two composers with this surname:
    1. Lorenzo Palafuti (fl 1779)
    2. Vincenzo Palafuti (fl 1783-88)
Both were cembalists in Florence

PAR, C.F.
Composer of "Das Alphabet", attributed to W. A. Mozart
as K.Anh.294d.

PARRY, Joseph (1841-1903)
The entry in S.8 is under Charles Hubert Hastings
Parry.

PARTCH, Harry (1901-1974)
Died 3 Sept. 1974, not 3 Sept. 1976 as stated in R.1.
His orbituary appeared in the New York Times 6 Sept.
1974.

PEARSALL, Robert Lucas [?pseud: G. BERTHOLD]
(1795-1856) - Duetto for two cats.
According to R.88 this piece, which is sometimes
attributed to Rossini was published in c1825 under the
pseudonym of G. Berthold, with an introduction by
Edgar Hunt and a facsimile of Pearsall´s autograph.

POLIAKIN, F. - Le Canari (Concert-polka)
POLIAKIN, Miron (1895-1941)
Diapason attributes "Le Canari" to Miron Poliakin.
This is incorrect. See R.89.

*** REGNART, Jacob François (1530-1600) or (1540?-1599)
This hybrid name appears in the Bielefelder catalogue
and copied by Croucher. It is a combination of:
    1. Jacob Regnart (1540/45-1599)
    2. François Regnart (fl 1579).
The pieces with French titles listed in Bielefelder
and Croucher under this name - "Si je trépasse" and
"Petite Nymfe folatre" - are by #2.

*** ROSSI, Francesco (1627-c1700) or (b c1645)
- Mitrane - Opera: Ah! rendimi quel core.
This entry appears in S.4 and S.18. But as R.1
explains, the opera "Mitrane" never existed and the
aria comes from an opera staged in the second half of
the 18th century. R.1 goes on to say that the music
is probably by Francesco Bianchi (c1752-1810).

SCHEPERS, Geleyn (fl 1660)
The piece listed under this name in S.8 - "Allegro
carillon in F major" - is attributed in the University
of Toronto card catalogue to Boudewijn Schepers
(d.1781).

SHRÖDER, Friedrich (1910-1972)
R.1, published 1980, makes no reference to the
composer's death.

SCHRÖDER, Hermann (1843-1909)
The choral prelude "Schönster Herr Jesu" attributed to
this composer in S.8 is actually by Hermann Schroeder
(1904-   ).

SCHULTZ/SCHULTZE
Since 1969 there has been a great deal of confusion in
the Bielefelder catalogue concerning composers with
the surname Schultz or Schultze. From the entries in
the University of Toronto card catalogue the correct
attributions of the pieces in question are:
    Johannes Schultz (1582-1653)
    - Musikalischer Lustgärte (1617)
    Johann Christoph Schultze (c1733-1813)
    - Overture, 2 recorders & continuo, no.1 in F major.
The variety of names, both real and imaginary, that
these two pieces have appeared under in the
Bielefelder catalogue (and copied by Croucher) since
1969 is quite astonishing.

SERINI, Giovanni Battista (b c1710)
In 1919 three keyboard sonatas by Serini were edited
by F. B. Pratella. For some reason he attributed them
to an earlier Serini. This error can be seen in R.90
which has the entry:
    SERINI, Giuseppe (164...).
See Musical Times, cv (1964), 581.

SHEREMETIEV, Alexander Dmitriyevich (1859-1931)
S.10 attributes the song "I loved you" to this
composer.   S.18 and R.89 attribute it to Boris
Sergeyevich Sheremetiev (1822-1906).

SMYTH, William (c1550-1600)
R.1 states that William Smith (1603-1645) has often
been confused with this composer. The recording of
"Preces and Responses" attributed to William Smyth
(c1550-1600) may be an example of this confusion.

SOLLBERGER, Harvey
  Date of birth varies: R.1: 11 May 1939
                        R.6: 11 May 1938
                        R.19: 11 May 1938

SOMERSET, Henry Richard Charles (1849-1932)
  At least some of the songs attributed in R.91 to Henry
  Vere Fitzroy Somerset (1898-   ) are by this
  composer. See R.44,88.

SOTO
  Confusion surrounds composers with this name in record
  catalogues and discographies. From R.1 and R.9 three
  people with this name emerge:
    1. Francisco de Soto (fl first half of 16th Cent)
    2. Pedro de Soto (fl 1591)
    3. Francisco Soto de Langa (1534-1619).
  The names appearing in record catalogues and discographies seem to be varying combinations of the above
  three names, e.g:
    Pedro de Soto (1539-1619) [S.17] seems to be #2
      with the dates for #3.
    Pedro Francisco Soto de Langa (1534-1619) [Biel-
      efelder] could be a combination of all three.
  Croucher has evidently copied this hybrid name.
  The confusion surrounding the names extends to the
  music. Angles in his article in R.9 and in his
  commentary in Monumentos de la Música Española (ii La
  Música en La Corte de Carlos V) casts doubt on the
  assumption made by Pedrell in 1908 that Pedro de Soto
  was a composer. Angles suggests that the music attributed by Pedrell to Pedro de Soto should be attributed
  to Francisco de Soto. These doubts about attribution
  are combined with confusion regarding names. Thus we
  may see in the Diapason catalogue the entry:
    Soto de Langa, Francisco (c1533-1619)
    - Tiento (organ)
  This Tiento may be one of the pieces that Pedrell
  attributed to #2 but which Angles believes to be by #1
  listed here under #3.

STACHOWICZ, Damian (?-1729)
  Listed in the Bielefelder catalogue as composer of
  "Veni Consalator". According to R.2 this piece is by
  Damian Stachowicz (1658-1699) who at one time was
  identified with Damian Torzyński (1673-1729).

STAMITZ
In view of the problems of identification and
attribution that exist with composers bearing this
name the information contained in discographies and
record catalogues is probably of little value.

STEWART, Charles Hylton (1884-1932)
STEWART, Haldane Campbell (1868-1942)
The confusion between these two gentlemen is
understandable as they share the same initials, both
were associated with Magdalen College, Oxford, and
both were organists. Two pieces have appeared in
record catalogues under the name "H. C. Stewart":
"On this day Earth shall ring" and "Veni, Sancte
Spiritus". The former is attributed in R.112 to
Charles Hylton.

*** TESSIER, Georg (Charles Guillaume?)
This hybrid name appears in the Bielefelder catalogue.
It is a combination of:
     1. Charles Tessier (fl c1600)
     2. Guillaume Tessier (fl c1582).

THAYER, Pat
According to R.91 Pat Thayer also wrote a song with
the name "A childs prayer". A piece with this name
appears in S.10 attributed to M. C. Thayer.

THÉRÉSA
R.7, using R.10s as his source, gives her real name as
Giovana Emma Valadon, whereas R.200 gives it as Emma
Eugene Rose Valladon.

TORELLI, Giacomo (1608-1678)
An Italian stage designer, engineer and architect.
The music attributed to him in the Bielefelder
catalogue is by Giuseppe Torelli (1658-1709).

VALERIUS, Adriaen (c1575-1625)
S.54(324) is a recording of the Dutch national anthem
"Wilhelmus van Nassouwe". It first appeared
"Neder-landtsche gedenck-clanck" which was compiled by
Adriaen Valerius. According to R.1 Valerius possibly
composed a few of the melodies himself.

VALE, Francisco (1869-1906)
The often recorded Heifetz arrangement of "Ao pe da
fogueira (preludio XV)" is always attributed to
"Francisco L. Valle". Could this be the same person
as the above Brazilian composer?

*** VECCHI, Orazio Orfeo (1540?-1604?)
This hybrid name appears in the Bielefelder catalogue.
It is a combination of:
1. Orfeo Vecchi (c1550-<1604)
2. Orazio Vecchi (1550-1605).

WEBER, Bernhard Anselm (1764-1821)
- Bruder, steckt nun
- Drei Sterne
- Frühlingsahnung
- Wanderers Nachtgebet
These titles appear in S.2 and S.5 under Carl Maria
von Weber. In S.5 they are noted as "unidentified"
and "perhaps by B.A. Weber".

WILKINSON (fl ?1579-96)
The Gramophone Classical Catalogue attributes a piece
"Salve regina" to this composer. From R.1 it would
appear that this piece is by Robert Wilkinson
(c1450-1515).

WYBICKIEGO - Polish National Anthem
According to R.94 the music to the Polish National
Anthem is traditional with words by Jozef Wybicki
(1747-1822).

WYLIE, Betty Jane
Named in S.52 as joint composer with Victor Davies of
the rock opera "Beowulf". R.81 states that she wrote
the lyrics only.

ZACAR [Zacharias, Zachara, Zacharie]
R.1 states that this name, in its various forms, is
associated with at least two and possibly three
musicians who flourished in late 14th- and early
15th-Century, Italy. Two of them are Antonio Zachara
da Teramo and Nicola Zacharie of Brindis.

ZHUBANOVA, Gaziza Akhmetovna
Date of birth: R.47: 2 Dec 1927
               R.7: 2 Dec 1928
S.18 gives her Christian name as Marger.

ZIMBALIST, Efrem (1889-1985)
Reference sources published prior to 1980 give his
date of birth as 9 April 1889 (eg R.3,4,6,19,23,100).
In addition R.99 states that this date was confirmed
by the composer in a letter to the editor. James
Creighton, compiler of S.24, has informed me that he

discussed the date of birth with the composer's son,
Efrem Zimbalist Jr. The latter confirmed that 1889
is the correct year. However, since the publication
of R.1 in 1980 the composer's date of birth has been
changed to 9 April 1890. This new date can be seen
in R.25 and in the obituaries published by the New
York Times (23 Feb 1985) and the Times of London (27
Feb 1985). In addition, R.19 states that he died in
1970. This is incorrect; it is probably a reference
to the death of his wife, Mary Louise Curtis Bok Zimbalist, who died 4 Jan 1970. Efrem Zimbalist died
22 Feb 1985, in Reno, Nevada.